THE WORLD WAS GOING OUR WAY

CHRISTOPHER ANDREW
and VASILI MITROKHIN

THE WORLD WAS GOING OUR WAY

The KGB and the Battle for the Third World

BASIC
BOOKS

A Member of the Perseus Books Group
New York

In Memory of

Vasili Nikitich Mitrokhin
(1922–2004)
and
Nina Mikhailovna Mitrokhina
(1924–1999)

Contents

The Evolution of the KGB, 1917–91

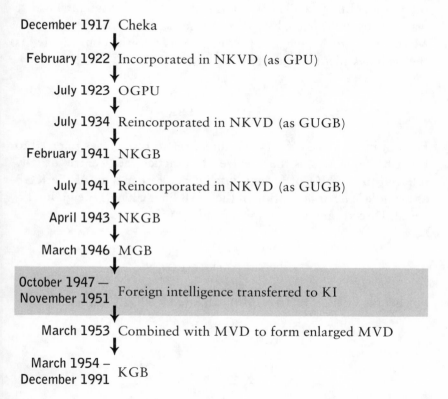

December 1917 Cheka
↓
February 1922 Incorporated in NKVD (as GPU)
↓
July 1923 OGPU
↓
July 1934 Reincorporated in NKVD (as GUGB)
↓
February 1941 NKGB
↓
July 1941 Reincorporated in NKVD (as GUGB)
↓
April 1943 NKGB
↓
March 1946 MGB
↓
October 1947 –
November 1951 Foreign intelligence transferred to KI
↓
March 1953 Combined with MVD to form enlarged MVD
↓
March 1954 –
December 1991 KGB

The functions, unlike the nomenclature, of the Soviet security and intelligence apparatus remained relatively constant throughout the period 1917–91. In recognition of that continuity, KGB officers frequently described themselves, like the original members of the Cheka, as Chekisty. The term KGB is sometimes used to denote the security and intelligence apparatus of the whole Soviet era, as well as, more correctly, for the period after 1954.

FOREIGN INTELLIGENCE

Founded in 1920, the foreign intelligence department of the Cheka and its inter-war successors was known as the Inostranni Otdel (INO). From 1941 to 1947 it was succeeded by the Inostrannoye Upravlenie (INU), also known as the First Directorate. From 1947 to 1951, the main foreign intelligence functions were taken over by the Komitet Informatsii (KI). From 1952 to 1991 foreign intelligence was run by the First Chief Directorate (save for the period from March 1953 to March 1954, when it was known, confusingly, as the Second Chief Directorate).

HEADQUARTERS

Foreign intelligence officers and directives to residencies referred to KGB headquarters as the 'Centre'. In practice the 'Centre' usually referred to the HQ of foreign intelligence rather than of the KGB as a whole. The organization of the KGB First Chief (Foreign Intelligence) Directorate is given in Appendix D.

KGB TERMINOLOGY

For detailed definitions, see Mitrokhin (ed.), *KGB Lexicon.*

Abbreviations and Acronyms

AFSA	Armed Forces Security [SIGINT] Agency (USA)
ANC	African National Congress
ARA	American Relief Association
ASA	Army Security [SIGINT] Agency (USA)
AVH	Hungarian security and intelligence agency
AVO	predecessor of AVH
AWACS	airborne warning and control system
BfV	security service (FRG)
BND	foreign intelligence agency (FRG)
BNS	Bureau of National Security (Syria)
CCP	Chinese Communist Party
CDR	Committee for the Defence of the Revolution (Cuba)
CDU	Christian Democratic Union (FRG)
Centre	HQ of the KGB (or FCD) and their predecessors
Cheka	Vserossiiskaya Chrezvychainaya Komissiya po Borbe s Kontrrevolyutsiei i Sabotazhem: All-Russian Extraordinary Commission for Combating Counter-Revolution and Sabotage (predecessor of KGB (1917–22))
CI	counter-intelligence
CIA	Central Intelligence Agency (USA)
CISPES	Committee in Solidarity with the People of El Salvador (USA)
COCOM	Coordinating Committee for East–West Trade (NATO and Japan)
Comecon	Council for Mutual Economic Assistance (Soviet bloc)
Comintern	Communist (Third) International
CPC	Christian Peace Conference
CPC	Communist Party of Canada
CPCz	Communist Party of Czechoslovakia

CPGB	Communist Party of Great Britain
CPI	Communist Party of India
CPJ	Communist Party of Japan
CPM	Communist Party of India, Marxist
CPSA	Communist Party of South Africa (later SACP)
CPSU	Communist Party of the Soviet Union
CPUSA	Communist Party of the United States of America
CSU	Christian Social Union (FRG; ally of CDU)
DCI	Director of Central Intelligence (USA)
Derg	Co-ordinating Committee of the Armed Forces, Police and National Guard (Ethiopia)
DGI	Dirección General de Inteligencia (Cuba)
DGS	Portuguese security service
DGSE	French foreign intelligence service
DIA	Defense Intelligence Agency (USA)
DISA	Direção de Informação e Segurança de Angola
DLB	dead letter-box
DRG	*diversionnye razvedyvatelnye gruppy*: Soviet sabotage and intelligence groups
DRU	Dirección Revolucionaria Unida (El Salvador)
DS	Bulgarian security and intelligence service
DST	French security service
EPS	Ejército Popular Sandinista (Nicaragua)
F Line	'Special Actions' department in KGB residencies
FAPSI	Federalnoye Agentsvo Pravitelstvennoi Sviazi i Informatsii: Russian (post-Soviet) SIGINT agency
FBI	Federal Bureau of Investigation (USA)
FCD	First Chief [Foreign Intelligence] Directorate, KGB
FCO	Foreign and Commonwealth Office (UK)
FLN	Front de Libération Nationale (Algeria)
FMLN	Farabundo Martí de Liberación Nacional (El Salvador)
FNLA	Frente Nacional de Libertação de Angola
FRAP	Frente de Acción Popular (Chile)
FRELIMO	Frente de Libertação de Moçambique
FRG	Federal Republic of Germany
FSB	Federalnaya Sluzhba Bezopasnosti: Russian security and intelligence service
FSLN	Frente Sandinista de Liberación Nacional (Nicaragua)

GCHQ	Government Communications Head-Quarters (British SIGINT Agency)
GDR	German Democratic Republic
GKNT	Gosudarstvennyi Komitet po Nauke i Tekhnologii: State Committee for Science and Technology
GPU	Gosudarstvennoe Politicheskoe Upravlenie: Soviet security and intelligence service (within NKVD, 1922–23)
GRU	Glavnoe Razvedyvatelnoe Upravlenie: Soviet Military Intelligence
GUGB	Glavnoe Upravlenie Gosudarstvennoi Bezopasnosti: Soviet security and intelligence service (within NKVD, 1934–43)
Gulag	Glavnoe Upravlenie Lagerei: Labour Camps Directorate
HUMINT	intelligence from human sources (espionage)
HVA	GDR foreign intelligence service
ICBM	intercontinental ballistic missile
ICP	Iraqi Communist Party
IDF	Israeli Defence Force
IMINT	imagery intelligence
INO	Inostrannyi Otdel: foreign intelligence department of Cheka/GPU/OGPU/GUGB, 1920–41; predecessor of INU
INU	Inostrannoe Upravlenie: foreign intelligence directorate of NKGB/GUGB/MGB, 1941–47
IRA	Irish Republican Army
ISC	Intelligence and Security Committee (UK)
ISI	Pakistani Inter-Services Intelligence
JCP	Japanese Communist Party
JIC	Joint Intelligence Committee (UK)
JSP	Japanese Socialist Party
KDP	Kurdistan Democratic Party
KGB	Komitet Gosudarstvennoi Bezopasnosti: Soviet security and intelligence service (1954–91)
KHAD	Afghan security service
KI	Komitet Informatsii: Soviet foreign intelligence agency (1947–51), initially combining foreign intelligence directorates of MGB and GRU

KMT	Kuomintang (Chinese Nationalists)
Komsomol	Communist Youth League
KR Line	Counter-intelligence department in KGB residencies
KUTV	Kommunisticheskii Universitet Trudiashchikhsia Vostoka: Communist University of the Toilers of the East
LDP	Liberal Democratic Party (Japan)
LLB	live letter-box
MEISON	All-Ethiopian Socialist Movement
MGB	Ministerstvo Gosudarstvennoi Bezopasnosti: Soviet Ministry of State Security (1946–54)
MGIMO	Moscow State Institute for International Relations
MI5	UK security service
MI6	alternative designation for SIS (UK)
MITI	Ministry of International Trade and Industry (Japan)
MLSh	Mezhdunarodnaya Leninskaya Shkola: International Lenin School
MPLA	Movimento Popular de Libertação de Angola
MVD	Ministerstvo Vnutrennikh Del: Soviet Ministry of Internal Affairs
N Line	illegal support department in KGB residencies
NAM	Non-Aligned Movement
NATO	North Atlantic Treaty Organization
NKGB	Narodnyi Kommissariat Gosudarstvennoi Bezopasnosti: Soviet security and intelligence service (1941–46; within NKVD, 1941–43)
NKVD	Narodnyi Kommissariat Vnutrennikh Del: People's Commissariat for Internal Affairs (incorporated state security, 1922–23, 1934–43)
NPUP	National Progressive Unionist Party (Egypt)
NSA	National Security [SIGINT] Agency (USA)
NSC	National Security Council (USA)
NSS	National Security Service (Somalia)
NSZRiS	People's [anti-Bolshevik] Union for Defence of Country and Freedom
NTS	National Labour Alliance (Soviet émigré social-democratic movement)
OAU	Organization of African Unity
OGPU	Obedinennoe Gosudarstvennoe Politicheskoe

	Upravlenie: Soviet security and intelligence service, 1923–34)
Okhrana	Tsarist security service, 1881–1917
OMS	Comintern international liaison department
OSS	Office of Strategic Services (USA)
OT	Operational Technical Support (FCD)
OUN	Organization of Ukrainian Nationalists
OZNA	Yugoslav security and intelligence service; predecessor of UDBA
PAIGC	Partido Africano da Independência da Guiné e Cabo Verde
PCA	Algerian Communist Party
PCF	French Communist Party
PCI	Italian Communist Party
PCP	Portuguese Communist Party
PDP	Partido del Pueblo (Panama)
PDPA	Afghan Communist Party
PDRY	People's Democratic Republic of [South] Yemen
PFLP	Popular Front for the Liberation of Palestine
PLO	Palestine Liberation Organization
PPP	Pakistan People's Party
PR Line	political intelligence department in KGB residencies
PRI	Partido Revolucionario Institucional (Mexico)
PSOE	Spanish Socialist Party
PUK	Patriotic Union of Kurdistan
PUWP	Polish United Workers [Communist] Party
RCMP	Royal Canadian Mounted Police
RENAMO	Resistência Nacional Moçambicana
RYAN	*raketno-yadernoe napadenie* (nuclear missile attack)
SACP	South African Communist Party (previously CPSA)
SADUM	Central Asian Spiritual Directorate of Muslims
SALT	Strategic Arms Limitation Talks
SAM	Soviet surface-to-air missile
SB	Polish security and intelligence service
SCD	Second Chief [Internal Security and Counter-Intelligence] Directorate (KGB)
SDECE	French foreign intelligence service; predecessor of DGSE
SDI	US Strategic Defense Initiative ('Star Wars')

SDR	Somali Democratic Republic
SED	Socialist Unity [Communist] Party (GDR)
SIGINT	intelligence derived from interception and analysis of signals
SIN	Servicio de Inteligencia Nacional (Peru)
SIS	Secret Intelligence Service (UK)
SK Line	Soviet colony department in KGB residencies
SKP	Communist Party of Finland
SNASP	Serviço Nacional de Segurança Popular (Mozambique)
SNI	Serviço Nacional de Informações (Brazil)
SOE	Special Operations Executive (UK)
SPC	Sindh Provincial Committee
SPD	Social Democratic Party (FRG)
Spetsnaz	Soviet special forces
SR	Socialist Revolutionary
SRC	Supreme Revolutionary Council (Somalia)
SRSP	Somali Revolutionary Socialist Party
S&T	scientific and technological intelligence
Stapo	Austrian police security service
Stasi	GDR Ministry of State Security
Stavka	Wartime Soviet GHQ/high command
StB	Czechoslovak security and intelligence service
SVR	Sluzhba Vneshnei Razvedki: Russian (post-Soviet) foreign intelligence service
SWAPO	South-West Africa People's Association
TUC	Trades Union Congress (UK)
UAR	United Arab Republic
UB	Polish security and intelligence service; predecessor of SB
UDBA	Yugoslav security and intelligence service
UNITA	União Nacional para a Independência Total de Angola
VPK	Voenno-promyshlennaya Komissiya: Soviet Military Industrial Commission
VTNRP	Voenno-Trudovaya Narodnaya Revolyutsionnaya Partiya: Military-Labour People's Revolutionary Party; Russian name for anti-Chinese underground in XUAR

VVR	Supreme Military Council (anti-Bolshevik Ukrainian underground)
WCC	World Council of Churches
WPC	World Peace Council
X Line	S&T department in KGB residencies
XUAR	Xinjiang Uighur Autonomous Region of China
YAR	[North] Yemen Arab Republic
YSP	[South] Yemeni Socialist Party
ZANLA	Zimbabwe African Liberation Army
ZANU	Zimbabwe African National Union
ZAPU	Zimbabwe African People's Union
ZIPRA	Zimbabwe People's Revolutionary Army

The Transliteration of Russian and Arabic Names

For ease of reference to published sources, when referring to authors and titles of Russian publications in the notes and bibliography we have followed the Library of Congress system usually used in library catalogues.

In the text we have followed a simplified version of the more readable system used by the US Board on Geographic Names and BBC Monitoring Service. There are thus occasional discrepancies between the transliteration of names in the text and those of authors and titles in the notes and bibliography. Simplifications include the substitution in surnames of 'y' for 'ii' (Trotsky rather than Trotskii, as in the Library of Congress system) and 'yi' (Semichastny rather than Semichastnyi). For first names we have substituted 'i' for 'ii' (Yuri rather than Yurii). Instead of initial 'ia', 'ie' and 'iu' we use 'ya', 'ye' and 'yu'. Soft and hard signs have been omitted. In cases where a mildly deviant English version of a well-known Russian name has become firmly established, we have retained that version, for example: Beria, *Izvestia*, Joseph (Stalin) and the anglicized names of Tsars.

Since there is no generally accepted system of transliterating Arabic names into English, we have tried to follow what we believe is best current practice (for example, Ahmad and Muhammad rather than Ahmed and Mohammed). Where there is a well-established English version of an Arabic name, we use this rather than a more technically correct transliteration: for example, Gamal Abdel Nasser (rather than Abd al-Nasir) and Saddam Hussein (rather than Husain). The same applies to Anglophone and Francophone names of Arabic origin: for example, Ahmed (rather than Ahmad) Sékou Touré. Once again, occasional discrepancies will be found between the text and the notes/bibliography.

Foreword:
Vasili Mitrokhin and His Archive

On 9 April 1992 a scruffy, shabbily dressed seventy-year-old Russian arrived in the capital of a newly independent Baltic state by the overnight train from Moscow for a pre-arranged meeting with officers of the British Secret Intelligence Service (SIS, also known as MI6) at the offices of the new British embassy. He began by producing his passport and other documents which identified him as Vasili Nikitich Mitrokhin, a former senior archivist in the First Chief (Foreign Intelligence) Directorate of the KGB. SIS then took the unprepossessing (and hitherto unpublished) photograph of him which appears in the illustrations.

Mitrokhin's first visit to the embassy had taken place a month earlier when he arrived pulling a battered case on wheels and wearing the same shabby clothes, which he had put on before leaving Moscow in order to attract as little attention as possible from the border guards at the Russian frontier. Since he had an image of the British as rather stuffy and 'a bit of a mystery', he made his first approach to the Americans. Apparently overwhelmed by asylum seekers, however, US embassy staff failed to grasp Mitrokhin's importance and told him to return at a later date. Mitrokhin moved on instead to the British embassy and asked to speak to someone in authority. The junior diplomat who came to the reception area struck him as unexpectedly 'young, attractive and sympathetic', as well as a fluent Russian speaker. Used to the male-dominated world of Soviet diplomacy, Mitrokhin was also surprised that the diplomat was a woman. He told her he had brought with him samples of top-secret material from the KGB archives. Had the diplomat (who prefers not to be identified) dismissed him as a down-at-heel asylum seeker trying to sell bogus secrets, this book and its predecessor would probably never have been written. Happily, however, she asked to see some of the material which Mitrokhin had brought with him, concealed in his suitcase beneath the bread, sausages, drink and change of clothing which he had packed for his journey, and asked if he would like tea. While Mitrokhin drank his first ever cup of English tea, the diplomat read some of his notes, quickly grasped their potential importance, then questioned him about them. Since the embassy contained no intelligence station, he agreed to return a month later to meet representatives from SIS's London headquarters.

At his meeting with SIS officers on 9 April, Mitrokhin produced another 2,000 pages from his private archive and told the extraordinary story of how, while supervising the transfer of the entire foreign intelligence archive from the overcrowded offices of the Lubyanka in central Moscow to the new FCD headquarters at Yasenevo, near the outer ring road, between 1972 and 1982, he had almost every day smuggled handwritten notes and extracts from the files out of the archives in his pockets and hidden them beneath his family dacha. When the move was complete, he continued removing top-secret material for another two years until his retirement in 1984. The notes which Mitrokhin showed SIS officers revealed that he had had access even to the holy of holies in the foreign intelligence archives: the files which revealed the real identities and 'legends' of the elite corps of KGB 'illegals' living abroad under deep cover posing as foreign nationals. After a further meeting with SIS in the Baltic, Mitrokhin paid a secret visit to Britain in the autumn to discuss plans for his defection. On 7 November 1992, the seventy-fifth anniversary of the Bolshevik Revolution,* SIS exfiltrated Mitrokhin, his family and his entire archive, packed in six large containers, out of Russia in a remarkable operation the details of which still remain secret.

Those who have had access to the Mitrokhin archive since its arrival in Britain have been amazed by its contents. In the view of the FBI, it is 'the most complete and extensive intelligence ever received from any source'.[1] The CIA calls it 'the biggest CI [counter-intelligence] bonanza of the post-war period'. A report by the all-party British Intelligence and Security Committee (ISC) reveals that a series of other Western intelligence agencies have also proved

---

* The old Russian calendar was thirteen days behind the Western calendar which was adopted after the October Revolution. Since 1918 the anniversary of the Revolution has thus fallen on 7 November rather than 25 October.

'extremely grateful' for the numerous CI leads provided by Mitrokhin's material.[2] The Sluzhba Vneshnei Razvedki (SVR), the post-Soviet successor of the FCD, at first refused to believe that such a massive haemorrhage of top-secret intelligence records could possibly have occurred. When a German magazine reported in December 1996 that a former KGB officer had defected to Britain with 'the names of hundreds of Russian spies', the SVR spokeswoman, Tatyana Samolis, instantly ridiculed the story as 'absolute nonsense'. '"Hundreds of people"! That just doesn't happen!' she declared. 'Any defector could get the name of one, two, perhaps three agents – but not hundreds!'[3] In reality, as both the SVR and the internal security and intelligence service, the Federalnaya Sluzhba Bezopasnosti (FSB), now realize, the Mitrokhin Archive includes details not just of hundreds but of thousands of Soviet agents and intelligence officers around the globe.

The Mitrokhin Archive contains extraordinary detail on KGB operations in Europe and North America, which formed the subject of our first volume. But there is also much on the even less well-known Cold War activities of the KGB in the Third World,* which pass almost unmentioned in most histories both of Soviet foreign relations and of developing countries. The lucid synthesis of scholarly research on Soviet foreign policy by Caroline Kennedy-Pipe, *Russia and the World, 1917–1991*, for example, contains barely a mention of the KGB, save for a brief reference to its role in the invasion of Afghanistan.[4] By contrast, no account of American Cold War policy in the Third World omits the role of the Central Intelligence Agency (CIA). The result has been a curiously lopsided history of the secret Cold War in the developing world – the intelligence equivalent of the sound of one hand clapping. The generally admirable *Oxford Companion to Politics of the World*, for instance, contains an article on the CIA but none on the KGB or its post-Soviet successors.[5] As this volume of the Mitrokhin Archive seeks

---

* The 'Third World', despite a number of anomalies, remains 'a convenient shorthand' for the states of Africa, Asia, Latin America and the Middle East; Krieger (ed.), *The Oxford Companion to Politics of the World*, pp. 834–5. The attempt to replace 'Third World' by the concept of a North–South divide between an economically advanced Northern hemisphere and a less developed South creates significantly more anomalies – among them the fact that the Sahara, the Middle East and most of Asia lie in the Northern hemisphere, while Australasia is in the South.

to show, however, the role of the KGB in Soviet policy towards the Third World was even more important than that of the CIA in US policy. For a quarter of a century, the KGB, unlike the CIA, believed that the Third World was the arena in which it could win the Cold War.

Much of the story of Mitrokhin's career was told in *The Sword and the Shield: The Mitrokhin Archive and the Secret History of the KGB* (hereafter referred to as volume 1).[6] Some parts of it, however, can now be revealed for the first time. For fear that the FSB would make life uncomfortable for some of his surviving relatives, Mitrokhin was unwilling while we were working on volume 1 to include any details of his early life – even his exact date of birth. He was born, the second of five children, on 3 March 1922 in central Russia at the village of Yurasovo in Ryazan oblast (province). Ryazan is probably best known in the West as the birthplace of the Nobel laureate Ivan Petrovich Pavlov, discoverer of the 'conditioned reflex' through his work with what became known as 'Pavlov's dogs'. Unlike Mitrokhin, who became a secret dissident, Pavlov was often openly at odds with the Soviet authorities but, protected by his international renown, was allowed to carry on working in his laboratory until he died in 1936 at the age of eighty-seven. Most of Mitrokhin's childhood was spent in Moscow, where his father was able to find work as a decorator, but the family kept its links with Yurasovo, where, despite the bitter cold, he acquired a deep and abiding love of the Ryazan countryside and the forests of central Russia. English forests, by contrast, were a disappointment to him – too small, too few and insufficiently remote. In retirement near London there were few things he missed more on his long winter walks than the sight of a fresh snowfall in the forest.[7]

Mitrokhin's interest in archives started as a teenage fascination with historical documents. After leaving school, he completed his compulsory military service in the artillery, then began studying at the Historical Archives Institute in Moscow. Such was the extraordinary importance which the Stalinist regime attached to its files that, even after Hitler's invasion in the summer of 1941, Mitrokhin was allowed to continue training as an archivist instead of being conscripted to defend the Soviet Union in its hour of supreme peril. He thus took no part in the great battles at Moscow, Leningrad and Stalingrad which helped to make the Eastern Front both the longest and the bloodiest front in the history of warfare. Instead, he was sent with a group of trainee archivists to Kazakhstan, far beyond the furthest limit of the German advance, probably to work on some of the files of suspect national minorities and prisoners in the Gulag who were deported in wartime, usually in horrendous conditions, to central Asia. Losing his early ambition to become an archivist, Mitrokhin managed to enrol at the Kharkov Higher Juridical Institute, which was evacuated to Kazakhstan after the German conquest of Ukraine. After the liberation of Ukraine, he returned with the Institute to Kharkov. His memories of the brutal punishment of many thousands of 'anti-Soviet' Ukrainians sometimes gave him nightmares in later life. 'I was deep in horrors,' was all he would tell me about his experiences. After graduating in Kharkov in 1944, he became a lawyer first with the civil police (militia), then with the military procurator's office. He did well enough to attract the attention of the MGB (predecessor of the KGB), which in 1946 sent him for a two-year course at the Higher Diplomatic School in Moscow to prepare him for a career in foreign intelligence which he began in 1948.[8]

Mitrokhin's first five years as an intelligence officer coincided with the paranoid, final phase of the Stalin era, when he and his colleagues were ordered to track down Titoist and Zionist conspirators, whose mostly non-existent plots preyed on the disturbed mind of the ageing dictator. His first and longest foreign posting before Stalin's death in 1953 was to the Middle East, of which he was later reluctant to talk because it involved the penetration and exploitation of the Russian Orthodox Church – an aspect of KGB operations for which, like the persecution of the dissidents, he later developed an especial loathing.[9] Mitrokhin had happier memories of subsequent short tours of duty which took him to such diverse destinations as Iceland, the Netherlands, Pakistan and Australia.

The most memorable of these tours of duty was as a member of the KGB escort which accompanied the Soviet team to the Melbourne Olympics which opened in October 1956. For the KGB the Games threatened to be a security nightmare. Two years earlier the KGB resident in Canberra, Vladimir Petrov, had become the most senior Soviet defector since the Second World War. Photographs of his tearful wife, Evdokia, also a KGB officer, losing her shoe in a mêlée at Sydney airport as Soviet security guards hustled her on to a plane to take her back to Russia, then escaping from their clutches when the aircraft stopped to refuel at Darwin, had made front-page news around the world. As Mitrokhin was aware, both the Petrovs had been sentenced to death after a secret trial *in absentia* and plans had been made by KGB assassins to hunt them down (though the plans were never successfully implemented).[10] The Centre was determined that this recent embarrassment should not be compounded by defections from the Soviet competitors at Melbourne. Further anxieties arose from the fact that, as the Duke of Edinburgh formally opened the games on the Melbourne cricket ground, Soviet tanks had entered Budapest to crush the Hungarian rising. The Olympic water-polo match between Hungary and the Soviet Union had to be abandoned after a fracas in the pool. At the end of the games the KGB was alarmed by the sudden decision of the organizers that all the athletes should mingle together during the closing ceremonies (thus making it easier to defect) instead of parading, as at previous games, in their national teams. In the end, however, the KGB considered its Melbourne mission a qualified success. There were no defections and the Soviet team emerged as clear winners with ninety-eight medals (including thirty-seven golds) to the Americans' seventy-four and a series of individual triumphs which included easy victories by Vladimir Kuts in both the 5,000 and 10,000 metres.

The 1956 Olympics were to be Mitrokhin's last tour of duty in the West. In the aftermath of Khrushchev's 'Secret Speech' earlier in the year denouncing Stalin's 'cult of personality' and his 'exceedingly serious and grave perversions of Party principles, of Party democracy [and] of revolutionary legality', Mitrokhin had become too outspoken for his own good. Though his criticisms of the way the KGB had been run were mild by Western standards, he acquired a reputation as a malcontent and was denounced by one of his superiors as 'a member of the awkward squad'. Soon after returning from Melbourne, Mitrokhin was moved from operations to the FCD archives, where for some years his main job was answering queries from other departments and provincial KGBs. His only other foreign posting, in the late 1960s, was to the archives department of the large KGB mission at Karlshorst in the suburbs of East Berlin. While at Karlshorst in 1968, he followed with secret excitement the attempt just across the German border by the reformers of the Prague Spring to create what the Kremlin saw as an unacceptably unorthodox 'Socialism with a human face'. Like Khrushchev's 'Secret Speech' twelve years before, the invasion of Czechoslovakia by the forces of the Warsaw Pact in August 1968 was an important staging post in what Mitrokhin called his 'intellectual odyssey'. He was able to listen in secret to reports from Czechoslovakia on the Russian-language services of the BBC World Service, Radio Liberty, Deutsche Welle and the Canadian Broadcasting Company, but had no one with whom he felt able to share his outrage at the invasion. The crushing of the Prague Spring proved, he believed, that the Soviet system was unreformable.

After his return to Moscow from East Germany, Mitrokhin continued to listen to Western broadcasts, though, because of Soviet jamming, he had frequently to switch wavelengths in order to find an audible station. Among the news which made the greatest impression on him were items about the *Chronicle of Current Events*, a *samizdat* journal first produced by dissidents in 1968 to circulate news on the struggle against Soviet abuses of human rights. By the beginning of the 1970s Mitrokhin's political views were deeply influenced by the dissident struggle, which he was able to follow in KGB files as well as Western broadcasts. 'I was a loner', he later told me, 'but I now knew that I was not alone.' Though Mitrokhin never had any thought of aligning himself openly with the human rights movement, the example of the *Chronicle of Current Events* and other *samizdat* productions helped to inspire him with the idea of producing a classified variant of the dissidents' attempts to document the iniquities of the Soviet system. He had earlier been attracted by the idea of writing an in-house official history of the FCD. Now a rather different project began to form in his mind – that of compiling his own private unofficial record of the foreign operations of the KGB. His opportunity came in June 1972 when he was put in charge of moving the FCD archives to Yasenevo. Had the hoard of top-secret material which he smuggled out of Yasenevo been discovered, the odds are that, after a secret trial, he would have ended up in a KGB execution cellar with a bullet in the back of his head.

For those whose ideals have been corroded by the widespread cynicism of the early twenty-first-century West, the fact that Mitrokhin was prepared to risk his life for twenty years for a cause in which he passionately believed is almost too difficult to comprehend. Almost equally hard to grasp is Mitrokhin's willingness to devote himself throughout that period to compiling and preserving a secret archive which he knew might never see the light of day. For any Western author it is almost impossible to understand how a writer could devote all his or her energy and creative talent for many years to secret writing which might never be publicly revealed. Yet some of the greatest Russian writers of the Soviet era did precisely that. No biography of any Western writer contains a death-bed scene comparable to the description by the widow of Mikhail Bulgakov of how in 1940 she helped him out of bed for the last time so that he could satisfy himself before he died that his great, unpublished masterpiece, *The Master and Margarita*, was still in its hiding place. Against all the odds, *The Master and Margarita* survived to be published a quarter of a century later. Though Alexander Solzhenitsyn's greatest work was published in his own lifetime (initially mostly in the West rather than the Soviet Union), when he began writing he told himself, like Bulgakov, that he 'must write simply to ensure that [the truth] was not forgotten, that posterity might some day come to know of it. Publication in my own lifetime I must shut out of my mind, out of my dreams.'[11]

Though Mitrokhin never had any literary pretensions, the survival of his archive is, in its own way, as remarkable as that of *The Master and Margarita*. Once he reached Britain, he was determined that, despite legal and security difficulties, as much as possible of its contents should be published. After the publication in 1999 of *The Sword and the Shield,* the Intelligence and Security Committee held a detailed enquiry at the Cabinet Office to which both Vasili Mitrokhin and I gave evidence. As the ISC's unanimous report makes clear, it was left in no doubt about Mitrokhin's motivation:

The Committee believes that he is a man of remarkable commitment and courage, who risked imprisonment or death in his determination that the truth should be told about the real nature of the KGB and their activities, which he believed were betraying the interests of his own country and people. He succeeded in this, and we wish to record formally our admiration for his achievement.[12]

While in Britain, scarcely a week passed without Mitrokhin re-reading his papers, responding to questions on them and checking translations. On the eve of his death on 23 January 2004 he was still making plans for the publication of parts of his archive.

With his wife Nina, a distinguished medical specialist,[13] Mitrokhin was also able to resume the foreign travels which he had been forced to discontinue a generation earlier when he was transferred from FCD operations to archives. Mitrokhin's first visit to Paris made a particular impression on him. He had read the KGB file on the defection in Paris of the Kirov Ballet's greatest dancer, Rudolf Nureyev, and had followed with personal outrage the planning of operations (happily never successfully implemented) to break one or both of Nureyev's legs with the aim – absurdly expressed in euphemistic KGB jargon – of 'lessening his professional skills'.[14] In October 1992, while Mitrokhin was meeting SIS in Britain to make final plans for the exfiltration of his family and archive in the following month, Nureyev, by then seriously ill with Aids, was directing his last ballet, *Bayaderka*, at the Paris Opera. When, after the performance, Nureyev appeared on stage in a wheelchair, wrapped in a tartan rug, he received a standing ovation. Many in the audience wept, as did many of the mourners three months later during his burial at the Russian cemetery of Sainte Geneviève des Bois in Paris. On his visit to Paris, Mitrokhin visited Nureyev's tomb as well as the graves of other Russian exiles, among them both White Russian refugees from the Bolshevik Revolution and dissidents of the Soviet era. Though also deeply interested in other Western sites associated with Russian émigrés, from Ivy House in London, home of the great ballerina Anna Pavlova, to the New York Russian community at Brighton Beach, his travels ranged far more widely. After the death of Nina in 1999, he flew around the world on his British passport. Only a year before his own death in 2004, he went for a walking holiday in New Zealand.

Save for his love of travel, Mitrokhin mostly remained, as he had always been, a man of simple tastes, preferring his own home-cooked Russian cabbage soup, *shchi*, to the elaborate cuisine of expensive restaurants. His favourite London restaurants were 'The Stockpot' chain, which specialize in good-value 'home-cooked' menus. Though Mitrokhin himself drank little, he would usually produce wine when entertaining friends and liked to splash out for family birthdays and major celebrations. On a visit to the Ritz the family splashed out more than it intended, having failed to appreciate the cost of a round of vintage cognacs. Mitrokhin was no more motivated by fame than by money. It was only after long persuasion that he agreed to include any of his career in volume 1, and only a few months before publication that he consented to the use of his real name rather than a pseudonym. Strenuous efforts by the media to track Mitrokhin down after publication were, happily, unsuccessful. He was too private a person and had arrived in Britain too late in life with too little experience of the West to have coped with the glare of publicity. Mitrokhin had, however, perfected the art of being inconspicuous and travelled unnoticed the length and breadth of the United Kingdom on his senior citizen's rail-card. Until his late seventies he also remained remarkably fit. Intelligence officers from a number of countries were mildly disconcerted by his unselfconscious habit, when meetings dragged on, of dropping to the floor and doing a set of press-ups.

Mitrokhin was both an inspiring and, at times, a difficult man to work with while I wrote the two volumes of the Mitrokhin Archive.[15] In his view, the material he had risked his life to smuggle out of KGB archives revealed 'the truth'. Though he accepted the need to put it in context, he had little interest in the work of scholars however distinguished, which failed, in his view, to recognize the central role of the KGB in Soviet society. Mitrokhin tolerated, rather than welcomed, my use of such works and a wide range of other sources to complement, corroborate and fill gaps in his own unique archive.[16] My admiration for some of the books which neglected the intelligence dimension of twentieth-century international relations was beyond his comprehension. Though Mitrokhin did not, alas, live to see the publication of this volume, it was virtually complete by the time of his death and I am not aware of any interpretation by me of material in his archive with which he disagreed. The opportunity he gave me to work on his archive has been an extraordinary privilege.

Since the original material in the Mitrokhin archive remains classified, the content of this second volume, like that of the first, was examined in great detail by an 'interdepartmental working group' in Whitehall before clearance for publication received ministerial approval.[17] Though the complex issues involved caused extensive delays in publication, I am grateful to the working group for the time and care they have taken, and for clearing all but about two pages of the original text.

As in volume 1, codenames (also known as 'worknames' in the case of KGB officers) appear in the text in capitals. It is important to note that the KGB gave codenames not merely to those who worked for it but also to those whom it targeted and to some others (such as foreign officials and ministers) who had no connection with it. Codenames are, in themselves, no evidence that the individuals to whom they refer were conscious or witting KGB agents or sources – or even that they were aware of being targeted for recruitment or to influence operations. At the risk of stating the obvious, it should also be emphasized that the vast majority of those outside the Soviet Union who expressed pro-Soviet opinions had, of course, no connection with the KGB.

Christopher Andrew

Acknowledgements

I am very grateful to those colleagues who commented on parts of this book during the brief interval between the clearance of the text by the Whitehall interdepartmental working group and its delivery to the publishers: Mr Geoffrey Archer, Sir Nicholas Barrington, Professor Chris Bayly, Dr Susan Bayly, Mr Kristian Gustafson, Professor Jonathan Haslam, Mr Alan Judd, Professor John Lonsdale, Dr Gabriella Ramos, Dr David Sneath and Sir Roger Tomkys. I also owe a considerable debt to the intellectual stimulation provided by the remarkable group of young scholars from around the world in the Cambridge University Intelligence Seminar who are transforming the academic study of intelligence history. While writing this book, I have been especially fortunate to have the opportunity to supervise and learn from the doctoral research of the outstanding Australian historian and Gates Scholar Ms Julie Elkner, who is conducting path-breaking work on the image of the secret policeman in Soviet and post-Soviet culture. I have also benefited from her extensive knowledge of published sources.

Christopher Andrew

1

Introduction:
'The World Was Going Our Way'
The Soviet Union, the Cold War and
the Third World

Communism, claimed Karl Marx and Friedrich Engels, would change not simply the history of Europe and the West but the history of the world. Their *Communist Manifesto* of 1848, though chiefly directed to industrialized Europe, ended with a clarion call to global revolution: 'The proletarians have nothing to lose but their chains. They have a world to win. Working men of all countries, unite!' (Working women, it was assumed, would follow in the train of male revolutionaries.) After the Bolshevik seizure of power in October 1917, Vladimir Ilyich Lenin hailed not only the triumph of the Russian Revolution but the beginning of 'world revolution': 'Our cause is an international cause, and so long as a revolution does not take place in all countries . . . our victory is only half a victory, or perhaps less.' Though world revolution had become a distant dream for most Bolsheviks by the time Lenin died seven years later, he never lost his conviction that the inevitable collapse of the colonial empires would one day bring global revolution in its wake:

Millions and hundreds of millions – actually the overwhelming majority of the world's population – are now coming out as an independent and active revolutionary factor. And it should be perfectly clear that, in the coming decisive battles of the world revolution, this movement of the majority of the world's population, originally aimed at national liberation, will turn against capitalism and imperialism and will, perhaps, play a much more revolutionary role than we have been led to expect.[1]

The Third Communist International (Comintern), founded in Moscow in March 1919, set itself 'the goal of fighting, by every means, even by force of arms, for the overthrow of the international bourgeoisie and the creation of an international Soviet republic'. For the next year or more, Comintern's Chairman, Grigori Yevseyevich Zinoviev, lived in a revolutionary dream-world in which Bolshevism was about to conquer Europe and sweep across the planet. On the second anniversary of the Bolshevik Revolution, he declared his hope that, within a year, 'the Communist International will triumph in the entire world'. At the Congress of the Peoples of the East, convened at Baku in 1920 to promote colonial revolution, delegates excitedly waved swords, daggers and revolvers in the air when Zinoviev called on them to wage a *jihad* against imperialism and capitalism. Except in Mongolia, however, where the Bolsheviks installed a puppet regime, all attempts to spread their revolution beyond Soviet borders foundered either because of lack of popular support or because of successful resistance by counter-revolutionary governments.[2]

By the mid-1920s Moscow's main hopes were pinned on China, where the Soviet Politburo had pushed the Chinese Communist Party (CCP) into alliance with the Nationalist Kuomintang (KMT). The KMT leader, Chiang Kai-shek, declared in public: 'If Russia aids the Chinese revolution, does that mean that she wants China to apply Communism? No, she wants us to carry out the national revolution.' Privately, he believed the opposite, convinced that 'What the Russians call "Internationalism" and "World Revolution" are nothing but old-fashioned imperialism.' The Soviet leadership, however, believed that it could get the better of Chiang. He should, said Stalin, 'be squeezed like a lemon and then thrown away'. In the event, it was the CCP which became the lemon. Having gained control of Shanghai in April 1927 thanks to a Communist-led rising, Chiang began a systematic massacre of the Communists who had captured it for him. The CCP, on Stalin's instructions, replied with a series of armed risings. All were disastrous failures. Moscow's humiliation was compounded by a police raid on the Soviet consulate in Beijing which uncovered a mass of documents on Soviet espionage.[3]

In an attempt to generate new support for Lenin's vision of a liberated post-colonial world, the League Against Imperialism was founded early in 1927, shortly before the Chinese débâcles, by the great virtuoso of Soviet front organizations, Willi Münzenberg, affectionately described by his 'life partner', Babette Gross, as 'the patron saint of fellow travellers' with a remarkable gift for uniting broad sections of the left under inconspicuous Communist leadership. Those present at the inaugural congress in Brussels included Jawaharlal Nehru, later the first Prime Minister of independent India, and Josiah Gumede, President of the African National Congress and head of the League's South African section. One of the British delegates, Fenner Brockway of the British Independent Labour Party, wrote afterwards: 'From the platform the conference hall was a remarkable sight. Every race seemed to be there. As one looked on the sea of black, brown, yellow and white faces, one felt that here at last was something approaching a Parliament of Mankind.'

The League, Brockway believed, 'may easily prove to be one of the most significant movements for equality and freedom in world history'.[4] But it was not to be. Within a few years the League had faded into oblivion, and Comintern, though it survived until 1943 as an obedient, though drastically purged, auxiliary of Soviet foreign policy and Soviet intelligence,[5] achieved nothing of importance in the Third World. The colonial empires remained intact until the Second World War, and neither the foreign policy nor the intelligence agencies of Joseph Stalin made any serious attempt to hasten their demise. Under his brutal dictatorship, the dream of world revolution quickly gave way to the reality of 'Socialism in one country', a Soviet Union surrounded by hostile 'imperialist' states and deeply conscious of its own vulnerability.

During the xenophobic paranoia of Stalin's Terror, Comintern representatives in Moscow from around the world lived in constant fear of denunciation and execution. Many were at even greater risk than their Soviet colleagues. By early 1937, following investigations by the NKVD (predecessor of the KGB), Stalin had convinced himself that Comintern was a hotbed of subversion and foreign espionage. He told Georgi Dmitrov, who had become its General Secretary three years earlier, 'All of you there in the Comintern are working in the hands of the enemy.' Nikolai Yezhov, the head of the NKVD whose sadism and diminutive stature combined to give him the nickname 'Poison Dwarf', echoed his master's voice. 'The biggest spies', he told Dmitrov, 'were working in the Communist International.' Each night, unable to sleep, the foreign Communists and Comintern officials who had been given rooms at the Hotel Lux in the centre of Moscow waited for the sound of a car drawing up at the hotel entrance in the early hours, then heard the heavy footsteps of NKVD men echo along the corridors, praying that they would stop at someone else's door. Those who escaped arrest listened with a mixture of relief and horror as the night's victims were taken from their rooms and driven away, never to return. Some, for whom the nightly suspense became too much, shot themselves or jumped to their deaths in the inner courtyard. Only a minority of the hotel's foreign guests escaped the knock on the door. Many of their death warrants were signed personally by Stalin.[6] Mao's ferocious security chief, Kang Sheng, who had been sent to Moscow to learn his trade, enthusiastically co-operated with the NKVD in the hunt for mostly imaginary traitors among Chinese émigrés.[7]

The most enduring impact of Soviet intelligence on the Third World before the Second World War was thus the liquidation of potential leaders of post-war independence movements.[8] Ho Chi-Minh, Deng Xiaoping, Jomo Kenyatta and other future Third World leaders who studied in Moscow at the Comintern-run Communist University of the Toilers of the East between the wars[9] were fortunate to leave before the Terror began. Kenyatta, in particular, would have been an obvious target. His lecturers complained that 'his attitude to the Soviet Union verges on cynicism'.[10] When his fellow student, the South African Communist Edwin Mofutsanyana, accused him of being 'a petty bourgeois', Kenyatta replied, 'I don't like this "petty" thing. Why don't you say I'm a big bourgeois?'[11] During the Terror such outrageously politically incorrect humour would have been promptly reported (if only because those who failed to report it would themselves be suspect), and the career of the future first Prime Minister and President of an independent Kenya would probably have ended prematurely in an NKVD execution cellar.

After victory in the Second World War, the Soviet Union, newly strengthened by the acquisition of an obedient Soviet bloc in eastern and central Europe, initially showed less interest in the Third World than after the Bolshevik Revolution. During the early years of the Cold War Soviet intelligence priorities were overwhelmingly concentrated on the struggle against what the KGB called 'the Main Adversary', the United States, and its principal allies. Stalin saw the world as divided into two irreconcilable camps – capitalist and Communist – with no room for compromise between the two. Non-Communist national liberation movements in the Third World were, like capital-

4

ists, class enemies. The decolonization of the great European overseas empires, which had begun in 1947 with the end of British rule in India, persuaded Stalin's ebullient successor, Nikita Khrushchev, to revive the Leninist dream. At the Twentieth Party Congress in 1956, as well as secretly denouncing Stalin's 'cult of personality', he publicly abandoned the two-camp theory, setting out to win support from former Western colonies which had won their independence:

The new period in world history which Lenin predicted has arrived, and the peoples of the East are playing an active part in deciding the destinies of the whole world, are becoming a new mighty factor in international relations.

Though one of the few major world leaders of peasant origins, Khrushchev had no doubt that the Soviet Union's break-neck industrialization in the 1930s provided a model for the newly independent former colonies to modernize their economies. 'Today', he declared, 'they need not go begging for up-to-date equipment to their former oppressors. They can get it in the socialist countries, without assuming any political or military commitments.' Many of the first generation of post-colonial leaders in the 1950s and 1960s, who blamed all their economic ills on their former colonial rulers, were happy to accept Khrushchev's offer.[12]

'In retrospect', writes the economic historian David Fieldhouse, 'it is one of the most astonishing features of post-1950 African history that there should have been so general an expectation that independence would lead to very rapid economic growth and affluence.'[13] Kwame Nkrumah, the leader of the first black African colony to gain its independence, claimed that Africa's hitherto slow industrial development was entirely the fault of colonial powers which had deliberately held back 'local economic initiative' in order to 'enrich alien investors': 'We have here, in Africa, everything necessary to become a powerful, modern, industrialized continent ... Africa, far from having inadequate resources, is probably better equipped for industrialization than almost any other region in the world.'[14]

In the euphoria of liberation from colonial rule there were many who, like Nkrumah, were seduced by anti-imperialist fantasy economics. Convinced that heavy industry was the key to rapid economic development, they welcomed inefficient Soviet steel mills and other heavy plant as symbols of modernity rather than potential industrial white elephants. In the small African state of Guinea alone during the Khrushchev era, the Soviet Union constructed an airport, a cannery, a sawmill, a refrigeration plant, a hospital, a polytechnic and a hotel as well as carrying out geological surveys and a series of research projects. The report presented to the Central Committee plenum which ousted Khrushchev in 1964 stated that during his decade in power the Soviet Union had undertaken about 6,000 projects in the Third World.[15] Khrushchev, the report implied, had allowed his enthusiasm for strengthening Soviet influence in developing countries to run away with him – at enormous cost to the Soviet economy.

Khrushchev, however, was supremely confident that the Soviet command economy, despite the scale of its investment in the Third World, was rapidly overhauling capitalism. 'It is true that you are richer than we are at present', he told Americans during his flamboyant coast-to-coast tour of the United States in 1959. 'But tomorrow we will be as rich as you. The next day? Even richer! But is there anything wrong with that?'[16] Khrushchev's optimism seemed less absurd at the time than it does now. The deputy leader of the British Labour Party, Aneurin Bevan, told the 1959 party conference that the triumph of nationalization and state planning in the Soviet Union proved that they were vastly superior to capitalism as a means of economic modernization: 'The [economic] challenge is going to come from Russia. The challenge is not going to come from the United States.'[17] The early achievements of the Soviet space programme encouraged wildly exaggerated expectations in the West as well as in the East of the ability of the Soviet economy to pioneer new technology. In 1957 the Soviet success in putting into orbit Sputnik 1, the first man-made satellite, had created a global sensation. President Dwight D. Eisenhower was taken aback by the 'wave of near hysteria' which swept the United States. Amid claims that America had suffered a scientific Pearl Harbor, the Governor of Michigan, G. Mennen Williams, expressed his inner anguish in verse:

Oh Little Sputnik, flying high
With made-in Moscow beep
You tell the world it's a Commie sky
And Uncle Sam's asleep.[18]

'How can we not rejoice, comrades,' asked Khrushchev in 1958, 'at the gigantic achievements of our industry? . . . What other state has ever built on such a scale? There never has been such a country!'[19]

Khrushchev was also enthused by the fiery rhetoric of the new generation of Third World leaders against both their former colonial masters and American imperialism. During his visit to the United States in 1959, he gave a speech to the General Assembly in New York, basking in the applause after his 'warm greetings from the bottom of my heart' to the independent states which had freed themselves from colonial rule:

Coming generations will highly appreciate the heroism of those who led the struggle for the independence of India and Indonesia, the United Arab Republic and Iraq, Ghana, Guinea and other states, just as the people of the United States today revere the memory of George Washington and Thomas Jefferson, who led the American people in their struggle for independence.

Khrushchev went on to denounce the imperialist exploitation which continued after the formal end of colonial rule:

The peoples of many of these countries have won political independence, but they are cruelly exploited by foreigners economically. Their oil and other natural wealth is plundered, it is taken out of the country for next to nothing, yielding huge profits to foreign exploiters.

Khrushchev's call for the plundered wealth to be returned as economic aid was music to the ears of many of his Third World listeners.[20]

The fact that neither the United States nor the European colonial powers yet took seriously the problems of racism within their own societies increased the popularity of anti-imperialist rhetoric. It now almost passes belief that, during the decade when most African colonies gained their independence, it was still legal for British landlords to put 'No Coloured' notices in their windows and illegal for African delegates to the United Nations in New York to travel on seats reserved for whites on the segregated buses of the Deep South. Because of Russia's lack of either African colonies or a black immigrant community, the racism of Russian society was far better concealed.[21]

Following the success of his brief visit to the United Nations in

1959, Khrushchev took the unprecedented decision to spend a month in New York as leader of the Soviet delegation at the autumn 1960 meeting of the UN General Assembly, which welcomed seventeen newly independent members, sixteen from Africa. While Khrushchev was bear-hugging the new African leaders, President Dwight D. Eisenhower went on a golfing holiday. With new African embassies opening in Washington, the President's chief of protocol became notorious for complaining about having to invite 'these niggers' to White House receptions.[22] Khrushchev, meanwhile, became joint sponsor of a draft UN declaration subsequently adopted in modified form as a 'Declaration on the Granting of Independence to Colonial Countries and Peoples', which denounced colonialism in all its forms and demanded immediate independence for all subjugated peoples. The abstention of the main Western powers merely served to enhance Moscow's prestige.[23] The fact that most still 'subjugated peoples' did not receive immediate independence meant that the Soviet Union was regularly able henceforth to complain that the colonial powers were defying a UN resolution.[24]

Khrushchev so enjoyed his time at the UN in the autumn of 1960 that he beat all previous records for loquacity, making a dozen speeches to the General Assembly totalling 300 pages of typescript. His performance was not, however, an unalloyed success. He was so outraged on 13 October by the speech of a delegate from the Philippines, who turned the issue of decolonization against him and claimed that eastern Europe had been 'swallowed up by the Soviet Union' and 'deprived of political and civil rights', that he began angrily pounding the table with his shoe. Afterwards Khrushchev told a member of the Soviet delegation who had missed his performance, 'Oh, you really missed something! It was such fun!' Despite their embarrassment, no one in the delegation dared to remonstrate with him.[25] With the heady experience of hearing Western imperialism publicly denounced by Third World leaders in the heartland of American capitalism still fresh in his mind, Khrushchev gave a secret speech in Moscow to Soviet ideological and propaganda 'workers' in January 1961, in which he declared that, by supporting the 'sacred' anti-imperialist struggle of colonies and newly independent states, the Soviet Union would both advance its own progress to Communism and 'bring imperialism to its knees'.[26]

The belief that the Cold War could be won in the Third World transformed the agenda of Soviet intelligence in ways that most Western historians have found difficult to credit. Eric Hobsbawm's brilliant history of the twentieth century concludes, like many others, that 'there is no real evidence that [the Soviet Union] planned to push forward the frontiers of communism by revolution until the middle 1970s, and even then the evidence suggests that the USSR made use of a favourable conjuncture it had not set out to create'.[27] KGB files show, however, that in 1961 there was already such a plan, though it was not of course publicly revealed. The Soviet Communist Party (CPSU) Programme of that year praised 'the liberation struggles of oppressed peoples' as one of 'the mainstream tendencies of social progress'. This message was enthusiastically received in the Centre (KGB headquarters). The youthful and dynamic chairman of the KGB, Aleksandr Shelepin, won Khrushchev's support for the use of national liberation movements and the forces of anti-imperialism in an aggressive new grand strategy against the 'Main Adversary' (the United States) in the Third World.[28] Though Khrushchev was soon to replace Shelepin with the more compliant and less ambitious Vladimir Semichastny, the KGB's grand strategy survived.

Grasping the extent of the KGB's ambitions in the Third World has been complicated by the legacy of McCarthyism. Just as the fraudulent inventions of Senator Joseph McCarthy's self-serving anti-Communist witch-hunt helped to blind liberal opinion to the reality of the unprecedented Soviet intelligence offensive against the United States,[29] so simplistic conspiracy theories of Soviet plans for world conquest made most non-conspiracy theorists sceptical of even realistic assessments of Soviet designs in the Third World. McCarthy and America's other anti-Communist conspiracy theorists were, albeit unconsciously, among the KGB's most successful Cold War agents of influence. Reaction against their risible exaggerations helps to account for the remarkable degree to which the KGB has been left out of Cold War history.

After Khrushchev himself was forced to step down in 1964 and replaced by Leonid Brezhnev, the belief that the Cold War could be won in the Third World was held with greater conviction in the Centre than in the Kremlin or the Foreign Ministry. The future head of KGB intelligence assessment, Nikolai Leonov, then a young foreign intelligence officer in the FCD Second (Latin American)

Department, was later to recall: 'Basically, of course, we were guided by the idea that the destiny of world confrontation between the United States and the Soviet Union, between Capitalism and Socialism, would be resolved in the Third World. This was the basic premise.'[30]

That strategy was enthusiastically supported by Yuri Andropov from the moment he succeeded Semichastny as KGB chairman in 1967. He told a meeting of the Second Chief Directorate (Internal Security and Counter-Intelligence) a year later:

One must understand that the struggle between the organs of state security and the special [intelligence] organs of the opponent in the present conditions reflect the present stage of a heightening of the class struggle. And this means that the struggle is more merciless. Today the same question is being decided as in the first days of Soviet power: who prevails over whom? Only today this question is being decided not within our country but within the framework of the whole world system, in a global struggle between two world systems.[31]

The initiative for the 'global struggle' came from the KGB rather than the Foreign Ministry. At the most dramatic moments of Soviet penetration of the Third World, from the establishment of the first Communist 'bridgehead' in the Western hemisphere (to use the KGB codename for Castro's Cuba) to the final, disastrous defence of the Communist regime in Afghanistan, the Centre had greater influence than the Foreign Ministry.

Andrei Gromyko, the long-serving Soviet Foreign Minister, is remembered by his almost equally long-serving ambassador in Washington, Anatoli Dobrynin, as 'a cautious man who opposed any serious confrontation with the United States':

. . . The Third World was not his prime domain. He believed that events there could not decisively influence our fundamental relations with the United States; that turned out to be a factor which he definitely underestimated. More than that, our Foreign Ministry traditionally was not really involved with the leaders of the liberation movements in the Third World, who were dealt with through the International Department of the party, headed by Secretary Boris Ponomarev. He despised Gromyko; the feeling was mutual.

The Soviet Union's forward policy in the Third World was thus led by the KGB with the support of the International Department of the CPSU Central Committee.[32] Khrushchev had nicknamed the Department's rigidly doctrinaire head 'Ponomar' (sacristan in the Orthodox Church). 'Ponomar', he said, 'is a valuable Party official but as orthodox as a Catholic priest.' Within the Politburo, the forward policy was also supported by the Party's leading ideologue, Mikhail Suslov, whose prestige during the 1970s was second only to Brezhnev's. 'Cloaked in the robe of doctrinal infallibility', recalls one Soviet diplomat, '[Suslov] regularly issued reminders of what he saw as the correct Marxist-Leninist policy.' Speaking *ex cathedra*, Suslov declared that the collapse of what remained of the Western colonial empires and the weakening of the capitalist system in the face of the onward march of socialism and progressive, anti-imperialist forces was 'historically inevitable'.[33]

Gromyko's frequent willingness for Andropov to take the initiative in the Third World reflected his own lack of interest in it. As Leonov later recalled:

The USSR [Foreign Ministry] and its head A. A. Gromyko were openly scornful with regard to the 'third world'. Andrei Andreyevich [Gromyko] visited and received his colleagues from small European states with greater pleasure than the disturbers of the peace from the countries of the 'third world'. Even the Politburo failed to convince him to visit the Near East, Africa, or Latin America. Trips to the countries of these regions were isolated incidents in his seemingly endless career as minister for foreign affairs.[34]

When taking initiatives in the Third World, Andropov was always careful not to appear to be treading on Gromyko's toes. 'Their personal relations', noted Dobrynin, 'were not bad, because Andropov was cautious enough not to interfere in Gromyko's everyday management of foreign policy, and Gromyko for his part respected Andropov's growing influence in the Politburo.' The two men gradually became co-sponsors of the major foreign policy proposals put before Brezhnev's Politburo.[35]

Further encouragement for a forward policy in the Third World came from the shift in the balance of power at the United Nations during the 1960s. With the rapid increase in newly independent states, the West lost its previous majority in the General Assembly. The Non-Aligned Movement (NAM) tended increasingly to vote with the Soviet bloc rather than the West, some of whose leading states were tainted by their imperial past. At the NAM conference which met at Belgrade in July 1969, the final communiqué pledged 'support for the heroic people of Vietnam' who were resisting American aggression, but made no significant mention of the Soviet invasion of Czechoslovakia in the previous year.[36] For the remainder of the Cold War, the KGB saw the Non-Aligned Movement as 'our natural allies'. 'The essential trend of their activities', declared the head of the First Chief (Foreign Intelligence) Directorate (FCD), Vladimir Aleksandrovich Kryuchkov, in 1984, 'is anti-imperialist.'[37]

The United States' defeat in Vietnam reinforced the Centre's confidence in its Third World strategy. The unprecedented TV coverage from Vietnam brought the horrors of war into the living rooms of Middle America and much of the world. It also gave dramatic global publicity to the anti-war movement in the United States, whose daily refrain, 'Hey, Hey, LBJ, How Many Kids Did You Kill Today?', helped to persuade President Lyndon B. Johnson not to run for re-election in 1968. Both Johnson and his successor, Richard Nixon, believed – wrongly – that an international Communist conspiracy lay behind American anti-war protest, particularly on university campuses. Richard Helms, the Director of Central Intelligence (DCI), later testified that, 'President Johnson was after this all the time.' So was Nixon. Though sceptical about the White House's conspiracy theories, Helms began operation CHAOS to discover the real extent of foreign influence on domestic dissent. In the course of the operation, the Agency began to spy illegally on American campus radicals. As Helms acknowledged: 'Should anyone learn of [CHAOS's] existence, it would prove most embarrassing for all concerned.' Though the negative findings of CHAOS failed to convince either Johnson or Nixon, it did lasting damage to the reputation of the CIA when the operation was revealed in the mid-1970s and provided further ammunition for KGB 'active measures'.[38]

Only a fortnight before the final American withdrawal from Saigon on 30 April 1975, Andropov still found it difficult to credit that the United States had really been defeated. He told a specially convened meeting on Vietnam in the FCD's Yasenevo headquarters:

Do you remember the Korean War and the course of its development? Then too the North Korean troops had occupied almost the whole territory of South Korea ... Then the Americans organized a major landing operation in the rear of the North Koreans, cutting off and devastating the main section of the North Korean army. In a matter of days the course of the war had changed. Now an extremely similar situation is taking shape. All the forces of North Vietnam have been sent to the south, to help the patriots. To all intents and purposes North Vietnam is defenceless. If the Americans undertake something similar to the Korean manoeuvre, then things may take a bad turn ... To all intents and purposes the road to [Hanoi] is open.

Not till Andropov saw the extraordinary TV pictures a fortnight later of Americans and some of their South Vietnamese allies being hurriedly rescued by helicopter from the roof of the US embassy as the Communist Vietcong made a triumphal entry into Saigon did he accept that the United States had really been defeated.[39]

The unprecedented humiliation of the United States at the end of a war which had divided its society as no other conflict had done since the Civil War seemed to demonstrate the ability of a Third World national liberation movement, inspired by Marxist-Leninist ideology, to defeat even an imperialist superpower. As Nixon's successor, President Gerald Ford, acknowledged, 'Our allies around the world began to question our resolve.' Among the foreign media reports which made a particular impression on Ford – and, doubtless, also on the KGB – was a front-page editorial in the *Frankfurter Allgemeine Zeitung*, headed 'America – A Helpless Giant'.[40]

Identifying the United States with the Western colonial powers, despite strong American support for decolonization after the Second World War,[41] was assisted by creative use of Lenin's definition of imperialism as 'the highest stage of capitalism'. It was thus possible for Soviet commentators to argue that the whole of the Third World, whether politically independent or not, was under imperialist attack: 'Having found it impossible to reshape the political map of the world as it did in the past, imperialism is striving to undermine the sovereignty of liberated states in roundabout ways, making particularly active use of economic levers ...'[42]

Such arguments found no shortage of supporters in the West as well as the Third World. Broadcasting on Radio Hanoi during the

Vietnam War, the great British philosopher Bertrand Russell told American GIs that they were being used 'to protect the riches of a few rich men in the United States': 'Every food store and every petrol station in America requires, under capitalism, the perpetuation of war production.' Vietnam popularized around the world the idea of the United States as the leader of world imperialism, bent on crushing the freedoms of the Third World in the interests of Western capitalism of which it was the leading exemplar. Russell declared:

The United States today is a force for suffering, reaction and counter-revolution the world over. Wherever people are hungry and exploited, wherever they are oppressed and humiliated, the agency of this evil exists with the support and approval of the United States . . . [which went to war in Vietnam] to protect the continued control over the wealth of the region by American capitalists.[43]

The 'Ballad of Student Dissent', made famous by Bob Dylan on American campuses during the Vietnam War, mocked Washington's incomprehension of the growing hostility in the Third World to US 'imperialism':

> Please don't burn that limousine,
> Don't throw tomatoes at the submarine.
> Think of all we've done for you.
> You've just got those exploitation blues.

Before the Vietnam War Western denunciations of Western imperialism were largely confined to limited numbers of academics and Marxist parties and sects. The Marxist political scientist, Bill Warren, was, however, right to claim that in the course of the war, the concept of imperialism became 'the dominant political dogma of our era':

Together with its offspring, the notion of 'neo-colonialism', it affords the great majority of humanity a common view of the world as a whole. Not only the Marxist-educated masses of the Communist world, but also the millions of urban dwellers of Latin America, the semi-politicized peasants of Asia, and the highly literate professional and working classes of the industrialized capitalist countries, are steeped in this world-view and its ramifications. It represents, of course, not simply a recognition of the existence of modern empires, formal or informal, and of their living heritage. More important, it embodies a set of quite specific (albeit often vaguely articulated) theses about the domination of imperialism in the affairs of the human race as a whole and in particular about the past and present economic, political, and cultural disaster imperialism has allegedly inflicted and continues to inflict on the great majority of mankind.[44]

Though Soviet writers contributed little of significance by comparison with Western Marxists to the serious study of imperialism during the Cold War,[45] the anti-imperialist mood which accompanied and followed the Vietnam War created fertile ground for KGB active measures in the Third World. During the 1970s, wrote Bill Warren:

... Bourgeois publishers have devoted more resources to the topic of anti-imperialism than to any other social, political or economic theme, with the possible exception of inflation. If to this we add the literature of the masochistic modern version of the White Man's Burden, more or less directly inspired by the view of imperialism as uniformly disastrous, then Marxism can record the greatest publication and propaganda triumph in its history ... In no other field has Marxism succeeded in so influencing – even dominating – the thought of mankind.[46]

The final stages of the Vietnam War were, ironically, accompanied by an unprecedented level of détente between Washington and Moscow. For the Nixon administration, anxious to extricate itself from Vietnam with as little damage to US prestige as possible, there were obvious advantages in lessening tension with the Soviet Union as well as the longer-term benefit of stabilizing the Cold War. A majority of the Politburo saw the Strategic Arms Limitation Talks (SALT) with the United States as a way of preventing further escalation in the already huge Soviet arms budget. In May 1972 Nixon became the first US president to visit Moscow, where, in the ornate surroundings of the Grand Kremlin Palace, he and Brezhnev signed agreements freezing their nuclear strike forces (SALT 1) and limiting their anti-ballistic missile defences. Brezhnev paid a return visit to Washington the following year. 'Soviet–American relations', wrote Dobrynin, 'reached a level of amity in 1973 never before achieved in the post-war era.' Though no Soviet policy-maker ever accepted that the progress of détente should prevent the Soviet Union extending its influence in the Third World at the expense of the United States, there was disagreement about how vigorously that influence should be increased. Brezhnev, who adored the pomp and ceremony of his meetings with Nixon in both Russia and the United States, was among the doves. In private talks with the President, he criticized some of his own colleagues in the Politburo by name and later sent the President a personal note of sympathy and support 'from the depths of my heart' as the Watergate scandal began to threaten his survival in office.[47] The Centre took a much less sentimental view. During 1973–74 there seems to have been disagreement within the Soviet leadership between the advocates of a more vigorous ideological offensive against the Main Adversary in the Third World (including the increased use of active measures) and those who feared the likely damage to détente with the United States.[48] The advocates of the offensive, Andropov probably chief among them, won the argument.[49]

Over the next decade there was a new wave of revolution in parts of Africa, Central America and Asia – most of it actively supported, though not originated, by the KGB.[50] The complex detail of events in the Third World was simply too much for Brezhnev to take in. As his eyesight deteriorated he found it increasingly difficult to read all but the briefest texts, and his staff first asked for the print size of intelligence reports sent to him to be as large as possible, then for them to be produced in capital letters. Telegrams were read out to him increasingly often.[51] From the mid-1970s he took little active part in the government of the country. At the rear of the cavalcade of black limousines in which he travelled around Moscow was a resuscitation vehicle.[52] At a summit in Vienna in 1979 the future DCI, Robert Gates, 'couldn't get over how feeble Brezhnev was':

Going in and out of the embassies, two huge – and I mean *huge* – KGB officers held him upright under his arms and essentially carried him. [William] Odom, a Soviet expert [later head of the US SIGINT agency, NSA], and I were trapped in a narrow walkway at one point, and as the KGB half-carried Brezhnev by we were nearly steamrollered.[53]

Despite his shuffling gait, disjointed speech and dependence on sleeping pills, Brezhnev thrived on a constant diet of flattery and remained convinced that his 'great experience and wisdom' made his continued leadership indispensable. He was also constantly reassured about the success of Soviet policy in the Third World and the enormous respect in which he was supposedly held by its leaders. Brezhnev opened the Twenty-sixth Party Congress in 1981 by announcing, without any sense of the absurd:

At its first Central Committee plenum, which passed in an atmosphere of exceptional unity and solidarity, the leading organs of our Party have been elected unanimously. The plenum has unanimously appointed as General Secretary of the Central Committee of the CPSU Comrade L. I. Brezhnev.

The entire audience jumped to its feet to deliver the usual sycophantic 'storm of applause'.[54] Despite the war in Afghanistan, Brezhnev exuded confidence in Soviet policy in the Third World as he stumbled through his speech, hailing the increased number of states with a 'socialist orientation' since the previous Congress five years earlier, the triumph of the Ethiopian, Nicaraguan and Afghan revolutions, and the conclusion of friendship treaties with Angola, Ethiopia, Mozambique, Afghanistan, Syria and the People's Democratic Republic of Yemen.[55]

The Centre had no doubt that its 'active measures' to influence operations had made a major contribution to turning most Third World opinion against the United States. In 1974, according to KGB statistics, over 250 active measures were targeted against the CIA alone, leading – it claimed – to denunciations of Agency abuses, both real and (more frequently) imaginary, in media, parliamentary debates, demonstrations and speeches by leading politicians around the world.[56] Though Mitrokhin did not record the statistics for subsequent years, the volume of active measures almost certainly increased, assisted by startling American revelations of skulduggery at the White House and the Agency. The Watergate scandal which forced Nixon's resignation in 1974 was followed in 1975, the 'Year of Intelligence', by sensational disclosures of CIA 'dirty tricks' – among them operation CHAOS and assassination plots against foreign statesmen. Helms's successor as DCI, William Colby, complained that, 'The CIA came under the closest and harshest public scrutiny that any such service has ever experienced not only in this country but anywhere in the world.' Though sympathetic to the Agency, President Ford faced a difficult dilemma. The best way to defend the CIA would have been to emphasize that, in the words of a later Congressional report, 'far from being out of control', it had been 'utterly responsive to the instructions of the President and the Assistant to the President for National Security Affairs'. Defending the CIA, however, would have conflicted with Ford's primary aim of rehabilitating the presidency. To restore confidence in the White House after the trauma of Watergate, the President and his advisers thus took the decision to distance themselves from the charges levelled against the Agency, which continued to multiply.[57]

In reality, the CIA's assassination plots, all undertaken with presidential approval, had either failed or been abandoned – partly because, unlike the KGB, it did not possess a group of trained assassins. Shocked by the revelations of the 'Year of Intelligence', however, a majority of Americans were taken in by conspiracy theories, which the KGB did its best to encourage, purporting to show that the CIA had been involved in the assassination of President John F. Kennedy.[58] If, as most of the world as well as most Americans continued to believe,[59] the CIA had been involved in the killing of its own president, it was reasonable to conclude that there were no limits to which the Agency would not go to subvert foreign regimes and assassinate other statesmen who had incurred its displeasure. KGB active measures successfully promoted the belief that the methods which the CIA had used to attempt to kill Fidel Castro and destabilize his regime were being employed against 'progressive' governments around the world. One active-measure operation in the Middle East in 1975 purported to identify forty-five statesmen from around the world who had been the victims of successful or unsuccessful Agency assassination attempts over the past decade.[60] Indira Gandhi was one of a number of prominent Third World leaders who were unconsciously influenced by disinformation fabricated by Service A (the FCD active-measures specialists) and who became obsessed by supposed CIA plots against them.[61]

The KGB's active-measures doctrine improbably insisted that its influence operations were 'radically different in essence from the disinformation to which Western agencies resort in order to deceive public opinion':

KGB disinformation operations are progressive; they are designed to mislead not the working people but their enemies – the ruling circles of capitalism – in order to induce them to act in a certain way, or abstain from actions contrary to the interests of the USSR; they promote peace and social progress; they serve international détente; they are humane, creating the conditions for the noble struggle for humanity's bright future.[62]

KGB active-measures campaigns were extensively supported by its allies in the Soviet bloc. According to Ladislav Bittman of the Czechoslovak StB:

Anti-American propaganda campaigns are the easiest to carry out. A single press article containing sensational facts of a 'new American conspiracy' may be sufficient. Other papers become interested, the public is shocked, and government authorities in developing countries have a fresh opportunity to clamour against the imperialists while demonstrators hasten to break American embassy windows.[63]

KGB active measures were also intended to serve a domestic political agenda by encouraging the support of the Soviet leadership for a forward policy in the Third World. The Centre supplied the Kremlin with regular reports designed to demonstrate its success in influencing Third World politicians and public opinion. The 'successes' listed in these reports seem to have changed little from Brezhnev to Gorbachev. Among documents liberated from the Central Committee archives in the aftermath of the abortive 1991 Moscow coup was a 1969 report from Andropov, boasting of the KGB's ability to organize large protest demonstrations outside the US embassy in Delhi for $5,000 a time, and a quite similar letter to Gorbachev twenty years later from the then KGB chairman, Vladimir Kryuchkov (formerly head of the FCD), reporting with much the same satisfaction the recruitment of an increased number of agents in the Sri Lankan parliament and the 'sincere gratitude to Moscow' allegedly expressed by the leader of the Freedom Party for Soviet 'financial support'.[64]

Given the tight control over the Soviet media and the virtual impossibility of mounting dissident demonstrations in Moscow, the Politburo was unsurprisingly impressed by the KGB's apparent ability to influence Third World opinion. Some KGB active measures were designed less to influence the rest of the world than to flatter the Soviet leadership and the Party apparatus. Unable to report to Moscow that the only aspect of CPSU congresses which made much impression on the world outside the Soviet bloc was the mind-numbing tedium of their banal proceedings, foreign residencies felt forced to concoct evidence to support the official doctrine that, 'The congresses of the CPSU are always events of major international importance: they are like beacons lighting up the path already traversed and the path lying ahead.'[65] Mitrokhin noted in 1977 that throughout the year residencies around the world were busy prompting local dignitaries to send congratulations to the Soviet leadership on the occasion of the sixtieth anniversary of the 'Great October Revolution' and the introduction of the supposedly epoch-making (but in fact insignificant) 'Brezhnev' Soviet constitution.[66] These carefully stage-managed congratulations, as well as featuring prominently in the Soviet media, were doubtless included in the daily intelligence digests prepared by FCD Service 1 (intelligence assessment), signed by Andropov, which were delivered to members of the Politburo and Central Committee Secretariat by junior KGB officers, armed with the latest Makarov pistols, travelling in black Volga limousines.[67]

In the Third World as elsewhere, KGB officers had to waste time pandering to the whims and pretensions of the political leadership. Khrushchev, for example, had been outraged by photographs in the American press showing him drinking Coca-Cola, which he regarded as a symbol of US imperialism, and demanded that further 'provocations' be prevented. Residencies thus kept a close watch for Coca-Cola bottles during the numerous foreign visits of Yuri Gagarin and Valentina Tereshkova, respectively the first man and the first woman into space. All went well until a banquet in Mexico in 1963, when an alert KGB officer noticed a news photographer about to take a picture of Tereshkova with a waiter holding a bottle of Coca-Cola in the background. A member of the Mexico City residency wrote later: 'The "provocation" prepared with regard to the cosmonauts did not slip past our vigilant eyes. The first female cosmonaut, a Soviet woman, featuring in an advertisement for bourgeois Coca-Cola! No, we could not permit this. We immediately turned to our Mexican colleagues for help.' The 'Mexican colleagues' (presumably local security officials) successfully prevented the photograph from being taken.[68]

Brezhnev's increasingly preposterous vanity, which was undiminished by his physical decline, had to be fed not merely by more medals than were awarded to all previous Soviet leaders combined[69] but also by a regular diet of praise from around the world, some of it manufactured by the KGB. In 1973, for example, a paid Moroccan agent codenamed AKMET, who regularly wrote articles based on material provided by Service A, published a book extolling Soviet assistance to African countries. At the prompting of the local residency, he sent a signed copy to Brezhnev as a token of his deep personal gratitude and respect. Trivial though this episode was, it was invested with such significance by the Centre that the book and dedication were forwarded to Brezhnev with a personal covering letter from Andropov – who doubtless did not mention that they had originated as a KGB active measure.[70] Brezhnev was, of course, carefully protected from any sense of how absurd his personality cult appeared to much of the outside world – as, for example, to Joan Baez, who in 1979 composed and sang a satirical birthday tribute to him:

> Happy birthday, Leonid Brezhnev!
> What a lovely seventy-fifth
> We watched the party on TV
> You seemed to be taking things casually
> What a mighty heart must beat in your breast
> To hold forty-nine medals on your chest![71]

As well as manufacturing evidence of the global popularity of the Soviet leadership, the KGB fed it a carefully sanitized, politically correct view of the outside world. Throughout the Soviet era there was a striking contrast between the frequent success of intelligence collection and the poor quality of intelligence analysis. Because analysis in all one-party states is distorted by the insistent demands of political correctness, foreign intelligence reports do more to reinforce than to correct the regime's misconceptions. Though the politicization of intelligence sometimes degrades assessment even within democratic systems, it is actually built into the structure of all authoritarian regimes. Soviet intelligence reports throughout the Stalin era, and for some years after, usually consisted only of selective compilations of relevant information on particular topics with little attempt at interpretation or analysis for fear that it might contradict the views of the political leadership. Though intelligence analysis improved under Andropov, it remained seriously undeveloped by Western standards. Leonov, who was dismayed to be appointed in 1971 as deputy head of the FCD assessment section, Service 1, estimates that it had only 10 per cent of the importance occupied by the Directorate of Intelligence (Analysis) in the CIA. Its prestige was correspondingly low. A general air of depression hung over Service 1, which was usually regarded as 'a punishment posting'. To be transferred there from an operational section, as happened to Leonov, was 'equivalent to moving from a guards regiment in the capital to the garrison in a provincial backwater'.[72]

In 1973 Leonov was promoted to head Service 1 and was soon able to resist the traditional pressure to accept rejects from operational departments. Freedom of debate, he claims, came to his department much earlier than to foreign intelligence as a whole, let alone to the rest of the KGB.[73] That debate, however, was coloured by Leonov's conspiracy theories about the United States which were still in evidence during the final years of the Soviet Union.[74] There was also little change in the standards of political correctness required in intelligence reports to the Soviet leadership:

All the filtration stages . . . were concerned with making sure that alarming, critical information did not come to the attention of the bosses. [Such information] was provided in a sweetened, smoothed form, with all the thorns removed in advance.[75]

Vadim Kirpichenko, who later rose to become first deputy head of foreign intelligence, recalls that during the Brezhnev era, pessimistic intelligence was kept from him on the grounds that it would 'upset Leonid Ilyich'.[76]

When Soviet policy in the Third World suffered setbacks which could not be concealed, analysts knew they were on safe ground if they blamed imperialist machinations, particularly those of the United States, rather than failures of the Soviet system. As one FCD officer admitted at the end of the Cold War, 'In order to please our superiors, we sent in falsified and biased information, acting on the principle "Blame everything on the Americans, and everything will be OK".'[77] Within the Centre it was possible during the Andropov era to express much franker opinions about Third World problems – for example, about Soviet prospects in Egypt after the death of Nasser or economic collapse in Allende's Chile[78] – than were communicated to the political leadership. From the moment that the KGB leadership had taken up a position, however, FCD dissidents kept their heads down. When, for example, Andropov concluded that the first Reagan administration had plans for a nuclear first strike against the Soviet Union, none of the probably numerous sceptics in KGB residencies around the world dared to breathe a word of open dissent.[79]

Despite the sanitized nature of the Centre's reports to the political leadership, however, its optimism about the Third World was genuine. By the mid-1970s, the KGB was confident that it was winning the Cold War in the Third World against a demoralized and increasingly discredited 'Main Adversary'. As Henry Kissinger later acknowledged:

It is doubtful that Castro would have intervened in Angola, or the Soviet Union in Ethiopia, had America not been perceived to have collapsed in Indochina, to have become demoralized by Watergate, and to have afterward retreated into a cocoon.[80]

But while Washington was stricken by self-doubt, Moscow was in economic denial. The severe structural problems of the Soviet economy and the military might which depended on it were far more serious than the transitory loss of American self-confidence which followed Vietnam. In June 1977 the Soviet government was forced to purchase 11.5 million tonnes of grain from the West. In August it concluded that another 10 million tonnes would be needed to meet the shortfall in Soviet production. Yet at the celebration three months later of the sixtieth anniversary of the October Revolution, Brezhnev declared to thunderous applause, 'This epoch is the epoch of the transition to Socialism and Communism . . . and by this path, the whole of mankind is destined to go.' Though the naive economic optimism of the Khrushchev era had largely evaporated, the ideological blinkers which constricted the vision of Brezhnev, Andropov and other Soviet true believers made it impossible for them to grasp the impossibility of the increasingly sclerotic Soviet command economy competing successfully with the market economies of the West.

Despite all the evidence to the contrary, Andropov passionately believed that, 'Everything that has been achieved here [in the Soviet Union] has long put socialism far ahead of the most democratic bourgeois states.'[81] While the Soviet system would solve its problems, those of the capitalist West were insoluble. The onward march of socialism in the Third World pointed to the inevitability of its ultimate global triumph. In the confident words of Karen N. Brutents, first deputy head of the International Department: 'The world was going our way.'[82] The CIA feared that Brutents might be right. It reported to the White House in June 1979 that, 'Part of the Soviet mood is a sense of momentum in the USSR's favour in the Third World.' Brezhnev and the Soviet leadership, it concluded, 'can view their position in the world with considerable satisfaction'.[83]

How the KGB set out to win the Cold War in the Third World, and with what consequences, is the subject of this book.

Latin America

Latin America

1. Mexico
2. Guatemala
3. Belize
4. Honduras
5. El Salvador
6. Nicaragua
7. Costa Rica
8. Panama
9. St Kitts & Nevis
10. Dominica
11. Martinique
12. St Lucia
13. St Vincent
14. Barbados
15. Grenada

N

Havana

CUBA
HAITI
JAMAICA   Kingston
DOMINICAN REP.

NORTH

ATLANTIC

OCEAN

Caribbean Sea

9
10
11
12
13   14
15

1
3
2
4
5
6
7
8

Caracas

VENEZUELA

GUYANA

SURINAM

FRENCH GUIANA

Bogota

COLOMBIA

Galapagos Is.

Quito

ECUADOR

BRAZIL

Lima

PERU

La Paz

BOLIVIA

Brasilia

PARAGUAY

Rio de Janeiro

PACIFIC

OCEAN

Asuncion

CHILE

ARGENTINA

URUGUAY
Santiago   Buenos Aires
Montevideo

Falkland Is.

South Georgia
(UK)

2

Latin America: Introduction

President Ronald Reagan was fond of quoting what he claimed was Lenin's description of the Soviet master-plan to take over the Western hemisphere:

First, we will take over Eastern Europe, then we will organize the hordes of Asia ... then we will move on to Latin America; once we have Latin America, we won't have to take the United States, the last bastion of capitalism, because it will fall into our outstretched hands like overripe fruit.[1]

Reagan was so impressed by this quotation that he repeated it twice in his memoirs. Lenin, however, said no such thing. His only published reference to Latin America, in *Imperialism: The Highest Stage of Capitalism*, was to cite approvingly a German economist who claimed that 'South America, and especially Argentina, was under the financial control of London' and was 'almost a British commercial colony'.[2]

For over forty years after the Bolshevik Revolution, Moscow doubted its own ability to challenge American influence in a continent which it regarded as the United States' backyard. By far the most important Soviet intelligence operation in Latin America during the Stalin era was aimed not at subverting any of the ruling regimes but at assassinating the great Russian heretic Leon Trotsky, who had taken refuge near Mexico City.[3] In 1951, two years before Stalin's death, he scornfully dismissed the twenty Latin American republics, most of them traditionally anti-Communist, as the 'obedient army of the United States'.[4] For the remainder of the decade the Soviet Union maintained diplomatic missions and 'legal' KGB residencies in only three Latin American capitals – Mexico City, Buenos Aires and Montevideo. Though the KGB began delivering secret Soviet subsidies to a handful of pro-Moscow Communist parties in 1955, the amounts remained small by comparison with those given to the leading parties in the West and Asia.[5]

The serious interest of the Centre (KGB headquarters) and subsequently of the Kremlin in the possibility of challenging the United States in its own backyard was first aroused by the emergence of a new generation of charismatic Latin American revolutionary leaders, chief among them Fidel Castro. The KGB's leading Latin American expert, Nikolai Leonov, who was the first to make contact with Castro, wrote later, 'Cuba forced us to take a fresh look at the whole continent, which until then had traditionally occupied the last place in the Soviet leadership's system of priorities.'[6] The charismatic appeal of Castro and 'Che' Guevara extended far beyond Latin America. Though the Western 'New Left' of the 1960s had little interest in the increasingly geriatric leadership of the Soviet Union, it idolized both Castro and Guevara, lavishing on them the uncritical adulation which much of the Old Left had bestowed on Stalin's supposed worker-peasant state in the 1930s. Che Guevara T-shirts on American campuses comfortably outnumbered, even in presidential election years, those bearing the likeness of any US politician alive or dead. Though there was much that was genuinely admirable in Cuban health-care and educational initiatives, despite the increasingly authoritarian nature of the Cuban one-party state, the radical pilgrims to Havana in the 1960s were as uncritical as those to Moscow in the 1930s of whom Malcolm Muggeridge had written, 'Their delight in all they saw and were told, and the expression they gave to that delight, constitute unquestionably one of the wonders of our age.' One of the wonders of the 1960s was delight such as that expressed by the political economist Paul Sweezy after his pilgrimage to Cuba:

To be with these people, to see with your own eyes how they are rehabilitating and transforming a whole nation, to share their dreams of the great tasks and achievements that lie ahead – these are purifying and liberating experiences. You come away with your faith in the human race restored.

Though sympathetic to the Cuban Revolution, Frances Fitzgerald accurately noted that 'many North American radicals who visit Cuba or who live there have performed a kind of surgery on their critical faculties and reduced their conversation to a kind of baby talk, in which everything is wonderful, including the elevator that does not work and the rows of Soviet tanks on military parade that are in the "hands of the people"'.

Similar examples of self-administered brain surgery proliferated across both the West and the Third World. Even Jean-Paul Sartre, despite his global reputation for rigorous philosophical analysis, became for a period almost incoherent in his hero-worship:

Among these fully awake men, at the height of their powers, sleeping doesn't seem like a natural need, just a routine of which they had more or less freed themselves ... They have excluded the routine alternation of lunch and dinner from their daily programme.

... Of all these night watchmen, Castro is the most wide awake. Of all these fasting people, Castro can eat the most and fast the longest ... [They] exercise a veritable dictatorship over their own needs ... they roll back the limits of the possible.[7]

Castro's emergence, after some hesitations, as a reliable pro-Moscow loyalist was of immense importance for both Soviet foreign policy and KGB operations. Had he shared much of the New Left's scornful attitude to the bloated Soviet bureaucracy and its increasingly geriatric leadership, siding instead with the Prague Spring and other manifestations of 'Socialism with a human face' (as many expected him to do after the tanks of the Warsaw Pact invaded Czechoslovakia in August 1968), Castro would have added to Moscow's problems instead of becoming one of its greatest international assets. With Castro and other charismatic Latin American revolutionaries on its side against American imperialism, the prestige of the Soviet Union in the Third World was enormously enhanced and its ageing revolutionary image rejuvenated.

It was often the KGB, rather than the Foreign Ministry, which took the lead role in Latin America. As Khrushchev later acknowledged, the first Soviet ambassador to Castro's Cuba 'turned out to be unsuited for service in a country just emerging from a revolution' and had to be replaced by the KGB resident, who proved to be 'an excellent choice'.[8] Nikolai Leonov later described how he had also 'worked with many [other] Latin American leaders ... to help them as far as possible in their anti-American stance'.[9] The first contacts with Salvador Allende before his election as President of Chile in

1970 and with Juan and Isabel Perón before their return to Argentina in 1973 were also made by the KGB rather than by a Soviet diplomat. KGB contacts with the Sandinistas began almost two decades before their conquest of power in Nicaragua in 1979. As Leonov acknowledged, the initiative frequently came from the Centre's Latin American experts:

We ourselves developed the programme of our actions, orienting ourselves . . . I might as well admit that sometimes we also wanted to attract attention to ourselves, to present our work as highly significant. This was to protect the Latin American direction in intelligence from withering away and dying out. On the whole we managed to convince the KGB leadership that Latin America represented a politically attractive springboard, where anti-American feeling was strong . . .[10]

KGB operations were greatly assisted by the clumsy and sometimes brutal American response to Latin American revolutionary movements. The poorly planned and ineptly executed attempt to overthrow Castro by a CIA-backed landing at the Bay of Pigs in April 1961 was probably the most farcically incompetent episode in Cold War US foreign policy. Humiliation at the Bay of Pigs, however, did not prevent Kennedy authorizing subsequently a series of plans to assassinate Castro which, mercifully, also degenerated into farce. Some, like the proposal to place an explosive seashell on the sea bed when Castro went snorkelling, probably never progressed beyond the drawing board. The most practicable scheme devised during Kennedy's presidency seems to have been the plan for one of Castro's lovers to slip two poison capsules into his drink. While waiting for an opportunity, she hid them in a jar of cold cream. When she came to retrieve them, the capsules had melted. It is doubtful in any case that she would actually have used them.

Investigative journalism and official investigations in the mid-1970s gave global publicity to a series of such homicidal farces. Also revealed were CIA attempts on presidential instructions to destabilize the regime of Chile's Marxist President Salvador Allende in the early 1970s. Among the revelations was that of an apoplectic President Richard M. Nixon ordering his Director of Central Intelligence, Richard Helms, to 'make the [Chilean] economy scream'.

KGB active-measures specialists could not have hoped for more promising raw material to use as the basis of their campaigns than the series of scandalous revelations of American dirty tricks in Latin America from the Bay of Pigs to Iran-Contra a quarter of a century later. Service A was also able to exploit a much older tradition of resentment at *Yanqui* imperialism, which was kept alive during the Cold War by a recurrent US tendency to claim that its determination to root out Communist influences in Latin America wherever possible was in reality a high-minded attempt to defend democratic values in the interests of Latin Americans themselves. Having persuaded himself in 1965, contrary to the advice of the State Department, that a coup in the Dominican Republic was Communist-inspired, President Johnson sought to justify US military intervention by the sanctimonious rhetoric which rarely failed to enrage much of Latin American opinion: 'The purpose of America is never to suppress liberty, but always to save it. The purpose of America is never to take freedom, but always to return it.'

American intervention, however, had little to do with democratic renewal. When Johnson's extravagant claims of 'headless bodies lying in the streets of Santo Domingo' were challenged by opponents of US intervention, he phoned the US ambassador and appealed to him, 'For God's sake, see if you can find some headless bodies.' The left-wing regimes overthrown with American assistance or approval in Guatemala in 1954, in the Dominican Republic in 1965 and in Chile in 1973 were replaced by military dictatorships.[11]

The Sandinista victory in Nicaragua in 1979 revived much the same hopes and fears of Central American revolution created by Castro's triumph in Cuba twenty years earlier. As one of their supporters noted, the Sandinistas had inspired 'a renewal of belief in the possibility of a revolution'. 'Backwater Nicaragua', said the left-wing writer Paul Berman, became 'the world center of the New Left'. For the journalist Claudia Dreifus: 'To be in Managua was like being in a time machine. Here was a place seemingly run by the kind of people who were Sixties radicals. Wherever one went, people were young, singing political folk songs and chanting "Power to the People".'[12]

The Reagan administration's campaign against the Sandinista regime was a public-relations disaster on a global scale. Just as the Bay of Pigs invasion was remembered by President John F. Kennedy as 'the most excruciating period of my life', so the lowest point in Ronald Reagan's generally popular presidency came as a result of the revelation that the profits from secret arms sales to Iran, then a state sponsor of terrorism, had been illegally diverted to support the Nicaraguan Contra rebels in their attempt to overthrow the Marxist Sandinista regime. When Reagan was informed in 1985 that this episode had been uncovered by the Attorney General, his chief of staff noted that 'the color drained from [the president's] face'.[13]

A survey in the mid-1980s found that the two most 'unappealing countries' in the view of Mexican academics were the United States and Pinochet's Chile. Though the USSR came in third place, 72 per cent of those polled believed that reports of 'repression' in the Soviet Union had been exaggerated. Clearly the most admired country was Castro's Cuba.[14] Estimating how much Service A's disinformation contributed to the Latin American distrust of *Yanqui* imperialism is an almost impossible task. It is, however, possible to identify some causes of widespread anti-American indignation which were clearly of Soviet origin. Among them was the 'baby parts' fabrication which alleged that wealthy Americans were buying up and butchering Latin American children in order to use their bodies for organ transplants. The story was taken up by a Soviet front organization, the International Association of Democratic Lawyers (IADL), and publicized extensively in the press of over fifty countries. Those taken in by the fabrication included groups as remote from the KGB as the Jehovah's Witnesses, who published the story in 1989 in their magazine *Awake*, which had a world-wide circulation of 11 million copies printed in fifty-four languages.[15] In 1990 an American correspondent in Mexico noted that the 'baby parts' story was still current even in 'the respectable press':

It was reported that Mexican children routinely were being kidnapped, spirited across the US border, and murdered for their vital organs, which were then transplanted into sick American children with rich parents ... Millions of educated and uneducated people – particularly in Latin America – firmly believe that the United States has created, in essence, an international network of child murderers, backed by gruesome teams of medical butchers.[16]

Despite their many differences, KGB active measures and American policy to Latin America thus had one strikingly similar effect – to strengthen the traditional distrust of *Yanqui* imperialism.

3

'The Bridgehead', 1959–1969

One of the most striking news photographs of 1960 showed the tall, youthful, bearded 'Maximum Leader' of the Cuban Revolution, Fidel Castro Ruz,[1] being greeted with a bear hug by the short, podgy, beaming Soviet leader Nikita Khrushchev at the United Nations in New York. Khrushchev's boisterous embrace symbolized a major shift in both Soviet foreign policy and KGB operations. Moscow had at last a charismatic revolutionary standard-bearer in the New World.

Castro later claimed that he was already a Marxist-Leninist when he began his guerrilla campaign against the corrupt pro-American Cuban dictatorship of Fulgencio Batista in 1953: 'We felt that Lenin was with us, and that gave us great strength in fighting.' That claim, however, was one of a number of attempts by Castro, once in power, to rewrite the history of his unorthodox early career. The word 'socialism' did not appear in any of Castro's speeches until 1961.[2] Castro had a privileged upbringing in an affluent Cuban landowning family, and drew his early political inspiration not from Lenin but from the radical nationalist Partido del Pueblo Cubano and the ideals of its anti-Marxist founder, Eduardo Chibás. Until 1958 the Cuban Communist Party – the Partido Socialista Popular (PSP) – continued to insist, with Moscow's backing, that Batista could only be overthrown not by Castro's guerrillas but by a popular uprising of Cuban workers led by the Communists. As late as October 1958, three months before Batista fled and Castro entered Havana in triumph, Khrushchev spoke pessimistically of 'the heroic but un-equal struggle of the Cuban people' against imperialist oppression.[3] Not until 27 December did the Kremlin approve a limited supply of arms by the Czechs to Castro's guerrillas. Even then it insisted that only German weapons of the Second World War era or arms of Czech design be handed over, for fear that a Soviet arms shipment, if discovered, might provoke a crisis with the United States. The arms, however, arrived too late to make a difference. At the stroke of midnight on New Year's Eve 1958, Batista fled from Cuba, leaving Castro and his guerrillas to enter Havana in triumph.[4]

The KGB's foreign intelligence arm, the First Chief Directorate (FCD), had realized Castro's potential earlier than either the Soviet Foreign Ministry or the International Department of the Communist Party Central Committee. The first of its officers to do so was a new recruit, Nikolai Sergeyevich Leonov, who was sent to Mexico City in 1953 in order to improve his Spanish before entering the KGB training school. *En route* to Mexico, Leonov became 'firm friends' with Fidel's more left-wing younger brother, Raúl Castro, at a socialist youth congress in Prague, then crossed the Atlantic with him aboard an Italian freighter bound for Havana. To his later embarrassment, on arrival at Havana Leonov insisted that Raúl hand him the negatives of all the photographs he had taken of him during the crossing for fear that they might be used for 'provocations'.[5] Soon after Leonov's arrival in Mexico, Fidel Castro led an unsuccessful attack on an army barracks which was followed by the imprisonment of himself and Raúl for the next two years. After his release, Fidel spent a year in exile in Mexico and appealed to the Soviet embassy for arms to support a guerrilla campaign against Batista. Though the appeal was turned down, Leonov met Castro for the first time in 1956, was immediately impressed by his potential as a charismatic guerrilla leader, began regular meetings with him and gave him enthusiastic moral support. Leonov privately regarded Castro's politics as immature and incoherent, but noted that both Fidel's closest advisers, Raúl Castro and the Argentinian Ernesto 'Che' Guevara, appeared to be committed Marxists.[6] 'I am one of those', wrote Che in 1957, '. . . who believes that the solution to the problems of this world lies behind what is called the Iron Curtain.'[7]

Leonov's far-sightedness and early association with the Castro brothers launched him on a career which led eventually to his appointment in 1983 as deputy head of the FCD, responsible for KGB operations throughout North and South America. His early assessments of Fidel, however, made little impression in the Centre (KGB headquarters).[8] Even when Castro took power in January 1959, Moscow still doubted his ability to withstand American pressure. Lacking a residency in Havana, the KGB obtained much of its

Cuban intelligence from the PSP,[9] which looked askance at the apparently moderate complexion of the new regime. By midsummer, however, the moderates had been ousted from the government, leaving the cabinet as little more than a rubber stamp for policies decided by Castro, the 'Maximum Leader', and his advisers. Though initially restrained in his public utterances, Castro privately regarded the United States as 'the sworn enemy of our nation'. He had written a few months before coming to power, 'When this war [against Batista] is over, I'll start a much longer and bigger war of my own: the war I'm going to fight against [the Americans]. I realize that will be my true destiny.' While American hostility was later to reinforce Castro's alliance with the Soviet Union, it did not cause it. The initiative for the alliance came from Havana.[10]

From the outset the KGB was closely involved in establishing the Soviet–Cuban connection. In July 1959 Castro sent his first intelligence chief, Ramiro Valdés, to Mexico City for secret talks with the Soviet ambassador and KGB residency.[11] Three months later, a Soviet 'cultural delegation' headed by the former KGB resident in Buenos Aires, Aleksandr Ivanovich Alekseyev, arrived in Havana to establish the first Cuban residency. Alekseyev presented Fidel Castro with a bottle of vodka, several jars of caviar and a photographic portfolio of Moscow, then assured him of the Soviet people's 'great admiration' both for himself and for the Cuban Revolution. Castro opened the bottle and sent for biscuits on which to spread the caviar. 'What good vodka, what good caviar!' he exclaimed. 'I think it's worth establishing trade relations with the Soviet Union!' Castro then 'stunned' his visitor by declaring that Marx and Lenin were his intellectual guides. 'At that time', said Alekseyev later, 'we could not even imagine that [Castro] knew Marxist theory.'[12]

During his meeting with Alekseyev, Castro proposed a visit to Cuba by Deputy Prime Minister Anastas Mikoyan, Khrushchev's favourite personal emissary and elder statesman of his regime, whose career stretched back to the Bolshevik Revolution. Under Brezhnev, Mikoyan's career was summed up behind his back as 'From Ilyich to Ilyich [from Lenin to Brezhnev], without a heart attack or paralysis.' Before leaving for Havana as the most senior Soviet representative ever to visit Latin America, Mikoyan summoned Leonov to his presence and asked him if it was really true that he knew the Castro brothers. Among the evidence which persuaded Mikoyan to take him as his interpreter were the photographs taken by Raúl while crossing the Atlantic seven years earlier. The main Cuban–Soviet talks took place not around a Havana conference table but after dark at Fidel's hunting cabin by a lagoon, the night air punctuated by croaking tropical frogs and buzzing mosquitoes. Most of their meals were of fish they caught in the lagoon and cooked themselves or else taken in workers' dining halls. They slept on concrete floors at an unfinished campsite, wrapped in soldiers' greatcoats for warmth, occasionally warming up with strong aromatic coffee. Mikoyan felt transported back from life as a top-ranking Moscow bureaucrat to his revolutionary origins. 'Yes, this is a real revolution,' he told Leonov. 'Just like ours. I feel as though I've returned to my youth!' By a trade agreement signed during his visit, the Soviet Union agreed to purchase about one-fifth of Cuba's sugar exports, supply oil at well below world prices and make Cuba a low-interest loan of $100 million for economic development projects.[13]

On 15 March 1960, soon after Mikoyan's return, Khrushchev sent his first personal message to Castro. Instead of putting it in writing, however, he instructed that it should be delivered verbally by the KGB. Alekseyev informed Castro that Khrushchev wanted him to have no doubt about 'our sympathy and fellow-feeling'. To flatter Castro personally, he was told that he was to receive honoraria for the publication of his speeches and articles in Russian. According to Alekseyev, the Maximum Leader was 'visibly moved' by the news that his words were held in such esteem in Moscow. Khrushchev also announced that Cuba was free to purchase whatever arms it wished from Czechoslovakia – 'and, if necessary, then directly from the Soviet Union'.[14] The Cuban arms purchases were negotiated in Prague by a delegation headed by Raúl. Despite sleeping with his boots on and demanding the services of blonde prostitutes, he displayed a Marxist-Leninist fervour which made a good impression on his hosts. According to the Czech general responsible for hosting the Cuban delegation, 'The[ir] villa was of course tapped but we learned nothing from our bugs that our guests would have been unwilling to tell us.'[15] During Raúl's visit to Prague, Leonov was personally instructed by the foreign intelligence chief, Aleksandr Mikhailovich Sakharovsky, head of the FCD, to travel to Prague, stay with the KGB resident and, without the knowledge of either the Czechs or the Soviet embassy, discover a way of passing on a personal invitation from Khrushchev to visit Moscow. An older and experienced KGB colonel was sent to assist him. Making contact with Raúl Castro proved more difficult than Leonov had expected. Raúl's villa was in a closed area of the city, he travelled constantly surrounded by armed guards, and no advance timetable of his movements was available. In the end Leonov decided to sit on a street bench on a route which Raúl's car was bound to pass on its way to the villa. Raúl would recognize Leonov, and tell the car to stop. Beyond this point, Leonov would improvise. The plan worked; Raúl picked Leonov up, and took him to the villa which the guards only allowed him to enter when he produced his Soviet diplomatic passport. Leonov waited for a moment when the guards were out of earshot, then whispered to Raúl that he had brought with him a personal invitation from Khrushchev. Two days later, on 17 July, they flew to Moscow, so deep in conversation that Leonov forgot that, for reasons of protocol, he was not supposed to accompany Raúl off the plane at the airport, where a reception committee of military top brass was waiting for him on the airport tarmac. As Leonov emerged with Raúl at the top of the aircraft steps, he was dragged away by burly KGB bodyguards who were probably unaware of his role in arranging the visit and, he believes, would have beaten him up had Raúl not shouted after him, 'Nikolai, we must see one another again without fail!' In the course of Raúl's visit, further arms supplies were negotiated along with the sending to Cuba of Soviet military advisers, some of them Spanish Republican exiles living in Moscow who had fought in the Red Army during the Great Patriotic War.[16]

As in arranging Raúl Castro's visit to Moscow, the KGB played a much more important role than the Foreign Ministry in developing the Cuban alliance. Fidel Castro regarded Alekseyev, the KGB resident, as a personal friend, telling him of his pleasure that they 'are able to meet directly, bypassing the Ministry of Foreign Affairs and every rule of protocol'. The Maximum Leader did not take to Sergei Kudryavtsev, who arrived as Soviet ambassador in Havana following the formal establishment in May 1960 of diplomatic relations between Cuba and the Soviet Union. Kudryavtsev repelled the Cubans by behaving – according to Alekseyev – as arrogantly as 'one of Batista's generals'. He also appeared constantly preoccupied with his own security, frequently wearing a bullet-proof vest as he travelled round Havana. Castro continued to use the KGB as his main channel of communication with Moscow. Alekseyev, not Kudryavtsev, remained his chief contact within the Soviet embassy.[17] The FCD set up a new section (which became its Second Department) to specialize in Latin American affairs, hitherto the responsibility of its First (North American) Department. Leonov was appointed to run the Cuban desk.[18]

Despite the influential KGB presence in Havana, Khrushchev's policy to Castro's Cuba was distorted by woefully inaccurate KGB and GRU intelligence reports from the United States. For most of the Cold War, the Washington and New York legal residencies had little success in providing the intelligence from inside the federal government which had been so plentiful during the Second World War. Their limitations were clearly exposed during the two years which led up to the most dangerous moment of the Cold War, the Cuban missile crisis of 1962. Conspiracy theory became a substitute for high-grade intelligence. On 29 June 1960 the KGB Chairman, Aleksandr Shelepin, personally delivered to Khrushchev an alarmist assessment of American policy, based on a horrifically misinformed report from an unidentified NATO liaison officer with the CIA:

In the CIA it is known that the leadership of the Pentagon is convinced of the need to initiate a war with the Soviet Union 'as soon as possible' . . . Right now the USA has the capability to wipe out Soviet missile bases and other military targets with its bomber forces. But over the next little while the defence forces of the Soviet Union will grow . . . and the opportunity will disappear . . . As a result of these assumptions, the chiefs at the Pentagon are hoping to launch a preventive war against the Soviet Union.

Khrushchev took this dangerously misguided report at its improbable face value. On 9 July he issued a public warning to the Pentagon 'not to forget that, as shown at the latest tests, we have rockets which can land in a pre-set square target 13,000 kilometres away'. 'Soviet artillerymen', he declared, 'can support the Cuban people with their rocket fire should the aggressive forces in the Pentagon dare to start intervention in Cuba.' During his visit to Moscow later in July, Raúl Castro conveyed Fidel's gratitude for Khrushchev's speech. He also expressed his personal admiration for the KGB and asked for some of its officers to be sent to Havana to help to train Cuban intelligence. In August 1960 the Centre decided on a new codeword for Cuba – AVANPOST ('Bridgehead'). Thanks chiefly to Castro and the KGB, the Soviet Union now had, for the first time in its history, a foothold in Latin America.[19]

Castro and his chief lieutenants made no secret of their desire to inspire the rest of Latin America with their own revolutionary example. As early as April 1959 eighty guerrillas set sail from Cuba in a comic-opera attempt to 'liberate' Panama which ended with their own surrender to the Panamanian National Guard.[20] Che Guevara, whose revolutionary fantasies were on an even grander scale than Castro's, told Kudryavtsev in October 1960, 'Latin America is at boiling point, and next year we can expect revolutionary explosions in several countries . . .'[21] Though the explosions turned out to be damp squibs, they generated far less publicity than the CIA's inept attempt, approved by the White House, to topple the Castro regime by landing an American-backed 'Cuban brigade' at the Bay of Pigs in April 1961, which gave the Maximum Leader an international reputation as a revolutionary David engaged in a heroic struggle with the imperialist American Goliath. Throughout the Bay of Pigs operation, Leonov was in the office of Shelepin's inexperienced successor as KGB Chairman, Vladimir Semichastny, briefing him every two to three hours on the latest developments. On the Chairman's wall he put up two large maps: one showing the course of events as reported by the Americans, the other based on Soviet sources in Cuba.[22] It can scarcely have occurred to either Leonov or Semichastny that the CIA operation would end so rapidly in humiliating defeat. More than 1,000 prisoners captured at the Bay of Pigs were taken to a sports stadium in Havana where for four days Castro flamboyantly interrogated and harangued them on television. At one point, broadcast on TV news programmes across the world, the prisoners applauded the man they had come to over-throw. The abortive invasion served both to raise Castro's personal popularity to new heights and to speed Cuba's transformation into a one-party state. In front of cheering crowds at May Day celebrations of the Cuban victory over American imperialism, Castro announced that Cuba was now a socialist state which would hold no further elections. The revolution, he declared, was the direct expression of the will of the people.

In Washington, President John F. Kennedy, who had been in office for only three months at the time of the Bay of Pigs débâcle, despairingly asked his special counsel, Theodore Sorensen, 'How could I have been so stupid?' At a summit meeting with Kennedy at Vienna in June, Khrushchev belligerently demanded an end to the three-power status of West Berlin and a German peace treaty by the end of the year. Kennedy said afterwards to the journalist James Reston: 'I think [Khrushchev] did it because of the Bay of Pigs. I think he thought anyone who was so young and inexperienced as to get in that mess could be taken, and anyone who got into it and didn't see it through had no guts. So he just beat the hell out of me.'[23]

Taking its cue from Khrushchev, the KGB also set out 'to beat the hell' out of the United States by exploiting the Cuban bridgehead. On 29 July 1961 Shelepin sent Khrushchev the outline of a new and aggressive global grand strategy against the Main Adversary, designed 'to create circumstances in different areas of the world which would assist in diverting the attention and forces of the United States and its allies, and would tie them down during the settlement of the question of a German peace treaty and West Berlin'. The first part of the plan proposed to use national liberation movements in the Third World to secure an advantage in the East–West struggle and 'to activate by the means available to the KGB armed uprisings against pro-Western reactionary governments'. At the top of the list for demolition Shelepin placed 'reactionary' regimes in the Main Adversary's own backyard in Central America. His master-plan envisaged creating a second anti-American bridgehead in Nicaragua, where the newly founded Frente Sandinista de Liberación Nacional (FSLN) was dedicated to following the example of the Cuban Revolution and overthrowing the brutal pro-American dictatorship of the Somoza dynasty. President Franklin Roosevelt was said to have justified his support for the repellent founder of the dynasty with the cynical maxim, 'I know he's a son of a bitch but he's our son of a bitch.' To the Centre the Somozas probably appeared as vulnerable to guerrilla attack as Batista had proved in Cuba. Shelepin proposed that the KGB secretly co-ordinate a 'revolutionary front' in Central America in collaboration with the Cubans and the Sandinistas. On 1 August, with only minor amendments, his grand strategy was approved as a Central Committee directive.[24]

The FSLN leader, Carlos Fonseca Amador, codenamed GIDRO-LOG ('Hydrologist'), was a trusted KGB agent.[25] In 1957, at the age of twenty-one, Fonseca had been the only Nicaraguan to attend the Sixth World Youth Festival in Moscow, and he had stayed on in the USSR for another four months. His book, *A Nicaraguan in Moscow*, which he wrote on his return, was full of wide-eyed admiration for the Soviet Union as a people's democracy with a free press, total freedom of religion, and – even more improbably – magnificently efficient state-run industries. Fonseca was equally enthusiastic about Fidel Castro. 'With the victory of the Cuban Revolution', he said later, 'the rebellious Nicaraguan spirit recovered its brightness . . . The Marxism of Lenin, Fidel, Che [Guevara] and Ho Chi-Minh was taken up by the Sandinista National Liberation Front which has started anew the difficult road of guerrilla warfare . . . Guerrilla combat will lead us to final liberation.'[26]

Within weeks of the victory of Castro's guerrillas in January 1959, Tomás Borge, one of the founders of the FSLN, and a group of Sandinistas arrived in Havana, where they were promised 'all possible support' by Che.[27] Much though he admired Fidel and Che Guevara, Fonseca was a very different kind of personality – remembered by one of his admirers as 'almost always serious' and by his son as 'Super austere, very disciplined, methodical, cautious. He didn't drink or smoke.' Fonseca was a dedicated revolutionary with little sense of humour and a solemn expression. Only one published photograph shows him with a smile on his face.[28]

The KGB's second major penetration of the Sandinistas was probably the recruitment by the Mexico City residency in 1960 of the Nicaraguan exile Edelberto Torres Espinosa (codenamed PIMEN), a close friend of Fonseca as well as General Secretary of the anti-Somoza Nicaraguan United Front in Mexico, and President of the Latin American Friendship Society. Initial contact with Torres had been established when his daughter approached the Soviet embassy with a request to study at the Patrice Lumumba Friendship University in Moscow. The Mexico City residency reported to the Centre that Torres was committed to the liberation of the whole of Latin America and saw revolution in Nicaragua as simply one step along that path.[29] An admiring biographer of Fonseca describes the older Torres as his 'mentor'. Among the projects on which they had worked together was a study of the anti-imperialist nineteenth-century

Nicaraguan poet Rubén Darío. Fonseca was later married in Torres's house in Mexico City.[30]

Shelepin reported to Khrushchev in July 1961:

In Nicaragua . . . at the present time – via KGB agents and confidential contacts* PIMEN, GIDROLOG and LOT[31] – [the KGB] is influencing and providing financial aid to the Sandino [Sandinista] Revolutionary Front and three partisan detachments which belong to the Internal Revolutionary Resistance Front, which works in co-ordination with its friends [Cuban and Soviet bloc intelligence services]. In order to obtain weapons and ammunition, it is proposed that an additional $10,000 be allocated to these detachments from KGB funds.[32]

The main early objective of KGB penetration of the Sandinista FSLN was the creation within it of what the Centre called 'a sabotage-terrorism group' headed by Manuel Ramón de Jesus Andara y Ubeda (codenamed PRIM), a Nicaraguan surgeon working in Mexico.[33] On 22 November 1961 Aleksandr Sakharovsky, the head of the FCD, reported to Semichastny, the KGB Chairman:

In accordance with the long-term plan for the KGB's intelligence operations in Latin America and Decision No. 191/75-GS of the highest authorities dated 1 August 1961 [approving Shelepin's grand strategy in the Third World], our Residency in Mexico has taken measures to provide assistance in building up the national liberation movement in Nicaragua and creating a hotbed of unrest for the Americans in this area. The Residency, through the trusted agent GIDROLOG [Fonseca] in Mexico, selected a group of Nicaraguan students (12 people), headed by the Nicaraguan patriot-doctor PRIM [Andara y Ubeda], and arranged for their operational training. All operations with PRIM's group are conducted by GIDROLOG in the name of the Nicaraguan revolutionary organization 'The Sandinista Front', of which he, GIDROLOG, is the leader. The supervision of the group's

---

* According to KGB rules, agents were required to agree 'to co-operate secretly with an official intelligence representative' and to carry out 'consciously, systematically and secretly' his intelligence assignments. 'Confidential contacts' were defined as those who 'communicate to intelligence officers information of interest to them and carry out confidential requests which in substance are of an intelligence nature'; unlike agents, however, they had not accepted a formal obligation to carry out intelligence assignments. Mitrokhin (ed.), *KGB Lexicon*, pp. 3, 34.

future activities and financial aid given to it will also be provided through GIDROLOG. At the present time PRIM's group is ready to be despatched to Honduras, where it will undergo additional training and fill out its ranks with new guerrillas, after which the group will be sent to Nicaraguan territory. During the initial period PRIM's group will be tasked with the following assignments: the organization of a partisan detachment on Nicaraguan territory, filling out its ranks with the local population, and creating support bases of weapon and ammunition supplies. In addition, the detachment will make individual raids on government establishments and enterprises belonging to Americans, creating the appearance of a massive partisan struggle on Nicaraguan territory. In order to equip PRIM's group and provide for its final training in combat operations, assistance amounting to $10,000 is required. The highest authorities have given their consent to using the sum indicated for these purposes.

I request your approval.

Though Semichastny had only just been appointed KGB Chairman and had been selected by Khrushchev for his political reliability rather than his understanding of intelligence, he did not hesitate. The day after receiving Sakharovsky's report, he gave his approval.[34] Semichastny would not have dared to do so unless he had been confident of Khrushchev's support. There can be little doubt that Khrushchev shared the KGB's exaggerated optimism on the prospects for a second bridgehead in Nicaragua on the Cuban model.

Having gained Semichastny's approval, Sakharovsky directed the KGB residency in Mexico City to give Andara y Ubeda (PRIM) $6,000 to purchase weapons and instruct him to despatch an initial group of seven guerrillas, later to be increased to twenty-two, from Mexico to Nicaragua. His guerrilla group was to be assembled at a camp in Nicaragua by 1 March 1962, ready to begin sabotage operations against American bases a fortnight later. Andara y Ubeda, however, insisted, no doubt correctly, that his men were too poorly armed and trained to launch attacks on the well-defended US bases. Instead, they engaged in guerrilla and intelligence operations against the Somoza regime, non-military American organizations and anti-Castro Cuban refugees. Between November 1961 and January 1964 Andara y Ubeda's guerrillas received a total of $25,200 through the Mexico City residency. Andara y Ubeda, however, was not at first aware that he was being funded by the KGB. Torres (PIMEN) told him that the money came from members of the 'progressive bourgeoisie' who wished to overthrow the Somoza dictatorship. Andara y Ubeda was asked – and agreed – to sign a political manifesto, supposedly prepared by his progressive bourgeois backers (in reality drafted by the KGB), which called for a Nicaraguan revolution as part of a socialist struggle against imperialism.[35]

Torres also kept the KGB informed on the activities of other small Sandinista guerrilla groups, who were being trained with varying success in the jungles of Honduras and Costa Rica. The Mexico City residency reported to the Centre that he saw himself not as a Soviet agent but as a member of a national liberation movement working with the Soviet Union to emancipate the peoples of Latin America from economic and political enslavement by the United States. Torres's case officers, V. P. Nefedov and V. V. Kostikov, none the less regarded him as 'a valuable and reliable KGB agent', who never failed to fulfil his assignments.[36]

In the heady early years of the Cuban Revolution, the Centre seems to have believed that its example was capable of inspiring movements similar to the Sandinistas in much of Latin America. Guerrilla groups sprang up in Colombia, Venezuela, Peru and Guatemala. In 1961 Castro's intelligence organization was reorganized as the Dirección General de Inteligencia (DGI), under the Ministry of the Interior. With Ramiro Valdés, Castro's first intelligence chief, in overall charge as Interior Minister, Manuel Piñeiro Losada, nicknamed 'Barba Roja' because of his luxuriant red beard, became head of the DGI. Piñeiro's chief priority was the export of the Cuban Revolution. The DGI contained a Dirección de Liberación Nacional with three 'Liberation Committees' responsible, respectively, for exporting revolution to the Caribbean, Central and South America. Piñeiro and Che Guevara spent many evenings, usually into the early hours and sometimes until daybreak, discussing the prospects for revolution with would-be revolutionaries from Latin America and the Caribbean. Always spread out on the table while they talked was a large map of the country concerned which Che examined in detail, alternately puffing on a cigar and drinking strong Argentinian tea – *mate* – through a straw.[37]

While Che and Piñeiro dreamed their revolutionary dreams and traced imaginary guerrilla operations on their maps into the early hours, the KGB sought methodically to strengthen its liaison with and influence on the DGI. Among the most striking evidence of the closeness of the DGI's integration into the intelligence community of the Soviet bloc was its collaboration in the use of 'illegals', intelligence officers and agents operating under bogus identities and (usually) false nationalities. In 1961 the Spanish-speaking KGB illegal Vladimir Vasilyevich Grinchenko (successively codenamed RON and KLOD), who ten years earlier had obtained an Argentinian passport under a false identity, arrived in Cuba, where he spent the next three years advising the DGI on illegal operations.[38]

Further KGB exploitation of the Cuban 'bridgehead', however, was dramatically interrupted by the missile crisis of October 1962. In May Khrushchev summoned Alekseyev, the KGB resident in Havana, unexpectedly to Moscow and told him he was to replace the unpopular Kudryavtsev as Soviet ambassador. A fortnight later Khrushchev astonished Alekseyev once again by saying that he had decided to install offensive nuclear missile sites in Cuba targeted against the United States. A small delegation, including Alekseyev, was sent to Havana to secure Castro's approval. 'If the issue had been only our defence', said Castro later, 'we would not have accepted the missiles.' He agreed to the building of the missile sites, he insisted, in the broader interests of solidarity with the Soviet bloc – or, as Moscow preferred to call it, 'the socialist commonwealth'. Though Khrushchev sought the KGB's assistance in cementing the alliance with Castro, he did not trouble to seek its assessment of the likely American reaction to the building of the Cuban missile bases. Acting, like Stalin, as his own intelligence analyst, he rashly concluded that 'the Americans will accept the missiles if we install them before their [mid-term Congressional] elections in November'. Few world leaders have been guilty of greater foreign policy misjudgements. The discovery of the construction of the missile sites by US U-2 spy planes in October 1962 led to the most dangerous crisis of the Cold War.[39]

Khrushchev's decision to resolve the crisis by announcing – without consulting Castro – the unilateral withdrawal of 'all Soviet offensive arms' from Cuba caused outrage in Havana. Castro angrily told students at Havana University that Khrushchev 'had no balls'. Privately, he denounced the Soviet leader as a 'sonofabitch', a 'bastard' and an 'asshole'. In a bizarre and emotional letter to Khrushchev, Castro declared that the removal of the missile bases brought tears to 'countless eyes of Cuban and Soviet men who were willing to die with supreme dignity'. Alekseyev warned Moscow in the aftermath of the missile crisis that 'one or two years of especially careful work with Castro will be required until he acquires all of the qualities of Marxist-Leninist party spirit'.[40]

In an attempt to shore up the Cuban bridgehead, Khrushchev issued a personal invitation to Castro to visit the USSR in order to 'become acquainted with the Soviet Union and the great victories achieved by its peoples', and 'to discuss matters concerning relations between the peoples of the Soviet Union and Cuba, and other matters of common interest'. In April 1963, accompanied by Alekseyev, Castro and his entourage arrived in Moscow, intending to stay only a few days. Castro was persuaded, however, to stay on for a forty-day tour of the Soviet Union which, amid almost continuous applause, took him from Leningrad to the Mongolian border. Old Bolsheviks in Leningrad told him that no one since Lenin had received such a hero's welcome. Wearing his olive-green battle fatigues when the weather was warm enough, Castro addressed enthusiastic crowds at sports stadiums, factories and town centres across the Soviet Union. He inspected a rocket base and the Northern Fleet, reviewed the May Day parade with Khrushchev from the top of the Kremlin wall, was made a Hero of the Soviet Union, and received the Order of Lenin and a gold star.[41] Castro responded with effusive praise for the achievements of Soviet Communism and its support for the Cuban Revolution. He told a mass rally in Red Square:

The Cuban Revolution became possible only because the Russian Revolution of 1917 had been accomplished long before. (*Applause*) Without the existence of the Soviet Union, Cuba's socialist revolution would have been impossible ... The might of the Soviet Union and of the whole socialist camp stopped imperialist aggression against our country. It is quite natural that we nourish feelings of profound and eternal gratitude to the Soviet Union. (*Applause*) ... From the bottom of their hearts the peoples of the entire world, all the peoples of the world, must regard your success as their own. (*Applause*)[42]

Khrushchev told the Presidium that his personal talks with Castro had lasted several days: '... As soon as I finished breakfast, he would come and wait for me. We would sit down together until 2:00. Then we would have lunch and more time together . . . He was left very satisfied.'[43] Throughout his forty-day triumphal progress across the Soviet Union, Castro was escorted both by Alekseyev and by Nikolai Leonov, the young KGB officer who had first identified Castro's revolutionary potential in the mid-1950s. Leonov acted as Castro's interpreter and, when the visit was over, boasted in the Centre that he and the Maximum Leader were now firm friends for life. In the wake of the visit, the Centre received the first group of Cuban foreign intelligence officers for training by the KGB.[44]

Scarcely had Castro returned to Cuba, however, than doubts returned in the minds of his Russian hosts about his reliability and political maturity. Moscow was particularly disturbed by the increasing public emphasis in Havana on 'exporting the revolution'. In September 1963, Che Guevara published a new, much-quoted article on guerrilla warfare. Previously, he had insisted on the importance of a series of preconditions for the establishment of guerrilla bases, such as the absence of an elected, constitutional government. Now he appeared to be arguing that no preconditions were necessary. 'Revolution', he declared, 'can be made at any given moment anywhere in the world.' Worse still, in Moscow's eyes, was the fact that Che's revolutionary heresies seemed to have the blessing of the Castro regime. Despite his personal closeness to Castro, even Alekseyev was shocked. A cable from the Soviet embassy in Havana to Moscow accused Che of ignoring 'basic tenets of Marxism-Leninism' and denounced his essay as 'ultrarevolutionary bordering on adventurism'. Che paid no heed either to the criticism from Moscow or to the opposition to his ideas from Latin American Communist parties. Henceforth he was to be personally involved in the export of the Cuban Revolution.[45]

As well as being increasingly alarmed by Cuban 'adventurism', Moscow was also dismayed by the failure of the Sandinistas to live up to its early expectations. The first FSLN guerrilla force, inadequately dressed in olive-green uniforms (which, though unsuitable for the climate, were chosen to preserve its self-image as freedom fighters), endured a miserable existence at its mountainous base on the Honduras–Nicaragua border. As Borge later recalled, 'There was nothing to eat, not even animals to hunt . . . It wasn't just hunger that was terrible, but constant cold twenty-four hours a day . . . We were always wet through with the clinging rain of that part of the country . . .' In order to survive, the guerrillas were reduced to appealing to local peasants for food. In 1963 the demoralized guerrilla force was routed with heavy loss of life by the Nicaraguan National Guard. For the next few years, in the words of one of its supporters, the FSLN had 'neither the arms, the numbers nor the organization to confront the National Guard again'.[46] In 1964, with the assistance of Torres,[47] the Mexico City residency reconstituted a sabotage and intelligence group (DRG) from the remnants of Andara y Ubeda's (PRIM's) guerrillas. The group was given one of the great historic codenames of Soviet history, chosen by Lenin as the title of the newspaper he had founded in 1900: ISKRA – 'Spark'.[48] By 1964, however, the extravagant optimism in the Centre at the prospects for Latin American revolution which had inspired Shelepin's 1961 master-plan had faded. The KGB plainly expected that it would be some years before the Sandinista 'spark' succeeded in igniting a Nicaraguan revolution.

During his summer leave in 1964, Alekseyev was told by Shelepin to discuss Cuban affairs with Leonid Brezhnev. This was the first hint he received of preparations for the KGB-assisted coup which led to Khrushchev's overthrow in October and Brezhnev's emergence as Soviet leader.[49] Soon after the coup, Mikhail Suslov, the chief Party ideologist, told the Central Committee that Khrushchev had been profligate in the promises he had made to other nations. Though he did not identify the states concerned, Suslov probably had Cuba chiefly in mind.[50] The Kremlin watched aghast as its Cuban allies squandered its economic aid on such frivolities as the giant Coppelia ice-cream emporium. Resentment at the cost of supporting Cuba's mismanaged economy combined with growing annoyance at Castro's revolutionary indiscipline. In the mid-1960s, despite opposition from Latin American Communist parties as well as from Moscow, Cuba made unsuccessful attempts to set up guerrilla bases in Peru, Argentina, Venezuela, Guatemala and Colombia.[51]

The main emissaries of the Cuban Revolution were illegals belonging to, or controlled by, the DGI. Cuban illegals were trained far more rapidly than their KGB counterparts: partly because the DGI was less thorough and paid less attention to devising secure 'legends', partly because it was far easier for a Cuban to assume another Latin

American nationality than for a Russian to pose as a west European. Instead of going directly to their Latin American destinations, most Cuban illegals were deployed via Czechoslovakia. According to statistics kept by the Czechoslovak StB (and handed over by it to the KGB), from 1962 to 1966 a total of 650 Cuban illegals passed through Czechoslovakia. The great majority carried Venezuelan, Dominican, Argentinian or Colombian passports and identity documents. In most cases the documents were genuine save for the substitution of a photograph of the illegal for that of the original owner.[52] One probable sign that the KGB had begun to distance itself from the Cuban attempt to export revolution, however, was the return to Moscow in 1964 of Grinchenko, who for the past three years had been advising the DGI on illegal operations.[53] He does not appear to have been replaced. In 1965, however, in an attempt to reinforce collaboration with the DGI, Semichastny (travelling under the pseudonym 'Yelenin') led a KGB delegation to Cuba. When they met in the country house of the Soviet ambassador, the easy rapport between Alekseyev and Castro quickly created an atmosphere conducive to convivial discussion over a shashlik dinner. Semichastny was struck by Castro's personal fascination with intelligence tradecraft. Later, as they watched a KGB film on the tracking down and interrogation of Oleg Penkovsky, the senior GRU officer who had given SIS and the CIA crucial intelligence on Soviet missile site construction before the Cuban missile crisis, Castro turned to Valdés, his Interior Minister, and the DGI officers who accompanied him, and exhorted them to learn as much as possible from the KGB delegation during their stay.[54] Despite his enthusiasm for KGB tradecraft, however, Castro continued to alarm the Centre by what it regarded as his excess of revolutionary zeal. In January 1966, undeterred by Moscow's reservations, Havana hosted a Trilateral Conference to support the onward march of revolution in Africa, Asia and Latin America. 'For Cuban revolutionaries', Castro declared, 'the battleground against imperialism encompasses the whole world . . . And so we say and proclaim that the revolutionary movement in every corner of the world can count on Cuban combat fighters.'[55]

Castro's confident rhetoric, however, was belied by the lack of success of the revolutionary movement in Latin America. In the summer of 1967 the Sandinistas launched a new offensive which the Centre condemned as premature.[56] Their guerrilla base in the mountainous jungle on the Honduran border was far better organized than at the time of the débâcle in 1963, thanks largely to much greater support from local peasants. According to one of the guerrillas, 'They took on the job of wiping out tracks where the [FSLN] column had passed; the compañeros hung out coloured cloths to warn us of any danger; they invented signals for us with different sounds . . . We had a whole team of campesino brothers and sisters who knew the area like the back of their hand.'[57] At the mountain of Pancasan in August 1967, however, the Sandinistas suffered another disastrous defeat at the hands of the Nicaraguan National Guard. Among those killed was the ISKRA leader, Rigoberto Cruz Arguello (codenamed GABRIEL). The Centre blamed this disaster on 'disloyalty' in the FSLN leadership (all of which had gathered at the guerrilla base), inadequate resources with which to take on the National Guard and the 'unprepared state' of the local population.[58] The jubilant Nicaraguan dictator, Tachito Somoza, boasted that the Sandinistas were finished. The late 1960s and early 1970s were 'a period of silence' for the FSLN during which it continued to rob banks to finance its underground existence but avoided open clashes with the National Guard.[59]

The rout of the Sandinistas was quickly followed by a major setback in the Cuban attempt to 'export the revolution'. In 1966 Che Guevara devised a hopelessly unrealistic plan to set up a base in Bolivia, the poorest country in Latin America, to train guerrillas from all parts of the continent and spread revolution across the Western hemisphere. Che convinced himself that he would turn Bolivia into another Vietnam. Argentina and Brazil would intervene and provoke mass protest movements which would bring down their military regimes. According to Che's fantasy master-plan for continental revolution, the United States would then also be drawn in. The strains of fighting guerrillas in both Vietnam and Latin America would force Washington to set up a dictatorship whose inevitable disintegration would destroy the bourgeois state and open the way to revolution in the United States.[60]

To conceal his journey to, and presence in, Bolivia for as long as possible, Che employed some of the techniques used by the DGI Illegals Directorate. He shaved off his beard and moustache, had his long hair cut short, put on a suit, disguised himself as a Uruguayan bureaucrat and had his photograph inserted in two false Uruguayan passports, each made out in a different name. In October 1966 Che flew to Moscow, then – like most Cuban illegals – returned to Latin America via Prague on one of his passports. In November he arrived in Bolivia, where his grandiose scheme for setting the continent ablaze rapidly reduced itself to guerrilla operations in a small area of the Rio Grande basin.[61] Only a few years earlier, before his revolutionary rhetoric lost all touch with Latin American reality, Che had insisted, 'A guerrilla war is a people's war . . . To attempt to conduct this kind of war without the support of the populace is a prelude to inevitable disaster.'[62] Che's Bolivian adventure ended in 'inevitable disaster' for precisely that reason. Not a single peasant in the Rio Grande basin joined his guerrillas. Even the Bolivian Communist Party (accused of treachery by Che) failed to support him. He wrote gloomily in his diary, 'The peasant masses are no help to us whatever, and they are turning into informers.'

During a visit to Havana in July 1967 the Soviet Prime Minister, Aleksei Kosygin, complained that Cuban attempts to export revolution were 'playing into the hands of the imperialists and weakening and diverting the efforts of the socialist world to liberate Latin America'. Castro's refusal to heed Soviet advice caused a significant setback to the hitherto high-flying career of his friend, Aleksandr Alekseyev, the former KGB resident turned Soviet ambassador in Havana, who was accused in the Centre of going native and failing to restrain Castro's adventurism. Alekseyev was recalled to Moscow, allegedly for medical treatment, in the summer of 1967. His successor as ambassador was a tough career diplomat, Aleksandr Soldatov, who did not arrive in Havana until the following year. The chief KGB adviser in the DGI, Rudolf Petrovich Shlyapnikov, was also recalled in the summer of 1967 after being accused by the DGI of conspiring with a pro-Moscow 'microfaction' in the Cuban Communist Party.[63]

Che's guerrilla operations ended in October 1967 with his capture and execution by US-trained Bolivian forces. Death enormously enhanced his reputation, replacing the reality of the brave but incompetent guerrilla with the heroic image of the revolutionary martyr. Castro declared in an emotional address to the Cuban people that 8 October, the day of Che's capture, would henceforth be for ever celebrated as the Day of the Heroic Guerrilla Fighter:

As all of us pay him homage, as all our thoughts are turned to the Che, as we look forward confidently to the future, to the final victory of the people, we all say to him and to all the heroes who have fought and fallen at his side: 'Ever onward to victory!'

Moscow initially failed to see the symbolic value of the martyred Che as a weapon in the propaganda war against US imperialism. *Pravda* published instead an article by an Argentinian Communist denouncing the futility of the Cuban policy of exporting revolution. Leonid Brezhnev clearly had Guevara in mind when publicly condemning the idea that 'a conspiracy of heroes' could make a socialist revolution.[64]

The KGB was later to recognize the world-wide popularity of the Che Guevara myth as a useful element in active-measures campaigns against American imperialism. In October 1967, however, the only commemoration in Moscow of Che's death was by a small, forlorn congregation of Latin American students who gathered outside the US embassy. In Washington, by contrast, over 50,000 Americans, most from various factions of the New Left which spread across American campuses in the late 1960s, assembled in front of the Lincoln Memorial and bowed their heads in silent homage to the great opponent of US imperialism. A poll of US university students in 1968 discovered that more identified with Che than with any other figure, alive or dead.

In the immediate aftermath of Che's martyrdom and the thinly veiled Soviet criticism of Cuban adventurism, Castro showed little inclination to mend his fences with Moscow. When in January 1968 he scornfully dismissed some of the ideas 'put forward in the name of Marxism' as 'real fossils', it was obvious that he had Soviet ideas in mind: 'Marxism needs to develop, overcome a certain sclerosis, interpret the realities of the present in an objective and scientific way, behave like a revolutionary force and not like a pseudo-revolutionary church.'

It was clear to Castro's listeners that Cuba was the 'revolutionary force' and the Soviet Union the 'pseudo-revolutionary church' which had succumbed to ideological sclerosis. Soon afterwards the Maximum Leader staged a show trial of a 'microfaction' of pro-Soviet loyalists within the Cuban Communist Party, who were found guilty of 'ideological diversionism' prejudicial to the 'unity and firmness of the revolutionary forces'. During the trial, the head of the DGI, Manuel Piñeiro, gave evidence that members of the microfaction had been in contact with the KGB.[65]

With the threatened collapse of the Soviet 'bridgehead' in Cuba, the KGB's grand strategy conceived in 1961 to orchestrate 'armed uprisings against pro-Western reactionary governments' in Latin America seemed in tatters. The Centre's early optimism about the prospects for a Sandinista revolution in Nicaragua had faded away. During the later 1960s the Centre was more interested in using FSLN guerrillas in operations to reconnoitre sabotage targets in the southern United States than in helping them prepare for revolution in Nicaragua. In 1966 a KGB sabotage and intelligence group (DRG) based on the ISKRA guerrilla group was formed on the Mexican–US border with support bases in the area of Ciudad Juárez, Tijuana and Ensenada. Its leader, Andara y Ubeda (PRIM), travelled to Moscow for training in Line F operations. Among the chief sabotage targets were American military bases, missile sites, radar installations, and the oil pipeline (codenamed START) which ran from El Paso in Texas to Costa Mesa, California. Three sites on the American coast were selected for DRG landings, together with large-capacity dead-drops in which to store mines, explosive, detonators and other sabotage materials. A support group codenamed SATURN was tasked with using the movements of migrant workers (*braceros*) to conceal the transfer of agents and munitions across the border.[66]

The year 1968 was a difficult one for the KGB in both Europe and Latin America. The show trial of the pro-Soviet microfaction in Havana was quickly followed by what Moscow considered an outrageous display of ideological subversion in Czechoslovakia. The attempt by the reformers of the Prague Spring to create 'Socialism with a human face' was interpreted by the KGB as counter-revolution. The near-collapse of official censorship culminated in a Prague May Day parade with banners proclaiming such irreverent messages for Moscow as 'Long live the USSR – but at its own expense!' The KGB played a major role both in assisting the invasion of Czechoslovakia by the forces of the Warsaw Pact in August 1968 and in the subsequent 'normalization' which ensured the country's return to pro-Soviet orthodoxy.[67]

Castro was widely expected to side with Prague reformers and to condemn the August invasion of Czechoslovakia. He began his first broadcast speech after the invasion, however, by saying that some of what he had to say would 'run counter to the feelings of many people'. Castro acknowledged that the invasion had no legal basis but insisted that, in the greater interests of 'the people's struggle against imperialism', it was fully justified:

In short, the Czechoslovak regime was moving toward capitalism and it was inexorably marching toward imperialism. About this we did not have the slightest doubt . . . The essential thing, whether we accept it or not, is whether the socialist bloc could permit the development of a political situation which led to the breakdown of a socialist country and its fall into the arms of imperialism. From our viewpoint, it is not permissible and the socialist bloc has the right to prevent it in one way or another.[68]

All this was music to Moscow's ears. The Maximum Leader's emergence over the next few months as a dependable Moscow loyalist made it possible for the Soviet Union to shore up its crumbling Cuban bridgehead.

Probably the main reason for Castro's ideological somersault only months after the show trial and imprisonment of Moscow loyalists within the Cuban Communist Party was a severe economic crisis which served to emphasize Cuba's dependence on Soviet economic aid. Cuban industry and power stations ran on Soviet oil shipped from the Black Sea. When Moscow began to cut back its oil exports as a sign of its displeasure early in 1968, there were power cuts in Havana, and Cuban sugar mills and factories began to grind to a halt. Castro himself worsened the crisis by an economically disastrous 'revolutionary offensive' in March designed to destroy the remnants of free enterprise by nationalizing 55,000 small businesses which accounted for a third of Cuba's retail sales. As a reward for the Maximum Leader's newfound loyalty, the Soviet Union effectively bailed out the Cuban economy. By the end of 1969, Cuba owed the Soviet Union $4 billion.[69]

Castro's decision to side with Moscow against the Czechoslovak reformers also reflected his own authoritarian leadership style and distaste for the political freedoms of the Prague Spring. By the mid-1960s the real achievements of the Cuban Revolution – the reforms in health and education and the end of *gangsterismo* chief among them – were increasingly overshadowed by an empty revolutionary rhetoric which bore little relation either to the regime's shambolic economic mismanagement or to its intolerance of dissent. In 1965 Castro himself admitted that Cuban jails contained 20,000 political prisoners.[70] A huge network of surveillance kept close watch for any sign of ideological dissidence. The DGI was assisted by the Committees for the Defence of the Revolution (CDRs), a nationwide network of neighbourhood associations which reported all suspicious activities. Founded in 1960, the CDRs expanded over the next decade to include almost a third of the adult population. Immediately after Castro's endorsement of the crushing of the Prague Spring, the CDRs, acting on instructions from the DGI, arranged for a series of 'spontaneous' demonstrations to support his speech. Cuba thus developed a vast system of social control similar to, but more conspicuous than, those operated by the KGB and its east European allies. By the late 1960s, Castro was using the CDRs to dictate even the length of men's hair and women's dresses. In November 1968 the parents of long-haired youths and miniskirted girls were summoned to appear before the local authorities.[71] Castro had a particular dislike of homosexuals and instructed that they 'should not be allowed in positions where they are able to exert an influence on young people'. Gays were routinely refused tenancies in new housing projects and frequently singled out for service in forced-labour units.[72]

Just as some of the Old Left of the 1930s, seduced by the myth-image of the Soviet Union as the world's first worker-peasant state, had been blind to the savage reality of Stalin's Russia, so a generation later many of the New Left of the 1960s shut their eyes to the increasingly authoritarian (though much less homicidal) nature of Castro's rule and his sometimes brutal disregard of basic human rights. The heroic image of Castro as a revolutionary David in battle fatigues blockaded on his island by the Goliath of American imperialism had a global appeal exploited by Soviet as well as Cuban propagandists. Among Castro's most naively enthusiastic Western supporters were the Americans of the Venceremos ('We Shall Overcome') Brigade, who from 1969 onwards came to cut sugar cane in Cuba and show their solidarity with the Cuban Revolution. Castro paid public tribute to the courage of the *brigadistas* 'in defying the ire of the imperialists'.[73]

Privately, however, he looked askance at the presence of gay and women's liberation movements among his American New Left supporters. Venceremos feminists, for their part, were taken aback by the behaviour of the Cuban female singers sent to entertain the Brigade: 'They frequently had bleached hair and tight-fitting skirts, and relied on sexual gestures and flirtation with the audience. We knew that, when not entertaining, these women were probably dedicated revolutionaries, doing hard work. The incongruity was hard to deal with.'[74]

Doubtless reflecting the views of the Maximum Leader, the DGI complained to the KGB that many of the New Left *brigadistas* were homosexuals and drug addicts. Venceremos gays, the DGI bizarrely reported, saw 'the possibility of using homosexuality to bring about the physical degeneration of American imperialism'. The Brigade, however, proved a valuable source of US identity documents for use in illegal intelligence operations.[75] The *brigadistas* were also regarded as an important propaganda asset.

Castro's return to Moscow loyalism had an immediate effect on the DGI's relations with the KGB. As a DGI officer later acknowledged, its role 'was always limited by the fact that Fidel Castro's strategic assumptions, personal convictions and intuitions were effectively off limits. Cuban intelligence was unable to challenge or contradict these.'[76] In accordance with the wishes of the Maximum Leader, during the winter of 1968–69 all heads of DGI overseas stations were recalled to Havana to be given new instructions on co-operation with the KGB. The DGI chief, Manuel Piñeiro, informed them that there had been a 'lessening of contradictions' between Cuba and the Soviet Union, and that they were to participate in a major new drive to collect scientific and technological intelligence (S&T) for the USSR. Piñeiro, however, had incurred the displeasure of the Centre as a result of his earlier investigation of KGB contacts with the pro-Moscow 'microfaction' before its show trial in January 1968. Early in 1969 KGB pressure led to his replacement by the more reliably pro-Soviet José Méndez Cominches. Henceforth the main priority of the DGI was intelligence collection rather than the export of revolution. Assistance to national liberation movements was hived off to the newly independent Dirección de Liberación Nacional (DLN), later the Departamento de América (DA), headed by Piñeiro.[77] Following a trip by Raúl Castro to

Moscow in the spring of 1970, there was a purge of those DGI officers who still appeared reluctant to co-operate with the KGB. A senior KGB adviser was given an office next door to the DGI chief, Méndez.[78]

The Soviet 'bridgehead' in Cuba seemed once again secure.

4

'Progressive' Regimes and 'Socialism with Red Wine'

At the beginning of the 1970s the greater part of Latin America was still, in Andropov's phrase, 'a new field for Soviet foreign policy activity'. He wrote in an unusually frank memorandum to the FCD, 'Our leaders know very little about Latin America. We must write more about these countries, and draw attention to them.' Andropov was determined that the lead in expanding Soviet influence in Latin America should be taken not by the Foreign Ministry but by the KGB:

We must remember that, when it comes to shedding light on the situation in the countries of Latin America, without us neither the Ministry of Foreign Affairs nor the Ministry of Foreign Trade will be able to undertake any effective action. We must be the first to establish contacts with important individuals in those countries where we do not have embassies, and to send our officers there on short or long-term visits.[1]

Andropov was anxious to exploit the new opportunities for KGB operations offered by the emergence of 'progressive' military regimes in Peru and Bolivia, and by the election of a Marxist President of Chile. Rather than attempting the high-risk strategy of trying to recruit Latin American Presidents and other leading politicians as Soviet agents, Andropov's preferred strategy was to turn as many as possible into 'confidential contacts', willing to have clandestine meetings with KGB officers who attempted to influence their policies, particularly towards the United States.[2] Agent recruitment was pursued only at a lower level of the Latin American political and official hierarchies, as well as in the media and other professions.

The KGB's greatest asset in recruiting both confidential contacts and an agent network was the popular resentment in Latin America at the arrogance of the *Yanqui* colossus of the North. The Centre's leading Latin American expert, Nikolai Leonov, who had been the first to identify Fidel Castro's revolutionary potential, later acknowledged:

All political efforts by the Soviet government, and hence by our country's intelligence service, were aimed at causing the greatest possible harm to North American dominance in this part of the world. So we supported politically, sometimes by sending weaponry or other aid, anyone who was against United States dominance – any government, any national liberation movement, any revolutionary group. However, with few exceptions, the extreme left [other than pro-Moscow Communist parties] did not enjoy great popularity in the Kremlin at that time. They were feared, and for that reason were always sidelined. But reasonable patriotic centre-left forces in Latin America always found strong support in the USSR. I personally took part in many operations of this type. I worked with many Latin American leaders, trying at least to encourage them, to help them as far as possible in their anti-American stance.[3]

Moscow's suspicion of 'the extreme left' was due, in large part, to fear that it was contaminated with Maoist heresy. A subsidiary theme in KGB operations in Latin America was to defeat the Chinese challenge to Soviet Communism. Alistair Horne wrote in 1972:

It is not in South-east Asia, the Middle East or Africa that *the* ideological battle of the seventies seems likely to be waged, but in South America. Here, one feels, may well be the battleground where the orthodoxy of Soviet communism will triumph definitively over Maoism or vice-versa.[4]

That estimate proved to be exaggerated, though at the beginning of the twenty-first century the main vestiges of Maoist revolutionary movements – in particular the Peruvian Sendero Luminoso (Shining Path) – were located in Latin America. At the beginning of the 1970s, however, Horne's prophecy seemed highly plausible.

The first 'progressive' junta to attract the attention of the Centre in Latin America was in Peru. To Marxist-Leninists, class conflict in Peru seemed to make it ripe for revolution. Since the foundation of the Peruvian Republic in 1821, vast wealth had been concentrated in the hands of an urban élite, while the mass of the rural population

– mostly aboriginals – lived in grinding poverty. Land ownership was more unequal than anywhere else in Latin America. In the 1960s 9 per cent of landowners owned 82 per cent of the land, while millions of peasants had none at all. The slums which ringed Lima, mostly inhabited by peasants unable to make a living in the country-side, were among the most wretched on the continent. Half-hearted land reform was halted in the mid-1960s by a hostile, conservative Congress.[5] Dependency theory, which became popular in the 1950s and 1960s, blamed Peru's backwardness on American imperialism. In order to maintain its own prosperity, the United States was alleg-edly promoting the 'underdevelopment' or 'dependency' of Latin America by controlling access to major natural resources, by main-taining financial and military control, and by other methods designed to prevent its southern neighbours escaping from their poverty. The US-owned International Petroleum Company, an Exxon subsidiary which dominated Peru's petroleum industry, seemed to the Latin American left to symbolize the way in which the power of American capital undermined Peruvian national sovereignty.[6]

Peru's political history had been punctuated by military coups. However, the junta headed by General Juan Velasco Alvarado, which seized power in October 1968, broke with precedent. It was the first Peruvian coup led by left-wing radicals, many of them with a background in military intelligence. 'Intelligence', claimed one of the radicals, '. . . opened our eyes and made us see the urgency for change in our country.' Within days of his coup, on what became known as 'National Dignity Day', Velasco nationalized the Inter-national Petroleum Company without compensation,[7] and began preparations for a series of other nationalizations. The junta went on to announce a radical programme of land reform and sought to pre-vent the flight of capital to Swiss bank accounts by giving itself the power to inspect bank deposits. Its policies combined radical reform with military discipline. The junta banned the riotous annual Lima carnival on the grounds of public safety and arrested those who trans-gressed traditional standards of sexual propriety in public parks.[8]

Since the Soviet Union did not have diplomatic relations with Peru at the time of the coup, it had no embassy or legal residency capable of reporting on the new regime. Nikolai Leonov, who had recently been given accelerated promotion to the post of deputy head of the FCD Second (Latin American) Department, was sent to investigate, staying at a Lima hotel posing as a correspondent of the Novosti Press Agency. With the help of the press office at the Peruvian Foreign Ministry, Leonov succeeded in making contact with a number of members and supporters of the new regime. His stay was none the less a difficult one – chiefly, he believed, because the CIA had revealed his real identity to a number of its local contacts. As a result, Leonov later claimed, he received threatening phone calls in Russian and the unwanted attentions of a photographer who took numerous pictures of him while he was dining in restaurants. On one occasion, he was 'followed along the street by a carload of semi-naked girls' – possibly festival dancers whose playful intentions Leonov misconstrued as a CIA provocation. A further difficulty was the fact that the only way that he could communicate with the Centre from Lima was by post. When he went to the main post office, he was told not to seal his letters with sticky tape, doubtless in order to make them easier to open. On one occasion early in 1969, when he felt it necessary to send a top-secret cipher telegram to Moscow, he had to travel to the KGB residency in Chile to do so. Though Mitrokhin did not note the text of Leonov's report, its tone was clearly optimistic. 'We were', Leonov said later, 'working politically against the United States and we put all our heart into this task.'[9] The Centre could not fail to be impressed by the new opportunities in Peru for operations against the United States. In February 1969, after an unbroken period of co-operation between American and Peruvian armed forces stretching back to the Second World War, all US military missions were expelled. For the first time, Peru began to turn for military assistance to the Soviet Union. In an attempt to strengthen popular support for its reform policies, the Velasco regime became the first Latin American military junta to form an undeclared tactical alliance with the Communists. Though the previously outlawed Peruvian Communist Party remained illegal, it was permitted to operate openly from its Lima headquarters and to publish its own newspaper.[10]

In August 1969, following the establishment of Peruvian–Soviet diplomatic relations, the KGB set up its first residency in Lima, headed for the next seven years by Arseni Fyodorovich Orlov.[11] Orlov reported optimistically that the military government was adopting 'a progressive, anti-imperialist line' with the support of the Communist Party.[12] When armed Communists took over the headquarters of the Bankworkers' Union in June 1970, the government failed to intervene. The most popular manifestation of Peru's new Soviet connection was the arrival of the Moscow State Circus, which performed in Lima's Plaza de Toros for an entire month.[13]

The Lima residency quickly acquired several 'confidential contacts' in the junta. One was reported to be President Velasco's 'most trusted confidant' and a 'firm supporter' of collaboration between the Peruvian intelligence community and the KGB.[14] Orlov reported that, thanks to the good offices of another member of the junta, 'the Residency has established contact with the President.'[15] One of Velasco's senior advisers (identified by name in Mitrokhin's notes) was recruited as a KGB agent. According to a 1971 report from the residency, which records a payment to him of $5,000: 'He enjoys the trust of President Velasco Alvarado. Through [him] influence is exerted on the President and on members of the Peruvian government, and public opinion is shaped through him. Two government newspapers are under his control.'[16]

In order to impress Soviet leaders, the KGB commonly exaggerated its ability to 'shape' foreign public opinion, and it may well have done so in this case. However, the Lima residency undoubtedly approved the Velasco regime's censorship of media opposition to it. In January 1972 there were world-wide protests at the sequestration of Peru's leading newspaper, La Prensa, the most influential of the junta's critics. The nineteenth-century house of its proprietor, Don Pedro Beltrán, an important part of Lima's cultural heritage, was demolished on the pretext of street-widening. The New York Times denounced the 'savage vendetta against one of the most respected journalists in the Americas'.[17]

Encouraged by the Lima residency's contacts with the junta, the KGB proposed formal co-operation with its Peruvian counterpart, the Servicio de Inteligencia Nacional (SIN), codenamed KONTORA. Negotiations between KGB and SIN representatives produced a draft agreement providing for an exchange of intelligence, co-operation in security measures, KGB training for SIN officers and the provision to SIN of KGB 'operational technical equipment'. In June 1971 the CPSU Central Committee approved the draft agreement. Two operations officers and one technical specialist were stationed in Lima to liaise with SIN. Meetings between Soviet and Peruvian intelligence officers took place about once a week, usually in SIN safe apartments. The Lima residency noted with satisfaction that one of the immediate consequences of the agreement was the ending of SIN surveillance of the embassy and other Soviet offices.[18] With KGB assistance, SIN set up a surveillance post near the US embassy which secretly photographed all those entering and leaving, and recorded their names in a card index. SIN later used KGB equipment to record embassy phone calls and intercept radio messages.[19] The Centre claimed that co-operation with SIN led to 'the neutralization of an American agent network in the [Peruvian] trade unions and the liquidation of an American intelligence operational technical group'. It also claimed the credit for 'the exposure of the conspiratorial activity' of the Minister of Internal Affairs, General Armando Artola, who appears to have opposed the Soviet connection and was sacked in 1971.[20]

Initially, KGB liaison officers found some members of SIN 'guarded' in their dealings with them. According to KGB files, however, many were won over by items of current intelligence, gifts, birthday greetings, 'material assistance', invitations to visit the Soviet Union and other friendly gestures.[21] Mitrokhin concluded from his reading of KGB files that intelligence both from 'confidential contacts' in the junta and from SIN was 'highly valued' in the Centre.[22] In 1973 the new head of SIN, General Enrique Gallegos Venero, visited Moscow for discussions with Andropov, Fyodor Mortin, head of the FCD, and other senior KGB officers. During his visit it was agreed to extend intelligence co-operation to include Peruvian military intelligence (codenamed SHTAB by the KGB).[23] Though apparently satisfied with the results of Gallegos's visit, the Centre took a somewhat censorious view of the behaviour of SIN officers, ranging in rank from captain to lieutenant-colonel, who were invited to Moscow at its expense (air travel included) to take part in FCD training courses. One KGB report primly concluded:

The Peruvians who were studying at the special P-2, P-3, and P-4 departments at the FCD's Red Banner [later Andropov] Institute were active in making contact with girls and women of loose behaviour in Moscow, and had intimate relations with them, after which these acquaintances were handed over to another group of students for intimate relations. The students did not heed the attempts of the course supervisors to enlighten them.[24]

In general, however, the Centre congratulated itself on the success of intelligence collaboration with Peru. A 1975 report gave the work of the Lima residency 'a positive evaluation'.[25] Intelligence on 'the situation in Peru's ruling circles', some of it passed on to the Politburo, was assessed as 'especially valuable'.[26] KGB co-operation with SIN against US targets led to the expulsion of a series of CIA officers and the curtailment of Peace Corps activities and US-sponsored English-language courses.[27] A relative of President Velasco's wife, occupying 'a high position' in the administration, was exposed as, allegedly, a CIA agent.[28] The Lima residency also carried out 'wide-ranging active measures' against US targets.[29] 'Operational technical' experts were sent from the Centre to instruct SIN officers in the use of KGB surveillance, eavesdropping and photographic equipment in operations against the US, Mexican and Chilean embassies in Lima.[30] With financial assistance from the KGB, SIN agents were sent to carry out KGB assignments in Chile, Argentina and other parts of Latin America.[31]

From 1973 onwards Peru made a series of massive Soviet arms purchases, totalling more than $1.6 billion over the next twelve years. In the Western hemisphere only Cuba received more.[32] The Centre's claims that it also succeeded in 'increasing the progressive measures of Velasco's government',[33] however, were probably made chiefly to impress the Soviet leadership. The KGB's influence on the military government's security, defence and foreign policy did not extend to its domestic reform programme. In 1972, for example, the Interior Minister, General Pedro Richter Prado, was dismayed by much of what he saw on a tour of collective farms in Poland and Czechoslovakia. Soviet bloc agriculture, he told Alistair Horne, was 'going backwards'. The junta publicly declared that, 'Peru stands for neither Communism nor Capitalism'. Horne concluded that, by this time, its confused ideological preferences lay somewhere between Tito's Yugoslavia and Gaullist France. Its heavy-handed economic mismanagement was compounded by the problems of financing the imports of Soviet arms. Almost a quarter of the national budget went on the armed forces, double the proportion in neighbouring Colombia. The revenues from the massive newly discovered oil reserves in the Amazon basin were frittered away.[34]

The Centre did not usually make reports to the Politburo which undermined its own previous claims to be able to influence foreign leaders. It is therefore unlikely that it reported to the political leadership on the declining prospects of the 'progressive' Peruvian junta as it struggled to cope with the consequences of its economic mismanagement. The coup toppling Velasco in August 1975, led by General Francisco Morales Bermúdez, began a more conservative phase of military rule.[35] The KGB was, however, able to claim an apparently striking victory over Peruvian Maoism. In June 1975 the Lima residency made 'operational contact' with one of the leaders of the pro-Chinese Marxist-Leninist Party of Peru, codenamed VANTAN. The KGB claimed the credit for disrupting, with VANTAN's assistance, the Party's 1976 Congress. According to a file summary noted by Mitrokhin: 'At its Congress, the Party sharply criticized Peking's policy, including its line of splitting the Communist and Workers' movement, and decided to break with Maoism and to dissolve itself. This operation produced great repercussions in Latin-American countries.'[36]

The next Latin American state after Peru to acquire what the KGB considered a 'progressive' military government was Bolivia, its landlocked southern neighbour. Bolivia's turbulent political history had been punctuated by more military coups than anywhere else in the world. At the beginning of the 1970s the presidential palace in La Paz (at 12,000 feet, the highest on the continent) was still pockmarked with bullet holes from previous coups which, given the likelihood of further violent regime changes, were not thought worth repairing. In front of the palace was a lamp-post with an inscription recording that a president had been hanged from it in 1946.

The leader of the junta which took power in April 1969, General Alfredo Ovando Candía, had been commander-in-chief of the Bolivian army at the time of Che Guevara's capture and death eighteen months earlier. It was widely believed, however, that he had since been at least partly seduced by the Che revolutionary myth and felt a deep sense of guilt at having ordered his execution. Once in power, Ovando followed the Peruvian example, nationalizing American-owned companies, establishing diplomatic relations with the Soviet Union and seeking support from workers, peasants and students. In October 1970, following a failed coup by right-wing army officers and riots by left-wing university students, Ovando was overthrown by the vociferously anti-imperialist General Juan José Torres González, who had been sacked as commander-in-chief for what Ovando considered his excessive adulation of Fidel Castro.[37]

The resident in La Paz, Igor Yevgenievich Sholokhov, was instructed to gain access to Torres (codenamed CAESAR by the KGB) 'in order to use him to carry out measures to rally anti-American forces in Bolivia'.[38] In the excitable aftermath of the 'October Revolution' which had brought Torres to power, students at San Andrés University in La Paz led violent demonstrations against American imperialism. Torres took no action as US offices were broken into and pillaged and the *Yanqui* community was reduced to living in a state of semi-siege. US diplomats removed the CD plates from their cars for fear of attack; even the Clínica América in La Paz was forced to change its name to Clínica Metodista.[39] The KGB was encouraged by Torres's close relations with the Communists as well as by his hostility to the *Yanquis*. Soon after he became President, the First Secretary of the Bolivian Communist Party, Jorge Kolle Cueto, reported to Sholokhov that Torres was 'taking steps to involve the Left in co-operation with the government', and had offered to help the Communists establish paramilitary groups to meet the threat of a right-wing coup.[40]

In July Andropov wrote to Brezhnev:

Considering the progressive nature of the change occurring in Bolivia, Torres's desire to develop multifaceted co-operation with the USSR, and the Bolivian friends' [Communists'] positive attitude towards the President, it would be worthwhile examining the possibility of supplying arms to Bolivia, as well as providing Torres with economic aid . . . , for the purpose of increasing his influence in the army and assisting in frustrating the conspiratorial plans of the reactionaries, thus gaining the time needed by the country's democratic forces to strengthen their position.[41]

Andropov's assessment, however, proved far too optimistic. By the time he wrote his report Torres's prospects of survival were already slim. 'Progressive change' in Bolivia was rapidly collapsing into anarchy. The army was deeply divided between right- and left-wing factions. In June 1971 the unoccupied Congress building next to the presidential palace was seized by the various factions of the left who declared themselves the Asamblea del Pueblo and began to function as a parallel government. Inevitably the factions quickly fell out among themselves, with the Communist Party denouncing the Maoists as 'petit bourgeois dedicated to leading the working class on a new adventure'. The extravagant if confused revolutionary rhetoric of the Assembly and Torres's apparent impotence in the face of it helped to provoke in August 1971 Bolivia's 187th coup, led by the right-wing Colonel Hugo Banzer Suárez, who had been sacked by Torres as commandant of the Military Academy. After the discovery of the large quantities of arms from the Soviet Union and Czechoslovakia despatched at Torres's request, Banzer ordered a mass expulsion of Soviet diplomats and intelligence officers.[42]

Despite the disappointment of Torres's overthrow, the KGB continued to seek opportunities to cultivate other Latin American leaders. Before the 1970 presidential election in Costa Rica, it had secret discussions with the successful candidate, José Figueres Ferrer (codenamed KASIK).[43] Figueres was the leading Costa Rican politician of his generation. As head of the founding junta of the post-war Second Republic, he had taken the lead in abolishing the army and turning Costa Rica into an unarmed democracy – a unique event in the history of the Americas. Figueres's first contact with Soviet intelligence, though he did not realize it, went back to 1951, when he had unwittingly appointed as envoy in Rome (and non-resident envoy in Belgrade) a KGB illegal, Iosif Grigulevich, posing as Teodoro Castro, the illegitimate son of a dead (and, in reality, childless) Costa Rican notable. Unknown to Figueres, early in 1953 Grigulevich had been given a highly dangerous mission to assassinate Marshal Tito. When his mission was aborted after Stalin's death in March, 'Teodoro Castro' disappeared – so far as Figueres was concerned – into thin air, beginning a new life in Moscow under his real name, Grigulevich, as an academic expert on Latin America.[44]

Figueres was first elected President in 1953, serving until 1958. His long-running feud with the US-backed Somoza dictatorship in neighbouring Nicaragua, which continued after his presidency, appears to have attracted the favourable attention of the KGB. When President Luis Somoza challenged him to a duel, Figueres agreed – provided it was fought on the deck of a Soviet submarine which Somoza falsely claimed to have captured.[45] Despite his anti-militarism, Figueres became a strong supporter of the Sandinistas. Before the 1970 presidential election the KGB secretly transmitted to him via the Costa Rican Communist Party a 'loan' of US $300,000 to help finance his campaign in return for a promise, if elected, to establish diplomatic relations with the Soviet Union. Once reinstalled as President, Figueres kept his promise.[46] In 1971 the CPSU Central Committee authorized A. I. Mosolov, head of the newly established San José residency, to establish contact with him.[47]

Mosolov and Figueres agreed on regular secret meetings to be arranged through the intermediary of a confidant of the President. Before each meeting, the confidant would meet Mosolov at a pre-arranged rendezvous in San José, then drive him in his own car to see Figueres.[48] Some of Mosolov's reports on these meetings were considered sufficiently important by the Centre to be passed on to the Politburo. The KGB's motives in doing so probably had less to do with the intrinsic importance of the reports' contents than with the further evidence they provided of the high level of its foreign contacts. As in Peru and Bolivia, the Centre wished to demonstrate to the Soviet leadership that in a continent formerly dominated by American imperialism, it now had direct access even to presidents and juntas. It claimed, probably with some exaggeration, that the KGB was able 'to exert useful influence' over Figueres.[49]

As well as providing confidential reports on other countries in Central America and the Caribbean, Figueres discussed his own political future with the KGB residency, probably in the hope of obtaining further Soviet financial support. He told Mosolov that he intended to stay in control of his political party and influence government decisions even after he ceased to be president in 1974. 'In order to do this', Mosolov reported, 'he has acquired a radio station and television channel, and is preparing to publish his own newspaper.' All were regarded by the KGB as useful vehicles for active measures.[50]

The Soviet ambassador in San José, Vladimir Nikolayevich Kazimirov, like his colleagues in a number of other capitals, deeply resented the fact that the resident's political contacts were superior to his own. While on leave in Moscow in August 1973, he demanded a meeting with Andropov and complained that Mosolov did not even bother to inform him about his contacts with Figueres. On one occasion he had called on the President, only to discover that Mosolov had met him an hour earlier. Kazimirov claimed that American agents in Costa Rica were seeking to use the President's contacts with the KGB to compromise him.[51] The ambassador's objections appear to have had little effect. KGB meetings with, and subsidies to, Figueres continued. The Centre informed Brezhnev in January 1974: 'In view of the fact that Figueres has agreed to publish materials advantageous to the KGB, he has been given 10,000 US dollars under the guise of stock purchases in his newspaper. When he accepted this money, Figueres stated that he greatly appreciated Soviet support.'[52]

Relations with Figueres, however, gradually cooled. In 1976 Manuel Piñeiro, head of the Cuban Departamento de América (DA), told a senior KGB officer that Figueres was 'an arrant demagogue', who kept a private armoury of weapons including machine guns and bazookas at his villa outside San José.[53] A KGB assessment concluded that Figueres's 'views and actions' were inconsistent.[54]

By far the most important of the KGB's confidential contacts in South America was Salvador Allende Gossens (codenamed LEADER by the KGB),[55] whose election as President of Chile in 1970 was hailed by a Moscow commentator as 'second only to the victory of the Cuban Revolution in the magnitude of its significance as a revolutionary blow to the imperialist system in Latin America'. Allende was the first Marxist anywhere in the world to win power through the ballot box. His victory in Chile, following the emergence of 'progressive' military governments in Peru and Bolivia, was cited by *Pravda* and other Soviet official organs as proof of 'the multiplicity of forms within the framework of which Latin America is paving its way to true independence'.[56]

Allende had first attracted KGB attention in the early 1950s when, as leader of the Chilean Socialist Party (Partido Socialista), he had formed an alliance with the then banned Communist Party. In 1952 he stood with its support at the presidential election but won only 6 per cent of the vote. Though there was as yet no KGB residency in Chile, a Line PR (political intelligence) officer, Svyatoslav Fyodorovich Kuznetsov (codenamed LEONID), probably operating under cover as a Novosti correspondent, made the first direct contact with Allende in the following year.[57] At the presidential election of 1958, standing as the candidate of a left-wing alliance, the Frente de Acción Popular (FRAP), Allende was beaten into second place by only 35,000 votes. What Allende's KGB file describes as 'systematic contact' with him began after the establishment in 1961 of a Soviet trade mission in Chile, which provided cover for a KGB presence. Allende is reported to have 'stated his willingness to co-operate on a confidential basis and provide any necessary assistance, since he considered himself a friend of the Soviet Union. He willingly shared political information . . .' Though he became a KGB 'confidential contact', however, he was never classed as an agent. The KGB claimed some of the credit for Allende's part in the campaign which led to the establishment of Soviet–Chilean diplomatic relations in 1964.[58] The new Soviet embassy in Santiago contained the first KGB legal residency on Chilean soil.[59]

At the 1964 presidential election, standing once again as the candidate of the FRAP alliance, Allende was further from victory than six years earlier, being soundly beaten by a strong centrist candidate in what became virtually a two-horse race. But, with 39 per cent of the vote, he did well enough to show that, if the anti-Marxist vote were to be divided at the next election, he would stand a good chance of victory.[60] The glaring social injustices of a country in which half the population lived in shanty towns or rural poverty also seemed to favour the electoral prospects of the left. The Archbishop of Santiago told the British ambassador that, 'considering the appalling conditions which the mass of the population had to put up with, it was not surprising that there were many Communists in Chile; what was . . . surprising was that the poorer classes were not Communist to a man.' The high birth-rate and level of immigration added to Chile's social tensions. During the 1960s the population grew by nearly a third.[61]

Though recognizing the advantages of electoral alliance with Allende, the leadership of the Chilean Communist Party made clear to the KGB that it regarded him as both 'a demagogue' and 'a weak and inconsistent politician' with Maoist sympathies:

His characteristic traits were arrogance, vanity, desire for glorification and a longing to be in the spotlight at any price. He was easily influenced by stronger and more determined personalities. He was also inconsistent in his attitude to the Communist Party. LEADER explained his attitude to the Communist Party by referring to his position as leader of the Socialist Party to which, as a party member, he was bound to be loyal. He had visited China a number of times and ranked Mao Zedong on the same level as Marx, Engels and Lenin.

The Santiago residency also reported that Chilean Communists were concerned by Allende's close connections with Freemasonry. His paternal grandfather had been Serene Grand Master of the Chilean Masonic Order, and Allende himself had been a Mason since before the Second World War. His Masonic lodge, the Communists complained to the KGB, had 'deep roots among the lower and middle bourgeoisie'.[62] Allende was unlike any existing stereotype of a Marxist leader. During his visits to Havana in the 1960s, he had been privately mocked by Castro's entourage for his aristocratic tastes: fine wines, expensive objets d'art, well-cut suits and elegantly dressed women. Allende was also a womanizer. The Nobel laureate in literature, Gabriel García Márquez, described him as 'a gallant with a touch of the old school about him, perfumed notes and furtive rendezvous'. Despite the private mockery which they aroused in Allende's Communist allies, however, his bourgeois appearance and expensive lifestyle were electoral assets, reassuring middle-class voters that their lives would continue normally under an Allende presidency. As even some of Allende's opponents acknowledged, he also had enormous personal charm. Nathaniel Davis, who became US ambassador in Santiago in 1971, was struck by his 'extraordinary and appealing human qualities . . . He had the social and socializing instincts of a long-time, top-drawer political personality.'[63]

In 1970 Allende stood again for the presidency as the candidate of an enlarged left-wing coalition: the Unidad Popular (UP) of the Communist, Socialist and Radical parties (and three smaller left-wing groups – the API, MAPU and SDP). His chances of success were strengthened by the division of the anti-Marxist vote between rival Christian Democrat and National Party candidates. Allende's original KGB case officer, Svyatoslav Kuznetsov, then serving in the Mexico City residency, was sent to Chile to maintain contact with him throughout the election campaign and co-ordinate covert operations designed to ensure his success.[64]

Both the CIA, acting on instructions from the White House and the 40 Committee (which oversaw US covert action), and the KGB spent substantial amounts of money in an attempt to influence the outcome of the election. Though the CIA spent $425,000 trying to ensure Allende's defeat,[65] its money was targeted far less effectively than that of the KGB. The 40 Committee approved a covert propaganda campaign 'to alert Chileans to the dangers of Allende and a Marxist government' but forbade support for either of the candidates opposing Allende. The Director of Central Intelligence, Richard Helms, was sceptical of the effectiveness of a CIA operation based on the assumption that it was possible to 'beat somebody with nobody'.[66] KGB money, by contrast, was precisely targeted. Allende made a personal appeal, probably via Kuznetsov, for Soviet funds.[67] Like other 'fraternal' parties around the world, the Chilean Communists received annual subsidies from Moscow, secretly transmitted to them by the KGB. Throughout the 1960s they were paid more than any other Communist Party in Latin America. Their original allocation for 1970 was $400,000.[68] However, doubtless on KGB advice, the Politburo made an additional allocation to the Party on 27 July to assist its role in the election campaign. It also approved a personal subsidy of $50,000 to be handed directly to Allende.[69] The Chilean Communist Party provided Allende with an additional $100,000 from its own funds.[70] The KGB also gave $18,000 to a left-wing Senator to persuade him not to stand as a presidential candidate and to remain within the Unidad Popular coalition. Given the closeness of the result, even the small vote which he might have attracted could have tipped the balance against Allende. That, at least, was the view of the KGB.[71]

On 4 September 1970 Allende won the presidential election with 36.3 per cent of the vote; his Nationalist and Christian Democrat opponents gained, respectively, 35 and 27.8 per cent. In its report to the Central Committee, the KGB claimed some of the credit for Allende's victory.[72] Though it doubtless did not underestimate the importance of its role, the closeness of the result suggests that the KGB may indeed have played a significant part in preventing Allende being narrowly beaten into second place. Allende won by only 39,000 votes out of a total of 3 million cast. Given the failure of any candidate to gain 50 per cent of the vote, the election of the President passed to a joint session of the two houses of the Chilean Congress on 24 October. Though precedent dictated that Allende would be elected, Andropov remained anxious about the outcome. He reported to the Central Committee on 23 September:

As the question of the election of the President will finally be decided by a vote in Congress on 24 October, Allende is still faced with a determined struggle with his political opponents, and substantial material resources may still be required for this purpose. With the aim of strengthening confidential relations with Allende and creating conditions for continuing co-operation with him in the future, it would be expedient to give him material assistance amounting to 30,000 dollars if the need arises.

At the same time, the Committee of State Security [KGB] will carry out measures designed to promote the consolidation of Allende's victory and his election to the post of President of the country. The International Department of the CPSU Central Committee (Comrade V. V. Zagladin) supports this proposal.[73]

The KGB's anxiety about parliamentary confirmation of Allende's electoral victory was understandable. The result of the presidential election left President Richard Nixon, according to his National Security Advisor, Henry Kissinger, 'beside himself' with rage. Having berated the Democrats for over a decade for allowing Cuba to go Communist, Nixon now faced the prospect as a Republican President of seeing Chile follow suit. There was, he angrily told Kissinger and the DCI, Richard Helms, 'only a one in ten chance, perhaps' of preventing Allende's confirmation, but the attempt must be made in order to 'save Chile' from Communism. The CIA drew up a two-track plan. Track I was to find some method of persuading the Chilean Congress not to vote Allende into office. Track II was to engineer a military coup.[74] Both failed. On 24 October Allende was formally elected President by vote of the Chilean Congress.

Regular Soviet contact with Allende after his election was maintained not by the Soviet ambassador but by Kuznetsov, who was instructed by the Centre to 'exert a favourable influence on Chilean government policy'. According to LEADER's KGB file:

In a cautious way Allende was made to understand the necessity of reorganizing Chile's army and intelligence services, and of setting up a relationship between Chile's and the USSR's intelligence services. Allende reacted to this positively.

The KGB devoted its attention to strengthening Allende's anti-American leanings. To this end, information obtained by the KGB Residency in Chile on the activities of American intelligence officers trying to penetrate the leaders of the army and intelligence services was conveyed to Allende. Important and goal-directed operations were conducted according to plan.[75]

CIA covert action against Allende continued during his presidency. Immediately after the September presidential election, Nixon gave instructions to 'make the [Chilean] economy scream', though in the event economic mismanagement by the Allende regime almost certainly did far more damage than the CIA.[76] The intelligence supplied by Kuznetsov to Allende about CIA operations in Chile included a certain amount of disinformation, such as the claim that Nathaniel Davis, who arrived in Santiago as US ambassador in October 1971, was a CIA officer.[77] There is no evidence that Allende realized he was being deceived. In 1971 he presented Kuznetsov with a Longines watch as a mark of his personal esteem.[78]

Kuznetsov arranged his regular meetings with Allende through the President's personal secretary, Miria Contreras Bell, known as 'La Payita' and codenamed MARTA by the KGB.[79] 'La Payita' appears to have been Allende's favourite mistress during his presidency. According to Nathaniel Davis:

Apparently it was for La Payita, and in her name, that Allende purchased El Cañaveral, a property in El Arrayán suburb outside Santiago. This estate also served as a training site for the president's bodyguards, a political meeting place, and, allegedly, an intimate hideaway where sex films were shown and the president, UP bigwigs, and their girlfriends cavorted – and had themselves photographed as they did so.[80]

Kuznetsov reported more discreetly that, 'according to available information', Allende was spending 'a great deal of time' in La Payita's company: 'Allende is very attentive to ladies, and tries to surround himself with charming women. His relationship with his wife has more than once been harmed as a result.'[81] Despite Allende's affairs, however, his wife Hortensia remained intensely loyal to him. Kuznetsov did his best to cultivate her as well as her husband.[82]

Cuban intelligence also established close relations with the Allende family. Allende's personal guard, the black-beret Grupo de Amigos Personales, contained numerous Cubans. His daughter, Beatriz, who oversaw presidential security, married a Cuban intelligence officer, Luis Fernández Oña, with the disconcerting nickname 'tiro fijo' ('quick-on-the-trigger').[83] One of the CIA officers stationed in Chile recalls that he had 'a lot of respect for the Cuban Intelligence. They were a lot more effective than the Russians in the sense that they still had revolutionary fervour, they were prepared to make sacrifices, they spoke the language, and they were prepared to mix it up with the *campesinos*.'[84]

In May 1971 FCD Service 1 (Intelligence Analysis), of which Leonov had become deputy head,[85] sent Kuznetsov a lengthy list of topics on which it instructed him to obtain Allende's views:

- The President's assessment of the internal political situation in the country, and his plans to hinder the subversive activities of the right-wing opposition.

- The President's assessment of the economic situation in the country and measures planned to strengthen the economy.

- Relations between the government and the parties in the Popular Unity coalition.

- The President's attitude towards unilateral actions by parties within the bloc, especially the Communist Party.

- The possibility of and conditions necessary for the unification of the Communists and socialists into a single party.

- Decisions by the President to strengthen the leadership of the Chilean armed forces and government with supporters of the left-wing parties.

- Prospects for the development of economic, political and military relations between Chile and the USSR, Cuba, other socialist countries, and China.

- Relations between Chile and the United States.

- Chile's policy with respect to the countries of Latin America.

It was a tribute to Kuznetsov's access to the President that he was able to obtain full responses on all these topics. Nikolai Leonov, was full of praise for the quality of Allende's information. Reports based on it were forwarded to the Politburo.[86] In October 1971, on instructions from the Politburo, Allende was given $30,000 'in order to solidify the trusted relations' with him.[87] Allende also mentioned to Kuznetsov his desire to acquire 'one or two icons' for his private art collection. He was presented with two icons, valued by the Centre at 150 rubles, as a gift.[88]

On 7 December, in a memorandum to the Politburo personally signed by Andropov, the KGB proposed giving Allende another

$60,000 for what was euphemistically termed 'his work with [i.e. bribery of] political party leaders, military commanders, and parliamentarians'. Allende was to be urged to strengthen his authority by establishing 'unofficial contact' with Chilean security chiefs and 'using the resources of friends [Communists]' in the Interior Ministry. The KGB also proposed giving an additional $70,000 to a Chilean monthly already subsidized by the KGB, to 'make it more combative and sharp in its defence of the interests of Popular Unity and in its exposure of the local reactionaries' and imperialists' intrigues'. The proposals were approved by the Politburo.[89]

In June 1972 Kuznetsov's close relationship with Allende was disturbed by the arrival in Santiago of a tough new Soviet ambassador, Aleksandr Vasilyevich Basov, whose membership of the Central Committee indicated both his high rank within the nomenklatura and the importance attached by Moscow to relations with Allende's Chile. Unlike his predecessor, Basov was not prepared to play second fiddle to a KGB officer. His relations with the residency worsened, apparently soon after his arrival in Santiago, after the discovery in the walls of both his office and apartment of American listening devices with miniature transmitters which could be activated from some distance away.[90] Basov doubtless blamed the KGB for failing to protect the security of the embassy. The KGB in turn blamed the Chilean Communist Party for recommending the firm which had been employed for building work at the embassy. The Party leader, Luis Corvalán Lepe (codenamed SHEF), was secretly informed by the KGB that the firm was untrustworthy and had been penetrated by 'hostile agents' who had installed the devices.[91]

Basov initially insisted on accompanying Kuznetsov to meetings with Allende, thus hampering the conduct of KGB business which the resident was reluctant to discuss in the presence of the ambassador.[92] Within a few months, however, Basov was seeking to replace Kuznetsov as the main Soviet contact with Allende. The Santiago residency complained to the Centre:

The ambassador intends to set the line himself for meetings with LEADER [Allende], and he goes to the meetings with LEADER accompanied not by LEONID [Kuznetsov] but by other officials. The ambassador is 'jealous' of LEONID's visits to LEADER, because he is taking away his bread [most important business]. Therefore, he demands detailed meeting plans and reports on the meetings. He is trying to supervise us on this matter.

Basov's ultimate aim was to reduce most Soviet contact with Allende to 'a single channel' controlled by himself. The residency complained that one channel 'is insufficient for conducting active measures and other special operations'. Hitherto Kuznetsov had built up a close relationship with Allende's wife and his daughter Beatriz. Both, according to the KGB, 'turn[ed] directly to LEONID with various requests'. Basov, however, assigned contact with the Allende family to a member of his staff and tried to make it impossible for Kuznetsov to continue his meetings with Allende's wife.[93] In December 1972, Kuznetsov was able to renew contact with Hortensia and Beatriz Allende while they were staying at the Barvikha Sanatorium in the Soviet Union. During their stay, almost certainly without informing Basov, the Centre made, at its own expense, a two-week booking at the sanatorium for Kuznetsov and his wife Galina.[94] It is clear from the tone of subsequent KGB reports that, once again probably without the ambassador's knowledge, Kuznetsov succeeded in establishing a secret channel 'for handling the most confidential and delicate matters' directly with Allende.[95]

The tone of KGB reporting on Chile during 1972 was somewhat more cautious than during the previous year. Nixon's visit to Moscow in 1972 and Brezhnev's return visit to Washington in the following year represented the high point of a period of Soviet–American détente. Andropov, like the Soviet leadership in general, was anxious not to provoke the Nixon administration by too ostentatious a challenge to American influence in Latin America – all the more so because the United States seemed tacitly to accept that the Soviet Union was free to act as it wished within its own sphere of influence in eastern and central Europe. 'Latin America', wrote Andropov, 'is a sphere of special US interests. The US has permitted us to act in Poland and Czechoslovakia. We must remember this. Our policy in Latin America must be cautious.'[96]

A further reason for caution in the level of Soviet support for Allende was the general instability of Latin American regimes – as evidenced recently in Bolivia, where President Torres had been overthrown in August 1971, only a month after Andropov had suggested supplying him with arms and economic aid. When the

FCD suggested renewing contact with Torres in January 1972, Andropov gave his unenthusiastic approval:

Apparently, this is something that must be done, although experience in other countries has shown that it is almost impossible for a deposed president to regain the position he has lost. This is some sort of irreversible law of history. Perhaps it is better to turn our attention to the new leaders who will undoubtedly appear in Bolivia.[97]

During Torres's exile in Chile and Argentina, the local KGB residencies maintained secret contact with him, using him for active-measures campaigns (of which Mitrokhin's notes give no details) and giving him financial assistance.[98] Andropov's forecast that Torres would never return to power, however, turned out to be entirely correct.

There was growing anxiety in the Centre at Allende's failure to consolidate his position by bringing the armed forces and security system under his control. Andropov decreed that the FCD's main Latin American priorities in 1972 were to strengthen – discreetly – the Soviet footholds in Chile and Peru. Both footholds, he had concluded, were insecure:

The main thing is to keep our finger on the pulse of events, and obtain multi-faceted and objective information about the situation there, and about the correlation of forces. It is necessary to direct the course of events, and make sure that events do not catch us unawares, so that we don't have any surprises, and will be aware of the very first tremors of approaching changes and events – thus enabling us to report them to the leadership in a timely manner.

There is one particular question which perhaps does not affect us [the KGB] directly, but which cannot be avoided, and that is the interpretation that the events in Chile and Peru have received in our press, and the emphasis that has been placed on the role of the Soviet Union there. One gets the impression that the [Soviet] press is doing too much boasting and bragging. I don't think that the friends [the Chilean and Peruvian Communist parties] have liked this.

While anxious to bolster the Allende regime by establishing close KGB liaison with Chilean intelligence, Andropov instructed that any attempt to force the pace would be counterproductive:

Do not permit anything that would cause complaints about our activity in Chile and Peru.

Do not force the establishment of liaison with the [intelligence] service in Chile. Arouse their interest by passing them intelligence of a topical nature through LEADER.[99]

In the course of 1972 Moscow substantially downgraded its assessment of the prospects of the Allende regime. In July a leading Soviet journal was still maintaining, 'The record of Chile shows that a number of Latin American countries can adopt a form of socialist construction.' In October, however, the 'Truckers' Strike', allegedly backed by CIA funding, virtually paralysed the economy for three weeks, providing dramatic evidence of the weakness of the Popular Unity government and the power of its opponents. At a meeting of the CPSU Central Committee in November, Chile was officially said not to be building socialism but merely to be seeking 'free and independent development on the path of democracy and social progress'. The mounting evidence of chronic economic mismanagement also made Moscow reluctant to provide large-scale support. Allende returned from a visit to Moscow in December with much less than he had hoped for. Simultaneously the *Sunday Times* published a report by its leading foreign correspondent, David Holden, headlined 'Chile, Collapse of a Marxist Experiment?' 'Allende's own survival is in doubt', predicted Holden. '. . . Anger, fear and a determination to fight are now more evident on the Right as well as the Left.'[100]

Andropov was anxious none the less that the KGB should do what it could to prevent the defeat of the Allende regime either at the polls or by military coup. On 25 December 1972 he sent the Politburo a memorandum giving a rather exaggerated impression of the KGB's ability to influence Chilean politics:

The KGB maintains confidential relations with Allende and [a left-wing senator], and also with prominent individuals in the Socialist, Radical, and Christian Democratic Parties.

Parliamentary elections will take place in March 1973.

Considering the situation during the pre-election period, it is planned to take measures to strengthen relations with the above-mentioned people, and also to make new contacts in government, party, and parliamentary circles, including certain representatives of the right-wing opposition and the extremist organization, the Leftist Revolutionary Movement (MIR).

Through unofficial contacts with the country's influential people and other ways, it is planned to concentrate [the KGB's] efforts on the following: helping to consolidate the forces supporting Chile's government; creating obstacles to any co-operation between the Christian Democratic and the National parties within the framework of the opposition; exerting an influence on the armed forces in order to prevent them from being used against Popular Unity.

The KGB also is planning to use its capabilities to carry out a series of active measures in Latin American and other countries for the purpose of exposing the imperialists' interference in Chile's internal affairs, and to exert the necessary influence on public opinion, thus inducing the anti-imperialist and progressive elements to support Popular Unity more actively.

In order to finance these measures, in addition to operations against government and political figures (including influencing some of them through financial means), the sum of $100,000 is required. Part of this money is to be given to Allende for work with his own contacts in political and military circles.

Approval for the payment of $100,000 from the Council of Ministers reserve fund for KGB 'special measures' in Chile was given by the Politburo on 7 February 1973.[101] An additional 'monetary reward' of $400 was made to Allende for unspecified 'valuable information' he had provided.[102]

A further report to the Politburo by Andropov in February 1973 gave an optimistic assessment of the KGB's influence on Allende during his meetings with Kuznetsov:

Allende set this channel apart from the usual unofficial governmental contacts and used it for handling the most confidential and delicate matters (establishing contact between Chile's and the USSR's armed forces, consulting on the use of Chilean atomic raw materials, organizing co-operation between the Chilean and Soviet security services, and other matters) by handing over information and discussing current political issues. [The KGB] is succeeding in exerting a definite influence on Allende. This is aiding, in particular, a more correct understanding on the President's part of China's policies, as well as a decision on his part to strengthen contact between the Chilean and Peruvian military for the purpose of exerting a positive influence on the leadership of Chile's armed forces. In turn, Allende is systematically informing us on the situation in the country and in Popular Unity, on his own personal plans, and so forth.

Our officer's meetings with Allende, during which they discussed business matters, were conducted in private. The President invited him to pay a visit at any time – either at work or at his home – without prior notice, whenever there was an urgent necessity for this.

The strengthening of our officer's relations with Allende was facilitated by material aid given to him, personal attention, and the fulfilment of his personal requests.

In order to make more effective and beneficial use of our contact with Allende, the following is suggested:

- help in strengthening Allende's position and authority both within the country and on the Latin American continent through the unofficial channels available to us;

- broader use of Allende's ability to assess the situation in Latin American countries, bearing in mind that he can send his own emissaries to several of them;

- measures to obtain information through Allende on the policies of the Chinese government, including the use of the President's trusted persons, whom he can send there;

- material assistance to Allende for his work with contacts in political and military circles, especially during the pre-election period, up to the sum of $50,000 – taken from funds allocated to the KGB via CPSU Central Committee Resolution No. P-78/31, dated 13 February 1973.

The flaws in Andropov's report were characteristic of many similar documents. Its chief purpose was to impress the Politburo with the KGB's ability to gain clandestine access to a foreign leader and exert influence on him. Characteristically, it avoided mentioning any problems which might take the gloss off the KGB's success. Privately, the Centre was increasingly worried about Allende's prospects of survival. Andropov, however, gave no hint of those concerns to the Politburo. His memorandum, including the request for additional funding, was duly approved.[103]

Privately, the Centre was worried by the deficiencies of Allende's security and intelligence system, which increased his vulnerability to a military coup. Once again, it gave the political leadership a rose-tinted view of the improvements which were under way. The Centre reported to Brezhnev that on 17 February 1973 the KGB operations officer responsible for liaison with the Chilean security services (not identified in Mitrokhin's notes) met Allende secretly at a villa in the suburbs of Santiago:

Allende expressed certain of his views regarding the reorganization of the security services. According to his plan, an efficient apparatus with both intelligence and counter-intelligence functions would be created to report directly to him. As the basis for this apparatus, he planned to use one component of the Servicio de Investigaciones [the Chilean security service] and recruit reliable personnel from the Socialist and Communist parties. The main efforts of this organ would be directed at uncovering and suppressing subversive activity on the part of Americans and local reactionary forces, and in organizing intelligence work within the armed forces, since the position taken by the armed forces was a decisive factor that would determine the fate of the Chilean revolutionary process.

Allende is very much counting on Soviet assistance in this matter.[104]

The attempted reorganization achieved little. The Servicio de Investigaciones successfully intimidated some of the regime's opponents and gained a reputation for turning the cellars at its headquarters into torture chambers. Nathaniel Davis, the US ambassador, noted, however, that the Servicio 'was consumed by personal squabbles between the Socialists and the Communists'. Any attempt to strengthen the civilian intelligence community faced an almost impossible dilemma. The measures necessary to forestall a coup – in particular, any attempt to gather intelligence on plotting within the armed services – were likely to provoke the military into the very action they were designed to prevent.[105]

In the March congressional elections Allende's Unidad Popular won 44 per cent of the vote as compared with the opposition's 56 per cent. Nathaniel Davis summed up the result as 'discouraging for both sides . . . Unidad Popular found itself a continuing minority for the foreseeable future, and the opposition found its majority insufficient to force legitimate change'.[106] There is no evidence that the KGB tried to explain to the Politburo why its 'confidential relations' with leading Chilean politicians across the political spectrum had failed to produce the UP victory which it had led the Politburo to expect three months earlier. Preferring as usual to concentrate on its successes, it emphasized instead the President's willingness to provide further assistance to its operations. Andropov wrote to Brezhnev to request approval for funding intelligence collection by Allende in other South American countries on the KGB's behalf:

Our officer had a discussion with [Allende] about receiving information on Latin America by enlisting the President's assistance. Allende showed an interest in this matter and expressed several specific ideas of his own. In particular, he expressed a willingness to send his own trusted people to Latin American countries, where they would be able to establish contacts with his friends and political supporters, and obtain useful information from them.

In the near future the President will be able to send his emissary to Venezuela for the purpose of ascertaining the situation in that country on the eve of the presidential elections coming up in November of this year. Among his trusted personal contacts, Allende named [Luis] Beltrán Prieto [Figueroa], the leader of the progressive Venezuelan party called the People's Election Movement [Movimento Electoral del Pueblo].

In addition, the President is willing to co-operate in obtaining information on Argentina and Ecuador, where the situation is characterized by complexities and contradictions.

Brezhnev wrote 'Approved' at the bottom of Andropov's request.[107]

Andropov, however, was increasingly pessimistic about Allende's prospects of survival. One day in the spring of 1973, he made an unexpected visit to FCD headquarters at Yasenevo. According to Nikolai Leonov:

He summoned everyone who had anything to do with Latin America and put a single question to us: How did we view the Chilean case? Did it have a chance or not? Should we commit all our resources, or was it already too late to risk them? The discussion was quite profound . . . We came to the conclusion that the measure being planned for making a cash loan – I believe 30 million US dollars was being talked about – would be unable to rescue the situation in Chile. It would be like putting a patch on a worn-out tyre.

In the KGB's view, Allende's fundamental error was his unwillingness to use force against his opponents. Without establishing complete control over all the machinery of the state, his hold on power could not be secure. 'All our sympathies were with [Allende's] experiment', recalls Leonov, '. . . but we did not believe in its success.'[108] Over the next few months the Santiago residency reported what it considered 'alarming signs of increased tension'.[109]

The first attempt to overthrow the regime was made by activists of the extreme right-wing Patria y Libertad movement, who hatched a plot with disaffected officers of the Second Armoured Regiment to kidnap Allende on 27 June. The Santiago residency informed the Centre that it had obtained intelligence on plans for the coup and warned Allende.[110] Its achievement, however, was rather less impressive than it probably appeared in Moscow. The security of the coup plotters was so poor that their plans leaked and the coup planned for the 27th was postponed. On the 29th, however, three combat groups of tanks and armoured cars with about a hundred troops left their barracks and headed for the centre of Santiago. The coup petered out in farce. As Nathaniel Davis noted, 'the column obeyed all the traffic lights and at least one tank stopped to fill up at a commercial gas station'. The most significant aspect of the failed coup was the apathetic response to it by Chilean workers, the supposed bedrock of Allende's support. Allende broadcast an appeal for 'the people . . . to pour into the centre of the city' to defend his government. They did not do so. That highly significant fact was duly noted by the Army Chief of Staff, General Augusto Pinochet Ugarte.[111]

The next ten weeks were a period of continuous political, economic and military crisis. Since Allende's election in 1970, Chile's currency had been devalued on the open market by the staggering figure of 10,000 per cent. David Holden headlined a report from Santiago, 'Chile: Black Market Road to Socialism', and reported that, 'Anyone who can afford the time to queue for petrol legally can become a rich man by selling his daily intake at 30 times the official price . . . To an outsider, it seems a mighty peculiar road to Socialism – or to anywhere else for that matter.'[112]

In his unsuccessful appeal to Chilean workers on 29 July to come to the defence of the regime, Allende had declared, 'If the hour comes, the people will have arms' – his first public statement that he would mobilize left-wing paramilitary groups if faced with military revolt. During August the armed forces mounted an increasingly intensive search for illegal arms dumps – predictably concentrating on those held by the left.[113] The KGB later complained that Allende paid too little attention to its warnings of an impending coup.[114] When Pinochet and a military junta launched the coup in the early hours of 11 September,[115] Corvalán and the Communist leadership, who had also been kept informed by the KGB,[116] were better prepared than Allende. The Communist Party newspaper that morning carried the banner headline, 'Everyone To His Combat Post!' 'Workers of city and countryside' were summoned to combat 'to repel the rash attempt of the reactionaries who are determined to bring down the constitutional government'. While Corvalán and the leadership moved underground, Communist factory managers began to mobilize workers in the industrial belt.

Allende, however, failed to live up to his promise six weeks earlier to summon the people to arms to defend his regime. When the coup began on 11 September, instead of seeking support in the working-class areas of Santiago, he based himself in the presidential offices in La Moneda, where he was defended by only fifty to sixty of his Cuban-trained GAP and half a dozen officers from the Servicio de Investigaciones. Allende's lack of preparation to deal with the coup partly derived from his preference for improvisation over advance planning. His French confidant, Régis Debray, later claimed that he 'never planned anything more than forty-eight hours in advance'. But Allende was also anxious to avoid bloodshed. Convinced that popular resistance would be mown down by Pinochet's troops, he bravely chose to sacrifice himself rather than his followers. Castro and many of Allende's supporters later claimed that he was gunned down by Pinochet's forces as they occupied La Moneda. In reality, it seems almost certain that, faced with inevitable defeat, Allende sat on a sofa in the Independence Salon of La Moneda, placed the muzzle of an automatic rifle (a present from Castro) beneath his chin and blew his brains out.[117]

Allende, wrote David Holden, was 'instantly canonized as the western world's newest left-wing martyr', becoming overnight 'the most potent cult figure since his old friend, Che Guevara'. Devotees of the Allende cult quickly accepted as an article of faith Castro's insistence that, instead of committing suicide, Allende had been murdered in cold blood by Pinochet's troops. The *Guardian* declared on 17 September, 'For Socialists of this generation, Chile is our Spain ... This is the most vicious Fascism we have seen in generations.' Pinochet's regime was as loathed in the 1970s as Franco's had been in the 1930s.[118]

As well as doing what it could to promote the Allende cult, KGB active measures also sought to establish a secondary cult around the heroic figure of the Communist leader Luis Corvalán, who had been captured after the coup and, together with some of Allende's former ministers, imprisoned in harsh conditions on Dawson Island in the Magellan Straits. As well as seeking to promote international appeals for Corvalán's release, the KGB also tried to devise a method of rescuing him and other prisoners from Dawson Island by a commando raid organized by the FCD Special Actions Directorate V, which was approved in principle by Andropov on 27 March 1974.[119] Satellite photographs were taken of Dawson Island and used by Directorate V to construct a model of the prison. The rescue plan eventually devised was for a large commercial cargo vessel to enter the Magellan Straits with three or four helicopters concealed beneath its hatches. When the vessel was fifteen kilometres from Dawson Island, the helicopters would take off carrying commandos who would kill the relatively small number of prison guards, rescue Corvalán and other prisoners, and transfer them to a submarine waiting nearby. The helicopters would then be destroyed and sunk in deep water, thus leaving no incriminating evidence to prevent the Soviet cargo vessel continuing on its way. The rescue plan, however, was never implemented. According to Leonov: 'When this plan was presented to the leadership, they looked at us as if we were half-crazy, and all our attempts to persuade them to study it in greater detail proved fruitless, although the military did agree to provide the means to carry it out.'[120]

Schemes were also devised to kidnap a leading member of the Chilean military government, or one of Pinochet's relatives, who could then be exchanged for Corvalán.[121] These schemes too were abandoned and Corvalán was eventually exchanged for the far more harshly persecuted Soviet dissident Vladimir Bukovsky.

For the KGB, Pinochet represented an almost perfect villain, an ideal counterpoint to the martyred Allende. Pinochet himself played into the hands of hostile propagandists. Marxist books were burnt on bonfires in Santiago as Pinochet spoke menacingly of cutting out the 'malignant tumour' of Marxism from Chilean life. The Dirección de Investigaciones Nacionales (DINA) set out to turn Pinochet's rhetoric into reality. From 1973 to 1977 its Director, General Manuel Contreras Sepulveda, reported directly to Pinochet. Official commissions established by Chile's civilian governments after the end of military rule in 1990 documented a total of 3,197 extra-judicial executions, deaths under torture and 'disappearances' during the Pinochet era. Since not all could be documented, the true figure was undoubtedly higher.[122] A Chilean government report in 2004 concluded that 27,000 people had been tortured or illegally imprisoned.[123]

KGB active measures successfully blackened still further DINA's deservedly dreadful reputation. Operation TOUCAN, approved by Andropov on 10 August 1976, was particularly successful in publicizing and exaggerating DINA's foreign operations against left-wing Chilean exiles. DINA was certainly implicated in the assassination of Allende's former Foreign Minister, Orlando Letelier, who was killed by a car bomb in the United States in 1976, and may also have been involved in the murder of other former Allende supporters living in exile. Operation TOUCAN thus had a plausible basis in actual DINA operations. TOUCAN was based on a forged letter from Contreras to Pinochet, dated 16 September 1975, which referred to expenditure involved in the expansion of DINA's foreign operations, chief among them plans to 'neutralize' (assassinate) opponents of the Pinochet regime in Mexico, Argentina, Costa Rica, the United States, France and Italy. Service A's forgers carefully imitated authentic DINA documents in their possession and the signature of its Director. The letter was accepted as genuine by some major newspapers and broadcasters in western Europe as well as the Americas (see appendix, p. 88). The Western media comment which caused most pleasure in the Centre was probably speculation on links between DINA and the CIA. The leading American journalist Jack Anderson, who quoted from the KGB forgery, claimed that DINA operated freely in the United States with the full knowledge of the CIA. The Senate Foreign Affairs Committee, he reported, was investigating DINA's activities.[124]

Pinochet's military government was far more frequently denounced by Western media than other regimes with even more horrendous human-rights records. KGB active measures probably deserve some of the credit. While operation TOUCAN was at the height of its success, Pol Pot and the Khmer Rouge were in the midst of a reign of terror in Cambodia which in only three years killed 1.5 million of Cambodia's 7.5 million people. Yet in 1976, the *New York Times* published sixty-six articles on the abuse of human rights in Chile, as compared with only four on Cambodia.[125] The difficulty of obtaining information from Cambodia does not provide a remotely adequate explanation for this extraordinary discrepancy.

APPENDIX: THE SERVICE A FORGERY USED IN OPERATION TOUCAN[126]

Secret to the Intelligence Service of Chile
To the Secretariat of the President of the Republic Copy 1
DINA /R/ No.1795/107
Explanation of the request for an increase in estimated expenditure
DINA Santiago 16 September 1975
From the Director of National Intelligence to the President of the Republic

In accordance with our agreement with you, I am giving the reasons for the request for the expenditure of DINA to be increased by 600,000 American dollars in the current financial year.

1 An additional ten members of DINA are to be sent to our missions abroad: two to Peru, two to Brazil, two to Argentina, one to Venezuela, one to Costa Rica, one to Belgium and one to Italy.
2 Additional expenditure is required to neutralize the active opponents to the Junta abroad, especially in Mexico, Argentine, Costa Rica, the USA, France and Italy.
3 The expense of our operations in Peru supporting our allies in the armed forces and the press (*Equise* and *Opinion Libre*).
4 Maintenance costs for our workers taking a course for anti-partisan groups at the SNI centre at Manaus in Brazil.

Yours sincerely,

Colonel Manuel Contreras Sepulveda
Director of National Intelligence

Official stamp of DINA

5

Intelligence Priorities after Allende

In February 1974 the Politburo carried out what appears to have been its first general review of Latin American policy since the Chilean coup. It defined as the three main goals of Soviet policy: 'to steadily broaden and strengthen the USSR's position on the continent; to provide support to the progressive, anti-American elements struggling for political and economic independence; and to provide active opposition to Chinese penetration'. Significantly, there was no mention either of encouragement to revolutionary movements in Latin America or of any prospect, outside Cuba, of a new Marxist-led government on the Allende model. The KGB's main priorities were 'to expose the plans of the US and its allies against the progressive, patriotic forces and the USSR'; to provide 'full and timely intelligence coverage' of the whole of Latin America (including what the Centre called 'white [blank] spots' in those countries which had no diplomatic relations with the Soviet Union); to expand the number of confidential contacts in Latin American regimes without resorting to the more risky process of agent recruitment; and to maintain clandestine contact with nineteen Communist parties, two-thirds of which were still illegal or semi-illegal.[1]

The five main targets for KGB operations identified in 1974 were Cuba, Argentina, Peru, Brazil and Mexico. Significantly, neither Nicaragua nor Chile any longer ranked as a priority target. In Nicaragua, the prospects for a Sandinista revolution were no longer taken seriously in the Centre. In Chile the firm grip established by the Pinochet military regime seemed to exclude any further experience of 'Socialism with red wine' for the foreseeable future.

As the only surviving Marxist regime in Latin America after the overthrow of the Allende regime, Cuba ranked clearly first in the

KGB's order of priorities. In the view of both the Centre and the Polit-buro: 'Cuba is taking on an important role as a proponent of socialist ideas. F. Castro's reorientation in important political issues (dis-claiming the policy of exporting the revolution, accepting a single form of socialism based on Marxist-Leninist doctrine) is of great importance.'[2]

At the Twenty-fourth Congress of the CPSU, held in the great palace of the Kremlin in 1971, Fidel Castro had received louder applause than any of the other fraternal delegates – to the deep, though private, irritation of some of them.[3] To many foreign Party bureaucrats in their sober business suits, it must have seemed very unfair that, after many years of never straying from the Moscow line, they should arouse less enthusiasm than the flamboyant Castro who had so recently dabbled in revisionism.

Castro's popularity in Moscow was due partly to the fact that he had established himself as the Soviet Union's most persuasive advo-cate in the Third World. He was the star performer at the Fourth Conference of the Non-Aligned Movement which met in Algiers in 1973, arguing the Soviet case more eloquently than any Soviet spokesman could have done. The host nation, Algeria, supported the traditional non-aligned policy of equidistance between East and West, arguing that there were 'two imperialisms': one capitalist, the other Communist. Castro insisted, however, that the countries of the Soviet bloc were the natural and necessary allies of the non-aligned:

How can the Soviet Union be labelled imperialist? Where are its monopoly corporations? Where is its participation in multinational companies? What factories, what mines, what oilfields does it own in the underdeveloped world? What worker is exploited in any country of Asia, Africa or Latin America by Soviet capital?

. . . Only the closest alliance among all the progressive forces of the world will provide us with the strength needed to overcome the still-powerful forces of imperialism, colonialism, neocolonialism and racism, and to wage a successful fight for the aspirations to peace and justice of all the peoples of the world.

The delegates were at least partly persuaded. The conference rejected the views of its Algerian hosts, failed to brand the Soviet Union as imperialist and denounced the 'aggressive imperialism' of the West as 'the greatest obstacle on the road toward emancipation and progress of the developing countries'.[4]

As well as proving an eloquent advocate of the Soviet cause in the international arena, Cuba was also an important intelligence ally. The Centre established what it regarded as 'good working relations' with the head of the DGI, José Méndez Cominches.[5] By 1973, if not earlier, Méndez Cominches was attending conferences of the intelligence chiefs of the Soviet bloc. At that time seventy-eight Cuban intelligence officers were at KGB training schools. Technical equipment valued by the Centre at 2 million rubles was provided free of charge to the DGI. The KGB liaison mission in Havana contained experts in all the main 'lines' of intelligence operation who provided the Cubans with 'assistance in the planning of their work'.[6] After the mass expulsion of Soviet intelligence officers from London in 1971, the DGI's London station took over the running of some KGB operations in Britain.[7] By, and probably before, 1973, the KGB maintained 'operational contact' with the DGI in six foreign capitals as well as in Havana.[8] During the 1970s the KGB made increasing use of DGI assistance in operations against the Main Adversary both inside and outside the United States. In 1976, for example, the KGB and DGI agreed on 'joint cultivation' of targets in the National Security Agency, the Pentagon and US military bases in Latin America and Spain. The DGI was thought particularly useful in cultivating Hispanics and blacks. Two of the five 'talent-spotting leads' in the United States selected by the KGB for 'joint cultivation' with the DGI in 1976 were African-American cipher clerks.[9]

In Latin America during the 1970s the DGI had fewer legal residencies than the KGB, chiefly because of the smaller number of states with which Cuba maintained diplomatic relations. In 1976–77 there appear to have been DGI residencies only in Ecuador, Guyana, Jamaica, Mexico, Panama, Peru and Venezuela.[10] Though Mitrokhin's notes provide only fragmentary information, all appear to have assisted KGB operations in various ways. In 1977 the DGI informed the KGB liaison office in Havana that it had a series of agents in 'high official positions' in Mexico, including the Interior Ministry and police force, and suggested that they be run jointly.[11] Mitrokhin's notes do not mention whether this offer was accepted.

The Centre seems to have been well informed about even the most highly classified aspect of DGI activity – its illegal operations. In the early 1970s the DGI had about forty-five illegals, all of whom went on year-long KGB training courses in Moscow.[12] Some KGB illegals with bogus Latin American identities were sent to Cuba to perfect their language skills and acclimatize themselves to living in a Latin American environment before being deployed to their final destinations. In 1976 a senior KGB delegation including both the head and deputy head of the FCD illegals directorate, Vadim Alekseyevich Kirpichenko and Marius Aramovich Yuzbashyan, went to Havana to discuss co-operation with their counterparts in the DGI. Agreement was reached on the joint training of several Latin American illegals for deployment against US, Latin American, Spanish and Maoist targets. The DGI agreed that the KGB could use its radio communications system to relay messages to its illegals operating in the United States and Latin America. During a return visit to Moscow the following year, the head of the DGI illegals directorate agreed to recruit two or three illegals for the KGB.[13]

Cuba was also one of the most important bases for KGB SIGINT operations, chiefly against US targets. The KGB file on the 1979 running costs of intercept posts in KGB residencies around the world shows that the Havana post (codenamed TERMIT-S) had the third largest budget; only the Washington and New York posts were more expensive to operate.[14] An even larger intercept post, also targeted on the United States, was situated in the massive SIGINT base set up by the GRU at Lourdes in Cuba in the mid-1960s to monitor US Navy communications and other high-frequency transmissions.[15] On 25 April 1975 a secret Soviet government decree (No. 342–115) authorized the establishment of a new KGB SIGINT station (codenamed TERMIT-P) within the Lourdes base, which began operations in December 1976. Run by the Sixteenth Directorate, TERMIT-P had a fixed 12-metre dish antenna and a mobile 7-metre dish antenna mounted on a covered lorry, which enabled it to intercept microwave communications 'downlinked' from US satellites or transmitted between microwave towers.[16]

As well as co-operating closely with the DGI in a variety of intelligence operations, the KGB maintained an undeclared residency in Havana which kept close watch on the Castro regime and the mood of the population; in 1974 it sent 205 reports by cable and sixty-four by diplomatic bag. Its sources included sixty-three agents and sixty-seven co-optees among the large Soviet community.[17] The aspect of Cuban intelligence which gave greatest concern to the Havana residency was its internal security. Though brutal by Western standards, Cuban internal surveillance struck the Centre as unacceptably feeble. The department charged with combating ideological subversion had a total establishment of only 180, many of them – in the KGB's view – poorly qualified. According to a report from the Havana residency in 1976, one Cuban anti-subversion officer had recruited five out of fourteen members of a Cuban orchestra simply 'in case the orchestra went on tour abroad'.[18] The Centre was particularly disturbed by the fact that it could not persuade the DGI to share its own obsession with Zionist 'subversion'. The KGB liaison office drew the DGI's attention to the presence of seventeen Zionist organizations in Cuba but complained to the Centre that no action had been taken against any of them.[19]

By Soviet standards, the Cuban surveillance department was also seriously understaffed. With a total of 278 staff in Havana and 112 in the provinces in 1976, the KGB residency calculated that it could deploy only about twelve surveillance groups of nine or ten people per day. Because of the two-shift system, this meant that it was able to keep full-time surveillance of only six moving targets.[20] The KGB was also dissatisfied with the scale of Cuban eavesdropping and letter-opening. The 260 people employed to monitor telephone conversations and eavesdropping devices listened in to a daily average of only about 900 international phone calls.[21] Cuban censorship monitored about 800 addresses on a full-time basis and translated 300 to 500 foreign-language letters a day.[22]

The Centre's concern at the Cuban failure to reproduce its own absurdly labour-intensive systems of surveillance and obsessive pursuit of even the most trivial forms of ideological subversion was most evident in the months before Brezhnev's visit to Cuba early in 1974. The Havana residency was also worried by what it believed was lax treatment of Cuban political prisoners. Of the 8,000 'sentenced for counter-revolutionary activity', many were reported to be allowed home once a month and on public holidays. Particular concern was caused by the fact that some of the 'counter-revolutionaries' given this comparatively lenient treatment had in the past made 'anti-Soviet statements' and might be on the streets during Brezhnev's visit.[23]

No dissident, however, disturbed the stage-managed welcome given to the vain and decrepit Soviet leader in Havana's Revolution Square by a crowd officially estimated at over a million people. Castro's own words of welcome plumbed new depths of platitudinous sycophancy. 'No other foreign visitor to Cuba', he declared, 'has ever been welcomed by our people so joyfully or with such rapturous enthusiasm as was Comrade Brezhnev.' Castro eulogized Brezhnev's own stumbling banalities as 'major political statements of tremendous importance' for the entire world:

It must be remembered that we attach paramount importance to the history of the Soviet Union itself and to the role played by the CPSU. I refer to both the USSR's role in the development of the history of all mankind and to the role which the USSR and the CPSU have played in the cause of solidarity with Cuba ... For us, Comrade Brezhnev – the most eminent Soviet leader – personifies, as it were, the entire policy of the USSR and the CPSU. And it was for this reason that our people looked forward to his arrival and were eager to express their feelings of friendship, profound respect and gratitude towards the Soviet Union.[24]

Castro did not feel it necessary, however, to display the same level of sycophancy to other Soviet bloc leaders. The KGB reported that the visit to Cuba shortly after Brezhnev's by Erich Honecker, the East German leader, had gone extremely badly. In private meetings Castro accused East Germany and other 'socialist countries' of doing little to help Cuba and 'profiteering' at Cuban expense by refusing to pay a fair price for its sugar. Honecker was said to have responded 'in an angry and intemperate manner'. 'If I had known that Castro would react in this manner to our visit', he told his staff, 'I would not have gone.' The atmosphere at Havana airport on Honecker's departure was said to have been 'extremely cold'. His entourage spent much of the flight home trying to calm him down, fearful – according to the KGB – that news of his row with Castro might leak to the West.[25] Behind the scenes, however, the conflict continued. In 1977 the East German Ministry of State Security (Stasi) liaison officer in Havana, Johann Münzel, told one of his KGB colleagues that the Cuban leadership were doing little to address their economic problems and simply expected other socialist countries to bail them out in the name of 'proletarian internationalism'. The DGI simultaneously complained to the KGB that Stasi officers were inclined to lecture them rather than treat them as colleagues.[26]

Moscow, however, judged Cuba's private quarrels with some member states of the Warsaw Pact in the mid-1970s as of far less significance than its public contribution to the establishment of new Marxist regimes in Africa. The FCD declared in a report to Andropov in 1976, 'Africa has turned into an arena for a global struggle between the two systems [communism and capitalism] for a long time to come.'[27] Cuban assistance in that struggle was of crucial importance. The nearly simultaneous break-up of the Portuguese Empire and the overthrow of the Ethiopian Emperor Haile Selassie brought to power self-proclaimed Marxist regimes in Angola, Mozambique and Ethiopia. In Angola, the richest of Portugal's colonies, the end of Portuguese rule was followed in 1975 by a full-scale civil war in which the Marxist Popular Movement for the Liberation of Angola (MPLA) was opposed by the National Front for the Liberation of Angola (FNLA) and the National Union for the Total Independence of Angola (UNITA). Though small-scale Soviet support for the MPLA, led by Agostinho Neto, had begun a decade earlier, the decisive factor in the struggle for power was the arrival of Cuban troops beginning in the autumn of 1975. Disappointed by the declining prospects for revolution in Latin America, Castro looked on Angola as an opportunity both to establish himself as a great revolutionary leader on the world stage and to revive flagging revolutionary fervour at home.[28] According to Castro's friend, the Colombian writer Gabriel García Márquez:

He personally had picked up the commanders of the battalion of special forces that left in the first flight and had driven them himself in his Soviet jeep to the foot of the plane ramp. There was no spot on the map of Angola that he hadn't memorized. His concentration on the war was so intense and meticulous that he could quote any figure on Angola as if it were Cuba, and he spoke of Angolan cities, customs and people as if he had lived there his entire life.[29]

Though the initiative for intervention in Angola was Cuban, from October 1975 it was enthusiastically encouraged by Moscow. During the next three months, the Soviet General Staff arranged the transport of over 12,000 Cuban troops to Africa by sea and air, as well as supplying them with advanced military hardware. Moscow was delighted with Castro's willingness to respect its political primacy in Angola. The Soviet chargé d'affaires in Luanda, G. A. Zverev, reported in March 1976, 'Close [Soviet–Cuban] coordination in Angola during the war has had very positive results.' The Luanda embassy demonstrated its missionary zeal by distributing huge amounts of Soviet propaganda. By the summer it had run out of portraits of Lenin and requested a further airlift.[30]

The Centre was also delighted by the level of Cuban intelligence collaboration. Castro sent the head of the DGI, Méndez Cominches, to take personal charge of intelligence operations in Angola, where, according to KGB files, he regularly provided 'valuable political and operational intelligence'. Vladimir Kryuchkov, the head of the FCD, gained Andropov's approval to send Méndez Cominches regular food parcels from Moscow, each valued by the Centre at 500 rubles, to encourage his continued co-operation.[31] Pedro Pupo Pérez, the acting head of the DGI in Havana during Méndez Cominches's absence, also provided intelligence on Africa and Latin America, and was rewarded with a gift valued at 350 rubles which was intended to 'consolidate confidential relations'.[32] Among the DGI operations in Angola carried out to assist the KGB was a penetration of the Brazilian embassy to obtain intelligence on its cipher system. A technical specialist from the KGB's Sixteenth (SIGINT) Directorate flew out from Moscow with equipment which enabled a DGI agent to photograph the wiring of the embassy's Swiss-made TS-803 cipher machine.[33] The KGB regularly showed its appreciation to the Cuban Interior Minister, Sergio del Valle, who was responsible for the DGI, for keeping it informed about 'important political and operational questions'. During a visit to Moscow in 1975, he was presented by Viktor Chebrikov, Deputy Chairman (and future Chairman) of the KGB, with a gift valued at 160 rubles.[34] In January 1977, during another visit to Moscow, Andropov approved the presentation to del Valle by Kryuchkov of a gift worth up to 600 rubles 'in return for information and in order to consolidate relations'.[35] Del Valle's relations with senior KGB officers became so close that he was even willing, on occasion, to complain to them about Castro's delusions of grandeur as a great international revolutionary leader.[36]

Late in 1977 Soviet–Cuban collaboration in Angola was extended to Ethiopia in support of the vaguely Marxist military junta headed by Lieutenant-Colonel Mengistu Haile Mariam in its war against Somalia. During the winter of 1977–78 Soviet military aircraft, as well as shipping huge quantities of arms, transported 17,000 Cuban troops to Addis Ababa.[37] The Cuban forces worked closely with Soviet military advisers to co-ordinate troop movements and military tactics. Their presence in Ethiopia, initially kept secret, was publicly admitted by Castro on 15 March 1978. 'The Cuban internationalist fighters', he declared, 'stood out for their extraordinary effectiveness and magnificent combat ability.' It was 'really admirable' to see 'how many sons of our people were capable of going to that distant land and fighting there as if fighting in their own country'. In both Moscow and Havana, Cuban military intervention and the decisive defeat of the Somali forces were celebrated as a triumph of proletarian internationalism.[38] A joint report in April by the Soviet Foreign Ministry and the International Department of the Central Committee noted with satisfaction: 'The Soviet Union and Cuba are in constant contact aimed at co-ordination of their actions in support of the Ethiopian revolution.'[39]

The level of Cuban intelligence and military collaboration during the mid- and late 1970s met and probably exceeded the expectations of the Centre and the Politburo during the policy review of 1974. A KGB delegation to Cuba in 1978, headed by Deputy Chairman Vadim Petrovich Pirozhkov, presented Fidel and Raúl Castro with PSM pistols and ammunition. Raúl was also given a dinner service and food parcel valued at 450 rubles.[40] By contrast, KGB operations in the other four priority Latin American targets agreed in 1974 – Argentina, Peru, Mexico and Brazil – failed to achieve as much as the Centre had hoped.

In the immediate aftermath of the Pinochet coup in Chile, the main opportunity identified by the KGB for the expansion of Soviet influence in South America was in Argentina. Twelve days after Allende's death, Juan Domingo Perón was elected President. Perón's third wife, María Estela (Isabel) Martínez, a confidential contact of the KGB, became Vice-President. Peronist nationalism, once regarded in Moscow as a 'fascist' phenomenon, now fitted in well with the KGB strategy of undermining US preponderance in Latin America by cultivating anti-American leaders.

First elected as President of Argentina in 1946, Perón had been forced into exile in Spain and his under-age mistress sent to a reformatory after a military coup in 1955. Eighteen years later his political fortunes revived with the election in May 1973 of a Peronist candidate, Héctor José Cámpora, as President. The only foreign heads of state to attend Cámpora's inauguration, which was boycotted by most other political leaders, were Latin America's two Marxist presidents: Salvador Allende of Chile and Osvaldo Dorticós of Cuba. Within a few days Cámpora had established diplomatic relations with Cuba, East Germany and North Korea. He also moved quickly to legalize the previously outlawed Argentinian Communist Party (CPA). Aware that Cámpora had been elected chiefly to pave the way for Perón himself, the Centre gained Brezhnev's permission to use a Peronist deputy, who had been recruited as a confidential contact by the Buenos Aires residency, to approach Perón while he was still in exile in Spain, sound him out on his policy towards the Soviet Union and propose 'unofficial contacts with Soviet representatives' once he became President. Though Perón was not told, the 'Soviet representatives' were to be KGB officers.[41] Isabel Perón received a more direct approach from the KGB. Vladimir Konstantinovich Tolstikov (codenamed LOMOV), who had succeeded Leonov as head of the Second (Latin American) Department in 1971, travelled to Spain to make personal contact with her, apparently posing as a representative of the Soviet film export agency and bringing with him a number of gifts.[42]

On 13 July Cámpora resigned the presidency in order to make it possible for Perón to stand in new presidential elections in September. The CPA immediately offered him an electoral alliance. Though Perón rejected the offer and purged Marxists from the Peronist movement, he none the less received Communist support during the campaign.[43] His inauguration as President in October was attended by a Soviet delegation which included Tolstikov, travelling under the alias Sergei Sergeyevich Konstantinov. Rather than drawing attention to himself by a direct approach to Vice-President Isabel Perón, Tolstikov made indirect contact with her through the leading Chilean exile in Argentina, General Carlos Prats González, a former commander-in-chief of the Chilean army whom Allende had made Interior Minister a year before the coup. Prats was given $10,000 from the funds allocated by the Central Committee for 'work with the Chilean resistance and émigré community' after the overthrow of the Allende regime. At Tolstikov's request, Prats reminded Isabel Perón of their meetings in Spain and the gifts she had received from Tolstikov, and asked her to arrange a meeting between him and her husband after the departure of the rest of the Soviet delegation. Tolstikov did not identify himself as a KGB officer. Instead he posed as a senior Latin American specialist in the Foreign Ministry who could henceforth provide a direct confidential channel to the Soviet leadership. Isabel Perón arranged for Tolstikov to be received by the President at his private residence at 9 a.m. on 21 October.

The KGB had no illusion about the prospects of turning Juan Perón into an Argentinian Allende. His secret meeting with Tolstikov, however, confirmed his potential as an ally against the Main Adversary. Perón denounced the United States' 'predatory economic policy towards Argentina' and the high-handed behaviour of American companies: 'Like an infection, American capital penetrates through all the cracks.' He told Tolstikov not to be misled by his public expressions of 'friendship toward the United States': 'If one is not in a position to defeat the enemy, then one must try to deceive him.' Perón also subjected Tolstikov to an exposition of his confused political philosophy, claiming that his 'concept of *justicialismo*, or a society based on fairness, differed very little from socialism'. However, 'the transformation of society proceeds harmoniously and in stages, changing the social structure gradually and not subjecting it to a radical break, which causes great disruption and economic ruin'. Tolstikov then had to listen patiently as Perón subjected him to a rambling disquisition of his views on a variety of other subjects. To the Centre, however, the meeting between Tolstikov and Perón must have seemed an important success. For the first time since Allende's death, the KGB had opened a direct, covert channel to the President of a major South American state.[44]

Tolstikov also held talks with Perón's influential Economics Minister, José Gelbard (codenamed BAKIN), a confidential contact of the Buenos Aires residency since 1970 who would, the Centre hoped, 'exert useful influence' on Perón. According to KGB files, Gelbard was described by Castro as an undeclared Communist. Together with two other Jewish businessmen, he secretly helped to finance the Argentinian Communist Party and held regular meetings with the KGB resident, Vasili Mikhailovich Muravyev, in one of the businessmen's houses. Before each meeting the businessman picked up the resident in his car at a pre-arranged location in Buenos Aires, then drove him to his house to meet Gelbard, who entered through the back door and supplied what the KGB considered 'important political and economic information'. Meetings of the Communist leadership also sometimes took place in the same house.[45]

In December 1973 Tolstikov reported to the Centre that Gelbard was, as expected, 'in favour of strengthening political and economic relations with the USSR'. 'He believes that co-operation with the USSR in the fields of hydro-electric energy, petrochemicals, ship-building, and fishing will help put an end to Argentina's dependence on the US, and will reinforce progressive tendencies in government policy.'

Gelbard asked Tolstikov for a Soviet trade delegation to be sent to Argentina. His request was reinforced by the general secretary of the Argentinian Communist Party, Arnedo Alvarez, who told Tolstikov that the delegation would reinforce Perón's links with 'democratic forces'. Tolstikov's meeting with Gelbard was considered of such importance that the Centre sent a report on it to Brezhnev, who speedily approved the sending of a trade mission.[46] Perón turned the arrival of the Soviet delegation in January 1974 into a public relations circus which was in striking contrast to the cool reception accorded to a US delegation a few months later.[47] The Centre judged many of the reports it received from the Buenos Aires residency in 1974 'especially valuable', and passed some of them on to Brezhnev.[48]

In May 1974 Gelbard and a 140-strong Argentinian trade delegation made a highly publicized return visit to the Soviet bloc. The importance attached to the visit was demonstrated by the numerous red carpets laid out for Gelbard in Moscow, where he was successively received in private audience by Brezhnev, Aleksei Kosygin, the Prime Minister, and Nikolai Podgorny, the Soviet President. Radio Moscow congratulated Argentina for having 'shown other countries in South America how to strengthen their independence and how to free themselves from the shackles of the multi-national corporation'. While in Moscow, Gelbard signed trade and economic co-operation agreements by which the Soviet Union agreed to long-term credits of $600 million – about twice those granted to Allende's Chile. Similar agreements with other countries in the Soviet bloc added long-term credits worth another $350 million. There were advantages to both sides in the agreements. The Soviet Union, obliged by the failure of its collective agriculture to import massive amounts of grain, had an obvious interest in increasing the number of its suppliers and in particular to limit its dependence on US imports. Argentina, faced with the protectionism of the European Community and contracting demand elsewhere as a result of the dramatic oil price rise of 1973, was anxious to find new markets.[49]

The hopes raised in the Centre for its Argentinian operations by Juan Perón's election in September 1973, however, declined rapidly after his sudden death from a heart attack on 1 July 1974. Though his widow and successor, Isabel, was a KGB confidential contact, she lacked both the personal authority and political skill of her husband. Gelbard was sacked as Economics Minister in 1975. In March 1976 Isabel Perón was ousted in a right-wing military coup led by General Jorge Videla, who began a campaign against Communist 'subversion'. Moscow did its best to salvage what it could of the Argentinian connection. By refraining from public denunciation of the Videla regime, the Argentinian Communist Party managed to remain relatively unmolested. The Soviet delegation at the United Nations went to the extraordinary lengths of vetoing American attempts to secure UN condemnation of the regime's appalling human-rights record. Politically, all that was achieved was a face-saving exercise. There were, however, real economic benefits. In 1980 80 per cent of Argentina's grain exports went to the Soviet Union.[50]

During the later 1970s, the KGB also lost much of the foothold it had acquired in Peru earlier in the decade. In 1974 the Centre still considered many of the reports from the Lima residency 'especially valuable', and passed some of them to Brezhnev, no doubt in order to demonstrate the continuing strength of its contacts with the junta.[51] The junta's economic policies, however, despite their ideological appeal in Moscow, led to chronic inflation, economic stagnation and repeated debt crises. After a coup in August 1975 by General Francisco Morales Bermúdez, the military government drifted to the right.[52] As in Argentina, Moscow tried to salvage what it could of the relationship built up over the previous few years. With Andropov's approval, the KGB presented Morales Bermúdez with a Makarov pistol and 200 cartridges.[53] In December 1975 the Centre sent the Peruvian intelligence service, SIN, a gift of operational equipment valued at about $300,000.[54] In the following year the new heads of SIN and Peruvian military intelligence were each presented, like Morales Bermúdez, with Makarov pistols; they also received further gifts valued, respectively, at 300 and 150 hard-currency rubles. Ten SIN officers were trained, at the KGB's expense, at the FCD Red Banner Institute during 1976.[55]

Such gestures achieved little. In August 1976 Tolstikov was informed by the Cuban ambassador to Peru and Deputy Interior Minister Abrahantes that Morales Bermúdez had assured Castro that he was 'a supporter of revolutionary changes in Peru' and prepared to collaborate in the struggle against the CIA. Simultaneously, however, he was removing 'progressive' officials and moving to the right. The Cuban regime concluded that Morales Bermúdez was not to be trusted and suspended aid to Peru.[56] By 1976 Cuban intelligence was pessimistic about the prospects for challenging American influence in South America. Manuel Piñeiro, head of the Departamento de América, which was responsible for the export of revolution, told Tolstikov in August that since the tour of five Latin American states earlier in the year by Henry Kissinger, 'one can begin to observe the onset of reaction and the fascistization of the regimes there'. On the South American mainland, said Piñeiro, only Guyana was following 'an anti-imperialist course': '[Forbes] Burnham, the Prime Minister of Guyana, shares some of the ideas of Marxism-Leninism, but for tactical reasons is forced to conceal this.'[57]

Mexico's presence on the list of the KGB's five priority Latin American targets in 1974 was due both to its strategic importance as a large state on the southern border of the United States and to the apparent opportunities created by the election as President in 1970 of Luis Echeverría Alvarez. Under the Mexican constitution, Echeverría served for a non-renewable six-year term, controlling during that period vast political patronage and having the final word on all major policy issues. Like his predecessors, though legitimized by a presidential election, he owed his position as President to a secret selection process within the Partido Revolucionario Institucional (PRI), which had dominated Mexican politics for the past forty years.

Echeverría's ultimate ambition (which he never came close to realizing) was, the KGB believed, to follow his term as President by becoming Secretary-General of the United Nations. He thus sought to establish himself during his presidency as a champion of Third World causes, became the first Mexican President to visit Cuba, was frequently publicly critical of the United States and in 1973 made a well-publicized trip to the Soviet Union. The KGB did not succeed in establishing direct access to Echeverría in the way that it did to Juan and Isabel Perón in Argentina and to some members of the military junta in Peru. From 1972 onwards, however, the Mexico City residency claimed to have one agent and two confidential contacts who provided 'stable channels for exercising influence on the President'. The agent, codenamed URAN, was a former Chilean diplomat of the Allende era. Of the two confidential contacts who were also said to influence Echeverría's foreign policy, MARTINA was the Rector of a Mexican university and OLMEK a leading member of the Partido Popular Socialista, one of a handful of small parties usually prepared to do deals with the ruling PRI. The Mexico City residency claimed the credit for persuading Echeverría to break off relations with the Pinochet regime, for much of his criticism of the United States, and for his decision to recognize the Marxist MPLA regime in Angola. It reported that its contacts had told Echeverría that these actions would strengthen his reputation in the Third World and enhance his prospects of becoming UN Secretary-General.[58] In 1975 he signed a mutual co-operation agreement with Comecon. In the same year, to the delight of Moscow, Echeverría instructed the Mexican representative at the UN to support an anti-Israeli resolution condemning Zionism as a form of racism – though he had second thoughts when this provoked Jewish leaders in the United States to promote a tourist boycott of Mexico.[59]

The KGB may well have exaggerated its ability to influence Echeverría's policy. When foreign statesmen or media made pronouncements in line with Soviet policy, it was quick to claim the credit for its own active measures. The KGB probably also exaggerated its influence on the press. In 1974, for example, the Mexico City residency reported that it had planted 300 articles in Mexican newspapers, among them *Excélsior*, then Mexico City's leading paper, the *Diario de México* and *Universal*.[60]

One of the KGB's most spectacular active measures, however, backfired badly. In 1973 the CIA defector Philip Agee (subsequently codenamed PONT by the KGB) had approached the residency in Mexico City and offered what the head of the FCD Counter-Intelligence Directorate, Oleg Kalugin, described as 'reams of information about CIA operations'. The residency, wrongly suspecting that he was part of a CIA deception, turned him away. According to Kalugin, 'Agee then went to the Cubans, who welcomed him with open arms . . . [and] shared Agee's information with us.'[61] Service A, the FCD active-measures department, claimed much of the credit for the publication in 1975 of Agee's sensational memoir, *Inside the Company: CIA Diary*, most of which was devoted to a denunciation of CIA operations in Latin America, identifying approximately 250 of its officers and agents. *Inside the Company* was an instant best-seller, described by the CIA's classified in-house journal as 'a severe body blow to the Agency'.[62]

Before publication, material on CIA penetration of the leadership of Latin American Communist parties was removed at Service A's insistence.[63] Service A seems to have been unaware, however, that KGB residencies were currently attempting to cultivate several of those publicly identified in *Inside the Company* as CIA agents or contacts. Among them was President Echeverría who, while the minister responsible for internal security, was alleged to have had the CIA codename LITEMPO-14, to have been in close contact with the CIA station in Mexico City and to have revealed to it the undemocratic processes by which, well in advance of his election in 1970, he had been selected by the ruling PRI as the next President.[64] The Mexican Foreign Minister told the Soviet ambassador that President Echeverría had been informed of the KGB's involvement in the publication of Agee's book and regarded it as an unfriendly act against both Mexico and the President personally. On instructions from Andropov and Gromyko, the ambassador claimed unconvincingly that the Soviet Union had no responsibility for the book.[65]

Brazil owed its place in the KGB's 1974 list of its five priority targets in Latin America simply to its size and strategic importance:

Special significance is ascribed to Brazil – a huge country with great wealth and claims to becoming a major power in the future, which is acquiring the characteristics of an imperialist state and actively entering the international arena. But the residency there is weak due to quota limitations [by the

Brazilian government on the size of the Soviet embassy] and thus has modest capabilities.[66]

For most of its existence, the military regime which held power from 1964 to 1985 made Brazil a relatively hostile environment for KGB operations. There was little prospect during the 1970s either of acquiring confidential contacts within the government, as in Argentina and Peru, or of finding contacts with direct access to the President, as in Mexico. The KGB's best intelligence on Brazil probably came from its increasing ability to decrypt Brazil's diplomatic traffic. By 1979 the radio-intercept post (codenamed KLEN) in the Brasilia residency was able to intercept 19,000 coded cables sent and received by the Foreign Ministry as well as approximately 2,000 other classified official communications.[67]

SIGINT enabled the Centre to monitor some of the activities of probably its most important Brazilian agent, codenamed IZOT, who was recruited while serving as Brazilian ambassador in the Soviet bloc.[68] As well as providing intelligence and recruitment leads to three other diplomats, IZOT also on occasion included in his reports information (probably disinformation) provided by the KGB. Assessed by the KGB as 'adhering to an anti-American line and liberal views concerning the development of a bourgeois society', IZOT was a paid agent. His remuneration, however, took a variety of forms, including in 1976 a silver service valued by the Centre at 513 rubles. The Centre had increasing doubts about IZOT's reliability. On one occasion it believed that he was guilty of 'outright deception', claiming to have passed on information provided by the KGB to his Foreign Ministry when his decrypted cables showed that he had not done so.[69]

The presidency of Ernesto Geisel (1974–79) made the first tentative moves towards democratization of the authoritarian and sometimes brutal Brazilian military regime. It remained, however, resolutely anti-Communist. In 1976 the official censor banned even a TV broadcast of a performance by the Bolshoi Ballet for fear of Communist cultural contagion. When Geisel revoked the banishment orders on most political exiles in 1978, he deliberately excluded the long-serving Secretary-General of the Brazilian Communist Party, Luis Carlos Prestes.[70] The inauguration as President in March 1979 of General João Batista Figueiredo, chief of the Serviço

Nacional de Informações (SNI), Brazil's intelligence service, para-
doxically made life somewhat easier than before for both the Communist Party and the KGB residency. The Brazilian intelligence
community was divided between reformers who favoured a gradual
transition to democracy and hard-liners who were preoccupied by
the danger of subversion. Figueiredo sided with the reformers. So,
even more clearly, did his chief political adviser and head of his
civilian staff, General Golbery do Couto e Silva, who fifteen years
earlier had been the chief architect and first head of SNI.[71] Despite
hard-line opposition, Figueiredo issued an amnesty for most of
Brazil's remaining political exiles, including Prestes and other leading Communists.[72]

While accepting that, in the East–West struggle, Brazil was ultimately on the side of the 'Giant of the North', Golbery argued
publicly in favour of a pragmatic foreign policy which avoided
subordination to the United States: 'It seems to us only just that
[, like the US,] we should also learn to bargain at high prices.'[73]
That, Golbery seems to have believed, involved dialogue with the
Soviet Union. In the spring of 1980 a Soviet parliamentary delegation
headed by Eduard Shevardnadze, then a candidate (non-voting)
member of the Politburo, visited Brasilia. Unknown to their hosts,
the plane (Special Flight L-62) carried new radio interception equipment to improve the performance of the residency's SIGINT station,
and took the old equipment with it when it left. Among the delegation was Brezhnev's personal assistant, Andrei Mikhailovich
Aleksandrov. The detailed instructions given to the resident on the
entertainment of Aleksandrov provide a good example of the pains
taken by the Centre to impress the political leadership. He was told
to ensure that the KGB officer selected to show Aleksandrov the
sights during his visit was smartly but soberly dressed, had his hair
neatly cut, and expressed himself lucidly, concisely and accurately
at all times.[74]

The pampered parliamentary delegation paved the way for other,
more covert contacts by the KGB with the Brazilian leadership. In
December 1980 Nikolai Leonov travelled to Brazil for talks with
General Golbery. Though Leonov posed as an academic working as
a Soviet government adviser, Golbery's background in intelligence
makes it highly unlikely that he failed to identify him as a senior
KGB officer. In June 1981, with Figueiredo's approval, Golbery sent

a member of his staff for further discussions in Moscow, where it was agreed that a 'counsellor' (in fact a KGB officer) would be added to the embassy staff in Brasilia, whose chief duty would be to conduct regular 'unofficial' meetings with the President.[75] Further, public evidence of a new era in Soviet–Brazilian relations was the signing in 1981 of a series of trade agreements worth a total of about $2 billion.[76]

The chief opposition to Golbery's support for democratic reforms at home and better relations with the Soviet bloc came from military hard-liners led by General Octávio Aguiar de Medeiros, the current chief of SNI. Golbery also opposed the austerity programme of the Minister of Economy, António Delfim Neto. In August 1981 he resigned in protest at the failure to prosecute military extremists involved in bomb attacks against the political opposition. Golbery was replaced as head of Figueiredo's civilian staff by João Leitão de Abreu, a lawyer more acceptable to military hard-liners.[77] Since the Brazilian files noted by Mitrokhin end in 1981, there is no indication of whether or not the meetings arranged by Golbery between Figueiredo and a KGB officer went ahead.

The KGB sought to compensate for the declining success of its operations against the priority targets established in 1974 by trying to make new 'confidential contacts' among 'progressive', anti-American political leaders. Among its targets in the mid-1970s was Alfonso López Michelson (codenamed MENTOR), leader of the Colombian Movimiento Revolucionario Liberal (MRL), who was elected President in 1974, declared an economic state of emergency and announced that Colombia would henceforth reject US economic assistance because 'foreign aid breeds an unhealthy economic dependency and delays or undermines measures that should be taken for development'.[78] In March 1975 the Politburo approved a KGB operation, codenamed REDUT, aimed at establishing 'unofficial relations' with President López.[79] A senior KGB officer was despatched to Bogotá, met López on 29 May and gained his agreement to future meetings. Though Mitrokhin's notes do not identify the officer concerned, he was almost certainly the head of the FCD Second (Latin American) Department, Vladimir Tolstikov, who also met López on subsequent occasions. As in his earlier meetings with Perón, Tolstikov identified himself during visits to Bogotá as Sergei

Sergeyevich Konstantinov, a senior Latin American specialist in the Foreign Ministry, and claimed to be able to provide a direct confidential channel to the Soviet leadership. At his first meeting with Tolstikov, unaware of his KGB connection, López handed him an album of pictures of Colombia which he asked to be presented to Brezhnev with a personal message from himself – a minor diplomatic gesture which was doubtless given an enhanced significance when reported to Brezhnev.[80]

The Centre's exaggerated hopes of establishing 'unoffical relations' with López derived from his distrust of the United States which, like many other Latin Americans, he blamed for the economic exploitation of Latin America. After Jimmy Carter's election as US President in November 1976, López was reported to have dismissed him as 'a provincial politician with a pathological stubbornness and the primitive reasoning of a person who produces and sells peanuts – an accidental figure on the American political horizon'.[81]

Operating under his diplomatic alias, Tolstikov established good personal relations with López, who in 1976 awarded 'Sergei Sergeyevich Konstantinov' the Order of San Carlos 'for active participation in strengthening relations between the USSR and Colombia'.[82] A rather more substantial achievement of the Bogotá residency was to establish covert contact at a senior level with the Colombian intelligence service, the Departamento Administrativo de Securidad (DAS) and, it claimed, to influence its intelligence assessments.[83]

Alfonso López was the first Colombian President to visit the neighbouring Republic of Panama, which had split from Colombia in 1903 after an uprising engineered by the United States. The new Republic had promptly been bullied into accepting a treaty leasing the Panama Canal Zone in perpetuity to the United States. López gave public support to the campaign for the abrogation of the treaty by the President of Panama, General Omar Torrijos Herrera (codenamed RODOM by the KGB), and agreed to Tolstikov's request to arrange a meeting for him with Torrijos.[84] In the event, the Centre selected for the meeting an even more senior officer operating under diplomatic cover, Nikolai Leonov, who over twenty years earlier had been Castro's first KGB contact and had since risen to become head of FCD Service No. 1 (Analysis and Reports). On 28 June 1977 Torrijos sent his personal aircraft to Bogotá to fly Leonov to a former US airbase in Panama, where they continued discussions for four days. Though Leonov brought with him gifts valued by the Centre at 1,200 rubles, he initially found Torrijos in a difficult mood. A few days earlier Guatemala had broken off diplomatic relations with Panama after Torrijos had incautiously told an American journalist that he rejected Guatemalan claims to sovereignty over Belize. He told Leonov angrily, 'I'm not going to receive any more foreigners – not even the Pope!'

Torrijos's anger, however, quickly refocused on the United States. He told Leonov that he was determined to restore Panama's sovereignty over the Canal Zone and eliminate every trace of the American presence. 'This', he declared, 'is the religion of my life!' He gave Leonov a film entitled *The Struggle of the People of Panama for the Canal* which he asked him to pass on to Brezhnev. In return Leonov presented Torrijos with a hunting rifle and a souvenir selection of vodkas, and gave his wife an enamel box. Torrijos declared his willingness to continue 'unofficial contact' with Soviet representatives and gave Leonov the direct phone numbers of his secretary, through whom future meetings could be arranged. He also gave orders for Leonov to be given a visa allowing him to visit Panama at any time over the next year. Leonov gave Torrijos his home telephone number in Moscow – a somewhat irregular proceeding which, as Leonov later acknowledged, disconcerted both the Centre and those members of his family who took calls from Torrijos.[85] Shortly after he returned to Moscow, Torrijos phoned him, said that he wanted to check that he had returned safely and discussed with him the negotiation of a Soviet–Panamanian trade treaty.[86] Torrijos believed his phone conversations with Leonov were probably intercepted by NSA, the American SIGINT agency, but – according to Leonov – looked on them as a way of putting pressure on the Carter administration, which he knew to be nervous about his Soviet contacts.[87]

Despite the diplomatic cover used by Leonov, there is no doubt that Torrijos realized that he was a KGB officer.[88] After reviewing the results of Leonov's mission, the Centre decided to arrange meetings with Torrijos every six to eight months, chiefly in an attempt to influence his policy (mainly, no doubt, to the United States). A KGB officer operating under cover as a correspondent with Tass, the Soviet news agency, was given responsibility for making the detailed arrangements for these meetings. In order to flatter Torrijos another operations officer, also under Tass cover, was sent to deliver to him a personal letter from Brezhnev.[89] To reinforce Torrijos's suspicion of the Carter administration he was also given a bogus State Department document forged by Service A which discussed methods of dragging out the Panama Canal negotiations and removing Torrijos himself from power.[90]

On 7 September 1977 Torrijos and President Jimmy Carter met in Washington to sign two treaties: a Canal Treaty transferring the Canal Zone to Panamanian control in stages to be completed by 2000 and a Neutrality Treaty providing for joint US–Panamanian defence of the Canal's neutrality. At another meeting in Washington on 14 October, however, Carter told Torrijos that the administration had only about fifty-five of the sixty-seven Senate votes required for ratification of the treaties.[91] For the next few months Torrijos had to spend much of his time acting as a jovial host in Panama to US senators whom he privately detested. According to the US diplomat Jack Vaughn:

[Torrijos] had an uncanny ability, looking at a VIP, to know whether he was the raunchy type who wanted girls around or if he was prudish and straitlaced, or maybe he wanted a more intellectual presentation. And, where do you want to go, what can I show you? He'd take them in a helicopter for short sightseeing trips, and they'd get off and go around and meet the natives. A very carefully orchestrated, devastatingly effective show . . . The effect on a gringo politician was, 'This guy has real power, he can make things happen.' He really did a job on the Senate.[92]

Ratification remained in doubt until the last moment. At the end of 1977, Torrijos asked for a meeting with Leonov to discuss the state of the negotiations with the United States. What probably most concerned him were the charges by leading Republican senators opposed to ratification that he was involved in drug trafficking. Carter, however, was convinced that the charges were false. In mid-February 1978 the Senate went into secret session to hear evidence from the Senate Intelligence Committee refuting the charges.[93] Ironically, the KGB believed the charges which Carter and the Senate Intelligence Committee dismissed.[94]

There is little doubt that the charges were correct. According to Floyd Carlton Caceres, a notable drug smuggler as well as personal pilot to Torrijos and his intelligence chief, Manuel Noriega Morena (later President), Torrijos had made contact with drug traffickers almost as soon as he took power. By 1971 his diplomat brother Moisés 'Monchi' Torrijos was providing drug couriers with official Panamanian passports to enable them to avoid customs searches.[95] In 1992 Noriega was to become the first foreign head of state to face criminal charges in a US court; he was sentenced to forty years' imprisonment on eight counts of cocaine trafficking, racketeering and money laundering.

Had the drug-trafficking charges against Torrijos stuck in 1978, there would have been no prospect of ratifying the treaties with the United States. On 16 March, however, the Neutrality Act passed the Senate by one vote more than the two-thirds majority required. Carter later recalled, 'I had never been more tense in my life as we listened to each vote shouted out on the radio.'[96] Apparently unknown to Carter and US intelligence, Leonov arrived in Panama City on 22 March for six days of talks with Torrijos, bringing with him presents for the Torrijos family with a total value of 3,500 rubles. Torrijos used the secret talks with Leonov partly to get off his chest in private the loathing of the *Yanquis* which he dared not express in public. 'I hate the United States', he told Leonov, 'but my position forces me to tolerate a great deal. How I envy Fidel Castro!'

The biggest strain of all had been dealing with the US Senate:

From November of last year up to March of this year, there have been 50 senators in Panama at our invitation. I worked with all of them personally, and it was a heavy cross for me to bear. Almost all of the senators are crude, arrogant, and unwilling to listen to any arguments from the other side . . . They are cavemen whose thought processes belong to the previous century.

Torrijos also had a personal scorn for Carter, whose inadequacy as President was 'a painful thing to see'.[97] Carter, by contrast, had a somewhat naive admiration for Torrijos. 'No one', he believed, 'could have handled the affairs of Panama and its people more effectively than had this quiet and courageous leader.'[98]

Though the KGB flattered Torrijos skilfully, they did not share Carter's unreciprocated respect for him. Torrijos's KGB file contains a description of him by Allende as 'a lecher'.[99] Given his own promiscuity, Allende presumably intended to imply that Torrijos's sexual liaisons were conducted with less dignity than his own. Torrijos's current girlfriend at the time of his sudden death in 1981 was a student friend of one of his own illegitimate daughters.[100] The Torrijos file also includes Cuban intelligence reports about his involvement, along with some members of his family and inner circle, with the drug trade and other international criminal networks.[101] Torrijos's Panama began to rival Batista's Cuba as a magnet for Mafia money-laundering, arms smuggling and contraband.[102] The KGB regarded many of Torrijos's personal mannerisms as somewhat pathetic imitations of Castro's. Like Castro, he dressed in military fatigues, carried a pistol and smoked Cuban cigars (presented to him by Castro, each with a specially printed band inscribed with his name). Also like Castro, he kept his daily schedule and travel routes secret, and pretended to make spontaneous gestures and decisions which were in reality carefully premeditated. Torrijos regularly sought Castro's advice on his negotiations with the United States, though the advice was so secret that it was concealed even from the Panamanian ambassador in Havana. The KGB reported that Noriega flew frequently to Havana in a private aircraft. As the KGB was aware, however, Noriega was also in contact with the CIA.[103]

On 18 April 1978 the Canal Treaty finally passed by the US Senate by the same slim majority as the Neutrality Act a month earlier. Doubtless after prior agreement with the Centre, Leonov suggested to Torrijos that the best way of depriving the United States of any pretext for claiming special rights to defend the Canal would be to turn Panama into 'a permanently neutral state on the model of Switzerland, Sweden, and Austria'. Torrijos was hostile to the idea – chiefly, Leonov believed, because he feared the effect of neutrality on his own authority. 'Would [a neutral] Panama be able to conduct its own foreign policy?' he asked Leonov. 'Would it be possible to assist the anti-imperialist movement? Would I become a political eunuch?'[104] Though Torrijos was succeeded as President in 1978 by Education Minister Aristedes Royo, he retained real power as head of the National Guard, resisting gentle pressure from Leonov to end military rule. He gave three reasons for being reluctant to follow Leonov's advice to set up his own political party:

In the first place, I would then cease to be the leader of the entire nation, and would be the leader of only a political party. In the second place, after creating one party, I would then have to permit the formation of other opposition parties. And third, I do not want to do this because this is what the Americans are always trying to get out of me.[105]

Torrijos told Leonov he was none the less convinced that by the year 2000 the majority of Latin American states would have adopted 'socialism in one form or another'.[106] Within Panama the pro-Moscow Communist Partido del Pueblo (PDP) was the only political party allowed to operate; the rival Maoist Communist Party was brutally persecuted and several of its leaders murdered.

In its early stages the corrupt, authoritarian Torrijos regime had made reforms in land distribution, health care and education. Progress towards Panamanian socialism, however, was largely rhetorical. The PDP unconvincingly declared the regime *la yunta pueblo-gobierno* – a close union of people and government. The corrupt and brutal National Guard became *el brazo armado del pueblo*, the people's weapon arm.[107] According to KGB reports, the PDP leadership maintained 'clandestine contact' with two ministers in the Torrijos government.[108] PDP influence was particularly strong in the Education Ministry. Communist-inspired educational reforms in 1979, however, collapsed in the face of teachers' strikes and demonstrations. Economic bumbling and corruption together left Panama with one of the highest per capita national debts anywhere in the world.[109]

On 31 July 1981, while Torrijos was *en route* with his girlfriend to a weekend retreat, his plane flew into the side of a mountain killing all on board.[110] The KGB, always prone to conspiracy theories, concluded that he was the victim of a CIA assassination plot.[111] A few years earlier, by resolving the great historic grievance against the United States which dated back to the birth of the state, Torrijos had given Panamanians a new sense of identity and national pride. By the time he died, however, many were pleased to see him go. The celebrations in some *cantinas* which followed his plane crash became so boisterous that they were closed down by the National Guard. The KGB had little left to show for the effort it had put into cultivating the Torrijos regime.

The same was true of most of the KGB's efforts during the 1970s to cultivate anti-American and 'progressive' regimes in Latin America. The series of short-term successes which the Centre proudly reported to the Politburo failed to establish a stable basis for the expansion of Soviet influence in Latin America. The KGB itself had lost confidence in the staying power of the Allende regime well before it was overthrown. Covert contacts with the 'progressive' junta in Peru, Torres in Bolivia, Perón in Argentina and Torrijos in Panama lasted only a few years until those leaders were deposed or died. At the end of the decade, however, the KGB's fortunes suddenly revived. The revolution in Central America of which it had been so hopeful in the early 1960s, and in which it had subsequently lost faith, unexpectedly became a reality at the end of the 1970s.

6

Revolution in Central America

For Fidel Castro 1979 was a year of both economic failure and international triumph. After two decades in power, his regime was as dependent as ever on large subsidies which the ailing Soviet economy could ill afford. Popular disaffection was more visible than ever before. Ten times as many Cubans fled to Florida in small boats during 1979 as in the previous year.[1] Castro, however, seemed more interested by increasing international recognition of his role on the world stage, newly signalled by his election as Chairman of the Non-Aligned Movement. The KGB liaison office in Havana reported growing concern at Castro's delusions of grandeur:

The personal influence of F. Castro in [Cuba's] politics is becoming stronger. His prestige as an 'outstanding strategist and chief commander' in connection with the victories in Africa (Angola, Ethiopia), and as a far-sighted politician and statesman, is becoming overblown. F. Castro's vanity is becoming more and more noticeable.

Cuba's Revolutionary Armed Forces are extolled. Castro's approval is needed on every issue, even insignificant ones, and this leads to delays, red tape, and the piling up of papers requiring Castro's signature. Everyone sees that this is an abnormal situation, but everyone remains silent for fear that any remark could be interpreted as an encroachment on the chief's incontestable authority. Cuba's revolutionary spirit is becoming more and more dissipated, while there is an emergence of servility, careerism, and competition between government agencies, and their leaders' attempts to prove themselves to Fidel in the best possible light. There is competition between the MVD [Ministry of Internal Affairs] and the RVS [Revolutionary Armed Forces] within the government to challenge MVD Minister Sergio del Valle's subservient position with respect to R. Castro. Their former friendly relationship has cooled.

MVD Minister Valle [whose responsibilities included the DGI], in an outburst of open exasperation, told P. I. Vasilyev, a representative of the KGB, the following:

'You might think that I, as the Minister of Internal Affairs and a member of the Politburo, can decide everything, but I cannot – I cannot even give an apartment to a Ministry employee. For this too, it is necessary to have the approval of the Commander-in-Chief [Fidel Castro].'[2]

Castro's self-importance was further inflated by the long-delayed spread of revolution in Central America. In March 1979 the Marxist New Jewel Movement, led by Maurice Bishop, seized control of the small Caribbean island of Grenada. A month later fifty Cuban military advisers arrived by ship, bringing with them large supplies of arms and ammunition to bolster the new regime. In September 400 Cuban regular troops arrived to train a new Grenadan army. In December 300 Cubans began the construction of a large new airport with a runway capable of accommodating the largest Soviet and Cuban military transport planes.[3] The once-secret documents of the New Jewel Movement make clear that, as well as being inspired by the Cuban example, Bishop's Marxism also had a good deal in common with the variety once described by French student revolutionaries as 'the Groucho tendency'. Bishop, however, was determined to stamp out opposition. As he told his colleagues: 'Just consider, Comrades . . . how people get detained in this country. We don't go and call for no votes. You get detained when I sign an order after discussing it with the National Security Committee of the Party or with a higher Party body. Once I sign it – like it or don't like it – it's up the hill for them.'

Once satisfied that the Bishop regime was solidly established, Moscow also began supplying massive military aid. A Grenadan general, Hudson Austin, wrote to Andropov as KGB Chairman early in 1982 to thank him 'once again for the tremendous assistance which our armed forces have received from your Party and Government', and to request KGB training for four Grenadan intelligence officers. Austin ended his letter 'by once again extending our greatest warmth and embrace to you and your Party – Sons and Daughters of the heroic Lenin'.[4]

Of far greater significance than Bishop's seizure of power in Grenada was the ousting of the brutal and corrupt Somoza regime in Nicaragua in July 1979 by the Sandinistas. Until less than a year earlier the Frente Sandinista de Liberación Nacional (FSLN) had had few major successes. On 25 August 1978, however, the Terceristas (or 'Insurrectional Tendency'), the dominant faction within the FSLN, pulled off one of the most spectacular coups in guerrilla history. Twenty-four Terceristas, disguised as members of an élite National Guard unit, seized control of the Managua National Palace where the Somoza-dominated National Congress was in session, and took all its members hostage. KGB files reveal that the guerrillas had been trained and financed by the Centre, which gave them the codename ISKRA ('Spark') – the same as that of the Sandinista sabotage and intelligence group founded by the KGB fourteen years earlier. On the eve of the ISKRA attack on the National Palace, Vladimir Kryuchkov, the head of the FCD, was personally briefed on plans for the operation by officers of Department 8 ('Special Operations') of the Illegals Directorate S.[5] In return for the release of the hostages, the Somoza regime was forced to pay a large ransom and free fifty-nine Sandinista prisoners. On their way to Managua airport, where a plane was waiting to take them to Cuba, the guerrillas and the freed prisoners were cheered by enthusiastic crowds. But though the FSLN was winning the battle for hearts and minds, Somoza still retained an apparently firm grip on power. Urban insurrections by the Sandinistas in September were brutally crushed by the National Guard.[6]

In Havana Castro and other Cuban leaders had a series of meetings with the three most influential Sandinistas: the Tercerista leaders Humberto and Daniel Ortega Saavedra, and the only surviving founder of the FSLN, Tomás Borge, who had been freed from a Nicaraguan prison by the ISKRA operation. It was thanks largely to Cuban pressure on them that the three factions of the FSLN formally reunited by an agreement signed in Havana in March 1979.[7] Simultaneously, the Cuban Departamento América (DA) helped the Sandinistas set up a base in Costa Rica from which to prepare an offensive against the Somoza regime. At the end of May FSLN forces crossed into Nicaragua. The arms and tactical advice provided by the DA's operations centre in San José made a major contribution to the rapid Sandinista victory. The former Costa Rican President, José Figueres, said later that, but for arms from Cuba and Costa Rican support for Sandinista operations, the victory over

Somoza 'would not have been possible'. The speed with which the resistance of Somoza's National Guard crumbled took both the CIA and the KGB by surprise. When the Sandinista offensive began, the CIA reported to the White House that it had little prospect of success. On 19 July, however, dressed in olive-green uniforms and black berets, the FSLN entered Managua in triumph.[8]

Cuban advisers quickly followed in the Sandinistas' wake. The most influential of them, the former head of the DA operations centre in San José, Julián López Díaz, was appointed Cuban ambassador in Managua. A week after their seizure of power, a Sandinista delegation, headed by their military commander, Humberto Ortega, flew to Havana to take part in the annual 26 July celebrations of the attack on the Moncada Barracks which had begun Castro's guerrilla campaign against the Batista regime. Amid what Radio Havana described as mass 'demonstrations of joy', a female Sandinista guerrilla in battle fatigues presented Cuba's Maximum Leader with a rifle captured in combat against Somoza's National Guard.[9] Castro paid emotional tribute to 'this constellation of heroic, brave, intelligent and capable commanders and combatants of the Nicaraguan Sandinista National Liberation Front':

They gained victory along a path similar to our path. They gained victory the only way they, like us, could free themselves of tyranny and imperialist domination – taking up arms [*applause*], fighting hard, heroically. And we must say and emphasize that the Nicaraguan revolution was outstanding for its heroism, its perseverance, the perseverance of its combatants – because it is not the victory of a single day, it is a victory after twenty years of struggle [*applause*], twenty years of planning [*applause*].[10]

In early August CIA analysts correctly forecast that the Sandinistas would seek Cuban help to 'transform the guerrilla forces into a conventional army', the Ejército Popular Sandinista (EPS). According to the same intelligence assessment, 'The Cubans can also be expected in the months ahead to begin using Nicaragua to support guerrillas from countries in the northern tier of Central America.'[11]

Castro's apotheosis as an international statesman, already enhanced by the Nicaraguan Revolution, came in September 1979 at the Havana conference of the Non-Aligned Movement. Active measures to exploit the conference proceedings in the Soviet interest had been co-ordinated in advance at meetings between Pedro Pupo Pérez of the DGI and Oleg Maksimovich Nechiporenko and A. N. Itskov of the KGB.[12] In his opening speech as Chairman of the Non-Aligned Movement, Castro denounced not merely the '*Yanqui* imperialists' but 'their new allies – the Chinese government'. He then paid fulsome tribute to the Soviet Union:

We are thankful to the glorious October Revolution because it started a new age in human history. It made possible the defeat of fascism and created conditions in the world which united the unselfish struggle of the peoples and led to the collapse of the hateful colonial system. To ignore this is to ignore history itself. Not only Cuba, but also Vietnam, the attacked Arab countries, the peoples of the former Portuguese colonies, the revolutionary processes in many countries of the world, the liberation movements which struggle against oppression, racism, Zionism and fascism in South Africa, Namibia, Zimbabwe, Palestine and in other areas have a lot to be thankful for regarding socialist solidarity. I ask myself if the United States or any country in NATO has ever helped a single liberation movement in our world.

According to the official transcript of Castro's speech, this passage was followed by applause.[13] Though ninety-two other heads of state were present, Castro was never out of the spotlight. For the next three years he continued as Chairman of the Non-Aligned Movement.

The first Soviet official to arrive in Managua in the immediate aftermath of the Sandinista seizure of power was the Centre's senior Latin American specialist, Nikolai Leonov, head of FCD Service No. 1 (Analysis and Reports). 'The city', Leonov recalls, 'was still smoking and we had no embassy, but I was there under the cover of a journalist.'[14] As after the Cuban Revolution twenty years earlier, the KGB played a far more important role than the Soviet Foreign Ministry in conducting relations with the new regime. The Soviet ambassador from another Latin American country who arrived in Managua to conduct the formal procedures of establishing diplomatic relations created an even worse impression than the first Soviet ambassador to Castro's Cuba.[15] On arrival at the airport, the ambassador staggered down the aircraft steps, his breath reeking of alcohol, and collapsed into the arms of his aides in front of the outraged Sandinista welcoming party. It was officially announced that he had been 'taken ill as a result of a difficult flight', and he was driven to hospital where attempts were made to revive him in time for the official ceremonies which were due to take place that evening on the stage of a Managua theatre. The ambassador made it to the theatre but collapsed once more and was forced to depart in the middle of the speeches. His aides had scarcely taken off his shoes and put him to bed when an irate Sandinista minister arrived to demand an explanation. Leonov attended a meeting next morning at the house of the Cuban ambassador where senior Sandinistas sought to register an official protest.

After giving my outraged hosts the opportunity to speak their minds fully, I said as calmly as possible that I shared their assessments and feelings. However, it was hardly worth starting the history of our relations with a protest and a diplomatic conflict. The ambassador was a human being with weaknesses, illnesses, [infirmities of] age ... An official note of protest (which lay before me on the desk) was unnecessary, because it did not reflect the real climate of our relations but, on the contrary, might spoil them. I gave a firm promise to inform the Politburo of what had taken place, but would prefer to do this orally. It would be awkward for me to accept the note since [as an undercover KGB officer] I had no official status, and the embassy was not yet open. I talked and talked, to buy time for passions to cool down.

Leonov reported the incident to Andropov by a telegram marked strictly 'personal', and Andropov informed Gromyko, also on a personal basis. Before long, however, it seemed to Leonov that half the Foreign Ministry knew about the ambassador's disgrace. Leonov as well as the Sandinistas bore the brunt of the anger of the Ministry, which, he was told, was 'offended' by his report and refused to see him on his return to Moscow.[16]

After delivering a preliminary report in person to the Centre, Leonov returned to Managua on 12 October for a week of secret talks with the Ortega brothers and Borge, the three dominating figures in the new regime, as well as with five other leading Sandinistas.[17] Leonov reported to the Centre that:

The FSLN leadership had firmly decided to carry out the transformation of the FSLN into a Marxist-Leninist Party, including within it other leftist parties and groups on an individual basis. The centrist and bourgeois mini-parties already existing in the country would be kept only because they presented no danger and served as a convenient facade for the outside world.

Daniel Ortega told Leonov:

We do not want to repeat Cuba's mistakes with regard to the United States, whereas the United States is clearly avoiding a repetition of the mistakes it made with regard to Cuba. Our strategy is to tear Nicaragua from the capitalist orbit and, in time, become a member of the CMEA [Comecon].

According to Leonov, Ortega 'regarded the USSR as a class and strategic ally, and saw the Soviet experience in building the Party and state as a model to be studied and used for practical actions in Nicaragua'. Ortega agreed to 'unofficial contacts' with Soviet representatives (a euphemism for meetings with KGB officers) in order to exchange information. He gave Leonov a secret document outlining the FSLN's political plans for transmission to the CPSU Central Committee.[18] Though Mitrokhin did not note its contents, this was, almost certainly, the so-called 'Seventy-Two-Hour Document', officially entitled the 'Analysis of the Situation and Tasks of the Sandinista People's Revolution', prepared by the Sandinista leadership in two secret seventy-two-hour meetings in September. It denounced 'American imperialism' as 'the rabid enemy of all peoples who are struggling to achieve their definitive liberation' and proclaimed the intention of turning the FSLN into a Marxist-Leninist 'vanguard party' which, in alliance with Cuba and the Soviet bloc, would lead the class struggle not merely in Nicaragua but across its borders in Central America.[19]

The first country to which the Sandinista leadership hoped to export their revolution was El Salvador, the smallest and most densely populated state in Latin America, ruled by a repressive military government. The KGB reported that a meeting of the Central Committee of the Partido Comunista Salvadoreño (PCS) in August 1979, after discussing events in Nicaragua, had agreed to make preparations for revolution. It was even thought likely that, following the flight of the Nicaraguan dictator, Anastasio Somoza, the Salvadoran President, General Julio Rivera, might surrender power without a fight. In September the PCS leader, Schafik Handal, visited Nicaragua and was promised arms by the Sandinistas.[20] Leonov also met Handal, probably soon after his own talks with Sandinista leaders in October, and discussed with him plans for Soviet bloc countries to supply Western-manufactured arms in order to disguise their support for the Salvadoran revolution.[21] These plans, however, were overtaken by a coup in El Salvador led by army officers anxious to maintain the dominant position of the armed forces. The political situation stabilized temporarily at the beginning of 1980 when the Christian Democrat Party agreed to form a new junta with the military and their exiled leader, José Napoleón Duarte. But while Duarte's government attempted to inaugurate a programme of social reform, right-wing death squads pursued a campaign of terror against their political opponents.

The Soviet attitude towards the prospects for revolution in Central America was ambivalent. The invasion of Afghanistan in December 1979 made Moscow both wary of further military commitments and anxious to repair the damage to its international reputation by successes elsewhere. Its desire to exploit the Sandinista revolution was balanced by nervousness at the likely reaction of the United States. The Carter administration, however, though expressing concern at the Sandinistas' left-wing policies, none the less gave them economic aid. In an attempt to diminish the risks inherent in the challenge to US influence in Central America, Moscow was happy to leave the most visible role to Fidel Castro.[22]

During the year after the Sandinista victory, Castro flew secretly to Nicaragua on a number of occasions, landing on the private airstrip at one of the estates of the deposed dictator, Anastasio Somoza. In July 1980 he made his first public visit to Managua to celebrate the first anniversary of the revolution and was greeted at the airport by the nine Sandinista *comandantes*, each in battle fatigues virtually identical to his own. 'Because you are a profoundly revolutionary people', he told a cheering crowd, 'we Cuban visitors feel as if we were in our own fatherland!'[23] During the Sandinistas' early years in power, military and economic assistance to the new regime was jointly discussed by tripartite Soviet–Cuban–Nicaraguan committees. In May 1980 a Sandinista delegation visited Moscow to ask for the large-scale military aid required to turn the Ejército Popular Sandinista into the most powerful force in Central America. Though the Soviet Union agreed to arm and equip the EPS over the next few years, it cautiously left the details to be decided by a tripartite committee which was not due to convene in Managua for another year.[24]

El Salvador, meanwhile, was slipping into civil war. During 1980 right-wing death squads carried out a series of well-publicized atrocities, among them the killing of Archbishop Oscar Arnulfo Romero during a church service, the assassination of several leading Christian Democrats, and the rape and murder of three American nuns and a church worker. In March the PCS decided to support the 'armed road' to revolution.[25] Three months later, at a secret meeting in Havana attended by Castro and Humberto Ortega, Schafik Handal and the leaders of El Salvador's four other Marxist factions united as the Dirección Revolucionaria Unida (DRU). The KGB reported that the two dominating figures in the DRU were Handal, the PCS leader, and a former PCS General-Secretary, Cayetano Carpio, leader of a breakaway movement.[26] The DRU was given a secure base in Nicaragua and, in consultation with Ortega, agreed to imitate the Sandinistas' strategy against the Somoza regime by seeking to create a military machine powerful enough to defeat the army of the state.[27] Thousands of Salvadoran revolutionaries were given rapid military training in Cuba; several hundred more were trained in Nicaragua.[28] The DRU agreed with its Cuban and Sandinista allies on the importance of striking 'a decisive blow' before the end of the Carter administration in January 1981 for fear that, if Ronald Reagan were elected President, he would provide more active military assistance to the Duarte government (as indeed he decided to do).[29]

In accordance with the strategy he had agreed with Leonov, Handal toured the Soviet bloc and two of its allies in June and July 1980 in search of arms and military equipment of Western manufacture for use in El Salvador. On Soviet advice, his first stop was in Hanoi where the Communist Party leader Le Duan gave him an enthusiastic welcome and provided enough US weapons captured during the Vietnam War to equip three battalions. Handal's next stop was East Berlin where Honecker promised 3 million Ostmarks to pay for equipment but was unable to supply any Western arms. In Prague Vasil Bil'ak agreed to supply Czech weapons of types available on the open market. The Bulgarian Communist Party leader, Dimitur

Stanichev, gave 300 reconditioned German machine guns from the Second World War, 200,000 rounds of ammunition, 10,000 uniforms and 2,000 medical kits. Hungary had no Western weapons but the Party leader, Janos Kadar, promised 10,000 uniforms as well as medical supplies. Handal's final stop was in Ethiopia whose army had been completely re-equipped by the Soviet Union over the previous few years. Lieutenant-Colonel Mengistu promised to supply 700 Thompson automatic weapons and other Western arms left over from the Haile Selassie era.[30] According to a KGB report, Handal acknowledged that the success of his arms mission had been possible only because of Soviet support:

We are clearly aware of the fact that, in the final analysis, our relations with the other countries in the socialist camp will be determined by the position of the Soviet Union, and that we will need the advice and recommendations of the leadership of the CPSU Central Committee. We cannot let out a war cry and lead trained personnel into battle without being sure of the full brotherly support of the Soviet Communists.

After Handal's return to Central America, the various guerrilla factions in El Salvador united as the Farabundo Martí de Liberación Nacional (FMLN). The KGB reported that the Cubans were confident that revolution would succeed in El Salvador by the end of the year.[31] The Salvadoran government was regarded as so divided and corrupt and its army as so poorly equipped and motivated that the guerrilla victory appeared certain.[32]

In January 1981, however, a supposedly 'final offensive' by the FMLN, approved by the Cubans, failed, forcing the guerrillas to take refuge in the mountains.[33] Simultaneously the new Reagan administration made clear that it intended to take a much tougher line in Central America. Using strikingly undiplomatic language, Reagan's first Secretary of State, Alexander Haig, delivered a blunt warning to Moscow that 'their time of unrestricted adventuring in the Third World was over'. 'Every official of the State Department, in every exchange with a Soviet official' was instructed to repeat the same message.[34] Wary of publicly provoking the new administration, Moscow sought to distance itself from the bloodshed in El Salvador. At the Twenty-sixth Congress of the CPSU in February, attended by Communist leaders and other fraternal delegates from around the world, Handal and the PCS were conspicuous by their absence – no doubt on instructions from Moscow.

While cautious in its public statements, however, the Soviet leadership authorized an increase in arms shipments to Cuba, some of them secretly intended for other destinations in Central America. According to US officials, more Soviet arms were sent to Cuba during the first eight months of 1981 than at any time since the missile crisis of 1962.[35] In May 1981 a Nicaraguan–Soviet–Cuban commission met in Managua to discuss the supply of Soviet arms to the Sandinista EPS. Following agreement in June, the first heavy weapons (tanks and artillery) began to arrive at Port Bluff in July.[36] Castro subsequently complained that, instead of continuing to discuss all their arms requirements with Cuba, the Sandinistas were now approaching the Soviet Union directly.[37] On 21 November Humberto Ortega and Marshal Ustinov signed an arms treaty in Moscow ratifying the agreement reached in Managua in June.[38] Within a few years the EPS was over 100,000 strong and had become the most powerful military force in Central American history.

Castro somewhat hysterically compared the inauguration of Ronald Reagan as US President in January 1981 to Adolf Hitler's appointment as German Chancellor in January 1933. After Reagan's election two months earlier, Castro had summoned the Cuban people to organize themselves into territorial militia to defend their fatherland against American attack. To pay for weapons, workers 'volunteered' to give up a day's wages. The *Yanqui* invaders, Castro declared, would 'face an anthill, an armed anthill . . . invincible and unyielding, and never, never surrendering!' In addition to the private warnings which he instructed American diplomats to deliver, Alexander Haig publicly denounced Cuba and the Soviet Union for acting as both 'tutors and arms suppliers' to Central American revolutionaries. Cuba's activities, he declared, were 'no longer acceptable in this hemisphere'. The United States would 'deal with this matter at source'. To Castro that appeared as an invasion threat.[39] Privately, he was annoyed that Moscow did not take a stronger line in public towards the new Reagan administration. According to a KGB report, he told a Soviet military delegation which visited Cuba in February, headed by the chief-of-staff of the Soviet armed forces, Marshal Nikolai Ogarkov, that the Soviet Union should toughen its policy towards the United States. In particular, it should refuse to accept the deployment of American cruise missiles in Europe. Castro made the extraordinary proposal that, if the deployment went ahead, Moscow should seriously consider re-establishing the nuclear missile bases in Cuba dismantled after the missile crisis nineteen years earlier. The new Cuban militia, he boasted, now numbered 500,000 men.[40]

The KGB reported that Castro's fears of American attack were strengthened by the crisis in Poland, where the authority of the Communist one-party state was being eroded by the groundswell of popular support for the Solidarity movement. Though he had no more (and probably even less) sympathy for Solidarity than he had had for the reformers of the Prague Spring in 1968, Castro told 'a Soviet representative' (probably a KGB officer) that if the Red Army intervened in Poland in 1981, as it had done in Czechoslovakia in 1968, there might be 'serious consequences for Cuba in view of its immediate proximity to the USA'. Castro, in other words, was afraid that a Soviet invasion of Poland might provoke an American invasion of Cuba.[41] When General Wojciech Jaruzelski became Polish Party leader in October, Castro insisted on the need for him to take 'decisive measures' which would make Soviet intervention unnecessary: 'Otherwise he will be finished both as a military leader and as a political figure.' The only solution, Castro argued, was for Jaruzelski to declare martial law, even if Solidarity responded by calling a general strike: 'One should not be afraid of strikes, since in themselves they are incapable of changing the government.'[42] Castro seems to have been aware that Moscow's policy was essentially the same as his. Andropov told the Politburo that Soviet military intervention was too risky to undertake. The veiled threats of intervention, which Castro took seriously, were intended to persuade the irresolute Jaruzelski to declare martial law and outlaw Solidarity, which he duly did in December 1981.[43]

Despite Castro's impeccable ideological orthodoxy and denunciation of Polish revisionism, his delusions of grandeur as a major statesman on the world stage continued to cause concern in Moscow. The KGB reported in 1981 that the Cuban presence in Africa was giving rise to 'complications': 'Leading personalities in Angola and Ethiopia doubt the desirability of the Cuban troops' continuing presence on the territory of these countries. The Cubans' efforts to influence internal processes in developing countries are turning into interference in their internal affairs.'

Cuban interference was all the more resented because its own mismanaged economy made it impossible for it to offer economic aid. The KGB also reported that Castro was in danger of being carried away by the prospects for revolution in Central America:

The victory of the Sandinista National Liberation Front in Nicaragua and of progressive forces in Grenada, the increasing number of incidents in El Salvador, and the mobilization of left-wing groups in Guatemala and Honduras give some Cuban leaders the impression that the historic moment has now come for a total revolution in Central Latin America, and that this must be expedited by launching an armed struggle in the countries of the region.

Raúl Castro reports that some members of the Central Committee of the Cuban Communist Party – [Manuel] Piñeiro, head of the American Department [Departamento América] and Secretary of the Central Committee, together with [José] Abr[ah]antes, the First Deputy Minister of Internal Affairs – are prompting Fidel Castro to take ill-considered action and calling for the export of revolution.[44]

Castro's first target for 'the export of revolution' remained El Salvador. He told Ogarkov in February 1981 that he had called a secret meeting in Havana of DRU and FMLN leaders in order to work out an agreed strategy for continuing the revolutionary struggle after the failure of what had been intended as the 'final offensive' in January.[45] Though Mitrokhin's notes do not record the results of that meeting, Schafik Handal later informed a KGB operations officer that the PCS had adopted a policy of guerrilla warfare and sabotage operations, with the aim of forcing the junta into negotiations with the DRU. In October the DRU held a meeting in Managua with representatives of the Sandinista regime and six revolutionary groups from Honduras. They jointly agreed to prepare for a guerrilla uprising in Honduras in case this proved necessary to prevent action by the Honduran army against FMLN guerrillas. According to KGB reports, pressure had been put on the President of Honduras, General Policarpo Paz García, to prevent his troops from being drawn into the civil war in El Salvador. Guerrilla forces in Guatemala were also allegedly strong enough to deter intervention by the Guatemalan army. Costa Rican Communists were said to have 600 well-trained and equipped guerrillas who were prepared to intervene on the side of the FMLN. Colombian revolutionaries had received over 1.2 million dollars' worth of weapons and ammunition via the Sandinistas and were reported to be 'capable of initiating combat actions in Colombia upon command'. The Libyan leader, Colonel Qaddafi, was providing large sums of money for the transport of weapons to guerrilla groups.[46]

Late in 1981, the FMLN agreed with Castro on a strategy designed to disrupt the elections due to be held in El Salvador in March 1982. Soviet arms supplies channelled by the Cubans through Honduras and Belize were used to block roads, destroy public transport and attack polling booths and other public buildings.[47] Ogarkov, among others, appears to have believed that the strategy might succeed. According to the Grenadan minutes of his meeting in Moscow shortly before the elections with the Chief of Staff of the People's Revolutionary Armed Forces of Grenada:

The Marshal [Ogarkov] said that over two decades ago there was only Cuba in Latin America, today there are Nicaragua, Grenada and a serious battle is going on in El Salvador. The Marshal of the Soviet Union then stressed that United States imperialism would try to prevent progress but that there were no prospects for imperialism to turn back history.[48]

The FMLN strategy, however, failed. The turnout at the El Salvador elections, witnessed by hundreds of foreign observers and journalists, was over 80 per cent. Henceforth the DRU and FMLN were resigned to a protracted 'people's war' on the Vietnamese model, epitomized by the slogan, 'Vietnam Has Won! El Salvador Will Win!'[49] Civil war continued in El Salvador for another decade.

Since Moscow appears to have seen little prospect of an early FMLN victory, the KGB's main priority became to exploit the civil war in active measures designed to discredit US policy. In particular it set out to make military aid to the El Salvador government (increased more than five-fold by the Reagan administration between 1981 and 1984) so unpopular within the United States that public opinion would demand that it be halted. Mitrokhin's notes on KGB active measures consist of only a brief file summary: 'Influence was exerted on US public opinion: about 150 committees were created in the United States which spoke out against US interference in El Salvador, and contacts were made with US Senators.'[50]

As often happened, the Centre seems to have exaggerated its ability to influence Western opinion. The majority of US protesters required no prompting by the KGB to oppose the policy of the Reagan administration in El Salvador. Both the KGB and the Cuban Departamento América, however, undoubtedly played a significant and probably co-ordinated role in expanding the volume of protest. A tour of the United States by Schafik Handal's brother, Farid, early in 1980 led to the founding of the Committee in Solidarity with the People of El Salvador (CISPES), an umbrella group co-ordinating the work of many local committees opposed to US involvement. Farid Handal's most important contacts in New York were Alfredo García Almedo, head of the DA's North American department, who operated under diplomatic cover as a member of the Cuban Mission to the UN, and the leadership of the Communist Party of the United States, which was also in touch with the KGB.[51]

Soon after its foundation, CISPES disseminated an alleged State Department 'Dissent Paper on El Salvador and Central America', which purported to reflect the concerns of many 'current and former analysts and officials' in the National Security Council, State Department, Pentagon and CIA. In reality, the document was a forgery, almost certainly produced by FCD Service A. It warned that continued military aid to the El Salvador government would eventually force the United States to intervene directly, and praised the political wing of the FMLN as 'a legitimate and representative political force' with wide popular support. Among the journalists who quoted the document were two columnists on the *New York Times*. One, Flora Lewis, later apologized to her readers for having been deceived by a forgery. The other, Anthony Lewis (no relation), did not.[52]

Soviet caution about the 'export of revolution' in Central America was reinforced by the increased risks of confrontation with the United States. On 1 December 1981 Reagan authorized covert support for the 'Contra' opposition, initially approving the expenditure of $19 million to train 500 'resistance fighters'. Support for the Contras rapidly ceased to be secret and turned into a public relations disaster which KGB active measures sought to exploit around the world.[53] As the 'Great Communicator' later acknowledged in his memoirs, 'One of my greatest frustrations . . . was my inability to communicate to the American people and to Congress the seriousness of the threat we faced in Central America.'[54] On 10 March

1982 the *Washington Post* revealed the covert action programme approved three months earlier and disclosed that the 500 Contras were being secretly trained to destroy Nicaraguan power plants and bridges, as well as to 'disrupt the Nicaraguan arms supply line to El Salvador'. Six months later the Contras numbered almost 3,500. On 8 November the lead story in *Newsweek*, headlined 'America's Secret War: Target Nicaragua', revealed the use of the Contras in a CIA covert operation intended to overthrow the Nicaraguan government and the involvement of the US ambassador to Honduras in their training and organization. The Reagan administration was forced to admit its secret backing for the Contras, but claimed implausibly that the purpose was merely to put pressure on, rather than to overthrow, the Sandinistas.

Congress was unconvinced. On 8 December, by a majority of 411 to 0, the House of Representatives passed the 'Boland Amendment', prohibiting both the Defense Department and the CIA from providing military equipment, training or advice for the purpose of overthrowing the Sandinista regime. The experience of the US-backed attempt to overthrow the Castro regime by the landing at the Bay of Pigs in 1961 should have made clear that paramilitary operations on the scale planned against the Sandinistas twenty years later in an era of more investigative journalism could not reasonably be expected to remain secret. 'A *covert* operation', writes George Shultz, who succeeded Haig as Secretary of State in 1982, 'was being converted to *overt* by talk on Capitol Hill and in the daily press and television news coverage.' By the summer of 1983, the CIA favoured making public American support for Contra operations, and transferring management of it to the Defense Department. The Pentagon, however, successfully resisted taking responsibility for such a controversial programme. Reagan's covert action in Central America had thus become riddled with contradictions which were easily exploited by both his political opponents and Soviet active measures. What had become in practice an overt programme of support to the Contras was still being implemented as a covert operation – with the result, as Shultz complained, that 'the administration could not openly defend it'. Reagan himself added to the contradictions by publicly proclaiming one policy while secretly following another. The stated aim of support for the Contras was to prevent the Sandinistas undermining their neighbours 'through the export of subversion and violence'. 'Let us be clear as to the American attitude toward the Government of Nicaragua,' the President told a joint session of Congress on 27 April. 'We do not seek its overthrow.' The KGB was well aware, however, that Reagan's real aim was precisely that – the overthrow of the government of Nicaragua.[55]

Though Soviet commentators continued to express 'unswerving solidarity' with the Nicaraguan people and 'resolute condemnation' of US aggression towards them, they failed to include Nicaragua on their list of Third World 'socialist-oriented states' – a label which would have implied greater confidence in, and commitment to, the survival of the Sandinista revolution than Moscow was willing to give. Both the Soviet Union and Cuba made clear to Sandinista leaders that they would not defend them against American attack. During Daniel Ortega's visit to Moscow in March 1983, he was obliged – no doubt reluctantly – to assent to Andropov's declaration as Soviet leader that 'the revolutionary government of Nicaragua has all necessary resources to defend the motherland'. It did not, in other words, require further assistance from the Soviet Union to 'uphold its freedom and independence'.[56]

Ortega's visit coincided with the beginning of the tensest period of Soviet–American relations since the Cuban missile crisis. Since May 1981 the KGB and GRU had been collaborating in operation RYAN, a global operation designed to collect intelligence on the presumed (though, in reality, non-existent) plans of the Reagan administration to launch a nuclear first strike against the Soviet Union. For the next three years the Kremlin and the Centre were obsessed by what the Soviet ambassador in Washington, Anatoli Dobrynin, called a 'paranoid interpretation' of Reagan's policy. Residencies in Western capitals, Tokyo and some Third World states were required to submit time-consuming fortnightly reports on signs of US and NATO preparations for nuclear attack. Many FCD officers stationed abroad were much less alarmist than the Centre and viewed operation RYAN with scome scepticism. None, however, was willing to put his career at risk by challenging the assumptions behind the operation. RYAN thus created a vicious circle of intelligence collection and assessment. Residencies were, in effect, required to report alarming information even if they were sceptical of it. The Centre was duly alarmed and demanded more. Reagan's announcement of the SDI ('Star Wars') programme in March 1983, coupled with his almost simultaneous denunciation of the Soviet Union as an 'evil empire', raised Moscow's fears to new heights. The American people, Andropov believed, were being psychologically prepared by the Reagan administration for nuclear war. On 28 September, already terminally ill, Andropov issued from his sickbed an apocalyptic denunciation of the 'outrageous military psychosis' which, he claimed, had taken hold of the United States: 'The Reagan administration, in its imperial ambitions, goes so far that one begins to doubt whether Washington has any brakes at all preventing it from crossing the point at which any sober-minded person must stop.'[57]

The overthrow of the Marxist regime in Grenada a few weeks later appeared to Moscow to provide further evidence of the United States' 'imperial ambitions'. In October 1983 a long-standing conflict between Prime Minister Maurice Bishop and his deputy, Bernard Coard, erupted in violence which culminated in the shooting of Bishop, his current lover and some of his leading supporters in front of a mural of Che Guevara. Ronald Reagan and Margaret Thatcher disagreed in their interpretation of the killings. The new regime, Mrs Thatcher believed, though it contained more obvious thugs, was not much different from its predecessor. Reagan, like Bill Casey, his DCI, regarded the coup as a serious escalation of the Communist threat to the Caribbean. Grenada, he believed, was 'a Soviet–Cuban colony, being readied as a major military bastion to export terror and undermine democracy'. Reagan was also concerned at the threat to 800 American medical students in Grenada. On 25 October a US invasion overthrew the regime and rescued the students. The operation further fuelled Soviet paranoia. Vice-President Vasili Kuznetsov accused the Reagan administration of 'making delirious plans for world domination' which were 'pushing mankind to the brink of disaster'. The Soviet press depicted Reagan himself as a 'madman'. The Sandinistas feared that Nicaragua might be the next target for an American invasion. So did the KGB.[58]

The impact of the Grenada invasion in Moscow was heightened by the fact that it immediately preceded the most fraught phase of operation RYAN. During the NATO command-post exercise, Able Archer 83, held from 2 to 11 November to practise nuclear release procedures, paranoia in the Centre reached dangerous levels. For a time the KGB leadership was haunted by the fear that the exercise might be intended as cover for a nuclear first strike. Some FCD officers stationed in the West were by now more concerned by the alarmism of the Centre than by the threat of Western surprise attack. Operation RYAN wound down (though it did not end) during 1984, helped by the death of its two main protagonists, Andropov and Defence Minister Ustinov, and by reassuring signals from London and Washington, both worried by intelligence reports on the rise in Soviet paranoia.[59]

The period of acute US–Soviet tension which reached its peak late in 1983 left Moscow in no mood to raise the stakes in Central America. The Soviet–Nicaraguan arms treaty of 1981 had provided for the delivery of a squadron of MiG-21s in 1985. Moscow was well aware, however, that the supply of MiG-21s would be strongly opposed by the United States. Early in 1984 Castro began trying to persuade the Sandinista leadership that they should accept a squadron of helicopters instead. Humberto Ortega reacted angrily, telling a meeting of the Sandinista National Directorate: 'It doesn't seem at all unlikely to me that the Soviets, lining up their international interests, have asked Castro to persuade us to give up the MiG-21s. But we must never renounce them, nor must we allow Cuba to continue being an intermediary between ourselves and the Soviets.' The MiG-21s, however, were never delivered.[60] In the mid-1980s Soviet bloc support for the Nicaraguan economy fluctuated between $150 and $400 million a year, all in bilateral trade credits rather than hard-currency loans – a significant drain on Soviet resources but a small fraction of the aid it gave to Cuba.[61]

For different reasons, Central America turned into a major policy failure for both the United States and the Soviet Union. The disorganized Contras (whose numbers, even on the most optimistic estimate, were never more than one-fifth those of the EPS) had no prospect of defeating the Sandinistas. Their inept guerrilla campaign served chiefly to discredit themselves and their American supporters. On 24 May 1984 the House voted another Boland Amendment, more drastic than the first. Signed into law by Reagan in October, Boland II (as it became known) prohibited military or paramilitary support for the Contras by the CIA, Defense 'or any other agency or entity involved in intelligence activities' for the next year. The Deputy Director for Intelligence (and future DCI), Robert Gates, wrote to the DCI, Bill Casey, on 14 December 1984:

The course we have been on (even before the funding cut-off) – as the last two years will testify – will result in further strengthening of the regime and a Communist Nicaragua which, allied with its Soviet and Cuban friends, will serve as the engine for the destabilization of Central America. Even a well-funded Contra movement cannot prevent this; indeed, relying on and supporting the Contras as our only action may actually hasten the ultimate unfortunate outcome.

The only way to bring down the Sandinistas, Gates argued, was overt military assistance to their opponents, coupled with 'air strikes to destroy a considerable portion of Nicaragua's military buildup'. Covert action could not do the job. Neither Casey nor Reagan was willing to face up to this uncomfortable truth.[62]

The attempt to circumvent the congressional veto on aid to the Contras led the White House into the black comedy of 'Iran-Contra' – an illegal attempt to divert to the Contras the profits of secret arms sales to Iran, followed by an attempted cover-up. Though the word 'impeachment' was probably never uttered either by the President himself or by his advisers in their conversations with him during the Iran-Contra crisis, it was in all their minds after the affair became public knowledge at a press conference on 25 November 1986. White House reporters, Reagan's chief-of-staff believed, were 'thinking a single thought: another Presidency was about to destroy itself'. That evening Vice-President George Bush dictated for his diary a series of staccato phrases which summed up the despondency in the White House: 'The administration is in disarray – foreign policy in disarray – cover-up – Who knew what when?' US support for the Contras had proved hopelessly counterproductive, handing a propaganda victory to the Sandinistas and reducing the Reagan presidency to its lowest ebb.[63]

Though the failures of US policy in Central America were eagerly exploited by Soviet active measures, however, Moscow was beginning to lose patience with the Sandinistas. In May 1986, despite the fact that Nicaragua already owed the Soviet Union $1.1 billion, the Politburo was still willing 'to supply free of charge uniforms, food and medicine to seventy thousand servicemen of the Sandinista army'.[64] By 1987, with economic problems mounting at home, Gorbachev was increasingly reluctant to throw good money after bad in Central America. The Nicaraguan Minister of External Co-operation, Henry Ruiz, ruefully acknowledged that Soviet criticism of the Sandinistas' chronic economic mismanagement was 'legitimate'.[65] The economic pressure created by the decline of Soviet bloc support was heightened by a simultaneous US embargo. According to the secretary-general of the Sandinista Foreign Ministry, Alejandro Bendaña, Moscow told Managua bluntly that it was 'time to achieve a regional settlement of security problems'. After three years of tortuous negotiations, continued conflict and missed deadlines, a peace plan chiefly devised by the Costa Rican President, Oscar Arias Sánchez, finally succeeded. According to Bendaña, 'It wasn't the intellectual brilliance of Oscar Arias that did it. It was us grabbing frantically onto any framework that was there, trying to cut our losses.'[66] As part of the peace plan, the Sandinistas agreed to internationally supervised elections in February 1990, and – much to their surprise – lost to a broad-based coalition of opposition parties.

With the demise of the Sandinistas, Cuba was, once again, the only Marxist-Leninist state in Latin America. During the later 1980s, however, there was a curious inversion of the ideological positions of Cuba and the Soviet Union. Twenty years earlier, Castro had been suspected of heresy by Soviet leaders. In the Gorbachev era, by contrast, Castro increasingly saw himself as the defender of ideological orthodoxy against Soviet revisionism. By 1987 the KGB liaison mission in Havana was reporting to the Centre that the DGI was increasingly keeping it at arm's length. The situation was judged so serious that the KGB Chairman, Viktor Chebrikov, flew to Cuba in an attempt to restore relations. He appears to have had little success.[67] Soon afterwards the Cuban resident in Prague, Florentino Aspillaga Lombard, defected to the United States and publicly revealed that the DGI had begun to target countries of the Soviet bloc. He also claimed, probably correctly, that Castro had a secret Swiss bank account 'used to finance liberation movements, bribery of leaders and any personal whim of Castro'.[68] At the annual 26 July celebration in 1988 of the start of Castro's rebellion thirty-five years earlier, the Soviet ambassador was conspicuous by his absence. In his speech Castro criticized Gorbachev publicly for the first time. Gorbachev's emphasis on *glasnost* and *perestroika* was, he declared, a threat to fundamental socialist principles. Cuba must stand guard over the ideological purity of the revolution. Gorbachev's visit to Cuba in April 1989 did little to mend fences.

The rapid disintegration of the Soviet bloc during the remainder of the year, so far from persuading Castro of the need for reform, merely reinforced his conviction that liberalization would threaten the survival of his regime. Gorbachev, he declared in May 1991, was responsible for 'destroying the authority of the [Communist] Party'. News of the hard-line August coup was greeted with euphoria by the Cuban leadership. One Western diplomat reported that he had never seen Castro's aides so happy. The euphoria, however, quickly gave way to deep dismay as the coup collapsed. The governments of the Russian Federation and the other states which emerged on the former territory of the Soviet Union quickly dismantled their links with Cuba. The rapid decline of Soviet bloc aid and trade had devastating consequences for the Cuban economy. Castro declared in 1992 that the disintegration of the Soviet Union was 'worse for us than the October [Missile] Crisis'.[69] Never, even in his worst nightmares, had he dreamt that Cuba would be the only Marxist-Leninist one-party state outside Asia to survive into the twenty-first century.

The Middle East

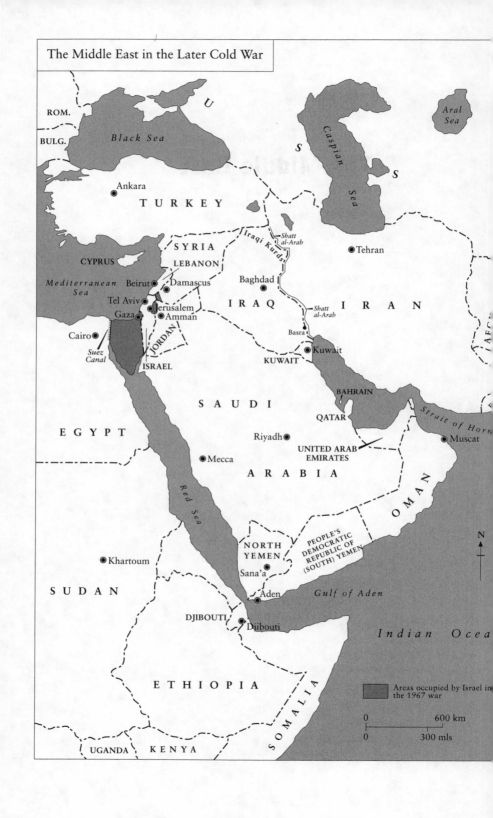

The Middle East in the Later Cold War

7

The Middle East: Introduction*

For much of the Cold War, Soviet policy-makers believed they had an in-built advantage in the struggle with the Main Adversary and its allies for power and influence in the Middle East. If Latin America was the United States' 'backyard', the Middle East was that of the Soviet Union. Israel's special relationship with the United States made its Arab enemies, in Moscow's view, the natural allies of the Soviet Union. Gromyko and Ponomarev jointly denounced Israel and international Zionism as 'the main instrument of US imperialism's assault on Arab countries'.[1] Hatred of Israel multiplied hostility to the United States in the rest of the Middle East.[2] The dramatic loss of America's confidence in dealing with the Muslim world after the fall of its ally, the Shah of Iran, and the rise of the Ayatollah Khomeini was epitomized by the decision of the Carter administration not to send any congratulations to Muslim leaders to celebrate the 1,400th anniversary of Islam in 1979, for fear that it would somehow cause offence. The Soviet Union, by contrast, despite its official atheism, flooded Arab capitals with messages of congratulation.[3]

The greatest volume of Soviet intelligence on the Middle East, as on much else of the Third World, came from SIGINT rather than HUMINT. By 1967 KGB codebreakers were able to decrypt 152 cipher systems used by a total of seventy-two states. Though no later statistics are available, the volume of decrypts doubtless continued to increase. Every day an inner circle within the Politburo – consisting in 1980 of Brezhnev, Andropov, Gromyko, Kirilenko, Suslov and Ustinov – were sent copies of the most important decrypts. The heads of the KGB's First and Second Chief Directorates were sent a

* For a summary of the conventions adopted in the transliteration of Arabic names see p. xxi.

larger selection. Though none of the decrypts have yet been declassified, they will one day be a source of major importance for historians of Soviet foreign policy.[4]

The task of KGB and GRU codebreakers was greatly simplified by the vulnerability of Middle Eastern cipher systems, which was also exploited by British and American intelligence. During the Suez crisis of 1956 the British Foreign Secretary, Selwyn Lloyd, wrote to congratulate GCHQ on both the 'volume' and the 'excellence' of the Middle Eastern decrypts it had produced and to say 'how valuable' they had proved to be.[5] Soviet codebreakers also benefited from the KGB's remarkable success in obtaining intelligence on cipher systems by penetrating Moscow embassies. Though Mitrokhin had no access to the decrypts themselves,[6] he and other defectors have provided an important insight into the extent of these penetrations. Ilya Dzhirkvelov has revealed his part during the early 1950s in successful break-ins at the Egyptian, Syrian, Iranian, Turkish and other Middle Eastern embassies in Moscow for which he and his colleagues were rewarded with engraved watches and the title of 'Honoured Chekist'.[7] The files noted by Mitrokhin reveal that in the later stages of the Cold War, at least thirty-four KGB agents and confidential contacts took part in a highly successful operation to penetrate the Moscow embassy of Syria, then the Soviet Union's main Middle Eastern ally. Middle Eastern states had little idea of the extent to which, because of the vulnerability of their cipher systems and embassy security, they were – so far as Moscow was concerned – conducting open diplomacy.[8]

SIGINT provided only a partial insight into the secretive policy-making of the region. Because of the autocratic nature of Middle Eastern regimes, the decrypted telegrams of their diplomats did not always disclose their real intentions. Anwar al-Sadat was one of a number of rulers in the region whose secret diplomacy was sometimes at variance with his country's official foreign policy. The KGB, however, may well have been able to break his presidential cipher as well as to decrypt Egyptian diplomatic traffic. It remains unclear whether the KGB discovered his secret contacts with the Nixon administration from SIGINT or HUMINT – or both. The discovery caused serious alarm within the Politburo.[9]

Penetrating the inner circles of the mostly suspicious rulers of the Middle East was more difficult than penetrating their Moscow embassies and diplomatic ciphers. The KGB, none the less, had close links with the intelligence services of Gamal Abdel Nasser, the Soviet Union's first major Middle Eastern ally. His main intelligence adviser, Sami Sharaf, was profuse in his protestations of gratitude and friendship to 'Comrade Brezhnev', and claimed to be convinced that, as the disciple of 'the great leader, Gamal Abdel Nasser, he occupies a special position in relation to his Soviet friends'. Probably the KGB's longest-serving agent in Syria was the diplomat and lawyer Tarazi Salah al-Din (codenamed IZZAT), who had been recruited by the KGB in 1954, became Director-General of the Foreign Ministry in the early 1970s, and was a member of the International Tribunal in The Hague at the time of his accidental death in 1980. The KGB also claimed for a time to be able to influence President Asad's youngest brother, Rif'at, who commanded Asad's élite 'Defence Companies', the best armed and trained units in the Syrian army, as well as the hit squads who operated against Syrian dissidents abroad. Despite, or perhaps partly because of, Saddam Hussein's fascination with the career of Joseph Stalin, he seems to have made Baghdad a more difficult operating environment for the KGB than Cairo or Damascus.[10]

In the Middle East, unlike Latin America, there was no realistic prospect of the emergence of a major Marxist-Leninist regime which would act as a role model for the Arab world and spread revolution through the region. Though the People's Democratic Republic of [South] Yemen claimed to be such a regime, its almost continuous and frequently homicidal internal power struggles made it, from Moscow's point of view, more of a liability than an asset. Moscow thus sought to base its strategy in the Middle East on alliance with one of the leading 'progressive' Arab powers which, it was hoped, would progress gradually to Marxism-Leninism. Its main hopes from 1955 to 1970 were pinned on Nasser, by far the most charismatic Arab leader of the Cold War as well as ruler of the largest Middle Eastern state. During the halcyon years of Nasser's special relationship with Moscow, he was one of the most eloquent advocates of the Soviet role in the Middle East. '[The Russians]', he told an American interviewer in 1957, 'helped us survive. Yes, and they helped us escape domination by the West.'[11] After Nasser's sudden death in 1970, Moscow was never able to find an Arab ally of remotely equal stature. His successor, Sadat, expelled all Russian advisers and opted instead for a special relationship with the United States and peace with Israel. Though Iraq became in the mid-1970s the chief recipient of Soviet military aid to the Third World, Saddam Hussein's suspicions of Soviet policy – despite his admiration for Stalin – ensured that the Soviet bridgehead in Baghdad was never secure. All that remained thereafter was an alliance with Asad's Syria, increasingly notorious as a state sponsor of terrorism as well as an increasing drain on the Soviet economy. No wonder that even the usually unsentimental Gromyko looked back nostalgically at the end of his long career on the special relationship with Nasser, arguing unconvincingly that, had he lived only 'a few years longer', the subsequent history of the Middle East might have been very different.[12]

During the Cold War, the KGB maintained secret links with, and channelled secret subsidies to, most if not all Middle Eastern Communist parties. None of these parties, however, possessed a popular charismatic leader to compare with Castro, Guevara, Allende or the leading Sandinistas, and all were liable to be sacrificed to Soviet strategic interests. In 1965, at a time when Moscow was pursuing its courtship of Nasser, the Egyptian Communist Party was persuaded to dissolve itself and tell its members to join the ruling Arab Socialist Union.[13] When Khrushchev made Nasser a Hero of the Soviet Union, one of his Presidium privately complained that he was honouring a leader who 'drove Communists into concentration camps'.[14] In 1972 Moscow put pressure on a somewhat reluctant Iraqi Communist Party to reach an accommodation with the Ba'th regime. When thousands of Party members were imprisoned and many tortured at the end of the decade, however, Moscow stayed silent for fear of antagonizing Baghdad at a time when it was at the forefront of the Arab campaign to prevent the United States brokering a peace treaty between Egypt and Israel. In Syria there was a growing breach between the long-serving Party leader and dogmatic neo-Stalinist, Khalid Bakdash, and the majority of the Party Politburo who resented both Bakdash's autocratic leadership and Moscow's support for the equally autocratic Asad.[15]

Since the Soviet Union was itself a Middle Eastern power bordering some of the other main states of the region, the Middle East was a greater preoccupation of Gromyko and the Foreign Ministry than Latin America. For that reason the role played by KGB residencies in most major Middle Eastern states, though important, was less central than that of Soviet embassies. The main exception was Israel, with which – to the subsequent dismay of the Foreign Ministry – the Soviet Union broke off diplomatic relations in 1967. Soviet policy to Israel thereafter became entangled with and was often driven by the KGB's anti-Zionist obsessions. 'Zionist subversion' was a particular obsession of Yuri Andropov who, as KGB Chairman, interpreted every protest by Jewish 'refuseniks' who were denied the right to emigrate to Israel as part of an international Zionist conspiracy against the Soviet Union. In a stream of reports to the Politburo he insisted on the need for resolute action to 'neutralize' the most minor protests. Even Brezhnev occasionally complained about the lack of proportion evident in the KGB campaign against refuseniks. After one wearisome discussion in the Politburo in 1973, he complained, 'Zionism is making us stupid'. Gromyko washed his hands of much of the anti-Zionist campaign, telling his staff 'not to bother him with . . . such "absurd" matters'.[16] Moscow none the less considered its role in 1975 in the adoption of UN Resolution 3379 denouncing Zionism as a form of racism as a major diplomatic victory, which demonstrated the Soviet Union's 'enormous support for the struggle of the Arab peoples'.[17] The Zionist obsession of the KGB leadership came close to, and at times arguably crossed, the threshold of paranoid delusion. A KGB conference concluded absurdly in 1982 that 'virtually no major negative incidents took place [anywhere] in the socialist countries of Europe without the involvement of Zionists'. Andropov insisted that even the sending of *matsos* (unleavened bread) from the West to Soviet Jews for their Passover celebrations represented a potentially serious act of ideological sabotage.[18]

The unexpected surge of international terrorism in the early 1970s and the precedent set a few years before by the KGB's use of Sandinista guerrillas against US targets in Central and North America[19] encouraged the Centre to consider the use of Palestinian terrorists as proxies in the Middle East and Europe. In 1970 the KGB began secret arms deliveries to the Marxist-Leninist Popular Front for the Liberation of Palestine (PFLP).[20] The secret was remarkably well kept. Though there were a series of Western press reports on support for the PFLP from Syria, Iraq and Libya, there were none of any significance on its Soviet connection. The KGB's willingness to use other terrorist proxies was inhibited by fear that the proxies would fail to conceal its involvement[21] – just as during the second half of the Cold War it failed to implement any of its numerous and detailed plans for the assassination of KGB defectors for fear that it would be blamed for their demise.[22] After the death of the two main Soviet agents within the PFLP in 1978, the KGB's direct connection with it appears to have died away.[23] Nor does the KGB seem to have established a connection with any other Palestinian terrorist group which was nearly as close as that with the PFLP for most of the 1970s. The Centre appears to have regarded the two most active terrorist leaders of the later 1970s and 1980s, Ilich Ramírez Sánchez (better known as 'Carlos the Jackal') and Sabri al-Banna (better known as 'Abu Nidal'), as mavericks with whom it was prudent to avoid all direct connection. Its judgement proved right in both cases. Carlos was a champagne terrorist with a passion for killing, high living and self-important revolutionary rhetoric.[24] As well as attacking European and US targets, the increasingly paranoid Abu Nidal became obsessed with the hunt for mostly imaginary Palestinian traitors, whom he subjected to horrific torture and execution.[25] While refusing to deal directly with either Carlos or Abu Nidal, however, Andropov was content for other Soviet bloc intelligence agencies to do so. With Andropov's knowledge (and doubtless his blessing), East Germany became what its last interior minister, Peter-Michael Diestel, later called 'an Eldorado for terrorists'.[26] By the mid-1980s, however, both Carlos and Abu Nidal had become such an embarrassment to their Soviet bloc hosts that their east European bases were closed down. Both continued to receive assistance from the Soviet Union's main Middle Eastern ally, Hafiz al-Asad. Carlos later claimed, in a characteristic transport of semi-reliable rhetoric, to be 'a senior officer of the Syrian secret service'.[27] Abu Nidal died in Baghdad in 2002, allegedly by his own hand, more probably murdered on the instructions of his former protector, Saddam Hussein.[28]

The KGB's dealings with Yasir Arafat and the PLO were ambivalent. Moscow gave strong support to an Arab initiative in the UN General Assembly recognizing the PLO as the lawful representative of Palestinian Arabs and giving it observer status at the UN. A Palestinian delegation to Moscow in 1975, headed by Arafat, expressed profound gratitude to the Soviet Union 'for its unfailing support of the just struggle of the Palestinian people for their national aspirations, against the intrigues of imperialism, Zionism and reaction'.[29] But despite Moscow's public praise for the PLO and the secret training for its guerrillas provided by the KGB, Arafat never gained the trust of either the Kremlin or the Centre. When PLO forces in Lebanon were defeated by an Israeli invasion in 1982, the Soviet Union offered no assistance. Though Moscow was embarrassed by the homicidal feud which broke out between Asad and Arafat in 1983, the closeness of its alliance with Syria was unaffected by it. In the final years of the Cold War Arafat was almost as unpopular in Moscow as in Washington.[30]

8

The Rise and Fall of Soviet Influence
in Egypt

The first Arab leader to be courted by the Kremlin was Gamal Abdel Nasser, who in 1954, at the age of only thirty-six, became the first native Egyptian ruler of an independent Egypt since Persian invaders had overthrown the last of the pharaohs almost 2,500 years earlier. Nasser's campaign against imperialism went back to his childhood protests against the British occupation of Egypt. 'When I was a little child', he recalled, 'every time I saw aeroplanes flying overhead I used to shout:

> "O God Almighty, may
> A calamity overtake the English!" '[1]

Despite his hostility to the British, neither the Kremlin nor the Centre immediately warmed to Nasser. As Khrushchev later acknowledged: 'We were inclined to think that Nasser's coup was just another one of those military take-overs which we had become so accustomed to in South America. We didn't expect much to come of it.'[2] Ivan Aleksandrovich Serov, who became KGB Chairman in 1954, knew so little about Egypt that he believed Egyptians were black Africans rather than Arabs. His Middle Eastern specialists appear to have been too embarrassed by his ignorance to point his error out to him.[3]

Moscow began to pay serious attention to Nasser when, only six months after taking power, he successfully put pressure on the British to withdraw their troops from the Suez Canal zone. Two months later, in December 1954, the youthful FCD high flier, Vadim Kirpichenko, arrived in Cairo as head of political intelligence with the principal ambition of penetrating Nasser's entourage. He had an early success, though neither Kirpichenko's memoirs (unsurprisingly) nor the files noted by Mitrokhin reveal the identity of the individual involved. Kirpichenko identifies him only as 'a firm friend [who] provided interesting information', without making clear whether he was an agent or a confidential contact. Given that Nasser's entourage was aware that the individual was sometimes in contact with Kirpichenko, it seems more likely that he was a confidential contact. At a time when the Soviet ambassador in Cairo, Daniil Semenovich Solod, was still inclined to dismiss Nasser as a reactionary nationalist, Kirpichenko's contact provided the first reliable evidence of 'where Nasser intended to lead his country' – towards a special relationship with the Soviet Union.[4] In September 1955 Nasser delighted Moscow and shocked the West by signing an agreement to purchase large quantities of Soviet arms via Czechoslovakia – an agreement concluded in such secrecy that even the Egyptian ambassador in Moscow was kept in ignorance of negotiations for it.[5]

Kirpichenko's contact also proved his worth during the visit to Cairo of Khrushchev's private envoy (shortly to become his foreign minister), Dmitri Shepilov, on a fact-finding mission in May 1956. After Solod had tried and failed for several days to arrange a meeting between Shepilov and Nasser, Kirpichenko went round to his contact's house at 1 a.m., failed to find him in but eventually tracked him down around dawn. At 9.30 a.m. the contact rang to say that a presidential motorcade would shortly arrive to conduct Shepilov to a meeting with Nasser at 10 o'clock.[6] Two Soviet defectors, the KGB officer Vladimir Kuzichkin and the diplomat Vladimir Sakharov (a KGB co-optee), both Middle Eastern specialists, later identified Kirpichenko's confidential contact or agent as Sami Sharaf, a pot-bellied man with a drooping moustache and the flattering codename ASAD ('Lion') who in 1959, as Director of the President's Office of Information, was to become Nasser's chief intelligence adviser.[7] Kirpichenko insists that 'Sami Sharaf was never our agent, and I did not even know him'.[8] He does, however, acknowledge that Sharaf was an 'ardent supporter' of Egyptian–Soviet friendship who, after Nasser's death, had repeated unauthorized discussions of official business at the Soviet embassy[9] – the kind of man, in other words, whom the KGB would almost certainly have attempted to recruit as at least a 'confidential contact'. When Sharaf finally met Brezhnev a year after Nasser's death, he was profuse in his protestations of gratitude and friendship:

I must thank Comrade Brezhnev for giving me this opportunity to see him in spite of all his preoccupations. I am sure . . . that this is a special favour for me personally. I trust relations between us will be everlasting and continuous, and that the coming days and the positions which we adopt will be taken as a sincere witness to the friendship which exists between [Egypt] and the Soviet Union, parties, peoples and governments . . . I firmly believe that, since Sami Sharaf is the son of the great leader, Gamal Abdel Nasser, he occupies a special position in relation to his Soviet friends.[10]

In July 1956 Nasser caused an international sensation by nationalizing the Suez Canal, hitherto a concession run by the Paris-based Suez Canal Company – in Arab eyes, the supreme symbol of Western imperialist exploitation. He then urgently sought Soviet advice on how to respond to Western opposition.[11] The black comedy of the failed Anglo-French attempt, in collusion with Israel, to reclaim control of the Suez Canal by force of arms in November played into the hands of both Khrushchev and Nasser. Within the Middle East the balance of power shifted decisively against the conservative, pro-Western regimes in Iraq and Jordan and in favour of the radical forces led by Egypt. Nasser emerged as the hero of the Arab world. Suez also drove him closer to Moscow and to the KGB. On the eve of the Anglo-French invasion Nasser received intelligence about plans to assassinate him, apparently drawn up by the British Secret Intelligence Service (SIS) on the orders of the temporarily unbalanced British Prime Minister, Sir Anthony Eden, who was obsessed by his determination to 'knock Nasser off his perch'.[12] Kirpichenko received a request from his contact in Nasser's entourage for help in improving his personal security. Two senior officers of the KGB Ninth (Protective Security) Directorate flew to Cairo and, together with Kirpichenko, were invited to lunch with Nasser in what Kirpichenko calls 'a very warm domestic setting'. Subsequent investigation quickly revealed that Nasser's only security consisted of a group of bodyguards. There was no alarm system in any of the buildings where he lived and worked. His cook bought bread at a bakery opposite the presidential residence, and meat and vegetables at the nearest market. Having rectified these security failings, the KGB advisers were then asked to provide protection against radiation and poison gas. The best method, they explained, was to keep a caged bird on all premises used by Nasser. If any of the birds died, the building concerned should be evacuated. Egyptian intelligence asked in vain for higher-tech systems of detection which the KGB was reluctant to provide.[13]

In 1958 Nasser received a hero's welcome on his arrival in Moscow for a triumphal three-week tour of the Soviet Union which both the Kremlin and the Centre intended to cement the special relationship with him. The entire Soviet leadership turned out to welcome Nasser at the airport and made him guest of honour at the annual May Day parade, standing beside a beaming Khrushchev on the reviewing platform above the Lenin mausoleum. The important role the KGB had assumed in Soviet–Egyptian relations was shown by the choice of Kirpichenko, rather than a diplomat, as interpreter during Nasser's trip – much as Leonov was later chosen to interpret for Castro. Kirpichenko found Nasser already tired when he arrived in Moscow and felt increasingly sorry for him as he worked his way through the long list of official engagements prepared for his visit. Since, however, all the engagements had been approved by Khrushchev, Kirpichenko felt powerless to cut any of them. Khrushchev, unlike his guest, was in ebullient form throughout the visit. During an evening at the Bolshoi Ballet to see *Swan Lake*, when the evil black swan appeared on stage Khrushchev exclaimed, 'That's Dulles [US Secretary of State]! But don't worry, Comrade Nasser, don't worry! At the end of the act we'll break his wings . . .' Kirpichenko duly translated.[14] Nasser seems to have been impressed as well as exhausted by the series of effusive welcomes to which he was subjected during his visit. On his return to Cairo, he told a huge, cheering crowd that the Soviet Union was 'a friendly country with no ulterior motive' which held the Arab nation 'in great esteem'.[15]

The main advantage derived by the KGB from the state visit was the liaison established between Kirpichenko and the head of the main Egyptian intelligence service, Salah Muhammad Nasr, who accompanied Nasser on his tour. 'Salah Nasr', writes Kirpichenko, 'was attentive to me and tried in all sorts of ways to show that he assigned important significance to our contact.' It was agreed that, after their return to Cairo, Kirpichenko would renew contact under the pseudonym 'George'. The female receptionist to whom he spoke on arrival at Nasr's office, however, told him, ' "Mister George", we all know who you are. You were interpreting for our president. You were in the newsreels every day in all the cinemas!' Despite this minor contretemps, Kirpichenko and Nasr maintained good personal and working relations for the next nine years until Nasr was arrested for plotting against Nasser.[16]

The special relationship with Nasser had moments of tension, due chiefly to his persecution of Communists in Egypt and in Syria (during the union of the two countries in the United Arab Republic from 1958 to 1961), and his denunciation of Communists in Iraq caused serious friction. By the early 1960s, however, Khrushchev and the Centre, though not all of the Presidium, were convinced that a new 'correlation of forces' existed in the Middle East which had to be exploited in the struggle against the Main Adversary. The aggressive global grand strategy devised by KGB Chairman Aleksandr Shelepin and approved by Khrushchev in the summer of 1961 envisaged the use of national liberation movements as the basis of a forward policy in the Third World.[17] Castro's victory in Cuba also encouraged the new policy of allying with anti-imperialist but ideologically unorthodox Third World nationalists, instead of relying simply on orthodox Communist parties which unfailingly toed the Moscow line. As well as supporting Cuba and the Sandinistas, Shelepin also conceived a remarkable scheme to support a Kurdish rebellion in northern Iraq and tell Nasser through 'unofficial' (probably KGB) channels that, if the rebellion succeeded, Moscow 'might take a benign look at the integration of the non-Kurdish part of Iraqi territory with the UAR [United Arab Republic] on the condition of Nasser's support for the creation of an independent Kurdistan'.[18] Unrealistic though the scheme was, particularly during the final months of the UAR's existence, the hugely ambitious plan for a Nasserite union of Egypt, Syria and the greater part of Iraq which Shelepin put to Khrushchev gives some sense of the Centre's hopes for exploiting both his enormous prestige as the most popular Arab leader of the twentieth century and his willingness to enter a special relationship with the Soviet Union.

Throughout the 1960s more Soviet hopes were pinned on Nasser than on any other Third World leader outside Latin America. Soviet ideologists devised the terms 'non-capitalist path' and 'revolutionary democracy' to define a progressive, intermediate stage between capitalism and socialism. Nasser's decision to nationalize much of Egyptian industry in 1961 provided encouraging evidence of his own progress along the 'non-capitalist path'.[19] Among the Soviet agents in the media who eulogized his achievements was the former SIS officer Kim Philby, who until his defection to Moscow early in 1963 was the Beirut correspondent for the *Observer* and *The Economist*. In an article entitled 'Nasser's Pride and Glory' on the tenth anniversary of the Egyptian Revolution in the summer of 1962, Philby declared that he had successfully turned Egypt into a 'co-operative socialist democracy': 'It is now as difficult to conceive an Egypt without Nasser as a Yugoslavia without Tito or an India without Nehru – and Nasser is still a young man.'[20] Of all Soviet aid to the Third World between 1954 and 1961 43 per cent went to Egypt. In 1964 Nasser was made a Hero of the Soviet Union, the USSR's highest decoration. A year later, the Egyptian Communist Party dissolved itself and its members applied for membership of the ruling Arab Socialist Union.[21]

By the mid-1960s the majority view among Moscow's Middle Eastern experts was that Soviet equipment and training had transformed the Egyptian armed forces. They were sadly disillusioned by the humiliating outcome of the Arab–Israeli Six-Day War in 1967. The Israeli attack on Egypt at 8.45 a.m. (Cairo time) on 5 June took the Centre as well as Nasser by surprise. The Soviet news media learned of the attack before the KGB, which only discovered the outbreak of war from intercepted Associated Press reports.[22] The war was virtually decided during the first three hours when Israeli air-raids destroyed 286 of 340 Egyptian combat aircraft on the ground, leaving the Egyptian army without air cover during the ensuing land battles in the Sinai desert.

On 28 June 1967, in one of his first speeches as KGB Chairman, Yuri Andropov addressed KGB Communist Party activists on the subject of 'The Soviet Union's Policy regarding Israel's Aggression in the Near East'. In order to avoid similar intelligence failures in future and have 'timely information and forecasts of events', the KGB 'must draw highly qualified specialists into intelligence work from a variety of academic fields'.[23] Among the Soviet journalists and academic experts sent on missions to increase the Centre's understanding of the Middle East was Yevgeni Primakov, code-named MAKS (later head of the post-Soviet foreign intelligence agency, the SVR, and one of Boris Yeltsin's prime ministers). In the late 1960s Primakov succeeded in getting to know both Hafiz al-Asad in Syria and Saddam Hussein in Iraq.[24] Intelligence analysis, which had scarcely existed hitherto in a KGB frightened of offering opinions uncongenial to the political leadership, made modest – though always politically correct – strides during the Andropov era.

In public, the Kremlin stood by Nasser and the Arab cause after the humiliation of the Six-Day War, denounced imperialist aggression and (to its subsequent regret) broke off diplomatic relations with Israel. Privately, however, there was savage criticism of the incompetence of the Arab forces and outrage at the amount of Soviet military equipment captured by the Israelis. Within the Centre there was grudging admiration for both the Israelis' military skill and the success of Israeli propaganda which sought to create an impression of Arab cowardice in battle by photographing Egyptian PoWs in their underwear and other unheroic poses standing next to undamaged Soviet tanks.[25] The débâcle of the Six-Day War left Moscow with only two options: either to cut its losses or to rebuild the Arab armies. It chose the second. President Podgorny visited Egypt with an entourage which included Marshal Matvei Zakharov, chief of the Soviet general staff, Kirpichenko, then working at the Centre, and Primakov.[26] Zakharov stayed on to advise on the reorganization and re-equipment of the Egyptian army. Desperate to resurrect his role as the hero of the Arab world, Nasser proved willing to make much larger concessions in return for Soviet help than before the Six-Day War. He told Podgorny:

What is important for us is that we now recognize that our main enemy is the United States and that the only possible way of continuing our struggle is for us to ally ourselves with the Soviet Union ... Before the fighting broke out, we were afraid that we would be accused by the Western media of being aligned [with the Soviet Union], but nothing of that sort concerns us any longer. We are ready to offer facilities to the Soviet fleet from Port Said to Salloum and from al-Arish to Gaza.[27]

Soviet advisers in Egypt eventually numbered over 20,000. In 1970, at Nasser's request, Soviet airbases, equipped with SAM-3 missiles and combat aircraft with Russian crews, were established to strengthen Egyptian air defences.

Nasser's most striking political gifts were his powerful rhetoric and charismatic stage presence, which enabled him to survive the military humiliation of 1967, for which he bore much of the responsibility, and inspired the Arab street with a seductive but unrealizable vision of Pan-Arab unity which would restore the pride and honour of which imperialism had robbed them. He left behind few practical achievements. The celebrated Aswan Dam and vast Helwan steel works, both financed by the Soviet Union and praised as models of socialist construction, were built in defiance of local conditions. Egyptian socialism had failed. As Nasser once admitted, 'The people can't eat socialism. If they weren't Egyptian they'd beat me with their shoes [almost the ultimate Arab humiliation].' The main growth area during Nasser's eighteen years in power was the civil service, which increased from 325,000 to 1.2 million mostly inefficient bureaucrats. Cairo, built to accommodate 3 million people, was close to meltdown with a population almost three times as large. Water pipes and sewage systems regularly collapsed, flooding parts of the city. Politically, Nasser left behind him a one-party state with an ailing economy built on the twin foundations of rigged elections and concentration camps to terrorize his opponents.[28]

The vast Soviet investment in Nasser's Egypt during the 1950s and 1960s rested on a far more precarious base than Moscow was willing to acknowledge. The influx of Soviet advisers served only to underline the gulf between Soviet and Egyptian society. Russians and Egyptians rarely visited each other's homes. Though almost half of the 15,000 Arabs who studied in the United States during the late 1950s and 1960s married Americans, marriage between Soviet advisers and their Egyptian hosts was virtually unknown.[29] Resentment at the aloofness of the advisers was compounded by the arrogance of the Soviet ambassador, Vladimir Mikhailovich Vinogradov. 'The Soviet Union', complained Vice-President Anwar al-Sadat, 'had begun to feel that it enjoyed a privileged position in Egypt – so much so that the Soviet ambassador had assumed a position comparable to that of the British High Commissioner in the days of the British occupation of Egypt.'[30]

With Nasser's sudden death in September 1970 and his replacement by Sadat, the imposing but fragile edifice of Soviet influence in Egypt began to crumble. Almost two decades later, the Soviet Foreign Minister, Andrei Gromyko, was still insisting that 'had [Nasser] lived a few years longer, the situation in the region might today be very different'.[31] Aleksei Kosygin, the Soviet Prime Minister, told Sadat soon after he became President, 'We never had any secrets from [Nasser], and he never had any secrets from us.'[32] The first half of the statement, as Kosygin was well aware, was nonsense; the second half, thanks to Sami Sharaf and others, may at times have been close to the truth. On his first day as President, Sadat had an immediate confrontation with Sharaf in his office. According to Sadat:

He had a heap of papers to submit to me. 'What is this?' I asked.

'The text of tapped telephone conversations between certain people being watched.'

'Sorry,' I said, 'I don't like to read such rubbish ... And, anyway, who gave you the right to have the telephones of these people tapped? Take this file away.' I swept it off my desk.[33]

There were times when Sadat took a greater interest in 'such rubbish' than he cared to admit to Sharaf. Kirpichenko, who returned to Cairo as resident in 1970, discovered that Sadat was 'listening in' to the conversations of a group of pro-Soviet plotters against him: chief among them Vice-President Ali Sabry, Interior Minister Sha'rawi Gum'a, War Minister Muhammad Fawzi and Minister for Presidential Affairs Sami Sharaf. The group, which Sadat privately called the 'crocodiles' (an expression adopted by the Cairo residency), had frequent meetings with Vinogradov and, in Kirpichenko's euphemistic phrase, 'shared with him their apprehensions regarding Sadat's line'[34] – in other words their plans to overthrow him.[35] The plotters sought Vinogradov's support but, according to Nikolai Leonov, the ambassador was 'overcome by fear' and gave no reply.[36]

The reports from Cairo which most alarmed the Politburo were what Kirpichenko claims was 'reliable' intelligence on Sadat's secret contacts with President Nixon, raising the suspicion that he was planning to loosen Egyptian links with the Soviet Union and move closer to the United States.[37] In January 1971 Fawzi, whose responsibilities included Cairo security, received a report of unauthorized radio transmissions. The triangulation techniques used to locate the source of the transmissions revealed that they came from Sadat's house. Further investigation showed that he was exchanging secret messages with Washington – despite the fact that diplomatic relations with the United States had been broken off by Nasser. According to Fawzi, he confronted Sadat, who told him that the secret contacts were no business of his. Fawzi allegedly retorted that it was the business of intelligence services to discover such things.[38] Kirpichenko may well have been informed of the confrontation between Fawzi and Sadat either by one of the 'crocodiles' or by one of his informants within Egyptian intelligence. It is equally likely that Sadat's radio messages to and from Washington were intercepted by the SIGINT station (codenamed ORION)[39] in the Cairo residency. The KGB's remarkable success with Third World ciphers made its codebreakers better able to decrypt Sadat's presidential cipher than any Egyptian intelligence agency.[40] Given the anxieties aroused in Moscow by Sadat's policies, decrypting his communications must have had a particularly high priority. Just as worrying from Moscow's point of view were the secret conversations in Cairo during March and April between the US diplomat Donald Bergus and Sadat's emissaries. Tapes of the conversations, recorded without Sadat's knowledge by a section of Egyptian intelligence, were passed on to the 'crocodiles' and, almost certainly, revealed by them to the Soviet embassy.[41]

On 28 April 1971, for the only time in Kirpichenko's career as a foreign intelligence officer, he was suddenly summoned back to Moscow, together with Vinogradov and the senior military adviser in Egypt, General Vasili Vasilyevich Okunev, to give his assessment of Sadat's intentions direct to a meeting of the Politburo. Vinogradov was criticized by Suslov for what he claimed were the contradictions between the 'quite optimistic' tone of his oral assessment (which was similar to that of Okunev) and some of the evidence contained in his diplomatic despatches. Kirpichenko, by contrast, bluntly declared that Sadat was deceiving the Soviet Union. Andropov told him afterwards, 'Everything you said was more or less correct, but a bit sharply expressed.' He was also informed that President Podgorny had said of his comments on Sadat, 'It's not at all appropriate . . . to speak of presidents in such a manner!' What also stuck in Kirpichenko's memory was the fact that while the table around which the Politburo sat had on it red and black caviar and a selection of fish delicacies, he and those seated around the walls were offered only sausage and cheese sandwiches.[42]

The events of the next few weeks fully justified Kirpichenko's pessimism. On 11 May a young police officer brought Sadat a tape recording showing, according to Sadat, that the 'crocodiles' 'were plotting to overthrow me and the regime'.[43] (Though Sadat's memoirs do not mention it, he had doubtless received similar tapes before.) At a meeting with Vinogradov, the chief plotters had sought Soviet support for a plot to overthrow Sadat and establish 'socialism in Egypt'. Moscow, however, dared not take the risk of promising support and Sadat struck first.[44] The timing of the arrest of the 'crocodiles' on the evening of 13 May took the Cairo residency by surprise. Kirpichenko spent the evening, like many other Soviet representatives, at a reception in their honour in the garden of the East German embassy. At the high point of the evening, just as suckling pigs appeared on the table, news arrived of the arrests, forcing Kirpichenko to abandon the meal and return to his embassy.[45]

Sadat, however, still went to great lengths to conceal his real intentions from the Russians. Only a fortnight later, he signed with President Podgorny in Cairo a Soviet–Egyptian Treaty of Friendship and Co-operation. His main motive, as he later acknowledged, was 'to allay the fears of the Soviet leaders' by seeking to persuade them that he was engaged in an internal power struggle rather than a reorientation of Egyptian foreign policy away from Moscow. As he saw Podgorny off at the airport, Sadat appealed to him to tell the Politburo, 'Please have confidence in us! Have confidence! Confidence!'[46] His disingenuous pleading had little effect. The Centre's confidence in Sadat was already almost gone. The Cairo residency had little doubt that he 'was aiming to cut down Soviet–Egyptian relations and would take active steps to curtail the activity of Soviet Intelligence in Egypt'.[47] For the moment, however, Moscow did not voice its suspicions, fearing that open opposition to Sadat would only undermine still further its remaining influence and huge investment in Egypt.

The Centre's irritation at its declining influence in Cairo was balanced by its hope of a Communist take-over in Khartoum. The leaders of the Sudanese Communist Party were considered by the KGB to be the most loyal and dedicated in the Middle East.[48] In July 1971 a coup by Sudanese army officers, supported by the Communists, briefly succeeded in toppling President Gaafar Muhammad al-Nimeiri. Vinogradov called on Sadat to urge him to recognize the new regime. An angry argument followed during which Sadat declared, 'I cannot allow a Communist regime to be established in a country sharing my borders.'[49] With Sadat's assistance, the coup was brutally suppressed and Nimeiri restored to power. Among those executed for their part in the coup was the General Secretary of the Sudanese Communist Party, Abdel Maghoub. Simultaneously the Centre discovered that a Soviet diplomat in the Middle East co-opted by the KGB, Vladimir Nikolayevich Sakharov, was working for the CIA. Alerted by a pre-arranged signal – a bouquet placed by the Agency on the back seat of his Volkswagen – Sakharov defected just in time. Among the secrets he had betrayed to the CIA was Sharaf's involvement with the KGB.[50]

As Soviet influence declined under Sadat's rule, Egyptian Communists increasingly regretted the decision to dissolve their Party in 1965. In 1971 the Soviet embassy in Cairo, probably through the KGB residency, paid the relatively modest sum of 1,000 Egyptian pounds to a leading Egyptian Communist, codenamed SOYUZNIK ('Ally'), to support left-wing candidates for the People's Assembly.[51] Moscow, however, remained anxious not to provoke Sadat by reviving the defunct Egyptian Communist Party and discouraged attempts to do so. In April 1972 the three main underground Marxist groups united and began producing critical reports on the current state of Egypt under the name Ahmad 'Urabi al-Misri.[52] SOYUZNIK and the other leaders of the newly unified underground movement secretly asked the Soviet embassy in Cairo to put them in contact with the leadership of the Soviet Communist Party. Moscow replied that the time was not yet ripe for setting up an open Marxist organization in Egypt. SOYUZNIK responded that the Soviet comrades plainly did not understand the real state of affairs in Egypt but that the new movement would none the less count on financial aid from fraternal Communist parties.[53] Two years later the KGB began channelling money to SOYUZNIK via the Iraqi Communist Party.[54]

By the summer of 1972, Sadat had secretly decided to expel all Soviet military advisers. On 8 July he summoned the Soviet ambassador to see him. According to Vinogradov, 'Sadat suddenly announced that our military advisers could return home, as they were "very tired"! I was absolutely furious. "Tired, Mr President!" I then challenged [him], "If you don't need them any more, then say it more directly!"'[55] According to Sadat's version of the same episode, he simply announced that he had 'decided to dispense with the services of all Soviet military experts', and ordered them to leave within a week.[56] Moscow, however, still could not bring itself to sacrifice what remained of its hard-won position in Egypt by an open breach with Sadat. The Soviet leadership concluded that it had no choice but to continue political and military support for Egypt for fear that Sadat might otherwise throw in his lot with the United States. It therefore opted for a face-saving official statement which claimed improbably that, 'After an exchange of views, the [two] sides decided to bring back the military personnel that had been sent to Egypt for a limited period.' Relations with Egypt, the statement maintained, continued to be 'founded on the solid basis of the Soviet–Egyptian Treaty of Friendship and Co-operation in the joint struggle for the elimination of the results of Israeli aggression'. After a brief interruption Soviet arms supplies to Egypt resumed. Sadat declared in April 1973, 'The Russians are providing us now with everything that's possible for them to supply. And I am now quite satisfied.'[57]

Sadat's arrest of the pro-Soviet faction within the Egyptian leadership and the expulsion of Soviet advisers damaged the morale of the KGB agent network and complicated the work of the Cairo residency. Fearful of discovery, a number of Egyptian agents began to distance themselves from their case officers.[58] In January 1973, as a security measure, the Centre ordered the residency to cease operations against Egyptian targets 'from agent positions'.[59] Its existing agents, however, though downgraded to 'confidential contacts', continued in some instances to provide significant intelligence on Sadat's military planning.

Like Western intelligence agencies, the KGB was confused about Sadat's intentions towards Israel. On twenty-two occasions in 1972–73 Egyptian forces were mobilized for periods of four or five days, then sent home. In the spring of 1973 war appeared to be imminent and Israel mobilized its forces. On Andropov's instructions, the FCD prepared a report on the crisis in the Middle East which was submitted to the Politburo on 7 May:

According to available information, steps are being taken in the Egyptian army to raise its battle readiness. To raise morale, Sadat and the top military leadership are going out to visit the troops. The General Staff of the Arab Republic of Egypt Armed Forces has drawn up an operational plan to force [cross] the Suez Canal.

Similar measures are being taken in Syria, whose leadership has taken a decision to prepare for aggressive military operations against Israel together with the Egyptian army.

The military intentions of Egypt and Syria are known, not only to the leading circles of other Arab countries, but also in the West, and in Israel.

According to available information, the Americans and the British are inclined to believe that the statements of Egyptian and Syrian leaders about the forthcoming confrontation with Israel are intended for internal consumption, but also aim to exert a certain psychological effect on Western countries and Israel. At the same time, they do not rule out the possibility that Sadat will carry out specific military operations.

Analysis of the available information indicates that the actions of Sadat with the support of [Colonel] Qaddafi [of Libya] and [President] Asad [of Syria] could lead to an uncontrolled chain of events in the Near East.

It is not impossible that with the aim of involving world opinion in the Near East problem and exerting pressure on the USSR and the USA, Sadat might opt to resume limited military operations on the eve of the forthcoming meeting between Comrade Leonid Ilyich Brezhnev and Nixon.[60]

It was of supreme importance that no Middle Eastern conflict interfere with Brezhnev's visit to Washington in June. To Brezhnev, notorious for his love of pomp and circumstance, his reception on the immaculately groomed South Lawn of the White House was, according to Dobrynin, the Soviet ambassador in Washington, 'the moment of his highest triumph. What could be greater than his being placed on a footing equal to the American president . . . ?'[61]

'In order to influence Sadat in our favour' and dissuade him from going to war with Israel, the KGB suggested sending a senior Soviet representative to hold talks with both him and Asad, as well as delaying the despatch to Egypt of missiles which the Soviet Union had agreed to supply. It also proposed using 'unofficial channels', in particular the head of the CIA station in Cairo, to persuade the Americans 'that the resumption of military operations in the Near East at the present time would not be in the interests of either the Soviet Union or the USA' and that they should bring pressure to bear on Israel.[62]

In the event, no conflict in the Middle East disturbed Brezhnev's Washington apotheosis as a world leader. 'Even the brilliant sunshine', Dobrynin nostalgically recalled, 'seemed to accentuate the importance of the event': 'The solemn ceremony, with both countries' national anthems and a guard of honor, the leader of the Soviet Communist Party standing side by side with the American president for the whole world to see – all this was for the Soviet leadership the supreme act of recognition by the international community of their power and influence.'[63]

The war scare of May 1973 none the less served Sadat's purpose. Even more than previous false alarms, it persuaded both the American and Israeli intelligence communities that his repeated mobilizations and threats of war were bluff. The simultaneous attack by Egyptian and Syrian forces on 6 October 1973, the Jewish holy day of Yom Kippur, caught Israel as well as the United States off guard.[64] The future DCI, Robert Gates, recalled that day as 'my worst personal intelligence embarrassment'. While he was briefing a senior US arms negotiator on the improbability of conflict, the news of the outbreak of war was broadcast over the radio. Gates 'slunk out of his office'. The KGB did very much better. Still conscious of having been caught out by the previous Arab–Israeli War six years earlier, it was able to provide advance warning to the Politburo before Yom Kippur – probably as a result of intelligence both from SIGINT and from penetrations of the Egyptian armed forces and intelligence community.[65]

After the humiliation of the six-day defeat in 1967, the early successes of the Yom Kippur War restored Arab pride and self-confidence. Militarily, however, though the war began well for Egypt and Syria, it ended badly with Israeli forces sixty miles from Cairo and twenty from Damascus. Sadat drew the conclusion that, because of its influence on Israel, only the United States could mediate a peace settlement. While Soviet influence declined, Henry Kissinger became the dominating figure in the peace process. Until his visit to the Middle East in November 1973 the globe-trotting Kissinger had never visited a single Arab state. Over the next two years of shuttle diplomacy he made eleven further visits and conducted four major rounds of negotiations. The Centre tried desperately to devise active measures to persuade Sadat that Kissinger would double-cross him. In operation IBIS, Service A in the FCD forged a despatch from the Swiss ambassador in Washington to his foreign ministry, reporting that he had been told by a Middle Eastern specialist in the State

Department that the United States would not infringe any of Israel's interests. The forgery was shown to Sadat late in 1973 but had no discernible influence on him.[66]

The Centre's anxiety at its loss of Middle Eastern influence to the United States was reflected in instructions from Andropov to the FCD on 25 April 1974 to devise active measures to prevent any further worsening in Soviet–Arab relations, force anti-Soviet Arab politicians onto the defensive and undermine the influence of the West and China, which was currently increasing at Soviet expense.[67] The Centre was particularly outraged by Sadat's links with the CIA. It reported in October 1974 that the Director of Central Intelligence, William Colby, had visited Egypt as Sadat's personal guest. The KGB set out to take revenge on the thirty-year-old Presidential Secretary for Foreign Relations, Ashraf Marwan (Nasser's son-in-law), who it believed had overall charge of the Egyptian intelligence community and was responsible for liaison with the Agency.[68] Section A devised an active-measures campaign which was designed to portray Marwan as a CIA agent. The Centre attached such importance to the campaign that in May 1975 it sent the head of the First (North American) Directorate, Vladimir Kazakov, to oversee final preparations for its implementation at the Cairo residency.[69] Articles denouncing Marwan's alleged links with the CIA were placed in Lebanese, Syrian and Libyan newspapers.[70] In the course of the KGB disinformation campaign against him, Marwan was accused of taking bribes and embezzling large sums of money given to Egypt by Saudi Arabia and Kuwait for arms purchases. The Cairo residency also planted rumours that Marwan was having an affair with Sadat's wife, Jihan, and reported that these had reached Sadat himself. Predictably, the KGB claimed the credit in 1976 when Sadat replaced Marwan as his Secretary for Foreign Relations.[71]

Service A's active measures against Sadat made much of his early enthusiasm for Adolf Hitler.[72] Sadat himself acknowledged in his autobiography that, as a fourteen-year-old when Hitler became Chancellor of Germany, he had been inspired by the way the Führer set out to 'rebuild his country': 'I gathered my friends and told them we ought to follow Hitler's example by marching forth . . . to Cairo. They laughed and went away.'[73] During the Second World War Sadat was also a great admirer of Rommel's campaign against the British in the Western Desert, and later established a museum in his memory at El-Alamein. As late as 1953 he said publicly that he admired Hitler 'from the bottom of my heart'.[74] The KGB claimed the credit for inspiring publications with titles such as 'Anwar Sadat: From Fascism to Zionism', which portrayed him as a former Nazi agent who had sold out to the CIA.[75] Sadat's control of the press meant that within Egypt active measures against him were mostly confined to spreading rumours and leaflets. In other Arab countries the KGB claimed to be able to inspire press articles denouncing Sadat as an accomplice in the attempts of both the United States and Israel to keep the occupied territories under Israeli control. Among the allegations fabricated by Service A was the claim that Sadat's support had been purchased by secret accounts in his name in Jewish-controlled banks.[76] Other Soviet-bloc intelligence agencies collaborated in the active-measures campaign. In an operation codenamed RAMZES, the Hungarian AVH forged a despatch to the State Department from the US ambassador in Cairo containing a psychological evaluation of Sadat which concluded that he was a drug addict who no longer had sexual relations with his wife and was exhibiting a marked deterioration in his mental faculties.[77]

Despite the priority given to active measures against Sadat in and beyond the Arab world during the years after the Yom Kippur War, the KGB remained extremely cautious about operations in Egypt itself. Its caution extended to the illegal Egyptian Communist Party which on May Day 1975 announced its rebirth in fraternal messages to other Communist parties around the world.[78] Andropov instructed the Centre to inquire into the leadership and composition of the Party, then prepare jointly with the International Department of the CPSU Central Committee a proposal for giving it financial assistance. 'Handing over money directly to the Egyptian Communist Party', he added, 'is dangerous for us because of the possibility of a leak.' It was therefore decided to continue passing money to the Egyptian Communists via the Iraqi Party.[79] Sadat's introduction of a limited form of multi-party democracy in 1976 made it somewhat easier for leading members of the still-illegal Communist Party to campaign in public – and easier also for the KGB to maintain contact with them. Three opposition 'platforms' were allowed to contest the general election of that year – among them the left-wing National Progressive Unionist Party (NPUP)[80] headed by the Communist leader, Khaled Mohieddin, to whom the KGB gave the codename

LYUBOMIR. In 1976 the Cairo residency handed over to a Communist contact two sums of $50,000 (slightly more than 18,000 Egyptian pounds): one for the Communist Party, one for the NPUP election campaign.[81]

At a meeting with Aleksandr Sergeyevich Kulik, Kirpichenko's successor as Cairo resident, and the leadership of the FCD Eighteenth (Arab States) Department in 1975, Andropov reaffirmed the ban on running Egyptian agents in Egypt itself. He also gave instructions that documents were not to be accepted from confidential contacts – probably for fear that KGB officers might be caught in the act of receiving them. There is little doubt that the Cairo residency was frustrated by the restrictions imposed on it. In May 1976 Vladimir Kryuchkov and N. A. Dushin, head of the KGB Third (Military Counter-Intelligence) Directorate, signed a joint submission to Andropov requesting permission to recruit a senior Egyptian military intelligence officer, codenamed GERALD. Andropov replied, 'By order of the highest authority [*Instantsii*] it is forbidden to carry on agent work in the Arab Republic of Egypt.' GERALD remained a confidential contact.[82] FCD files noted by Mitrokhin contain a number of examples of former Egyptian agents, downgraded to confidential contacts, who broke contact with the Cairo residency – among them, in 1976, FEDOR, a colonel in the Egyptian army recruited in Odessa in 1972,[83] and MURTARS, an employee of the Presidential Office recruited in Moscow in 1971.[84] A Centre report in 1977 concluded that the Cairo residency had no sources in 'most targets of penetration'. Later in the year it was discovered that KHASAN, an employee of the Soviet Cultural Centre in Cairo whom the residency had used to channel disinformation to Egyptian intelligence, had in reality been operating under Egyptian control.[85]

Sadat's unilateral denunciation of the Soviet–Egyptian Friendship Treaty in March 1976 caused little surprise but predictable indignation in the Centre. The FCD claimed that this indignation was more widely shared. It reported in November, probably with some exaggeration, 'According to information from Egyptian business circles, the curtailment of relations with the USSR is creating dissatisfaction in a considerable section of the Egyptian bourgeoisie . . .': 'In an effort to lessen the dissatisfaction in the country with its biased policy towards the West, the Egyptian leadership is taking certain steps which are intended to give the impression that it is interested in the normalization of relations with the Soviet Union.' However, the FCD quoted with approval the opinion of the former Egyptian Prime Minister, Aziz Sidqi (codenamed NAGIB, 'Baron'): 'The readiness of Sadat to seek a reconciliation with the USSR is a mere manoeuvre based on expediency.' Sadat, the Centre believed, was bent on moving closer to the United States.[86]

Though the Centre sought to improve the appearance of its Middle Eastern reports by quoting from confidential conversations with prominent Egyptians, the intelligence access of the Cairo residency had diminished considerably since the early 1970s. One sign of its limitations was the fact that it was taken by surprise by the mass popular protests in January 1977 against the reduction of government subsidies on basic foodstuffs and cooking gas.[87] In two days of rioting 160 were killed and hundreds more wounded before the army restored order. Sadat's government blamed the riots on an 'odious criminal plot' by 'leftist plotters'. 'Many Communist elements', it charged, had infiltrated the NPUP and tried to use it to 'overthrow the government and install a Communist regime'. Over a period of three months, 3,000 Egyptians were arrested and charged with 'subversive conspiracy'.[88] During the campaign against 'leftist plotters' a counsellor at the Soviet embassy, O. V. Kovtunovich, visited its main Communist contact in his office. Fearing that his office was bugged, the contact said little but wrote on a sheet of paper, 'About 35 members of our organization have been arrested, and 17 are in hiding. The printing press of the organization has not been affected, nor have most of the district leaders of the organization. Assistance must be given to the families of those who have been arrested or are in hiding. We need urgent material assistance, amounting to 3,000 Egyptian pounds.' Apparently afraid even to hand over the note in his office, the contact waited until Kovtunovich was leaving, then passed it to him in a corridor.[89] Probably as a result of this and similar experiences, three Egyptian Communists were sent for counter-intelligence training in the Soviet Union to enable them to set up a Party security service.[90] The Cairo residency's main Communist contact sent his thanks to the Soviet leadership. Only their support, he told them, had kept the Party afloat during 1977.[91]

On 1 October 1977, the Soviet Union and the United States signed a joint statement on the need to resolve the Arab–Israeli conflict.

Moscow believed that it had recovered much of the diplomatic ground it had lost in the Middle East since the Yom Kippur War and at last secured US recognition of the Soviet role in peace negotiations. Almost immediately, however, according to an official history of Soviet foreign policy, 'Under pressure from Israel, the [US] Carter Administration treacherously violated the agreement.'[92] Only seven weeks after the agreement was signed, Sadat travelled to Jerusalem to begin a dialogue with the Israelis. His visit was one of the most stunning diplomatic *coups de théâtre* of modern times. As Sadat stepped off the plane at Tel Aviv airport on 20 November, an Israeli radio reporter gasped over the air, 'President Sadat is now inspecting a guard of honour of the Israeli Defence Force. I'm seeing it, but I don't believe it!' The former Israeli Prime Minister, Golda Meir, said of Sadat and the current Israeli Prime Minister, Menachem Begin, at the end of the visit, 'Never mind the Nobel Peace Prize [which Sadat and Begin were to be awarded a year later]. Give them both Oscars!'

With its habitual tendency to conspiracy theory, never more marked than in its attitude to Zionism and the Jewish lobby in the United States, the Centre interpreted Sadat's visit less as a piece of theatre than as a deep-laid plot. Sadat, it believed, had arranged the trip with the Americans, who had known that it was imminent even when treacherously signing the agreement with the Soviet Union. The 'Framework for Peace in the Middle East' signed by Sadat, Begin and Carter at Camp David in September 1978 was instantly denounced by *Pravda* as 'a sell-out transacted behind the back of the Arab nation, one which serves the interests of Israel, America, imperialism and the Arab reactionaries'. The Centre believed that Carter and the CIA had lured Sadat into an American–Zionist plot intended to oust Soviet influence from the Middle East. It responded with an intensified active-measures campaign accusing Sadat of being a CIA agent with a villa in Montreux waiting for him with round-the-clock Agency protection when he was finally forced to flee from the wrath of the Arab nation he had betrayed.[93]

In March 1979 Sadat returned to the United States to sign a peace treaty with Israel in a ceremony on the South Lawn of the White House attended by distinguished guests and television reporters from around the world. As after the Camp David agreement six months earlier, Sadat was welcomed on his return to Cairo by huge enthusiastic crowds convinced that they were witnessing the dawn of a new era of peace and prosperity. There were authenticated reports of Egyptian taxi drivers offering free rides to Israeli visitors. Initially the opposition of the NPUP leadership to Camp David caused resentment even among some of its own rank and file. In much of the Arab world, however, Sadat was treated as a pariah who had sold out to Israel. Egypt was expelled from the Arab League, which moved its headquarters from Cairo to Tunis. Perhaps as many as 2 million Egyptians working in other Arab countries were sent home. Within Egypt, as the new era of prosperity failed to arrive, euphoria gave way to disillusion.[94] Though an Israeli–Egyptian peace treaty was signed in March 1979, the plans made at Camp David for a broader settlement of the Arab–Israeli conflict came to nothing. Sadat's opponents accused him of having betrayed the Palestinian people and reinforced Israeli control of the occupied territories.

The Cairo residency claimed that during 1979, thanks to its Communist contacts, it had been able to inspire press articles, public meetings and questions in the People's Assembly.[95] The trials in 1978–79 of those accused of complicity in the 'conspiracy' of January 1977 offered the NPUP a platform for attacks on the Sadat regime which it would not otherwise have been able to voice publicly. Mohieddin announced that the NPUP constituted 'a democratic committee for the defence of liberties, including lawyers who were non-party members, coming together around the principle of providing all the guarantees of legal defence to those imprisoned for their opinions and supporting their families'. The evidence against most of those arrested was too flimsy even for them to be brought to trial. In most other cases, defendants were found not guilty or received lenient sentences. There were only twenty jail sentences, none longer than three years. Mohieddin himself successfully sued the pro-government press when he was accused of unpatriotic behaviour because of his opposition to Sadat's peace policy with Israel, and was awarded damages of 20,000 Egyptian pounds.[96]

As well as receiving at least $100,000 a year for the Egyptian Communist Party, the Cairo residency's main Communist contact also requested – and probably received – a similar annual sum for the NPUP.[97] One of its leaders privately acknowledged in 1978 that, without $100,000 a year from Moscow, the NPUP 'was in danger of falling apart. The fate of the left-wing movement in Egypt depended on this money.'[98] The Centre had grandiose plans for the formation of an 'anti-Sadat front', based on the NPUP, which, it believed, would organize popular opposition to his 'pro-imperialist' policies.[99] Its plans, however, achieved nothing of significance. Despite tactical successes, the NPUP was incapable of mobilizing mass support. At the elections to the People's Assembly in 1983 it gained only 4 per cent of the vote.[100]

Probably no other Third World leader inspired as much loathing in Moscow as Sadat. While stationed at the Centre at the end of the 1970s, Oleg Gordievsky heard a number of outraged KGB officers say that he should be bumped off. Though there is no evidence that the Centre was ever implicated in such a plot, it was aware that some of its contacts were. In December 1977 it received information that a secret meeting in Damascus between leaders of Syrian intelligence and the Popular Front for the Liberation of Palestine had discussed plans for assassinating both Sadat and Ashraf Marwan.[101] On 6 October 1981, the anniversary of the outbreak of the Yom Kippur War, Sadat was assassinated by fundamentalist fanatics while reviewing a military parade. Though there is no indication in files noted by Mitrokhin that the KGB had advance warning of the assassination plot, the news that it had succeeded was greeted with jubilation in the Centre[102] – and doubtless in the Kremlin.

Almost a decade after Sadat's death, Gromyko could still barely contain his hatred of him: 'He has been called the "Egyptian darkness", after the biggest dust cloud in human history which settled on Egypt 3,500 years ago when the volcanic island of Santorini erupted ... All his life he had suffered from megalomania, but this acquired pathological proportions when he became President.'[103] Underlying Gromyko's cry of rage was his consciousness that the Sadat era had witnessed the complete failure of Soviet policy in Egypt and the loss of the largest military, economic and political investment Moscow had made in any Third World country – extending to the unprecedented lengths of approving in 1965 the dissolution of the Egyptian Communist Party. But the political system which had made it possible for Sadat to carry out what he termed the 'corrective revolution' of the early 1970s and remove the pro-Soviet group from positions of power had been put in place by Hero of the Soviet Union Gamal Abdel Nasser. The presidential system developed by Nasser was a thinly disguised structure of personal rule which survived virtually intact into the twenty-first century. The main effect of the supposedly democratic reforms introduced by Sadat and by his successor, former Vice-President Hosni Mubarak, was to reinforce the clientelism on which presidential rule was based. Even the NPUP, on which in the early 1980s Moscow had pinned its hopes for a return to the Soviet–Egyptian alliance, eventually succumbed to the clientelism of the Mubarak regime. The NPUP's move from confrontation to co-operation was epitomized in 1995 by Mubarak's appointment of one of its leaders, Rifa'at al-Sa'id, to the Consultative (Shura) Council. 'It was', declared Sa'id, 'crazy to isolate ourselves from the system of which we are part.'[104]

9

Iran and Iraq

During the Second World War the Red Army, together with forces from its Western allies, had occupied Iran. Soviet intelligence used the occupation to establish its largest presence so far beyond its borders with nearly forty residencies and sub-residencies. The main residency in Tehran had 115 operations officers. Their principal task, as in neighbouring areas of the Soviet Union, was the identification, abduction and liquidation of those whom Stalin considered 'anti-Soviet' elements.[1] Only strong post-war pressure from both the United States and Britain persuaded the Soviet Union to end its military occupation in 1946. For almost two decades thereafter Moscow hoped, and the West feared, that an Iranian revolution would bring a pro-Soviet regime to power. Muhammad Reza Pahlavi, who had become Shah in 1941 shortly before his twenty-second birthday, remained uneasy on the 'peacock throne'. In 1949 a group of Tudeh (Communist) Party members in the Iranian officer corps made an attempt on his life.[2] Though the Shah survived, his authority was weakened two years later when he yielded to public pressure and appointed the eccentric nationalist, Dr Muhammad Mossadeq, as his Prime Minister. Mossadeq promptly nationalized the oil industry – to the outrage of the British government which owned 50 per cent of the shares in the Iranian Oil Company.

Both Britain and, still more, the United States greatly exaggerated Mossadeq's susceptibility to Communist influence. When Dwight D. Eisenhower became President in January 1953, Sir Anthony Eden, the Foreign Secretary in Winston Churchill's government, found him 'obsessed by the fear of a Communist Iran'. Six months later the CIA and SIS jointly organized a coup which overthrew Mossadeq, and restored the authority of the Shah. According to Kermit Roosevelt, the CIA officer chiefly responsible for planning the coup, an emotional Shah told him afterwards, 'I owe my throne to God, my people, my army – and to you!' He then reached into his inside pocket and presented Roosevelt with a large gold cigarette case. On his way back to Washington, Roosevelt called at London to brief Churchill in person. He found the Prime Minister propped up in bed, recovering from a stroke but eager to hear a first-hand account of the coup. 'Young man,' said Churchill, when Roosevelt had finished his briefing, 'if I had been but a few years younger, I should have loved nothing better than to have served under your command in this great venture!' Eisenhower was equally enthusiastic. He wrote in his diary that Roosevelt's exciting report 'seemed more like a novel than a historical fact'. The short-term success of the coup, however, was heavily outweighed by the long-term damage to American and British policy in Iran.[3] It was easy for KGB active measures to encourage the widespread Iranian belief that the CIA and SIS continued to engage in sinister conspiracies behind the scenes. Even the Shah from time to time suspected the Agency of plotting against him. The Centre tried hard to encourage his suspicions.

For a quarter of a century after the 1953 coup, none the less, the CIA's influence in Tehran comfortably exceeded that of the KGB. The banning of the Tudeh Party and the exile of its leadership meant that the Centre was unable to rely in Iran on the assistance it received from fraternal Party leaders in a number of other Middle Eastern countries. In 1957, in order to both monitor and intimidate domestic opposition, the Shah created with help from both the CIA and Mossad a new state security and intelligence organization, better known by its acronym SAVAK, which rapidly acquired a fearsome reputation for brutality. Two years after its foundation, Iran and Israel signed a secret agreement on intelligence and military co-operation.[4]

The KGB retaliated with a series of active measures to which it seems to have attached exaggerated importance. Late in 1957 the head of the Soviet department of the Iranian Foreign Office was trapped by a KGB agent into – allegedly – changing money illegally during a visit to Moscow and reported to the Iranian ambassador. According to a KGB report, he was dismissed on the personal orders of the Shah and replaced by a less anti-Soviet successor.[5] The Centre's most effective tactic, however, was to exploit the Shah's continuing sense of insecurity and recurrent fears of US double-dealing. In February 1958, Service A forged a letter from the American Secretary of State, John Foster Dulles, to his ambassador in Tehran, belittling the Shah's ability and implying that the United States was plotting his overthrow. The Tehran residency circulated copies of the letter to influential Iranian parliamentarians and editors in the confident expectation that one would come to the attention of the Shah – which it duly did. According to the KGB file on the operation, the Shah was completely taken in by the fabricated Dulles letter and personally instructed that a copy be sent to the US embassy with a demand for an explanation. Though the embassy dismissed it as a forgery, the Tehran residency reported that its denials were disbelieved. Dulles's supposedly slighting references to the Shah were said to be a frequent topic of whispered conversation among the Iranian élite.[6] The impact of these insults on the Shah's insecure personality was all the greater because of the court culture of 'shadulation' which normally protected him from any hint of criticism.

The Shah's irritation with the United States was increased by its failure to provide as much military aid as he wanted. During 1959 he flirted with the idea of signing a non-aggression pact with the Soviet Union unless his demands were met by Washington. Dulles privately complained that the Shah was coming close to 'blackmail tactics'.[7] Friction between Tehran and Washington was skilfully exacerbated by the Centre. In 1960 Service A fabricated secret instructions from the Pentagon ordering US missions in Iran and other Third World countries to collaborate in espionage operations against the countries to which they were accredited and to assist in operations to overthrow regimes of which Washington disapproved. Copies of the forged instructions were sent in November to the Tehran embassies of Muslim states by a supposedly disaffected Iranian working for the US military mission. Once again, as the Centre had intended, the forgery was believed to be genuine by the Iranian government and came to the attention of the Shah. The US ambassador was summoned by the Iranian foreign minister and asked for an explanation. As a result of the active measures, according to the Tehran residency, in 1961 the Shah personally ordered the replacement of a number of pro-American Iranian officers.[8]

The KGB also claimed to have influenced the Shah's choice of his third (and last) wife, the twenty-one-year-old Farah Diba, whom it wrongly believed had Communist sympathies. The Centre boasted that, while Ms Diba was an architecture student in Paris, a KGB agent had persuaded the Iranian cultural attaché, Djahanguir Tafazoli, to introduce her to the Shah.[9] Though she was unaware of the KGB's interest in her, Farah Diba's correspondence with her mother shows that there was some truth to the Centre's boast. Her first meeting with the Shah took place at a reception at the Iranian embassy during his visit to Paris in the spring of 1959. Tafazoli took Ms Diba's hand and tried to take her to meet the Shah. The shy Ms Diba hung back but when the Shah spoke to her later in the reception, she told her mother that, 'Tafazoli added immediately, "Mademoiselle is a very good student. She is first in her class and she speaks French very well."' Ms Diba added that it was 'very nice of [Tafazoli] to have said so many nice things about me'. A cousin who was at the reception told her that the Shah clearly liked her and had his eyes on her as she left the room. 'Of course', wrote Ms Diba, 'all of that is just talk.'[10] Only a few months later, however, she and the Shah became engaged. The KGB's misplaced interest in the future Empress appears to have derived from the fact that she had a circle of Communist student friends within the Paris Left Bank café society which she frequented. A friend who persuaded her to attend a demonstration in support of Algerians 'fighting French imperialism' was later imprisoned in Iran as a member of the Tudeh Party.[11] The Centre was also encouraged by the fact that, unknown to Farah Diba, one of her relatives was a KGB agent codenamed RION.[12] The KGB, however, failed to realize that she remained, as she had been brought up, a convinced royalist.

Though Farah Diba went to the pro-Algerian demonstration to counter taunts that she lacked the courage to do so, she recalls finding the world-view of her Communist and fellow-traveller friends 'grim and deeply depressing': 'They were so young, but already they seemed to be against the whole world, extremely sour and bitter. You would have thought that, in their view, there was nothing worth keeping on this planet apart from the Soviet Union.'[13]

As soon as Farah Diba became Empress of Iran in December 1959, it became clear that the KGB had misjudged her. The new Empress's radicalism showed itself not in her politics but in her artistic tastes. Farah Diba scandalized both Shia clergy and conservative Iranians by her patronage of avant-garde Western art. At a time when, as one Iranian businessman put it, 'we were only just beginning to listen to Bach', the Empress's interest in Stockhausen seemed shocking.[14]

For some years after his marriage to Farah Diba the Shah's position still appeared far from secure. At his summit meeting with John F. Kennedy in Vienna in 1961, Khrushchev confidently predicted that Iran would fall like a rotten fruit into Soviet hands. The CIA also thought that an Iranian revolution was on the cards. A National Intelligence Estimate of 1961 concluded, 'Profound political and social change in one form or another is virtually inevitable.' Among those plotting against the Shah was the brutal head of SAVAK, General Teimur Bakhtiar, whom the Shah sacked after receiving a warning from the CIA.[15] The Shah also had to endure several further assassination attempts. According to the KGB defector, Vladimir Kuzichkin, one of the attempts was organized by the KGB and personally approved by Khrushchev. In February 1962 a Volkswagen Beetle packed with explosive by a KGB illegal was parked on the route taken by the Shah as he drove to the Majlis (the Iranian parliament). As the Shah's motorcade passed the VW, the illegal pressed the remote control but the detonator failed to explode.[16] There was no further plot by the KGB to assassinate the Shah, due in large part to a dramatic scaling down of its foreign assassinations after the damaging international publicity given to the trial in West Germany later in the year of one of the Centre's leading assassins, Bogdan Stashinsky.[17]

During the Khrushchev era sabotage replaced assassination as the most important of the 'special actions' for which the FCD was responsible. At the heart of its sabotage planning was the identification of foreign targets, mostly in the West, and preparations for their destruction in time of war or other crises by Soviet sabotage and intelligence groups (*diversionnye razvedyvatelnye gruppy* or DRGs) operating with local Communist or other partisans.[18] Greater preparations for sabotage were made in Iran than in any other non-Western country. Between 1967 and 1973 a series of landing sites, bases and arms dumps for DRGs in Iranian Kurdistan, Iranian Azerbaijan and Abadan were selected, photographed and reconnoitred in detail, mostly by KGB illegals. The Azerbaijani, Kazakh and Kyrgyz KGBs were ordered to assist in recruiting illegals who could pass as members of one of Iran's ethnic groups and help in setting up illegal residencies on Iranian territory.[19] Following Andropov's call in 1967 for a new 'offensive to paralyse the actions of our enemies', the main priority of FCD Department V became the planning of 'special actions of a political nature' – the peacetime use of sabotage and other forms of violence in the furtherance of Soviet policy. Line F officers in residencies, who reported to Department V, were instructed to show greater ingenuity in devising 'special actions' in which the hand of the KGB would be undetectable.[20] In Tehran alone detailed preparations were made for the bombing of twenty-three major buildings (among them royal palaces, major ministries, the main railway station, police and SAVAK headquarters, TV and radio centres) as well as key points in the electricity supply system and fifteen telephone exchanges.[21] None of these elaborate schemes, however, ever proceeded beyond the planning stage. In September 1971 the defection of a Line F officer in the London residency, Oleg Adolfovich Lyalin, compromised many of Department V's plans and led to the recall of most other Line F officers. Though the planning of 'special actions of a political nature' by the KGB continued, they never again had the same priority.[22]

During the later 1960s the Shah's regime seemed to stabilize. The United States, whose military aid was on a much larger scale than a decade earlier, saw partnership with Iran and Saudi Arabia as the key to preserving Western access to the oil of the Persian Gulf. The Shah acquired the image in the West of an enlightened despot gallantly pursuing liberal reforms in the teeth of bigoted opposition. Washington and other Western capitals preferred to turn a blind eye when the Shah used SAVAK to crush protests from left-wing militants, independent-minded liberals and Islamic activists, chief among them the Ayatollah Khomeini.[23] A brief for President Lyndon Johnson before the visit to Washington in 1968 by the Iranian Prime Minister, Amir Abbas Hoveyda, warned, 'Queries about party politics should be avoided because the Iranian parliament is a one-party body, hand-picked by the Shah in an effort at "guided democracy". Freedom of the press is similarly a touchy subject.'[24] Though the Soviet Union maintained a tone of official cordiality in its relations with Iran, it was well aware that it was losing the struggle for influence in Tehran to the United States. The appointment in 1973 of the former Director of Central Intelligence, Richard Helms, as US ambassador in Tehran seemed to demonstrate that the special relationship between the Shah and the CIA had survived disruption by KGB active measures.

The Soviet ambassador, Vladimir Yerofeyev, said sneeringly to Hoveyda, 'We hear the Americans are sending their Number One spy to Iran.' 'The Americans are our friends,' Hoveyda retorted. 'At least they don't send us their Number Ten spy!'[25]

During the early 1970s the Soviet Union's most reliable major ally in the Middle East increasingly appeared to be Iran's main regional opponent, Iraq. The preoccupation of the Ba'thist regime in Baghdad with plots against it, probably even greater than that of the Shah, was skilfully exploited by the KGB, which claimed much of the credit for alerting President Ahmad Hasan al-Bakr and other Iraqi leaders to a conspiracy against them in January 1970. The Iraqi government declared that the conspirators had been acting in collusion with 'the reactionary government in Iran', with which it had a serious border dispute over the Shatt el-Arab waterway, and expelled the Iranian ambassador. In December Iran in turn accused Iraq of plotting to overthrow the Shah. Diplomatic relations between the two states were broken off in the following year. The Baghdad residency reported with satisfaction that, as a result of its active measures, many 'reactionary' army officers and politicians had been arrested and executed – among them a former military governor of Baghdad whom it blamed for a massacre of Iraqi Communists seven years earlier.[26] In 1972 another active-measures operation, code-named FEMIDA, compromised further Iraqi 'reactionaries' who were accused of contact with SAVAK and SIS.[27] Simultaneously Moscow put pressure on a somewhat reluctant Iraqi Communist Party (ICP) to reach an accommodation with the Ba'th regime.[28] In April 1972 the Soviet Union and Iraq signed a fifteen-year Treaty of Friendship and Co-operation. A month later two Communists entered the Iraqi cabinet. In July 1973 the Ba'th and ICP joined in a Ba'th-dominated Progressive National and Patriotic Front (PNPF).[29]

Simultaneously the KGB maintained covert contact in northern Iraq with the leader of the Kurdistan Democratic Party (KDP), Mullah Mustafa Barzani (codenamed RAIS), who had spent over a decade in exile in the Soviet Union after the Second World War. From 1968 to 1972 the KGB carried out twenty-three operations to pass funds to Barzani.[30] In 1973, after a series of clashes with Iraqi forces, Barzani publicly accused the Baghdad government of duplicity and double-dealing. Forced to choose between the Ba'th regime and the Kurds, Moscow opted for the Ba'th. Betrayed by the

Soviet Union, Barzani turned instead to Iran, the United States and Israel, who provided him with covert support. In 1974 full-scale war broke out between the Kurds and the Ba'th regime. At its peak, 45,000 Kurdish guerrillas succeeded in pinning down over 80,000 Iraqi troops, 80 per cent of the total. According to a UN report, 300,000 people were forced to flee their homes. The war ended in victory for Baghdad in 1975 when Iran and Iraq settled their differences and the Shah withdrew support for the Kurds. Barzani was forced into exile in the United States, where he died four years later. In July 1975 Iraq became the first Middle Eastern country to be admitted to Comecon with the status of observer.[31]

Since 1969, the British embassy in Baghdad had correctly identified Saddam Hussein as President Bakr's 'heir apparent'. The embassy found him a 'presentable young man' with 'an engaging smile' who, despite his reputation as a 'Party extremist', might 'mellow' with added responsibility. Speaking 'with great warmth and what certainly seemed sincerity', Saddam assured the British ambassador that Iraq's relationship with the Soviet bloc 'was forced upon it by the central problem of Palestine', and expressed an apparently 'earnest' hope for improved ties with Britain and the United States. The ambassador summed up Saddam as 'a formidable, single-minded and hard-headed member of the Ba'athist hierarchy, but one with whom, if only one could see more of him, it would be possible to do business'.[32] Moscow, however, was impressed by a quite different side of the Iraqi heir apparent's devious personality. Saddam Hussein's fascination with the career of Joseph Stalin appeared to offer an unusual opportunity to strengthen Soviet–Iraqi relations. Saddam's henchmen had frequently to listen to his tedious descriptions of Stalin's powers of dictatorial leadership. A Kurdish politician, Dr Mahmoud Othman, who visited his private apartments, was struck not merely by the crates of Johnnie Walker whisky but also by his bookshelf of works on Stalin translated into Arabic. 'You seem fond of Stalin,' Othman told him. 'Yes,' replied Saddam, 'I like the way he governed his country.' The KGB arranged secret visits by Saddam to all the villas which had been reserved for Stalin's private use along the Black Sea coast. Stalin's biographer, Simon Sebag Montefiore, has plausibly argued that among the qualities which Saddam so admired was Stalin's sadistic pleasure in disposing of his enemies. 'My greatest delight', Stalin once admitted, 'is to mark one's enemy, avenge oneself thoroughly, then go to sleep.' Saddam shared a similar mindset.[33]

Moscow's hopes of turning Iraq into its major Middle Eastern bridgehead were reflected in its growing military investment. From 1974 to 1978 Iraq was the chief recipient of Soviet military aid to the Third World. The Soviet bridgehead in Baghdad, however, was always insecure. With Kurdish resistance apparently broken in 1975, the brutal Ba'th regime had less need thereafter of Communist support and set about achieving the complete subordination of the ICP. Desperate to avoid an open breach with Baghdad, Moscow made no public protest at the open persecution of Iraqi Communists which began in 1977. The Iraqi leader most suspicious of the Soviet–ICP connection was probably Saddam Hussein, whose admiration for Stalin did not extend to sympathy for Iraqi Communists. Saddam's suspicions of a plot to prepare a Communist take-over in Iraq were fuelled by Soviet support for a coup in Afghanistan in April 1978 which brought to power a Marxist regime headed by Nur Muhammad Taraki. The Ba'th regime in Iraq swiftly denounced the ICP's 'subservience to Moscow'. Twenty-one Party members were executed on charges of 'forming secret groups inside the Iraqi armed forces'. 'The Soviet Union', declared Saddam Hussein, 'will not be satisfied until the whole world becomes Communist.'[34]

With the Party forced into an underground existence, an ICP Politburo member, Zaki Khayri (codenamed SEDOY, 'Bald'), asked the KGB resident in Baghdad to take the Party archives into safekeeping. In an elaborate operation on 18 August 1978 approved by the Centre, an ICP car containing three trunks of Party documents followed a pre-arranged route through Baghdad, kept under surveillance by KGB officers, to a secret rendezvous where the archives were transferred to a residency car.[35] In November, A. A. Barkovsky, the Soviet ambassador to Iraq, reported to Moscow that three of the seven-man Politburo, including the general secretary, Aziz Muhammad (codenamed GLAVNY, 'Head'), had gone abroad some months earlier. According to the ambassador, their absence had aroused great suspicion within the Ba'th regime, which doubtless suspected that a plot was being hatched.[36] Its suspicions would have been all the greater had it known that Muhammad was in exile in Moscow and communicating with the ICP via the Baghdad residency.[37]

Early in 1979 the purge of ICP members intensified. Writing in the March issue of the *World Marxist Review*, the Iraqi Communist Nazibah Dulaymi declared that, in addition to executions of Party militants, 'more than 10,000 persons have been arrested and subjected to mental and physical torture'. She naively expressed her confidence that 'fraternal Communist and workers' parties' would demand 'an immediate end to the repression against Communists and their friends in Iraq'. The Soviet Communist Party, however, remained silent. At a time when Iraq was at the forefront of the Arab campaign to prevent the Carter administration brokering a peace treaty between Egypt and Israel, Moscow was cravenly anxious not to antagonize Baghdad. The torture and execution of Iraqi Communists counted for less in Soviet eyes than Iraqi attempts to disrupt the Middle Eastern peace process.[38]

The brutal persecution of Iraqi Communists in 1978–79 coincided with the rapid decline and fall of the Shah in Iran. Like Western intelligence agencies, the KGB was taken by surprise. During Hoveyda's twelve years as Prime Minister (1965–77), the Tehran residency had limited success in penetrating the regime. Its two most important Iranian agents during this period, General Ahmad Mogarebi, codenamed MAN,[39] and a relative of Hoveyda, codenamed ZHAMAN, had both been recruited, apparently as ideological agents, in the early years of the Cold War. Mogarebi was responsible during the final years of the Shah's rule for arms purchases from the United States and other Western states. According to Vladimir Kuzichkin, who later defected from the Tehran residency, he was 'regarded as the Residency's best agent' and had 'innumerable connections in various spheres of Iranian life, including the court of the Shah, the government and SAVAK'.[40] Mogarebi became an increasingly mercenary agent whose growing importance was reflected in his monthly salary, raised in 1972 from 150–200 to 330 convertible rubles a month and in 1976 to 500 rubles. In 1976 he was awarded the Order of the Red Banner. Because of the shortage of high-grade intelligence from other sources, in 1976–77 the residency breached normal security procedures by contacting Mogarebi every two weeks.[41] The habitual method of contact was by radio communication from a residency car, usually parked within 1,500 metres of his home.[42] For meetings with his controller, Boris Kabanov (remembered by Kuzichkin as 'Everybody's favourite, with a sense of humour, good natured, quiet, always smiling . . .'),[43] Mogarebi would leave his house and rendezvous with the nearby car. The fact that a residency car with diplomatic number plates was to be seen in the vicinity of Mogarebi's house every fortnight might well have led to his arrest by SAVAK in September 1977.[44]

The KGB found ZHAMAN far less reliable than Mogarebi. When recruited as an ideological agent in 1952, he eulogized the Soviet Union as 'the stronghold of progress in the struggle against Imperialism and Anglo-American dominance in Iran'. His KGB file, however, complains that he was sometimes 'uncontrollable'. In 1956 he shocked his controller by condemning the Soviet suppression of the Hungarian Uprising. By the time his relative Amir Abbas Hoveyda became Prime Minister, ZHAMAN's ideological commitment to the Soviet cause had faded away. Though his file claims that he adopted a more pro-Western outlook for careerist reasons, it also acknowledges that he became genuinely devoted to the Shah, to whom he owed his career in the official bureaucracy. The Tehran residency reported that, because of his personal wealth, it had no means of putting financial pressure on him. In the mid-1970s, ZHAMAN none the less took part in KGB active-measures operations, passing disinformation prepared by Service A to the Shah as well as to American, Egyptian, Pakistani and Somali contacts. In 1977 ZHAMAN was presented by the KGB with a thousand-dollar pair of cufflinks for his assistance in promoting Soviet active measures.[45]

In the summer of 1977 economic crisis and growing discontent at rising prices and daily power cuts in Tehran led to the resignation of Hoveyda as Prime Minister. Over the next year the newly arrived Soviet ambassador, Vladimir Vinogradov, formerly stationed in Cairo, paid regular calls on Hoveyda at home. SAVAK, predictably, took a close interest in his movements. On one occasion Hoveyda told Vinogradov that he had seen a SAVAK report to the Shah complaining that they were having 'long political discussions'.[46] As unrest spilled into the Tehran streets, the slogans used by demonstrators were mostly religious rather than political: *Allahu Akhbar!*, then increasingly *Allahu Akhbar! Khomeini Rakhbar!* ('God is Great! Khomeini is Our Leader!'). The Mujahidin and Fedayin, left-wing groupings who organized demonstrations and strikes, chose the same slogans to win popular support.[47] The KGB residency failed to take seriously the religious fervour of the Tehran demonstrations and pinned its hopes instead on the prospect of a left-wing revolution sweeping the Shah from power. The Centre was much less optimistic about the prospects of the Iranian left. 'The most likely alternative to the Shah if he were to leave the political stage', it believed, 'would be the military. The opposition to the regime in Iran is weak and uncoordinated. In general the opposition in Iran is not a threat to the present regime . . .'[48] It did not yet occur either to the KGB or to most Western intelligence services that the seventy-five-year-old Shi'ite fundamentalist Ayatollah Khomeini, who had lived in exile for the past thirteen years, represented any serious threat to the Shah.[49] Gary Sick, the desk officer for Iran in the US National Security Council, noted in retrospect, 'The notion of a popular revolution leading to the establishment of a theocratic state seemed so unlikely as to be absurd.' On that point both the White House and the Kremlin were agreed. Visiting Tehran at the beginning of 1978, President Jimmy Carter declared in a New Year toast, 'Iran is an island of stability in one of the more troubled parts of the world.' Only a year later, the Shah was forced to abdicate.[50]

The well-publicized arrest of Mogarebi in September 1977 produced what Kuzichkin described as 'an intelligence vacuum' in the Tehran residency. As a security precaution, it was ordered to suspend agent operations and prepare a damage assessment. With ZHAMAN abroad, the residency had in any case no other agent capable of providing high-grade intelligence during this critical period.[51] The residency's problems were compounded by the Iranian refusal to grant visas for a number of FCD officers whom the Centre had intended to station in Tehran. During a visit to Hoveyda's house in February 1978, Vinogradov asked if he could intervene with the authorities to help obtain the visas. Hoveyda declined. 'I will tell you frankly what is happening,' he replied. 'The point is that SAVAK does not want to let the KGB into Iran.'[52] By this time, operating conditions in Tehran had become so difficult and the surveillance of the Soviet embassy so tight that the residency appealed to the Centre to retaliate against the Iranian embassy in Moscow. Its suggestions for the harassment of Iranian embassy personnel included draining the brake fluid from their cars and slashing their tyres.[53]

Though operations officers under diplomatic cover in the Tehran residency were barely able to operate, KGB illegals succeeded in 1977 in hiding a secret weapons cache of twenty-seven Walther pistols and 2,500 rounds of ammunition in a dead letter-box (DLB) in the Tehran suburbs.[54] In accordance with common KGB practice, the DLB was probably fitted with a Molniya ('Lightning') booby-trap which was intended to destroy the contents if any attempt was made to open it by non-KGB personnel. Since the KGB is unlikely to have taken the risk of trying to retrieve the arms later, the cache may still be there and in a dangerous condition. (A booby-trapped KGB communications equipment cache in Switzerland whose location was identified by Mitrokhin exploded when fired on by a water cannon. According to the Swiss Federal Prosecutor's Office, 'Anyone who tried to move the container [in the cache] would have been killed.')[55] Though the purpose of the arms cache is not recorded in Mitrokhin's brief note on the illegal operation which put it in place, the arms were probably intended for use in the event of a popular rising against the Shah's regime. In the spring of 1978 a Line PR officer at the Tehran residency under diplomatic cover, Viktor Kaza-kov, confidently told an American contact that the Shah would be toppled by 'oppressed masses rising to overthrow their shackles'.[56] The still banned Tudeh (Communist) Party, operating through front organizations, began to show renewed signs of life, distributing anti-Shah leaflets and a news-sheet covertly produced with the help of the Tehran residency and Tass, the Soviet news agency.[57] During the summer of 1978, however, most Middle Eastern experts in the Centre still believed that the Shah's regime was too strong to be overthrown in the foreseeable future.[58] In July 1978, at a meeting in Moscow with the Tehran resident, Ivan Anisimovich Fadeykin, Andropov was less concerned by the possible consequences of toppling the Shah than by the threat posed to the southern borders of the Soviet Union by the Shah's alliance with the United States. Andropov instructed Fadeykin to step up active measures designed to destabilize the Shah's regime and to damage its relations with the United States and its allies.[59]

As the Shah's position worsened, he increasingly resorted to conspiracy theories to account for his misfortunes. KGB active measures probably had at least some success in strengthening his suspicions of the United States. 'Why do [the Americans] pick on me?' he plaintively asked his advisers in the summer of 1978.[60] The KGB fed disinformation to the Shah that the CIA was planning to create disturbances in Tehran and other cities to bring him down and that Washington was searching for a successor who could stabilize the country after his overthrow with the help of the army and SAVAK.[61] There were moments when the Shah did indeed fear that Washington intended to abandon him and turn instead to Islamic fundamentalism to build a barrier against Soviet influence in the Middle East. Not all the Shah's conspiracy theories, however, conformed to those devised by Service A. At times he feared that the United States and the Soviet Union were jointly conspiring to divide Iran between them. Some of the Shah's family had even more bizarre theories. According to his son and heir, Reza, the Americans bombarded the Shah with radiation which brought on the malignant lymphoma that eventually killed him.[62]

The Tehran residency remained resolutely hostile to Khomeini. He had, it reported, denounced Iranian Communists as unpatriotic puppets of Moscow and was incensed by the Communist coup in Afghanistan in April which he believed had cut short its transformation into an Islamic regime. Though noting increasing popular support for Khomeini, the residency believed that he did not plan to step into the shoes of the Shah himself.[63] It was badly mistaken. Though Khomeini had started his revolt against the Shah without political ambitions of his own, fourteen years of exile had changed his mind. His aim now was to preside over Iran's transformation into an Islamic republic ruled by Shia religious scholars.[64] The KGB's failure to understand Khomeini's intentions derived not from any lack of secret intelligence but from the fact that it had not bothered to study his tape-recorded sermons which drew such an emotional response in Iranian mosques. The CIA made the same mistake.[65] The middle-class Iranian liberals who had wanted to be rid of the autocracy and corruption of the Shah's regime were equally surprised by the consequences of his overthrow.

On 16 January 1979 the Shah left Iran for Egypt, vainly hoping that the military would take control and enable him to return. Instead, on 1 February Khomeini returned in triumph from exile in Paris to a delirious welcome from 3 million supporters who thronged the airport and streets of Tehran. Within a week Khomeini's supporters had taken control of the police and administration in a number of cities across the country. On 9 February a pro-Khomeini mutiny began among air-force technicians and spread to other sections of the armed forces. The Tehran residency was able to follow the dramatic transfer of allegiance to the new Islamic regime by monitoring the radio networks of the police and armed services. While on duty in the residency's IMPULS radio interception station on 10 February, Kuzichkin listened to government and rebel-controlled police stations exchanging sexual insults over the air. Next day, it became clear that the rebels had won. The government resigned and Khomeini's nominee, Mehdi Bazargan, became acting Prime Minister.[66] Among the most prominent early victims of Khomeini's revolution was Amir Abbas Hoveyda, who was sentenced to death by a revolutionary tribunal headed by the 'Hanging Ayatollah', Hojjat al-Islam Khalkhali, in May 1979. Khalkhali kept the pistol used to execute Hoveyda as a souvenir. The front pages of Tehran newspapers carried gruesome pictures of his bloodstained corpse.[67] The FCD officer who closed Hoveyda's file in the Centre wrote on it, 'A pity for the poor man. He was harmless and useful for us.'[68]

The Ayatollah Khomeini (codenamed KHATAB by the KGB)[69] was even more prone than the Shah to conspiracy theories. All opposition to the Islamic revolution was, he believed, the product of conspiracy, and all Iranian conspirators were in the service of foreign powers. He denounced those Muslims who did not share his radical views as 'American Muslims' and many left-wingers as 'Russian spies'. Since Khomeini claimed to be installing 'God's government', his opponents were necessarily enemies of God Himself: 'Revolt against God's government is a revolt against God. Revolt against God is blasphemy.'[70] At least during the early years of the new Islamic Republic, the KGB found Iran even more fertile ground for active measures than under the Shah. Its chief targets included both the US embassy in Tehran and members of the new regime who were judged to have 'anti-Soviet tendencies'.[71] KGB operations against the US embassy, however, paled into insignificance by comparison with those of the new regime. On 4 November 1979 several thousand officially approved militants, claiming to be 'students following the Imam [Khomeini]'s line', overran the American embassy, declared it a 'den of spies', and took hostage over fifty US diplomatic personnel. But if the United States was denounced as the 'Great Satan' by Iran's fundamentalist revolutionaries, the Soviet Union was the 'Small Satan'. After the Soviet invasion of Afghanistan at the end of the year, Leonid Shebarshin (codenamed SHABROV), who had become Tehran resident a few months earlier,[72] feared an attack on the Soviet embassy. A first incursion on New Year's Day 1980 did little damage and was repulsed by the local police. By the time a second attack took place on the first anniversary of the invasion of Afghanistan, so many bars and metal doors had been fitted to the embassy that it resembled, in Shebarshin's view, 'something between a zoo and a prison'. No hostages were taken and no documents seized.[73] The world's attention remained focused on the American hostages, who were finally freed in January 1981.

The large cache of diplomatic and CIA documents discovered in the US embassy, many painstakingly reassembled by the Iranians from shredded fragments, provided further encouragement both for the new regime's many conspiracy theorists and for Service A. Among the victims of the conspiracy theorists was the relatively moderate first President of the Islamic Republic, Abolhassan Bani-Sadr, one of Khomeini's former companions in exile. Captured CIA cables and reports showed that the Agency had given him the codename SDLURE-1 and tried to 'cultivate and recruit' him in both Tehran and Paris. Though there was no evidence that Bani-Sadr ever had any conscious dealings with the CIA, the mere fact of its interest in him damned him in the eyes of many militants.[74] Bani-Sadr was simultaneously a target for KGB active-measures operations.[75] Though Mitrokhin's notes give no details, the purpose of the operations was probably to reinforce suspicions that he had been a US agent. Bani-Sadr was forced to step down as President in June 1981.

Not content with the compromising documents plundered by Iranian militants from the US embassy, the KGB conducted a joint operation (codenamed TAYFUN, 'Typhoon') with the Bulgarian intelligence service during 1980, using a series of far more sensational forgeries purporting to come from a (fictitious) underground Military Council for Salvation plotting the overthrow of Khomeini and the restoration of the monarchy. The Centre claimed that the Khomeini regime was taken in by the forgeries and blamed the non-existent Military Council for a number of attacks on its supporters. Further disinformation on plots against the Islamic revolution (including an alleged attempt to assassinate Khomeini) by the CIA, SIS, Mossad, the French SDECE and the German BND was fed by the KGB resident in Beirut, codenamed KOLCHIN,[76] to the leader of the PLO, Yasir Arafat. According to KGB reports, Arafat personally passed the disinformation on to Khomeini. Service A fabricated a report to the CIA from a fictitious Iranian agent providing further apparent evidence of an Agency-sponsored attempt on Khomeini's life.[77]

Among the chief targets of KGB active measures within the Khomeini regime, besides Bani-Sadr, was Sadeq Qotbzadeh, who had also been in Khomeini's inner circle during his years in exile and became Foreign Minister soon after the occupation of the US embassy. In the spring of 1980 Qotbzadeh told Moscow that if it failed to withdraw its troops from Afghanistan, Iran would give military assistance to the Mujahidin. In July he ordered the Soviet embassy in Tehran to cut its staff.[78] Though neither of these episodes was mentioned in the Soviet press, Moscow took a secret revenge. Service A forged a letter to Qotbzadeh from US Senator Harrison Williams, who had met him twenty years earlier while Qotbzadeh was a student in the United States. The letter advised Qotbzadeh not to release the American hostages in the immediate future and also contained information intended to compromise Qotbzadeh personally. In July 1980 the Iranian ambassador in Paris was fed further disinformation alleging that Qotbzadeh was plotting with the Americans to overthrow Khomeini. Qotbzadeh was also said to have received a bribe of $6 million for helping to smuggle out of Iran six American diplomats who had taken refuge in the Canadian embassy in Tehran.[79] Though proof is lacking, these active measures probably helped to bring about Qotbzadeh's dismissal in August.

The KGB considered Qotbzadeh such an important target that its attempt to discredit him continued even after he ceased to be Foreign Minister. Fabricated evidence purporting to show that he was a CIA agent probably contributed to his arrest in April 1982 on a charge of plotting to assassinate Khomeini. Service A continued to forge documents incriminating him after his arrest. The Tehran residency regarded as the 'final nail in his coffin' a bogus CIA telegram prepared by Service A in an easily broken code and addressed to an agent readily identifiable as Qotbzadeh.[80] He and about seventy army officers accused of conspiring with him were shot in September.

Another target of KGB active measures, Grand Ayatollah Kazem Shari'atmadari,[81] a senior religious scholar seen as a rival by Khomeini, was also accused of complicity in the plot. Threatened with the execution of his son, Shari'atmadari was forced to humiliate himself on television and plead for Khomeini's forgiveness. Subsequently he became the first Ayatollah ever to be defrocked, and spent the last four years of his life under house arrest.[82]

Despite its success in incriminating a number of senior figures in the new Islamic Republic, however, the KGB had only a minor influence on the bloodletting as a whole. The impact of the bogus conspiracies devised by Service A was far smaller than that of the actual attempt to overthrow the Khomeini regime in June 1981 by the Iranian Mujahidi yi Khalq (Holy Warriors), who drew their inspiration from both Islam and Marxism. Of the 2,665 political prisoners executed by the Revolutionary Tribunals between June and November 1981, 2,200 were Mujahidi and about 400 members of various left-wing groups – a total seven times as great as that of the monarchists, real and alleged, executed over the previous sixteen months. The Mujahidi death toll continued to mount over the next few years.[83]

The KGB's intelligence collection in the early years of the Khomeini era had less impact than its active measures. When Shebarshin became Tehran resident in 1979, he criticized some of his operations officers for lack of energy in trying to cultivate contacts among the army and the mullahs, and for attempting to conceal their lack of high-grade sources. Ironically, one of those in whom he had most confidence was Vladimir Kuzichkin, who, as he later discovered, made secret contact in Tehran with SIS. Shebarshin's problems were compounded when the head of the residency's Line PR was arrested in 1981 while meeting a foreign businessman whom he had targeted for recruitment; next day he was expelled from Iran. In the residency reorganization which followed, Kuzichkin was promoted. After his defection in the following year, Shebarshin concluded that the head of Line PR had been deliberately compromised by Kuzichkin to assist his own promotion.[84]

Shebarshin also had problems with the special commission on Iran set up by the Politburo after the fall of the Shah, nominally chaired by Brezhnev but with Andropov as its most influential member.[85] The Tehran residency sent what Shebarshin considered valuable reports from four non-Russian FCD officers whose ethnic origins – Armenian, Azeri, Turkmen and Uzbek – allowed them daily to mingle undetected with the local population. The Politburo Commission, however, was not satisfied with the residency's lack of high-level sources in the Khomeini regime and its coverage of the hostage crisis in the American embassy. On 24 April 1980 (a day remembered by President Jimmy Carter as 'one of the worst of my life') a secret US attempt to rescue the hostages was aborted after a series of mechanical failures and accidents to the helicopters and aircraft involved in the rescue mission. At 1 a.m. Washington time on the 25th, the White House announced the failure of the rescue attempt. Shebarshin was severely reprimanded by the Centre when he failed to send a report until the following day. He reasonably believed that the residency should not be expected to compete with the immediacy of the media reporting, and that it was better to wait twenty-four hours before producing a considered assessment. On several occasions Shebarshin also – probably unwittingly – committed the politically incorrect error of sending a report which contradicted Andropov's misguided views on Iran. He reported correctly that news of the Shah's death in exile in July 1980 had no significant impact on the still-fervent popular support for Khomeini, and that the monarchist cause was dead. Andropov made clear his disapproval of the report. In Shebarshin's view, he, like a number of others on the Politburo who had met the Shah, 'greatly overestimated his significance'.[86]

The fall of the Shah and Khomeini's rise to power in Iran were swiftly followed by the triumph of Saddam Hussein in Iraq. On 16 July 1979, at the climax of a long-prepared coup, Iraq's Revolutionary Command Council relieved President Bakr of all his offices and installed Saddam, his former deputy, in his place. Six days later Saddam celebrated his conquest of power by arranging a filmed conference of senior Ba'thist officials which might have been conceived as a tribute to his role model, Joseph Stalin. The proceedings began with the announcement of 'a painful and atrocious plot' and a rehearsed, fabricated confession, reminiscent of Stalin's show trials, by one of Saddam's opponents, Muhi al-Din 'Abd al-Husain Mashhadi, who declared that for the past four years he had been part of a Syrian plot aimed at removing Bakr and Saddam. Saddam, however, took a more direct role in the proceedings than Stalin had ever done. After Mashhadi had completed his confession, Saddam read out the names of sixty-six supposed traitors, all present at the conference, pausing occasionally to light his cigar. As those he had named were led away to be executed by their Party comrades, the audience erupted into hysterical chants of support for Saddam and demands of death for traitors.[87] Much of the energy of Saddam's intelligence services, like those of Stalin, was to be expended on the hunting down of 'traitors' both at home and abroad. Saddam's admiration for Stalin as a role model, however, did not diminish his suspicion of current Soviet policy. Among the victims of his first purge were those he suspected of favouring close ties with the Soviet Union, chief among them Murtada Sa'd 'Abd al-Baqi, Iraqi ambassador to Moscow.[88]

By the time Saddam Hussein seized power, the ICP had been driven underground. Though Moscow remained anxious to avoid an open breach with Baghdad, the Politburo agreed on secret support to the Party to enable it to organize opposition to Saddam. In April 1979 a member of the ICP Politburo codenamed STOGOV had two secret meetings in Tehran with the deputy head of the FCD Eighth (Iran and the non-Arab Middle East) Department, Lev Petrovich Kostromin, to report on the measures taken by the Party to prepare for 'armed struggle'.[89] A camp for 100 partisans had been set up in the mountains of Iraqi Kurdistan with the help of the Marxist-oriented Patriotic Union of Kurdistan (PUK) headed by Jalal Talabani. STOGOV claimed that three more partisan groups were in the process of formation and that talks were being held with Talabani in the hope of forming a united front against the Iraqi regime.[90] On 19 July the Soviet Politburo authorized the KGB to supply the ICP with the equipment for a secret radio station at its base in Iraqi Kurdistan. Free training for three Iraqis chosen to operate the station was provided in the Soviet Union.[91] At a meeting with the deputy head of the FCD Eighteenth (Arab states) Department, G. P. Kapustyan, on 19 October, the ICP leader, Aziz Muhammad, reported that calls for resistance to Saddam were being broadcast by the two Kurdish movements, the PUK and the nationalist Kurdistan Democratic Party (KDP), headed by Mas'ud Barzani (son of the KDP's founder, Mullah Mustafa Barzani). Muhammad asked for ten relay stations to extend the station's broadcasting range.[92]

Soviet hostility to Saddam Hussein was reinforced by his immediate denunciation of the Soviet invasion of Afghanistan in December 1979. The following month Czechoslovakia secretly agreed to supply the ICP base in Kurdistan with 1,000 anti-tank rockets and several thousand Skorpion sub-machine guns with ammunition.[93] Further military supplies followed from the Soviet Union and Hungary.[94] Apart from acting as a conduit for Soviet-bloc arms, however, the ICP added little to the strength of Kurd resistance. Aziz Muhammad admitted to a KGB contact that Party organization inside Iraq had largely broken down. His plan to move the ICP Politburo to Kurdistan was being resisted by 'some leading comrades' who preferred to stay in exile in the Soviet bloc. Muhammad acknowledged that the Party needed to rectify the 'low level of its ideological work', resolve internal differences, reorganize its security and intelligence system, and improve central direction.[95]

The outbreak of the Iran–Iraq War in September 1980 reduced Soviet–Iraqi relations to their lowest point since the establishment of the Ba'th regime. Saddam's invasion of Iran, whose immediate pretext was the long-running border dispute over the Shatt al-Arab waterway, was motivated by a mixture of fear and aggression: fear that Khomeini would rouse Iraq's Shia majority to revolt, combined with a desire to take advantage of the confusion in the Iranian armed forces brought about by the Islamic revolution. Moscow declared its neutrality in the conflict and cut off all military supplies to Iraq, including those due under existing contracts. Saddam's delusions of grandeur made him confident, none the less, of an easy victory. A popular joke put Iraq's population at 28 million: 14 million Iraqis and 14 million portraits of Saddam Hussein. Oil export revenues, which had risen from $1 billion in 1972 to $21 billion in 1979, fed Saddam's ambitions. 'Iraq', he boasted, 'is as great as China, as great as the Soviet Union and as great as the United States.'[96] Among the greatest of Saddam's delusions was his absurd belief, despite his complete lack of military experience, in his own military genius.[97] His inept generalship helped to ensure that, instead of ending in a quick victory, the war with Iran was to drag on for eight years and end with fighting inside Iraq.

The Kurds, as well as the Iranians, benefited from Saddam's military incompetence. At the end of 1980 Aziz Muhammad sent an optimistic message to the Soviet Politburo via the KGB resident in

Damascus. War with Iran had forced Saddam to reduce his forces in Kurdistan. The ICP, Muhammad reported, was making progress in bringing together the Kurdish factions into a unified military campaign to overthrow Saddam's dictatorship. Armed ICP partisan units in Iraqi Kurdistan, including some members of the Central Committee, were ready to join the armed struggle. Significantly, however, Muhammad spoke not of thousands but only of 'hundreds' of Communist partisans. In reality, though Muhammad refused to recognize it, the ICP units had no prospect either of posing a significant threat to Saddam Hussein or of providing leadership for the much more numerous Kurdish detachments. 'You, dear Comrades', he told the Soviet Politburo, 'remain our main support and hope.' He asked for $500,000 to support 'the struggle of our partisan detachments and the work of our Party within Iraq' during the coming year.[98]

Soviet support for Kurdish partisans in Iraq remained secret. During the Twenty-sixth Congress of the CPSU in the spring of 1981 Aziz Muhammad denounced the campaign of 'savage repression' conducted against the ICP and the Kurdish people by the Iraqi Ba'th regime. But, at least in the *Pravda* version of his speech, he was allowed to make no reference to the partisan war to overthrow Saddam Hussein. Muhammad was permitted only to say, vaguely, that the ICP was employing 'diverse methods for the struggle for the establishment of a democratic regime and autonomy for the Kurdish people'.[99] In the last resort Moscow was unwilling to give large-scale support to the Kurds for fear of helping Khomeini achieve victory in the Iran–Iraq War.

In the summer of 1981, having lost hope of a quick victory over Iran, Saddam abandoned his opposition to the Soviet invasion of Afghanistan. The Soviet Union responded by inconspicuously ending its arms embargo. Soviet arms deliveries during the remainder of the year, however, fell far short of Iraqi requirements. In 1982 the tide of war shifted in favour of Tehran. During the spring Iran recovered almost all the territory lost since the beginning of the conflict. In June Iraq announced a unilateral withdrawal from Iranian territory. Iran, however, failed to respond to Saddam's peace moves and carried the war onto Iraqi territory. Anxious to prevent an Iranian victory, Moscow resumed large-scale arms exports to Iraq for the first time since the start of the war. In return Saddam declared a general amnesty for Iraqi Communists and released many from jail.[100] The Soviet Union no longer had any illusions about the prospects of turning Iraq into its main Middle Eastern bridgehead. The prospect of an Iranian victory over Iraq, however, followed by a triumphant Khomeini inciting Soviet Muslims to revolt, was totally unacceptable. The scale of Soviet military supplies to Baghdad was thus carefully calculated to prevent decisive victory by either side. Kissinger's celebrated comment, 'What a pity they can't both lose!', probably evoked some sympathy in Moscow.

The partial mending of bridges between Moscow and Baghdad coincided with a Soviet intelligence disaster in Tehran. On 5 June 1982 Shebarshin was on holiday at a KGB sanatorium re-reading *War and Peace* when he received an urgent summons to Moscow, where he was told that Kuzichkin had disappeared from Tehran three days earlier. A KGB investigation eventually concluded, correctly, that Kuzichkin had been working for SIS and had fled across the Turkish border using a British passport. The next two months, Shebarshin wrote later, were 'the most difficult, the most bitter period of my life': 'It is painful for me to recall that I had once got on well with [Kuzichkin] and facilitated his promotion.' Shebarshin was forced to return to Tehran to close down agent networks which Kuzichkin might have compromised.

The final humiliation, so far as Shebarshin was concerned, was an order from the Centre to call on the head of the British diplomatic mission, Nicholas Barrington (later knighted), to ask how a British passport had come into Kuzichkin's possession: 'The absurdity of this plan was clear to me, but someone in the Centre had imagined that the Englishman would reveal the whole truth to me. This was one of those stupid orders which I was forced to carry out periodically throughout the entire course of my service in the KGB.'[101]

Shebarshin and Barrington had been on friendly terms since they had met while on diplomatic postings in Pakistan in the mid-1960s before Shebarshin joined the KGB – though Barrington's wide range of Pakistani contacts had led Shebarshin to conclude wrongly that he was an SIS officer. On leaving the Soviet embassy in Tehran for the appointment made by his secretary with Barrington in the summer of 1982, Shebarshin had only to cross the road to enter the British embassy. Since the beginning of the hostage crisis at the US embassy, however, the Swedish, not the Union, flag had flown over the embassy. To protect those of its staff who remained in Tehran, it had become the British interests section of the Swedish embassy. Instead of following the Centre's absurd instructions to ask Barrington about the British passport given to Kuzichkin to help him escape across the Turkish frontier, a question which no British diplomat would have dreamt of answering, Shebarshin merely reported that Kuzichkin had disappeared and asked if Barrington had any news. The two men then had a general discussion on the dangers of diplomatic life in Khomeini's Iran.[102] 'Barrington', Shebarshin later recalled, 'was courteous, even sympathetic, and promised to consult London.'[103]

During his debriefing in Britain, Kuzichkin provided voluminous information on Soviet intelligence operations in Iran, which SIS shared with the CIA. Early in 1983 the CIA passed much of it on to Tehran. The Khomeini regime reacted swiftly, expelling Shebarshin and seventeen other Soviet intelligence officers, and arresting 200 leading Tudeh militants, including the entire Central Committee, on charges of spying for Moscow.[104] On May Day the KGB residency was further embarrassed to see both the Tudeh secretary general, Nureddin Kianuri, and its leading ideologue, Ehsan Tabari, make grovelling televised confessions of 'treason', 'subversion' and other 'horrendous crimes', later repeated in even greater detail at show trials where they obsequiously thanked the authorities for their 'humane treatment'. Though both were spared, largely because of the propaganda value of their regular acts of public contrition, many other Party militants were executed or imprisoned. Tudeh disintegrated as a significant force in Iranian politics. Tehran newspaper headlines declared, 'Members of the Central Committee Confess to Spying for the KGB', 'Tudeh Created for the Sole Purpose of Espionage' and 'Confessions Unprecedented in World History'.[105]

KGB operations in both Iran and Iraq thus ended in strategic failure. Their main priority for what remained of the Soviet era was damage limitation. In the final stages of the Iran–Iraq War, Gorbachev agreed to supply Iraq with the Scud-B missiles whose use in rocket attacks on Iranian cities helped to persuade Khomeini in 1988 to, as he put it, 'drink poison' and agree to a cease-fire. Despite the loss of perhaps a million lives, the Iran–Iraq border remained precisely where it had been when Saddam began the war eight years before.

Saddam's invasion of Kuwait on 2 August 1990 – the first international crisis of the post-Cold War era – produced a sharp division of opinion among Gorbachev's advisers. Next day Eduard Amrosievich Shevardnadze, the Soviet Foreign Minister, and James Baker, the US Secretary of State, jointly condemned the invasion and called on 'the rest of the international community to join with us in an international cut-off of all arms supplies to Iraq'. A fortnight later Gorbachev made a televised defence of Soviet co-operation with the United States: 'For us to have acted in a different way would have been unacceptable since the [Iraqi] act of aggression was committed with the help of our weapons, which we had agreed to sell to Iraq to maintain its defence capability – not to seize foreign territories . . .'

On 25 August the United States began a naval blockade of Iraq, an implied warning that it was prepared to go to war unless Saddam withdrew from Kuwait. The Centre, however, was deeply concerned that co-operation with the United States would weaken Soviet influence in the Middle East. With the support of the KGB Chairman Vladimir Kryuchkov and the Defence Minister Dmitri Yazov, Yevgeni Primakov, the Middle Eastern expert on Gorbachev's Presidential Council whose links with the KGB went back thirty years, persuaded Gorbachev to send him on a mission to Baghdad. James Baker was impressed by Primakov's 'skill and cunning' as well as his knowledge of Arab history, but regarded him as 'an apologist for Saddam Hussein'. Primakov's declared aim was to find a compromise which would leave Saddam with two disputed islands and an oil field in return for his withdrawal from the rest of Kuwait and the promise of an international conference on the Palestinian question. In Baker's view, Primakov's proposals were 'more capitulation than compromise'. 'And he had abetted Saddam's strategy to weaken the Arab coalition [against him] by linking the Kuwaiti crisis with the larger Arab–Israeli conflict.'[106] Like Baker, the CIA was deeply suspicious of Primakov's 'game of footsie' with Saddam.[107] So too was Shevardnadze, who privately communicated his suspicions to Baker. In October Shevardnadze told Primakov, in the presence of Gorbachev and Kryuchkov, that his proposals would be disastrous both for the Middle East and for Soviet foreign policy. Primakov, as he later acknowledged, lost his temper, ridiculing the Foreign Minister's knowledge of Iraq. 'How dare you,' he sneered, 'a graduate of a correspondence course from a teachers' college in Kutaisi, lecture me on the Middle East, the region I've studied since my student days!' 'Yevgeni,' interrupted Gorbachev, 'stop right now!'[108] 'Shevardnadze', writes Baker, 'felt betrayed by Primakov and humiliated by Gorbachev, who by allowing Primakov to peddle a peace initiative, had permitted him to usurp Shevardnadze's authority as Foreign Minister.'[109] In December 1990, deeply depressed at the increasing power of the Moscow hard-liners, whom he rightly suspected of planning a coup, Shevardnadze resigned as Foreign Minister, publicly declaring his support for Gorbachev but calling his resignation 'my protest against the onset of dictatorship'.[110]

Primakov's mission to Baghdad, however, achieved little. Saddam had become so deeply distrustful of Soviet intentions that he failed to show much interest in the lifeline which Primakov was trying to throw him. He told his advisers that Primakov's warning that Iraq faced attack by a multinational coalition if there was no negotiated settlement was simply a Soviet attempt to intimidate him. Saddam refused to believe, until the last minute, that the US-led air attack would be followed by a ground offensive.[111] His suspicions of Soviet policy also led him to disregard intelligence of great importance. Just before the beginning of the ground offensive, operation DESERT STORM, in February 1991, satellite imagery shown by Soviet military experts to the Iraqi leadership provided convincing evidence that coalition forces were about to launch a flanking attack (the so-called 'Hail Mary' strategy) instead of – as was widely expected – an amphibious operation directly against the occupying army in Kuwait. Saddam, however, interpreted this intelligence as an attempted Soviet deception agreed with the United States, and made no attempt to reinforce his positions against the flanking attack.[112] Partly as a result, his forces were routed in only a hundred hours of ground warfare.

10

The Making of the Syrian Alliance

The Ba'th regime in Syria, dominated by Hafiz al-Asad from 1970 until his death thirty years later, emerged during the 1970s as the Soviet Union's only reliable ally among the major states of the Middle East. In the immediate aftermath of the coup d'état, masquerading as a 'revolution', which had brought the Ba'th party to power in March 1963, Moscow had viewed the new regime with deep suspicion – despite its declared commitment to socialism as well as Arab unity. Syria's new rulers publicly pledged to crush the Communist Party and 'other enemies of the Revolution'. Moscow retaliated in kind. The Soviet *New Times* dismissed the Ba'th Party as 'a synonym for brutality cloaked by shameless demagogy'. By the spring of 1964, however, encouraged by the nationalization of the main Syrian textile factories and other large industries, Moscow had begun to distinguish between 'progressive' and right-wing forces in the new regime. It was also attracted by the Ba'th's uncompromisingly anti-Western rhetoric. Despite the continuing ban on the Syrian Communist Party, the Soviet Union agreed to supply Syria with both arms and military advisers.[1]

The KGB had from the outset significant penetrations of the new regime's foreign service and intelligence community. The diplomat and lawyer Tarazi Salah al-Din (codenamed IZZAT) had been recruited by the KGB in 1954 and went on to become one of its longest-serving Soviet agents. By the early 1970s he was Director-General of the Foreign Ministry.[2] A further senior official in the Foreign Ministry, codenamed KARYAN, was recruited in 1967. Files noted by Mitrokhin also identify one major penetration of Syrian intelligence: KERIM, who had been recruited by the KGB in East Berlin in the early 1960s. The Damascus residency claimed the credit for helping him obtain a job in the main Syrian civilian intelligence agency, the Bureau of National Security (BNS), after his return to Syria. In 1964 KERIM played the central role in operation RUCHEY during which the KGB successfully bugged some of the BNS offices.[3]

Just as KGB active measures in Iran were able to exploit memories of CIA and SIS covert action during the 1953 coup to overthrow Mossadeq and restore the authority of the Shah, so they benefited in Syria from the deep suspicions left by abortive CIA/SIS attempts during 1956–57 to promote a coup in Damascus to undermine the growing influence of the Ba'th.[4] In Damascus, as in other Middle Eastern capitals, the prevailing culture of conspiracy theory also offered fertile ground for Service A's fabrications. The KGB's first major disinformation success after the Ba'th 'revolution' was operation PULYA ('Bullet'): a series of active measures during 1964–65 designed to unmask a supposed plot by the CIA, in collusion with the West German BND, to undermine the Ba'th regime. In the summer of 1964 the Soviet military attaché in Damascus visited General Amin al-Hafiz, the commander-in-chief of the Syrian army and increasingly the dominating figure in the Ba'th regime, to show him a forged BND intelligence report which purported to identify Syrian army officers in contact with both the BND and the CIA, as well as the CIA officers involved in their recruitment. The attaché was given strict instructions not to leave the report in Hafiz's possession on the pretext of protecting the security of his sources – in reality in order to prevent the forgery being exposed. However, he allowed Hafiz to write down the names of the Syrian officers and CIA personnel mentioned in it. It does not seem to have occurred to Hafiz to challenge the authenticity of the report. Instead, he assured the attaché that he would keep the existence of the document secret and take 'effective measures' against those named in it. Soon afterwards the KGB residency sent an anonymous letter to the Bureau of National Security, purporting to give information on the activities of the CIA Damascus station. Posing as an American well-wisher, a residency operations officer also made an anonymous telephone call to a pro-American Syrian army officer to warn him that his links with the United States were about to be exposed. Shocked by the warning, the officer asked whether he should go into hiding or visit the US embassy to seek political asylum. As the KGB had expected, the whole telephone conversation was monitored by the BNS. The officer was removed from the staff of a Syrian military delegation which was about to visit Moscow.[5] His subsequent fate, however, is not recorded in Mitrokhin's notes.

The KGB claimed the credit for the announcement by the Ba'th regime in February 1965 of the discovery of 'an American spy organization . . . whose assignment was to gather information on the Syrian army and several kinds of military equipment'. Soon afterwards, against the background of furious denunciations of American policy by the Syrian media and angry demonstrations outside the US embassy, two Syrians were tried and executed on charges of spying for the CIA. A State Department protest was rejected by the Ba'th regime on the grounds that 'American policy in Syria is based on espionage and the creation of conspiracy and sabotage networks in the country'.[6] The KGB also believed that its active measures convinced the regime in 1966 that the US ambassador was preparing a coup, and led it to make over 200 arrests in mid-September.[7]

On 23 February 1967 a military coup, publicly praised by Moscow as the work of 'patriotic forces', brought to power a left-wing Ba'th regime headed by the austere Salah Jadid, who rarely appeared in public. High on the list of Soviet aid sought by the new regime was finance for the construction of the Euphrates Dam. Moscow appears to have set three conditions, all quickly accepted by Damascus: the return to Syria of the exiled Communist leader Khalid Bakdash; the inclusion of a Communist in the cabinet; and permission for the Syrian Communist Party to publish a daily newspaper.[8] With the Party once again able to function, though not yet formally legalized, the Damascus residency made arrangements for regular clandestine contact with it. The Communist intermediary, codenamed RASUL, selected by the Party leadership was sent for training in Moscow, where he was taught various forms of secret communication, radio transmission, document photography, use of dead letter-boxes, how to signal danger and arrange emergency meetings with the Damascus residency. He was given a small radio signal transmitter, codenamed ISKUL-2, concealed in a briefcase, which enabled him to send secret signals to the residency from up to 500 metres away. From 1968 until at least the early 1980s a residency operations officer met RASUL once or twice a month.[9]

The humiliation of the Six-Day War in June 1967,[10] less than four months after the February coup, dealt a shattering blow to the prestige of the Jadid regime. Amid the recriminations which followed, the Defence Minister and future Syrian leader, Hafiz al-Asad, kept his portfolio only because he had the support of the brutal and much-feared head of the BNS, 'Abd al-Karim al-Jundi.[11] A serious rift followed between Asad and Jadid. Jadid's main concern remained the internal Ba'th 'revolution'. For Asad, by contrast, the overwhelming priority was the conflict with Israel and the recovery of the Golan Heights, lost in the Six-Day War. Syria had entered the war with poorly trained forces equipped with out-of-date weaponry being phased out of the Red Army. It had no air-defence missiles to protect it against the crack Israeli air force and only half its 500 tanks were operational. Asad was well aware that, to take on Israel, Syria required not merely far better-trained troops but also massive arms supplies from the Soviet Union.[12]

During the clash between Jadid and Asad, KERIM continued to operate as a KGB agent inside the BNS. Among the operations recorded in KGB files in which KERIM took part was a secret night-time entry into the West German embassy in Damascus to abstract (and presumably photograph) classified documents. The operation, which began at 10 p.m. on 20 April 1968 and was concluded at 4 a.m. the following day, was assisted by a Syrian BNS agent inside the embassy. On 24 April the German embassy was burgled again in a similar operation probably also involving KERIM.[13]

In November 1970, with the support of both the army and security forces, Asad deposed Salah Jadid and seized power. 'I am the head of the country, not of the government,' Asad used to claim. In reality, the fear of taking any decision which might displease him meant that even the most trivial issues were frequently referred to President Asad for a decision. The KGB seems to have found his immediate entourage difficult to penetrate. Within the inner circle of his authoritarian regime Asad placed a premium on personal loyalty. Even the clerks and coffee makers on his presidential staff were rarely changed. The key members of his regime – his foreign and defence ministers, chief of the general staff and intelligence chief – remained in power for a quarter of a century or more.[14] During the early 1970s Muhammad al-Khuly, previously head of air-force intelligence, built up what was in effect a presidential intelligence service answerable only to Asad, who began each day with security and intelligence briefings.[15] The fact that Asad, like a majority of his high command

and intelligence chiefs, came from the 'Alawi sect (whose beliefs fused Shi'ite doctrine with elements of nature worship), in defiance of the tradition that power was held by Sunni Muslims, strengthened his anxiety for regular intelligence reports on the mood in the country. (Even Jadid, an 'Alawi like Asad, had chosen a Sunni to act as nominal President.) Asad eventually had fifteen different security and intelligence agencies, all relatively independent of each other, with a total personnel of over 50,000 (one Syrian in 240) and an even larger number of informers. Each agency reported to the President alone and was instructed by the deeply suspicious Asad to keep watch on what the others were up to. Though brutal and above the law, routinely abusing, imprisoning and torturing its victims, Asad's security system was also cumbersome. A Human Rights Watch investigation concluded:

A casual visitor to Damascus cannot fail to notice the confusion at airport immigration, the piles of untouched official forms, and the dusty, unused computer terminal. Local security offices convey the same disorderly impression with their yellowing stacks of forms piled on tables and officials chatting on the phone while supplicants wait anxiously to be heard. The atmosphere is one of chaos mixed with petty corruption and the exercise of bureaucratic power, not of a ruthlessly efficient police state.[16]

The disorderly appearance of Syrian security offices was, however, somewhat misleading. Very few dissidents escaped their huge network of surveillance. Obsessed with his own personal security, Asad was protected by a presidential guard of over 12,000 men. Though his image was ubiquitous – on the walls of public buildings, on trucks, trains and buses, in offices, shops and schools – Asad's leadership style became increasingly remote. By the 1980s most cabinet ministers met him only at their swearing in.[17] Only a handful of key figures had the right to telephone him directly. Foremost among them were his security chiefs. As British ambassador in Damascus in the mid-1980s, Sir Roger Tomkys once had occasion to ring up the head of one of the Syrian intelligence agencies, who replied half an hour later, having just spoken to Asad.[18]

During the early 1970s the KGB residency in Damascus succeeded in establishing what it claimed was 'semi-official contact' with Asad's youngest brother, Rif'at, codenamed MUNZIR, who was a member of his inner circle until the early 1980s. Rif'at's importance in the KGB's view, according to a report of 1974, was that he commanded Asad's élite 'Defence Brigades', the best armed and trained units in the Syrian army, as well as – it believed – having a leading role in the intelligence community.[19] Unlike his relatively reclusive and austere elder brother, Rif'at al-Asad acquired a taste for foreign travel and Western luxuries, acting with little regard for the law and using his position to accumulate private wealth. Under his command the Defence Brigades held a weekly market in Damascus to sell black-market goods smuggled in from Lebanon. Rif'at was sometimes referred to by the Lebanese as 'King of the Oriental Carpets' because of the frequent confiscation of these prized objects by his personal Lebanese militia, popularly known as the 'Pink Panthers'.[20] Access to the corrupt, high-living Rif'at was thus very much easier than to the reclusive Asad. The KGB claimed in 1974 that, through its active measures, it succeeded in using Rif'at 'unconsciously', but Mitrokhin's brief note on the report does not indicate how it did so.[21] A further KGB report of 1974 also identifies as a confidential contact a relative of Asad (codenamed KARIB) with Communist sympathies who was a senior official in the Syrian Council of Ministers. According to KARIB's file, he provided 'valuable and reliable' intelligence on Asad's entourage as well as on his policies.[22] KGB files also claim that SAKR, a department head in military intelligence recruited in 1974, was used to channel disinformation to Asad and the Syrian high command.[23]

Other KGB contacts in, or close to, the Syrian government during the early years of the Asad regime continued to include the long-standing agent IZZAT, Tarazi Salah al-Din, director-general of the Syrian foreign ministry and later a member of the International Tribunal in The Hague.[24] Other KGB contacts included two generals in the Syrian army, OFITSER and REMIZ;[25] SARKIS, an air-force general;[26] PREYER and NIK, both Syrian ministers;[27] PATRIOT, adviser to Asad's first Prime Minister, 'Abd al-Ra'hman Khulayfawi (1970–74);[28] SHARLE ('Charles'), adviser to Asad's second Prime Minister, Mahmud al-Ayyubi (1974–76);[29] VATAR, who provided copies of cipher telegrams obtained by Syrian intelligence from the US embassy in Beirut;[30] BRAT, an intelligence operations officer;[31] FARES and GARGANYUA, both proprietors and editors-in-chief of Syrian newspapers;[32] VALID, a senior official in the Central

Statistical Directorate;[33] and TAGIR, a leading official of the Syrian Arab Socialist Union.[34] There is no indication, however, that any had significant direct access to Asad. Mitrokhin's brief notes on them also give very little indication of the intelligence which they supplied and whether most were agents or confidential contacts.[35]

The KGB's best opportunities to penetrate Asad's entourage almost certainly came during his travels to the Soviet Union, which he visited six times during his first three years as Syrian leader. 'He might look slightly ineffectual', Andrei Gromyko later recalled, 'but in fact he was highly self-controlled with a spring-like inner tension.'[36] While in Moscow, Asad was housed in luxurious apartments in the Kremlin which were inevitably bugged – 'with a view', according to a report to Andropov by Grigori Fyodorovich Grigorenko, head of the KGB Second Chief Directorate, 'to obtaining information about the plans and reactions of Hafiz Asad and his entourage'.[37] The information of most interest to the KGB probably concerned Asad's response to the pressure put on him to sign a Friendship Treaty. Though anxious for Soviet arms, Asad wished to avoid the appearance of becoming a Soviet client. It may well have been from bugging Asad's Kremlin apartment during his visit in July 1972 that the KGB discovered that he was so annoyed by Brezhnev's pressure for a Friendship Treaty that he had ordered his delegation to pack their bags. Alerted to his imminent departure, Brezhnev visited Asad in his apartment and assured him that there would be no further mention of the treaty during their talks. On the last day of Asad's visit, Brezhnev admitted that, despite the Soviet–Egyptian Friendship Treaty, Egypt had just expelled all Soviet advisers: 'I know you will tell me that our treaty with Egypt has not saved us from embarrassment there.' Asad resisted pressure from Sadat to expel Soviet advisers from Syria also, declaring publicly, 'They are here for our own good.'[38]

Though unwilling to sign a Friendship Treaty, Asad had given the still-illegal Syrian Communist Party two posts in his cabinet. In March 1972 the Party was allowed to join the Ba'th-dominated National Progressive Front, thus giving it *de facto* legality, and permitted to publish a fortnightly newspaper, *Nidal al-Sha'b* ('The People's Struggle'). Membership of the Front, however, strengthened the growing breach between Khalid Bakdash (codenamed BESHIR by the KGB), a dogmatic Soviet loyalist who had been Party leader for the past forty years, and the majority of the Party Politburo who resented both Bakdash's autocratic leadership and Moscow's support for Asad. In April 1972 Bakdash's critics within the Party leadership took advantage of his temporary absence in Moscow for medical treatment to pass resolutions accusing him of Stalinist methods. In July pro- and anti-Bakdash factions were summoned to Moscow to resolve their differences at a meeting hosted by senior officials of the CPSU International Department. Though one of Bakdash's critics complained that he had created a personality cult and suffered from 'ideological sclerosis' which made him 'unable to identify the new phenomena in our Arab Syrian society', *Pravda* announced that the meeting had taken place in 'a warm, friendly atmosphere' and had agreed on the importance of 'the ideological, political and organizational unity of the Syrian Communist Party'. Bakdash outmanoeuvred his opponents by playing the role of a loyal supporter both of the Soviet Union and of the Asad regime. The 'Moscow Agreement' papered over the cracks within the Party, and lauded both Soviet–Arab friendship and Syria's achievements under Asad's leadership. For the remainder of the Soviet era, however, the conflict between Bakdash and his Party critics continued to complicate Soviet policy towards Syria.[39]

The most successful KGB penetration during the Asad era recorded in the files noted by Mitrokhin was of the Syrian embassy in Moscow. As well as bugging the ambassador's office and several other parts of the embassy, the KGB regularly intercepted diplomatic bags in transit between the embassy and Damascus, and opened, among other official correspondence, personal letters from Asad's first ambassador in Moscow, Jamil Shaya, to the Foreign Minister, 'Abd al-Halim Khaddam, marked 'MOST SECRET, ADDRESSEE ONLY'. As usual, the KGB's letter-openers paid meticulous attention to replicating the glues, adhesive tapes and seals used on the envelopes and packets in the diplomatic bag. Though Shaya asked for all his envelopes to be returned to him so that he could check personally for signs that they had been tampered with, he seems to have detected nothing amiss.[40]

Mitrokhin's notes from KGB files include the codenames (and a few real names) of thirty-four agents and confidential contacts used in the penetration of the Syrian embassy. Though this total may well be incomplete, it is sufficient to indicate the considerable scale of

KGB operations. The majority of the agents used were Soviet citizens; only six can be clearly identified as Syrian. The operational methods were similar to those employed against many other Moscow embassies. As in the case of other embassy penetrations, the agents were tasked to report on the personalities as well as the opinions of the diplomats. Ambassador Shaya's file, for example, recorded that he was somewhat lax in his Islamic observance and contained such trivial details as a report from Agent MARIYA that he was planning to send a piano he had purchased in Moscow back to Damascus. Soviet female employees of the embassy from interpreters to maids were expected to assess the vulnerability of Syrian diplomats to sexual seduction. Agent SOKOLOVA, who worked in the chancery, reported that the ambassador was showing interest in her. VASILYEVA was planted on Shaya at a reception in the Egyptian embassy in the hope, according to a KGB report, that she would 'be of interest to the ambassador as a woman'. Though there is no evidence in the files noted by Mitrokhin that any Syrian ambassador (unlike a number of his Moscow colleagues) fell for the KGB's 'honey trap', one KGB 'swallow' so successfully seduced another Syrian diplomat that they began living together. Unofficial currency exchange was another common method of compromising foreign diplomats. NASHIT reported that an official of the Syrian military procurement office in Moscow had illegally changed $300 for Shaya on the black market. The KGB drew up plans to arrest and expel the official, probably as a means of putting pressure on the ambassador.

One of the KGB officers involved in operations against the Syrian embassy had the responsibility of organizing hunting expeditions for the ambassador and other senior diplomats. The KGB's hospitality was elaborate. On one expedition to the Bezborodovsky State Hunting Ground, Shaya had the opportunity to shoot elk, wild boar and hares. The entertainment concluded with a visit to a dacha and sauna situated in an orchard on the Volga. The purpose of these expeditions was two-fold: both to ensure that the ambassador was away from the embassy during 'special operations' such as the photography of classified documents and to encourage confidential discussions with his hunting companions. One undercover KGB officer codenamed OSIPOV, who accompanied Shaya on hunting expeditions, reported that on 12 September 1973 the ambassador had confided in him that the Arab states had no prospect of destroying the state of Israel for at least ten, perhaps fifteen years. However, within the next few years they would launch an attack on Israel with the more limited aim of destroying the myth of Israeli invincibility and deterring both foreign investment and Jewish immigrants. The KGB subsequently concluded that Shaya had had advance knowledge of the outbreak of the Yom Kippur War less than a month later on 6 October.[41]

Asad was deeply dissatisfied with the performance of Syria's MiG-19s and MiG-21s during the Yom Kippur War, and angry that the Soviet Union had refused to supply the more advanced MiG-23. He showed his displeasure by declining to send the usual congratulations to Moscow on the anniversary of the October Revolution.[42] A visit to Syria in February 1974 by Air Marshal A. Pokryshkin to assess Syria's military needs failed to resolve the friction with Moscow. An official communiqué after Asad's visit to Moscow in April described the atmosphere as one of 'frankness' (a codeword for serious argument) as well as, less convincingly, 'mutual understanding'. Moscow's desire to settle the dispute with Asad, however, was greatly increased by Sadat's apostasy and turn towards the United States. A week after Asad's April visit, Marshal Viktor Kulikov, chief-of-staff of the Soviet armed forces, flew to Damascus to carry out a fresh assessment of Syrian needs. In the course of 1974 Syria was supplied with over 300 Soviet fighter aircraft, including 45 MiG-23s with Cuban and North Korean pilots, over 1,000 tanks, 30 Scud missiles (with a range of up to 300 kilometres), 100 shorter-range Frog missiles and other military equipment. By the end of the year 3,000 Soviet military advisers had been despatched to Syria and training had begun in the Soviet Union for Syrian pilots of MiG-23s.[43]

In June 1975 the head of the International Department of the CPSU, Boris Ponomarev, told a Ba'th delegation in Moscow 'how much the Soviet people and its Party valued the existence in Syria of a progressive national front with the participation of the Syrian Communist Party'.[44] Simultaneously, however, without Asad's knowledge, the KGB was using the Bakdash wing of the Party leadership to recruit illegals. At a meeting in Moscow with P. D. Sheyin, a senior officer in the FCD Illegals Directorate S on 19 March 1975, Bakdash and a close associate (codenamed FARID) agreed to begin the search for suitable candidates as soon as they returned to Damascus.[45] They were given the following criteria to guide their selection:

[Candidates] were to be dedicated and reliable members of the Communist Party, firmly holding Marxist-Leninist Internationalist positions, with experience of illegal Party work, not widely known within the country as belonging to the Communist Party, bold, determined, resourceful, with organizational aptitude, highly disciplined and industrious, in good physical health, preferably unmarried, aged between 25 and 45. They were to have a good understanding of international affairs, and be capable of analysing and summarizing political information.

These candidates were intended for work in Saudi Arabia and Iran. Besides a native command of English or Persian (for Iran), they had to have a real possibility of obtaining an entry visa for Saudi Arabia or Iran on their own, for the purpose of working and long-term settlement; they had to have a qualification which was needed in the above countries (such as engineer, or technician in the petro-chemical field, in civil engineering related to road construction or housing construction, water and gas supply, electronics, civil aviation, or service industries).

It was desirable that the candidates should have relatives or personal contacts who could help them to enter the country and settle by finding a job or starting their own trading or production businesses; or that they should have the possibility of getting a job in their own country or in a third country with a company or enterprise which was represented in or had a branch in Saudi Arabia or Iran, and could thus go out to work there. Only the [Party] General Secretary or a trusted assistant of his should be aware of the use to which these people were being put.

Bakdash probably welcomed the KGB's request as a reaffirmation of the special relationship with the Soviet leadership which his rivals within the Syrian Communist Party leadership lacked.[46]

In his keynote address to the Twenty-fifth CPSU Congress in February 1976, Brezhnev singled out Syria as the Soviet Union's closest Middle Eastern ally and declared that the two countries 'act in concert in many international problems, above all in the Middle East'.[47] Asad was unaware that 'through agent channels' the KGB was simultaneously planting on him Service A forgeries designed to reinforce his suspicion of Sadat and the United States. Among them was a bogus despatch from the French Foreign Ministry to its embassies in Arab capitals in 1976 reporting that Sadat's decision to terminate the Soviet–Egyptian Friendship Treaty had been taken under US pressure and was part of his strategy to solicit American investment and turn Egypt into a conduit for US influence in the oil-producing countries of the Middle East.[48]

The public celebration of Soviet–Syrian amity suffered a serious setback in June 1976 when Syria intervened in the Lebanese civil war in favour of the Maronite Christians against their PLO and left-wing opponents, with some of whom the KGB had close contacts. The left-wing leader, Kamal Jumblatt, was one of only a handful of Arabs to have been awarded the Lenin Peace Prize. Talks in Moscow in July between Khaddam, the Syrian Foreign Minister, and his Soviet counterpart, Gromyko, ended in such disarray that no joint communiqué was issued. *Pravda* declared that Syria was plunging 'a knife into the back' of the Palestinian movement.[49] Asad would have been further outraged had he known that the KGB residency in Damascus was secretly providing funds to support the Lebanese Communist Party which opposed Syrian intervention. On 26 July a KGB Buick Apollo motor car with diplomatic number plates set out from Damascus to the Lebanese border ostensibly to collect correspondence and foodstuffs sent by the Soviet embassy in Beirut. In reality it was carrying $50,000 concealed between a tyrewall and inner tube for transmission to the Lebanese Communist Party.[50] Two months later a further $100,000 was handed over.[51]

The main practical effect of the Soviet–Syrian quarrel during the second half of 1976 was an apparently drastic cutback in Soviet arms supplies. Asad retaliated by refusing an invitation to visit Moscow and by expelling about half the Soviet military advisers (then more numerous in Syria than anywhere else in the world). In January 1977 he instructed the Soviet navy to remove its submarines and support craft from the port of Tartus. Over the next few months, however, the winding down of Syrian involvement in the Lebanese civil war made possible the mending of the rift with Moscow. After the assassination of Kamal Jumblatt in March 1977, his son and successor Walid called on Asad at the end of the forty-day period of mourning – despite widespread and apparently well-founded suspicions that Asad had ordered his father's death. In April Asad decided to mend his fences with the Soviet Union and flew to Moscow where he was greeted personally at the airport by Brezhnev. At a banquet in the Kremlin, Asad declared that Soviet–Syrian relations had 'overcome all the difficulties in their way': 'We have always been convinced that the relations between our two countries are based on identity of principled outlook and on friendship and common interests . . .' During 1977 Soviet arms exports to Syria totalled $825 million. In the following year they exceeded $1 billion for the first time.[52]

Asad's extreme hostility to both Sadat's visit to Jerusalem in November 1977 (a day of national mourning in Syria) and the Camp David Agreement of September 1978[53] reinforced his desire for Soviet support, and even produced a short-lived reconciliation between Syria and Iraq. Asad later admitted that, when Sadat visited him in Damascus shortly before his visit to Jerusalem, he thought briefly of locking him up to prevent him going to Israel.[54] KGB files reveal that in December 1977 Asad authorized a secret meeting in Damascus between his intelligence chiefs and the Popular Front for the Liberation of Palestine (PFLP) which discussed plans for assassinating Sadat.[55]

In the later 1970s, Moscow once again made the mistake of trying to force the pace in strengthening its alliance with Asad. In an obvious reference to renewed Soviet proposals for a Treaty of Friendship and Co-operation, Brezhnev told him during a Moscow banquet in his honour in October 1978 that the Soviet Union was prepared to expand co-operation with Syria still further, 'particularly in the field of politics'. A month later, during a visit to Moscow by the Chief of the Syrian General Staff, General Hikmat Shihabi, there was an attempt to pressure him to conclude a trilateral pact with the Soviet Union and Iraq. He was also told that, to avoid the risk of exposing further Syrian MiG-27s to Israeli surprise attack, they would be better stationed in Iraq. Shihabi took deep offence and returned home two days ahead of schedule. Soon afterwards the Syrian ambassador in Moscow was recalled to Damascus.[56]

Once again, however, the rift was mended, due chiefly to the common Soviet and Syrian opposition to both Camp David and Israeli support for the Maronite Phalangists in southern Lebanon. Encouraged by KGB active measures[57] which played on his own penchant for conspiracy theory, Asad saw the Camp David agreements as part of a gigantic US–Israeli conspiracy. In March 1980

Asad publicly accused the CIA of encouraging 'sabotage and subversion' in Syria in order to bring 'the entire Arab world under joint US–Israeli domination'.[58] Asad repeatedly claimed and almost certainly believed that a central part of the plan for the subjection of 'the entire Arab world' was a secret Zionist conspiracy, with American support, to create a greater Israel. His close friend and Defence Minister, Mustafa Talas, later claimed absurdly that, 'Had it not been for Hafiz al-Asad, Greater Israel would have been established from the Nile to the Euphrates.'[59]

During 1979 Moscow supplied more MiG-27s and other advanced weaponry, as well as writing off 25 per cent of Syria's estimated $2 billion military debt. After the Soviet invasion of Afghanistan in December, Asad was one of the very few leaders outside the Soviet bloc not to join the world-wide chorus of condemnation. His Foreign Minister, Khaddam, told an interviewer: 'We have studied the situation and have come to the conclusion that the fuss about Afghanistan is meaningless theatrics, designed to reshuffle the cards in the Arab region, to end Sadat's isolation, and to assist in bringing success to the Camp David agreements.'

In January 1980, in a further attempt to please Moscow, Asad included two members of the Bakdash faction of the Syrian Communist Party in his new government. He also allowed the exiled leader of the Iraqi Communist Party, Aziz Muhammad,[60] to base himself in Syria. In October, Asad finally agreed to sign a twenty-year Treaty of Friendship and Co-operation with the Soviet Union. During 1980 Syrian arms imports from the Soviet bloc exceeded $3 billion.[61]

While reinforcing its alliance with Asad, Moscow secretly strengthened its covert relationship with Bakdash. In 1978 Bakdash had assured one of his KGB contacts that, while he remained Party leader, 'there would never be a Carrillo or even a Marchais' – in other words, that the Party would remain uncompromisingly loyal to Moscow and ideologically orthodox.[62] He told the Party Congress in 1980: 'I firmly believe that it is not enough [merely] to declare friendship for the Soviet Union. Rather, we must support every action in Soviet foreign policy which has always been, still is, and always will be in harmony with the interests of all people.'[63]

Bakdash also benefited from the support of Asad. Immediately after the signature of the Friendship Treaty in October 1980, Asad began a campaign of intimidation and terror against a Communist breakaway group, led by Bakdash's opponent, Riyadh al-Turk. Most of al-Turk's supporters were jailed, forced to leave the Party, driven underground or went into exile. Some were tortured. According to reports by Amnesty International and human rights groups during the 1980s, al-Turk was systematically tortured throughout the decade, and was rushed to hospital at least six times on the verge of death to be resuscitated for further abuse, which included breaking bones in all his limbs.[64]

During 1978 108 Syrian Communists went on training courses (doubtless at Soviet expense) in the Soviet Union. The KGB noted that most were the friends or relatives of Party leaders.[65] During 1979 the KGB Damascus residency made five payments to the Party leadership totalling $275,000.[66] Bakdash informed the residency that over $50,000 had been spent on setting up an underground printing press and requested an additional allocation.[67] Payments in 1980 amounted to at least $329,000 and were probably higher.[68] Far more substantial sums, however, were paid to the Party as a result of lucrative Soviet contracts with trading companies controlled by the Party. In 1982, for example, the Damascus residency reported that one of the companies set up with Party funds would contribute during the year 1,200,000 Syrian pounds to the Party.[69] At Bakdash's personal request, the Damascus residency also secretly supplied the Party with arms: 150 Makarov pistols and ammunition were handed over in June 1980. As a security precaution, in case the arms were subsequently discovered, they were wrapped in Syrian packaging obtained by the KGB on the black market.[70] A further consignment of seventy-five Makarov pistols with ammunition was handed over in March 1981. Bakdash thanked the KGB for 'their fraternal assistance and constant concern for the needs of the Syrian Communist Party'.[71] At a meeting in a safe apartment a year later with two operations officers from the Damascus residency, Bakdash enumerated one by one the residents with whom he had established close and friendly collaboration over the quarter of a century since he had returned from exile. He ended by eulogizing the KGB: 'You are the only Soviet authority with which we have always enjoyed, and still enjoy, full mutual understanding on the most varied issues. Please convey to Comrade Andropov the profound gratitude of our Party.'[72]

The KGB, however, was increasingly concerned by the growing

divisions within the Syrian Communist Party. Late in 1982 Nikolai Fyodorovich Vetrov of the Damascus residency had a series of meetings with Bakdash, then seventy years old, who had been Party leader for half a century. Bakdash complained that 'not all Party members were totally dedicated to the Marxist-Leninist cause', and that his age and poor health made it increasingly difficult for him to keep full control over all Party activities. Bakdash was also becoming increasingly suspicious of his associate FARID. He told Vetrov that, though a good Party official, FARID 'had been unable to break finally with the petit-bourgeois environment from which he came'. Bakdash's real objection to FARID, however, was fear that he was plotting against him. He told Vetrov that, as well as 'promoting people who were personally loyal to him', FARID had become corrupt, borrowing 50,000 Syrian pounds (which he had not repaid) to buy a house in Damascus from a businessman who had made a fortune from Soviet contracts but had ceased to support the Party.[73] By the mid-1980s, however, Bakdash caused the Centre greater concern than FARID. For all his past protestations of Soviet loyalism, Bakdash was unable to adapt to the new era of *glasnost* and *perestroika*. As the Soviet Union fell apart, Bakdash defended Stalin and denounced Gorbachev.[74]

Israel's invasion of Lebanon in June 1982 in an unsuccessful attempt to destroy the PLO and strengthen its Maronite allies caused a new crisis in Syrian–Soviet relations. From 9 to 11 June Israel and Syria fought one of the largest air battles of the twentieth century over the Biqa' valley. The Israeli air force destroyed all Syria's SAM-6 missile sites on both sides of the Syrian–Lebanese border and shot down twenty-three Syrian MiGs without losing a single aircraft.[75] When further SAM sites were installed in the course of the summer the Israelis demolished those too. Behind the scenes the Syrians blamed their defeat on the shortcomings of Soviet equipment, while the Russians blamed Syrian incompetence in using it. Both sides, however, needed each other. 'Asad needed arms', writes Patrick Seale, 'while the Russians needed to restore the reputation of their high-performance weapons as well as their overall political position in the Arab world.' Asad's visit to Moscow for Brezhnev's funeral in November 1982 provided an opportunity to mend fences with the new Soviet leader, Yuri Andropov. Despite opposition from both Gromyko and Ustinov, the Defence Minister, Andropov agreed to provide Syria with advanced weapons systems which were supplied to no other Third World country, some of them operated by Soviet personnel.[76]

The memoirs of Vadim Kirpichenko, one of the Centre's leading Middle Eastern experts, contain a curiously fulsome tribute to Asad. During two meetings and five hours of discussions on security and intelligence matters, in the course of which Asad asked many detailed questions about the structure and functions of the KGB,[77] Kirpichenko claims to have found him 'a good-natured, mild, proper and attentive person. No neurosis whatsoever, no haste, no posing whatsoever.' Asad strongly reminded Kirpichenko of the legendary KGB officer Ivan Ivanovich Agayants, who had been wartime resident in Tehran and post-war resident in Paris: 'Old intelligence hands still remember this good-natured and wise man.' (Kirpichenko does not mention that Agayants was a specialist in deception, also a strong interest of Asad's.)[78]

Kirpichenko's rose-tinted recollections give some sense of the cosmetically enhanced view of Asad's Syria passed on to the Soviet leadership at the time of the conclusion of the Treaty of Friendship and Co-operation. In reality, Asad was, by any standards, an unattractive ally. The signing of the treaty coincided with the beginning of the most homicidal period of Asad's rule. During the early 1980s his regime killed at least 10,000 of its own citizens and jailed thousands more in usually atrocious conditions. Most of the Sunni stronghold of Hama, Syria's most beautiful city and a centre of opposition to the 'Alawi regime, was destroyed, its magnificent Great Mosque reduced to rubble. Many Lebanese from Syrian-controlled areas of Lebanon disappeared into Syrian prisons never to re-emerge.[79] Like Saddam Hussein and Muammar al-Qaddafi, Asad also used his intelligence agencies to hunt down his enemies abroad. As well as becoming notorious for providing safe haven for some of the Middle East's most ruthless terrorists, his regime also failed to cover its tracks when carrying out its own terrorist operations against émigré dissidents and other Arab critics. Early in 1981 a Syrian hit squad, operating on the orders of Asad's brother Rif'at, whom the KGB had once claimed to be able to influence,[80] entered Jordan with instructions to assassinate the Jordanian Prime Minister, Mudar Badran, whom Asad had publicly condemned for being in league with Americans, Zionists and Syrian dissidents. The entire group was caught and made a humiliating three-hour public confession on Jordanian television, which could be seen by many Syrian viewers. Despite this embarrassment, Rif'at declared publicly that 'enemies' who had fled abroad would be dealt with. In March 1982 there were reports in the British press, based on briefings by 'Western diplomatic sources in Damascus', that six well-armed 'hit squads' had been despatched to Europe to assassinate dissidents. One such three-man squad arrested in Stuttgart, Germany, was found to be carrying sub-machine guns and explosives. A month later a bomb attack on the Paris offices of an Arab newspaper well known for its hostility to the Asad regime killed a pregnant woman passing by and injured sixty-three others, twelve seriously. The French government, which made little secret of its belief that the Asad regime was responsible, promptly expelled two Syrian 'diplomats' for 'unacceptable activities'.[81] It is highly unlikely that Brezhnev's final years were disturbed by reports of such embarrassing bad behaviour by a regime with which he had just signed, after years of persuasion, a Friendship Treaty.

Unattractive though Syria had become as an ally, all other Soviet options for alliance with a major Middle Eastern power had disappeared. Syria's attempt over the next few years to achieve strategic parity with Israel made it more dependent than ever before on advanced Soviet weaponry, among them fighter planes, surface-to-air and surface-to-surface missiles, and electronic and air-control battle systems. General Dmitri Volkogonov, then of the GRU, later recalled: 'No country ever had as many Russian-speaking advisers as Syria . . . Everyone lived in a state of half-war, half-peace. The Soviet Union and its ideology were not wanted by anyone there, but its tanks, guns and technicians were highly valued.'[82]

By the end of 1985 the Syrian economy was collapsing under the weight of a military budget which accounted for half the gross national product. With Gorbachev unwilling to bail him out, Asad reluctantly accepted in 1986 that strategic parity with Israel was beyond Syria's reach. The British ambassador in Damascus, Sir Roger Tomkys, found Asad brutally realistic about the changed balance of power in the Middle East. 'If I were Prime Minister of Israel,' Asad told him, 'with its present military superiority and the support of the world's number one power, I would not make a single concession.'[83]

During the later 1980s, Moscow rejected most Syrian requests for advanced weaponry. Asad none the less regarded the disintegration of the Soviet bloc and the Soviet Union as a disaster. Despite all his disputes with Moscow over the previous two decades, he had come to regard the Soviet alliance as essential to Syria's security. A senior Damascus official said mournfully as power in the Kremlin passed from Gorbachev to Yeltsin at the end of 1991, 'We regret the Soviet collapse more than the Russians do.'[84]

11

The People's Democratic Republic of Yemen

The Soviet Union's closest ideological ally in the Arab world was the People's Democratic Republic of [South] Yemen (PDRY), founded in 1970, three years after gaining independence from Britain. As in Cuba, the ruling National Liberation Front (NLF) gained power as the result of a guerrilla campaign and thereafter declared itself a Marxist-Leninist party. As the Soviet presence in the Indian Ocean expanded during the 1970s, the Soviet fleet also made increasing use of port facilities at Aden and Socotra Island.[1] According to the Soviet ambassador to the PDRY, O. G. Peresypkin:

We proceeded from the assumption that scientific socialism was a universal theory and we wanted to prove that a small underdeveloped Arab country, a former British colony, would advance with seven-league strides towards the bright future provided it was armed with the slogans of scientific socialism.

The slogans failed. The Soviet advisers seconded to Yemeni ministries imbued them with the cumbersome inefficiency of the command economy in which they had been trained. Aleksandr Vassiliev, one of the Soviet officials who visited the PDRY, noted later: 'When I visited Aden before collectivization . . . the Aden market and all the waterfronts were full of fish and fish products. When the fishermen were subjected to [collectivization], the fish immediately disappeared.' In retrospect, Peresypkin was 'inclined to forgive the South Yemeni leaders who brought their country to deadlock. They were simply following blindly along behind their "elder brothers" who had "built socialism" . . .'[2]

Despite its early hopes of turning the PDRY into an Arab beacon of 'scientific socialism', Moscow found South Yemen an almost constant headache. One of the main tasks of the Aden residency was to monitor the nearly continuous intrigues and power struggles which rent the NLF and its successor (from October 1978), the Yemeni Socialist Party (YSP). It could do little to control them. From 1969 to 1978 there was a prolonged power struggle between 'Abd al-Fattah Isma'il, the staunchly pro-Soviet leader of the NLF, and Salim Rubai' Ali, the more pro-Chinese head of state. In June 1978, with Soviet and Cuban assistance, Isma'il led a successful coup against Rubai' Ali, who was executed on charges of plotting an armed coup of his own with the support of the West and Saudi Arabia.[3]

The main supporters of the PDRY within the Centre during the mid-1970s were Nikolai Leonov and Service 1 (Intelligence Analysis). In 1975 Leonov submitted a report to Andropov arguing that the Soviet Union was getting a poor return for its vast investment in the Middle East. Egypt, Syria and Iraq had no intention of paying their huge debts. Egypt had ceased to be a reliable ally, the Iraqi connection was insecure and Syria was then unwilling to commit itself to a Friendship Treaty. Service 1 therefore proposed concentrating on the PDRY, which did not require large amounts of aid. Its regime was 'the most Marxist-Leninist', Aden was of major strategic significance, and its oil distillery could meet the needs of both the Soviet navy and the air force. The report cited the way in which the British Empire had used Aden as one of the key points in its global strategy. The PDRY was also well away from the main Middle Eastern conflict zones. Its only – achievable – strategic need was to make peace with North Yemen. Service 1's revival of the idea of turning the PDRY into an Arab beacon of 'scientific socialism' found little favour with Andropov. After keeping the report for several days, he returned it with a request for it to be shortened. Then he returned the shortened version asking for all the proposals to be deleted, leaving only the information it contained on the current position in the PDRY. In Leonov's view, all that was of interest in the original document had now been removed from it. He had no doubt that Andropov's demands for cuts derived from his personal discussions of its proposals with Politburo members who disliked the idea of increasing contact with a regime cursed with apparently ineradicable internecine warfare.[4]

From 1972 onwards, however, the Centre maintained close links with the PDRY intelligence service, which proudly called its officers 'Chekists' in honour of its Soviet allies.[5] On 12 May 1972 Andropov had a meeting in Moscow with the Yemeni Interior Minister, Muhammad Salih Mutiya, during which the KGB agreed to provide free training for PDRY intelligence officers and cipher personnel. The fact that Mutiya also accepted an offer of free Soviet ciphers presumably enabled the FCD Sixteenth Directorate to decrypt PDRY intelligence radio traffic.[6] From July 1973 a KGB liaison officer was stationed in Aden (in addition to the undeclared staff of the Aden residency). In May 1974 the KGB and PDRY intelligence agency signed a secret agreement on collaboration in intelligence operations against the United States, United Kingdom and Saudi Arabia. As part of the agreement the PDRY was supplied with 'special equipment', probably for use in bugging and surveillance operations. In 1976 the two agencies collaborated in operation KHAMSIN to bug the Saudi Arabian embassy in Aden.[7]

Just as the Politburo disliked dealing with the divided Yemeni regime, however, so the KGB despised some of its PDRY intelligence allies. A prime example was a senior Yemeni intelligence officer codenamed AREF,[8] who was given a free holiday in 1978 at the Dubovaya Roscha Sanatorium at Zheleznovodsk, where he was diagnosed as suffering from cardiac insufficiency, diabetes, insomnia, nervous and physical exhaustion, as well as from excessive alcohol consumption. These ailments were not AREF's main concern. His first priorities were treatment for incipient baldness and plastic surgery to improve his appearance. His Soviet doctor concluded that many of his problems stemmed from obsessive masturbation and a 'passive' homosexual relationship with a senior Yemeni minister which had produced nervous and sexual debility. AREF, however, turned out to be bisexual and pestered his interpreter, V. Konavalov, a KGB operations officer, to persuade a woman he had met at the clinic to have sexual relations with him. When Konavalov refused, saying that his duties were limited to providing translation and arranging medical treatment, AREF replied, 'Comrade "Aleksandrov" [Kryuchkov, the head of the FCD] paid for the tickets, gave me a free pass to the Sanatorium, and I am convinced that he would not object to my having women.' When Konavalov still refused, AREF accused him of being a racist. Konavalov also reported that, though AREF had brought with him some of the works of Marx and Lenin, he did not read them and used them only for display purposes.[9]

In Kirpichenko's view, the PDRY 'Chekists' also became increasingly demanding:

[They] were often aggressive in their conduct of negotiations, especially when they needed to hammer out various kinds of material-technological assistance from us. 'Since we're in the same boat (the beloved argument of our Arab allies), then you must help us.' We provided, of course, the minimum, mostly operational technology, and taught the Yemeni free of charge at our short courses . . . But the South Yemen partners sometimes demonstrated immoderate appetites. In the final years they insistently asked us to build them a Ministry for State Security building in Aden, buildings for security services in all the provincial centres and even a prison.[10]

The KGB's main concern, however, was the [North] Yemen Arab Republic (YAR) rather than the PDRY.[11] In July 1972 the YAR became the first member of the Arab League to resume the diplomatic relations with the United States which had been broken off after the Six-Day War five years earlier. Moscow's anxieties increased when a military regime headed by the pro-Saudi Lieutenant Colonel Ibrahim al-Hamdi took power in June 1974 and sought arms from the United States, paid for by the oil-rich Saudis. Al-Hamdi was dissatisfied with the American response. As the US military attaché in the YAR capital, Sana'a, reported to Washington, Saudi Arabia wanted a North Yemen that was 'strong enough but not too strong'. The United States, in turn, was anxious not to offend its main ally in the region, Saudi Arabia, by meeting all al-Hamdi's requests for military assistance.[12] The relationship of the al-Hamdi regime with Washington and Riyadh thus never became as close as the Centre feared. The KGB none the less embarked on a prolonged active-measures campaign designed to discredit the three men it saw as the main pro-American and pro-Saudi influences within the YAR government: 'Abd Allah al-Asnadji, Minister of Foreign Affairs, M. Khamis, Minister of Internal Affairs and Chief of the Central National Security Directorate, and Muhammad Salim Basindawa, Minister of Culture and Information. In 1976 the KGB sent an anonymous letter to al-Hamdi, accusing Khamis of being a CIA agent and enclosing a forged document acknowledging his receipt of American money. Khamis, however, succeeded in persuading al-Hamdi that the receipt was a forgery, though – according to KGB files – he blamed the forgery on the Saudis or rebellious sheikhs rather than on the KGB.[13]

On 12 October 1977 al-Hamdi was assassinated in circumstances which still remain obscure.[14] KGB active measures sought to persuade his successor, Ahmad al-Gashmi, that Khamis was responsible for al-Hamdi's assassination. Soviet agents informed al-Gashmi that Khamis was also plotting his overthrow and conspiring to seize power himself.[15] On 24 June 1978 al-Gashmi was assassinated, though not by Khamis. The previous day President Salim Rubai' Ali of the PDRY had telephoned al-Gashmi to tell him he was despatching a special envoy to meet him in Sana'a on the following day. When the envoy arrived in al-Gashmi's office he opened a briefcase which exploded, killing both men. Two days later Salim Rubai' Ali was executed in Aden, ostensibly for organizing the assassination of al-Gashmi and plotting a coup in the PDRY with the support of the West and Saudi Arabia. Rubai' Ali's supporters later claimed that the explosive had been put in the briefcase on orders from his pro-Soviet rival, 'Abd al-Fattah Isma'il, who later in the year succeeded him as President.[16] Moscow immediately began a propaganda offensive in support of Isma'il, denouncing an alleged Saudi and American threat to the PDRY and flying in Cuban troops from Ethiopia to support the new regime while Soviet warships patrolled the Gulf of Aden.[17]

Al-Gashmi's successor as President of the YAR, Ali Abdullah Salih, survived an assassination attempt a few days after taking power.[18] One of the objectives of Soviet policy was to exploit President Salih's discontent with what he considered was the inadequate level of US arms supplies to the YAR. In November 1978 and January 1979, Salih held well-publicized talks with the Soviet ambassador on 'ways to strengthen relations' – including the supply of Soviet arms.[19] Soviet attempts to cultivate Salih, however, were complicated by an attack on the YAR in late February 1979 by the PDRY, which for some time had cast envious eyes over its wealthier and more populous neighbour. A leading South Yemeni Communist told the Soviet ambassador, doubtless to Moscow's displeasure, 'Yes, it's us who've started the war. If we win, we'll create Great Yemen. If we lose, you'll intervene and save us.'[20] The war, however, ended bizarrely on 27 March with a meeting in Kuwait between Presidents Salih and Isma'il which concluded with a hopelessly optimistic agreement to produce within four months a draft constitution for the unification of North and South Yemen.[21] (Unification did not actually occur until 1990.)

Immediately after his meeting with Isma'il, Salih announced the dismissal of his Foreign Minister, al-Asnadji, and the Minister of Culture and Information, Basindawa. The Centre claimed the credit for both dismissals, which – it reported – had been strongly opposed by Saudi Arabia. Ever since Salih had become President, the KGB had been using its agents and confidential contacts to feed him disinformation that a pro-Saudi group, led by al-Asnadji and including Basindawa, had been plotting his overthrow with Saudi and American support and planning his assassination.[22] The KGB's victory, however, was far from complete. Despite his dismissal as Foreign Minister, al-Asnadji remained one of Salih's chief political advisers. In June 1979 al-Asnadji visited Washington to appeal for 'a more direct US military role in the Arabian Peninsula and Gulf Region' and the despatch of senior US military advisers to train YAR armed forces.[23]

In April 1980 Soviet policy in Yemen suffered another setback when a coup in the PDRY overthrew its staunch ally, President Isma'il. Among the causes of the coup was dissatisfaction with the amount of Soviet aid – far smaller than that given to other ideological allies in the Third World. Power cuts in Aden were blamed by Yemenis on the Soviet failure to complete the construction of a promised power station. Unlike his immediate predecessor, Isma'il survived his overthrow. Probably due to the intervention of the Soviet ambassador, he was allowed to go into exile in Moscow instead of being executed or imprisoned as his main opponents had intended. The Soviet Union was quick to mend its fences with the new regime in the PDRY, inviting Isma'il's successor, Ali Nasir Muhammad, on a state visit to Moscow only a month after the coup. The visit led to a new agreement on Soviet economic aid (including construction of the promised power station) and a joint communiqué condemning US policy in the Middle East and supporting the pro-Soviet regime in Afghanistan.[24]

In September 1980 the KGB obtained from agents in the YAR intelligence services a copy of a tape recording of a confidential discussion between Presidents Salih and Muhammad which had been made without their knowledge on Khamis's instructions. The tape was then handed to Salih as evidence of Khamis's treachery. Attempts were also made to persuade Salih that Khamis had links with the CIA. Khamis was dismissed in October and, according to KGB files, 'physically eliminated' in January 1981. The KGB also passed reports to Salih alleging that al-Asnadji was having an affair with a woman in the US Peace Corps, had $30 million in a London bank account and also owned a hotel and three houses in the London suburbs. In March 1981 al-Asnadji and some of his supporters were arrested on charges of preparing a coup. Salih seems to have been influenced by KGB active measures suggesting that the plotters had conspired with the CIA. He told his advisory council on 21 March that 'if an improper role on the part of the Americans in organizing the conspiracy is confirmed, then questions will be raised about the American presence in Northern Yemen'. The KGB also claimed the credit for persuading Salih to order the expulsion of an American military adviser on a charge of espionage.[25]

The KGB's tactical successes in the YAR, however, had little strategic significance. From 1982 onwards the discovery of oil fields in North Yemen led to a series of concessions to US companies. In April 1986 President Salih and Vice-President George Bush attended the ceremonial opening of the YAR's first oil refinery. Collaboration in oil production, Bush declared, meant greater US 'partnership with the Yemeni people'.[26] The PDRY, meanwhile, was in turmoil. On 13 January 1986 several of President Muhammad's opponents were machine-gunned in the Politburo meeting room. The Aden residency appears to have given no advance warning of the renewed bloodshed. In the fortnight's civil war which followed thousands of YSP members, militia and armed forces were killed. The cost of the damage done to buildings and the economic infrastructure in Aden was estimated at $140 million. Muhammad lost power and was forced to flee with some thousands of his supporters to the YAR.[27] The Soviet Commander-in-Chief Ground Forces, General Yevgeni Ivanovsky, who was despatched to Aden on a 'peacemaking' mission, reported that about one third of the Yemeni officers killed in the fighting had been trained at Soviet military academies.[28] A few weeks later, representatives of the YSP attended the Twenty-seventh Congress of the Soviet Communist Party in Moscow. Fidel Castro is said to have put to the Yemeni delegation a question which summed up much of the frustration of Soviet policy to the PDRY over the previous quarter of a century. 'When', he reportedly asked, 'are you people going to stop killing each other?'[29]

In May 1990, after prolonged negotiations, the PDRY and YAR finally merged as the Republic of Yemen, whose 16 million inhabitants accounted for more than half the population of the Arabian peninsula. In April 1994 the more powerful Northern leadership launched an attack on the South which brought the whole of a still-unstable country under Northern control.

12

Israel and Zionism

'Zionist subversion' was one of the KGB's most enduring conspiracy theories. The Stalinist era bequeathed to the KGB a tradition of anti-semitism masquerading as anti-Zionism still clearly visible even in the mid-1980s. In 1948, however, the Soviet Union had been the first to recognize the state of Israel, seeing its creation as a blow to British imperialism in the Middle East inflicted by 'progressive' Jews of Russian and Polish origin. Moscow also counted on Zionist gratitude for the leading role of the Red Army in defeating Hitler. The arms supplied to the Zionists from Czechoslovakia with Moscow's blessing during the first Arab–Israeli War (known to Israelis as the War of Independence and to Arabs as *al-Nakbah*, 'the Disaster'), as well as Soviet diplomatic support, were of crucial importance to the birth of Israel. Within the new state the left-wing Mapam (United Workers) Party described itself on its foundation in 1948 as 'an inseparable part of the world revolutionary camp headed by the USSR'. Dr Moshe Sneh, member of the Mapam executive committee and head of the Israeli League for Friendly Relations with the USSR, said in his speech of welcome on the arrival of the Soviet legation in Tel Aviv:

Our people love the Soviet Union and trust the Soviet Union, which has supported us and never let us down. For our part, we swear that we shall never let the Soviet Union down, and shall devote all our energies to strengthening the friendship and unbreakable alliance with our great friend and the defender of mankind – the Soviet Union.[1]

Late in 1947 Andrei Mikhailovich Otroshchenko, head of the Middle and Far Eastern Department of the Committee of Information (KI), which then ran foreign intelligence, called an operational conference to announce that Stalin had given the KI the task of ensuring that Israel became an ally of the Soviet Union. To counter American attempts to exploit Israeli links with the Jewish community in the United States, the KI was to ensure that large numbers of its agents were included in the ranks of the Soviet Jews allowed to leave for Israel. The head of the Illegals Directorate in the KI (and later in the FCD), Aleksandr Mikhailovich 'Sasha' Korotkov, who had a Jewish wife, was put in charge of the selection of agents. His chief assistant, Vladimir Vertiporokh, was appointed as the first resident in Israel in 1948 under diplomatic cover with the alias 'Rozhkov'. Vertiporokh told one of his colleagues that he was anxious about his new posting – partly because he disliked the 'crafty Jews', partly because he doubted whether he could fulfil the mission entrusted to the KI by Stalin of turning Israel into a Soviet ally: 'The work the residency will have to do is so serious and important that, quite simply, I am afraid of not being able to cope with it, and you know what that would mean.'[2]

Probably the most successful of the first generation of Soviet agents infiltrated into Israel was the epidemiologist Avraham Marcus Klingberg, who, at the age of thirty, was recruited by Israel's first Prime Minister in April 1948 to work on chemical and biological weapons. Klingberg was later one of the founders and deputy director of the Israel Institute of Biological Research in Ness Ziona, south-east of Tel Aviv. He continued to work for Soviet and East German intelligence for the remarkable period of thirty-five years.[3] Soviet-bloc intelligence services co-operated with the KI in the agent penetration of the new state of Israel; thirty-six of the Jews who left Bulgaria for Israel in the period 1947–50, for example, were Bulgarian agents. Though Mitrokhin's notes on KGB files give very little detail on their activities, it is clear that they achieved at least a few significant successes. KHAIMOV, for example, obtained a job in the secretariat of Israel's first President, Chaim Weizmann.[4] Contact with another Bulgarian agent, PERETS, whose role is not recorded, continued until 1975.[5]

Satisfaction in the Centre at the early successes of agent penetration in Israel, however, was overshadowed by alarm at the enthusiasm of Soviet Jews for the new state and at the evidence of Israel's growing links with the United States. Within a year of Israel's foundation, there had been a volte-face in Soviet policy. Henceforth, Zionism was officially condemned as part of an imperialist plot to subvert the Soviet Union. Much of Vertiporokh's work as resident in Tel Aviv appears to have been taken up by the pursuit of anti-Zionist conspiracy theories rather than by conventional intelligence collection. In 1949 he had three lengthy meetings with Yitzhak Rabinovich, formerly a member of the Jewish Agency's Soviet Liaison Committee, to discuss in detail the nature of Zionism. A year later Rabinovich produced, at Vertiporokh's request, a fifty-page summary of the main points covered in their conversations.[6]

During the final years of Stalinist rule the anti-semitic campaign against imaginary Zionist conspiracies in Russia spread throughout the Soviet bloc. In Czechoslovakia the trial in 1952 of the 'Leadership of the Anti-State Conspiratorial Centre', led by a former Party leader, Rudolf Slánský, identified eleven of the fourteen defendants, including Slánský himself, as 'of Jewish origin'. The simultaneous purge of Jews from the Soviet nomenklatura was nowhere more energetically pursued than at the Centre. By early 1953 all had been removed from the MGB (predecessor of the KGB), save for a small number of 'hidden Jews': people of partly Jewish origin who were registered as members of other ethnic groups. In the winter of 1952–53 the MGB crushed a non-existent 'Jewish doctors' plot' to murder Stalin and the Soviet leadership, denouncing a group of innocent doctors as 'monsters and murderers' working for a 'corrupt Jewish bourgeois nationalist organization' in the service of Anglo-American intelligence. Following the fabrication of the doctors' plot, the Tel Aviv legation complained that 'anti-Soviet hysteria' had reached unprecedented heights. Since the legation could not admit the reality of Soviet anti-semitism, it absurdly blamed the 'hysteria' on the Israeli government's desire both to convince the United States that it could count on Israeli support for its 'aggressive plans' and 'continue to use Israel as a centre of espionage in the countries of the socialist camp', and 'to divert the attention of the Israeli population from the economic difficulties' at home.[7]

Though the level of anti-Zionist and anti-semitic paranoia in the Centre dropped sharply after Stalin's death in March 1953, it did not disappear. None of the Jews sacked from the MGB at the height of the anti-semitic witch-hunt was reinstated. Over forty years later, at the beginning of the Gorbachev era, Jews were still excluded (along with a number of other minorities) from the KGB. The only exceptions were a handful of recruits with Jewish mothers and non-Jewish fathers, registered as members of other ethnic groups. Even the Central Committee was less rigid than the KGB about rejecting applicants of Jewish origin.

Despite the anti-semitic paranoia of Stalin's final years, the Israeli security service, Shin Bet, suspected that Mapam was passing classified material to the Soviet Union and placed a bugging device with a battery-operated radio transmitter beneath the desk of the Party's general secretary. In January 1953 two Shin Bet officers were caught red-handed breaking into the Mapam headquarters to change the radio batteries.[8] Shin Bet's suspicions were, however, fully justified. The files of the Soviet Foreign Ministry show that two leading Mapam politicians in the Knesset were providing the Soviet embassy with classified material. Yaakov Riftin, who served on the Knesset Foreign Affairs and Security Committee and was described by Prime Minister David Ben-Gurion as 'a preacher from the Cominform', regularly supplied the embassy with Committee documents, including those from sessions held *in camera*. Moshe Sneh provided a probably smaller amount of intelligence on Israeli foreign policy. The material furnished by Riftin and Sneh served to reinforce Soviet suspicion of Israel's special relationship with the United States. In August 1952, for example, the Tel Aviv legation reported to Moscow that, according to Sneh, Foreign Minister Moshe Sharett had declared 'that Israel's situation was such that it must follow the US without any preliminary conditions or reservations'.[9]

By the mid-1950s, if not earlier, the KGB had an agent group inside Mapam, codenamed TREST (one of the most prestigious codenames in KGB history, originally used in the 1920s for a highly successful deception operation against White Russian émigrés and Western intelligence services[10]). In 1956 a courier codenamed BOKER was recruited to maintain contact with the group. The fact that he had three successive controllers over the years which followed indicates that the operation was considered of some importance.[11] Though Mitrokhin's notes do not identify the members of the agent group, they probably included Aharon Cohen, Mapam's main expert on Arab affairs. Cohen's contacts with the Tel Aviv residency were discovered after a car with diplomatic number plates, registered in the name of a known KGB operations officer, Viktor Sokolov, was spotted by a policeman outside the main gate of Cohen's kibbutz near Haifa in April 1958. Shin Bet surveillance of further meetings between Cohen and KGB officers led to his arrest. Though Cohen claimed that his dealings with the Russians were limited to academic discussions, he was sentenced to five years in jail for unauthorized contacts with a foreign agent; he was released after serving seventeen months. Isser Harel, the head of Israel's foreign intelligence service, Mossad, declared dramatically that Mapam had been 'born with a malignant growth in its belly – the Soviet Dybbuk [evil spirit]'.[12]

Mossad itself, however, suffered one serious Soviet penetration in the mid-1950s. Potentially the most important KGB agent during Israel's first decade was Ze'ev Avni, born Wolf Goldstein, a multilingual economist and ardent Communist who had spent the Second World War in Switzerland where in 1943 he had been recruited by the GRU. Avni was a committed ideological agent. 'There was no doubt in my mind', he wrote later, 'that I belonged not only to the vanguard of the revolution, but to its very élite.' In 1948 he emigrated to Israel, joined a kibbutz and contacted the Soviet embassy to try to renew his links with the GRU. He was disappointed to receive a lukewarm, non-committal welcome – possibly because of his lack of security at the kibbutz, where he had made no secret of his Communist convictions and told a senior Mapam member that he would be happy to help the Party establish 'a direct link to Moscow'. In 1950 Avni entered the Israeli Foreign Ministry, where he behaved with much greater discretion. A later security enquiry 'had no difficulty finding people who had known Avni as a militant Communist' at his kibbutz but found 'practically universal admiration' for him among his fellow diplomats, who were entirely unaware that his real loyalty was to the Soviet Union.

In 1952 Avni had his first foreign posting as Israeli commercial attaché in Brussels, where he was also appointed security officer and given the keys to the legation's only safe, in which classified documents were kept. Having successfully renewed contact with the GRU, he began photographing the contents of the safe. After his arrest four years later, he admitted to his interrogator, 'I gave them everything I had.' Remarkably, Avni's enthusiasm for the Soviet Union survived even the paranoia of the 'Jewish doctors' plot'. He later told his interrogator that Stalin had been a 'genius' and initially refused to believe that Khrushchev's 'Secret Speech' of 1956 denouncing Stalin was genuine.[13]

While in Brussels, Avni also began to be employed by Mossad, using his fluent German to pose as a German businessman and make contact with former Nazis. Late in 1953, Avni was offered both a full-time position in Mossad and the post of commercial attaché in Belgrade and Athens. It was agreed that during his next posting he would combine espionage for Mossad with work as commercial attaché, based chiefly in Belgrade, and thereafter move to a permanent position in Mossad. Once in Belgrade, Avni was assigned a new controller operating under diplomatic cover as first secretary at the Soviet embassy.[14] Though he believed himself still to be working for the GRU, he had – without his knowledge – been transferred to the KGB with the codename CHEKH. His KGB file identifies him, while in Belgrade, as acting head of Mossad operations in West Germany and Greece.[15] Among the operations which he personally conducted for Mossad, using his cover as a German businessman, was to penetrate the ranks of the former Wehrmacht officers employed by Gamal Abdel Nasser, after his 1954 coup, as military advisers in Egypt.[16] In 1955–56 Avni supplied the KGB residency in Belgrade with the ciphers used by Mossad for communications with its Belgrade and Athens stations (probably enabling them to be decrypted), as well as details of Mossad personnel (probably both officers and agents) in France, Germany, Greece, Italy, Switzerland and Yugoslavia.[17] As in Brussels, he gave his controller 'everything I had'.

Avni was caught early in 1956 and sentenced to fourteen years' imprisonment. When he finally came to terms with the fact that Khrushchev's 'Secret Speech' denouncing Stalin was not – as he initially believed – a fabrication, he lost the uncompromising Communist faith which had inspired him since the age of fifteen. His experience, he recalls, closely resembled that memorably described by Arthur Koestler: 'I went to Communism as one goes to a spring of fresh water, and I left Communism as one clambers out of a poisoned river strewn with the wreckage of flooded cities and the corpses of the drowned.'[18]

Probably at about the time of Avni's arrest, the KGB made initial contact with Yisrael Beer, Professor of Military History at Tel Aviv University as well as a well-known military commentator and lieutenant colonel in the Israeli Defence Force (IDF) reserves, who was subsequently recruited as a Soviet agent. Beer had arrived in Palestine from Austria on the eve of the Anschluss in 1938, claiming to have been a member of the Schutzbund, the paramilitary defence organization of the Austrian Social Democratic Party, and to have taken part in the 1934 Viennese workers' rising against the pro-Nazi Chancellor Engelbert Dolfuss. In 1936 the Party had, allegedly, sent him to fight in the International Brigades in the Spanish Civil War, where he had taken the pseudonym José Gregorio and risen to the rank of colonel, subsequently receiving further military training in Moscow at the Frunze Military Academy. Beer claimed that early in 1938 he had picked up by chance a biography of the founder of modern Zionism, Theodor Herzl: 'I read it the whole night without stopping, and in the morning I . . . decided to go to Palestine.' After his arrest in 1961, Beer's account of his early career turned out to be wholly fraudulent. He had never been a member of the Schutzbund, fought in the Spanish Civil War or enrolled at the Frunze Military Academy. In reality, before leaving for Palestine in 1938 he had been only a clerk in the Austrian Zionist Federation.[19] During Beer's interrogation by Shin Bet, the British embassy in Tel Aviv reported to London that there was 'some doubt about whether Beer really is a Jew, since he is uncircumcised, a feature uncommon even in assimilated Jewish circles in Austria'.[20]

There has since been speculation that Beer's bogus autobiography was a 'legend' fabricated for him by Soviet intelligence. It is inconceivable, however, that the KGB or its predecessors would have devised a cover story which could be so easily disproved. Beer's fantasy career in the Schutzbund and the International Brigades was his own, rather than Moscow's, invention. The fact that Beer's claims went unchallenged during the twenty-three years between his arrival in Palestine in 1938 and his arrest in 1961 reflected, as the British embassy told the Foreign Office, 'the perpetual problem of security which Israel by its very nature is bound to face': 'It is a country of immigrants about whose origins and past in many cases nothing is known except for what they themselves reveal. It has been pointed out that hundreds of people in responsible positions in theory offer the same kind of risk as Beer.'[21]

On his arrival in Palestine in 1938, Beer had succeeded in joining the Jewish settlement police. Soon afterwards he became a member of the Planning Bureau of the Haganah (the forerunner under the British mandate of the IDF), distinguishing himself in the first Arab–

Israeli War and becoming a founder member of Mapam.[22] The British military attaché later reported that Beer had become 'a fairly close friend of Shimon Peres', the ambitious young Deputy Minister of Defence.[23] Among the most important intelligence provided by Beer early in his career as a KGB agent was information on Peres's secret attempts in 1957 to obtain military assistance from West Germany and buy reconditioned German submarines. When the news was leaked to the press, possibly by Beer, there was such a public outcry that the Prime Minister, David Ben-Gurion, with whom Beer had also established a close relationship, threatened to resign. Shin Bet burgled Beer's Tel Aviv apartment but failed to find incriminating evidence.

It has been plausibly suggested that Shin Bet was slow to follow up its suspicions about Beer after 1957 because of his links with the Prime Minister. Early in 1961, however, a surveillance team took up residence opposite Beer's apartment. On 30 March he was observed apparently handing over a briefcase to Viktor Sokolov, previously identified as one of Aharon Cohen's case officers. By the time a warrant had been obtained and Beer had been arrested in the early hours of the following morning, the briefcase was back in his possession. Inside, doubtless photographed by the Tel Aviv residency, were a classified military report and extracts from Ben-Gurion's diary. It was later discovered that the Prime Minister's diary for the period January to July 1956 was missing. The probability is that this had been among the first documents supplied by Beer to the KGB.[24] The British embassy informed the Foreign Office that, 'Not only was Beer closely concerned with the Ministry of Defence but he was also a friend of many people in high positions in the Government. The Police have already interviewed over one hundred persons and many of them have admitted that they have spoken to him more freely than they should have done.'[25] Beer was sentenced to fifteen years' imprisonment in 1962 and died in jail four years later.

None of the Israeli agents recruited in the mid-1960s whose files were noted by Mitrokhin appears to have compared in importance with either Avni or Beer.[26] The best indication of the KGB's lack of high-level Israeli sources was its complete surprise at the outbreak of the Six-Day War in June 1967. Before the war, the Soviet embassy had been contemptuous of Israel's capacity to take on its Arab neighbours. In May one of the embassy's leading informants, Moshe

Sneh, formerly a Mapam politician but now leader of the Israeli Communist Party, told the Soviet ambassador, Dmitri Chubakhin, that if there was another Arab–Israeli war, Israel would win. Chubakhin replied scornfully, 'Who will fight [for Israel]? The espresso boys and the pimps on Dizengoff [Tel Aviv's main] Street?'[27] The Centre first discovered the Israeli surprise attacks on Egyptian, Jordanian and Syrian targets early on 5 June not from the Tel Aviv residency but from intercepted news reports by Associated Press.[28] In the immediate aftermath of the stunning Israeli victory, the residency itself seemed stunned. According to a Shin Bet officer responsible for the surveillance of residency personnel:

They were like scared mice. They didn't understand what was going on, had no idea how this attack had fallen on them from out of the clear blue sky, or who was up against whom. They made a few attempts to leave the embassy to meet with their agents and ascertain what Israel's goals were. They didn't get a thing. This was the position until they were pulled out.[29]

Moscow's decision (which it later regretted) to break off diplomatic relations with Israel and thus to close the legal residency in the legation caused further disruption to KGB operations. Since 1964 the Centre had had plans to base a group of operations officers at the Russian Orthodox Church mission in Jerusalem.[30] After the closure of the Soviet embassy, Shin Bet quickly realized that the KGB residency had moved to the mission.[31] But the mission offered a much smaller and less secure base for KGB operations than the legation. The fact that its budget was only a fraction of those of the major Middle Eastern residencies is testimony to the decline of intelligence operations inside Israel after 1967.[32] The KGB lost contact with a number of the agents it had recruited before the Six-Day War.[33]

In the aftermath of the Six-Day War, Markus Wolf, the head of the East German HVA, found the KGB, despite the decline in its operations inside Israel, 'fixated on Israel as an enemy'.[34] The Centre, like the Politburo, was particularly alarmed by the effect of the war on Jewish communities in the Soviet Union. One Russian Jew, Anatoli Dekatov, later wrote in an article which he dared to send for publication in the *Jerusalem Post*:

The victory of the tiny Israeli state over the hosts of the Arab enemies sent a thrill through the hearts of the Jews in Russia, as it did, I suppose, for Jews all over the world. The feeling of deep anxiety for the fate of Israel with which Soviet Jewry followed the events was succeeded by boundless joy and an overpowering pride in our people. Many, and especially the young, realized their Jewish identity for the first time ... The anti-Israel campaign in the Soviet mass media served only to spread further Zionist feeling among the Jews.[35]

Immediately following the Six-Day War, Moscow banned all emigration to Israel. A year later, however, irritated by Western denunciations of the ban as a breach of Jewish human rights, Andropov and Gromyko jointly proposed to the Politburo a limited resumption of emigration 'in order to contain the slanderous assertions of Western propaganda concerning discrimination against the Jews in the Soviet Union'. The KGB, they added, would continue to use this emigration 'for operational goals' – in other words to infiltrate agents into Israel.[36] In 1969 a record number of almost 3,000 Jews were allowed to emigrate. Though the number fell to little more than 1,000 in 1970, it rose sharply to 13,000 in 1971 – more than in the whole of the previous decade. In both 1972 and 1973 over 30,000 Jews were allowed to leave for Israel.[37]

The sharp rise in exit visas, however, fell far short of keeping pace with demand. The unprecedented surge in Jewish applications for permits to emigrate to Israel was confronted with bureaucratic obstructionism and official persecution. All applicants from technical professions, even those employed as clerks, were dismissed from their jobs. Students whose families applied for exit visas were expelled from their universities and required to perform three years' military service, after which they could not apply for visas for another five years. The KGB reviewed every application and was usually responsible for deciding the outcome. In the case of individuals well known either in the Soviet Union or in the West, the decision taken always carried Andropov's personal signature. In August 1972 a 'diploma tax' was introduced, obliging all those emigrants who had received higher education to refund the cost. All applicants for exit visas were branded in effect as enemies of the Soviet Union.[38]

During the early 1970s the 'refuseniks', those who had been denied exit visas, formed themselves into groups, contacted Western journalists and organized a series of protests ranging from demonstrations to hunger strikes. The KGB sent a stream of reports, often signed personally by Andropov, to the Politburo and the Central Committee, reporting the resolute action taken to 'neutralize' even the most minor protests. Every protest was interpreted as part of an international Zionist conspiracy against the Soviet Union:

With the growing aggressiveness of international imperialism, the data received indicate that subversive activity by foreign Zionist centres against the socialist countries has substantially increased. At the present time, there are more than 600 Zionist centres and organizations in the capitalist states, possessing significant propaganda resources. Since Israel's aggression against the Arab countries in June 1967, it has begun a campaign of widespread and open provocation against the Soviet Union and other socialist countries.

Zionist circles, in trying to deflect the attention of world public opinion away from the aggressive actions of the US in Indochina and of Israel in the Middle East, and toward the non-existent 'problem' of the Jews in the USSR, have unleashed on our country a broad campaign of slander, and to this end are organizing abroad anti-Soviet meetings, assemblies, conferences, marches and other hostile acts.

. . . Along with the cultivation of anti-Soviet world opinion, the Zionists are striving to exert ideological influence on the Jewish population of the Soviet Union, in order to provoke negative manifestations and create a nationalist underground in our country.

. . . The KGB organs have been focusing on operations for curtailing hostile and specially organized activity of Jewish nationalists, in particular methods of dismantling, separating and dividing groups, compromising their spiritual leaders and isolating deluded individuals from them.[39]

Soviet policy oscillated between the desire to deter Jewish emigration to Israel and intermittent anxiety at the impact on foreign opinion of the persecution of the refuseniks. Brezhnev was in a particularly nervous mood for several months before his visit to Washington in June 1973. He told the Politburo in March, 'In the last few months, hysteria has been whipped up around the so-called education tax on individuals emigrating abroad. I have thought a lot about what to do.' Unusually he criticized Andropov by name for failing to implement his instructions to end collection of the tax. 'It was my fault that we delayed implementing your instructions for six days,' Andropov confessed. 'It was simply the unwieldiness of our apparatus.' As Brezhnev carried on complaining, his tone became increasingly self-pitying. 'On Saturday and Sunday I didn't even go outside', he told the Politburo, 'and now I will have to devote even more time to these questions.' He concluded the discussion with a bizarre, rambling monologue which epitomized the broader confusion of Soviet policy:

Why not give [the Jews] some little theatre with 500 seats for a Jewish variety show that will work under our censorship with a repertoire under our supervision? Let Auntie Sonya sing Jewish wedding songs there. I'm not proposing this, I'm just talking . . . I'm speaking freely because I still have not raised my hand for anything I'm saying. For now, I'm simply keeping my hands at my sides and thinking things over, this is the point . . . Zionism is making us stupid, and we [even] take money from an old lady who has received an education.[40]

The outbreak of the Yom Kippur War enabled Andropov to recoup some of his personal prestige within the Politburo. The simultaneous attack by Egyptian and Syrian forces on 6 October 1973 caught Israel and the United States, but not the KGB, off guard. Still conscious of having been caught out by the beginning of the Six-Day War six years earlier, the KGB was able to provide advance warning to the Politburo before Yom Kippur – probably as a result of intelligence from its penetrations of the Egyptian armed forces and intelligence community.[41]

The KGB appears to have achieved no similar penetration of the Israeli Defence Force and intelligence agencies, despite the inclusion of large numbers of agents among those allowed to emigrate to Israel. According to Oleg Kalugin, head of FCD Counter Intelligence:

Many promised to work for us abroad, but almost invariably forgot their pledges as soon as they crossed the Soviet border. A few did help us, keeping the KGB informed about the plans and activities of Jewish émigré and refusenik groups. Our ultimate goal was to place these Jewish émigrés, many of whom were scientists, into sensitive positions in Western government, science or the military-industrial complex. But we enjoyed little success, and by the time I stepped down as head of Foreign Counter-Intelligence in 1980 I didn't know of a single valuable [Jewish émigré] mole in the West for the KGB.[42]

Other Soviet-bloc intelligence services were probably no more successful than the KGB. Markus Wolf later acknowledged that during his thirty-three years as head of the East German HVA, 'We never managed to penetrate Israeli intelligence.'[43]

The KGB found it far easier to infiltrate agents into Israel than to control them once they were there. The small residency in the Russian Orthodox Church mission in Jerusalem, which was kept under close surveillance by Shin Bet, could not cope with the demands made of it by the Centre. In October 1970 the Centre approved a plan to expand intelligence operations in Israel by sending a series of illegals on short-term missions as well as preparing the establishment of a permanent illegal residency.[44] Among the illegals despatched to Israel in 1971–72 both to contact existing agents and to cultivate potential new recruits were KARSKY, PATRIYA, RUN and YORIS, posing as – respectively – Canadian, Spanish, Mexican and Finnish nationals.[45] In 1972 an illegal residency in Israel also began operating, run by the thirty-four-year-old Yuri Fyodorovich Linov (codenamed KRAVCHENKO), posing as the Austrian Karl-Bernd Motl. Plans were made to give Linov control of a network of five agents:[46] LEON, a medical researcher with Israeli intelligence contacts who had been recruited in 1966 while on a visit to the Soviet Union;[47] KIM, a bogus Jewish refugee sent to Israel in 1970, where he enrolled at the Hebrew University in Jerusalem to penetrate organizations such as the Prisoners of Zion Association which campaigned for the release of Jewish refuseniks in the Soviet Union;[48] PETRESKU, another KGB Jewish agent who arrived in Israel in 1970;[49] GERDA, an employee of the German embassy;[50] and RON, a foreign ambassador in Israel.[51]

Linov's new illegal residency, however, survived for only a year. The first danger signal, the significance of which was apparently not appreciated by the Centre, was KIM's sudden unauthorized appearance in West Berlin in February 1973, where he complained to the KGB that Shin Bet was showing an interest in him.[52] A month later Linov was arrested while in the middle of an intelligence operation. The Centre concluded that he had been betrayed by

LEON, who may well have been a double agent controlled by Shin Bet.[53] PETRESKU was also suspected of having been turned by Israeli intelligence.[54] Though contact with RON (and probably GERDA) continued, the Centre noted that RON was 'inclined to be extortionate' in his financial demands.[55]

Following Linov's arrest, the Centre shelved plans for an illegal residency and cancelled all visits by illegals to Israel.[56] Plans by the Hungarian AVH to send their illegal YASAI to Israel posing as a French-born Jew were also shelved after he refused to be circumcised.[57] Two FCD officers, V. N. Okhulov and I. F. Khokhlov, took part in protracted secret negotiations with Israeli intelligence officers to secure Linov's release. Throughout the negotiations he was referred to by his Austrian alias 'Motl'. The Israelis requested in exchange the release of Heinrich Speter, a Bulgarian Jew sentenced to death on a probably spurious charge of espionage, and of sixteen Soviet Jews imprisoned for an alleged attempt to hijack a Soviet aircraft. The KGB insisted at first on a straight swap of Linov for Speter, claiming that both men had been found guilty on similar charges of espionage. In the end, however, the Centre also agreed to free Silva Zalmonson, one of the alleged hijackers, and to allow two of her companions to emigrate to Israel at the end of their prison sentences. As a condition of the exchange, the Israeli negotiators insisted that no mention be made in public of the release of 'Motl' – probably to avoid the impression that Israel was willing to exchange captured Soviet spies for persecuted Jews in the Soviet bloc.

The arrival in Israel of Speter and Zalmonson in September 1974 was thus interpreted by some Western observers as evidence that the Kremlin had decided on a more conciliatory policy towards Jewish emigration. *Time* magazine's Moscow correspondent saw their release as a Soviet attempt to influence the US Congress by making a humanitarian gesture. Andropov appeared delighted with the outcome of the negotiations for Linov's release and presented Okhulov and Khokhlov with formal letters of congratulation.[58] The Centre was less pleased with Linov. Officers in the FCD Illegals Directorate believed that he had given away more than he should have done under Israeli interrogation.[59]

During the mid-1970s Soviet policy towards Jewish emigration hardened once again. The immediate cause was the passage through Congress in 1974 of the Jackson–Vanik and Stevenson amendments to the 1972 US/Soviet Trade Agreement, making most-favoured-nation status dependent on the relaxation of curbs on emigration. The numbers of exit visas given in the mid-1970s declined from the record numbers of over 30,000 a year in 1972–73 to 20,000 in 1974 and less than 15,000 a year in 1975–76. Andropov continued to take a close, even obsessive, personal interest in the surveillance of would-be Jewish emigrants and all contacts between Soviet Jews and their foreign supporters.[60] He regarded even the sending of *matsos* (unleavened bread) from the West to Soviet Jews for the *seder* (the Passover meal) as an issue of such grave importance that it needed to be brought to the attention of the Politburo, writing in March 1975:

From the experience of previous years, it is clear that the delivery of such parcels [of *matsos*] to the addressees gives rise to negative processes among the Jewish population of the USSR, and reinforces nationalist and pro-emigration feelings.

In view of this, and in view of the fact that at the present time Jewish communities are fully supplied with locally baked *matsos*, the Committee of State Security considers it essential for parcels containing *matsos* sent from abroad to be confiscated . . .[61]

The claim that Soviet Jews were already well supplied with Passover *matsos* was disinformation designed to pre-empt opposition to Andropov's proposal from those Politburo members who, like Brezhnev, occasionally grasped that the obsession with Zionist conspiracy was 'making us stupid'. Andropov regarded foreign telephone calls as an even greater danger than imported *matsos*, in view of the politically incorrect tendency of Soviet Jews to complain to foreigners about the various forms of persecution to which they were subject. In June 1975 he reported personally to the Politburo on the success of KGB measures 'to prevent the use of international communications channels for the transfer abroad of tendentious and slanderous information' by Soviet Jews. During the previous two years over a hundred telephone lines used by 'Jewish nationalists' to make phone calls abroad had been disconnected, 'thereby inflicting a noticeable blow on foreign Zionist organizations'. More recently, however, Jews had taken to using telephone booths in telegraph offices, giving the staff non-Jewish names in order not to arouse suspicion, and direct-dial international telephone lines where there was no operator to keep track of them.[62]

Zionism was second only to the United States ('the Main Adversary') as a target for KGB active measures. For some conspiracy theorists in the Centre and elsewhere in Moscow, the two targets were in any case closely linked. Arkadi Shevchenko, the Soviet Under Secretary-General of the United Nations in the mid-1970s, was struck by the puzzlement in Moscow at how the United States functioned with such technological efficiency despite so little apparent regulation: 'Many are inclined towards the fantastic notion that there must be a secret control centre somewhere in the United States.'[63] The power behind the scenes, they believed, was monopoly capital which, in turn, was largely identified in some Soviet imaginations with the Jewish lobby.

The Centre devoted enormous energy to anti-Zionist active measures within the United States which, it was hoped, would also discredit the Jewish lobby. Probably the Centre's most successful tactic was to exploit the activities of the extremist Jewish Defense League (JDL), founded by a Brooklyn rabbi, Meir Kahane, whose inflammatory rhetoric declared the need for Jews to protect themselves by 'all necessary means' – including violence. The JDL so perfectly fitted the violent, racist image of Zionism which the KGB wished to project that, had it not existed, Service A might well have sought to invent a similarly extremist US-based underground movement. In September 1969, six Arab missions at the UN received threatening telegrams from the League, claiming that they were 'legitimate targets' for revenge attacks for terrorist acts committed by Arabs.[64] A year later, on 4 October 1970, KGB officers in New York posted forged letters containing similar threats, purporting to come from the JDL and other Zionist extremists, to the heads of Arab missions. The Centre calculated that these letters would provoke protests by the missions to both U Thant, the UN Secretary-General, and the US government.[65]

In the early hours of 25 November 1970 there was a bomb attack on the Manhattan offices of the Soviet airline Aeroflot, followed by an anonymous phone call to Associated Press by a caller who claimed responsibility for the bombing and used the JDL slogan, 'Never again!' Another bomb attack on 8 January 1971, this time outside a Soviet cultural centre in Washington, was followed by a similar phone call and the use of the same slogan. A spokesman for the JDL denied the League's involvement in the bombing but refused to condemn it. Once again, the Centre decided to imitate the example of the League. On 25 July the head of the FCD First (North American) Department, Anatoli Tikhonovich Kireyev, instructed the New York residency to implement operation PANDORA: the planting of a delayed-action explosive device in 'the Negro section of New York', preferably 'one of the Negro colleges'. After the explosion, the residency was ordered to make anonymous phone calls to black organizations, claiming responsibility on behalf of the JDL. PANDORA was merely the most dramatic in a series of active measures designed to stir up racial hostility between the black and Jewish communities. Simultaneously Andropov approved the distribution of bogus JDL leaflets fabricated by Service A, which denounced the crimes perpetrated by 'black mongrels'. Sixty letters were sent to black student and youth groups giving lurid accounts of fictitious JDL atrocities and demanding vengeance. Other anti-semitic pamphlets, circulated in the name of a non-existent 'Party of National Rebirth', called on whites to save America from the Jews.[66]

The main data base used by Service A in its active-measures campaigns against Zionist targets from 1973 onwards was obtained during operation SIMON, carried out by an agent of the Viennese residency codenamed CHUB ('Forelock') against the Paris headquarters of the World Jewish Congress (WJC). Preliminary reconnaissance by CHUB established that the premises were unguarded at night and had no burglar alarm. Using a duplicate key to the main entrance, he entered the WJC Paris offices on the night of 12–13 February 1972 and removed the entire card index listing names and addresses of the WJC's 20,000 French supporters together with details of their financial contributions, address plates giving the 30,000 addresses in fifty-five countries to which the WJC French-language periodical *Information Juive* was despatched, finance files relating to the activities of the WJC European Executive and details of the financing of a book on anti-semitism in Poland. At 11 a.m. on 14 June CHUB delivered all this material, which filled two suitcases and a shopping bag, to the Soviet consulate in Paris, then returned to Vienna using a false passport.[67]

Service A spent much of the next year planning the production of forgeries based on the format of the stolen documents which were designed to discredit the WJC and Zionism. On 4 January 1973, N. A. Kosov, the head of Service A, submitted a large-scale plan for active measures based on the forgeries which was approved by Andropov on the following day. Many of the fabricated documents were posted to addresses in Europe and North America over the next few years in the name of a fictitious 'Union of Young Zionists': among them a letter from one of the leaders of the French branch of the WJC containing compromising information on the World Zionist Organization (WZO), which, through its executive arm, the Jewish Agency, was responsible for Jewish emigration to Israel; financial documents purporting to show that WJC leaders had embezzled large sums of money which had been collected to provide aid for Israel; evidence that a series of newspapers had been bribed to publish pro-Israeli propaganda; and material designed to show that the WJC had links with Jewish extremists who were secretly trying to provoke outbreaks of anti-semitism in order to encourage emigration to Israel.[68] There is no evidence, however, that this elaborate disinformation exercise had any significant impact. No KGB active-measures campaign was capable of countering the adverse publicity generated by the persecution of the refuseniks. The Centre's obsession with the menace of Zionist subversion also introduced into the campaign an element of sometimes absurd exaggeration. It decided, for example, to exploit the murder in October 1973 of a female relative of the future French President, Valéry Giscard d'Estaing, by distributing in the name of a fictitious French Israeli support group a ludicrous fabrication declaring that she had been killed by Zionists in revenge for Giscard's part in the prosecution some years earlier of a group of Jewish financiers. So far from grasping the pointlessness of this dismal active measure, the Centre was unaccountably proud of it.[69]

Though estimating the impact of KGB anti-Zionist and anti-Israeli active measures in Europe is inevitably difficult, they appear to have achieved no more than marginal successes. Among these marginal successes was the visit to the Soviet Union of the British Chief Rabbi, Immanuel (later Lord) Jakobovits, in December 1975. On his return he was greeted by the headline in the *Jerusalem Post*: 'Jakobovits "Duped" by Soviets, Say Those Who Have Lived There'. Though the headline was exaggerated, the Chief Rabbi had shown a degree of naivety when subjected during his visit to a succession of carefully prepared active measures. Even when he wrote an account of his visit in his memoirs nine years later, it seems not to have occurred to him that the Russian Jews with whom he had lengthy discussions during his visit inevitably included a series of well-trained KGB agents.[70] Mitrokhin's notes contain the code-names of eleven of them; their task included 'conveying slanted information about the situation in the Soviet Union'.[71]

Though Jakobovits met dissidents as well as official representatives during his visit, he returned with an inadequate grasp of the numbers who wished to emigrate, telling a packed audience in the St John's Wood Synagogue: 'Even if the doors of the Soviet Union were freely opened to emigration, the most optimistic estimate is that only about half a million Jews would avail themselves of the opportunity, while some believe that the figure would not be much above 100,000.'

The fact that Jakobovits even mentioned the highly implausible hypothesis that as few as 100,000 Soviet Jews might wish to emigrate strongly suggests that he had been influenced by the 'slanted information' passed on to him by KGB agents. In fact, within twenty years of his visit the total number of emigrants had risen to over a million. Convinced that 'the bulk of Soviet Jewry' did not wish to emigrate, the Chief Rabbi placed as much emphasis on improving the conditions of Jewish life in the Soviet Union as on supporting the refuseniks.[72] But if Jakobovits showed a degree of naivety, so too did the KGB. Agent SHCHERBAKOV was given the impossible task of cultivating the executive director of the Chief Rabbi's office, Moshe Davis, with a view to his recruitment by the KGB.[73]

Probably the greatest success of the Soviet anti-Zionist campaign was its role in promoting the passage in the UN General Assembly by sixty-seven to fifty-five votes (with fifteen abstentions) of Resolution 3379, denouncing Zionism as a form of racism, in November 1975. In Jakobovits's view, 'UN resolutions hostile to Israel had been commonplace, but none could compare in virulence to this one. Its impact on Jews everywhere was devastating . . .'[74] The anti-Western majority which voted for Resolution 3379, however, was achieved as much by the lobbying of the Arab states as by the Soviet bloc. Though the KGB officers operating under diplomatic cover in New York and elsewhere doubtless played their part in the lobbying, there is no indication in any of the files noted by Mitrokhin that the KGB made a substantial contribution to the success of the vote. Soviet diplomacy appears to have contributed far more than Soviet intelligence to the passage of Resolution 3379.

In 1977 the Soviet Union began a gradual increase in the number of exit visas granted to would-be Jewish emigrants in an attempt to demonstrate its compliance with the human rights provisions of the Helsinki Accords of 1975.[75] Almost 29,000 Jews emigrated in 1978, followed by a record 51,000 in 1979.[76] KGB pressure on the refuseniks, however, was unrelenting. In March 1977 the leading refusenik, Anatoli (Natan) Shcharansky, was arrested. For the next year he resisted all the attempts of his KGB interrogators to bully and cajole him into co-operating in his own show trial by admitting working for the CIA. Andropov refused to admit defeat. In June 1978 he falsely informed the Politburo that, 'Shcharansky admits his guilt; we have caught him in his espionage activities and can present the appropriate materials.' How long a sentence Shcharansky received, Andropov added, would 'depend on how he behave[d] himself' in court.[77] The trial, though almost unpublicized inside the Soviet Union, ended in a moral victory for Shcharansky, who made a movingly defiant final address:

For two thousand years the Jewish people, my people, have been dispersed all over the world and seemingly deprived of any hope of returning. But still, each year Jews have stubbornly, and apparently without reason, said to each other, 'Next year in Jerusalem!' And today, when I am further than ever from my dream, from my people and from my [wife] Avital, and when many difficult years of prisons and camps lie ahead of me, I say to my wife and to my people, 'Next year in Jerusalem!'

And to the court, which has only to read a sentence that was prepared long ago – to you I have nothing to say.[78]

Shcharansky was sentenced to thirteen years in prison and camps on trumped-up charges of espionage and betrayal of the motherland. There is little doubt that Andropov was personally responsible for his persecution. Despite their conspiracy theories about Zionism, some – perhaps most – other members of the Politburo barely knew the name either of Shcharansky or of any other refusenik. In September President Jimmy Carter raised the Shcharansky case at a meeting with Gromyko in the White House. Gromyko replied that he had never heard of Shcharansky. Dobrynin, who was present at the meeting, believed at the time that Gromyko 'had shown great diplomatic skill in handling such a sensitive subject by feigning ignorance of it'. After the meeting, however, Dobrynin discovered to his surprise that Gromyko's ignorance was genuine: 'He had instructed his subordinates in Moscow not to bother him with what he called such "absurd" matters.'[79]

With the breakdown in East–West relations which followed the Soviet invasion of Afghanistan in December 1979, there was a sharp cut-back in the number of exit visas given to Jewish emigrants. Emigrants fell from 51,000 in 1979 to 25,000 in 1980 – many probably on visas issued before the change in Soviet policy. In 1981 there were fewer than 10,000, in 1982 under 5,000, and for each of the next four years fewer than 2,000.[80] During the first half of the 1980s the refuseniks, like the rest of the dissident movements within the Soviet Union, seemed at their lowest ebb since their emergence in the late 1960s. Those who remained at liberty were under constant KGB surveillance. Andropov and his successors as KGB Chairman, Fedorchuk and Chebrikov, took pride in reporting to the Politburo and Central Committee on the success of their efforts to disrupt the refuseniks' 'anti-Soviet' activities. On a number of occasions, the KGB exploited popular anti-semitism in order to intimidate the refuseniks. Andropov reported in May 1981, for example, that an attempt by 'Jewish nationalists' to hold a meeting in a forest near Moscow to commemorate the Holocaust and protest against the refusal of exit visas had been prevented 'with the active participation of the Soviet public'.[81]

Andropov's term as Soviet leader from 1982 to 1984 witnessed the tensest period in Soviet–American relations since the Cuban missile crisis of 1962.[82] The Centre's conspiracy theories about Zionist–American collaboration to subvert the Soviet bloc gave added impetus to KGB operations against Zionist targets. In 1982 the KGB held a high-level in-house conference in Leningrad devoted to 'The main tendencies of the subversive activity of Zionist centres abroad and Jewish nationalists within the country, and topical questions relating to increasing the effectiveness of KGB agencies in combating this [activity] in present-day conditions.' Meeting soon after the suppression of the Polish Solidarity movement (whose minority of Jewish leaders attracted disproportionate interest in the Centre), the conference agreed that 'virtually no major negative incidents took place in the socialist countries of Europe without the involvement of Zionists'. A number of speakers claimed that the Zionists' penetration of the political leadership of much of the West had given them a major influence over Western policy which was exacerbating both East–West tension and 'treasonable tendencies' among Soviet Jews.[83] In the summer of 1982, probably as a result of this conference, residents were sent a detailed four-year 'Plan for Work against Zionism in 1982–1986', warning them that the Soviet bloc was threatened by 'all kinds of subversive operations' organized by Zionists in league with Israel and 'imperialist intelligence services', especially the CIA. These had to be countered by a major increase in intelligence collection on 'the plans, forms and methods of Zionist subversion' as well as by a wide range of active measures designed to weaken and divide the Zionist movement.[84]

In a review of foreign operations early in 1984, Vladimir Kryuchkov, the head of the FCD, claimed that during the previous two years, 'The subversive activity of émigré, nationalist and Zionist organizations and associations abroad has shown a marked increase.'[85] The FCD 'Plan of Work' for 1984 put first on its list of counter-intelligence targets: 'Plans for subversive action or secret operations by the adversary's special services and by centres for ideological diversion and nationalists, especially Zionists and other anti-Soviet organizations, against the USSR and other countries of the socialist community.'[86]

At the beginning of the Gorbachev era, there were still many in the Centre who believed that the American 'military-industrial complex' was dominated by the Jewish lobby. Proponents of even more extreme Zionist conspiracy theories included L. P. Zamoysky, deputy head of the FCD Directorate of Intelligence Information. Despite his reputation as one of the Centre's ablest analysts, Zamoysky maintained that Zionism had behind it not merely Jewish finance capital but also the occult power of Freemasonry whose rites, he maintained, were of Jewish origin. It was, he insisted, a 'fact' that Freemasons were an integral part of the Jewish conspiracy.[87]

During his early career, Mikhail Gorbachev absorbed at least some of the anti-Zionist prejudices which were part of the mindset of the CPSU. Those prejudices were clearly apparent at a Politburo meeting on 29 August 1985 which discussed the case of the leading dissident, Andrei Sakharov, and his Jewish wife, Elena Bonner, both of whom had been banished to Gorky five years earlier. Chebrikov, the KGB Chairman, declared (inaccurately) that Bonner had 'one hundred per cent influence' over her husband and dictated his actions. 'That's what Zionism does for you!' joked Gorbachev. It was Gorbachev, none the less, who over the next four years played the leading role in resolving the problem of the refuseniks. Gorbachev realized that neither democratic reform nor the normalization of East–West relations could continue so long as Sakharov's exile and the persecution of other dissidents continued. Because of the opposition of the KGB and the old guard within the Politburo, however, he was forced to proceed cautiously. It was not till December 1986, twenty-one months after he became General Secretary, that he judged that the Politburo was ready to accept Sakharov's and Bonner's return from internal exile.[88] The rearguard action against ending the persecution of the refuseniks was even stronger than in the case of non-Jewish dissidents. The release of Natan Shcharansky from the gulag in 1986 and his departure for Israel, where he arrived to a hero's welcome, none the less marked a turning point in the struggle for Jewish emigration.

In August 1987, at the request of the KGB leadership, the Politburo agreed to a propaganda campaign designed to deter would-be Jewish emigrants to Israel, as well as measures such as the foundation of Jewish cultural associations which would provide positive incentives to remain in the Soviet Union.[89] By this time, Gorbachev's own policy was to remove the obstacles to the emigration of the refuseniks while encouraging as many other Soviet Jews as possible to remain. Though he saw the departure of Jewish professionals as 'a brain drain' which threatened to slow the progress of *perestroika*, he abandoned the attempt to hold on to those who were determined to depart. Of the 8,000 Jewish emigrants in 1987, 77 per cent had previously been denied exit visas.[90]

The new Jewish cultural associations were subjected to a series of anti-semitic attacks. In 1988, for example, the refusenik Judith Lurye arrived for a meeting of one of the associations to find the door of the meeting hall padlocked and guarded by two KGB officers. A notice nailed to the door declared: 'Why do we – the great, intelligent, beautiful Slavs – consider it a normal phenomenon to live with

Yids among us? How can these dirty stinking Jews call themselves by such a proud and heroic name as "Russians"?'[91]

In 1989, with the campaign to deter Jewish emigration in visible disarray, the floodgates were opened at last. That year 71,000 Jews left the Soviet Union, followed over the next two years by another 400,000.[92] To the old guard in the KGB, bitterness at the collapse of the Soviet Union was compounded by what they saw as the triumph of Zionist subversion.

13

Middle Eastern Terrorism and the Palestinians

The precedent set by the KGB's use of Sandinista guerrillas against US targets in Central and North America during the later 1960s[1] encouraged the Centre to consider the use of Palestinian terrorists as proxies in the Middle East and Europe. The man chiefly responsible for exporting Palestinian terrorism to Europe was Dr Wadi Haddad, deputy leader and head of foreign operations of the Marxist-Leninist Popular Front for the Liberation of Palestine (PFLP), codenamed KHUTOR,[2] headed by Dr George Habash. On the day Israeli forces destroyed his family home in Galilee, Haddad had sworn that he would pursue the Israelis for the rest of his life.

Convinced of the futility of attacking Israeli military targets after the humiliation of the Six-Day War, Haddad devised a new strategy of aircraft hijacking and terrorist attacks on 'Zionist' targets in Europe which made front-page news across the world and attracted the favourable attention of the Centre. 'To kill a Jew far from the battlefield', he declared, 'has more effect than killing hundreds of Jews in battle.' The first hijack organized by Haddad was in July 1968 on board an El Al Boeing 707 bound for Tel Aviv which two PFLP hijackers renamed 'Palestinian Liberation 007' and forced to land in Algiers. Though Israel had publicly declared that it would never negotiate with terrorists, Haddad forced it to do just that. After more than a month's negotiations, the Israeli passengers on board were exchanged for sixteen Palestinians in Israeli jails.[3] It was probably in the aftermath of the hijack that the KGB made its first contact with Haddad.[4] The KGB remained in touch with him during the spate of PFLP hijackings and attacks on Jewish targets in European capitals over the next few years.

In 1970 Haddad was recruited by the KGB as Agent NATSIONALIST. Andropov reported to Brezhnev in May:

The nature of our relations with W. Haddad enables us to control the external operations of the PFLP to a certain degree, to exert influence in a manner favourable to the Soviet Union, and also to carry out active measures in support of our interests through the organization's assets while observing the necessary conspiratorial secrecy.[5]

Haddad's career as a KGB agent very nearly ended only a few months after it began. On the evening of 11 July, he had a meeting in his Beirut apartment with one of the PFLP hijackers, the twenty-four-year-old Laila Khalid, whose photogenic appearance had caught the attention of the media and helped to make her the world's best-known female terrorist. While they were talking, six Soviet-made Katyushka rockets – launched, almost certainly by Mossad, from the flat opposite – hit his apartment. Amazingly, Haddad and Khalid suffered only minor injuries.[6]

One of Haddad's reasons for becoming a KGB agent was probably to obtain Soviet arms for the PFLP. With Brezhnev's approval, an initial delivery of five RPG-7 hand-held anti-tank grenade launchers in July was followed by the elaborately planned operation VOSTOK ('East'), during which a large consignment of arms and ammunition were handed over to the PFLP at sea near Aden under cover of darkness. To prevent any of the arms and ammunition being traced back to the KGB if they were captured, the shipment consisted of fifty West German pistols (ten with silencers) with 5,000 rounds of ammunition; fifty captured MG-ZI machine guns with 10,000 rounds of ammunition; five British-made Sterling automatics with silencers and 36,000 rounds of ammunition; fifty American AR-16 automatics with 30,000 rounds of ammunition; fifteen booby-trap mines manufactured from foreign materials; and five radio-activated 'SNOP' mines, also assembled from foreign materials. The two varieties of mine were among the most advanced small weapons in the extensive Soviet arsenal, and, like some of the silencers, had never been previously supplied even to other members of the Warsaw Pact.[7]

The first use of Haddad as a KGB proxy was in operation VINT: the attempt, personally approved by Brezhnev, to kidnap the deputy head of the CIA station in Lebanon, codenamed VIR, and 'have him taken to the Soviet Union'. Andropov assured Brezhnev that no suspicion would attach to the KGB:

Bearing in mind that the Palestinian guerrilla organizations have recently stepped up their activities in Lebanon against American intelligence and its agents, the Lebanese authorities and the Americans would suspect Palestinian guerrillas of carrying out the [VINT] operation. The ultimate purpose of the operation would only be known to NATSIONALIST [Haddad], on the foreign side, and to the KGB officers directly involved in planning the operation and carrying it out, on the Soviet side.

Despite elaborate preparations, operation VINT failed. VIR varied his daily routine and Haddad's gunmen found it impossible to abduct him. A later KGB plan for the gunmen to assassinate him also failed.[8]

A number of other PFLP operations against Mossad and CIA targets succeeded. In 1970 an individual codenamed SOLIST, who was being cultivated by the KGB residency in Beirut, came under suspicion of working for the Israelis after his brother was arrested in Cairo, charged with being a Mossad agent. SOLIST was kidnapped by a PFLP snatch squad, headed by Ahmad Yunis (also known as Abu Ahmad), chief of the PFLP security service in Lebanon, and brought to the Beirut residency for interrogation. Soon afterwards Yunis became a KGB confidential contact (though not, like Haddad, a fully recruited agent) with the codename TARSHIKH.[9]

The KGB was complicit in a number of other abductions by Yunis. In August 1970 his security service kidnapped a US academic, Professor Hani Korda, whom it, and apparently the KGB, believed – quite possibly wrongly – to be a deep-cover CIA officer operating in Lebanon against Palestinian targets. In his Beirut apartment they found a notebook with the names and addresses of his contacts in Arab countries. Korda was smuggled across the Lebanese border to a PFLP base in Jordan, but, though brutally interrogated, refused to confess and succeeded in committing suicide.[10] In October the PFLP kidnapped Aredis Derounian, an Armenian-born American journalist in Beirut suspected of having links with the CIA. Though Derounian was best known for his attacks on US fascist sympathizers written under the pseudonym John Roy Carlson, the PFLP considered his work pro-Zionist and anti-Arab. In his apartment the PFLP found two passports and a mass of documents which it passed on to the KGB. Derounian was more fortunate than Korda. After being held prisoner for several days in a refugee camp in Tripoli, he managed to escape and take refuge in the US embassy.[11]

KGB collaboration with Haddad was even closer than with Yunis. To conceal his contacts with the Beirut residency from his colleagues, Haddad would send his secretary by car to rendezvous with a KGB operations officer who followed him, also by car, to a location chosen by Haddad, which was never the same from one meeting to the next.[12] The main purpose of these meetings for the KGB was to encourage Haddad to undertake 'special actions' proposed or approved by the KGB and to prevent PFLP operations which ran counter to Soviet interests.[13] Thanks to Haddad, the KGB almost certainly had advance notice of all the main PFLP terrorist attacks.

The most dramatic operation organized by Haddad in 1970 was a plan for the almost simultaneous hijack of four airliners bound for New York on 6 September and their diversion to a remote former RAF airbase in Jordan known as Dawson's Field. The most difficult assignment was given to Laila Khalid, still photogenic despite plastic surgery to change her appearance since her previous hijack, and the Nicaraguan-American Patrick Arguello. The pair posed as a newly married couple. Their aircraft, an El Al Boeing 707 departing from Tel Aviv, was the only one of the four which, as a result of previous PFLP hijacks, carried an armed air marshal. Though Khalid and Arguello succeeded in smuggling both handguns and grenades aboard, the hijack failed. Arguello was shot by the air marshal and Khalid, who was prevented by other passengers from removing the grenades hidden in her bra, was arrested after the plane made an emergency landing at Heathrow. The hijackers aboard a TWA Boeing 707 and a Swissair DC8, however, successfully diverted them to Dawson's Field, which they promptly renamed Revolution Airstrip. A hijacked Pan Am Boeing 747, which was discovered to be too large to land at the airstrip, landed instead at Cairo where passengers and crew were hastily evacuated and the aircraft blown up. A fifth plane, a BOAC VC10, was hijacked three days later and flown to Revolution Airstrip to provide British hostages to barter for Khalid. There the passengers were eventually exchanged for Khalid and Palestinian terrorists imprisoned in West Germany and Switzerland, and the aircraft were destroyed by the hijackers.[14]

Mitrokhin's material gives no indication of what advice FCD 'special actions' experts gave Haddad about the PLFP hijacks. Proof that they did advise him on terrorist attacks, however, is provided by the file on operation NASOS: an attack on the Israeli tanker *Coral Sea* while it was carrying Iranian crude oil under a Liberian flag of convenience to Eilat. The KGB advised Haddad on both the method and location of the attack in the straits of Bab al-Mandab close to the island of Mandaran. On 13 June 1971 two PFLP terrorists, codenamed CHUK and GEK by the KGB, boarded a speed-boat on the coast of South Yemen and launched an attack on the tanker using three of the RPG-7 hand-held anti-tank grenade launchers supplied by the KGB in the previous year. According to the KGB post-operation report, between seven and nine rockets were fired, of which five hit their target. Though the *Coral Sea* was set on fire, however, it did not sink. CHUK and GEK made their escape to the coast of North Yemen. The head of the FCD, Fyodor Mortin, was sufficiently encouraged by the partial success of operation NASOS to recommend to Andropov afterwards that the KGB 'make more active use of NATSIONALIST and his gunmen to carry out aggressive operations aimed directly against Israel'.[15] Relations with Haddad were complicated by turmoil within the PFLP. In 1972, Habash, as leader of the PFLP, publicly renounced international terrorism, provoking a bitter row with Haddad, who set up a new headquarters in Baghdad where he founded a PFLP splinter group, the Special Operations Group.[16] KGB support for Haddad, however, continued.

Moscow showed rather less interest in the Palestine Liberation Organization (PLO, codenamed KARUSEL),[17] the umbrella organization for all Palestinian movements which was based in Jordan until 1970, than in Haddad's faction of the PFLP. Disguised as an Egyptian technician, the PLO chairman, Yasir Arafat (initially codenamed AREF),[18] had accompanied Nasser on a visit to the Soviet Union in 1968 and, probably as a result of Nasser's backing, received a promise of weapons.[19] For the next few years, Arafat was cultivated without conspicuous success by an FCD officer, Vasili Fyodorovich Samoylenko.[20] Arafat, however, was unaware that since 1968 the KGB had had an agent, codenamed GIDAR, in the office of his personal intelligence chief and most trusted adviser, Hani al-Hasan.[21]

In September 1970 King Hussein of Jordan, infuriated by the recent PFLP hijacking of aircraft to a Jordanian airfield and by the emergence of the PLO as a virtually independent state within his kingdom, used his army to drive it out. Thousands of Palestinians were killed in what became known as Black September. A shadowy terrorist organization of that name was set up within Arafat's Fatah movement at the heart of the PLO when it regrouped in Lebanon. Among the atrocities committed by Black September, for which Arafat disingenuously disclaimed responsibility, was an attack on Israeli athletes competing in the August 1972 Munich Olympics, in which eleven were killed.

In 1972 Arafat paid his first official visit to Moscow at the head of a PLO delegation but failed to impress the Centre, which distrusted the 'slanted' nature of the information he provided and found him anxious to maintain contact with 'reactionary Arab regimes' as well as with the Soviet bloc.[22] Though Mitrokhin's notes do not mention it, the Centre was also doubtless well aware that Arafat's claims to have been born in Jerusalem were fraudulent; in reality, though his parents were Palestinian and he was deeply committed to the Palestinian cause, he had been born in Cairo and had spent his first twenty-eight years in Egypt. The Centre also knew that during the Suez War of 1956, when Arafat claimed to have been an officer in the Egyptian army fighting to defend Port Said, he had actually been attending a Communist-sponsored student conference in Czechoslovakia.[23] The fact that Arafat had friendly relations with the deviant Communist dictator of Romania, Nicolae Ceauşescu, strengthened Moscow's suspicion of him. Arafat was franker with Ceauşescu than with the Kremlin. According to the Romanian foreign intelligence chief, Ion Pacepa, during a visit to Bucharest in October 1972 Arafat claimed that Hani al-Hasan, who accompanied him, had been behind the Black September attack at the Munich Olympics.[24]

Arafat's visit to Bucharest led to the establishment of a close liaison between the PLO and the Romanian foreign intelligence service. Probably in response to the Centre's desire not to be upstaged by the Romanians, a Politburo resolution of 7 September 1973 instructed the KGB to maintain secret liaison with Arafat's intelligence service through the Beirut residency.[25] Arafat's international prestige, and hence Moscow's interest in him, increased in the following year after he became the first head of a nongovernmental organization to be invited to address a plenary session of the United Nations. 'I have come bearing an olive branch in one hand and a freedom fighter's gun in the other,' Arafat declared. 'Do not let the olive branch fall from my hand.' During a visit by Arafat to Moscow in 1974 an official communiqué recognized the PLO as 'the sole legitimate representative of the Arab people of Palestine'. In the course of the visit, Samoylenko, the KGB officer who had been cultivating Arafat since the later 1960s, was photographed with him at a wreath-laying ceremony.[26] Moscow officially announced that it was authorizing the PLO to establish a Moscow office – though it was another two years before it allowed the office to open. The only other national liberation movement given similar status in the Soviet Union was the National Liberation Front of Vietnam.[27]

The Centre, however, retained much greater confidence in Haddad than in Arafat. Soviet policy remained to distance itself from terrorism in public while continuing in private to promote Palestinian terrorist attacks. When seeking Politburo approval for Haddad's terrorist operations, Andropov misleadingly referred to them instead as 'special' or 'sabotage' operations. 'W. Haddad', he reported, 'is clearly aware of our negative attitude in principle towards terrorism and he does not raise with us matters connected with this particular line of PFLP activity.' There was, however, no coherent dividing line between the terrorist attacks which 'in principle' the Soviet leadership opposed and the 'sabotage operations' which it was willing in practice to support. On 23 April 1974 Andropov informed Brezhnev that Haddad had requested further 'special technical devices' for his future operations:

At the present time [Haddad's section of] the PFLP is engaged in preparing a number of special operations, including strikes against major petroleum reservoirs in various parts of the world (Saudi Arabia, the Persian Gulf, Hong Kong and elsewhere); the destruction of tankers and supertankers; operations against American and Israeli representatives in Iran, Greece, Ethiopia and Kenya; a raid on the building of the Tel Aviv diamond centre, among other [targets].

Andropov repeated his earlier assurances that, through Haddad, the KGB retained the ability 'to control to some extent the activities of the PFLP foreign operations department, [and] to influence it in ways favourable to the Soviet Union'. Three days later Brezhnev authorized the supply of 'special technical devices' to Haddad.[28] In June 1974 Andropov approved detailed arrangements for the secret supply of weaponry to Haddad and the training of PFLP Special Operations Group instructors in the use of mines and sabotage equipment. In September, Haddad visited Russia, staying with his wife, son and daughter in a KGB dacha (codenamed BARVIKHA-1). During discussions on his future operations he agreed to allocate two or three of his men to the hunting down of Soviet defectors. The weapons supplied to Haddad included foreign-manufactured pistols and automatics fitted with silencers together with radio-controlled mines constructed from foreign materials, at a cost of $50,000, in order to conceal their Soviet manufacture.[29] Further KGB arms shipments to Haddad, approved by the Politburo, included one in May 1975 of fifty-three foreign-produced automatics, fifty pistols (ten with silencers) and 34,000 rounds of ammunition. Brezhnev was informed that Haddad was the only non-Russian who knew the source of the arms, which, as in the first weapons delivery to the PFLP five years earlier, were handed over at sea near Aden under cover of darkness.[30] Among other assistance given by the KGB to Haddad during 1975 was $30,000.[31]

Through the Beirut residency the KGB also established contact with two other terrorist groups which gained publicity after attacks on Israeli civilians in the spring of 1974: the Democratic Front for the Liberation of Palestine (DFLP), led by Nayif Hawatmeh (codenamed INZHENER),[32] a Greek Orthodox Christian; and the Popular Front for the Liberation of Palestine-General Command (PFLP-GC), a breakaway from the PFLP headed by a former Syrian army officer, Ahmad Jibril (codenamed MAYOROV).[33] The Beirut residency arranged meetings with Hawatmeh two or three times a month (for how long is unclear) and planted Service A disinformation in the DFLP journal *Hurriya* at a cost of 700 Lebanese pounds per page.[34] Mitrokhin's notes contain no details of KGB contacts with Jibril.[35]

The most spectacular terrorist operation of the mid-1970s, of which the KGB was almost certainly given advance notice by Haddad, was a PFLP Special Operations Group raid on a meeting of OPEC oil ministers at its Vienna headquarters in December 1975 by a group of Palestinian and German gunmen led by Ilich Ramírez

Sánchez, better known as 'Carlos the Jackal'.[36] Carlos was the spoiled son of a millionaire Venezuelan Communist who had named his three sons Vladimir, Ilich and Lenin in honour of the leader of the October Revolution. The KGB had first encountered Carlos when he was given a place in 1968, with his brother Lenin, at the Lumumba University in Moscow for students from the Third World. According to a Venezuelan Communist leader, Carlos paid little attention to his studies: 'There was no control over him. He received a lot of money, he played the guitar, and he ran after young women.'[37] The KGB, it is safe to conclude, did not regard him as a suitable recruit.[38] In 1970 he and his brother were expelled from Lumumba University for 'anti-Soviet provocation and indiscipline'. After his expulsion Carlos flew to Jordan and joined the PFLP, later becoming one of its leading hitmen in London and Paris. Though he claimed to be a Marxist revolutionary, his passion for terrorism derived chiefly from his own vanity and bravado as 'the great Carlos'. 'Revolution', he declared in a characteristic transport of self-indulgent rhetoric, 'is my supreme euphoria.'[39]

The early stages of Carlos's attack on the poorly defended Vienna OPEC headquarters in December 1975 went remarkably smoothly. All the oil ministers were taken hostage and the Austrian government gave in to Carlos's demands for a plane to fly them out of the country. Haddad had instructed Carlos to fly around the world with the hostages, liberating most of the oil ministers one by one in their respective capitals in return for declarations of support for the Palestinian cause, but gave orders that the Saudi Arabian and Iranian ministers were to be executed as 'criminals'. Carlos, however, failed to kill either and freed both in exchange for a large ransom. An outraged Haddad told Carlos that he had disobeyed orders, and dismissed him from his 'operational teams'.

Over the next two years, Haddad suffered two humiliating defeats. In July 1976 PFLP Special Operations Group terrorists hijacked an Air France Airbus with over a hundred Israelis on board to the Ugandan airport of Entebbe. The hostages, however, were rescued and the terrorists killed in a daring Israeli commando raid. In October 1977 a Lufthansa Boeing 737 was hijacked to Mogadishu and its eighty-six passengers taken hostage. Though the captain was killed by the mentally unstable leader of the hijackers during a stop-over in South Yemen, the plane was stormed at Mogadishu by West German commandos and the remaining hostages freed.[40]

Despite these débâcles, Haddad remained in close contact with the KGB. In 1976 ten of his terrorists were sent on a three-month course at the FCD Red Banner Institute (later known as the Andropov Institute), which included training in intelligence, counter-intelligence, interrogation, surveillance and sabotage. Further courses were run in 1977–78.[41] In March 1977 Haddad visited Moscow for operational discussions with the head of the FCD 'special tasks' department, Vladimir Grigoryevich Krasovsky, and his deputy, A. F. Khlystov. The assistance given to Haddad included $10,000 and ten Walther pistols fitted with silencers. At the KGB's request, Haddad agreed to act as intermediary in making contact with the Provisional IRA representative in Algiers, codenamed IGROK ('Gambler'), who was believed to have useful information on British intelligence operations.[42] From 1974 the KGB had a second agent within the PFLP leadership, Ahmad Mahmud Samman (codenamed VASIT), an Arab born in Jerusalem in 1935. Mitrokhin's brief notes on Samman's file record that he supplied the KGB with information on PFLP operations, but give no details.[43]

In 1978 the Centre lost both its main agents within the PFLP. Haddad died of a brain haemorrhage while staying in East Germany. His KGB file records that, despite their earlier quarrel, the PFLP leader George Habash declared in an emotional oration at Haddad's funeral in Baghdad, 'Let our enemies know that he did not die, but is alive; he is in our hearts, and his name is in our hands; he is organically bound to our people and to our revolution.'[44] Samman, according to Mitrokhin's note on his file, was 'liquidated by the PFLP as the result of internal dissension [probably following Haddad's death] and the activities of the Syrian special services'.[45] The Beirut residency also lost probably its most important confidential contact in the PFLP, Ahmad Yunis, head of the PFLP security service in Lebanon. In 1978 Yunis was found guilty by a PFLP tribunal of the murder of one of his colleagues and the attempted murder of another, and executed.[46]

The final entry in Haddad's file noted by Mitrokhin was a decision by the Centre to make contact with his successor.[47] Mitrokhin found no evidence, however, that the KGB ever again established links with any major Palestinian terrorist as close as those which it had maintained with Haddad. Carlos, who had been expelled by Haddad from the PFLP Special Operations Group, used Haddad's death as an opportunity to found his own terrorist group, the Organization of Arab Armed Struggle, composed of Syrian, Lebanese, West German and Swiss militants, and to pursue his quest for international stardom as the world's leading revolutionary practitioner of terror. He obtained a diplomatic passport from the Marxist-Leninist regime of the People's Democratic Republic of [South] Yemen in the name of Ahmad Ali Fawaz, which showed his place of birth as Aden, and increased his credit with the Yemeni authorities by falsely claiming that he was a fully trained KGB officer operating on missions approved by the Centre. In February 1979, according to his KGB file, Carlos also began regular contact with the security agency of the PLO. During the remainder of the year he went on an extraordinary tour of the Soviet bloc, beginning in the spring in East Berlin, in order to make contact with the local intelligence agencies. Though Carlos was allowed to set up bases in East Berlin and Budapest, however, he was held at arm's length by the KGB. When Erich Mielke, the East German Minister of State Security, passed on to Moscow Carlos's claims, as reported to him by his South Yemeni counterpart, that he was working for the KGB, he received an official denial from Mikhail Andreyevich Usatov, the deputy head of the FCD, and Yakov Prokofyevich Medyanik, then head of the African Department.[48] Carlos eventually became an embarrassment to his Soviet-bloc hosts. According to Markus 'Mischa' Wolf, the head of the HVA, the Stasi's foreign intelligence arm, 'Carlos was a big mouth, an uncontrollable adventurer. He spent his nights in bars, with a gun hanging at his belt, surrounded by girls and drinking like a fish.' He was eventually expelled from his East Berlin and Budapest bases in 1985 and moved to Damascus in Syria, the most steadfast of his Arab allies.[49]

Moscow had also become cautious about collaborating with the Libyan leader, Colonel Muammar al-Qaddafi, probably the most active state sponsor of terrorist groups ranging from the PFLP to the Provisional IRA. In 1979 a secret Soviet–Libyan agreement had been signed on intelligence and security, followed by the posting of an FCD liaison officer to the Tripoli embassy. The KGB provided training for Libyan intelligence officers in Moscow, gave advice on security and surveillance inside Libya, and supplied intelligence on US activities in the eastern Mediterranean. In return, Libya provided intelligence on Egypt, North Africa and Israel, as well as assisting the KGB in targeting Western diplomatic missions in Tripoli. Collaboration, however, steadily declined as Moscow became increasingly concerned by Qaddafi's reputation as the godfather of international terrorism. Qaddafi's first visit to Moscow in 1981 further lowered his reputation. In the Centre his flamboyant posturing and extravagant uniforms were interpreted as an attempt to contrast his own virility with Brezhnev's visible decrepitude. At a private briefing for Soviet diplomats and KGB officers in London in 1984, Aleksandr Bovin, chief political commentator of *Izvestia*, denounced Qaddafi as 'a criminal and a fascist'.[50]

By the early 1980s the Centre seems to have abandoned the hopes it had placed a decade earlier in collaboration with the PFLP and its breakaway groups. Its contacts with the PLO (in particular with Arafat's dominant Fatah group), however, had somewhat improved. In June 1978 Abu Iyad (codenamed KOCHUBEY), a member of the Fatah Central Committee and head of Arafat's intelligence service, visited Moscow for talks with the KGB and the International Department.[51] Abu Iyad complained of the blunt, tactless behaviour of Lev Alekseyevich Bausin, the KGB officer under diplomatic cover at the Beirut residency who was responsible for contacts with the PLO and other Palestinian groups. Unusually, the Centre showed its desire for better relations by recalling Bausin and replacing him with Nikolai Afanasyevich Kuznetsov, who at his first meeting with Arafat identified himself as a KGB officer.[52]

Moscow welcomed Arafat's increasing attempts to win international respectability. In 1979 he was invited to a meeting of the Socialist International in Vienna and began a successful European diplomatic offensive. By 1980 the countries of the European Community, though not the United States, had agreed that the PLO must be party to peace negotiations in the Middle East. The British Foreign Secretary, Lord Carrington, declared: 'The PLO as such is not a terrorist organization.' Arafat's success in driving a wedge between the United States and its European allies further enhanced the Centre's interest in him.[53]

The military training courses provided by Moscow for the PLO, however, caused some ill feeling on both sides. A report on a course in 1981 for 194 officers from ten different PLO factions suggests serious deficiencies in both Soviet training and the quality of many

PLO recruits. According to the PLO commander, Colonel Rashad Ahmad, 'The participants in the courses did not correctly understand the political aspects of sending military delegations abroad. As a result, the upper echelon of the delegation, namely the participants in the battalion officer courses, refused to study and asked to return, using all sorts of illogical excuses.' Ahmad reported that he had been forced to expel thirteen officers from the training course for offences which included alcoholism, passing counterfeit money and sexual 'perversion'. Had he enforced the code of conduct strictly, he would, he claimed, have been forced to send home more than half the officers. Ahmad appealed for a higher standard of recruits for future courses in the Soviet Union.[54] East Germany provided additional training for the PLO in the use of explosives, mines and firearms with silencers.[55]

In 1981 Brezhnev at last gave the PLO formal diplomatic recognition. The limitations of Soviet support, however, were graphically illustrated in the following year when Israel invaded Lebanon in an attempt to destroy the PLO as an effective force and establish a new political order headed by its Maronite Christian allies. Moscow, complained Abu Iyad, responded with 'pretty words' but no practical assistance.[56] In the early stages of the Israeli assault, the Soviet embassy and the Beirut residency were almost unable to function. According to Markus Wolf:

With Beirut in ruins, there was an interval during which Moscow lost contact with its embassy and its KGB officers in the Lebanese capital. Our officers were the only ones able to maintain radio and personal contact with the leaders of the PLO and, acting as Moscow's proxies, our men were instructed to pass on the PLO's reaction to events. They ventured forth, risking their lives among the shooting and the bombings to meet their Palestinian partners.[57]

There were no clear winners in the war. After seventy-five days of savage fighting, the PLO was forced to leave Lebanon and establish a new base in Tunisia on the periphery of the Arab world. Israel, however, failed to achieve its aim of establishing a new pro-Israeli political order in Lebanon. By the time its troops withdrew in the summer of 1983, the war had weakened Israel's government, divided its people, and lowered its international standing. An official Israeli commission concluded that Israel bore indirect responsibility for the massacre of Palestinians by Christian militia in the Lebanese refugee camps of Sabra and Shatila. Far from relegating the Palestinian problem to the sidelines, as Israel had intended, the war focused international attention on the need to find a solution.[58]

Finding a solution, however, ranked low in the Soviet order of priorities. Moscow's difficulties in dealing with the PLO were compounded by the homicidal feud which broke out in 1983 between its main Middle Eastern ally, Asad, and Arafat. Asad expelled Arafat from Damascus, backed an unsuccessful armed rebellion within Fatah against his leadership, and actively supported the assassination campaign against Arafat's lieutenants being conducted by his sworn Palestinian enemy, Abu Nidal, an unstable terrorist who habitually referred to Arafat as 'the Jewess's son'.[59] Arafat, the great survivor, kept his position as leader of the PLO but failed to recover the confidence of Moscow. For Soviet as for many Western diplomats, his credibility was undermined by a deviousness born of ceaseless manoeuvring between the different factions within the PLO.[60] During the remainder of the Soviet era, Moscow was only peripherally involved in the search for a Palestinian settlement. Though Arafat eventually succeeded in gaining an invitation to Moscow in 1988, Gorbachev was reluctant to receive him. 'So what's the point in my meeting with him?' Gorbachev asked his aides. When persuaded to agree to a meeting, he told Arafat bluntly that the Arab–Israeli dispute was no longer linked to Soviet–American rivalry, and that armed conflict would do terrible damage to the Palestinian cause. The communiqué at the end of the meeting made no reference to the founding of a Palestinian state. 'The talks', wrote Gorbachev's aide, Anatoli Chernyaev, 'didn't really yield any results . . . It just gave Arafat the chance to strut all the more.'[61]

Asia

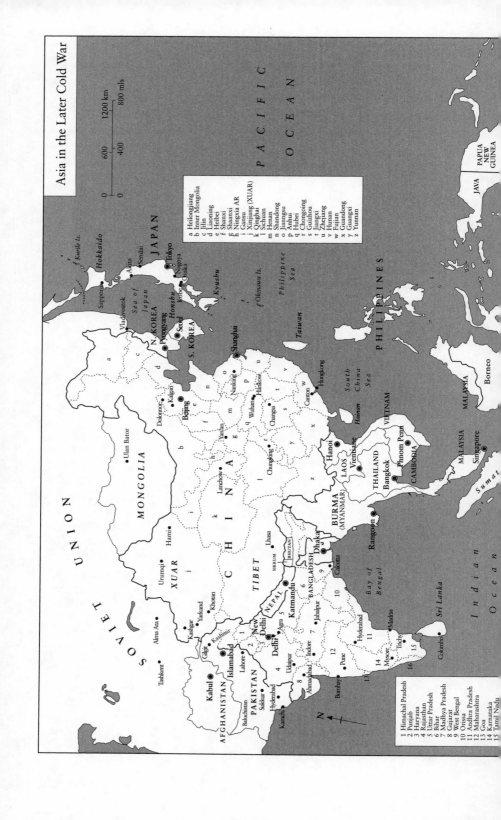

Asia in the Later Cold War

14

Asia: Introduction

By far the greatest advances of Communism during the Cold War were in Asia, where it conquered the world's most populous state, China, its neighbour North Korea, the whole of former French Indo-China (Vietnam north and south, Laos and Cambodia) and Afghanistan. Ironically, however, it was the heartland of Asian Communism which from the early 1960s onwards became the hardest target for Soviet foreign intelligence operations. Mao Zedong and Kim Il Sung turned their brutalized countries into security-obsessed societies where the KGB found it as difficult to operate as Western intelligence agencies had done in Stalin's Soviet Union.

Even the 'sickly suspicious' Stalin (as Khrushchev correctly called him) seems never to have imagined that Mao and Kim would one day dare to reject Moscow's leadership of world Communism.[1] When Mao visited Moscow late in 1949 after the declaration of the Chinese People's Republic (PRC), he won a standing ovation for delivering a deferential eulogy at Stalin's seventieth-birthday celebrations in the Bolshoi.[2] Kim Il Sung, though impatient to invade South Korea, did not launch his attack until Stalin gave him permission. Stalin allowed the Korean War to begin in June 1950 largely because he had misjudged US policy. Intelligence from the United States, following its failure to intervene to prevent the Communist victory in China, indicated, he believed, that 'the prevailing mood is not to interfere' in Korea. That erroneous conclusion seems to have been based on his misinterpretation of a US National Security Council document (probably supplied by the KGB agent Donald Maclean), which excluded the Asian mainland from the American defence perimeter. Having thus misinterpreted US policy, Stalin was prepared for the first time to allow Kim to attack the South.[3]

The Sino-Soviet split in the early 1960s brought to an acrimonious end the deference from the PRC which Stalin had taken for granted. The first public attack on Moscow was made by Mao's veteran security chief, Kang Sheng, whose ferocious purges during Mao's Great Leap Forward were largely modelled on techniques he had learned in Moscow during the Great Terror.[4] On the Soviet side, the ideological dispute with China was compounded by personal loathing for Mao – the 'Great Helmsman' – and a more general dislike of the Chinese population as a whole. Khrushchev 'repeatedly' told a Romanian delegation shortly before his overthrow in 1964 that 'Mao Zedong is sick, crazy, that he should be taken to an asylum, etc.'[5] An assessment of Chinese national character circulated to KGB residencies by the Centre twelve years later claimed that the Chinese were 'noted for their spitefulness'.[6]

What most outraged both the Kremlin and the Centre was Beijing's impudence in setting itself up as a rival capital of world Communism, attempting to seduce other Communist parties from their rightful allegiance to the Soviet Union. Moscow blamed the horrors of Pol Pot's regime (on which it preferred not to dwell in detail) on the take-over of the Cambodian Communist Party by an 'anti-popular, pro-Beijing clique'.[7] The decision by Asia's largest non-ruling Communist party in Japan to side with the PRC deprived the KGB of what had previously been an important intelligence asset and turned it into a hostile target. The Japanese Communist Party complained that its minority pro-Moscow faction was being assisted by Soviet spies and informants.[8] The Centre was so put out by the number of portraits of Mao appearing on public display in some African capitals that it ordered counter-measures such as the fly-posting of pictures of the Great Helmsman defaced with hostile graffiti on the walls of Brazzaville.[9]

To most Western observers, the least problematic of the Soviet Union's relations with the Asian Communist regimes appeared to be with the Democratic Republic of [North] Vietnam. As well as providing Hanoi with a majority of its arms during the Vietnam War,[10] Moscow was lavish in public praise for its 'heroic resistance' to American imperialism and support for the Vietcong guerrillas in the south: 'With determined military support from the Democratic Republic of Vietnam, the patriots in South Vietnam struck at the Saigon regime of generals, bureaucrats and landowners with such force that it could not be saved by the deep involvement in the war of the strongest imperial power.'

Even more than American attempts to topple Fidel Castro, the Vietnam War united most of the Third World as well as what Moscow called 'progressives in all nations', the United States included, in vocal opposition to US imperialism.[11] Both Presidents Kennedy and Johnson made the mistake of seeing the mainspring of the Vietnam War less in Hanoi than in Moscow. Johnson's conspiracy theories of manipulation by Moscow extended even to the US Senate. He claimed absurdly that Senators William Fulbright and Wayne Morse, two of the leading opponents of his Vietnam policy, were 'definitely under the control of the Soviet embassy' – by which he undoubtedly meant the KGB's Washington residency.[12]

In reality, the strongly nationalist Ho Chi-Minh (whose name was chanted in anti-American demonstrations around the world) and the North Vietnamese regime were determined not to be dictated to by either Moscow or Beijing. Despite paying lip service to fraternal co-operation with its Soviet ally, the North Vietnamese intelligence service held the KGB somewhat at arm's length. As KGB chairman in the mid-1960s, Vladimir Semichastny was never satisfied with the opportunities given to his officers to question American PoWs. On several occasions, interrogations were curtailed just as they seemed to be producing useful results. Semichastny was also frustrated by the reluctance of the North Vietnamese to allow Soviet weapons experts access to captured US military technology. On several occasions he raised the 'ticklish issue' of access to American prisoners and weaponry when the North Vietnamese Interior Minister (who was responsible for intelligence) came to visit his daughter who was studying in Moscow. Hanoi's only response was to present him with a couple of war souvenirs, one of which was a comb made from a fragment of a shot-down American bomber.[13]

The Kremlin was acutely aware of its lack of influence on North Vietnamese policy. In 1968 an *Izvestia* correspondent in Hanoi sent a report to the CPSU Central Committee on a conversation with a Vietnamese journalist, who had mockingly asked him: 'Do you know what is the Soviet Union's share of the total assistance received by Vietnam and what is the share of Soviet political influence there (if the latter can be measured in percentages)? The figures are, respectively, 75–80 per cent [for the former] and 4–8 per cent [for the latter].' The

Izvestia correspondent thought the first figure was probably 15–20 per cent too high but that the estimate of Soviet influence in North Vietnam was about right.[14] As well as conducting fraternal liaison, the KGB residency in Hanoi carried out much the same hostile operations as in a Western capital. In 1975 it was running a network of twenty-five agents and sixty confidential contacts tasked to collect intelligence on Vietnamese military installations, the internal situation and the frontier with China.[15] As in Western capitals, the residency contained an IMPULS radio station which monitored the movements of Vietnamese security personnel and their systems of surveillance in an attempt to ensure that these did not interfere with its KGB contacts or its agent network.[16] Though far less hostile than Beijing and Pyongyang, Hanoi was none the less a difficult operating environment. The highest-level Vietnamese source identified by Mitrokhin, ISAYEYEV, a senior intelligence officer probably recruited while he was stationed in Moscow, provided classified information on his intelligence colleagues in return for payment but refused to make any contact while in Hanoi for fear of detection.[17]

The Asian intelligence successes of which the Centre was most proud were in India, the world's second most populous state and largest democracy. It was deeply ironic that the KGB should find democratic India so much more congenial an environment than Communist China, North Korea and Vietnam. Oleg Kalugin, who in 1973 became the youngest general in the FCD, remembers India as both a prestige target and 'a model of KGB infiltration of a Third World government'. The openness of India's democracy combined with the streak of corruption which ran through its media and political system provided numerous opportunities for Soviet intelligence. In addition to what Kalugin termed 'scores of sources throughout the Indian government – in Intelligence, Counterintelligence, the Defence and Foreign Ministries, and the police', successful penetrations of Indian embassies (replicated in operations against Japan, Pakistan and other Asian countries) assisted the decryption of probably substantial – though as yet unquantifiable – amounts of Indian diplomatic traffic.[18]

The Soviet leadership regarded a special relationship with India as the foundation of its South Asian policy. Growing concern in both Moscow and New Delhi with the threat from China gave that relationship added significance. Gromyko and Ponomarev jointly declared: 'The Soviet Union and India march side by side in the struggle for détente, for peace and world security ... India has always relied on Soviet assistance on the international scene in safeguarding its rights against colonial schemes.'[19]

The primary purpose of KGB active measures in India was to encourage support for the special relationship and strengthen suspicion of the United States. According to Leonid Shebarshin, who served in the New Delhi residency in the mid-1970s, 'The CIA's hand could be detected in material published in certain Indian newspapers. We, of course, paid them back in the same coin ... Like us, [the CIA] diligently and not always successfully did what they had to do. They were instruments of their government's policy; we carried out the policy of our State. Both sides were right to do so.'[20]

Though the KGB tended to exaggerate the success of its active measures, they appear to have been on a larger scale than those of the CIA. By the early 1980s there were about 1,500 Indo-Soviet Friendship Societies as compared with only two Indo-American Friendship Societies.[21] The Soviet leadership seems to have drawn the wrong conclusions from this apparently spectacular, but in reality somewhat hollow, success. American popular culture had no need of friendship societies to secure its dominance over that of the Soviet bloc. No subsidized film evening in an Indo-Soviet Friendship Society could hope to compete with the appeal of either Hollywood or Bollywood. Similarly, few Indian students, despite their widespread disapproval of US foreign policy, were more anxious to win scholarships to universities in the Soviet bloc than in the United States.

In India, as elsewhere in the Third World, KGB active measures were intended partly for Soviet domestic consumption – to give the Soviet people, and in particular their leaders, an exaggerated notion of the international esteem in which the USSR was held. The New Delhi residency went to considerable lengths to give the Soviet political leadership an inflated sense of its own popularity in India. Before Brezhnev's official visit in 1973, recalls Shebarshin,

Together with the Embassy, the 'Novosti' [news agency] representatives and the Union of Soviet Friendship Societies, the Residency took steps to create a favourable public atmosphere in the country immediately before and during the visit, and to forestall possible hostile incidents by the opposition and the secret allies of our long-standing Main Adversary.

We had extensive contacts within political parties, among journalists and public organizations. All were enthusiastically brought into play.[22]

The priority given to KGB operations in India is indicated by the subsequent promotion of some of the leading officers in the New Delhi residency. A decade after Shebarshin left India, he became head of the FCD. Vyacheslav Trubnikov, who also served in New Delhi in the 1970s,[23] went on to become head of the post-Soviet foreign intelligence service, the SVR, with direct access to President Yeltsin.[24] He later also became a confidant of President Putin, serving successively as Deputy Foreign Minister and, from August 2004, as Russian ambassador in New Delhi. Trubnikov's return to India was attributed by Russian press commentators to the mutual desire of Russia and India 'to upgrade their strategic partnership'.[25]

Within the Muslim areas of Asia, the KGB's chief priority before the Afghan War was to monitor the loyalty to Moscow of the Soviet republics with predominantly Muslim populations. From the Second World War onwards the cornerstone of Soviet policy to its Muslim peoples, as to the Russian Orthodox Church,[26] was the creation of a subservient religious hierarchy. Despite the KGB's extensive penetration of and influence over the official hierarchy of Soviet Islam, however, the greater part of Muslim life remained outside the Centre's control. Islam was less dependent than Christianity and Judaism on official clergy. Any Muslim who could read the Quran and follow Islamic rites could officiate at ceremonies such as marriage and burial. Soviet rule in the Muslim republics was a politically correct façade which concealed the reality of a population which looked far more to Mecca than to Moscow, ruled by a corrupt political élite whose Marxism-Leninism was often little more than skin-deep. Even the local KGB headquarters were, in varying degree, infected by the corruption. The war in Afghanistan, as well as turning world-wide Muslim opinion against the Soviet Union, also undermined Moscow's confidence in the loyalty of its Muslim subjects. The Central Asian press switched from propaganda celebration of the supposed 'friendship' between Soviet Muslims and their Russian 'Elder Brother' to emphasizing the ability of the 'Elder Brother' to eliminate 'traitors' and maintain law and order.[27]

The decision to invade Afghanistan in December 1979 to ensure the survival of the Communist regime there was essentially taken by the four-man Afghanistan Commission – Andropov, Gromyko, Ponomarev and the Defence Minister, Marshal Ustinov – which obtained the consent of the ailing Brezhnev at a private meeting in his Kremlin office. Gromyko's influence on the decision, however, was clearly inferior to that of Andropov and Ustinov. KGB special forces played a more important role in the invasion than in any previous conflict and were charged with the assassination of the supposedly traitorous President Hafizullah Amin.[28] 'The Kremlin fantasy', recalls one senior KGB officer, 'was that a great breakthrough [in Afghanistan] would demonstrate [Soviet] effectiveness, showing the world that communism was the ascendant political system.'[29] The fantasy, however, originated with Andropov rather than with Brezhnev.

Andropov's emergence as the most influential member of the Politburo was demonstrated by his election as Party leader in 1982 after Brezhnev's death. By then, however, Afghanistan had become, in the words of one KGB general, 'our Vietnam': 'We are bogged down in a war we cannot win and cannot abandon.'[30] In the end, as Gorbachev recognized, abandonment was the only solution. But, whereas the US defeat in Vietnam had resulted in only a temporary loss of American self-confidence in world affairs, the Afghan war helped to undermine the foundations of the Soviet system. Many Soviet citizens took to referring to Afghanistan as 'Af-gavni-stan' ('Af-shit-stan').[31] Disastrous though the war was, it demonstrated, once again, the central role of the KGB in Soviet Third World policy. Just as the KGB's enthusiasm a generation earlier for Fidel Castro had helped to launch the Soviet forward policy in the Third World, so the disastrous military intervention in Afghanistan, for which the KGB leadership bore much of the responsibility, brought it to a halt.

15

The People's Republic of China
From 'Eternal Friendship' to 'Eternal Enmity'

Collaboration between Soviet intelligence and the Chinese Communist Party (CCP) went back to the 1920s. A police raid on the Soviet consulate at Beijing in 1927 uncovered a mass of documents on Soviet espionage in China, the involvement of the CCP and instructions to it from Moscow 'not to shrink from any measures, even including looting and massacres' when promoting clashes between Westerners and the local population.[1] The arrest in 1931 of the Comintern representative in Shanghai, Jakov Rudnik (alias 'Hilaire Noulens'), led to the capture of many more files on Soviet intelligence operations and the Communist underground. A British intelligence report concluded that the files 'afforded a unique opportunity of seeing from the inside, and on unimpeachable documentary evidence, the working of a highly developed Communist organization of the illegal order'. Among the documents which attracted particular attention were a large number of letters from 'the notorious Annamite Communist, Nguyen Ai Quac', later better known as Ho Chi-Minh. But the 'most outstanding' document, in the view of British intelligence, was a CCP report on the killing of members of the family of an alleged Communist traitor, Ku Shun-chang, carried out under the direction of Mao Zedong's future Prime Minister, Zhou Enlai.[2] In 1933 Mao's security chief, Kang Sheng, arrived in Moscow as deputy head of the Chinese delegation to the Comintern and spent the next four years learning from the example of the NKVD during its most paranoid phase. Kang proved an apt pupil. During the Great Terror, he founded an Office for the Elimination of Counter-Revolutionaries and purged the émigré Chinese Communist community with exemplary zeal for its mostly imaginary crimes. Late in 1937 he returned on a Soviet plane to the base established by Mao after the Long March in Yan'an, where he continued the witch-hunt he had started in Moscow and began the creation of China's gulag, the *laogai* (an abbreviation of *laodong gaizao*, 'reform through labour'). To his subordinates he became the 'Venerable Kang'; to others he was 'China's Beria'. Though a connoisseur of traditional Chinese art and a skilful, ambidextrous calligrapher, Kang surpassed even Beria in personal depravity, taking sadistic pleasure in supervising the torture of supposed counter-revolutionaries.[3] As well as helping Mao polish his poetry and prose, Kang also contributed to his personal collection of erotica.[4]

Nikolai Leonov later claimed that during the 1930s and 1940s Soviet intelligence had built up 'a very extensive and well-formed information network on Chinese soil'.[5] In the summer of 1949, however, on the eve of the victory of Mao's forces over the Nationalist Kuomintang, led by Chiang Kai-shek, a high-level CCP delegation in Moscow complained, probably with considerable exaggeration, that a large part of that network had been penetrated by Chiang and the Americans. Due at least in part to his addiction to conspiracy theory, Stalin took the complaint seriously. 'The situation', he declared, 'requires us to unify the efforts of our intelligence bodies, and we are ready to start this immediately . . . Let us act as a united front.'[6] On Stalin's instructions, the names of all those in the Soviet intelligence network in China were given to the CCP leadership.[7] Simultaneously the CCP demanded that all Chinese who had worked for Soviet intelligence should declare themselves to the Party.[8]

Yuri Tavrosky, a leading Sinologist in the International Department of the CPSU Central Committee, later described Sino-Soviet relations during the generation after the foundation of the People's Republic of China (PRC) in October 1949 as falling into two starkly contrasting phases: a decade of 'eternal friendship' between the world's two largest socialist states, followed from the early 1960s by the era of 'eternal enmity'.[9] For most of the decade of 'eternal friendship' there was close collaboration between Soviet and Chinese intelligence. On Khrushchev's instructions, the KGB continued to provide its Chinese allies with details of its Chinese intelligence networks.[10] Until 1957 a series of KGB illegals of Chinese, Mongolian, Turkic and Korean ethnic origin were given false identities in the PRC, mostly with the co-operation of the Chinese Ministry of Public Security, before being sent on their first foreign missions.[11]

Khrushchev's visit to Beijing in 1958, however, witnessed a visible chill in the 'eternal friendship'. Though Mao had to a degree been prepared to defer to Stalin, he was not in awe of Khrushchev, whose revolutionary experience he regarded as inferior to his own. As his Chinese hosts were doubtless aware, Khrushchev was a non-swimmer and he was made to look foolish during 'photo opportunities' in Mao's swimming pool. More importantly, Khrushchev's proposals for a joint Russian–Chinese fleet under a Russian admiral and for Russian listening posts on Chinese soil were angrily rejected.[12] The future KGB Chairman Yuri Andropov, then responsible for relations with foreign Communist parties, later complained to the Chinese that they had failed to warn Khrushchev during his visit that they had decided to begin shelling two off-shore islands in the Taiwan Straits still held by Chiang Kai-shek almost as soon as he left Beijing.[13]

By the later 1950s Kang Sheng, who had suffered a temporary eclipse during the earlier part of the decade, apparently due to mental illness, had re-emerged as a close adviser of (and procurer of teenage girls for) Mao. The purge of 'right deviationists' during the 'Great Leap Forward' begun in 1958 replicated many of the horrors of the Great Terror in which Kang had enthusiastically participated in Moscow two decades earlier. According to Mao's doctor, 'Kang Sheng's job was to depose and destroy his fellow party members, and his continuing "investigations" in the early 1960s laid the groundwork for the attacks of the Cultural Revolution to come.'[14] Between 1958 and 1962 perhaps as many as 10 million 'ideological reactionaries', real and imagined, were imprisoned in the *laogai*; millions more Chinese citizens died as a result of famine.[15]

Kang was the first to bring the Sino-Soviet quarrel out into the open. At a Warsaw Pact conference in February 1960, he made a speech attacking Soviet policy, then had a heated exchange with Khrushchev. 'You don't have the qualifications to debate with me,' Khrushchev shouted at Kang. 'I am General Secretary of the Communist Party of the Soviet Union . . .' 'Your credentials are much more shallow than mine!' Kang retorted in ungrammatical Russian. According to one of the Soviet participants, '[Kang] could freeze you with his stare. Everyone was afraid of him. On the Soviet side we compared him to Beria. You could see at first glance that he was a very evil and ruthless person.' Though Kang's speech was not published in Moscow, it appeared in full in Beijing.[16] In April a series of articles in the Chinese *People's Daily* and *Red Flag* on the ninetieth anniversary of Lenin's birth effectively accused Moscow of 'revising, emasculating and betraying' Lenin's teaching. Khrushchev replied in June by publicly denouncing Mao as 'an ultra-leftist, an ultra-dogmatist and a left revisionist'.[17]

A month later all Soviet experts in China were withdrawn. Over the next few years many of the China specialists in the KGB and the Soviet Foreign Ministry tried to transfer to other work for fear that a continuing reputation as Sinologists would blight their careers.[18] Moscow, however, still hoped to prevent the quarrel with Beijing turning into a major schism which would divide the Communist world. During the early 1960s the USSR and PRC usually limited themselves to attacking each other by proxy. While Moscow denounced Albanian hard-liners, Beijing condemned Yugoslav revisionists. Moscow made a final attempt to paper over the Sino-Soviet cracks by proposing a meeting between senior Party delegations in July 1963. The CCP delegation, led by the future Chinese leader Deng Xiaoping, showed no interest in reaching a settlement. The most vitriolic attacks on the Soviet leadership came once again from Kang Sheng, who made an impassioned defence of Stalin against the 'curses and swear words' with which he claimed that Khrushchev had defamed his memory:

Can it really be that the CPSU, which for a long time had the love and respect of the revolutionary peoples of the whole world, had a 'bandit' as its great leader for several decades? From what you have said it appears as if the ranks of the international Communist movement which grew and became stronger from year to year were under the leadership of some sort of 'shit'.

Kang then dared to say what perhaps no meeting of senior Communists in Moscow had ever heard said aloud since Khrushchev's 'Secret Speech' of 1956. He taunted Khrushchev by quoting some of his numerous past eulogies of Stalin as 'a very great genius, teacher, great leader of humanity', and recalled Khrushchev's active participation (along with Kang) in the attempt during the Great Terror 'to wipe all the Trotskyist-rightist carrion from the face of the earth'.[19] The impact of Kang's extraordinary speech on his shocked Soviet listeners was heightened by the fact that he delivered it through ferociously clenched teeth.[20]

The acrimonious collapse of the Moscow talks in the summer of 1963 was followed by the most strident polemics in the history of the international Communist movement. In April 1964 a senior Soviet official even accused Beijing of a racist attempt to set yellow and black races 'against the whites' – a policy which, he claimed, was 'no different from Nazism'. The PRC was also accused of selling drugs to finance the Great Leap Forward. The virulence of Soviet attacks reflected the deep indignation generated in Moscow by the Sino-Soviet schism. For almost half a century after the Bolshevik Revolution the Soviet Union had been able to depend on the unconditional loyalty of other Communist parties around the world. Now it stood accused of heresy by the Communist rulers of the world's most populous state. Moscow's alarm was heightened by Beijing's charm offensive in the Third World. In Asia the PRC established close links with Pakistan, Burma and Indonesia. During 1964 Beijing established diplomatic relations with fourteen African states, all of whom ceased to recognize the Chinese Nationalist regime on Taiwan, to which the PRC laid claim.[21] The Centre was outraged by reports that in some of these states pictures of Soviet-bloc leaders had been displaced or overshadowed by huge portraits of Mao, and demanded that a record be kept of when and where every such portrait appeared. Markus Wolf, the long-serving head of the East German HVA, complained that, at the request of the KGB, he was forced to conduct the 'senseless exercise' of counting the number of portraits of the Great Helmsman on public display in each of the African countries where his service operated.[22] The successful test of China's first atomic bomb in October 1964 both enhanced its international prestige in the Third World and dramatically increased the threat which China posed to the Soviet Union.

Once 'eternal friendship' had given way to 'eternal enmity', residencies in many parts of the world were told to regard Line K (K for Kitay, the Russian word for China) as a major operational priority, second only to operations against the 'Main Adversary' and its leading allies. Within China itself, however, Stalin's earlier decision to reveal the identities of the entire Soviet intelligence network to the CCP leadership had crippled KGB intelligence collection. Throughout the remainder of the Soviet era the Centre was left with what Nikolai Leonov called 'an unbridgeable gap in our information sources on China'.[23] Most of the KGB's former Chinese agents whose names had been given to the Ministry of State Security were executed or left to rot in the *laogai*.[24] The fact that the Beijing Ministry of Public Security knew the real names of the illegals given false Chinese identities in the PRC during the 1950s made it impossible to use them against Chinese targets. As a result most Line K operations were conducted outside the PRC. Chinese officials stationed abroad, however, were under strict instructions to go out only in groups of two or more. As a result, recalls one retired Western intelligence officer, 'You could never meet any of them alone.' Line K thus spent much of its time trying to recruit non-Chinese citizens with access to PRC officials. Among its leading agents during the 1960s was the Finnish businessman Harri Ilmari Hartvig (code-named UNTO), who was on the committee of the Finnish–Chinese Friendship Society and had frequent meetings with the Chinese ambassador and other PRC diplomats. Meetings between the Friendship Society committee and PRC diplomats took place in Hartvig's department, which, without his knowledge, had been bugged by a KGB listening device concealed in his sideboard. Extracts from the transcript of at least one meeting attended by the Chinese ambassador which discussed Sino-Soviet relations and PRC policy to Scandinavia and Yugoslavia were passed to the Politburo.[25] The fact that the intelligence obtained through Hartvig was accorded such importance, despite the fact that it appears to have included no classified documents, is further evidence of the general weakness of KGB intelligence collection on the PRC.

The 'Cultural Revolution' (officially 'A Full-Scale Revolution to Establish a Working-Class Culture') launched by Mao in 1966 made China a more difficult and dangerous place for the KGB to operate than anywhere else on earth. In an extraordinary attempt to re-fashion Chinese society on a utopian revolutionary model, Mao unleashed a general Terror. Millions of youthful, fanatical Red Guards were urged to root out revisionist and bourgeois tendencies wherever they found them – and they found them almost everywhere. Veteran Communist officials and intellectuals were paraded in dunces' hats, abused, imprisoned and in some cases driven to suicide. The leadership of the Soviet Union were denounced as 'the biggest traitors and renegades in history'. As during the Stalinist Great Terror thirty years earlier, most of the enemies of the people unmasked and persecuted by the Red Guards had committed only imagined crimes. And, as in Stalin's Russia, the bloodletting was accompanied by a repellent form of Emperor-worship. Mao was hailed as the 'Great Helmsman', 'the Reddest Red Sun in Our Hearts'. Each day began with a 'loyalty dance': 'You put your hand to your head and then to your heart, and you danced a jig – to show that your heart and mind were filled with boundless love for Chairman Mao.' Rival factions outdid themselves in terrorizing the Great Helmsman's imagined enemies, each claiming to be more Maoist than the others.[26]

Agent recruitment within China during the Cultural Revolution was, as KGB Chairman Semichastny later acknowledged, 'an impossible task'. In Beijing, 'Every one of our men, from diplomats to drivers, was as conspicuous as an albino crow.'[27] A September 1967 directive by Aleksandr Sakharovsky, the head of the FCD, noted that the Beijing residency was being forced to operate under siege conditions.[28] Soviet contact with Chinese officials was minimal and closely supervised. The spy-mania and xenophobia of the Red Guards made it difficult for diplomats even to walk round Beijing. Owners of foreign books were forced to crawl on their knees through the streets in shame; those caught listening to foreign broadcasts were sent to prison. As an official Chinese report later acknowledged, 'The ability to speak a foreign language or a past visit to a foreign country became "evidence" of being a "secret agent" for that country.' The road leading to the beleaguered Soviet embassy was renamed 'Anti-Revisionist Lane'. The families of Soviet diplomats and KGB officers were manhandled as they left Beijing airport for Moscow in 1967.

The best first-hand reporting to reach the Centre from Beijing during the Cultural Revolution came from KGB officers of Mongolian or Central Asian extraction who could pass as Chinese citizens and were smuggled out of the Soviet embassy compound after dark in the boots of diplomatic cars. Let out unobserved when the opportunity arose, they mingled with the vast crowds roaming through a city festooned with slogans, read the day's wall posters (which were declared off-limits for foreigners), attended political rallies and purchased 'little newspapers' with news from across China. Late in 1967 they saw the first wall posters denouncing the Head of State, Liu Shaoqi, as the 'Number One person in authority taking the capitalist road'. After Liu was jailed in the following year, more than 22,000 people were arrested as his alleged sympathizers. Even a night-soil collector, who had been photographed being congratulated by Liu at a model workers' conference, was paraded through the streets with an accusing placard around his neck and maltreated until he lost his reason. Acting on the principle that 'Revolutionaries' children are heroes, reactionaries' children are lice', Red Guards killed one of Liu's children by laying him in the path of an oncoming train. Brutally ill-treated and suffering from pneumonia and diabetes for which he was denied medical treatment, Liu himself died naked on a prison floor in 1969.

Deng Xiaoping, Party General Secretary and 'Number Two person in authority taking the capitalist road', was dismissed and sent to do manual labour but – probably on Mao's personal instructions – allowed to survive. The Red Guards took revenge on his eldest son, a physics student, by throwing him from a second-floor window at Peking University.[29] No fellow student dared to come to his aid, and no doctor was willing to operate on him. He was left paralysed from the waist down. Fed with a relentless series of reports of chaos and atrocity, the Centre interpreted the Cultural Revolution not as a convulsion in the life of a one-party state but as a peculiarly Chinese descent into oriental barbarism. Though perhaps 30 million Chinese were persecuted during the Cultural Revolution, however, the numbers killed (about a million) were fewer than the victims of the Stalinist Great Terror.[30]

The FCD plan for intelligence operations in the PRC and Hong Kong during 1966–67, approved by Semichastny as KGB Chairman in April 1966, made no reference to the hopeless task of recruiting agents in most of mainland China. Instead it concentrated on proposals for the use of illegals and agent infiltration across China's northern frontiers with the Soviet Union and the Soviet-dominated Mongolian People's Republic. Plans were made for the establishment of an illegal residency in Hong Kong and for short-term visits by illegals to the PRC (some of them in collaboration with the Mongolian intelligence agency), but it was recognized that planning for an illegal KGB residency in the PRC could not go beyond a preliminary stage. The most ambitious part of the plan for 1966–67 concerned preparations for cross-border operations in collaboration with KGB units in frontier regions and the Mongolian security service.[31]

The most vulnerable area for KGB penetration was the remote, sparsely populated Xinjiang Uighur Autonomous Region (XUAR) in north-west China, a vast expanse of mountain and desert on the borders of the Kazakh and Kyrgyz republics and Mongolia, with which it had far closer ethnic, cultural and religious ties than with the rest of the PRC. Though covering one-sixth of China's territory (an area the size of western Europe), the XUAR still accounts for only 1.4 per cent of the Chinese population (17 million out of 1.2 billion). Even today over half its population is composed of non-Chinese Muslim ethnic groups, by far the largest of which are the Muslim Uighurs. Before the foundation of the PRC the proportion was much larger. In 1944 a Uighur-led movement in northern Xinjiang had established the independent state of East Turkestan. Though its independence ended when it was forcibly incorporated by the PRC in 1950, Beijing remained concerned by the threat of XUAR separatism for the remainder of the century. Han Chinese immigration, promoted by Beijing and deeply resented by the Uighurs, increased their numbers from only 6 per cent of the population in 1949 to 40 per cent thirty years later. The leading Communist Party officials at almost all levels in the XUAR were, and remain, Chinese.[32] The horrors of the Cultural Revolution were arguably even worse for the non-Chinese minorities in the XUAR, Inner (Chinese) Mongolia and Tibet, whose whole way of life was threatened, than for the Han Chinese who constituted 94 per cent of the PRC population. The deputy director of religious affairs in Kashgar, one of the most devoutly Muslim cities of the XUAR, later admitted:

During the Cultural Revolution, I saw with my own eyes, before the Great Mosque in Kashgar, piles of Korans and other books being burnt. Some people ordered the Muslims to burn these copies themselves ... I also saw people trying to pull down the minarets beside the Great Mosque. The masses were very indignant, but they could do nothing.

Mosques in most of the XUAR were closed. Some were used as pork warehouses and Uighur families were forced to rear pigs.[33] The suffering of Tibetan Buddhists was even greater than that of Muslims in the XUAR, but Tibet was too remote and difficult of access for significant KGB operations (though the Centre investigated the possibility of penetrating the entourage of the exiled Dalai Lama).[34]

The XUAR, by contrast, had a 1,000-mile frontier with Kazakhstan and one of 600 miles with Mongolia.

In 1968 the Kazakhstan KGB was instructed to set up an illegal residency in Urumqi, the capital of the XUAR, and agent groups in a number of other areas, including the Lop Nor nuclear test site.[35] The Politburo also authorized the KGB to provide arms and training in Kazakhstan for the underground resistance to Chinese rule in the XUAR, which in Russian took the politically correct name of the Voenno-Trudovaya Narodnaya Revolyutsionnaya Partiya (Military-Labour People's Revolutionary Party) or VTNRP, code-named PATRIOTY. The Kazakhstan KGB was instructed to print anti-Chinese newspapers in Uighur, Kazakh, Kyrgyz, Dungan and the other XUAR languages to be smuggled across the border.[36] *Sherki Türkestan Evasi* ('The Voice of Eastern Turkestan'), published in Alma Ata, the capital of Kazakhstan, called on Uighurs 'to unite against Chinese chauvinism and to proclaim the establishment of "an independent free state" based on the principles of self-determination and the constitutional law of the United Nations'. Broadcasts by Radio Alma Ata and Radio Tashkent sought to convince XUAR Uighurs that living conditions for Soviet Uighurs were vastly superior to their own.[37]

In April 1968 the Politburo also approved a further reinforcement of Soviet forces along its 4,000-mile frontier with China, the longest armed border in the world.[38] About one third of Soviet military power was eventually deployed against the PRC.[39] Mao, Moscow feared, was intent on regaining large tracts of territory ceded to Tsarist Russia under the 'unequal treaties' of the nineteenth century.[40] During 1969 there were a series of armed clashes along the border. The first, on a remote stretch of the Ussuri river 250 miles from Vladivostok, does not seem to have been planned by either Beijing or Moscow. The trouble began when soldiers on the Chinese side of the river, offended by the allegedly aggressive behaviour of a Soviet lieutenant on the opposite bank, turned their backs, dropped their trousers and 'mooned' at the Soviet border guards. During the next 'mooning' episode, the Soviet soldiers held up pictures of Mao, thus leading the Chinese troops inadvertently to show grave disrespect to the sacred image of the Great Helmsman. These and other episodes led on 2 March to the Chinese ambush of a Soviet patrol on the small, disputed island of Damansky in the Ussuri river.[41]

Twenty-three of the patrol were killed. Both Moscow and Beijing responded with a furious denunciation of the other. This was the first occasion on which either side had reported an armed clash along the border. On 7 March a reported 100,000 Muscovites attacked the Chinese embassy and smashed its windows. Not to be outdone, Beijing Radio claimed that 400 million Chinese, half the country's population, had taken part in protest demonstrations.[42]

In mid-April 1969 there was fighting 2,500 miles farther west on the Kazakh–XUAR border, followed by further sporadic clashes in the same area over the next four months. Henry Kissinger, recently appointed as President Nixon's National Security Advisor, was originally inclined to accept Soviet claims that these clashes were started by the Chinese. When he looked at a detailed map of the frontier region, however, he changed his mind. Since the clashes occurred close to Soviet railheads and several hundred miles from any Chinese railway, Kissinger concluded that 'Chinese leaders would not have picked such an unpropitious spot to attack'.[43] His conclusion that Soviet forces were the aggressors is strengthened by the evidence in KGB files. On 4 June two KGB agents in the VTNRP, codenamed NARIMAN and TALAN, both based in Kazakhstan, crossed secretly into the XUAR to make contact with the underground Party leadership. On their return on 9 July, they reported, probably with considerable exaggeration, that the VTNRP had 70,000 members and a Presidium of forty-one (ten of whom were 'candidate', non-voting members). But it had not been a wholly successful mission. Within a few days of their arrival in the XUAR, the agents' automatic weapons and radio telephones had been stolen by TALAN's relatives. NARIMAN and TALAN also explained that they had been unable to set up a dead letter-box in an agreed location because of the presence of nomadic herdsmen. They reported that many former members of the VTNRP Presidium were in prison. The Mongolian security service concluded that the VTNRP was not ready for 'active operations' but should concentrate instead on strengthening its underground organization. Though Mitrokhin's notes do not record the Centre's assessment, it must surely have reached the same conclusion.[44]

In August and September Moscow began sounding out both Washington and European Communist parties on their reaction to the possibility of a Soviet pre-emptive strike against Chinese nuclear installations before they were able to threaten the Soviet Union. A series of articles in the Western press by a journalist co-opted by the KGB, Victor Louis (born Vitali Yevgenyevich Lui), mentioned the possibility of a Soviet air strike against the Lop Nor nuclear test site in the XUAR. Louis claimed that a clandestine radio station in the PRC had revealed the existence of anti-Mao forces (probably a reference to the XUAR) which might ask other socialist countries for 'fraternal help'. Even the KGB officers who spread such rumours were uncertain whether they were engaged simply in an active measure designed to intimidate the Chinese or warning the West of proposals under serious consideration by the Soviet general staff. In retrospect, the whole exercise looks more like an active-measures campaign.[45] Though the Soviet Defence Minister, Marshal Andrei Grechko, appears to have proposed a plan to 'get rid of the Chinese threat once and for all', most of his Politburo colleagues were not prepared to take the risk.[46]

As a result of the lack of any high-level Soviet intelligence source in Beijing, Moscow seems to have been unaware of the dramatic secret response by Mao to its campaign of intimidation after the border clashes. Mao set up a study group of four marshals whom he instructed to undertake a radical review of Chinese relations with the Soviet Union and the United States. Marshals Chen Yi and Ye Jianying made the unprecedented proposal that the PRC respond to the Soviet threat by playing 'the United States card'.[47] Fear of a pre-emptive Soviet strike seems to have been a major reason for the Chinese decision to enter the secret talks with the United States which led to Nixon's visit to Beijing in 1972 and a Sino-American *rapprochement* which only a few years earlier would have seemed inconceivable.[48] During Nixon's visit, Kissinger gave Marshal Ye Jianying an intelligence briefing on Soviet force deployments at the Chinese border which, he told him, was so highly classified that even many senior US intelligence officials had not had access to it.[49]

There was prolonged discussion in the Centre in the early 1970s as to whether the PRC now qualified for the title 'Main Adversary', hitherto applied exclusively to the United States. In the end it was relegated in official KGB jargon to the status of 'Major Adversary', with the United States retaining its unique 'Main Adversary' status.[50] For China, by contrast, it was clear that the Soviet Union had become the Main Adversary. Mao's suspicions of Moscow deepened as reports began to reach him of a plot by his heir apparent, Lin Biao. By the summer of 1970, according to his doctor, Li Zhisui, 'Mao's paranoia was in full bloom.' Li was afraid even to tell Mao that he had pneumonia for fear of being accused of being part of Lin Biao's conspiracy. 'Lin Biao wants my lungs to rot,' Mao told him. In August 1971 Mao was told that Lin's son had set up a 'secret spy organization in the air force' to prepare a coup. On the evening of 12 September Mao was informed that Lin Biao had fled by air from Shanhaiguan airport. Li noted that 'Mao's face collapsed at the news.' Lin's plane had taken off with such haste that it had not been properly fuelled and had no navigator, radio operator or co-pilot on board. It was also clear, since the aircraft had struck a fuel truck during the take-off and lost part of its landing gear, that it would have difficulty landing. As Chinese radar tracked Lin's plane, it first flew west across Inner Mongolia, then turned abruptly north across the frontier of the Mongolian People's Republic in the direction of the Soviet Union. Next day Mao received news that the plane had crashed before it reached the Soviet border, killing all on board.[51] Had the aircraft reached the Soviet Union, the public quarrel between Beijing and Moscow would doubtless have scaled new heights of hysteria. Even after the crash, there were Chinese charges of Soviet complicity in Lin Biao's treason.[52] Mao never admitted that the Cultural Revolution had been a disastrous mistake. 'But', according to Li, 'Lin Biao's perfidy convinced him that he needed to change his strategy. He put Zhou Enlai in charge of rehabilitating many of the leaders who had been overthrown.'[53]

For the remainder of the Soviet era the KGB sought, without much apparent success, to compensate for its inability to penetrate the government in Beijing by two other strategies: cross-border agent infiltration, particularly from Kazakhstan to the XUAR, and the penetration of PRC groups outside China. In 1969 the Kazakhstan KGB was given an additional fifty-five operations officers, followed by another eighty-one in 1970.[54] To assemble an appropriate wardrobe for KGB agents, clothes were taken from Chinese refugees crossing the Kazakhstan border.[55] In 1970 operation ALGA, mounted by the Kazakhstan KGB in collaboration with 'special actions' officers from the Centre, set out to create a sabotage base in the XUAR with caches to conceal arms and explosives. After a preliminary cross-border expedition by two agents ran into difficulty, however, the operation was suspended as premature and plans to infiltrate an armed group of seven or eight refugees back into the XUAR were cancelled.[56]

Over the next few years there were a series of other failed penetrations. Among them was the Chinese refugee MITOU, former head of the Department of Chinese Literature at a technical institute, who had fled to the Soviet Union in 1968 at the height of the Cultural Revolution when centres of higher education were closed for several years. After being recruited as a KGB agent and trained in the use of dead letter-boxes (DLBs), radio communication, ciphers and photography, he was smuggled into the XUAR across the Mongolian frontier in August 1971. Though MITOU collected money and food coupons which had been left for him in a DLB, no more was heard from him. His file concludes that he was probably too frightened to carry on working as an agent.[57] LIVENTSOV was another Chinese agent infiltrated into the XUAR through Mongolia. In 1972 he was used for operation STRELA which was intended to carry out visual reconnaissance of nuclear and defence industry plants. He was taught to distinguish different kinds of smoke and effluents from factory chimneys, take soil and water samples and make careful notes of what he observed. As in the case of MITOU, however, LIVENTSOV's deployment ended in complete failure.[58]

Probably because of the high failure rate among Chinese agents infiltrated over the border, the KGB devised an unusual method of testing their reliability under operational conditions. In operation ZENIT the agents being tested were told they would be crossing the Chinese border in an area near the Ussuri river first to locate a DLB and replace a malfunctioning radio which had been left in it with a working model, then to meet an agent operating inside China at a pre-arranged location in order to pass on instructions. The agents being tested, however, were unaware that the area where they were carrying out these operations was actually inside the Soviet Union and that they were being closely observed from surveillance posts equipped with night-vision equipment and tape recorders. ZENIT was one of five border zones in which similar tests took place. In 1974 sixty-six agents were put through their paces; in 1975 their number rose to 107.[59] In addition to sending agents on foot across remote areas of China's northern borders, the KGB also investigated two other methods of infiltration: by sea using inflatable dinghies which could be hidden after landing and, more ingeniously, by concealing an agent in the ventilation pipe of the mail carriages of trains crossing the Chinese border. The latter method was thought to be practicable only in summer because of the danger in winter that the agent would freeze to death.[60] The files seen by Mitrokhin do not make clear whether either of these methods was actually used.

Operational conditions in the PRC were simply too difficult for cross-border infiltration by any route to achieve significant success. As Jung Chang was later to write in *Wild Swans*, 'The whole of China was like a prison. Every house, every street was watched by the people themselves. In this vast land there was nowhere to hide.'[61] Strangers and strange behaviour quickly aroused suspicion. A Chinese agent smuggled across the Amur river in the Soviet Far East after a ten-year absence from the PRC discovered that the cigarettes he had been given to take with him were now available only in hard-currency shops reserved for foreigners. He made the further mistake, when out of cigarettes, of asking strangers for a smoke – a habit he had picked up in the Soviet Union which immediately attracted attention in the PRC. Having become accustomed to the metric system, the agent also ran into difficulties with Chinese weights and measures and found himself hesitating in mid-sentence while he attempted the necessary mental arithmetic. Even asking for directions caused problems. In Russia he had learned to think in terms of 'left' and 'right', instead of referring to points of the compass as was usual in China. On one occasion, when told that the entrance to an eating place was the south door, he asked where the south door was – only to be informed that it was opposite the north door.[62]

Probably late in 1973 the Centre sent a directive to residencies around the world entitled 'Measures designed to improve work against China from third countries' during the period 1974–78. Residencies were instructed to cultivate PRC citizens living abroad, as well as members of the Chinese diaspora, Taiwanese citizens and foreigners with contacts in the PRC. They were also told to penetrate Maoist groups and centres of Chinese studies, to plant 'operational devices' (bugs) on appropriate cultivation targets, identify active-measures channels and report on agents who could be sent on missions to the PRC.[63] The KGB residency in Prague reported in 1975 that it was using thirty agents to cultivate the Chinese embassy. Of seventy-two Czechoslovak citizens who attended a reception at the embassy in October 1975 to mark the anniversary of the foundation of the PRC, twenty-three were agents of the KGB or the Czechoslovak StB.[64] There is no evidence in any of the files noted by Mitrokhin that either this or any similar cultivation achieved any significant results. Most Chinese embassies appear to have proved as difficult targets as the PRC itself.

Unsurprisingly, the files seen by Mitrokhin do not identify a single KGB agent in Beijing with access to classified Chinese documents. The Beijing residency did, however, obtain some material from a senior disaffected North Korean diplomat codenamed FENIKS, who was privately critical of the Mao cult (and, no doubt, the even more preposterous cult of Kim Il Sung in North Korea). A Line PR officer under diplomatic cover, A. A. Zhemchugov, began cultivating FENIKS at diplomatic receptions and in the course of other routine diplomatic contacts. On several occasions Zhemchugov arranged for them to meet in his apartment. The residency reported that FENIKS showed great skill in disguising the purpose of his contacts with Zhemchugov, maintained careful security and appeared confident and calm during their meetings, which gradually increased in frequency. Due to the close relations between the Beijing and Pyongyang regimes in the mid-1970s, the North Korean embassy was given copies of a series of secret Chinese Central Committee documents, some of which were passed on by FENIKS. Among other material which he provided was a letter from the Politburo member Yao Wenyuan, later to become infamous after Mao's death as one of the disgraced 'Gang of Four'. Though documents supplied by FENIKS were cited in a number of KGB reports to the Politburo, he made clear to Zhemchugov that he wished to preserve his freedom of action and was not prepared to become a KGB agent. None the less, because of his willingness to supply classified material and from 1976 to have clandestine contact with a case officer, FENIKS was classed from that year as a confidential contact. From November 1976 he passed material to Zhemchugov during brush contacts in a Beijing department store.[65]

In the summer of 1976, with Mao's death correctly judged to be imminent, the Politburo set up a high-level commission to assess the future of Sino-Soviet relations. Chaired by the chief Party ideologist, Mikhail Suslov (then considered Brezhnev's most likely successor), the commission also included Gromyko, the Foreign Minister, Usti-nov, the Defence Minister, Andropov, the KGB Chairman, and Konstantin Chernenko, then head of the Central Committee General Department which, despite its innocuous name, controlled the Party's secret archives. Following Mao's death on 9 September, Soviet press attacks on China were suspended until the policy of his successors had been clarified. KGB residencies around the world were instructed to report any sign of changed attitudes towards the Soviet Union by Chinese officials[66] and sent a lengthy brief 'On certain national-psychological characteristics of the Chinese and their evaluation in the context of intelligence work' which was intended to improve the dismal level of agent recruitment:

Experience has shown that success in agent-operational work with persons of Chinese nationality depends to a large extent on the possession by intelligence personnel of a sound knowledge of their national-psychological peculiarities. A sound appreciation of the traits of the Chinese national character is essential for the study of potentially interesting sources of information, for progress towards a satisfactory recruitment, and for agent running.

Though emphasizing the importance of 'establishing a solid, friendly relationship with the Chinese based on respect for the individual and Chinese culture', the brief simultaneously made clear the Centre's loathing for the citizens of the PRC. They were, the brief reported, deeply imbued with an egocentric view of the world; became 'uncontrollable' when their pride was hurt; were 'distinguished by their hot temper, great excitability, and a tendency to sudden changes from one extreme to another'; possessed an innate ability to dissemble which made them 'a nation of actors'; had characters in which, in most cases, 'the negative qualities of perfidiousness, cruelty and anger are inherent'; were 'noted for their spitefulness'; and were indifferent to the misery and misfortunes of other people. Because of the obsession with 'loss of face', however, 'the use of compromising material is a strong lever to make a Chinese collaborate'.[67] Similar views, enlivened by the swear words in which the Russian language is unusually rich, were common in conversations about China at the Centre. Underlying the KGB's attitude to the PRC was thinly disguised racial loathing as well as ideological and strategic rivalry.

Less than a month after Mao's death, his widow Jiang Qing and her main radical associates, the so-called 'Gang of Four', were arrested and denounced as traitors in the service of the Chinese Nationalists. KGB officers must privately have recalled the equally absurd claim in Moscow after Beria's arrest and execution that he had been a British agent. Over the next few years, as the Cultural Revolution was finally brought to a conclusion, the Gang of Four became convenient if improbable scapegoats for all the horrors of the Mao regime which could be publicly acknowledged. As the BBC correspondent, Philip Short, noted:

Every Chinese official knew that the 'Gang of Four' had been Mao's closest followers; and every Chinese official without exception depicted them as Mao's most vicious enemies . . . Every official conversation began with the words, 'Because of the interference and sabotage of the Gang of Four . . .' – followed by a litany of the sins they were alleged to have committed.[68]

Service A attempted to cause confusion among Maoist parties outside China by fabricating a final testament from Mao to Jiang Qing calling on her to 'continue the work I had started'. The forgery was circulated in the name of supporters of the Gang of Four, calling on Marxist-Leninists everywhere to condemn the betrayal of Mao's legacy by the current regime.[69]

Though Moscow welcomed the disgrace of the Gang of Four, it remained pessimistic about the prospects for reconciliation with Mao's successors. The Centre's list of intelligence requirements for 1977 concluded that 'the ruling circle in China remains, as before, nationalistic, hegemonistic and anti-Soviet'. China, it admitted, remained a 'conundrum'. The FCD wanted intelligence on power struggles within the Party leadership and the People's Liberation Army, the future prospects of Deng Xiaoping (the most senior survivor of those purged in the Cultural Revolution) and policy changes in the post-Mao era. While it saw no prospect of major improvements in Sino-Soviet relations, it hoped for a 'gradual overhaul of Maoism and for a partial abstention from its more odious aspects', leading to 'a more sober approach' to China's dealings with the Soviet Union.[70]

In July 1977 a red wall poster sixty feet long with black characters two feet high placed on an official building announced that the

Central Committee had reinstated Deng Xiaoping. The broadcast of an official communiqué confirming his reinstatement was followed by the sound of firecrackers across Beijing and jubilant flag-waving, gong-banging, drum-beating demonstrations in Tiananmen Square. Though the demonstrations were orchestrated, the jubilation was genuine. To the demonstrators the diminutive figure of Deng, the shortest of the major world leaders, represented the hope of a better life after the horrors of the past.[71] Deng's rehabilitation and subsequent emergence as the dominant Chinese leader caused mixed feelings in the Centre. Though he was believed to be a pragmatist rather than an ideological fanatic, his past record suggested that he was also strongly anti-Soviet. The FCD concluded that Deng had two main foreign objectives: first, to gain concessions from the United States; second, to make a show of improving relations with the Soviet Union in order to blame Moscow for the lack of real progress. His economic modernization programme, with its initially heavy reliance on Western technology, capital and expertise, caused further distrust in Moscow.

In January 1978 KGB residents were informed by a circular from the Centre that the Deng regime was on 'a collision course with the USSR', and that the modernization of Chinese armed forces with Western help represented 'a particular danger'. Intelligence operations against the PRC, however, were seriously hampered by 'the continuous intensification of the counter-intelligence measures in Beijing'. It was therefore urgently necessary to compensate for the weakness of intelligence collection within the PRC by stepping up operations against Chinese targets abroad. Though some 'residencies in third countries' were said to have achieved 'positive' results, the 'lack of the essential agent apparatus' remained a severe handicap. Residents were admonished for their lack of energy in Line K work and ordered to redouble their efforts.[72]

The Centre gave particular emphasis to increasing operations against PRC targets in Hong Kong. In April 1978 residents were sent a detailed target list:

There has been a marked increase in the number of PRC official missions in Hong Kong over the past few years and, equally, of various local organizations and undertakings which are under the control of Beijing. Thus, the PRC controls more than forty Hong Kong banks, a large number of trading and industrial firms, together with a number of local newspapers. Chinese influence is also strong in the Hong Kong trades unions.

Additional targets included foreign missions in Hong Kong, British and American intelligence posts, and scientific institutions whose students were regarded as potential Line X agents. Though some of the potential targets were shrewdly chosen, there were also some curious omissions which suggested significant gaps in the KGB's information on Hong Kong. Its references to the Hong Kong newspapers 'best informed on the Chinese scene', for example, made no mention of the *Ming Pao*, which was considered by some Western Sinologists to be the best informed of all.[73]

Active measures as well as intelligence collection proved more difficult against Chinese than against Western targets. The KGB's failure to recruit agents able to provide authentic documents from the Chinese Ministries of Foreign Affairs, Defence and Public Security, for example, made it impossible for Service A to produce plausible fabrications of material from these ministries comparable to its forgeries of CIA, State Department and Pentagon documents. The Centre complained in January 1978 that, 'The future improvement of the level and efficiency of active measures on China is adversely affected by the lack of essential agent apparatus.'[74] The Party documents provided by FENIKS (and perhaps by others), however, enabled Service A to imitate the format of speeches by Deng Xiaoping and other Chinese leaders at closed Party meetings. In operation AUT transcripts of speeches supposedly made by Deng and a Deputy Foreign Minister in Beijing on 29 September 1977 to leading supporters of the PRC among the Chinese diaspora, which emphasized their role as the 'connecting link of world revolution' in undermining the 'reactionary regimes' of South-East Asia, were sent to the embassies of Indonesia, Thailand and Malaysia in Singapore.[75] To compensate for its lack of official Chinese documents to use as templates for forgeries, Service A also frequently fabricated hostile reports on the PRC from those foreign intelligence agencies and foreign ministries of which it had sample documents on file. In August 1978, for example, a bogus Malaysian intelligence report, purporting to contain details of the subversive activities of Chinese agents sent to Malaysia and Thailand by Beijing, was given to the ambassador of Thailand in Kuala Lumpur.[76] A month later further disinformation was fed to President Asad of Syria (apparently in the form of an Iranian report on talks with a Chinese delegation), supposedly revealing a secret meeting between the Chinese Foreign Minister, Huang Hua, and an emissary of the Israeli Prime Minister, Menachem Begin. Asad was reported to have been completely deceived. 'I always treat the Chinese with suspicion', he told his Soviet informant, 'but, even so, I didn't expect this of them.'[77]

The Centre also used active measures in an attempt to disrupt China's relations with Communist regimes outside the Soviet bloc. In 1967 it devised an operation to channel to the Romanian leader, Nicolae Ceauşescu, a bogus version of Zhou Enlai's private comments after his return from a visit to Bucharest in the previous year. Zhou was said to have praised the ability of the Romanian Prime Minister, Ion Gheorge Maurer, 'the real leader of the Party and government', his deputy Emil Bodnaraş, who 'hates Ceauşescu', and several other members of the Romanian Presidium. He dismissed Ceauşescu, by contrast, as 'an uncultured upstart' who, despite his notorious vanity, ranked only fifth in influence in the Presidium. The Centre had no doubt that Ceauşescu would be so outraged at this personal insult that there would be a 'sharp change in [Romanian] relations with the Chinese People's Republic'.[78]

Service A also attempted to drive a wedge between China and North Korea. In 1978, during the visit of General Zia ul-Haq to Beijing, the North Korean embassy in Islamabad was sent a forged Pakistani document produced by Service A reporting that he had been told that the Chinese leadership had informed the US Secretary of State, Cyrus Vance, that they accepted the need for American troops to remain in South Korea.[79] As the Centre had hoped, Chinese–North Korean relations deteriorated sharply at the end of the decade. The reasons, however, had far less to do with KGB active measures than with North Korean distrust of the Sino-American *rapprochement*. On 1 January 1979 the United States and the PRC commenced full diplomatic relations. In February Chinese forces invaded the Soviet Union's ally, Vietnam, and for the next month waged the world's first war between 'socialist' states. Soviet arms supplies to North Korea, which had been suspended in 1973, resumed during 1979. On Red Army Day in February 1980, Pyong-yang celebrated anew the 'militant friendship' between Soviet and North Korean forces.

The agent of influence who carried most authority in the KGB active-measures campaign in the West against the PRC during the later 1970s was probably Jean Pasqualini, also known as Bao Ruowang. The son of a Corsican father and a Chinese mother, Pasqualini was arrested in 1957, charged with imaginary 'counter-revolutionary activities' as 'an agent of the imperialists and a loyal running dog of the Americans', and spent the next seven years in the *laogai*. He first came to the attention of the Paris residency in the early 1970s while writing, in collaboration with an American journalist, a memoir of his harrowing experiences in labour camp, *Prisoner of Mao*. 'Over the years', wrote Pasqualini, 'Mao's police have perfected their interrogation methods to such a fine point that I would defy any man, Chinese or not, to hold out against them.' Though he later recovered from his brainwashing, at the time he was sentenced he felt that he 'truly loved Mao, his police and the People's Courts'. The KGB was doubtless impressed by the fact that, despite being 'employed as slave labour', Pasqualini did not emerge from the *laogai* as an anti-Communist. Though hostile to Mao's regime, he admired 'the honesty and dedication of most of the Communist cadres' and insisted that his book was not intended to give aid and comfort to the CIA.[80] First published in the United States in 1973, *Prisoner of Mao* was published in Britain two years later and translated into Chinese, French, German, Spanish and other languages. It remains a classic and is still listed prominently on the booklists of campaigners against the *laogai*. Pasqualini was first contacted by the Paris residency in 1972 and became a KGB agent in 1975 with the codename CHAN, paid 1,500 francs a month. As well as teaching at the Paris École des Langues Orientales, he was invited to give a series of lectures at Oxford University in 1978 on the abuse of human rights in the PRC. As in his Oxford lectures, Pasqualini proved willing to add to his authentic experience of the *laogai* information passed to him by the KGB, which included – according to his file – a number of Service A fabrications. Between June 1977 and December 1978 he had forty-eight meetings with his case officer, who was convinced of his 'sincerity'. In 1979, however, the KGB discovered that Pasqualini was under surveillance by the DST, the French security service.[81] The breach of security which led to the surveillance was probably the fault of the Paris residency. In June 1979 the residency's most important agent of influence,

Pierre-Charles Pathé, was arrested while meeting his case officer, who had been tailed by the DST.[82] Mitrokhin's notes on Pasqualini's file end in 1979, and it is unclear whether his contact with the KGB was later resumed.[83]

For the Chinese people the most dramatic indications of the new era which followed Deng's victory in the succession struggle after Mao's death were the posthumous rehabilitation of the most celebrated victim of the Cultural Revolution, Liu Shaoqi, in February 1980, followed in November by the beginning of the two-month trial of the Gang of Four. Liu was declared the victim of the 'biggest frame-up in the history of our Party' and given a belated state funeral. At their trial, to preserve the memory of Mao as unsullied as possible, the Gang of Four were made responsible for this and all other atrocities of the Cultural Revolution. It is probably a sign of the lack of high-grade Soviet intelligence on these political convulsions that a French Foreign Ministry report on President Giscard d'Estaing's visit to the PRC in October 1980, provided by Agent SEN in Paris, was forwarded to the Politburo as a document of special importance.[84]

In a report early in 1984 on KGB operations during the previous two years, Vladimir Kryuchkov, the head of the FCD, claimed that: 'Beijing is blocking normalization of Sino-Soviet relations . . . Beijing is counting on deriving political advantages for itself by manoeuvring between the West and the socialist countries, and trying to blackmail the West with the prospect of an improvement of relations with the Soviet Union.'

In general, Kryuchkov was dissatisfied with the performance of Line K:

The [FCD] has achieved some useful results over the past two years in its work against China, but the successes have been in general in the nature of isolated episodes. Many residencies are still slow in dealing with the specific tasks posed by [agent] recruitment. Insufficient attention is being given to promising categories of Chinese nationals abroad such as specialists, students and trainees. Little effort is being made to select agents for prolonged periods in the PRC or in Hong Kong or Taiwan.

Residencies must step up their endeavour to achieve solid results in recruiting Chinese nationals. The most highly trained officers and experienced agents must be directed into this work. We must not let slip the opportunities created by the changeover in personnel in the Chinese state administration, the process of discrediting Maoist ideology and the purge carried out in the Party.

Nowhere more than in working against China do we require circumspection, patience, endurance and accurate appreciation of the particular characteristics of the Chinese.[85]

The FCD Plan for 1984 ordered active-measures operations to 'counter the military and political *rapprochement* between the PRC and the USA and other imperialist countries on an anti-Soviet basis'.[86] Among them were active measures intended to disrupt Anglo-Chinese relations over the future of Hong Kong. In the 'Joint Declaration' signed in December 1984, Britain and the PRC agreed that Hong Kong would return to full Chinese sovereignty after the expiry of the British lease on the bulk of the colony in 1997 but that for the next half-century the capitalist system would continue in Hong Kong under the formula, 'One Country, Two Systems'. The KGB sought, without striking success, to disseminate through the media the 'thesis' that weak-kneed Britain had suffered a major humiliation at the hands of the Chinese.[87]

At the beginning of the Gorbachev era the KGB continued to find the PRC the most difficult of its major targets to penetrate. In April 1985 a review of operations against China by Directorate T (Scientific and Technological Espionage), one of the FCD's most successful sections, disclosed serious and persistent 'shortcomings'. Of the S&T collected by residencies only 1 per cent related to China and its quality was considered 'low'. Residents were informed of these findings during May in a circular which berated them for 'a number of negligences' – chief among them their lack of Chinese contacts, which was described as 'a source of extreme anxiety'.[88] This anxiety extended to all aspects of intelligence collection against Chinese targets. As Nikolai Leonov acknowledged after the collapse of the Soviet Union, 'We had an unbridgeable gap in our information sources on China.'[89]

One conundrum, however, remains. Mitrokhin had no access to the SIGINT archives of the KGB Eighth and Sixteenth Directorates, which house diplomatic decrypts.[90] The files noted by him contain few clues about the KGB's ability to intercept and decrypt PRC communications. As in other major capitals, the Beijing residency contained a SIGINT station, codenamed KRAB. Its budget for 1979, a fraction of that for the US residencies and significantly lower than that for the main European capitals, does not suggest, by KGB standards, a high level of activity.[91] Probably in the early to mid-1970s operation ALPHA succeeded in 'the technical penetration of the People's Republic of China embassy and other Chinese establishments in Ulan Bator', but Mitrokhin's notes give no indication of the intelligence which this generated.[92] Viktor Makarov, a former KGB officer who worked in the Sixteenth Directorate from 1980 to 1986, believes that the significance of Chinese SIGINT declined in the early 1980s. From 1981 he was permitted to enter the office used by Chinese cryptanalysts, which had hitherto been out of bounds. Makarov deduced, probably correctly, that its current success rate no longer merited the unusually high level of security previously accorded to the office within the directorate.[93] Though Chinese communications were also intercepted by other sections of the vast KGB and GRU SIGINT network, on present evidence it seems unlikely that cryptanalysis was able to compensate adequately for the relative failure of agent recruitment.

16

Japan

With the exception of Kim Philby, the most celebrated of all Soviet spies was the German GRU illegal Richard Sorge, who was stationed in Tokyo in 1933, posing so successfully as a Nazi newspaper correspondent for the next eight years that a Japanese journalist described him as 'a typical, swashbuckling arrogant Nazi . . . quick-tempered, hard-drinking'. He was also, according to the female Soviet agent Hede Massing, 'startlingly good-looking'. As well as penetrating the German embassy in Tokyo and seducing the ambassador's wife, Sorge also ran a Japanese spy ring headed by an idealistic young Marxist from a wealthy family, Hotsumi Osaki, a member of the brains trust of the leading statesman, Prince Konoye. Sorge correctly forecast both the Japanese invasion of China in 1937 and the German invasion of the Soviet Union in 1941, sending crucial reassurance on both occasions that the Japanese did not intend to invade Siberia. Until the Wehrmacht began its attack on 22 June 1941, Stalin refused to believe all intelligence warnings of the German invasion, dismissing Sorge as a lying 'shit who has set himself up with some small factories and brothels in Japan'. Shortly before his arrest in October 1941, however, Sorge received a belated message of thanks from Moscow. In 1964, twenty years after his execution by the Japanese, he was made a Hero of the Soviet Union, honoured by a series of officially approved hagiographies and – most unusually for a foreign agent – a special issue of postage stamps. Though Sorge had worked for the rival GRU, the Centre regarded him as the ideal role model to inspire a new generation of KGB illegals. At the Twenty-fourth CPSU Congress in Moscow in 1971, senior KGB officers approached a series of Western Communist Party leaders to seek help in recruiting illegals from their countries. In each case, as an indication of the kind of recruit they were looking for, they gave the example of Richard Sorge.[1] At that very moment, however, a series of agents in the Tokyo Foreign Ministry were providing a greater volume of classified documents on Japanese foreign policy (albeit at a less critical time in Soviet–Japanese relations) than Sorge's spy ring had obtained a generation earlier. Their names, unlike that of Sorge, have never been made public.[2]

Japan's defeat in the Pacific War in August 1945 was followed by an American military occupation which imposed on it a new democratic constitution. In September 1951 a peace treaty signed in the improbable setting of the San Francisco Opera House provided for the occupation to end in the following April. A US–Japanese Security Treaty signed on the same day, however, approved the maintenance of American military bases not merely to defend Japan from foreign attack and assist in maintaining the peace and security of the Far East but also, if requested by the Japanese government, to help 'put down large-scale internal riots and disturbances in Japan, caused through instigation or intervention of an outside Power or Powers'.[3] The Soviet Union refused to sign the San Francisco peace treaty and condemned the security treaty. Its refusal to give up the four islands in the southern chain of the Kuriles north of Hokkaido (known in Japan as the 'Northern Territories'), which it had occupied at the end of the war, made it impossible for the remainder of the century to conclude a peace treaty with Japan. A Soviet offer in 1956 to return the two southernmost islands (Shikotan and the Habomais[4]) in return for a peace treaty on its own terms failed to break the deadlock and was later withdrawn.

Throughout the Cold War one of the main priorities of the Tokyo residency's active measures was to drive a wedge between Japan and the United States. Its first major opportunity came with the negotiation of a revised security treaty in January 1960.[5] A campaign against ratification of the treaty begun by the Japanese Socialist Party (JSP), the Japanese Communist Party (JCP), the Trades Union General Council (Sohyo) and the Student Federation (Zengakuren) turned into the biggest mass movement in Japanese political history. At the height of the protest in May and June 1960, several million people in Tokyo and the main cities took part in street demonstrations and work stoppages, attended meetings and signed petitions. There were brawls in the Diet and riots in the streets, during which a female Tokyo University student was trampled to death.[6]

As usually happened with protest movements of which it approved, the KGB claimed excessive credit for it.[7] The Tokyo residency, however, at least partly inspired a number of anti-American incidents – among them an airport demonstration by Communist students in the Zengakuren against the arrival of President Dwight D. Eisenhower's press secretary, James Hagerty. In June the Liberal Democratic Party (LDP) government of Nobusuke Kishi suffered the humiliation of having to cancel a forthcoming visit by Eisenhower himself on the grounds that his personal safety could not be guaranteed. 'Viewed from any angle', wrote Eisenhower later, 'this was a Communist victory.'[8] The Centre, predictably, claimed the 'victory' for itself.[9] The Tokyo residency also succeeded in publicizing bogus secret annexes to the security treaty concocted by Service A, which purported to continue the 1951 agreement on the use of US troops to quell civil unrest and to extend US–Japanese military co-operation throughout the Far East from the Soviet Pacific to the Chinese coast.[10]

The KGB's tactical successes, however, had little strategic significance. A few days after the cancellation of Eisenhower's visit, the US–Japanese Security Treaty was ratified by the Japanese Diet. The resignation of the Kishi government shortly afterwards took the steam out of the protest movement. The left failed to make the treaty a major issue in the November elections at which the ruling LDP, which dominated Japanese politics from 1955 until 1993, gained another comfortable majority. The JCP received less than 3 per cent of the vote and won only three seats.[11]

The degree to which Japan was seen by the Centre as effectively a NATO member is indicated by the extensive activity during the 1960s by Line F ('special actions') at the Tokyo residency. In the event of war with NATO, Moscow planned a massive campaign of sabotage and disruption behind enemy lines. Each year residencies in NATO and some neutral European countries were expected to draw up detailed plans for the sabotage of four to six major targets.[12] The same applied in Japan, where both Japanese and US installations were targeted. In 1962, for example, Line F made preparations for the sabotage of four major oil refineries in different areas of Japan[13] as well as of US bases on Okinawa.[14] As in NATO countries, Line F in Tokyo was also instructed to reconnoitre possible wartime bases in remote parts of Japan for Soviet sabotage and intelligence groups (DRGs). In 1970, for example, Line F identified four possible DRG landing sites on the north-west coast of the island of Hokkaido.[15] As well as containing precise map references and detailed descriptions of the terrain, each file on a possible DRG base used a standardized coded jargon. Each DRG landing area was known as a DOROZHKA ('runway'); each site for a DRG base was termed a ULEY ('beehive').

The Tokyo residency also made plans for peacetime acts of sabotage intended to damage US–Japanese relations. In Line F jargon each act of sabotage was termed a 'lily' (*lilya*), the explosive device a 'bouquet' (*buket*), the detonator a 'little flower' (*tsvetok*), the explosion of the device a 'splash' (*zaplyv*), and the saboteur the 'gardener' (*sadovnik*).[16] Among the sabotage plans devised by Line F was operation VULKAN, an attack on the library of the American Cultural Center in Tokyo which was planned to coincide with demonstrations against the Vietnam War in October 1965. The illegal agent NOMOTO was to place a book bomb in a bookcase in the library shortly before it closed one evening, together with a detonator concealed in a pack of American cigarettes which was timed to go off in the early hours of the morning. In order to conceal the KGB's hand in the operation, Service A was to prepare leaflets purporting to come from Japanese nationalist extremists calling for attacks on US property.[17] The most dramatic scheme devised by Line F to cause a major crisis in US–Japanese relations was a 1969 plan to scatter radioactive material in Tokyo Bay in the expectation that it would be blamed on US nuclear submarines using the Yokosuka naval base and cause a national outcry. Though supported by the Tokyo resident, the plan was turned down by the Centre because of the difficulty of obtaining suitable radioactive material from the United States and the danger that the source of Soviet material might be detected.[18] Two years later KGB plans for 'special actions' were drastically scaled down after some of them were compromised by the defection in London of the Line F officer, Oleg Lyalin.[19]

The main problem encountered by Line PR during the 1960s was the loss of what had hitherto been its main intelligence asset, the assistance of the JCP, Asia's largest non-ruling Communist party. As the Sino-Soviet split developed, the Japanese Communist leadership sided more with Beijing than with Moscow. In 1964 Moscow, already engaged with Beijing in the most vitriolic polemics in the history of international Communism, accused the JCP of kowtowing to the Chinese Communist Party and declaring war on the CPSU. The JCP retaliated by denouncing the CPSU's 'brazen and unpardonable' attempts to dictate to its Japanese comrades: 'The chief cause for the disunity in the international Communist movement and the socialist camp today is precisely your self-conceit and the flagrant interference with, and attacks on, the fraternal parties unleashed brazenly by you as a result of this self-conceit.'

The JCP also complained of 'the destructive activities against our Party of Soviet Embassy staff members and special correspondents' – doubtless with the activities of the Tokyo residency particularly in mind. It correctly accused Moscow of using spies and informants to maintain contact with, and promote the interests of, those Japanese Communists pursuing 'anti-party [pro-Moscow] activities'.[20] The Chairman of the JCP Central Committee, Hakamadi Satomi, boasted of burning CPSU literature to heat his *ofuro* (Japanese bath).[21] In the space of a few years the JCP had changed from an important KGB intelligence asset into a hostile target.[22]

The Centre's Japanese operations suffered another major blow in 1963 with the loss of what seems to have been the main illegal KGB residency in Tokyo run by a veteran pro-Soviet Chinese Communist, JIMMY, who, with assistance from Communist Chinese intelligence, had succeeded in setting up an export–import company based in Hong Kong and Tokyo and in procuring bogus Hong Kong identity papers for other KGB illegals. When JIMMY failed to return from a visit to China to see his relatives after the Sino-Soviet split, the Centre decided to wind up his residency, probably fearing that it had been compromised.[23] The Tokyo residency's lack of major Japanese intelligence sources during the mid-1960s was reflected in the fact that its most productive agent from 1962 to 1967 was a journalist on the *Tokyo Shimbun*, codenamed KOCHI, who appears to have had access to high-level gossip from the cabinet and Foreign Ministry but probably not to classified documents.[24]

Line PR's main strategy after the breach with the JCP was to recruit leading members from the left wing of the main opposition party, the Japanese Socialist Party (JSP), which it codenamed KOOPERATIVA,[25] and to use them as agents of influence. On 26 February 1970 the Politburo approved the payment by the KGB of a total of 100,000 convertible rubles (35,714,000 yen) to a number of leading figures in the JSP and to subsidize the party newspaper.[26] Similar subsidies seem to have been paid each year.[27] Probably by the time the Politburo approved secret subsidies to the JSP, five influential party members had already been recruited as KGB agents: Seiichi Katsumata (codenamed GAVR), runner-up in the 1966 election for the post of JSP General Secretary, who in 1974 was given 4 million yen to strengthen his position in the party;[28] Tamotsu Sato (transparently codenamed ATOS), leader of a Marxist faction in the JSP, who was used to place active-measures material in four party periodicals;[29] ALFONS, who was paid 2.5 million yen in 1972, and used to place articles in the JSP daily *Shakai Shimpo*;[30] DUG, a JSP official close to the Party Chairman, who was given 390,000 yen in 1972 for his election campaign;[31] and DIK, paid 200,000 yen in 1972 to publish election leaflets and posters.[32] Other recruits in the 1970s included JACK, a JSP deputy and prominent trade unionist;[33] Shigero Ito (codenamed GRACE), also a deputy and a member of the party's Central Committee,[34] and DENIS, who had been a close aide of the former JSP Chairman Saburo Eda.[35] KGB confidential contacts included a former Communist codenamed KING, who had become one of the leading figures in the JSP,[36] and KERK, a member of Katsumata's JSP faction in the Diet.[37] Mitrokhin's notes on the files of DENIS and GRACE record that their motivation was both ideological and financial.[38] The same was probably true of most of the KGB's other agents in the JSP. The KGB's influence operations in the Diet were also assisted by the academic YAMAMOTO, who was described in his file as being 'ideologically close' to Moscow. After being recruited as an agent in 1977, he successfully prompted at least two parliamentary questions in each session of the Diet, which, according to the residency's possibly optimistic assessment, had a significant impact.[39]

Of the politicians recruited by the KGB outside the JSP, the most important was Hirohide Ishida (codenamed HOOVER), a prominent parliamentary deputy of the ruling Liberal Democratic Party (LDP), formerly Minister of Labour. In February 1973 Ishida became Chairman of the newly founded Parliamentary Japanese–Soviet Friendship Association (codenamed LOBBY),[40] and led a delegation to the Soviet Union from 27 August to 6 September, shortly before the visit of Kakuei Tanaka, the first by a Japanese Prime Minister for seventeen years. On this and subsequent visits to Moscow, Ishida was publicly fêted at the request of the Centre by Brezhnev, President Nikolai Podgorny, Prime Minister Aleksei Kosygin and other notables.[41] The KGB also went to great pains to flatter Ishida and assure him of the high regard in which he was held by the Soviet leadership. The leading Japanese newspaper, *Asahi Shimbun*, on which the KGB had at least one well-placed agent, reported after Ishida's visit to Moscow in the summer of 1973: 'The Soviet Union today said it would immediately release all forty-nine Japanese fishermen detained on charges of violating Soviet territorial waters. The announcement was made by the Chairman of the Presidium of the Supreme Soviet during his meeting with Hirohide Ishida, head of a visiting Japanese parliamentary delegation.'

According to Stanislav Levchenko, then working on the FCD Japanese desk, the Japanese fishermen released in honour of Ishida were among those 'routinely shanghaied and held for use as bargaining chips'. Ishida was also co-opted into the network of global flattery which the KGB used to service Brezhnev's voracious appetite for world-wide recognition. He was persuaded by Vladimir Pronnikov, head of Line PR at the Tokyo residency, to show his appreciation for the liberation of the fishermen by presenting Brezhnev with a maroon Nissan limousine to add to his considerable collection of luxury foreign cars. Levchenko, who suspected – probably correctly – that the Nissan had been purchased with KGB funds, was put in personal charge of the car, which was delivered in a crate to FCD headquarters, in order to prevent parts being stolen before its formal presentation to Brezhnev.[42] In 1974, already a KGB confidential contact, Ishida was recruited as an agent by Pronnikov, who was rewarded with the Order of the Red Banner.[43] Ishida became one of the Tokyo residency's leading agents of influence.

The priority attached by the Centre to operations in Japan in the early 1970s was reflected in the fact that the budget for them in 1973 was almost as large as for India and almost three times as large as for any of the eleven other Asian states which were then the responsibility of the FCD Seventh Department.[44] KGB active measures before and during Tanaka's visit to Moscow in 1973 were intended to promote a peace treaty and agreement on Japanese–Soviet relations on the lines agreed by the Politburo on 16 August. If progress was made during the negotiations, Tanaka was to be offered the return of the Habomais and Shikotan as well as concessions on fishing rights in return for the abrogation of the

US–Japanese Security Treaty and the closure of US military bases.[45] Though Tanaka was not expected to accept these terms, it was hoped to increase Japanese public support for an agreement on these lines.[46] The visit, however, achieved little. Tanaka insisted that return of all the Northern Territories was the pre-requisite for economic co-operation and other forms of improved relations with the Soviet Union.[47]

During the remainder of the 1970s, Ishida continued to be used as an agent of influence within both the LDP and the Parliamentary Japanese–Soviet Friendship Association. In 1977, at the request of the KGB, he complained personally to the LDP Prime Minister, Takeo Fukuda, that the Japanese ambassador in Moscow and his wife had made themselves unwelcome by their contacts with dissidents and to hint that it was time for him to be recalled.[48] During the 1970s there were at least two further recruitments within the LDP: FEN, a confidant of Kakuei Tanaka,[49] and KANI, a deputy whose career the Tokyo residency claimed to be actively promoting.[50] The key to the KGB's penetration of conservative politics was the corruption endemic in some factions of the LDP and other parts of Japanese society. Tanaka owed much of his phenomenal success in rising through the ranks to become a cabinet minister at the age of only thirty-nine, despite never having finished secondary school, to the consummate mastery of the politics of the pork barrel which helped to raise his remote prefecture of Niigata 'from rural obscurity to contemporary affluence'. All those who won contracts for the numerous public works in Niigata were expected to contribute handsomely to Tanaka's political war chest. In December 1974 he was forced to resign, allegedly on health grounds, after some details of his corruption appeared in the press. In 1976 much more damning evidence emerged that the US aircraft company Lockheed had paid Tanaka and other prominent LDP politicians large bribes to win a contract to supply its Tri-star planes to All Nippon Airways. Lockheed followed in an already long tradition of bribery by foreign firms.[51] The KGB, though able to exploit that tradition, was never able to compete financially with the kick-backs on offer from such major players as Lockheed and, partly for that reason, never truly penetrated the commanding heights of Japanese conservative politics.

Most KGB agents in the media probably also had mainly mercenary motives. Files noted by Mitrokhin identify at least five senior Japanese journalists (other than those on JSP publications) who were KGB agents during the 1970s: BLYUM on the *Asahi Shimbun*,[52] SEMYON on the *Yomiuri Shimbun*,[53] KARL (or KARLOV) on the *Sankei Shimbun*,[54] FUDZIE on the *Tokyo Shimbun*[55] and ODEKI, identified only as a senior political correspondent on a major Japanese newspaper.[56] The journalist ROY, who, according to his file, regarded his work for the KGB simply as 'a commercial transaction', was valuable chiefly for his intelligence contacts and was instrumental in the recruitment of KHUN, a senior Japanese counter-intelligence officer who provided intelligence on China.[57] Not all the paid agents in the Japanese media, however, were willing recruits. Mitrokhin's summary of SEMYON's file notes that, during a visit to Moscow in the early 1970s, 'He was recruited on the basis of compromising material': changing currency on the black market (probably in an ambush prepared for him by the SCD) and 'immoral' behaviour (doubtless one of the many variants of the KGB 'honey trap'). During his six years as a Soviet agent, SEMYON tried frequently to persuade the KGB to release him. The Centre eventually broke contact with him after he had been caught passing disinformation.[58]

Stanislav Levchenko later identified several other journalists used for KGB active measures,[59] of whom the most important seems to have been Takuji Yamane (codenamed KANT), assistant managing editor and personal adviser to the publisher of the conservative daily *Sankei Shimbun*. According to Levchenko, one of his controllers, Yamane skilfully concealed his pro-Soviet sympathies beneath a veneer of anti-Soviet and anti-Chinese nationalism and became one of the Tokyo residency's leading agents of influence. Among the Service A forgeries which he publicized was a bogus 'Last Will and Testament' of Zhou Enlai concocted soon after his death in 1976, which contained numerous references to the in-fighting and untrustworthiness of the rest of the Chinese leadership and was intended to disrupt negotiations for a Sino-Japanese peace treaty. The Centre doubtless calculated that the forgery would make more impact if published in a conservative rather than a JSP paper. It believed that even Beijing, which tried frantically to discover the origin of the document, was not at first sure whether or not the document was genuine.[60] After a detailed investigation, however, the Japanese intelligence community correctly identified Zhou's will as a forgery.[61] This and other active measures failed to prevent the signing on 12 August 1978 of a Sino-Japanese peace treaty which, to the fury of Moscow, contained a clause committing both signatories to opposing attempts by any power to achieve hegemony (a phrase intended by Beijing as a coded reference to Soviet policy).[62]

By the autumn of 1979 Line PR at the Tokyo residency had a total of thirty-one agents and twenty-four confidential contacts.[63] These statistics and examples of KGB disinformation planted in the media were doubtless used by the Centre to impress the Soviet political leadership – especially since the Japanese were the world's most avid newspaper readers.[64] The evidence of opinion polls demonstrates, however, that the KGB active-measures offensives in Japan against both the United States and China, though achieving a series of tactical successes, ended in strategic defeat. During the 1960s around 4 per cent of Japanese identified the Soviet Union as the foreign country they liked most. Despite the combined efforts of Service A, Line PR in Tokyo and a substantial network of agents of influence in both the JSP and the media, Soviet popularity actually declined during the 1970s, dipping below 1 per cent after the invasion of Afghanistan and never rising significantly above 2 per cent even during the Gorbachev era. By contrast, the percentage naming the United States as their favourite nation was usually over 40 per cent, save for a dip in the early 1970s due to the Vietnam War. After the normalization of Tokyo's relations with Beijing in 1972, China too, though never rivalling the appeal of the United States, was far more popular than the Soviet Union.[65]

Intelligence collection in Japan had much greater success than active measures. The Tokyo residency's most successful penetration was probably of the Foreign Ministry. From the late 1960s at least until (and perhaps after) Levchenko's defection in 1979, two Japanese diplomats, codenamed RENGO and EMMA, provided large amounts of classified material in both Tokyo and their foreign postings. Their files describe both as 'valuable agents'. Early in her career EMMA's controller gave her a handbag fitted with a concealed Minox camera which she regularly took to work to photograph diplomatic documents. RENGO also acted as a talent spotter.[66] The diplomat OVOD, who was the victim of two honey traps during postings in Moscow six years apart, was a far more reluctant recruit. On the second occasion, after he had been seduced by Agent MARIANA, who was employed as his language teacher, and – following usual KGB practice – had probably been confronted with photographs of their sexual encounter, OVOD gloomily told his case officer, 'Now I shall never be rid of the KGB for the rest of my diplomatic career.'[67]

The KGB's most successful diplomatic honey trap involving a Japanese target recruitment was almost certainly the seduction of the cipher clerk MISHA by the KGB 'swallow' LANDYSH while he was stationed in Moscow during the early 1970s.[68] MISHA is probably identical with the cipher clerk who in the late 1970s was working at the Foreign Ministry in Tokyo under the new KGB codename NAZAR.[69] NAZAR's intelligence was considered so important that his case officers in Tokyo, first Valeri Ivanovich Umansky, then Valentin Nikolayevich Belov, were taken off all other duties. For security reasons NAZAR rarely met either case officer, leaving his material in a dead letter-box or passing it on by brush contact. Whenever he was due to make a delivery, operations officers ringed the DLB or brush-contact location to ensure that it was not under surveillance and, if necessary, act as decoys if any suspicious intruder approached the area. The diplomatic telegrams supplied by NAZAR, which included traffic between Tokyo and its Washington embassy, were sometimes so voluminous that the residency found it difficult to translate them all before forwarding to the Centre. The assistance given to the Centre's codebreakers by NAZAR's cipher material was probably rated even more highly than his copies of Japanese diplomatic traffic.[70] There must have been moments when, thanks to NAZAR and Soviet codebreakers, the Japanese Foreign Ministry was, without knowing it, practising something akin to open diplomacy in its dealings with the Soviet Union.[71]

The other most striking success of the Tokyo residency during the 1970s was the increased collection of scientific and technological intelligence (S&T) by Line X which reported in the Centre to FCD Directorate T. During the 1960s Japan's annual growth rate had averaged over 10 per cent. The value of exports increased from $4.1 billion in 1960 to $19.3 billion a decade later. By 1970 Japan had the largest ship-building, radio and television industries in the world. Its consumer industries far outstripped those of the Soviet Union. In less than a decade Japan had passed from the era of the 'Three

Sacred Treasures' (washing machine, refrigerator, black and white TV) to that of the 'Three C's' (car, cooler, colour TV).[72] In 1971 the Ministry of International Trade and Industry (MITI) set out a new high-tech agenda for the Japanese economy, based on a shift to 'knowledge-intensive' industries such as semi-conductors and integrated circuits.[73]

In June 1971 Agent TONDA, the head of a high-tech company in the Tokyo region, supplied the residency with two volumes of secret documents on a new micro-electronic computer system intended for US air and missile forces.[74] Among the most highly rated of the agents who provided intelligence on, and samples of, Japanese and US semi-conductors was TANI, the owner of a company which specialized in semi-conductor design. TANI told his case officer that he regarded himself not as working for the KGB but as simply engaging in industrial espionage which, he seemed to imply, was a fact of modern business life.[75] Some, if not most, Line X agents probably took a similarly cynical view. Among the other agents who provided intelligence on state-of-the-art semi-conductor production was LEDAL, director of semi-conductor research in a Japanese university.[76] Mitrokhin's notes on KGB files identify a total of sixteen agents with senior positions in Japanese high-tech industry and research institutes during the 1970s.[77] This list, which does not include confidential contacts, is doubtless far from comprehensive. Even the equipment used by the KGB residency to monitor the communications exchanged between Tokyo police surveillance teams and their headquarters was based on technology stolen from Japan.[78]

According to Levchenko, it was not unusual for the fortnightly consignments sent by Line X to Moscow via diplomatic couriers 'to weigh as much as a ton'. They were transported to Aeroflot flights leaving Tokyo airport in an embassy minibus.[79] The statistics for S&T collection in 1980, provided by a French agent in Directorate T, tell a less dramatic story. Though Japan was the fifth most important source of S&T, it came far behind the United States.[80] In 1980 61.5 per cent of S&T came from American sources (not all in the US), 10.5 per cent from West Germany, 8 per cent from France, 7.5 per cent from Britain and 3 per cent from Japan. Though producing advanced technology used for military purposes, Japan did not possess the large defence industries which were the chief target of

Directorate T. Even 3 per cent of the vast global volume of Soviet S&T, however, indicates that Japanese material benefited approximately 100 Soviet R&D projects during 1980.[81] That statistic understates the significance of S&T operations in Japan. Japan was a major source for US as well as Japanese S&T. The Directorate T 'work plan' for 1978–80 instructed Line X officers:

- to cultivate and recruit American citizens in Japan;

- to cultivate and recruit Japanese working in American establishments in Japan, and in American organizations involved in Japanese/American co-operation in the scientific, technical and economic fields;

- to cultivate Japanese and individuals of other nationalities engaged in industrial espionage in the USA on behalf of Japanese monopolies;

- to train agent-recruiters and agent talent-spotters capable of working on American citizens in Japan and in the USA;

- to penetrate the Japanese colony in the USA;

- to obtain information of American origin;

- systematically to seek out, cultivate and recruit Japanese with the object of deploying them to the USA, and also to act as support agents.[82]

Line X also devised ways of evading the Co-ordinating Committee for East–West Trade (COCOM) embargo maintained by NATO and Japan on the export to the Soviet Union of technology with military applications. Directorate T regarded as a major coup the successful negotiation in 1977 of a major contract with a Japanese shipbuilder, Ishikawajima-Harima Heavy Industries, for a floating dock with a capacity of over 80,000 tonnes, supposedly for the exclusive use of the Soviet fishing fleet. Levchenko found it difficult to 'believe the Japanese were so naive as to accept those assurances as the literal truth'. It is possible that MITI, which approved the contract, simply turned a blind eye to the military significance of the floating dock in order not to lose a large export order. The Japanese Defence Ministry, which would doubtless have taken a different view, did not learn of the contract until after it was signed. Within a few months of its delivery in November 1978 to Vladivostok, the main base of the Soviet Pacific Fleet, the dry dock was being used to carry out repairs to nuclear submarines and the aircraft carrier *Minsk*.[83]

The Tokyo resident, Oleg Aleksandrovich Guryanov, told his staff in the late 1970s: 'The proceeds from the operations these [Line X] officers carry out each year would cover the expenses of our entire Tokyo residency with money still left over. In fact, worldwide, technical intelligence all by itself covers *all* the expenses of the whole KGB foreign intelligence service.'[84]

The dynamic and ambitious head of Directorate T, Leonid Sergeyevich Zaitsev, made similar claims and campaigned unsuccessfully for his directorate to become independent of the FCD.[85] Though S&T was of crucial importance in preventing Soviet military technology falling seriously behind the West, however, it made a much smaller contribution to the Soviet economy as a whole. The real economic benefit of Western and Japanese scientific and technological secrets, though put by Directorate T at billions of dollars, was severely restricted by the incurable structural failings of the command economy. Hence the great economic paradox of the 1970s and 1980s that, despite possessing large numbers of well-qualified scientists and engineers and a huge volume of S&T, Soviet technology fell steadily further behind that of the West and Japan.[86]

The defection of Stanislav Levchenko in the autumn of 1979 did major damage to KGB operations in Japan, particularly those of Line PR. Soon after 8 p.m. on the evening of 24 October, Levchenko approached a US naval commander in the Hotel Sanno near the US embassy in Tokyo and asked him to arrange an urgent meeting with a CIA officer. By dawn the next day Levchenko had a US visa in his passport and a first-class ticket on a Pan Am flight to Washington. After Levchenko refused to meet representatives of the Soviet embassy, he and his CIA escort, surrounded by Japanese policemen, made their way across the tarmac at Narita airport to a waiting aircraft.[87] The Centre, meanwhile, embarked on an immediate damage limitation exercise. Contact with a series of the Tokyo residency's agents was suspended[88] and planning begun for the creation of a new Line PR network.[89] The most important of the agents compromised by the defection was probably NAZAR. He and the other agents put on ice by the residency must have spent the next few years nervously wondering if they would be publicly exposed. The difficulties encountered by the Tokyo residency in finding replacements for the Line PR agents compromised by Levchenko was reflected in the directives sent in 1980 to residencies in twelve other countries instructing them to cultivate likely Japanese recruits.[90]

The disruption of the political intelligence network coincided with a worsening of Soviet–Japanese relations following an increase in the numbers of Soviet SS-20 medium-range missiles stationed in the Far East, the construction of new military bases on the Kuriles ('Northern Territories') and the beginning of the war in Afghanistan. Prime Minister Kenko Suzuki declared in 1980, 'If the Soviet Union wants to improve its relations with Japan, it must fulfil Japan's two requests for a withdrawal of Soviet troops from Afghanistan and the reversion of the Northern Territories.' He later added a third request for the removal of Soviet SS-20s from the Soviet Far East.[91] On 7 February 1981 the Suzuki government inaugurated an annual Northern Territories Day to promote public support for the return of the four islands.[92]

When Suzuki and his Foreign Minister, Yoshio Sakurauchi, visited Moscow to attend Brezhnev's funeral in November 1982, they invited Gromyko to visit Tokyo for talks aimed at improving relations but were firmly rebuffed. The Kuriles, Gromyko declared, were Soviet territory and 'the timing and atmosphere' were not right for a visit.[93] The atmosphere was further damaged in December by Levchenko's first public revelations of KGB operations in Japan since his defection three years earlier, among them the sensational disclosure that 'Among the most efficient [KGB] agents were a former member of the Japanese government, several leading functionaries of the Socialist Party of Japan, one of the most eminent Sinologists with close contacts with government officers, and several members of the Japanese Parliament.'[94] Though the Centre had doubtless been expecting such revelations, they were none the less a public relations disaster which undermined much of its active-measures offensive.

Given the US military bases in Japan, it was inevitable that Soviet relations with Tokyo in the early 1980s should suffer from the fear of both the Centre and the Kremlin that the Reagan administration was making preparations for a nuclear first strike. The main priority of the Tokyo residency, as of residencies in the West, was to collect intelligence on these non-existent preparations as part of operation RYAN.[95] Meanwhile, even the JSP, which only a few years earlier had been regarded by the Centre as an important vehicle for active measures, had become alarmed by the Soviet arms buildup in the Far East. In 1983 the JSP leadership officially informed the CPSU that the SS-20 missile bases in Soviet Asia were 'the cause of great concern to the Japanese people and to those in other regions of Asia'.[96] According to opinion polls the proportion of Japanese people concerned by 'a military threat coming from the Soviet Union' grew from 55 per cent in 1981 to 80 per cent in 1983.[97]

The foreign intelligence 'work plan' for 1984, circulated to Tokyo and other residencies in November 1983 at the height of operation RYAN, declared, 'The threat of an outbreak of nuclear war is reaching an extremely dangerous position. The United States is involving its NATO allies and Japan in pursuing its aggressive designs.' Japan was elevated, along with the United States, its NATO allies and China, to the status of one of the 'main targets' for KGB agent penetrations. Residencies were instructed to embark on an active-measures offensive 'exacerbating contradictions between the USA, Western Europe and Japan'.[98]

While the dawn of the Gorbachev era dissipated the dangerous tension of the early 1980s, it did little to bring closer the long-delayed peace treaty with Japan. As Gorbachev embarked on 'new thinking' in foreign policy, Georgi Arbatov, the Director of the US–Canada Institute, tried to persuade him that the Soviet Union 'should give back two or even all four of the [Kurile] islands to the Japanese, otherwise we'd never get anywhere with them'.[99] Gorbachev did not listen. In April 1991, eight months before the collapse of the Soviet Union, he complained during a speech in the Soviet Far East, on the eve of his first visit to Tokyo, 'Everybody keeps asking me . . . how many islands I am planning to give away.' When voices in the audience shouted, 'Don't give away a single one!' Gorbachev replied, 'I feel the same as you.'[100]

Despite the damage to the Line PR agent network as a result of Levchenko's defection, Line X appears to have been little affected and may well have expanded its activities at least until the spring of 1987. In May of that year, it was revealed that a Toshiba subsidiary had joined with a Swedish firm to sell to the Soviet Union sophisticated machine tools and computers which made it possible to manufacture submarine propellers whose low noise emissions made them difficult to detect. Almost simultaneously a Japanese spy ring working for Soviet intelligence was discovered to have supplied secret documents on AWACS technology to Soviet intelligence. The Japanese government responded by expelling an officer from the Tokyo residency. Moscow retaliated by expelling the Japanese naval attaché and a Mitsubishi executive.[101]

Though the KGB offensive in Japan generated many tactical operational successes, it ended in strategic failure. The enormous quantity of S&T collected by Line X from the West and Japan could not save the Soviet system from economic collapse. Nor were KGB active measures able to persuade Tokyo to sign a peace treaty acceptable to Moscow. At the beginning of the twenty-first century Russia and Japan were the only major combatants in the Second World War that had not yet 'normalized' their relations.

17

The Special Relationship with India

Part 1: The Supremacy of the Indian National Congress

The Third World country on which the KGB eventually concentrated most operational effort during the Cold War was India. Under Stalin, however, India had been regarded as an imperialist puppet. The *Great Soviet Encyclopedia* dismissed Mohandas 'Mahatma' Gandhi, who led India to independence in 1947, as 'a reactionary . . . who betrayed the people and helped the imperialists against them; aped the ascetics; pretended in a demagogic way to be a supporter of Indian independence and an enemy of the British; and widely exploited religious prejudice'.[1] Despite his distaste for Stalinist attacks Jawaharlal Nehru, the first Prime Minister of independent India, 'had no doubt that the Soviet revolution had advanced human society by a great leap and had lit a bright flame which could not be smothered'. Though later eulogized by Soviet writers as 'a leader of international magnitude' who ranked 'among the best minds of the twentieth century',[2] Nehru was well aware that until Stalin's death in 1953 he, like Gandhi, was regarded as a reactionary. During the early years of Indian independence, secret correspondence from Moscow to the Communist Party of India (CPI) was frequently intercepted by the Intelligence Branch (IB) in New Delhi (as it had been when the IB was working for the British Raj). According to the head of the IB, B. N. Mullik, until the early 1950s 'every instruction that had issued from Moscow had expressed the necessity and importance [for] the Indian Communist Party to overthrow the "reactionary" Nehru Government'.[3] Early in 1951 Mullik gave Nehru a copy of the latest exhortations from Moscow to the CPI, which contained a warning that they must not fall into government hands. Nehru 'laughed out loud and remarked that Moscow apparently did not know how smart our Intelligence was'.[4]

Neither Nehru nor the IB, however, realized how thoroughly the Indian embassy in Moscow was being penetrated by the KGB, using its usual varieties of the honey trap. The Indian diplomat PRO-KHOR was recruited, probably in the early 1950s, with the help of a female swallow, codenamed NEVEROVA, who presumably seduced him. The KGB was clearly pleased with the material which PRO-KHOR provided, which included on two occasions the embassy code-book and reciphering tables, since in 1954 it increased his monthly payments from 1,000 to 4,000 rupees.[5] Another Indian diplomat, RADAR, was recruited in 1956, also with the assistance of a swallow, who on this occasion claimed (probably falsely) to be pregnant.[6] A third KGB swallow persuaded a cipher clerk in the Indian embassy, ARTUR, to go heavily into debt in order to make it easier to compromise him. He was recruited as an agent in 1957 after being trapped (probably into illegal currency dealing) by a KGB officer posing as a black-marketeer.[7] As a result of these and other pen-etrations of the embassy, Soviet codebreakers were probably able to decrypt substantial numbers of Indian diplomatic communications.[8]

As KGB operations in India expanded during the 1950s and 1960s, the Centre seems to have discovered the extent of the IB's previous penetration of the CPI. According to a KGB report, an investigation into Promode Das Gupta, who became secretary of the Bengal Communist Party in 1959, concluded that he had been recruited by the IB in 1947.[9] Further significant IB penetrations were discovered in the Kerala and Madras parties.[10] By the 1960s KGB penetration of the Indian intelligence community and other parts of its official bureaucracy had enabled it to turn the tables on the IB.[11] After the KGB became the main conduit for both money and secret communications from Moscow, high-level IB penetration of the CPI became much more difficult. As in other Communist parties, this secret channel was known only to a small inner circle within the leadership. In 1959 the PCI General Secretary, Ajoy Gosh, agreed with the Delhi residency on plans to found an import–export business for trade with the Soviet bloc, headed by a senior Party member codenamed DED, whose profits would be creamed off for Party funds. Within little more than a decade its annual profits had grown to over 3 million rupees.[12] The Soviet news agency Novosti provided further subsidies by routinely paying the CPI publishing house at a rate 50 per cent above its normal charges.[13]

Moscow's interest in Nehru was greatly enhanced by his emergence (together with Nasser and Tito) as one of the leaders of the Non-Aligned Movement, which began to take shape at the Bandung Conference in 1955. An exchange of official visits in the same year by Nehru and Khrushchev opened a new era in Indo-Soviet relations. On his return from India in December, Khrushchev reported to the Presidium that he had received a warm welcome, but criticized the 'primitive' portrayal of India in Soviet publications and films which demonstrated a poor grasp of Indian culture. Khrushchev was, however, clearly pleased with the intelligence and personal security provided by the KGB during his trip and proposed that the officers concerned be decorated and considered for salary increases.[14]

American reliance on Pakistan as a strategic counterweight to Soviet influence in Asia encouraged India to turn to the USSR. In 1956 Nehru declared that he had never encountered a 'grosser case of naked aggression' than the Anglo-French invasion of Egypt, but failed to condemn the brutal Soviet suppression of the Hungarian Uprising in the same year. India voted against a UN resolution calling for free elections in Hungary and the withdrawal of Soviet forces. The Kremlin increasingly valued Indian support as, with growing frequency, the Non-Aligned Movement tended to vote in the UN with the Soviet bloc rather than the West. During the 1960s India and the Soviet Union found further common cause against Mao's China.[15]

Within Nehru's Congress Party government the KGB set out to cultivate its leading left-wing firebrand and Nehru's close adviser, Krishna Menon, who became Minister of Defence in 1957 after spending most of the previous decade as, successively, Indian High Commissioner in London and representative at the United Nations. To the Soviet Foreign Minister, Andrei Gromyko, 'It was . . . plain that [Menon] was personally friendly to the Soviet Union. He would say to me heatedly: "You cannot imagine the hatred the Indian people felt and still feel to the colonialists, the British . . . The methods used by American capital to exploit the backward countries may be oblique, but they're just as harsh."'[16]

In May 1962 the Soviet Presidium (which under Khrushchev replaced the Politburo) authorized the KGB residency in New Delhi to conduct active-measures operations designed to strengthen Menon's position in India and enhance his personal popularity, probably in the hope that he would become Nehru's successor.[17] During Menon's tenure of the Defence Ministry, India's main source of arms imports switched from the West to the Soviet Union. The Indian decision in the summer of 1962 to purchase MiG-21s rather than British Lightnings was due chiefly to Menon. The British High Commissioner in New Delhi reported to London, 'Krishna Menon has from the beginning managed to surround this question with almost conspiratorial official and ministerial secrecy combined with a skilful putting about of stories in favour of the MiG and against Western aircraft.'[18] Menon's career, however, was disrupted by the Chinese invasion of India in October 1962. Having failed to take the prospect of invasion seriously until the eve of the attack, Menon found himself made the scapegoat for India's unpreparedness. Following the rout of Indian forces by the Chinese, Nehru reluctantly dismissed him on 31 October. A fortnight later, the Presidium authorized active measures by the Delhi residency, including secret finance for a newspaper which supported Menon, in a forlorn attempt to resuscitate his political career.[19] Though similar active measures by the KGB in Menon's favour before the 1967 election[20] also had little observable effect, a secret message to Menon from the CPSU Central Committee (probably sent by its International Department) expressed appreciation for his positive attitude to the Soviet Union.[21]

KGB support did little to revive Menon's fortunes. Before he became Defence Minister, most of his political career had been spent outside India – including twenty-eight years in Britain, where he had served for more than a decade as a Labour councillor in London. As a result, despite the personal support of some ardent disciples within the Congress Party (at least one of whom received substantial KGB funding),[22] Menon lacked any real popular following in India itself. By the time he returned to India from foreign exile, the only language he spoke was English, he could no longer tolerate spicy Indian food and he preferred a tweed jacket and flannel trousers to traditional Indian dress. After failing to be renominated by Congress in his existing Bombay constituency for the 1967 election, Menon stood unsuccessfully as an independent. Two years later, with Communist support, he was elected as an independent in West Bengal. Some of the issues on which he campaigned suggest that he had been influenced by KGB active measures – as, for example, in his demand that American troops in Vietnam be tried for genocide and his claim that they were slitting open the wombs of pregnant women to expose their unborn babies.[23] Well before his death in 1974, however, Menon had ceased to be an influential voice in Indian politics.

Following Menon's political eclipse, Moscow's preferred candidate to succeed Nehru after his death in May 1964 was Gulzarilal Nanda, Home Minister and number two in the cabinet. The Delhi residency was ordered to do all it could to further his candidature but to switch support to Lal Bahadur Shastri, also a close associate of Nehru, if Nanda's campaign failed.[24] There is no indication in the files noted by Mitrokhin that the KGB was in contact with either Nanda or Shastri. Moscow's main reason for supporting them was, almost certainly, negative rather than positive – to prevent the right-wing Hindu traditionalist Morarji Desai, who began each day by drinking a glass of his own urine (a practice extolled in ancient Indian medical treatises), from succeeding Nehru. In the event, after Desai had been persuaded to withdraw reluctantly from the contest, Shastri became Prime Minister with the unanimous backing of Congress. Following Shastri's sudden death in January 1966, the cabal of Congress leaders (the 'Syndicate') chose Nehru's daughter, Indira Gandhi (codenamed VANO by the KGB), as his successor in the mistaken belief that she would prove a popular figurehead whom they could manipulate at will.[25]

The KGB's first prolonged contact with Indira Gandhi had occurred during her first visit to the Soviet Union a few months after Stalin's death in 1953. As well as keeping her under continuous surveillance, the Second Chief Directorate also surrounded her with handsome, attentive male admirers.[26] Unaware of the orchestration of her welcome by the KGB, Indira was overwhelmed by the attentions lavished on her. Though she did not mention the male admirers in letters to her father, she wrote to him, 'Everybody – the Russians – have been so sweet to me . . . I am being treated like everybody's only daughter – I shall be horribly spoilt by the time I leave. Nobody has ever been so nice to me.' Indira wrote of a holiday arranged for her on the Black Sea, 'I don't think I have had such a holiday for years.' Later, in Leningrad, she told Nehru that she was 'wallowing in luxury'.[27] Two years later Indira accompanied her father on his first official visit to the Soviet Union. Like Nehru, she was visibly impressed by the apparent successes of Soviet planning and economic modernization exhibited to them in carefully stage-managed visits to Russian

1. Vasili Mitrokhin, photographed by a British intelligence officer at his first meeting with SIS in the Baltic on 9 April 1992. His shabby appearance had been intended to deter border guards from opening his suitcase, which contained a substantial sample of his top-secret archive.

2. Vasili and Nina Mitrokhin during their early married life.

3. Mitrokhin at home in England after his exfiltration from Russia.

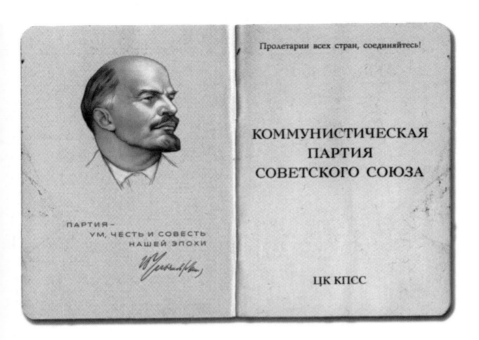

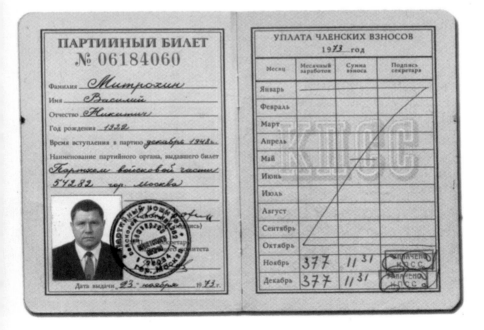

4. Mitrokhin's Communist Party card.

5. September 1960: Nikita Khrushchev, the most ebullient world leader of his time, embraces Fidel Castro, the 'Maximum Leader' of the Cuban Revolution, on the floor of the UN General Assembly.

6. June 1979: Leonid Brezhnev, by then the most decrepit world leader of his time, is helped down from the podium at a conference in Vienna by a KGB officer and US President Jimmy Carter.

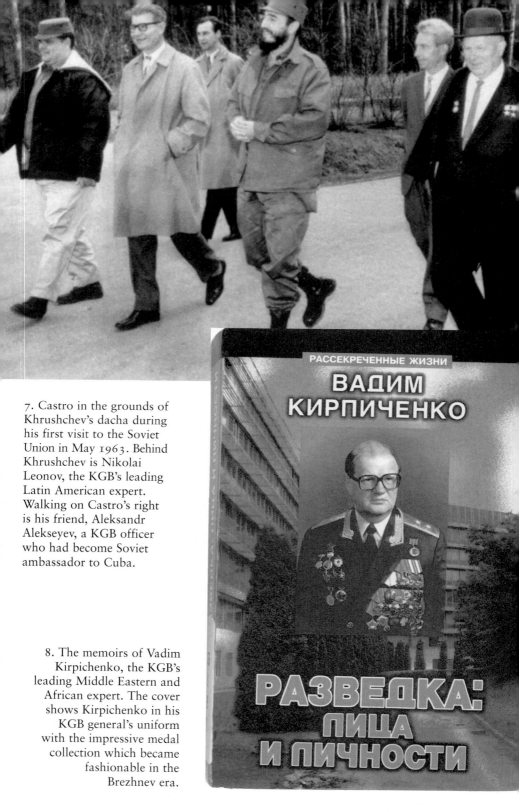

7. Castro in the grounds of Khrushchev's dacha during his first visit to the Soviet Union in May 1963. Behind Khrushchev is Nikolai Leonov, the KGB's leading Latin American expert. Walking on Castro's right is his friend, Aleksandr Alekseyev, a KGB officer who had become Soviet ambassador to Cuba.

8. The memoirs of Vadim Kirpichenko, the KGB's leading Middle Eastern and African expert. The cover shows Kirpichenko in his KGB general's uniform with the impressive medal collection which became fashionable in the Brezhnev era.

РАССЕКРЕЧЕННЫЕ ЖИЗНИ

ВАДИМ КИРПИЧЕНКО

РАЗВЕДКА: ЛИЦА И ЛИЧНОСТИ

Форма № 5
СЕКРЕТНО

«УТВЕРЖДАЮ»

Начальник _____

_____

«____»_____ 19__ г.

С П Р А В К А

Мною _____
(должность, звание, фамилия и инициалы)

_____

«____»_____ 198__ г. выдано _____
(агенту, резиденту, доверенному
или связи, их псевдоним)

единовременное   вознаграждение
ежемесячное   пенсия, пособие _____
(сумма цифрами и прописью)

за _____
(работу по делу №_____, полученную информацию)

Расписка в получении им указанной суммы (прилагается, не отбиралась
или находится в деле №_____)

Отметка в регистрационном листе в деле № _____ сделана.

Основание _____
(кто разрешил выдачу, номер и дата документа)

Подпись лица, вручившего деньги (подарок) _____

«ПОДТВЕРЖДАЮ»

Начальник _____   (_____)
(фамилия)

_____   _____
(звание)   (подпись)

«____»_____ 198__ г.   ТК 5609

---

9. The KGB form used in the 1980s to record payments to agents and other contacts. (original and translation)

Form No.5

SECRET

"I APPROVE"

Head of ....

....

"..........."......................19......

CERTIFICATE

I ....
(function, rank, surname and initials)

....

on "..........."........198... paid out to ....
(codename of agent, resident, cooptee or contact)

....

a <u>one-time</u>   <u>reward</u>   of ....
   monthly   pension,allowance   (sum in words and figures)

for................................
(work relating to file No. ...., or information supplied)

A receipt for the above sum ....
(is attached/was not obtained/is attached to file No....)

An entry has been made in the record sheet of file No............................

Signature of the individual who handed over the money (or gift)..............

"I CONFIRM"

Head of............................   ....
(surname)

....
(rank)   (signature)

"..............."..............198..   TK 5609

10. Aleksandr Shelepin, the youthful KGB Chairman who in 1961 devised a grand strategy to use national liberation movements as the spearhead of a forward policy in the Third World.

11. Vladimir Kryuchkov, the only foreign intelligence chief (1974–88) to become KGB Chairman, at the podium in 1990 at the Congress of People's Deputies. Behind him are Boris Yeltsin (left) and Mikhail Gorbachev (right). In August 1991 Kryuchkov was the leader of a hard-line coup whose failure hastened the collapse of the Soviet Union.

12. Yuri Andropov, the longest-serving KGB Chairman of the Cold War (1967–82) and the only one to become Soviet leader, gives a convincing impression of enjoying a joke by Brezhnev in 1975. The Foreign Minister, Andrei Gromyko, is less amused.

13. An episode in the prolonged charm offensive against Indira Gandhi. Viktor Cherkashin of the New Delhi residency (second from the right) at the presentation of a portrait of Mrs Gandhi by the Soviet artist Ilya Glazunov (next to Cherkashin).

14. Leonid Shebarshin, resident in New Delhi (1975–77) and the KGB's leading expert on the Indian sub-continent. He later became head of foreign intelligence (1988–91).

15. A rare picture of the KGB's favourite terrorist, Wadi Haddad, head of foreign operations in the Popular Front for the Liberation of Palestine, who was recruited in 1970 as Agent NATSIONALIST.

16. PLO leader Yasir Arafat laying a wreath in Moscow in 1974. Immediately behind him is Vasili Samoylenko, a KGB officer chosen by the Centre to cultivate him. He made little progress. Unlike Haddad, Arafat was never trusted by the KGB.

17. The KGB campaign against Jewish refuseniks seeking to emigrate to Israel. A plain-clothes officer (right) tears down a refusenik banner. 'Zionism', complained Brezhnev in 1973, 'is making us stupid.'

A girl's best friend

Claudia Wright explores the often secret relationship between US Ambassador to the UN, Jeane Kirkpatrick, and South Africa

THE UNITED STATES Ambassador to the United Nations, Jeane Kirkpatrick, celebrates her birthday on 19 November. Last year the South African government sent a special courier to the Ambassador's New York office to deliver a birthday greeting. It was signed by Pieter Swanepoel, the Information Counsellor at the South African Embassy in Washington, who had just arrived from Pretoria. There were also 'best regards and gratitude' from Lieutenant-General P. W. van der Westhuizen, head of South Africa's military intelligence. With the letter (see illustration) came a birthday gift, a 'token of appreciation', honouring Kirkpatrick's 'activity for freedom and democracy'.

Now birthday presents are normal enough among friends and Kirkpatrick has been a friend, if not of freedom and democracy, at least of the parody version practised in South Africa. According to United States law, Mrs Kirkpatrick is obliged to report any gift to the Protocol Office of the Department of State. If it is of more than nominal value, she may not keep it for herself.

Kirkpatrick has not reported her gift from the South African government. In the annual list of gifts to US officials – published in the Federal Register on 26 March 1982 – Kirkpatrick remembered to record a small rust and green rug, worth $300, given to her on 30 August 1981, by General Mohammed Zia of Pakistan – but that was all. When I asked the Ambassador's office about a gift from South Africa in 1981, the response was there had been none. Swanepoel and the South African ambassador, Brand Fourie, also say that they 'know nothing about such a gift'.

Forgetfulness in reporting gifts has caused trouble for exalted officials in the Reagan Administration, among them the President's first Assistant for National Security Affairs, Richard Allen, who lost his job because of a Japanese watch and honorarium. More important, however, in the case of Mrs Kirkpatrick are the reasons General van der Westhuizen and the Pretoria government felt so grateful to the ambassador.

DURING 1981, General van der Westhuizen had several reasons for being personally grateful to Kirkpatrick. She was, for example, the most senior US official to meet him and four other South African military intelligence men on 15 March (see *NS* April 3, 1981). Until that meeting, the US had barred official visits by South African officers of brigadier rank or above. Early reports about Kirkpatrick's meeting were denied. She then admitted there had been a meeting, but lied about her knowledge of van der

Westhuizen's identity. The then Secretary of State, General Alexander Haig, intervened to tell the press that Kirkpatrick's meeting with van der Westhuizen had his personal authorisation.

The South African general returned to the US again, on 23-24 November, to attend a negotiating session on Namibia which was held near Washington. The State Department admits that Assistant Secretary of State for Africa, Chester Crocker, was at this meeting. Kirkpatrick's office denies meeting van der Westhuizen at that time. He returned for another visit (his third at least), this time to the State Department in Washington, on 22-23 February, this year. In Kirkpatrick's absence, the meetings were monitored by an official from her office.

Each of van der Westhuizen's visits have preceded major shifts in US policy, and large, usually secret, concessions to South African demands. Kirkpatrick's role on each occasion has been that of a 'go-between', according to officials at the UN, relaying South African requests to Washington, and helping to coordinate joint American-South African positions and negotiating tactics. According to a State Department official, she is one of several members of 'President Reagan's entourage (whose) furtive association . . . with some foreign governments, the South African regime in particular . . . will inflict serious damage to the long-term interests of my country'.

After the March 1981 meeting with van der Westhuizen, the administration sent Assistant Secretary Crocker to Pretoria. Summaries of his talks there were leaked and

published by the *Covert Action Information Bulletin*. The documents reveal that Crocker told the South Africans that 'top US priority is to stop Soviet encroachment in Africa. US wants to work with SAG (South African Government) but ability to deal with Soviet presence severely impeded by Namibia . . . USG (US Government) assumes Soviet/Cuban presence is one of (SAG's) concerns and we are exploring ways to remove in the context of Namibia settlement.' This was the beginning of a US-South African shift on the terms of the settlement for Namibia, undermining the current UN resolution on Namibia and ending the effective negotiating role carried out so far by the Namibia 'contact group' – the US, UK, Canada, France and Germany. It was also the beginning of the 'linkage' in US and South African policy between the withdrawal of South African forces and the independence of Namibia on the one side, with a simultaneous withdrawal of Cuban forces from Angola to the north. According to South African officials, the idea of this 'linkage' was 'something the Americans initiated, wanted, and pursued'.

The Kirkpatrick and Crocker meetings in early 1981 were also the green light for General van der Westhuizen and his fellow generals to widen their military operations in Namibia and Angola and to escalate covert operations against Mozambique and Zimbabwe. As South African troops advanced into southern Angola in August 1981, Kirkpatrick played the role of public defender at the UN. The draft resolution requested by Angola condemning the South African invasion had overwhelming support in the Security Council on 31 August. But Britain abstained and Kirkpatrick cast the American veto. The justification she gave was that South Africa's attack was a legitimate reprisal for SWAPO raids from Angolan bases into Namibia – the same view Crocker had privately offered in Pretoria on 15 April.

Kirkpatrick was to play the same role protecting South Africa from UN votes on sanctions through the autumn of 1981, and

EMBASSY OF SOUTH AFRICA
3051 MASSACHUSETTS AVENUE, N. W.
WASHINGTON, D. C. 20008

December 1, 1981

H.E. Mrs. Jeane J. Kirkpatrick
Ambassador
United States Mission to the United Nations
NEW YORK, N.Y. 10017

Excellency,

I am pleased to announce my recent arrival as Counsellor (Infromation) at the South African Embassy, replacing Mr. W. Lotz in that position. My curriculum vitae is attached for your information.

I have the privilege of informing you that my Government as previously highly appreciates your activity for freedom and democracy. The bearer of this message has been authorised to present you with this gift on the occasion of your birthday as a token of appreciation from my Government.

I was also requested by Lt. Gen. P.W. van der Westhuizen to convey his best regards and gratitude.

Yours sincerely,

Pieter A. Swanepoel
COUNSELLOR (INFORMATION)

18. The KGB kept up a constant stream of forgeries designed to discredit US policy in Africa by providing bogus evidence of secret American agreements with the South African apartheid regime. One such forgery was the centrepiece of a *New Statesman* article attacking US policy in November 1982.

'US and S Africa in Angola plot'

by GODWIN MATATU

US officials say the secret memo is a forgery.

A CONFIDENTIAL memorandum, smuggled out of Zaire, claims that envoys of the United States and South Africa had a secret meeting to discuss destabilisation of the Cuban-backed Government of Angola.

Plans were drawn up to supply more arms and equipment to the rebel UNITA forces of Dr Jonas Savimbi.

The document, if proved genuine, will cause a storm in the United States, where aid for rebel Angola movements is prohibited by the Clark Amendment passed by Congress in 1977.

A spokesman at the US Embassy in London refused to believe that the document was genuine. 'I am positive that no such meeting took place,' he said.

'The document is a forgery. The people who are peddling it want to discourage the MPLA (the ruling party in Angola) from continuing negotiations with the United States.'

Sources close to Nguza Karl i Bond, a former Zaire Prime Minister who now lives in Brussels, have told *The Observer* that the meeting did indeed take place. It was, they claim, part of a series of discussions. As far as they could tell, the document was genuine.

The document is headed with the insignia of the Zairean National Security Council and is addressed to President Mobutu of Zaire. The memorandum is filed from the office of the President's special adviser, Seti Yale.

The document reports that the meeting in late November was attended by a US 'special envoy,' three representatives of UNITA movement, and military and intelligence officers from South Africa. An adviser from the Israeli military mission in Kinshasa was also present as an observer.

Among the topics discussed were:
● The supply by America and South Africa of arms and money for rebel groups in Angola.
● Ways of stirring up popular feeling against the Angolan regime of Eduardo dos Santos and 'destabilising the situation in the capital (Luanda).'
● Sabotage against factories and transport systems within Angola.
● The best means of bringing pressure to bear on Cuba to withdraw its troops.

The main aims of the meeting, according to the document, were to review the military and political situation in Angola and discuss aid for the rebels. Another was to forge a common front between the anti-government movements in the former Portuguese colony. The special US envoy, the document says, called on UNITA and other opposition groups to 'consolidate their authority and influence in the liberated areas.' They should also 'speed up social and political measures to deepen the population's discontent against the regime of dos Santos, the Cuban and Soviet presence and other Communist countries in Angola ; destabilise the situation in the capital ; organise acts of sabotage against principal economic installations and seize strategic points as well as important roads.'

The American official also stressed the need to disrupt joint Angolan and Soviet projects and undermine the relations between the dos Santos Government and the Cubans and Russians.

The rebel movements were also encouraged to sow divisions in the ranks of the MPLA leadership in Luanda and infiltrate agents into the Angolan Army. The aim is to force part of the Angolan leadership to negotiate with UNITA.

He also called for more military pressure against the Luanda regime by the South Africans, who did indeed launch a military operation, deep into Angola last December. The document says the US emissary suggested creation of a 'democratic government in the liberated areas which would include representatives of all the struggling movements.' The United States, for its part, would increase 'military and financial assistance' to the rebels and apply pressure to stem the flow of foreign investment in Angola.

Marcos Samondo, UNITA's representative in Washington, would neither confirm nor deny that the meeting took place. However, he said UNITA had 'contacts with US officials at all levels on a regular basis.' Savimbi visited Washington in 1981 and held discussions with top officials in the Reagan administration, including Mr Alexander Haig, then Secretary of State. UNITA's secretary for foreign affairs, Jeremiah Chitunda, is a regular lobbyist in Washington, Samondo said.

Chitunda left the jungle headquarters of UNITA early in November and later travelled to the United States. Zairean sources in Brussels say he travelled as usual through Kinshasa and may have been available to attend the meeting.

19. Another Service – A forgery was featured in a January 1984 *Observer* article headlined 'US and S Africa in Angola Plot'. Though reporting American claims that the document was fabricated, the *Observer* gave greater weight to supposed evidence for its authenticity.

20. President Hafizullah Amin of Afghanistan, assassinated by KGB special forces on 27 December 1979 at the start of the Soviet invasion and replaced by the reassuringly sycophantic Babrak Karmal, a long-standing KGB agent.

21. The brutal head of KHAD, the KGB-backed Afghan intelligence and security service, Dr Muhammad Najibullah, who sometimes executed prisoners himself by methods which included kicking them to death. In 1986, after Soviet pressure on Karmal to resign, Najibullah replaced him as President.

22. Soviet forces occupy Kabul in December 1979.

23. In March 2002 the restored Russian Orthodox Church of St Sofia in Central Moscow was consecrated by Patriarch Aleksi II as the parish church of the FSB, successor to the militantly atheistic KGB.

24. A triptych of St George ('the dragon-slayer') presented by the head of the FSB, Nikolai Patrushev, to St Sofia. As well as being the patron saint of England, St George is now sometimes described as the patron saint of Russian intelligence officers.

factories. During her trip, Khrushchev presented her with a mink coat which became one of the favourite items in her wardrobe – despite the fact that a few years earlier she had criticized the female Indian ambassador in Moscow for accepting a similar gift.[28]

Soviet attempts to cultivate Indira Gandhi during the 1950s were motivated far more by the desire to influence her father than by any awareness of her own political potential. Like both the Congress Syndicate and the CPI, Moscow still underestimated her when she became Prime Minister. During her early appearances in parliament, Mrs Gandhi seemed tongue-tied and unable to think on her feet. The insulting nickname coined by a socialist MP, 'Dumb Doll', began to stick.[29] Moscow's strategy during 1966 for the Indian elections in the following year was based on encouraging the CPI and the breakaway Communist Party of India, Marxist (CPM) to join together in a left-wing alliance to oppose Mrs Gandhi and the Congress government.[30] As well as subsidizing the CPI and some other left-wing groups during the 1967 election campaign, the KGB also funded the campaigns of several agents and confidential contacts within Congress. The most senior agent identified in the files noted by Mitrokhin was a minister codenamed ABAD, who was regarded by the KGB as 'extremely influential'.[31]

During the election campaign, the KGB also made considerable use of active measures, many of them based on forged American documents produced by Service A. An agent in the information department of the US embassy in New Delhi, codenamed MIKHAIL, provided examples of documents and samples of signatures to assist in the production of convincing forgeries.[32] Among the operations officers who publicized the forgeries produced for the 1967 election campaign was Yuri Modin, former controller of the Cambridge 'Magnificent Five'. In an attempt to discredit S. K. Patil, one of the leading anti-Communists in the Congress Syndicate, Modin circulated a forged letter from the US consul-general in Bombay to the American ambassador in New Delhi referring to Patil's 'political intrigues with the Pakistanis' and to the large American subsidies supposedly given to him. Though Patil was one of the most senior Congress politicians defeated at the election, it remains difficult to assess how much his defeat owed to KGB active measures.[33] Modin also publicized a bogus telegram to London from the British High Commissioner, John Freeman, reporting that the United States was giving vast sums to right-wing parties and politicians. The fact that the KGB appears to have had no agent like MIKHAIL in the High Commission, however, led Service A on this occasion to make an embarrassing error. Its forgery mistakenly described the British High Commissioner as *Sir* John Freeman.[34]

Other Service A fabrications had much greater success. Among them was a forged letter purporting to come from Gordon Goldstein of the US Office of Naval Research and revealing the existence of (in reality non-existent) American bacteriological warfare weapons in Vietnam and Thailand. Originally published in the Bombay *Free Press Journal*, the letter was reported in the London *Times* on 7 March 1968 and used by Moscow Radio in broadcasts beamed at Asia as proof that the United States had spread epidemics in Vietnam. The Indian weekly *Blitz* headlined a story based on the same forgery, 'US Admits Biological and Nuclear Warfare'. Goldstein's signature and official letterhead were subsequently discovered to have been copied from an invitation to an international scientific symposium circulated by him the previous year.[35]

After the elections of February 1967, the KGB claimed, doubtless optimistically, that it was able to influence 30 to 40 per cent of the new parliament.[36] Congress lost 21 per cent of its seats. The conflict between Indira Gandhi and her chief rival Morarji Desai made its forty-four-seat majority precarious and obliged her to accept Desai as Deputy Prime Minister. By 1968 Desai and Kamaraj, the head of the Syndicate, were agreed on the need to replace Mrs Gandhi.[37] Congress was moving inexorably towards a split.

During 1969 there were major policy reorientations in both Moscow and Delhi. The growing threat from China persuaded the Kremlin to make a special relationship with India the basis of its South Asian policy. Simultaneously, Mrs Gandhi set out to secure left-wing support against the Syndicate. In July 1969 she nationalized fourteen commercial banks. Desai was sacked as Finance Minister and resigned as Deputy Prime Minister. Encouraged by Moscow, the CPI swung its support behind Mrs Gandhi. By infiltrating its members and sympathizers into the left-wing Congress Forum for Socialist Action (codenamed SECTOR by the KGB), the CPI set out to gain a position of influence within the ruling party.[38] In November the Syndicate declared Mrs Gandhi guilty of defiance of the Congress leadership and dismissed her from the party, which then split in two: Congress (O), which followed the Syndicate line, and Congress (R), which supported Mrs Gandhi. The Syndicate hinted that Mrs Gandhi intended to 'sell' India to the Soviet Union and was using her principal private secretary, Parmeshwar Narain Haksar, as a direct link with Moscow and the Soviet embassy.[39]

From 1967 to 1973 Haksar, a former protégé of Krishna Menon, was Mrs Gandhi's most trusted adviser. One of her biographers, Katherine Frank, describes him as 'a magnetic figure' who became 'probably the most influential and powerful person in the government' as well as 'the most important civil servant in the country'. Haksar set out to turn a civil service which, at least in principle, was politically neutral into an ideologically 'committed bureaucracy'. His was the hand that guided Mrs Gandhi through her turn to the left, the nationalization of the banks and the split in the Congress Party. It was Haksar also who was behind the transfer of control of the intelligence community to the Prime Minister's Secretariat.[40] His advocacy of the leftward turn in Mrs Gandhi's policies sprang, however, from his socialist convictions rather than from manipulation by the KGB. But both he and Mrs Gandhi 'were less fastidious than Nehru had been about interfering with the democratic system and structure of government to attain their ideological ends'.[41] The journalist Inder Malhotra noted the growth of a 'courtier culture' in Indira Gandhi's entourage: 'The power centre in the world's largest democracy was slowly turning into a *durbar*.'[42]

At the elections of February 1971 Mrs Gandhi won a landslide victory. With seventy seats more than the undivided Congress had won in 1967, her Congress (R) had a two-thirds majority. The Congress Forum for Socialist Action had the support of about 100 MPs in the new parliament. Mrs Gandhi made its most vocal spokesman, the former Communist Mohan Kumaramangalam, Minister of Mines; one of his first acts was the nationalization of the coal industry. Kumaramangalam seemed to be implementing a 'thesis' which he had first argued in 1964: that since the CPI could not win power by itself, as many of its members and sympathizers as possible should join the Congress, make common cause with 'progressive' Congressmen and compel the party leadership to implement socialist policies.[43] Another leading figure in the Congress Forum for Socialist Action was recruited in 1971 as Agent RERO and paid about

100,000 rupees a year for what the KGB considered important political intelligence as well as acting as an agent recruiter. His controllers included the future head of the FCD, Leonid Shebarshin (codenamed VERNOV).[44]

In August 1971 Mrs Gandhi signed a Treaty of Peace, Friendship and Co-operation with the Soviet Union. According to the Permanent Secretary at the Indian Foreign Office, T. N. Kaul, 'It was one of the few closely guarded secret negotiations that India has ever conducted. On [the Indian] side, hardly half a dozen people were aware of it, including the Prime Minister and the Foreign Minister. The media got no scent of it.'[45] A delighted Gromyko declared at the signing ceremony, 'The significance of the Treaty cannot be over-estimated.' Mrs Gandhi's popularity among the Soviet people, he later claimed, was demonstrated by the 'large number of Soviet babies who were given the unusual name Indira'.[46] The Soviet Union seemed to be guaranteed the support of the leading power in the Non-Aligned Movement. Both countries immediately issued a joint communiqué calling for the withdrawal of US troops from Vietnam. India was able to rely on Soviet arms supplies and diplomatic support in the conflict against Pakistan which was already in the offing. According to Leonid Shebarshin, who was posted to New Delhi as head of Line PR (political intelligence) at a time when 'Soviet military technology was flowing into India in an endless stream', the Centre – unlike many in the Foreign Ministry – concluded that war was inevitable. Shebarshin realized that war had begun when the lights went out in the middle of a diplomatic reception at the Soviet embassy on 2 December. Looking out of the window, Shebarshin saw that the power cut affected the whole of the capital. Leaving the embassy hurriedly, he drove to a phone box some way away to ring a member of the residency's agent network who confirmed that hostilities had started.[47] Another member of the network arranged a meeting between Shebarshin and a senior Indian military commander:

It would be an understatement to say that the general's mood was optimistic. He knew precisely when and how the war would end: on 16 December with the surrender of Dacca [later renamed Dhaka] and capitulation of the Pakistani army [in East Pakistan] . . . They were in no state to resist and would not defend Dacca, because they had no one from whom to expect help. 'We know the Pakistani army', my interlocutor said. 'Any professional soldiers would behave the same way in their place.'[48]

Despite diplomatic support from both the United States and China, Pakistan suffered a crushing defeat in the fourteen-day war with India. East Pakistan gained independence as Bangladesh. West Pakistan, reduced to a nation of only 55 million people, could no longer mount a credible challenge to India. For most Indians it was Mrs Gandhi's finest hour. A Soviet diplomat at the United Nations exulted, 'This is the first time in history that the United States and China have been defeated together!'[49]

In the Centre, the Indo-Soviet special relationship was also celebrated as a triumph for the KGB. The residency in New Delhi was rewarded by being upgraded to the status of 'main residency'. Its head from 1970 to 1975, Yakov Prokofyevich Medyanik, was accorded the title of 'main resident', while the heads of Lines PR (political intelligence), KR (counter-intelligence) and X (scientific and technological intelligence) were each given the rank of resident – not, as elsewhere, deputy resident. Medyanik also had overall supervision of three other residencies, located in the Soviet consulates at Bombay, Calcutta and Madras. In the early 1970s, the KGB presence in India became one of the largest in the world outside the Soviet bloc. Indira Gandhi placed no limit on the number of Soviet diplomats and trade officials, thus allowing the KGB and GRU as many cover positions as they wished. Nor, like many other states, did India object to admitting Soviet intelligence officers who had been expelled by less hospitable regimes.[50] The expansion of KGB operations in the Indian subcontinent (and first and foremost in India) during the early 1970s led the FCD to create a new department. Hitherto operations in India, as in the rest of non-Communist South and South-East Asia, had been the responsibility of the Seventh Department. In 1974 the newly founded Seventeenth Department was given charge of the Indian subcontinent.[51]

Oleg Kalugin, who became head of FCD Directorate K (Counter-Intelligence) in 1973, remembers India as 'a model of KGB infiltration of a Third World government': 'We had scores of sources throughout the Indian government – in intelligence, counter-intelligence, the Defence and Foreign Ministries, and the police.'[52] In 1978 Directorate K, whose responsibilities included the penetration of foreign intelligence and security agencies, was running, through Line KR in the Indian residencies, over thirty agents – ten of whom were Indian intelligence officers.[53] Kalugin recalls one occasion on which Andropov personally turned down an offer from an Indian minister to provide information in return for $50,000 on the grounds that the KGB was already well supplied with material from the Indian Foreign and Defence Ministries: 'It seemed like the entire country was for sale; the KGB – and the CIA – had deeply penetrated the Indian government. After a while neither side entrusted sensitive information to the Indians, realizing their enemy would know all about it the next day.'

The KGB, in Kalugin's view, was more successful than the CIA, partly because of its skill in exploiting the corruption which became endemic under Indira Gandhi's regime.[54] As Inder Malhotra noted, though corruption was not new in India:

People expected Indira Gandhi's party, committed to bringing socialism to the country, to be more honest and cleaner than the old undivided Congress. But this turned out to be a vain hope. On the contrary, compared with the amassing of wealth by some of her close associates, the misdeeds of the discarded Syndicate leaders, once looked upon as godfathers of corrupt Congressmen, began to appear trivial.

Suitcases full of banknotes were said to be routinely taken to the Prime Minister's house. Former Syndicate member S. K. Patil is reported to have said that Mrs Gandhi did not even return the suitcases.[55]

The Prime Minister is unlikely to have paid close attention to the dubious origins of some of the funds which went into Congress's coffers. That was a matter which she left largely to her principal fundraiser, Lalit Narayan Mishra, who – though she doubtless did not realize it – also accepted Soviet money.[56] On at least one occasion a secret gift of 2 million rupees from the Politburo to Congress (R) was personally delivered after midnight by the head of Line PR in New Delhi, Leonid Shebarshin. Another million rupees were given on the same occasion to a newspaper which supported Mrs Gandhi.[57] Short and obese with several chins, Mishra looked the part of the corrupt politician he increasingly became. Indira Gandhi, despite her own frugal lifestyle, depended on the money he collected from a variety of sources to finance Congress (R). So did her son and anointed heir, Sanjay, whose misguided ambition to build an Indian popular car and become India's Henry Ford depended on government favours. When Mishra was assassinated in 1975, Mrs Gandhi blamed a plot involving 'foreign elements', a phrase which she doubtless intended as a euphemism for the CIA.[58] The New Delhi main residency gave his widow 70,000 rupees from its active-measures budget.[59]

Though there were some complaints from the CPI leadership at the use of Soviet funds to support Mrs Gandhi and Congress (R),[60] covert funding for the CPI seems to have been unaffected. By 1972 the import–export business founded by the CPI a decade earlier to trade with the Soviet Union had contributed more than 10 million rupees to Party funds. Other secret subsidies, totalling at least 1.5 million rupees, had gone to state Communist parties, individuals and media associated with the CPI.[61] The funds which were sent from Moscow to Party headquarters via the KGB were larger still. In the first six months of 1975 alone they amounted to over 2.5 million rupees.[62]

In the mid-1970s Soviet funds for the CPI were passed by operations officers of the New Delhi main residency to a senior member of the Party's National Council codenamed BANKIR at a number of different locations. The simplest transfers of funds occurred when KGB officers under diplomatic cover had a pretext to visit BANKIR's office, such as his briefings for visiting press delegations from the Soviet bloc. Other arrangements, however, were much more complex. One file noted by Mitrokhin records a fishing expedition to a lake not far from Delhi arranged to provide cover for a transfer of funds to BANKIR. Shebarshin and two operations officers from the main residency left the embassy at 6.30 a.m., arrived at about 8 a.m. and spent two and a half hours fishing. At 10.30 a.m. they left the lake and headed to an agreed rendezvous point with BANKIR, making visual contact with his car at 11.15. As the residency car overtook his on a section of the road which could not be observed from either side, packages of banknotes were passed through the open window of BANKIR's car.[63] Rajeshwar Rao, general secretary of the CPI from 1964 to 1990, subsequently provided receipts for the sums received. Further substantial sums went to the Communist-led All-India Congress of Trade Unions, headed by S. A. Dange.[64]

India under Indira Gandhi was also probably the arena for more KGB active measures than anywhere else in the world, though their significance appears to have been considerably exaggerated by the Centre, which overestimated its ability to manipulate Indian opinion. According to KGB files, by 1973 it had ten Indian newspapers on its payroll (which cannot be identified for legal reasons) as well as a press agency under its 'control'.[65] During 1972 the KGB claimed to have planted 3,789 articles in Indian newspapers – probably more than in any other country in the non-Communist world. According to its files, the number fell to 2,760 in 1973 but rose to 4,486 in 1974 and 5,510 in 1975.[66] In some major NATO countries, despite active-measures campaigns, the KGB was able to plant little more than 1 per cent of the articles which it placed in the Indian press.[67]

Among the KGB's leading confidential contacts in the press was one of India's most influential journalists, codenamed NOK. Recruited as a confidential contact in 1976 by A. A. Arkhipov, NOK was subsequently handled by two Line PR officers operating under journalistic cover: first A. I. Khachaturian, officially a *Trud* correspondent, then V. N. Cherepakhin of the Novosti news agency. NOK's file records that he published material favourable to the Soviet Union and provided information on the entourage of Indira Gandhi. Contact with him ceased in 1980 as a result of his deteriorating health.[68] Though not apparently aware of the KGB's involvement in the active-measures campaign, P. N. Dhar believed that the left was 'manipulating the press . . . to keep Mrs Gandhi committed to their ideological line'.[69] India was also one of the most favourable environments for Soviet front organizations. From 1966 to 1986 the head of the most important of them, the World Peace Council (WPC), was the Indian Communist Romesh Chandra. In his review of the 1960s at the WPC-sponsored World Peace Congress in 1971, Chandra denounced 'the US-dominated NATO' as 'the greatest threat to peace' across the world: 'The fangs of NATO can be felt in Asia and Africa as well [as Europe] . . . The forces of imperialism and exploitation, particularly NATO . . . bear the responsibility for the hunger and poverty of hundreds of millions all over the world.'[70]

The KGB was also confident of its ability to organize mass demonstrations in Delhi and other major cities. In 1969, for example, Andropov informed the Politburo, 'The KGB residency in India has the opportunity to organize a protest demonstration of up to 20,000 Muslims in front of the US embassy in India. The cost of the demonstration would be 5,000 rupees and would be covered in the . . . budget for special tasks in India. I request consideration.' Brezhnev wrote 'Agreed' on Andropov's request.[71] In April 1971, two months after Mrs Gandhi's landslide election victory, the Politburo approved the establishment of a secret fund of 2.5 million convertible rubles (codenamed DEPO) to fund active-measures operations in India over the next four years.[72] During that period KGB reports from New Delhi claimed, on slender evidence, to have assisted the success of Congress (R) in elections to state assemblies.[73]

Among the most time-consuming active measures implemented by Leonid Shebarshin as head of Line PR were the preparations for Brezhnev's state visit in 1973. As usual it was necessary to ensure that the General Secretary was received with what appeared to be rapturous enthusiasm and to concoct evidence that his platitudinous speeches were hailed as 'major political statements of tremendous importance'.[74] Since Brezhnev was probably the dreariest orator among the world's major statesmen this was no easy task, particularly when he travelled outside the Soviet bloc. Soviet audiences were used to listening respectfully to his long-winded utterances and to bursting into regular, unwarranted applause. Indian audiences, however, lacked the experience of their Soviet counterparts. Brezhnev would have been affronted by any suggestion that he deliver only a short address, since he believed in a direct correlation between the length of a speech and the prestige of the speaker. His open-air speech in the great square in front of Delhi's famous Red Fort, where Nehru had declared Indian independence twenty-six years earlier, thus presented a particular challenge. According to possibly inflated KGB estimates, 2 million people were present – perhaps the largest audience to whom Brezhnev had ever spoken. As Shebarshin later acknowledged, the speech was extraordinarily long winded and heavy going. The embassy had made matters even worse by translating the speech into a form of high Hindi which was incomprehensible to most of the audience. As the speech droned on and night began to fall, some of the audience started to drift away but, according to Shebarshin, were turned back by the police for fear of offending the Soviet leader. Though even Brezhnev sensed that not all was well, he was later reassured by the practised sycophants in his entourage.

Shebarshin was able to persuade both himself and the Centre that the visit as a whole had been a great success.[75] The KGB claimed much of the credit for 'creating favourable conditions' for Brezhnev's Indian triumph.[76]

Leonid Shebarshin's perceived success in active measures as head of Line PR almost certainly helps to explain his promotion to the post of main resident in 1975 and launched him on a career which in 1988 took him to the leadership of the FCD. In a newspaper interview after his retirement from the KGB, Shebarshin spoke 'nostalgically about the old days, about disinformation – forging documents, creating sensations for the press'. It was doubtless his days in India which he had chiefly in mind.[77] Among the KGB's most successful active measures were those which claimed to expose CIA plots in the subcontinent. The Centre was probably right to claim the credit for persuading Indira Gandhi that the Agency was plotting her overthrow.[78] In November 1973 she told Fidel Castro at a banquet in New Delhi, 'What they [the CIA] have done to Allende they want to do to me also. There are people here, connected with the same foreign forces that acted in Chile, who would like to eliminate me.' She did not question Castro's (and the KGB's) insistence that Allende had been murdered in cold blood by Pinochet's US-backed troops. The belief that the Agency had marked her out for the same fate as Allende became something of an obsession. In an obvious reference to (accurate) American claims that, in reality, Allende had turned his gun on himself during the storming of his palace, Mrs Gandhi declared, 'When I am murdered, they will say I arranged it myself.'[79]

Mrs Gandhi was also easily persuaded that the CIA, rather than the mistakes of her own administration, was responsible for the growing opposition to her government. Early in 1974 riots in Gujarat, which killed over 100 people, led to 8,000 arrests and caused the dissolution of the State Assembly, reinforced her belief in an American conspiracy against her.[80] Irritated by a series of speeches by Mrs Gandhi denouncing the ever-present menace of CIA subversion, the US ambassador in New Delhi, Daniel Patrick Moynihan, ordered an investigation which uncovered two occasions during her father's premiership when the CIA had secretly provided funds to help the Communists' opponents in state elections, once in Kerala and once in West Bengal. According to Moynihan:

Both times the money was given to the Congress Party which had asked for it. Once it was given to Mrs Gandhi herself, who was then a party official.

Still, as we were no longer giving any money to *her*, it was understandable that she should wonder to whom we *were* giving it. It is not a practice to be encouraged.[81]

A brief visit to India by Henry Kissinger in October 1974 provided another opportunity for a KGB active-measures campaign. Agents of influence were given further fabricated stories about CIA conspiracies to report to the Prime Minister and other leading figures in the government and parliament. The KGB claimed to have planted over seventy stories in the Indian press condemning CIA subversion as well as initiating letter-writing and poster campaigns. The Delhi main residency claimed that, thanks to its campaign, Mrs Gandhi had raised the question of CIA operations in India during her talks with Kissinger.[82]

On 28 April 1975 Andropov approved a further Indian active-measures operation to publicize fabricated evidence of CIA subversion. Sixteen packets containing incriminating material prepared by Service A on three CIA officers stationed under diplomatic cover at the US embassy were sent anonymously by the Delhi residency to the media and gave rise to a series of articles in the Indian press. According to KGB files, Mrs Gandhi sent a personal letter to the Prime Minister of Sri Lanka, Sirimavo Bandaranaike, enclosing some of the KGB's forged CIA documents and a series of articles in Indian newspapers which had been taken in by them. The same files report that Mrs Bandaranaike concluded that CIA subversion posed such a serious threat to Sri Lanka that she set up a committee of investigation.[83]

One of Mrs Gandhi's critics, Piloo Moody, ridiculed her obsession with CIA subversion by wearing around his neck a medallion with the slogan, 'I am a CIA agent'.[84] For Mrs Gandhi, however, the Agency was no laughing matter. By the summer of 1975 her suspicions of a vast conspiracy by her political opponents, aided and abetted by the CIA, had, in the opinion of her biographer Katherine Frank, grown to 'something close to paranoia'. Her mood was further darkened on 12 June by a decision of the Allahabad High Court, against which she appealed, invalidating her election as MP on the grounds of irregularities in the 1971 elections. A fortnight later she persuaded both the President and the cabinet to agree to the declaration of a state of emergency. In a broadcast to the nation on India Radio on 26 June, Mrs Gandhi declared that a 'deep and widespread conspiracy' had 'been brewing ever since I began to introduce certain progressive measures of benefit to the common man and woman of India'. Opposition leaders were jailed or put under house arrest and media censorship introduced. In the first year of the emergency, according to Amnesty International, more than 110,000 people were arrested and detained without trial.[85]

Reports from the New Delhi main residency, headed from 1975 to 1977 by Leonid Shebarshin, claimed (probably greatly exaggerated) credit for using its agents of influence to persuade Mrs Gandhi to declare the emergency.[86] The CPI Central Executive Committee voiced its 'firm opinion that the swift and stern measures taken by the Prime Minister and the government of India against the right-reactionary and counter-revolutionary forces were necessary and justified. Any weakness displayed at this critical moment would have been fatal.' Predictably, it accused the CIA of supporting the counter-revolutionary conspiracy.[87] KGB active measures adopted the same line.[88] The assassination of Sheikh Mujibur Rahman and much of his family in Bangladesh on 14 August further fuelled Mrs Gandhi's conspiracy theories. Behind their murders she saw once again the hidden hand of the CIA.[89]

According to Shebarshin, both the Centre and the Soviet leadership found it difficult to grasp that the emergency had not turned Indira Gandhi into a dictator and that she still responded to public opinion and had to deal with opposition: 'On the spot, from close up, the embassy and our [intelligence] service saw all this, but for Moscow Indira became India, and India – Indira.' Reports from the New Delhi residency which were critical of any aspect of her policies received a cool reception in the Centre. Shebarshin thought it unlikely that any were forwarded to Soviet leaders or the Central Committee. Though Mrs Gandhi was fond of saying in private that states have no constant friends and enemies, only constant interests, 'At times Moscow behaved as though India had given a pledge of love and loyalty to her Soviet friends.' Even the slightest hiccup in relations caused consternation.[90] During 1975 a total of 10.6 million rubles was spent on active measures in India designed to strengthen support for Mrs Gandhi and undermine her political opponents.[91] Soviet backing was public as well as covert. In June 1976, at a time when Mrs Gandhi suffered from semi-pariah status in most of the West, she was given a hero's welcome during a trip to the Soviet Union. On the eve of her arrival a selection of her speeches, articles and interviews was published in Russian translation.[92] She attended meetings in her honour in cities across the Soviet Union.[93] The visit ended, as it had begun, in a mood of mutual self-congratulation.

The Kremlin, however, was worried by reports of the dismissive attitude to the Soviet Union of Indira's son and anointed heir, Sanjay, an admirer of Ferdinand Marcos, the corrupt anti-Communist President of the Philippines.[94] Reports reached P. N. Dhar (and, almost certainly, the New Delhi main residency) that one of Sanjay's cronies was holding regular meetings with a US embassy official 'in a very suspicious manner'. Soon after his mother's return from her triumphal tour of the Soviet Union, Sanjay gave an interview in which he praised big business, denounced nationalization and poured scorn on the Communists. Probably annoyed by complaints of his own corruption, he said of the CPI, 'I don't think you'd find a richer or more corrupt people anywhere.' By her own admission, Indira became 'quite frantic' when his comments were made public, telling Dhar that her son had 'grievously hurt' the CPI and 'created serious problems with the entire Soviet bloc'. Sanjay was persuaded to issue a 'clarification' which fell well short of a retraction.[95]

The emergency ended as suddenly as it had begun. On 18 January 1977 Mrs Gandhi announced that elections would be held in March. Press censorship was suspended and opposition leaders released from house arrest. The New Delhi main residency, like Mrs Gandhi, was overconfident about the outcome of the election. To ensure success it mounted a major operation, codenamed KASKAD, involving over 120 meetings with agents during the election campaign. Nine of the Congress (R) candidates at the elections were KGB agents.[96] Files noted by Mitrokhin also identify by name twenty-one of the non-Communist politicians (four of them ministers) whose election campaigns were subsidized by the KGB.[97] The Soviet media called for 'unity of action of all the democratic forces and particularly the ruling Indian National Congress and the Communist Party of India'.[98] Repeated pressure was put on the CPI leadership by both the New Delhi main residency and Moscow to ensure its support for Mrs Gandhi. The CPI General Secretary, Rajeshwar Rao, and the Secretary of the Party's National Council, N. K. Krishna, were summoned to the Soviet embassy on 12 February to receive a message of exhortation from the CPSU Central Committee. Further exhortations were delivered in person on 15 February by a three-man Soviet delegation. KGB files report Rao and Krishna as saying that they greatly appreciated the advice of their Soviet colleagues and were steadfast in their support for Mrs Gandhi.[99] Their appreciation also reflected the unusually high level of Soviet subsidies during the CPI election campaign – over 3 million rupees in the first two months of 1977.[100]

Agent reports reinforced the New Delhi main residency's confidence that Indira Gandhi would secure another election victory. Reports that she faced the possibility of defeat in her constituency were largely disregarded.[101] In the event Mrs Gandhi suffered a crushing defeat. Janata, the newly united non-Communist opposition, won 40 per cent of the vote to Congress (R)'s 35 per cent. One of the KGB's *bêtes noires*, Morarji Desai, became Prime Minister. When the election result was announced, writes Mrs Gandhi's biographer, Katherine Frank, 'India rejoiced as it had not done since the eve of independence from the British thirty years before.' In Delhi, Mrs Gandhi's downfall was celebrated with dancing in the streets.[102]

18

The Special Relationship with India
Part 2: The Decline and Fall of Congress

The result of the Indian elections of March 1977 caused shock and consternation in both the Centre and the New Delhi main residency. Leonid Shebarshin, the main resident, was hurriedly recalled to Moscow for consultations.[1] As well as fearing the political consequences of Mrs Gandhi's defeat, the Centre was also embarrassed by the way the election demonstrated to the Soviet leadership the limitations of its much-vaunted active-measures campaigns and its supposed ability to manipulate Indian politics. The FCD report on its intelligence failure was largely an exercise in self-justification. It stressed that an election victory by Mrs Gandhi had also been widely predicted by both Western and Indian observers (including the Indian intelligence community), many of whom had made even greater errors than itself. The report went on to explain the FCD's own mistakes by claiming that the extreme diversity of the huge Indian electorate and the many divisions along family, caste, ethnic, religious, class and party lines made accurate prediction of voting behaviour almost impossible. This was plainly special pleading. The complexities of Indian politics could not provide a credible explanation for the failure by the KGB (and other observers) to comprehend the collapse of support for Mrs Gandhi in the entire Hindi belt, the traditional Congress stronghold, where it won only two seats, and its reduction to a regional party of South India, where it remained in control.

The FCD also argued, in its own defence, that Mrs Gandhi's previous determination to hold on to power had made it reasonable to expect that she would refuse to surrender it in March 1977, and would be prepared if necessary either to fix the election results or to declare them null and void (as, it alleged, Sanjay's cronies were urging). Indeed the FCD claimed that on 20 March, when the results were announced, Mrs Gandhi had tried to prevent the Janata Party taking power but had been insufficiently decisive and failed to get the backing of the army high command.[2] There was no substance to these claims, which probably originated in the Delhi rumour mill, then working overtime, and were passed on to the KGB by its large network of agents and confidential contacts. Contrary to reports to Moscow from the New Delhi main residency, the transfer of power after the election was swift and orderly. In the early hours of 21 March Mrs Gandhi summoned a short and perfunctory cabinet meeting, where she read out her letter of resignation, which was approved by the cabinet with only minor changes. At 4 a.m. she was driven to the home of the acting President, B. D. Jatti, and submitted her resignation. Jatti was so taken aback that, until prompted by Dhar, he forgot to ask Mrs Gandhi to stay on as acting Prime Minister until the formation of the next government.[3]

The tone of the Soviet media changed immediately after the Indian election. It blamed the defeat of Mrs Gandhi, hitherto virtually free from public criticism, on 'mistakes and excesses' by her government. Seeking to exempt the CPI from blame, a commentator in *Izvestia* claimed, 'It is indicative that Congress Party candidates were most successful in places where a pre-election arrangement existed between the Congress and the Communist Party of India, or where the Communist Party, with no official encouragement, actively supported progressive candidates of the Congress Party.' In reality the election was a disaster for the CPI as well as for Congress. Dragged down by the unpopularity of the Indira Gandhi regime, it lost all but seven of the twenty-five seats it had won in 1971, while its rival, the breakaway Communist Party of India, Marxist (CPM), won twenty-two. The Centre responded cautiously to the landslide victory of a CPM-led coalition in state elections in West Bengal in June 1977. Though Andropov was eager to set up covert communications with the new state government, he was anxious not to offend the CPI. It was therefore agreed after discussions between Shebarshin (recently promoted to become deputy head of the FCD Seventeenth Department) and a senior CPSU official that, though KGB officers could make contact with CPM leaders, they must claim to be doing so on a purely personal basis. According to FCD files, 'important information' about CPM policy was obtained by the Delhi main residency from its contacts with Party leaders.[4]

The KGB's main priority during the early months of the Janata government was damage limitation. In the course of the campaign Morarji Desai had charged Mrs Gandhi with doing 'whatever the Soviet Union does' and declared that, under a Janata government, the Indo-Soviet treaty might 'automatically go'.[5] The Centre feared 'a reinforcement of reactionary anti-Soviet forces'.[6] On 24 March the Politburo approved an FCD directive 'On measures in connection with the results of the parliamentary elections in India', whose main objectives were to preserve the Friendship Treaty and to deter Janata from seeking a *rapprochement* with the United States and China.[7] Though the Desai government did set out to improve relations with the United States and China, the Indo-Soviet treaty survived. A joint communiqué after a visit by Gromyko to New Delhi in April committed both countries to 'the further strengthening of equal and mutually beneficial co-operation in the spirit of the Indo-Soviet Treaty of Peace, Friendship and Co-operation'.[8] In August the Politburo approved a directive on KGB active measures entitled 'On measures to influence the ruling circles of India in new conditions to the advantage of the USSR'.[9]

The 'new conditions' of Janata rule made active-measures campaigns more difficult than before. Articles planted by the KGB in the Indian press declined sharply from 1,980 in 1976 to 411 in 1977.[10] The Centre, however, continued to make exaggerated claims for the success of its active measures in making the Janata government suspicious of American and Chinese policy.[11] The New Delhi main residency also claimed in June 1978 that it had succeeded in discrediting the Home Minister, Charan Singh, Indira Gandhi's most outspoken opponent in the Janata government, and forcing his dismissal.[12] In reality, Singh's dismissal was due to the fact that he had accused Desai and other ministers of being 'a collection of impotent men' because of their failure to bring Mrs Gandhi to trial.[13] He was later to return to the government and briefly succeeded Desai as Prime Minister in the later months of 1979.

The March 1977 KGB directive approved by the Politburo had instructed the Delhi main residency to 'influence [Mrs] Gandhi to renew the Indian National Congress on a democratic [left-wing] basis'. In order not to offend the Janata government, the Soviet embassy was wary of maintaining official contact with Mrs Gandhi after her election defeat.[14] Instead, the Delhi main residency re-established covert contact with her through an operations officer, Viktor Nikolayevich Cherepakhin (codenamed VLADLEN), operating under cover as a *Trud* correspondent, though there is no evidence that she realized he was from the KGB. The residency also set up an active-measures fund codenamed DEPO in an attempt to buy influence within the Committee for Democratic Action founded by Mrs Gandhi and some of her supporters in May 1977. Though there is no evidence that Mrs Gandhi knew of its existence, the fund had available in July 275,000 convertible rubles.[15] On New Year's Day 1978 Mrs Gandhi instigated a second split in the Congress Party. She and her followers, the majority of the party, reconstituted themselves as Congress (I) – I for Indira. Though she eventually admitted that things 'did get a little out of hand' during the emergency, she continued to insist that Janata's election victory owed much to 'foreign help'. 'The movement against us', she declared, 'was engineered by outside forces.'[16] As usual, Mrs Gandhi doubtless had the CIA in mind.

Janata's fragile unity, which had been made possible during the 1977 election campaign only by common hostility to Indira Gandhi, failed to survive the experience of government. At the general election in January 1980 Congress (I) won 351 of the 542 seats. 'It's Indira All The Way', declared the headline in the *Times of India*. Soon after her election victory, Mrs Gandhi tried to renew contact with Cherepakhin, only to discover that he had been recalled to Moscow.[17] While welcoming Mrs Gandhi's return to power, the Centre was apprehensive about the future. The power of Sanjay, whom it strongly distrusted, was at its zenith, his role as heir apparent appeared unassailable, and – despite the presence, unknown to Sanjay, of an agent codenamed PURI in his entourage[18] – the KGB seems to have discovered no significant means of influence over him. Though Sanjay's death in an air crash in June 1980 left Mrs Gandhi distraught, it was doubtless welcomed in the Centre.

Mrs Gandhi's relations with Moscow in the early 1980s never quite recaptured the warmth of her previous term in office. She particularly resented the fact that she could no longer count on the support of the CPI. During Brezhnev's state visit to India in December 1980, she said pointedly at a reception in his honour, 'Understandably, we face an onslaught from the "right" and, not so understandably, from the "left".'[19] According to KGB reports, some of the CPI attacks were personal. Indian Communist leaders spread rumours that Mrs Gandhi was taking bribes both from state ministers and from the French suppliers of the Mirage fighters which she decided to purchase for the Indian air force. During visits to India by both Brezhnev and the Soviet Defence Minister, Marshal Ustinov, she asked for Soviet pressure to bring the CPI into line.[20] When the pressure failed to materialize, Mrs Gandhi took her revenge. In May 1981 she set up a new Congress (I)-sponsored association, the Friends of the Soviet Union, as a rival to the CPI-sponsored Indo-Soviet Cultural Society – declaring that the time had come to liberate Indo-Soviet friendship from those who had set themselves up as its 'custodians'. It was, she said, the 'professional friends and foes of the Soviet Union who created problems for us'. She also set up a 'world peace and solidarity' organization to break the monopoly of the World Peace Council, headed by an Indian Communist and much used as a vehicle for Soviet active measures.[21]

Moscow's failure to bring the CPI into line, however, continued to rankle with Mrs Gandhi. In June 1983 she sent a secret letter to the Soviet leader, Yuri Andropov, attacking the CPI for having 'ganged up' against her with right-wing reactionaries. The letter was entrusted to Yogendra Sharma, a member of the Party Politburo who disagreed with Rajeshwar Rao's opposition to Mrs Gandhi. Once in Moscow, however, Sharma had second thoughts and 'confessed all' to a Party comrade. When the story was made public in India, Indira's critics accused her of 'inviting Soviet interference in India's internal affairs'. Mrs Gandhi refused to comment.[22] Though somewhat tarnished, however, the Indo-Soviet special relationship survived. When Mrs Gandhi visited Moscow for Brezhnev's funeral, she was the first non-Communist leader to be received by Yuri Andropov.[23]

The KGB continued to make large claims for the success of its active measures. When the Indian government refused in July 1981 to give an entry visa to an American diplomat named Griffin, who was due to take up a post as political counsellor at the US embassy, the KGB claimed that the decision was due to its success over the previous six months in linking him with the CIA. Vladimir Kryuchkov, the head of the FCD, reported to the Politburo:

According to information received, the initiative in making this decision came from I[ndira] Gandhi herself. A significant role was also played by anti-American articles which we inspired in the Indian and foreign press, which cited various sources to expose the dangerous nature of the CIA's subversive operations in India. Attempts by representatives of the USA and of the American press to justify the methods and to pretend that Griffin had been the victim of a Soviet 'disinformation' campaign were decisively rejected by the Minister for Foreign Affairs, N[arasimha] Rao, who stated that 'this action was taken independently and was in no way prompted by another country'.[24]

The greatest successes of Soviet active measures in India remained the exploitation of the susceptibility of Indira Gandhi and her advisers to bogus CIA conspiracies against them. In March 1980 Home Minister Zail Singh blamed the USA and China for fomenting unrest in Assam and the tribal areas of the north-east. Shortly afterwards Home Ministry officials claimed to have 'definite information' that the CIA was 'pumping money' into the region through Christian missionaries. Mrs Gandhi herself repeatedly referred to the 'foreign hand' behind this and other outbreaks of domestic unrest. Though she rarely identified the 'foreign hand' in public, it was clear that she meant the CIA.[25]

One of the main aims of KGB active measures in the early 1980s was to manufacture evidence that the CIA and Pakistani intelligence were behind the growth of Sikh separatism in the Punjab.[26] In the autumn of 1981 Service A launched operation KONTAKT based on a forged document purporting to contain details of the weapons and money provided by Pakistani Inter-Services Intelligence (ISI) to the militants seeking to bring about the creation of an independent Sikh state of Khalistan. In November the forgery was passed to a senior Indian diplomat in Islamabad. Shortly afterwards the Islamabad residency reported to the Centre that, according to (possibly optimistic) agents' reports, the level of anxiety in the Indian embassy about Pakistani support for Sikh separatists indicated that KONTAKT was having the alarmist effect that Service A had hoped for.

In the spring of 1982 the New Delhi residency reported that Agent 'S' (apparently a recent recruit) had direct access to Mrs Gandhi and had personally presented to her another forged ISI document fabricated by Service A, which purported to demonstrate Pakistani involvement in the Khalistan conspiracy.[27] Though there is no convincing evidence that Agent 'S' or the forgeries channelled through

him had any significant influence on Mrs Gandhi, the Centre succumbed to one of its recurrent bouts of wishful thinking about its
ability to manipulate Indian policy. On 5 May it congratulated
the recently installed main resident, Aleksandr Iosifovich Lysenko
(codenamed BOGDAN), on the supposed success of Agent 'S'[28] and
informed him that the Centre proposed to use 'S' as a major channel
for feeding future disinformation to Mrs Gandhi. Before the agent's
meeting with Mrs Gandhi, the Centre sent the following detailed
instructions:

(A) During meetings [with 'S'], acquaint the agent with the contents of the
[latest forged] document and show interest in his opinion regarding
the importance and relevance of the information contained in it for the
Indian authorities. Also it should be explained to the agent that the
document is genuine, obtained by us through secret channels.

(B) Work out a detailed story of how 'S' obtained the document. (This will
involve organizing a short trip to Pakistan for the agent.)

(C) Inform 'S' that, in accordance with the terms laid down by the source
[of the document], he must not leave the document with VANO [Mrs
Gandhi]. Recommend to the agent that he acts in the following way in
order not to arouse a negative reaction in VANO. If VANO insists
that the document is left with her, then 'S' should leave a previously
prepared copy of the document, without the headings which would
indicate its origin. Instruct 'S' to observe VANO's reaction to the
document.

(D) Point out to the agent that it is essential that he builds on his conversation with VANO in order that he can drop hints on what she can
expect from 'S' in the future and what information would be of special
interest to her.

'S' reported that he had shown the document to Mrs Gandhi on
13 May 1982. The fact that she did not ask for a copy suggests that
she did not attach much significance to it. The KGB, however,
preferred to credit the self-serving claims made by 'S' about his
supposed influence on the Prime Minister.[29]

Shortly after succeeding Brezhnev as Soviet leader in November
1982 Yuri Andropov approved a proposal by Kryuchkov to fabricate a further Pakistani intelligence document detailing ISI plans to
foment religious disturbances in Punjab and promote the creation

of Khalistan as an independent Sikh state. The Centre believed that the Indian ambassador in Pakistan, to whom this forgery was sent, would consider it so important that he was bound to forward it to Mrs Gandhi.[30] The KGB appeared by now supremely confident that it could continue to deceive her indefinitely with fabricated reports of CIA and Pakistani conspiracies against her.

Mrs Gandhi's importance as one of the Third World's most influential leaders was further enhanced, in Moscow's eyes, by her election as Chair of the Non-Aligned Movement in succession to Fidel Castro. The Indian press published photographs of a beaming Castro embracing her in a bear hug as he handed over to her in March 1983 at the seventh summit of the Movement in Delhi. On the eve of the summit the Delhi main residency succeeded in planting in the Indian press a forged secret memorandum in the name of the US representative at the United Nations, Jeane Kirkpatrick, which gave further bogus details of American plans to foster divisions in the Third World and undermine Indian influence.[31] Under Mrs Gandhi's chairmanship, the Non-Aligned summit devoted little time to the war in Afghanistan and concentrated instead on issues of disarmament and economic development, which offered ample scope for attacks on the United States. The post-summit communiqué condemned the United States fifteen times; the Soviet Union, by contrast, was only once bracketed with the United States as sharing responsibility for the arms race. Moscow was predictably delighted. *Pravda* declared that 'the Non-Aligned Movement has displayed devotion to its basic principles of struggle against imperialism, colonialism, racism and war'.[32]

The next stage in the Soviet cultivation of the Gandhi dynasty was the visit to Moscow in July 1983 by Indira's elder son, Rajiv, who had reluctantly entered politics at his mother's insistence after Sanjay's death and was being groomed by her for the succession. The high-level meetings and glittering receptions laid on for Rajiv showed, according to one Indian observer, that he had been 'virtually anointed by the Soviet commissars as the unquestioned successor to Mrs Gandhi'. During his visit Rajiv was plainly persuaded by his hosts that the CIA was engaged in serious subversion in the Punjab, where Sikh separatism now posed the most serious challenge to the Congress government. He declared on his return that there was 'definite interference from the USA in the Punjab situation'.[33]

In early June 1984 Mrs Gandhi sent troops into the Punjab where they stormed the Sikh holy of holies, the Golden Temple at Amritsar. The Soviet Union, like the CPI, quickly expressed 'full understanding of the steps taken by the Indian government to curb terrorism'. Once again, Mrs Gandhi took seriously Soviet claims of secret CIA support for the Sikhs.[34] A KGB active measure also fabricated evidence that Pakistani intelligence was planning to recruit Afghan refugees to assassinate her.[35] Though Mrs Gandhi, thanks largely to the KGB, exaggerated the threat from the United States and Pakistan, she tragically underestimated the threat from the Sikhs in her own bodyguard, countermanding as a matter of principle an order from the head of the IB that they be transferred to other duties. India, she bravely insisted, 'was secular'. One of the principles by which she had lived was soon to cost her her life. On 31 October she was shot dead by two Sikh guards in the garden of her house.[36] Predictably, some conspiracy theorists were later to argue that the guards had been working for the CIA.[37] Though the Centre probably did not originate this conspiracy theory, attempting to implicate the Agency in the assassination of Mrs Gandhi became one of the chief priorities of KGB active measures in India over the next few years.[38]

Rajiv Gandhi's first foreign visit after succeeding his mother as Prime Minister was to the Soviet Union for the funeral of Konstantin Chernenko in March 1985. He and Chernenko's successor, Mikhail Gorbachev, established an immediate rapport, which was reinforced during Rajiv's first official visit two months later. The KGB, meanwhile, pursued active-measures operations designed to persuade Rajiv that the CIA was plotting against him. Its fabrications, however, which included a forged letter in 1987 from the DCI, William Casey, on plans for his overthrow,[39] seem to have had little effect. The personal friendship between Rajiv and Gorbachev could not disguise the declining importance of the Indian special relationship for the Soviet Union. Part of Gorbachev's 'new thinking' in foreign policy was the attempt to extricate the Soviet Union from India's disputes with China and Pakistan. At a press conference during his visit to India in November 1986, Gorbachev was much more equivocal than his predecessors about Soviet support in a military conflict between India and China.[40]

The winding down of the Cold War also greatly decreased the usefulness of India as an arena for KGB active measures. One of the most successful active measures during Gorbachev's first two years in power was the attempt to blame Aids on American biological warfare. The story originated on US Independence Day 1984 in an article published in the Indian newspaper *Patriot*, alleging that the Aids virus had been 'manufactured' during genetic engineering experiments at Fort Detrick, Maryland. In the first six months of 1987 alone the story received major media coverage in over forty Third World countries. Faced with American protests and the denunciation of the story by the international scientific community, however, Gorbachev and his advisers were clearly concerned that exposure of Soviet disinformation might damage the new Soviet image in the West. In August 1987 US officials were told in Moscow that the Aids story was officially disowned. Soviet press coverage of the story came to an almost complete halt.[41] In the era of *glasnost*, Moscow also regarded the front organizations as a rapidly declining asset. In 1986 Romesh Chandra, the Indian Communist President of the most important of them, the World Peace Council, felt obliged to indulge in self-criticism. 'The criticisms made of the President's work', he acknowledged, 'require to be heeded and necessary corrections made.' The main 'correction' which followed was his own replacement.[42]

Rajiv Gandhi lost power in India at elections late in 1989 just as the Soviet bloc was beginning to disintegrate. New Delhi was wrong-footed by the final collapse of the Soviet Union two years later. On the outbreak of the hard-line coup in Moscow of August 1991 which attempted to overthrow Gorbachev, Prime Minister Narasimha Rao declared that it might serve as a warning to those who attempted change too rapidly. Following the collapse of the coup a few days later, Rao's statement was held against him by both Gorbachev and Yeltsin. When Gorbachev rang world leaders after his release from house arrest in the Crimea, he made no attempt to contact Rao. The Indian ambassador did not attend the briefing given by Yeltsin to senior members of the Moscow diplomatic corps after the coup collapsed.[43] The Indo-Soviet special relationship, to which the KGB had devoted so much of its energies for most of the Cold War, was at an end.

19

Pakistan and Bangladesh

The Soviet Union's special relationship with India drastically limited its influence in Pakistan. Gromyko complained of 'the insidious [Western] web into which Pakistan fell almost at the outset of her existence as an independent state'.[1] The KGB also found the authoritarian military regimes which governed Pakistan for most of the Cold War more difficult to penetrate than India's ruling Congress Party. The Communist Party of Pakistan, officially banned in 1951, was of much less significance than its large and influential Indian counterpart. According to KGB files, about twenty leading Karachi and Hyderabad Communists set up a small underground party with the cover name 'Sindh Provincial Committee' (SPC) which maintained secret contact with the KGB Karachi residency.[2] The SPC was kept going by an annual Soviet subsidy delivered by the KGB which by the mid-1970s amounted to $25–30,000.[3] Another small Communist underground in East Pakistan also received covert funding.[4] In addition, a number of SPC leaders made what the KGB considered handsome profits from privileged trading contracts with the Soviet Union.[5] Moscow, however, had realistically low expectations of the SPC which, it believed, tended to exaggerate its support.[6]

Despite the KGB's apparent inability to penetrate the entourage of Pakistan's first military ruler, Ayub Khan (1958–69), it was well informed on his foreign policy, chiefly as a result of a series of agents in the Pakistani Foreign Ministry and Diplomatic Corps: among them GNOM, KURI, GREM and GULYAM. For seven years GNOM ('Gnome') provided both ciphered and deciphered diplomatic cables which he was taught to photograph with a miniature camera. He was recruited in 1960 under a 'false flag' by an English-speaking Russian KGB agent posing as the representative of a US publishing company who claimed to be collecting material for a book on international relations. In 1965 he was finally told (though he may well have realized this much earlier) that he was working for a foreign intelligence agency and signed a document acknowledging that he had received a monthly salary from it for the past five years. When GNOM returned to Pakistan in 1967 after a series of foreign postings, however, he broke contact with his controller.[7] Like GNOM, the cipher clerk KURI was recruited under a false flag. In 1961 the KGB agent SAED, claiming to represent a large Pakistani company, persuaded KURI to supply Foreign Ministry documents on the pretext that these would help its commercial success in foreign markets. Again like GNOM, KURI probably realized subsequently that he was working for the KGB but continued to provide cipher material and other 'valuable documents' from both Pakistani embassies (including Washington) and the Foreign Ministry at least until the 1970s. His file also notes that he became 'very demanding' – presumably as regards the payment which he expected for his material.[8]

The most senior Pakistani diplomat identified in the files noted by Mitrokhin was GREM, who was recruited in 1965 and later became an ambassador. He is said to have provided 'valuable information'. The fact that, when he became ambassador, his controller was the local KGB resident is a further indication of his importance.[9] The only KGB agent in the Foreign Ministry whose identity can be revealed is Abu Sayid Hasan (codenamed GULYAM) who was recruited in 1966. At the time of, or soon after, his recruitment, he worked in the Soviet section of the Ministry. During the 1970s he worked successively as Third Secretary in the High Commission in Bombay, Second Secretary in Saudi Arabia and section chief in the Ministry Administration Department. In 1979, a year before his death, he moved to the Ministry of Culture, Youth and Sport.[10]

As a result of the KGB's multiple penetrations of the Pakistani Foreign Ministry and embassies abroad, the codebreakers of the Eighth, and later the Sixteenth, Directorate were almost certainly able to decrypt substantial amounts of Pakistan's diplomatic traffic.[11] Thanks in part to the recruitment of ALI, who held a senior position in the military communications centre in Rawalpindi, Soviet codebreakers were probably also able to decrypt some of the traffic of the Pakistani high command. ALI was recruited under false flag in 1965 by G. M. Yevsafyev, a KGB operations officer masquerading as a German radio engineer working for a West German company, and provided details of the high command's cipher machines. He later noticed the diplomatic number plates on Yevsafyev's car and realized that he was working for the KGB. The fact that a decade later ALI was still working as a Soviet agent, with the Karachi resident, S. S. Budnik, as his controller indicates the importance attached to his intelligence.[12]

The main purpose of KGB active measures in Pakistan both during and after the Ayub Khan era was to spread suspicion of the United States. At the outbreak of Pakistan's short and disastrous war with India over Kashmir in September 1965, the United States suspended military assistance to it. The KGB set out to exploit the bitterness felt at the American abandonment of Pakistan in its hour of need. The main target of its influence operations was Ayub Khan's flamboyant Foreign Minister, Zulfikar Ali Bhutto. Four years earlier, Bhutto, then Minister for Natural Resources, had invited the Soviet ambassador, Mikhail Stepanovich Kapitsa, and his wife to visit his family estate. With the Kapitsas, to act as translator, went a young Urdu-speaking diplomat, Leonid Shebarshin, who three years later was to transfer to the KGB. Bhutto made clear that he saw himself as a future foreign minister and that his ultimate ambition (also realized) was to become Prime Minister and President. Shebarshin found Bhutto's conversation 'desperately bold and even reckless'. He appeared obsessed with ending American influence in Pakistan and wanted Soviet assistance in achieving this.[13] Operation REBUS in the spring of 1966 was principally designed to reinforce Bhutto's hostility to the United States by passing to the Pakistani government forged documents produced by Service A which purported to show that the US ambassador, Walter McConaughy, was plotting the overthrow of Ayub Khan, Bhutto and other ministers.[14] The operation seems to have had some effect, at least on Bhutto, who was convinced for the rest of his life that his removal from office in June 1966 was the result of American pressure.[15]

Operation REBUS was followed in July 1966 by operation SPIDER, an active measure designed to convince Ayub Khan that the United States was using the West German Tarantel press agency to attack his government and its close links with China. A bogus agency report including an insulting anti-Ayub cartoon, prepared by Service A on genuine Tarantel office stationery, was posted by the Karachi residency to newspapers and opposition figures. To ensure that it came to the authorities' attention, Service A also prepared forged letters supposedly written by outraged Pakistanis to the police chiefs in Lahore and Karachi, enclosing copies of the agency report. The bogus letter from Lahore claimed that two named members of the US Information Service were distributing the Tarantel material. The covering letter sent with the Service A forgeries to the Karachi residency on 9 June by the head of the South Asian Department, V. I. Startsev (unusually copied in its entirety by Mitrokhin), serves as an illustration both of the remarkably detailed instructions sent to residencies involved in active measures, even including repeated reminders to affix the correct postage, and of the Centre's high expectations of what such operations were likely to achieve:

We hope that the two [forged] letters from well-wishers enclosing the Tarantel Press Agency information will serve as further proof to Pakistani counter-intelligence that the Americans are using this agency to spread anti-government material in the country. In order that operation SPIDER may be completed, you are requested to carry out the following operations:

1 Packet no. 1 contains envelopes containing Tarantel press agency material. They are to be sent to addresses of interest to us [newspapers and opposition figures]. You must stick on stamps of the correct value and post them in various post boxes in Karachi. This is to be done on July 21 or 22 this year. We are presuming that some of these addresses are watched by the police. We took most of them from the list of addresses used by the Tarantel press agency.

2 Packet no. 2 contains a letter from a well-wisher to the police headquarters in Karachi. You must stick a stamp of the correct value on the envelope and post it on July 23 this year.

3 Packet no. 3 contains a letter from a well-wisher to the police headquarters in Lahore. You must stick a stamp of the right value on this envelope too and post it in Lahore on August 2 or August 3 this year. We chose this date so that you would have time to arrange a trip to Lahore.

All these requests must be carried out, of course, with the utmost care and secrecy as otherwise the action could be turned against us. I would like you to inform us when the SPIDER actions have been carried out. We would also like you to observe the reactions of the Pakistani authorities to this action and to inform us accordingly. We consider it possible that the Pakistani government may make a protest to the West German embassy that anti-government material is being distributed by Tarantel press agency or that it might take some kind of action against the USA. The Pakistanis might even expel the Americans mentioned in our material. The local authorities might resort to organizing some kind of action against American institutions, such as demonstrations, disturbances, fires, explosions etc. For your personal information we are sending the texts of the SPIDER material in Russian and English in Packet no. 4. After reading them, we request you to destroy them.[16]

What effect, if any, operation SPIDER had on the Ayub Khan regime remains unknown. The Centre's hope that Pakistani authorities might bomb American buildings in revenge for US involvement in the circulation of 'anti-government material' was, however, based on little more than wishful thinking.

While operations REBUS and SPIDER were in full swing, the Karachi residency was in turmoil as a result of the appointment at the beginning of the year of a new and incompetent resident, codenamed ANTON, a veteran of the South Asian section. ANTON was one of those intelligence officers with severe drinking problems who were deployed by the FCD from time to time in Third World countries. According to Shebarshin, who had the misfortune to serve under him, he appeared not to have read a book for years, 'was incapable of focusing on an idea, appraising information, or formulating an assignment in a literate manner'. He was also frequently drunk and persistently foul-mouthed. Residency officers tried to avoid him. ANTON's one redeeming feature, in Shebarshin's view, was that he rarely interfered in their work. Eventually, after he collapsed at an embassy reception, the Soviet ambassador, M. V. Degtiar, insisted on his recall to Moscow. To the dismay of Shebarshin and his colleagues, however, ANTON continued working in the FCD. Within the often heavy-drinking culture of the Centre, alcoholism rarely led to dismissal.[17]

Late in 1967 Zulfikar Ali Bhutto took the initiative in founding the Pakistan People's Party (PPP) under the populist slogan, 'Islam is our faith, democracy is our polity, socialism is our economic policy; all power to the people.' 'To put it in one sentence', declared one of the PPP's founding documents, 'the aim of the Party is the transformation of Pakistan into a socialist society.'[18] During the winter of 1968–69, the PPP under Bhutto's charismatic leadership co-ordinated a wave of popular protest which in March 1969 finally persuaded Ayub Khan to surrender power. He did so, however, not, as the 1962 constitution required, to the Speaker of the Assembly but to the commander-in-chief of the armed forces, General Yahya Khan, who promptly abrogated the constitution and declared martial law.[19]

The Centre immediately embarked on a series of active measures designed to make Yahya Khan suspicious of both China and the United States. Operation RAVI was based on two Service A forgeries: a 'Directive' dated 3 June 1969 supposedly sent from the Central Committee of the Chinese Communist Party to the Chinese chargé d'affaires in India and a Chinese Foreign Ministry document outlining plans to turn Kashmir into a pro-Chinese independent state. On 28 June copies of both forgeries were sent to the Pakistani ambassadors in Delhi and Washington, doubtless in the hope that their contents would be reported to Yahya Khan.[20] Simultaneously, another active-measures operation, codenamed ZUBR, spread reports that Americans had lost faith in Yahya Khan's ability to hold on to power and were afraid that he would be replaced by a left-wing government which would nationalize the banks and confiscate their deposits. The United States embassy was said to have reported to Washington that Yahya Khan's regime was hopelessly corrupt and would squander any foreign aid given to it. The Karachi residency also claimed the credit for organizing a demonstration against the Vietnam War.[21]

After RAVI and ZUBR came operation PADMA, which was designed to persuade the Yahya Khan regime that the Chinese were inciting rebellion in East Pakistan. Service A fabricated a Chinese appeal to 'Bengali revolutionaries', urging them to take up arms against 'the Punjabi landowners and the reactionary regime of Yahya Khan'. The original intention was to write the appeal in Bengali but, since no KGB officer was sufficiently fluent in the language and the operation was considered too sensitive to entrust to a Bengali agent, it was written in English. A copy was posted to the Indian ambassador in November 1969 in the knowledge that it would be opened by Pakistani intelligence before arrival and thus come to the knowledge of the Pakistani authorities. A further copy was sent to the US ambassador in the hope that he too would personally bring it to the attention of the Pakistanis. Simultaneously, KGB agents in Kabul warned Pakistani diplomats of Chinese subversion in East Pakistan. The Pakistani representative in the UN was reported to be taking similar reports seriously. A post-mortem on PADMA concluded that the operation had been a success. The supposed Chinese appeal to Bengali revolutionaries was said to have become common knowledge among foreign diplomats in Pakistan. The Centre concluded that even the Americans did not suspect that the appeal was a KGB fabrication.[22]

New entrants to the FCD South Asian Department were often told that, when shown a map of the divided Pakistani state after the partition of India in 1947, Stalin had commented, 'Such a state cannot survive for long.'[23] By the late 1960s the Kremlin seems to have come to the conclusion that the separation of Pakistan's western and eastern wings would be in Soviet, as well as Indian, interests.[24] The KGB therefore set out to cultivate the leader of the autonomist Awami League, Sheik Mujibur Rahman ('Mujib'). Though Mujib was unaware of the cultivation, the KGB claimed that it succeeded in persuading him that the United States had been responsible for his arrest in January 1968, when he had been charged with leading the so-called 'Agartala conspiracy', hatched during meetings with Indian officials at the border town of Agartala to bring about the secession of East Pakistan with Indian help. Through an intermediary, Mujib was told in September 1969 that the names of all the conspirators had been personally passed to Ayub by the US ambassador. According to a KGB report, Mujib was completely taken in by the disinformation and concluded that there must have been a leak to the Americans from someone in his entourage.[25]

Late in 1969 Yahya Khan announced that, though martial law remained in force, party politics would be allowed to resume on 1 January 1970 in preparation for elections at the end of the year. The Centre's main strategy during the election campaign was to ensure the victory of Bhutto's PPP in the West and Mujib's Awami League in the East.[26] In June 1970 V. I. Startsev, head of the FCD South Asian Department, jointly devised with N. A. Kosov, the head of Service A, an elaborate active-measures campaign designed to discredit all the main opponents of the PPP and Awami League. The President of the Qaiyum Muslim League, Abdul Qaiyum Khan, who had been Chief Minister from 1947 to 1953, was to be discredited by speeches he had allegedly made before 1947 opposing the creation of an independent Pakistan. The founder and leader of the religious party, Jamaat-i-Islami, Maulana Syed Abul Ala Maudidi, was to be exposed as a 'reactionary and CIA agent'. The head of the Council Muslim League, Mian Mumtaz Daultana, was to be unmasked as a veteran British agent (presumably because of his past residence in London) and accomplice in political murders. The leader of the Convention Muslim League, Fazal Ilahi Chaudhry, was also to be implicated in past political murders as well as in plans to murder Bhutto. (Ironically, in 1973 he became President of Pakistan with Bhutto's backing.) The President of the Pakistan Democratic Party, Nurul Amin, in order to discredit him in West Pakistan, was to be unmasked as a leading figure in the 'Agartala conspiracy'.[27]

Though the elections of December 1970 produced the result for which the KGB had covertly campaigned, there is no evidence that active measures had any significant impact on the outcome. It would, however, have been out of character if the Centre had failed to claim substantial credit when reporting on the election to the Politburo. The PPP won 81 of the 138 seats allocated to West Pakistan; the runner-up in the West, the Qaiyum Muslim League, won only nine seats. In the East, the Awami League won an even more sweeping victory with 160 of the 162 seats. Though Mujib had failed to contest a single seat in West Pakistan, he thus won an overall majority in the National Assembly and was entitled to become Prime Minister. Bhutto colluded with Ayub and the army in refusing to allow Mujib to take power. On 25 March 1971 Yahya Khan ordered Mujib's arrest and began savage military repression in East Pakistan. The Centre reported to the Central Committee that the end of Pakistani unity was imminent.[28] While Bhutto naively – or cynically – declared, 'Pakistan has been saved', Bengal was overwhelmed by a bloodbath which compared in its savagery with the intercommunal butchery which had followed Indian independence in 1947. India provided a safe haven for Bengali troops resisting the Pakistani army. In November the civil war between East and West Pakistan turned into an Indo-Pakistani war. On 16 December Dhaka fell to Indian troops and East Pakistan became independent Bangladesh.

The political transformation of the Indian subcontinent caused by the divorce between East and West Pakistan suited Moscow's interests. The Indo-Soviet special relationship had been enhanced and Indira Gandhi's personal prestige raised to an all-time high. Pakistan had been dramatically weakened by the independence of Bangladesh. Moscow's preferred candidates (given the impossibility of Communist regimes) took power in both Islamabad and Dhaka. After defeat by India, Yahya Khan resigned and handed over the presidency to Bhutto. On 10 January 1972, Mujib returned from captivity in West Pakistan to a hero's welcome in Dhaka.

Despite the fact that Bhutto nationalized over thirty large firms in ten basic industries in January 1972 and visited Moscow in March, the Kremlin had far more reservations about him (initially as President, then, after the 1973 elections, as Prime Minister) than about Mujib. The most constant element in Bhutto's erratic foreign policy was friendship with China, which he visited almost as soon as he succeeded Yahya Khan. At his request, China vetoed Bangladesh's admission to the United Nations until it had repatriated all Pakistani personnel captured after the war (some of whom it was considering putting on trial for war crimes). China also helped to set up Pakistan's first heavy-engineering plants as well as supplying arms.

Somewhat incongruously in view of his largely Western lifestyle, Bhutto took to imitating Mao Zedong's clothes and cap. In 1976 he even had a book of his own sayings published in the various languages spoken in Pakistan, much in the manner of Mao's *Little Red Book*.[29] Mildly absurd though Bhutto's neo-Maoist affectations were, Moscow was not amused. As one of Bhutto's advisers, Rafi Raza, later acknowledged: 'The lack of importance attached by the Soviet Union to ZAB[hutto] was evidenced by the fact that no significant Soviet dignitary visited Pakistan during his five and a half years in government, despite his own two visits [to Moscow] . . .'[30]

So far as Moscow was concerned, Mujib's relations with China, in contrast to Bhutto's, were reassuringly poor. Bangladesh and China did not establish diplomatic relations until after Mujib's death. As in India and Pakistan, the KGB was able to exploit the corruption of newly independent Bangladesh. For politicians, bureaucrats and the military there were numerous opportunities to cream off a percentage of the foreign aid which flooded into the country.[31] Mujib once asked despairingly: 'Who takes bribes? Who indulges in smuggling? Who becomes a foreign agent? Who transfers money abroad? Who resorts to hoarding? It's being done by us – the five per cent of the people who are educated. We are the bribe takers, the corrupt elements . . .'[32]

Though overwhelmingly the most popular person in Bangladesh, Mujib was in some ways curiously isolated. Irritated by the personality conflicts within the Awami League, he increasingly saw himself as the sole personification of Bangladesh – the *Bangabandbu*. He was, it has been rightly observed, 'a fine *Bangabandbu* but a poor prime minister'.[33] The Dhaka residency acknowledged in its annual report for 1972, after Bangladesh's first year of independence, that it had failed to recruit any agent close to Mujib.[34] Among its successes during that year, however, was the recruitment of three agents in the Directorate of National Security (codenamed KOMBINAT).[35] The KGB also succeeded in gaining control of one daily newspaper (to which it paid the equivalent of 300,000 convertible rubles to purchase new printing presses) and one weekly.[36] On 2 February 1973 the Politburo instructed the KGB to use active measures to influence the outcome of Bangladesh's forthcoming first parliamentary elections.[37] The KGB helped to fund the election campaigns of Mujib's Awami League as well as its allies, the Communist Party and the left-wing National Awami Party. Probably with little justification, it claimed part of the credit for the predictable landslide victory of the Awami League.[38]

In June 1975, doubtless to the delight of Moscow, Mujib transformed Bangladesh into a one-party state whose new ruling party, BAKSAL, incorporated the three parties hitherto secretly subsidized by the KGB (Awami League, National Awami Party and Communist Party) and one other left-wing party.[39] By this time the Dhaka residency had recruited a senior member of Mujib's secretariat, MITRA, two ministers, SALTAN and KALIF, and two senior intelligence officers, MAKHIR and SHEF. All were used against US targets.[40]

The FCD's analytical department, Service 1, had forecast after the 1973 elections that the Awami League would retain power for the full five-year term and that the main opposition to it would come from the pro-Chinese left (always a *bête noire* of the KGB). A series of Service A forgeries were used in an attempt to persuade both Mujib and the Bangladeshi media that the Chinese were conspiring with the left-wing opposition.[41] The real threat to Mujib, however, came not from Maoists but from his opponents within the armed forces. On 15 August 1975 a group of army officers murdered both him and much of his family. The KGB immediately began an active-measures campaign, predictably inspiring newspaper articles in a series of countries claiming that the coup was the work of the CIA.[42] Within twenty-four hours of Mujib's murder, Zulfikar Ali Bhutto became the first to recognize the new military regime – deluding himself into believing that Bangladesh might now be willing to form a federation with Pakistan. Bhutto was later to repent of his early enthusiasm as it became clear that Bangladesh's links with New Delhi would remain far closer than those with Islamabad. It also dawned upon him that the coup in Bangladesh might set a bad example to the Pakistani military – as indeed it did.[43]

During the mid-1970s the KGB substantially increased its influence in the Pakistani media. In 1973, according to KGB statistics, it placed thirty-three articles in the Pakistani press – little more than 1 per cent of the number in India.[44] By 1977 the number had risen to 440,[45] and the KGB had acquired direct control of at least one periodical.[46] The main aim of active-measures operations was, once again, to increase Pakistani distrust of the United States. Disinformation fed to Bhutto's government claimed that the United States considered Pakistan too unreliable an ally to deserve substantial military aid. Washington was, allegedly, increasingly distrustful of Bhutto's government and regarded the Shah of Iran as its main regional ally. The Shah was said to be determined to become the leader of the Muslim world and to regard Bhutto as a rival. He was also reported to be scornful of Bhutto's failure to deal with unrest in Baluchistan and to be willing to send in Iranian troops if the situation worsened.[47]

By 1975 the KGB was confident that active measures were having a direct personal influence on Bhutto.[48] On 16 November the Soviet ambassador informed him that, in view of 'the friendly and neighbourly relations between our two countries', he had been instructed to warn him that the Soviet authorities had information that a terrorist group was planning to assassinate him during his forthcoming visit to Baluchistan. Bhutto was profuse in his thanks for the ambassador's disinformation:

I was planning to fly to Baluchistan tonight or tomorrow morning for a few days. I shall now cancel the visit to get to the bottom of this matter in order not to put my life at risk. I am particularly conscious of the genuine and friendly relations between our countries at this difficult stage in the political life of Pakistan which is also difficult for me personally. I am doubly grateful to your country and its leaders.[49]

The KGB reported that Bhutto had also been successfully deceived by disinformation claiming that Iran was planning to detach Baluchistan from Pakistan and had stated as fact supposed Iranian plans to destabilize Pakistan which, in reality, had been fabricated by Service A.[50] Agent DVIN was reported to have direct access to Bhutto to feed him further fabrications.[51]

Despite Bhutto's susceptibility to Soviet disinformation, however, Moscow continued to regard him as a loose cannon. As one of Bhutto's ministers and closest advisers, Rafi Raza, later acknowledged, 'Neither superpower considered him reliable.' Among the initiatives by Bhutto which annoyed the Kremlin was his campaign for a 'new economic world order . . . to redress the grave injustice to the poorer nations of the world'. Kept out of the Non-Aligned Movement (NAM) by what amounted to an Indian veto, Bhutto appeared to challenge its authority. On the eve of the NAM summit in Colombo in August 1976, Bhutto published an article entitled 'Third World – New Direction', calling for a Third World summit in Islamabad in the spring of 1976 to discuss global economic reform.[52] The Centre feared that, by bringing in non-NAM members under Bhutto's chairmanship, such a summit would damage the prestige of the NAM, which it regarded as an important vehicle for KGB active measures. Following a Politburo resolution condemning Bhutto's proposal,[53] the Centre devised an active-measures operation of almost global dimensions. KGB agents were to inform the current Chair of the NAM, Sirimavo Bandaranaike, and other Sri Lankan politicians that Bhutto's aim was to undermine her personal authority as well as to divide NAM members and weaken the movement's commitment to anti-imperialism. Disinformation prepared by Service A designed to discredit Bhutto's initiative was to be forwarded by the local KGB residencies to the governments of Somalia, Nigeria, Ghana, Cyprus, Yemen, Mexico, Venezuela, Iraq, Afghanistan and Nepal. The Centre was also confident that its active measures would persuade President Boumedienne of Algeria to spread the message that an Islamabad conference would weaken the NAM and diminish the influence of 'progressive' leaders in the movement. Delegates attending a NAM planning conference in Delhi were to be given statements by Indian groups prepared under KGB guidance condemning Bhutto's initiative as a threat to the unity of the NAM.[54]

In the event the Islamabad conference failed to materialize and on 5 July 1977 Bhutto was overthrown in a military coup led by the commander-in-chief of the army, General Zia ul-Haq. On 3 September Bhutto was charged with conspiracy to murder the father of a maverick PPP politician. By now, most of the popular enthusiasm which had swept him to power seven years earlier had been dissipated by his autocratic manner and the corruption of his regime. As one of his most fervent supporters noted in December, 'It was painful to see that while Bhutto stood trial for murder in Lahore, the people of the city were showing greater interest in the Test match being played there.'[55] Bhutto was sentenced to death on 18 March 1978 following a trial of dubious legality and executed on 4 April 1979 after the sentence had been narrowly upheld by the Supreme Court. KGB active measures predictably blamed Bhutto's overthrow and execution, like that of Mujib, on a CIA conspiracy.[56]

Neither General Ziaur Rahman (better known as Zia), who by the end of 1976 had emerged as the dominant figure in Bangladesh (initially as Chief Martial Law Administrator and from 1977 as President), nor Zia ul-Haq (also, confusingly, better known as Zia) was favourably regarded in the Kremlin. Both, in the Centre's view, were far better disposed to Washington than to Moscow. One of Ziaur Rahman's first actions was to change the constitution by replacing 'socialism' as a principle of state with a vaguer commitment to 'economic justice and equality'. His economic policy was based on encouraging the private sector and privatizing public enterprise. The increased foreign aid desperately needed by Bangladesh, Zia believed, could only be obtained by moving closer to the West (especially the United States), the Muslim world and China. Moscow was visibly affronted. *Izvestia* complained in 1977 that right-wing and Maoist forces in Bangladesh were conducting a campaign of 'provocation and vilification against the Soviet Union'.[57] The KGB claimed the credit for organizing a series of protest demonstrations in September and October 1978 against an agreement signed by the Zia regime with Washington permitting the US Peace Corps to operate in Bangladesh.[58]

According to KGB statistics, active measures in Bangladesh increased from ninety in 1978 to about 200 in 1979, and involved twenty agents of influence. The KGB claimed that in 1979 it planted 101 articles in the press, organized forty-four meetings to publicize disinformation and on twenty-six occasions arranged for Service A forgeries to reach the Bangladesh authorities.[59] The dominant theme of the forgeries was CIA conspiracy against the Ziaur Rahman regime. Operation ARSENAL in 1978 brought to the attention of the Directorate of National Security the supposed plotting of a CIA officer (real or alleged) named Young with opposition groups.[60] Service A drew some of the inspiration for its forgeries from real plots by the President's Bangladeshi opponents. During Zia's five and a half years in power he had to deal with at least seventeen mutinies and attempted coups. In August 1979, for example, a group of officers were arrested in Dhaka and accused of plotting to overthrow him. Two months later Andropov approved an FCD proposal for Service A to fabricate a letter supporting the plotters from Air Vice-Marshal Muhammad Ghulam Tawab, whom Zia had sacked as head of the air force. Other material planted in the Bangladeshi, Indian and Sri Lankan press purported to unmask Tawab as a long-standing CIA agent.[61] Service A also forged a letter from a CIA officer in Dhaka to the former Deputy Prime Minister, Moudud Ahmad, assuring him of US support for the right-wing opposition to Zia.[62] In 1981 another disinformation operation purported to show that the Reagan administration was plotting Zia's overthrow and had established secret contact with Khondakar Mustaque Ahmad, who had briefly become President after the assassination of Mujib and had been imprisoned by Zia from 1976 to 1980.[63] There is no evidence that KGB active measures had any success in undermining the Zia regime. At the 1979 general election, which was generally considered to have been fairly conducted, Zia's Bangladesh National Party won 207 of the 300 seats. Zia, however, never succeeded in resolving the problems posed by unrest in the armed forces. After several narrow escapes, he was assassinated while on a visit to Chittagong during an attempted coup led by the local army commander on 29 May 1981.[64]

Whatever successes were achieved by active-measures campaigns in Pakistan and Bangladesh during the late 1970s were more than cancelled out by the hostile reaction in both countries to the Soviet invasion of Afghanistan in December 1979 and the brutal war which followed. Hitherto Zia ul-Haq had been widely underestimated in both West and East. In the summer of 1978 *The Economist* had dismissed him as a 'well-intentioned but increasingly maladroit military ruler', while the *Guardian* declared that, 'Zia's name has a death-rattle sound these days. There's a feeling he can't last much longer.' Once war began in Afghanistan, however, it seemed to Zia ul-Haq's chief of army staff, General Khalid Mahmud Arif, that:

All eyes were focused on Pakistan. Would she buckle under pressure and acquiesce in superpower aggression? The Western countries quickly changed their tune. The arch critics of the autocratic military ruler of Pakistan began to woo him. They suddenly discovered Zia's hitherto unknown 'sterling qualities' and the special importance of Pakistan in the changed circumstances.[65]

Zia began pressing the Carter administration to provide arms and assistance to the *mujahideen* insurgents against the Communist regime in Afghanistan even before the Soviet invasion. The Pakistani Inter Services Intelligence Directorate (ISI) made similar approaches to the CIA. In February 1980 President Jimmy Carter's National Security Advisor, Zbigniew Brzezinski, visited Pakistan to agree with Zia US covert assistance to the Afghan *mujahideen* across the Pakistan border.[66] The meeting between Zia and Brzezinski inaugurated what was in effect a secret US–Pakistani alliance for covert intervention in Afghanistan which lasted for the remainder of the war. The KGB almost certainly deduced, even if they did not obtain detailed intelligence on, the purpose of Brzezinski's visit. After Brzezinski's departure from Islamabad, Gromyko declared that Pakistan was putting its own security at risk by acting as a 'springboard for further aggression against Afghanistan'.[67]

Andropov simultaneously approved an elaborate series of active measures designed to deter Zia from providing, or allowing the Americans or Chinese to provide, assistance to the *mujahideen*. The head of the Pakistani intelligence station in Moscow was to be privately warned that if Pakistan was used as a base for 'armed struggle against Afghanistan', the Oriental Institute (then headed by Yevgeni Primakov) would be asked to devise ways of assisting Baluchi and Pushtun separatist movements on the North-West Frontier in order to seal off the Afghan border.[68] The CIA concluded that there was a serious 'possibility of large-scale Soviet aid to the Baluchi'.[69] KGB active measures also sought to persuade Zia that some of his own senior officers, who opposed his Afghan policy, were plotting against him. Service A prepared leaflets in English and Urdu on Pakistani paper purporting to come from a secret opposition group to Zia within the Pakistani army. On the night of 28 February to 1 March 1980 KGB officers drove round Islamabad, Rawalpindi and Karachi distributing copies of the leaflets from a device attached to their cars. According to a KGB report, the leaflets were taken seriously by Pakistani security, which began an immediate investigation and wrongly incriminated the deputy army chief-of-staff, Lieutenant-General Muhammad Iqbal Khan (remembered by a British diplomat who knew him well as 'a decent and straightforward man'). The KGB claimed that this investigation provoked an unsuccessful coup by Iqbal Khan on 5 March, which led in turn to the removal or retirement of a series of senior officers and to the expulsion of two members of the US consulate in Lahore who had been in contact with them. On 25 March Andropov was informed that operation SARDAR had led the Zia regime to believe that the United States was conspiring with dissidents in the Pakistani army. Andropov approved the continuation of the operation. Several similar leaflets were distributed over the next year.[70]

Letters fabricated by Service A in the names of various informants and bogus conspirators were sent to American organizations and other addresses in Pakistan whose mail was believed to be intercepted by the local security services, as well as to the Pakistani ambassador in Washington, in order to spread the fiction of a CIA plot to overthrow the Zia regime. Disinformation planted on the Pakistani ambassador in Bangkok reported that the State Department regarded the regime as an unpopular, incompetent dictatorship which should be replaced as soon as possible.[71] Another active-measures operation sought to persuade the Pakistani authorities that the CIA was plotting with separatists in Baluchistan, promising to support their campaign for autonomy in return for help in conducting covert cross-border operations against the Khomeini regime. Among the more ingenious fabrications devised by Service A as part of this operation was a wallet containing a compromising document allegedly lost by a CIA officer operating under diplomatic cover. The wallet, supposedly found by a member of the Pakistani public, was handed in at a police station to ensure that it came to the attention of the authorities.[72] Simultaneously, the KGB orchestrated a large-scale campaign in the Pakistani and foreign press attacking Pakistani involvement in Afghanistan.[73] During the first eight months of the war the KGB claimed to have planted 527 articles in Pakistani newspapers.[74]

The Centre also went to elaborate lengths to exacerbate popular resentment against the Afghan refugees flooding across the border by planting agents in their midst with a mission to discredit them.[75] Its active measures, however, had no effect on Zia's policy. The Afghan refugee camps quickly became recruitment centres for the *mujahideen*. The ISI channelled the recruits into seven Islamic resistance groups, all with bases in Pakistan which directed operations across the Afghan border. The Hizb-i-Islami (Islamic Party) led by Gulbuddin Hekmatyar, the most important of the fundamentalist *mujahideen* groups, had particularly close links with the Zia ul-Haq regime. In 1978, in an attempt to bolster support for the regime, Zia had taken five members of the Pakistani wing of Hizb-i-Islami into his government. With Zia's support, the ISI replaced the Foreign Ministry as the main policy-making body on Afghanistan.[76]

Zia ul-Haq was well aware, even if he did not know many of the details, that the KGB was conducting a major active-measures offensive against him. Though the details remain classified, from an early stage in the war he received intelligence from the CIA as well as from his own agencies.[77] His response to the KGB offensive appears to have taken the Centre by surprise. In August and September 1980 Pakistan carried out the biggest expulsion of Soviet intelligence and other personnel since Britain had excluded 105 KGB and GRU officers in 1971.[78] Kryuchkov reacted to the expulsion and the problems created by the dramatic reduction in the size of the Pakistani residencies by setting up an interdepartmental working group within the FCD chaired by one of his deputies, V. A. Chukhrov, to try to devise ways of working with Pakistani opposition forces to destabilize and eventually overthrow the Zia regime.[79]

The most violent of Zia's opponents was Murtaza Bhutto, elder son of Zulfikar Ali Bhutto, who founded a small terrorist group, initially claiming to be the armed wing of the PPP, to avenge his father's death. While in jail, Bhutto senior had famously remarked, 'My sons are not my sons if they do not drink the blood of those who dare shed my blood today.'[80] In May 1979, a month after his father's execution, Murtaza visited Kabul to seek the help of the Taraki government in setting up a base in Afghanistan from which his guerrillas could launch attacks against the Zia regime.[81] Murtaza was allowed to receive a large arms shipment from Yasir Arafat and to house a small band of apprentice guerrillas, his so-called 'revolutionary army', in a derelict building which the volunteers called 'Dracula House'. His first attempt to smuggle some of his arms cache into Pakistan ended in disaster when the man chosen to take them across the border turned out to be a Pakistani agent. Murtaza was reduced to scouring Pakistani newspapers and claiming to his Afghan hosts that accidents and fires reported in them were the work of his guerrillas. After the Soviet invasion, however, Murtaza established a close relationship with Muhammad Najibullah, head of KHAD, the newly founded Afghan intelligence service, who as a goodwill gesture paid the costs of Murtaza's wedding to a young Afghan woman.[82]

Murtaza and Najibullah had a series of discussions on joint covert operations against Pakistan.[83] Since KHAD was operating under KGB direction, there is no doubt that their discussions were fully approved by the Centre.[84] Given the risks of operating with the volatile Murtaza, however, the Centre preferred to deal with him at one remove through KHAD. Murtaza may never have realized that, in his dealings with him, KHAD was acting as a KGB surrogate.[85] His first successful operations inside Pakistan, agreed with Najibullah, were a bomb attack on the Sindh high court and the destruction of a Pakistan International Airlines (PIA) DC-10 aircraft at Karachi airport in January 1981. He also planned to disrupt the visit of Pope John Paul II to Pakistan in February by exploding a bomb during the pontiff's address in a Karachi stadium. But the bomb went off prematurely at the entrance to the stadium, killing the bomber and a policeman.[86]

In December Murtaza Bhutto and Najibullah decided on what was to be their most spectacular joint operation, codenamed ALAMGIR

('Swordbearer') by the KGB.[87] It was agreed that Murtaza's guerrillas would hijack a PIA airliner over Pakistan and divert it to
Damascus or Tripoli. The three novice hijackers who boarded a
plane at Karachi on 2 March 1981, however, made the mistake
of choosing an internal flight which had insufficient fuel to reach
Damascus or Tripoli. The leading hijacker, Salamullah Tipu, ordered
the pilot to land at Kabul instead. As the plane landed, Tipu informed
the control tower that he was a member of the armed wing of the
PPP, which was fighting for the restoration of democracy in Pakistan, and wished to speak to 'Dr Salahuddin', Murtaza's codename
in Kabul. Murtaza, who chose the occasion to rename his terrorist
group Al-Zulfikar ('The Sword'), came to meet Tipu at the bottom
of the aircraft steps[88] and was joined by Najibullah, who was disguised in the clothes of an airport worker. Both the KGB mission
and the Kabul residency advised Najibullah on the best methods of
using the hijack to discredit the Zia regime.[89] On 4 March Anahita
Ratebzad, President of the Afghan–Soviet Friendship Association
and Minister of Education, who was a 'confidential contact' of the
KGB,[90] came to the airport surrounded by TV cameras, to express
support for the 'just demands' of the hijackers and to ask for the
release of the women and children on the aircraft to mark International Women's Day. In a pre-arranged gesture, Tipu announced
that he was happy to accede to Ratebzad's request. On 5 March the
Afghan leader and long-standing KGB agent, Babrak Karmal, who
had just returned from Moscow, conducted a live televised phone
conversation with Tipu from the control tower. Like Ratebzad,
Karmal gave strong backing to the hijackers' 'just demands'. Tipu
replied in an emotional voice that Karmal was the greatest man in
the whole of Asia.[91]

Among the hijackers' demands was the release of over fifty 'political prisoners' from Pakistani jails. When Zia refused, one of the
passengers was beaten, shot and thrown onto the tarmac, where he
writhed in agony as he lay dying. The victim, Tariq Rahim, was
a devoted former ADC to Zulfikar Ali Bhutto, but the paranoid
tendencies of both Tipu and Murtaza convinced them that Rahim
had really been in league with Zia.[92] This gruesome episode may
well have persuaded the KGB that it was time for the aircraft to
move on. Before the plane was refuelled for a flight to Syria, then
the Soviet Union's closest major ally in the Middle East, further

arms were taken on board unseen by the TV cameras. The three hijackers, who had arrived in Kabul armed only with pistols, left equipped with Kalashnikovs, grenades, explosives, a timing device and $4,500.[93] After the aircraft landed in Damascus, Zia initially continued to refuse to release political prisoners but was eventually persuaded to do so by Washington in order to save the lives of American hostages on board. Murtaza hailed the freeing of fifty-four PPP members from Pakistani jails as a triumph for Al-Zulfikar. KHAD and the KGB appeared to agree. Al-Zulfikar's base was moved from the derelict 'Dracula House' to new palatial headquarters, which received a steady stream of refugees from Zia's regime anxious to become guerrillas and fight for its overthrow.[94]

As well as supporting Al-Zulfikar, KHAD was also used by the KGB to channel arms to separatist and dissident groups in the Pakistani provinces of Baluchistan and Sindh. At the end of 1980 the leader of a Baluchi separatist group based in Afghanistan had secret talks with Najibullah who promised to provide the separatists with arms, 400 military instructors and three training camps. After talks between another Baluchi leader and the Afghan President, Babrak Karmal, in April 1982, KHAD opened two more camps to train Baluchi guerrillas to fight the Pakistani and Iranian regimes.[95]

The huge influx of Afghan refugees in Pakistan (eventually numbering perhaps as many as 3.5 million) offered numerous opportunities for agent infiltration. Since the agents were usually Afghan, in most instances the KGB used KHAD as its surrogate. According to statistics in FCD files, acting as a KGB surrogate, in the early 1980s KHAD's foreign intelligence directorate had 107 agents and 115 'trainee' agents operating inside Pakistan, mostly within the Afghan refugee community.[96] The FCD interdepartmental working group headed by Chukhrov made penetration of the *mujahideen* a major priority.[97] Twenty-six KHAD agents were said to have access to the headquarters of the rival *mujahideen* groups; fifteen were members of the Pakistani armed forces, intelligence community and official bureaucracy.[98] Their main achievement was to increase the existing tension and mistrust between the rival groups. Though this achievement did not change the course of the war in Afghanistan, it significantly diminished the effectiveness of *mujahideen* operations.[99]

The Centre also attempted to disrupt the links between Zia and the *mujahideen* groups in Pakistan by active measures designed to brand him as a traitor to Islam. On 18 April 1981 Kryuchkov submitted to Andropov a new proposal for disinformation designed 'to cause a deterioration in Pakistani–Iranian relations and to exacerbate the political situation in Pakistan':

1 Using [Service A's] samples in the Centre, leaflets should be written in Urdu by a fictitious opposition group calling for the overthrow of the regime of Zia ul-Haq and an Islamic Revolution in Pakistan. A large number of the leaflets should be printed and distributed in Pakistan. The text of the leaflet must make it clear that the writers are under the strong influence of Khomeini. The leaflet should quote Khomeini's criticisms of Zia ul-Haq and the present regime in Pakistan. The leaflet should be distributed by the residencies in Islamabad and Karachi and by our Afghan friends.
2 The residencies in Bangladesh and India should get the press in these countries to publish articles about a powerful opposition organization in Pakistan which was set up by the Iranian special services and which is actively working to overthrow Zia ul-Haq.

We await your approval.

Andropov gave his approval on 21 April.[100] Service A's leaflets attacking Zia as a traitor to Islam (operation ZAKHIR) took several forms. Some, such as the following example (unusually copied in its entirety by Mitrokhin), were intended to appear to be the work of Shi'ite groups inspired by Khomeini's example:

In the name of Allah, merciful and kind! Glory to Allah who made us Muslims and said in his Holy book: 'Is there anyone better than the man who calls on Allah to do good and says that he is obedient to him?' (S.41, A.33) Blessed is the prophet, his family and associates.

Brothers in faith!

Our enemies are not only those who openly oppose Islam, but also those who, under the cover of Islamism, do their dirty deeds. For it is written: 'Do not be afraid of your enemies, but of the day when you turn your back on Islam and the mosques.'

Zia ul-Haq is a hypocrite like the former Shah of Iran. He also prayed with Muslims, went on a pilgrimage to the Holy places and knew how to talk about the Holy Quran.

We are calling on the army and the people to rise up against the despot Zia ul-Haq, the servant of Satan – the United States of America – and to prepare him for the fate of the Shah. Satan is frightened that the Islamic Revolution, started in Iran, will spread to Pakistan. This is why Satan is generously supplying Zia ul-Haq with arms with which to kill believers. Zia ul-Haq has flooded our country with various unbelieving Americans and impure Chinese who are teaching him how to kill pure Muslims. He believes in their advice more than in the teachings of Allah. Zia ul-Haq is a mercenary dog who is living on Satan's dollars. He has ordered Zia ul-Haq to establish a cruel and bloody regime and to crush the Muslim people who are now living with no rights.

At the same time corruption and hypocrisy are eating away at our society. Crime is increasing. The reason is not only a lack of true belief, but the increasing gap between the rich and poor. As All-powerful Allah teaches us: 'A man will only receive when he is zealous.' Our prophet Muhammad, may Allah bless him, called on us Muslims to work honestly and hard in respect of the Almighty. This means that a Muslim must only receive what he has earned by his own labours. But Zia ul-Haq and his clique are unlawfully making themselves rich from other people's work. Even the Zekat [obligatory alms to the needy – one of the pillars of Islam] has become a thing of personal gain to them. Taking advantage of the fact that no one can control them, they award a large part of the Zekat. But the Most High ordered us that: 'Charity is for the poor and beggars, for the deliverance of slaves, for those in debt, for actions in the name of Islam and for travellers as declared by Allah. He is knowing and wise.' And our prophet Muhammad, and may He rest in peace, taught us that the Zekat must all be used for the needs of the poor, orphans and widows. Ask our poor people whether they have received much charity from the Zekat. Collecting the Zekat by force, Zia ul-Haq and his clique are not only insulting true Muslims. They are shamelessly ignoring the teachings of Islam. And they manage to hide their own money from the Zekat. All Muslims should know that Zia ul-Haq recently stole millions. He keeps his riches abroad as did the former Shah of Iran, knowing that sooner or later he will be forced to flee. He is hoping that Satan will protect him from the anger of the people. Meanwhile he is serving Satan faithfully by ensuring favourable conditions for the dominance of non-believers. He knows that this will lead to further theft from Muslims.

The clique of Zia ul-Haq has carried out a census of the population and its housing. This was also inspired by Satan as a way to introduce new taxes and labour conditions in contradiction of the teachings of Muhammad, may Allah bless him, for he said that anyone who oppresses a Muslim is not his follower.

Zia ul-Haq is leading the country to disaster. He wants to ride on the atomic devil and become a despot over all Muslims.

But Allah is great and just. Only dust remains from the enemies of Islam, but the warriors for the true faith are remembered for ever.

Everyone must join the fight in the name of Islam against the bloody dictator Zia ul-Haq.

Allah is great![101]

Other Service A leaflets purported to come from dissident Islamic officers, condemning Zia as a hypocritical traitor who, while professing friendship for Iran, was secretly plotting with the Americans to bring down the Islamic Republic. The Service A forgers threatened Zia with assassination. 'Next time', they told him, 'you will pay for it as Sadat did.'[102]

Murtaza Bhutto, meanwhile, with the assistance of Najibullah, acting as a KGB surrogate, was preparing a real plot to assassinate Zia. Though the evidence comes exclusively from former Al-Zulfikar sources, it appears that Zia narrowly escaped two assassination attempts early in 1982. The weapon in both cases was a Soviet SAM-7 (surface-to-air) missile. On the first occasion, in January, two Al-Zulfikar terrorists carried a SAM missile in the boot of a car to a deserted hillside in sight of Islamabad airport and awaited the arrival of a Falcon jet bringing Zia home from a visit to Saudi Arabia. But the poorly trained terrorist who fired the SAM did not wait for the red signal in his viewfinder to turn green, indicating that the missile had locked on to its target, and the attack failed. A few weeks later the Pakistani press revealed that on the morning of 7 February Zia would be arriving at Lahore aboard his personal plane. The two terrorists drove to a public park beneath Zia's flight path with another SAM in their boot, waited for the Falcon jet to come into view and fired the missile. Once again, however, they ignored some of the instructions in the SAM-7 manual. This time the terrorist who fired the missile waited for the green signal but failed to follow the manual's advice that the aircraft should be watched through the viewfinder until it was hit. The missile missed its target, though on this occasion the Falcon pilot saw the SAM-7 being launched and took what turned out to be unnecessary evasive action. The strict censorship imposed by Zia's regime prevented any mention of the assassination attempt appearing in the Pakistani press. The two terrorists escaped back to Kabul.[103] Two more SAM-7 missiles smuggled into Pakistan for a further attempt on Zia's life later in the year were seized by the police before they could be used. As Murtaza's paranoid strain became more pronounced, he suspected a bizarrely improbable plot between the Afghan regime and Zia to exchange him for the *mujahideen* leader, Gulbuddin Hekmatyar, and moved to New Delhi.[104]

Without any credible strategy to bring Zia down, the Centre could do little more than continue to publicize imaginary plots against him, chiefly from a supposedly secret Islamic opposition within the Pakistani armed forces. Some of Service A's fabrications appear to have deceived the Indian press. In 1983, for example, the Delhi *Patriot* published a text allegedly prepared by a clandestine cell calling itself the Muslim Army Brotherhood (Fauji Biradiri), which denounced the Zia regime as 'a despicable gang of corrupt generals ... more interested in lining their own pockets than in defending the nation', who had 'betrayed the ideas of Pakistan's founder, Mohammed Ali Jinnah, and were leading the country to ruin'. A recent history of Pakistan concludes: 'Nothing resembling the Muslim Army Brotherhood materialized in the more than ten years that Zia remained at the helm of state affairs, and it would appear to have been the invention of fertile minds in the neighbouring state [India].'[105]

In all probability, however, the 'fertile minds' were those not of the Indians but of Service A. Allegations of the Zia regime's corruption were also a regular theme in KGB disinformation. Zia was said to have large amounts of money in Swiss bank accounts, into which American arms manufacturers paid 10 per cent commission on their sales to Pakistan. KGB disinformation also claimed that Zia had a special plane in continual readiness in case he and his family had to flee the country.[106]

In Pakistan, as in India, some of the most effective active measures were based on fabricated evidence of US biological and chemical warfare.[107] Operation TARAKANY ('Cockroaches') centred on the claim that American specialists in this field had set up a base in the US bacteriological laboratory at the Lahore medical centre, which was secretly experimenting on Pakistani citizens. Outbreaks of bowel disease in the districts of Lishin, Surkhab and Muslim Bag and the neighbouring areas of Afghanistan, as well as epidemics and cattle deaths in Punjab, Haryana, Jammu, Kashmir and Rajasthan in western India were alleged to be the result of the movement across the Pakistani border of people and cattle infected by American germ-warfare specialists. On 11 February 1982 the Karachi *Daily News* reported that Dr Nellin, the American head of a research group at the Lahore medical centre, had been expelled by the Pakistani authorities. The Pakistani newspaper *Dawn* reported on 23 February:

Following the expulsion from Pakistan of Dr Nellin for dangerous experiments on the spread of infectious diseases, an American delegation of doctors is paying an urgent visit to Islamabad. Their aim is to hush up the scandal over the work of the Lahore medical centre and to put pressure on Pakistan not to make known the work which was carried out at the centre ... The fact that a group of American doctors has made such an urgent visit to Pakistan confirms that Washington is frightened that the dangerous experiments on new substances for weapons of mass destruction might be revealed. It supports the conclusion that Pakistan intends to allow the Americans to continue to carry out dangerous experiments, probably because these new weapons could be used against India, Iran and Afghanistan.

In May 1982 the KGB succeeded in taking the story a stage further by planting reports in the Indian press, allegedly based on sources in Islamabad, that the United States had stockpiled chemical and bacteriological weapons in Pakistan:

According to information received from local military sources, chemical reagents have recently been sent to Pakistan from the American chemical weapons arsenals on Johnston Island in the Pacific Ocean and in Japan. They will be positioned in areas not far from Islamabad, Karachi, Lahore, Quetta and Peshawar. According to the sources, these reagents are the same as those used by the Americans during the Vietnam War. According to the same reports, the reserve of American chemical and bacteriological weapons in Pakistan is intended for possible use by American rapid-deployment forces throughout South and South-West Asia. Agreement on the stationing of chemical and bacteriological weapons in Pakistan was reached between Washington and Islamabad as early as August 1980 when the agreement on the stationing of the American bacteriological service on Pakistani territory was officially prolonged. Point 2 of Article 5 of this agreement gives the Americans, in the form of the International Development Agency of the USA, the right to evaluate periodically the work and make suggestions for its improvement. In practice this means that the Americans have full control over all aspects of the work in Pakistan on new forms of chemical, bacteriological and biological weapons. This makes it possible for the USA independently to establish how chemical reagents must be stored and used in Pakistan. Confirmation of this is the well-known work in the medical centre in Lahore where American specialists have invented new forms of bacteriological and chemical weapons.

Within the Centre, Operation TARAKANY was considered such a success that Andropov made a special award to the resident in Pakistan.[108]

Anti-American black propaganda, however, failed to disrupt the increasing co-operation between Zia and Washington. Though Zia spurned the offer in 1980 of a $400-million economic and military aid package from the Carter administration as 'peanuts' (a mocking metaphor doubtless derived from Carter's background as a peanut farmer), in 1981 he accepted an offer from the incoming Reagan administration of $3.2 billion spread over six years.[109] During the war in Afghanistan the CIA supplied over $2 billion of covert assistance to the *mujahideen* through the Pakistani ISI. There was close liaison between the CIA and ISI with a series of exchange visits by their chiefs, Bill Casey and General Akhtar Abdul Rahman.[110] KGB active measures had no discernible effect in undermining either Zia or ISI support for the *mujahideen*. Until Zia's death in 1988 in an air crash whose cause has never been convincingly explained, his regime proved one of the most stable in Pakistani history.[111]

When Zulfikar Ali Bhutto's daughter, Benazir, became Prime Minister after Zia's death in 1988, she showed little enthusiasm for *mujahideen* operations in the final stages of the war.[112] Had she become Prime Minister earlier or Zia been assassinated in 1982, the history of the war in Afghanistan would have been significantly different. The KGB had been right to identify Zia's personal commitment to opposing the Soviet invasion as crucial to Pakistan's covert role in Afghanistan but had failed in its attempts to put effective pressure on him to diminish or end it.

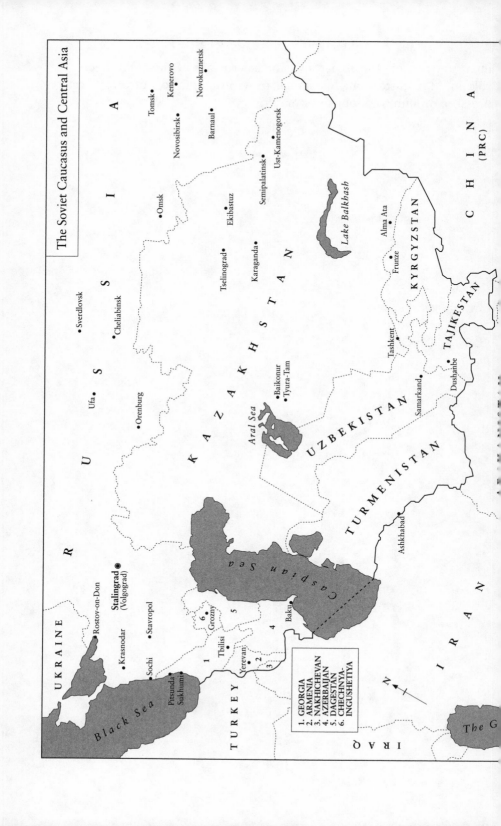

The Soviet Caucasus and Central Asia

20

Islam in the Soviet Union*

During the Cold War the Soviet Union contained the fifth largest Muslim population in the world – less than Indonesia, Pakistan, India and Bangladesh, but more than Egypt, Turkey or Iran.[1] Tsarist Russia's imperial expansion into the Muslim world had begun four centuries earlier with the conquest of Kazan by Ivan the Terrible's 'Soldiers of Christ'. The multicoloured onion domes on St Basil's Cathedral in Red Square supposedly represent the severed, turbaned heads of eight Muslim leaders killed during the conquest. Russia's occupation of Muslim territory continued at intervals for the next three and a half centuries. The Bolshevik Revolution, however, brought with it the promise of liberation for the Muslim peoples of the Tsarist Empire. Lenin and Stalin, then Commissar for Nationalities, jointly declared on 3 December 1917:

Muslims of Russia! Tatars of the Volga and the Crimean! Kyrgyz and Sarts of Siberia and of Turkistan! Turks and Tatars of Trans-Caucasus! Chechens and mountain peoples of the Caucasus! And all of you whose mosques and places of worship have been destroyed, whose customs have been trampled under foot by the tsars and the oppressors of Russia! Your beliefs, your customs, your national and cultural constitutions are from now on free and safe. Organize your national life freely and with no hindrance. You have the right to do so.

In reality, Soviet persecution during the generation which followed the Bolshevik Revolution was far worse than anything endured

---

* The transliteration of personal and place names from the Muslim areas of the Soviet Union poses complex problems. In the interests of simplicity and consistency, most have been transliterated from their Cyrillic versions.

by the Muslim subjects of the later Tsarist Empire. Islam was condemned as a relic of the feudal era which had no place in a society of 'advanced socialism' and was therefore 'doomed to disappear'.[2]

During the Great Patriotic War Stalin saw all Soviet Muslims, like the Volga Germans, as actual or potential traitors. The Muslim peoples whose territory had been invaded by the German army (Karachai, Kalmyks, Balkars and Crimean Tatars) as well as the Chechens and Ingush, whose republic had barely been reached by the Wehrmacht, were deported by the NKVD to Siberia and central Asia, mostly during 1943–44, in horrific conditions. One of the Balkar deportees later recalled, 'They only gave us fifteen minutes to gather a few belongings and we didn't even know what was going on. It was only when they put us in the train wagons that we realized we were going far away.' Though hundreds of thousands died from starvation and cold during the deportation and in the 'special settlements' in which they were dumped, Beria declared the whole operation a complete success and promoted a decree by the Supreme Soviet 'on decorations and medals for the most outstanding [NKVD] participants'. There was no word of official criticism until Khrushchev's 'Secret Speech' to the Twentieth Party Congress in 1956 denounced the deportations as 'crude violations of the basic Leninist principles of the nationality policies of the Soviet State'. Over the next few years most of the surviving deportees, except for the Crimean Tatars and Volga Germans, were allowed to return to their homelands. They found their houses occupied, most mosques demolished and many family gravestones ripped up for use as building materials.[3]

Public discussion of the deportations remained officially taboo until the final years of the Soviet era. As even Soviet analysts concluded, however, the experience of deportation and persecution, so far from weakening Islamic belief, actually reinforced it. The deportees who returned to the North Caucasus were the most religious group in Soviet society.[4] Until the late 1980s Moscow routinely described the Muslim population of central Asia and the Caucasus as 'backward peoples'.[5] A Turkmen woman educated in Russian schools later recalled being taught that her culture was as primitive as 'that of the Australian aborigines'.[6] The KGB, however, was struck by the tenacity with which this primitive culture was preserved. In the Muslim republics, it concluded in 1973, 'Religion

370

is identified with the nation. The fight against religion is seen as an attack on the national identity.'[7]

From the Second World War onwards the cornerstone of Soviet policy to its Muslim peoples, as to the Russian Orthodox Church,[8] was the creation of a subservient religious hierarchy. Moscow maintained firm control of the four Islamic 'directorates' (each headed by a mufti) established or re-established in 1943, at the same time as the revival of the Moscow Patriarchate of the Orthodox Church. The most important was the Central Asian Spiritual Directorate of Muslims (SADUM), with its headquarters in Tashkent, which covered the five central Asian republics (Kazakhstan, Uzbekistan, Kyrgyzstan, Tajikistan and Turkmenistan). Because SADUM was responsible for a majority of Soviet Muslims, its head was often referred to as the Grand Mufti. Both SADUM and the madrasahs which it administered in Tashkent and Bukhara were heavily penetrated by KGB agents.[9] Since only graduates of these madrasahs, which had a total enrolment limited to about eighty,[10] were legally entitled to conduct religious services, the KGB thus had an informal right of veto over the admission of 'undesirable' Muslim clerics. Those identified as KGB agents in files noted by Mitrokhin include imams at mosques in such major Muslim centres as Tashkent, Dushanbe and Chimkent.[11]

The selection of the eighty-two-year-old Ishan Babakhan ibn Abdul Mejid Khan as first head of SADUM in 1943 inaugurated a family dynasty of outwardly subservient Grand Muftis which endured until Soviet rule in central Asia began to crumble in 1989. Babakhanov's son, Ziautdin (Grand Mufti, 1957–82), proved 'slavishly loyal to the Soviet regime'. His series of *fatwahs* in the late 1950s condemning pilgrimages to traditional Muslim holy places within the jurisdiction of SADUM was doubtless prompted by the KGB's fear of their potential both for spreading Islam and encouraging anti-Soviet protest.[12] Ziautdin Babakhanov was also used both to host a series of international conferences and to head delegations abroad by Soviet Muslims, all of which faithfully promoted the Soviet worldview and suppressed evidence of Moscow's campaign to discourage Islamic practice. The pattern was set by the first conference chaired by Babakhanov at Tashkent in 1970 on 'Unity and Co-operation of Muslim Peoples in the Struggle for Peace', attended by delegates from twenty-four Muslim countries. Though there were strident denunciations of American, Israeli and South African 'imperialism', Moscow received fulsome praise for its supposed commitment to the welfare of its Muslim subjects.[13] The formula changed little for the remainder of the decade. At an international conference at Dushanbe in September 1979 convened by SADUM at the secret prompting of the KGB on 'The Contribution of the Muslims of Central Asia, the Caucasus and the Volga to the Development of Islamic Thought, Peace and Social Progress',[14] Babakhanov repeated his by now ritual attacks on 'US, Israeli and South African imperialism'.[15] Mingling at the conference with Muslim delegates from thirty countries were officers and agents of the KGB Fifth Directorate and the local KGBs of Azerbaijan, Uzbekistan, Kazakhstan, Tajikistan, Turkmenistan, Kyrgyzstan, Bashkiria and Tataria.[16] SADUM was also used to provide cover for KGB agents travelling abroad. Between 1953 and 1970 (the only period for which Mitrokhin's notes contain statistics), ten KGB officers and over fifty agents went on operational missions to Saudi Arabia on the pretext either of going on pilgrimage (Haj) to Mecca (a privilege allowed to very few Soviet Muslims) or of visiting Islamic theological schools.[17] In the 1970s at least one KGB agent, codenamed NASIB, was elected to a leading position in the World Islamic League.[18]

Despite the KGB's extensive penetration of and influence over the official hierarchy of Soviet Islam, however, the greater part of Muslim life remained outside the Centre's control. It has become clear since the main Muslim regions of the Soviet Union gained their independence that Islamic practice during the Soviet era was much more widespread than was realized at the time – even if most of it took place within the home rather than at the small number of officially approved mosques. Male circumcision, for example, remained almost universal.[19] As KGB reports complained, even Party and Komsomol (Communist Youth League) members saw no contradiction between their public profession of Marxism-Leninism and their private participation in Muslim religious rituals.[20] There were many reports also of popular resistance to campaigns to promote 'scientific atheism'. When, for example, an 'atheistic corner' was set up in School Number 2 in the Chechen town of Sernovodsk, it was destroyed by the children themselves, who threw the visual aids into the river. In 1973 the philosophy lecturer at the Grozny Institute of Higher Education was asked to give a lecture in the town of Nazran attacking religion. Fearing for his personal safety, the lecturer asked friends who lived locally to try to ensure his security. They replied that there was no need since no one would attend the lecture. No one did.[21]

Much of the strength of what Soviet officials termed 'unofficial Islam' derived, particularly in the northern Caucasus, from the underground mystical Sufi brotherhoods (tariqa) which as far back as the twelfth century had taken on the role of defenders of the faith when Islam was threatened by infidel invasion. Though the Naqshbandiya, founded in the fourteenth century and present throughout the twentieth-century Muslim world, were the largest Sufi brotherhood in the Soviet Union, the twelfth-century Qadiriya were the dominant group in the Chechen-Ingush Republic. The Qadiriya were more radical, more aggressive and more clandestine than the Naqshbandiya. The Naqshbandiya were chiefly concerned to preserve Islamic practice outside the constraints imposed by the state and official Islam, but showed little inclination to challenge directly the political and social dominance of the Soviet system. The Qadiriya, however, and in particular its most influential brotherhoods, the Vis Haji, were uncompromisingly hostile to the Soviet regime.[22]

Mitrokhin's notes include varying amounts of detail from KGB files on operations against Sufi brotherhoods. In 1962 the KGB claimed to have identified the leader of the Qadiriya brotherhood as an 'unofficial' mullah named Auaev from the Borchasvili clan which had refused to do the work expected of them on their collective farm. The KGB arranged a show trial of Auaev and seven of his associates, who were sentenced to five years' imprisonment. At the prompting of the KGB, the official muftiate (Spiritual Directorate of Muslims) of the northern Caucasus solemnly instructed all believers to have nothing to do with unauthorized 'sects' (Sufi brotherhoods) and mullahs. Though the Centre was doubtless able to present the case as a significant victory, it can have had no illusions that the instructions of the muftiate would have any perceptible effect.[23] The relatively mild sentence passed on Auaev is surprising. Other members of Sufi brotherhoods in the Caucasus arrested in the early 1960s were commonly sentenced to death on charges of 'banditism'.[24] Given Auaev's prominence, it is possible that the authorities preferred to keep him alive in miserable conditions and try to discredit him.

A further success recorded in KGB files was the shooting,

apparently in the mid-1960s,[25] of another leading figure in the Qadiriya brotherhood, Khamad Gaziev, who had been hunted by the KGB since leading an armed uprising in the northern Caucasus in the 1950s. Though the uprising was defeated and Gaziev forced underground, the KGB reported that he remained a charismatic leader who inspired his fanatical followers with the belief that he possessed supernatural powers. The KGB sought to undermine his reputation with an active-measures campaign in the north-Caucasian media which portrayed Gaziev as a criminal adventurer with no real commitment to Islam who used religion as a pretext for armed robbery and the murder of Soviet citizens. A KGB-inspired article on Gaziev entitled 'A Blood-Stained Turban' was published in all local newspapers, broadcast on radio and television, and read aloud in state enterprises and collective farms.

Eventually a KGB agent codenamed GORSKY penetrated Gaziev's network and reported that he was hiding in the house of his 'accomplice', Akhma Amriev, in the village of Chemulg in the Sunzhensk region of Ingushetiya. An attempt to arrest Gaziev led to a shoot-out in which both he and his bodyguard were killed. The trial of Amriev and his wife, Khamila Amrieva, in the Sunzhensk House of Culture, carefully orchestrated by the KGB, was used to expose the 'crimes' of the Qadiriya brotherhood. The KGB organized meetings in Chemulg and other villages which had hidden Gaziev at which some of his relatives and 'accomplices', as well as official Muslim clerics, also carefully rehearsed, denounced him as a fraud and condemned the activities of the Qadiriya. The mufti of the northern Caucasus issued *fatwahs* containing similar denunciations.[26] The elimination of individual Sufi leaders, however, did little to undermine the movement as a whole. Their names were added to the long list of Sufi saints and martyrs.

Among the episodes which caused particular concern in Moscow was a mass Ingush public demonstration which began in Grozny, the capital of Chechnya-Ingushetiya, on the morning of 16 January 1973. The occasion was a particular embarrassment for the KGB since it demonstrated how badly it had misjudged the level of local discontent. As crowds filed into Revolution Square in the heart of Grozny, there was no initial indication of the trouble which was to follow. The garishly coloured banners carried the usual politically correct slogans: among them 'Long live Soviet Ingushetiya!' and 'Long live Red Ingushetiya – the cradle of the Revolution in the northern Caucasus!' The ceremonies began with the placing on the statue of Lenin of wreaths adorned with the usual red ribbons loyally inscribed 'To Great Lenin from the Ingush People'. As the speeches continued, however, the authorities became increasingly anxious. Among those singled out for criticism by the Ingush speakers was the First Secretary of the Regional Party, Apryatkin, popularly known as *tryapkin* ('rag') or *pryatkin* ('someone in hiding') because of his reluctance to appear in public. To the horror of the local worthies, the meeting then demanded the return of land in Dagestan and northern Ossetia which had belonged to the Ingush before their expulsion in 1944.

At the end of the day, the demonstrators refused an official order to disperse. Fires were lit in Revolution Square, sheep were roasted and crates of vodka brought in. The meeting continued in freezing cold for three days and nights while speaker after speaker denounced the injustices suffered by the Ingush under Soviet rule. One of the former deportees described seeing his bewildered mother with a baby in her arms kicked out of her house in 1944 by a Russian officer. In exile in Kazakhstan the ground had been so hard that it was difficult to dig graves for the families who died of cold and starvation. 'I am glad', the speaker concluded, 'that I saw this with my own eyes so that my anger will never fade away.' According to the KGB transcript of the meeting, a woman shouted from the speakers' platform:

We have no mosques. We opened a mosque in Grozny but the authorities closed it. But this does not stop us praying. We Ingush believe in Allah. He listens to us and will help us. When we were in Kazakhstan, we prayed every day and asked Allah to punish those responsible for our misfortunes. He heard us. One after another they died or passed from the scene – Stalin, Beria, Malenkov, Molotov and Khrushchev. We will continue to pray secretly every day.

Two senior Party figures, Mikhail Solomentsev, the Russian Prime Minister, and Nikolai Shchelokov, the Soviet Interior Minister, were urgently despatched to Grozny to bring the demonstration to an end. At a meeting of Party activists, Solomentsev berated the local leadership for its inertia and cowardice. The regional Party Committee was disbanded and the local KGB and police chiefs dismissed.

Though Solomentsev declared that the Politburo wished to end the demonstration without violence, the demonstrators continued to refuse to disperse. In a show of force the square was surrounded by soldiers and the entrances blocked by troop carriers and lorries, but the demonstrators were assured that if they dispersed no action would be taken against them. A hundred or so KGB agents were sent to mingle with the crowd and persuade them to leave. Some did, but the majority remained. Fire engines then drenched the crowd with freezing water from their hoses, and a combination of soldiers, KGB units and militiamen drove most of the demonstrators from the square. About 400 initially stood firm in the centre of the square but were finally beaten with rifle butts and truncheons into buses to be driven to detention by the KGB. Other mass demonstrations in Chechnya-Ingushetiya took place in Nazran, Malgobek and Sunzhensk.[27]

The Centre ordered an immediate investigation. As when dealing with dissidents elsewhere in the Soviet bloc, a series of FCD illegals posing as outside sympathizers were sent to Grozny and other parts of Chechnya-Ingushetiya to make contact with leaders of the demonstrations. AKBAR, STELLA, SABIR, ALI and STRELTSOV were given Iranian passports, MARK, RAFIEV, DEREVLYOV and his wife DEREVLYOVA Soviet identity documents, KHALEF a Turkish passport, and BERTRAND a French passport.[28] A year earlier BERTRAND, posing as a French archaeologist, had succeeded in winning the confidence of the leading Russian dissident, Andrei Sakharov, privately described by Andropov as Public Enemy Number One.[29] In Grozny and Ordzhonokidze BERTRAND passed himself off as an academic from the University of Montpellier who had been invited by the Soviet Ministry of Higher Education to study the teaching of French and other foreign languages in the Soviet Union.[30] DEREVLYOV was later tasked with trying to penetrate the entourage of Pope John Paul II.[31]

Based on intelligence from the illegals and other sections of the KGB, Andropov made a preliminary report to the Politburo in April 1973 on the reasons for the January unrest. He paid a grudging tribute to the efficiency with which the protests had been organized. The discipline and secrecy preserved beforehand by thousands of demonstrators had meant that no advance warning had reached the authorities. Andropov acknowledged frankly that the influence of the official Islamic directorate of the northern Caucasus was 'minimal': 'As there are no official mosques, religious ceremonies are carried out secretly by believers.' Real influence lay with the unauthorized mullahs who 'do not stop believers joining the Party or the Komsomol as long as they remain true to the teachings of Islam. This they do.'

The KGB had successfully put pressure on many of the participants in the demonstration to make public statements of repentance. But, Andropov admitted, the vast majority of the population had been deeply impressed by the demonstration and were in favour of it:

The situation is such that [the January demonstration] could be repeated. The causes have not been eliminated. The local population is prejudiced against the Russians whom they hold responsible for all their troubles and misery. The expulsions in 1944 and the dominant influence of the Russians are the main causes of their hostility . . . There is also strong resistance to Russian culture and a feeling amongst the people that they do not want to mix with Russians. The palaces of culture, clubs, libraries, lecture rooms, theatres and other places of enlightenment are literally empty.[32]

The KGB believed that disciplined and secretive Sufi brotherhoods were present in every town, street and village of Chechnya-Ingushetiya. The only authority which the people respected was that of the religious elders. Disputes were settled in Islamic courts and Soviet law ignored.[33] In reality, though the Centre refused to admit it, most KGB officers had given up hope of extending to the northern Caucasus much of the system of social control which they exercised in Russia. As a former KGB officer in Chechnya-Ingushetiya has since acknowledged, except when pressured by the Centre, the local KGB usually accepted the traditional system of justice administered by the Chechens themselves rather than insisting on the enforcement of Soviet law: 'Otherwise, on the occasions when for some reason we really *had* to get a result, no one would even have talked to us.'[34]

The most visible sign of the strength of Sufism during the 1970s was continued mass pilgrimages, despite official attempts to prevent them, to the Sufi holy places which were particularly numerous in the northern Caucasus. Many pilgrimages were accompanied by religious songs and dances, often performed with a fervour which the authorities condemned as frenzy. A Soviet study concluded in 1975:

Collective fanaticism and religious exaltation may reach high levels of paroxysm when the pilgrims, believers and unbelievers alike, including the students, sing for hours the litanies of the *zikr* – 'There are no gods but God'. Pilgrims come from everywhere, from the villages and the cities, and when they return home, they sing religious songs and behave as active propagandists of holy places.[35]

The KGB reported one occasion on which 40,000 pilgrims gathered at the tomb of the Sufi saint Hay Imam in Azerbaijan.[36] Even the destruction of religious monuments did not always deter the pilgrims. When the Uzbek authorities blew up the holy rock at Parpiata, the Muslim faithful constructed a pyramid from the remains, which they continued to venerate.[37]

Moscow's concern about the loyalty of its Muslim subjects in both the Caucasus and central Asia was heightened at the end of the 1970s by the 'Islamic revolution' in Iran and the beginning of the war in Afghanistan. In February 1979 Ayatollah Kazem Shari'atmadari broadcast from Tehran, 'The Iranian people's triumphant struggle constitutes a turning point in the history of world struggles and the best model to follow by the oppressed Muslim peoples of the world.' As an Azeri Turk from Tabriz, Shari'atmadari probably had particularly in mind the oppressed Muslims of Azerbaijan.[38] The KGB active-measures campaign to discredit Shari'atmadari, prompted by his appeal to Soviet Muslims, probably contributed to his disgrace three years later.[39] In 1980 the Chairman of the Azerbaijani KGB, Yusif Zade, publicly denounced the 'infiltration of foreign agents across our borders' (an indirect reference to Iranian attempts to export the Khomeini brand of fundamentalism into Azerbaijan) and the 'anti-social activity' of 'sectarians' and 'reactionary Muslim clergy' (the traditional Soviet codewords for the Sufi brotherhoods and unauthorized mullahs).[40] The Azerbaijani journal *Kommunist* declared two years later that the rise in unauthorized 'religious activity' was 'a direct consequence of the political-religious movement taking place in Iran'.[41]

Reports from Azerbaijan and elsewhere in the Soviet Union[42] blaming Iran for an increase in 'anti-social' activity by Sunni as well as Shia Muslims cannot be taken entirely at face value. The KGB invariably tended to see foreign conspiracy as a major explanation for outbreaks of 'ideological subversion' within the Soviet Union. A special department was set up in the KGB Fifth Directorate 'to fight the ideological subversion from foreign Muslims and the activities of the Islamic clergy', as well as 'to expose the negative aspects of religious observance'.[43] In September 1981 the Politburo adopted a resolution proposed by the KGB on 'Measures to counter attempts by the adversary to use the Islamic factor for purposes hostile to the Soviet Union'.[44] An FCD directive approved by Andropov a month later instructed foreign residents 'to devise and carry out offensive active measures to eradicate the anti-Soviet actions of hostile Islamic forces abroad, to expose their ties with Western special [intelligence] services, to bring a halt to their anti-Soviet actions, and to expose the contradictions and disagreements amongst the leaders of the Islamic movement and to use them in active measures'. To achieve these tasks, it would be necessary to establish 'permanent surveillance' of leading foreign Muslims with 'strong anti-Soviet views' and to place agents in Islamic organizations of all kinds. A working group containing members of ten foreign intelligence departments was set up under the chairmanship of the FCD deputy head, Yakov Prokofyevich Medyanik, to draw up a detailed plan of action for the period 1982–85 to 'counter attempts by the West to use the Islamic factor against the USSR'.[45]

The Soviet invasion of Afghanistan in December 1979 and the war which followed (discussed in the next chapter), however, proved a fundamental obstacle to the KGB's attempts to extend Soviet influence in the Islamic world. On 14 January 1980 the UN General Assembly passed a resolution calling for 'immediate, unconditional and total withdrawal of foreign troops' from Afghanistan by a majority of 104 to 18 votes. KGB active measures proved powerless to prevent further hostile votes.[46] Similar UN resolutions were passed by massive majorities every year until Gorbachev finally agreed to withdraw Soviet troops in 1988.[47] The war also strengthened Moscow's doubts about the loyalty of its Muslim subjects. In late February 1980, after some central Asian troops in Afghanistan had gone over to the *mujahideen*, Moscow began withdrawing Muslim troops and replacing them with Russian units. The central Asian press switched from propaganda celebration of the supposed 'friendship' between Soviet Muslims and their Russian 'Elder Brother' to emphasizing the ability of the 'Elder Brother' to eliminate 'traitors' and maintain law and order. There was an unprecedented flood of articles and publications eulogizing 'our brave Chekisty' and the proud legacy of 'Iron Feliks'.[48] The deputy head of the Tajik KGB, A. Belousov, reported that the CIA's aim in the war in Afghanistan was not merely to defeat the Red Army and the Communist regime but 'to destabilize the central Asian republics of the USSR'.[49]

Abroad, the ambitious FCD programme to extend Soviet influence in the Islamic world rapidly degenerated into a damage limitation exercise designed to stifle as many Muslim protests against the war in Afghanistan as possible. The Centre was reduced to reporting as successes cases where its agents at international Islamic conferences had managed to prevent the tabling of critical resolutions on the war.[50] But the official Soviet representatives also suffered many setbacks. At the meeting in Mecca of the Supreme World Council of Mosques in 1983, the head of the Soviet delegation, Grand Mufti Shamsutdin Babakhanov, tried in vain to keep Afghanistan off the agenda. The Centre claimed that he had won the consent of delegates from Jordan, Libya, Tunisia and the United States, but that the Saudi royal family had insisted on discussing the role of Soviet troops in the war.[51] Vladimir Kryuchkov told a conference of FCD departmental heads early in 1984, '. . . Anti-Soviet pronouncements from reactionary Muslim organizations have intensified.'[52]

Despite the formidable problems created by the war in Afghanistan, the main threats to the maintenance of Soviet authority in the Muslim regions were internal. Islamic religious practice obstinately refused to go away, while the proportion of Muslims in the Soviet population increased steadily throughout the middle and later years of the Cold War. Until the 1950s ongoing Slav immigration had seemed to guarantee Moscow's continued dominance of Muslim areas. From the late 1950s onward, however, there was net Slav emigration from most of the Muslim republics. Simultaneously the Muslim birth rate began to outstrip that of the Slavs. Between 1959 and 1979 Muslims increased from less than one-eighth to one-sixth of the total Soviet population. By the 1988/89 academic year half of all primary schoolchildren came from Muslim backgrounds.[53]

Soviet rule in the Muslim republics was a politically correct façade which concealed the reality of a population which looked far more to Mecca than to Moscow, ruled by a corrupt political élite whose Marxism-Leninism was often little more than skin deep. Even the local KGBs were, in varying degree, infected by the corruption. The area of the Muslim Caucasus in which KGB control seemed most secure during the 1970s was Azerbaijan. During the previous decade the local Party leader, Muhammad Akhund-Zadeh, had turned corruption into an instrument of government under which a carefully calibrated system of bribery could purchase everything from university places to queue-jumping for apartments. In 1969, however, the local KGB chief, Geidar Aliyev, launched a 'crusade against corruption' which swept Akhund-Zadeh from office and led to his own appointment as Party boss. During the next decade Aliyev supposedly 'cleansed' Azerbaijan and clamped down on Muslim dissent by putting the republic under what appeared to be direct KGB rule. Baku, the capital and one of the main centres of the Soviet oil industry, became a propaganda showcase for 'advanced socialism' during the oil boom of the 1970s. In reality, claims the Pulitzer prize-winning journalist David Remnick, 'Aliyev ruled Azerbaijan as surely as the Gambino family ran the port of New York. The Caspian Sea caviar mafia, the Sumgait oil mafia, the fruits and vegetables mafia, the cotton mafia, the customs and transport mafias – they all reported to him, enriched him, worshiped him.'[54]

The Centre was well aware that corruption in many guises existed in much of Muslim central Asia,[55] but preferred to turn a blind eye when corruption reached the top. In the pre-Gorbachev era, noted Mitrokhin, 'only the small fry were caught'.[56] As Party First Secretary in the mid-1950s in Kazakhstan, the largest Islamic republic, Brezhnev had become convinced that 'a certain degree of corruption' was endemic in the national character of the peoples of central Asia and the Caucasus. The corruption, however, ran out of control. Brezhnev's crony, Dinmukhamed Kunayev, Party First Secretary in Kazakhstan from 1970 to 1985, headed what was later denounced as the 'Kazakh Mafia'; David Remnick found him 'all bravado and condescension ... He wore dark glasses and carried the sort of carved walking stick that gave Mobutu his authority.' The Kazakh novelist Abdul-Jamil Nurbeyev saw Kunayev as a traditional clan chieftain whose main ambition was to 'install his own relatives and friends at all key posts'.[57]

Corruption was probably worst in Uzbekistan, the most populous of the Muslim republics, with a population exceeded by only Russia and Ukraine. Just as the 'Kazakh Mafia' was led by Kunayev, so the 'Uzbek Mafia' (later accused of embezzling more than 5 billion rubles of public funds) was led by the Uzbek First Secretary, Sharaf Rashidov, holder of no fewer than ten Lenin prizes. In 1977 the Centre was confronted with damning evidence of Rashidov's corruption when it received reports that a former official in the Uzbek Ministry of Motor Transport named Ibrahim was planning to publish an exposé in the West. Rashidov, it was revealed, had bribed a deputy chairman of Gosplan (the State Planning Commission) with mink coats and other inducements to approve the building of an airport near his home in defiance of a plan already approved to site it elsewhere. Ibrahim himself complained that he had been forced to pay a bribe of 20,000 rubles to an Uzbek official to obtain the visa required for him to travel to the West.[58] Andropov was doubtless informed of the case but appears to have been more concerned by the prospect of the exposé than by the corruption it revealed. On a subsequent occasion, Rashidov sacked the head of the Uzbek KGB, Melkumov, for arresting corrupt Communist Party members without obtaining the consent of the Party district committees.[59] Like Kunayev, Rashidov was a Brezhnev crony. According to the Soviet procurators who later investigated the Uzbek scandal, 'Due to their "special relationship", Uzbekistan was out of bounds to any critics.'[60] Rashidov bought Brezhnev at least half a dozen luxury European sports cars as well as building extravagant hunting lodges for Brezhnev's occasional forays into Uzbekistan. Rashidov also indulged the weakness for diamonds of Brezhnev's daughter, Galina; Brezhnev's son-in-law, Yuri Churbanov, later admitted receiving, among other gifts, a suitcase stuffed with banknotes. Aliyev was not to be outdone. In 1982 he presented Brezhnev with a ring set with a huge jewel, representing him as the Sun King, surrounded by fifteen smaller precious stones representing the Union Republics – 'like planets orbiting the sun', Aliyev explained. Overcome with emotion, Brezhnev burst into tears in front of the TV cameras.[61]

Corruption in the Muslim republics was condoned in Moscow. In 1971 Kunayev was elected a full member of the Politburo. With the election of Aliyev in 1982, shortly after Andropov succeeded Brezhnev as Soviet leader, the Politburo had for the first time two full members of Muslim origin, as well as Rashidov as a candidate member. Though Andropov may have detested the Russian corruption of the Brezhnev era, his promotion of Aliyev (whom he made

First Deputy Chairman of the Council of Ministers), like his previous disinclination to take action over Rashidov, demonstrates that he had different standards for Muslim regions. It was not until 1983 that Andropov finally confronted Rashidov with evidence of his corruption. Soon afterwards Rashidov died from heart failure – or, according to some accounts, committed suicide.[62] A secret investigation into the 'Uzbek Mafia' revealed what has been described as 'one of the largest cases of public office corruption in contemporary history'.[63] It was left to Gorbachev to sack Kunayev[64] and Aliyev[65] in, respectively, 1986 and 1987, and to reveal some (but by no means all) of the investigation into the Uzbek scandal in 1988.

The crumbling of Soviet rule in central Asia began after Kunayev's replacement by a Russian First Secretary. Riots led by university students in the Kazakh capital, Alma Ata, left about thirty dead and there were protests elsewhere in Kazakhstan. At the same time, the authority of the official Muslim hierarchy began to erode. SADUM issued vaguely worded condemnations of 'attempts to lead the youth astray' but irritated the Centre by its reluctance to endorse the Russian repression which followed the riots. It caused even greater offence among the Muslims of central Asia by its failure to defend their rights. An *Islamizdat* (Muslim *samizdat*) leaflet accused Grand Mufti Shamsutdin Babakhanov of 'not knowing what the right path is to take': 'It is not enough to go abroad and speak out against the injustice of Zionist occupation of lands that belong to Muslim Arabs and to deny the right of [Kazakh] Muslims to reign in their own homeland here . . .' On 6 February 1989 Babakhanov was forced to resign after several days of demonstrations in Tashkent's main mosque accusing him of drunkenness and womanizing.[66]

The old guard in Moscow fell back once again on conspiracy theory to explain the crumbling of Soviet rule. A writer in the influential *Literaturnaya Gazeta* asserted in 1987:

[President Carter's National Security Adviser, Zbigniew] Brzezinski developed an Islamic 'Kriegspiel' against the Soviet Union . . . The objective was to create an 'Islamic bomb' in the Soviet republics of central Asia. The idea took flesh when an official report was prepared in 1979. [I]t indicated that specialized, secret Muslim organizations should be created with the aim of undertaking subversive operations in our country.[67]

There is no doubt that this bizarre article reflected some of the thinking in the Centre. Nikolai Leonov, head of KGB intelligence assessment, declared in April 1991, 'Read the articles and speeches of Zbigniew Brzezinski ... and you will see that his goal is to eliminate the Soviet Union as a united state.' The Bush administration, he insisted, was secretly following the same policy. 'The all-pervading tune' of US-financed broadcasts to the Caucasus and other parts of the Soviet Union was 'the incitement of hatred of the Russians'. Unlike previous KGB chairmen, Kryuchkov did not claim that imperialist plots were the principal cause of Soviet ills. 'The main sources of our trouble, in the KGB's view,' he declared, 'are inside our country.' But he accused the CIA and other Western intelligence services of promoting 'anti-socialist', separatist groups as part of their continuing 'secret war against the Soviet state'.[68]

Kryuchkov, however, did more than the CIA to assist the 'separatist groups'. By leading an abortive hard-line coup in August 1991 to preserve the Soviet Union, he inadvertently accelerated its demise. The first Muslim people to declare independence as the Soviet Union crumbled in the aftermath of the failed coup were, predictably, the Chechens, Moscow's most disaffected Islamic subjects. The KGB had long been aware of the buildup of arms in Chechnya-Ingushetiya but seemed powerless to prevent it. Andropov had told the Politburo in 1973, 'The men of Chechnya-Ingushetiya are mad on rifles. They will spend vast sums acquiring them and will even attack guards, the militia and members of the armed forces for this purpose.' Some of the Chechens' illegal armoury came from Georgia. Workers at the Tbilisi arms factory stole firearms components, assembled them at home, then sold them in Grozny. The Chechens also succeeded in stealing firearms, including machine guns, from Red Army depots.[69] As the arms buildup accelerated in 1991, many of the weapons went to the paramilitary National Guard of the leader of the Chechen independence movement, Djokhar Dudayev, a former Soviet air force general. Though the independence movement proclaimed, 'Chechnya is not a subject of Russia but a subject of Allah', Dudayev took some time to reacquaint himself with his Islamic roots. He told an interviewer that Muslims were obliged to pray three times a day. When told that it was five times rather than three, he replied nonchalantly, 'Oh well, the more the merrier.'[70]

On 6 September Dudayev's National Guard stormed the Supreme

Soviet in Grozny. The Russian head of the city administration threw himself, or was thrown, to his death from a third-floor window. Nine days later, surrounded by Dudayev's National Guard, the Supreme Soviet voted to dissolve itself. The climax of the struggle for power which followed was the seizure on Dudayev's orders of the KGB headquarters in Grozny in early October. By the time the building was stormed by the National Guard, it contained only three or four KGB personnel, of whom one at most was armed. The evidence from both Chechen and Russian sources strongly suggests that Boris Yeltsin had agreed in private simply to hand over the headquarters to Dudayev, together with advanced communications and other technical equipment hitherto used to control KGB operations in the whole of the northern Caucasus.[71] The long drawn-out conflict between Soviet intelligence and the Chechens, marked on the Soviet side by what some human rights groups claimed were crimes against humanity, thus ended in a humiliating retreat for the KGB.

Dudayev was elected President at chaotic elections on 27 October, and on 1 November issued a presidential decree proclaiming the 'state sovereignty of the Chechen Republic'. In December, at a meeting in the Kazakh capital, Yeltsin and the leaders of ten other Soviet republics signed the Alma Ata Declaration, formally ending the existence of the USSR. From that agreement emerged five newly independent central Asian republics, all recognized by Russia: Kazakhstan, Kyrgyzstan, Tajikistan, Turkmenistan and Uzbekistan. The conflict between Russia and Chechnya, however, was not over. During the Brezhnev era Chechnya-Ingushetiya had been forced into a 'voluntary union' with Russia which amounted in reality to annexation.[72] Yeltsin's government insisted on maintaining the union.[73] That insistence led first to cold war, then in 1994 to a Russian invasion of Chechnya and a war which still continues.[74]

21

Afghanistan

Part 1: From the 'Great April Revolution' to the Soviet Invasion

The Communist era in Afghanistan began on 27 April 1978 with a bloody military coup which the Afghan Communist Party (PDPA) subsequently dignified with the title, 'the Great *Saur* [April] Revolution'.[1] The KGB residency in Kabul was given advance warning of the coup by two of its Afghan military leaders, Sayed Gulabzoy (codenamed MAMAD) and Muhammad Rafi (NIRUZ), both of whom were Soviet agents. The Centre was alarmed by the news, telling the residency on 26 April that SAVAK, the Shah's intelligence service, might have tricked PDPA supporters in the armed forces into staging a rebellion which it expected to be crushed. There was no basis for the Centre's pessimistic conspiracy theory. Instead of being crushed, the rebels won a surprisingly easy victory. A single tank battalion, one air squadron and a few hundred PDPA militants, led by the Party leader, Nur Muhammad Taraki, were all that were required next day to seize the former royal palace and kill the President, Muhammad Daoud, together with his family. At a meeting with the KGB resident, Viliov Osadchy, and the Soviet ambassador, Aleksandr Puzanov, two days after the coup, Taraki complained that, but for Soviet discouragement, the PDPA could have seized power three years earlier. Osadchy and Puzanov reported to Moscow that they had dismissed his complaint.[2]

The KGB had been in contact with Nur Muhammad Taraki for almost thirty years. As a thirty-four-year-old Marxist journalist and writer, he had been recruited as a Soviet agent in 1951 with the surprisingly transparent codename NUR. In 1965 Taraki was elected First Secretary of the newly founded PDPA, then an underground movement, and was invited to Moscow, where he impressed the CPSU International Department and the other leading apparatchiks as serious, ideologically sound and ready to follow the Soviet lead. In keeping with the Centre's usual practice, having become a fraternal Party leader he was formally removed from the Soviet agent network but, like many other Party leaders, maintained secret contact with the KGB and continued to provide intelligence on Afghanistan, talent-spotted potential agents and assisted in operations against the US and Chinese embassies in Kabul and other targets. As well as being given secret subsidies for the PDPA, Taraki was also given a personal allowance and food supplies. Though the Kabul residency had no doubt about Taraki's loyalty, however, it found him increasingly difficult to deal with. Particularly since being given the red-carpet treatment in Moscow, he had become 'painfully vain', expected to be the centre of attention and was apt to interpret light-hearted conversation as jokes at his expense.[3]

The Centre was sufficiently concerned by Taraki's conduct to order the residency in September 1968 to vet him thoroughly by 'operational-technical means' (almost certainly the bugging of his home). Though Taraki appears to have passed this test, the KGB held him largely responsible for the growing split within the PDPA between his own mainly rural Pushtun-speaking Khalq ('Masses') faction and the predominantly urban Persian-speaking Parcham ('Banner') group, led by Babrak Karmal. The Kabul residency found Karmal somewhat easier to deal with than Taraki. Karmal was better educated, naturally sociable and, in the KGB's view, more flexible. Like Taraki, he had been recruited as a KGB agent, probably in the mid-1950s, and given the codename MARID.[4] Both Taraki and Karmal complained bitterly to the KGB about each other. Taraki claimed that the circumstances of Karmal's release from prison after serving a three-year term in 1952, ahead of other political prisoners, indicated that he had agreed to work for Afghan counter-intelligence. Despite its predilection for conspiracy theory, the Centre dismissed this allegation as disinformation devised to discredit Karmal and split the PDPA. Karmal in turn accused Taraki of taking bribes, owning four cars, having a large private bank account and being in secret contact with the Americans. The Centre dismissed these allegations also. It instructed the Kabul residency in 1974:

In the course of regular meetings and conversations with MARID (Karmal) and NUR (Taraki) you must carefully, in the form of friendly advice and without referring to instructions from Moscow, tell them not to take any steps without prior agreement by us which could be used by their enemies as a pretext for striking a blow at their groups or compromising them. MARID and NUR should also be warned that they must desist from attacking each other and accusing each other of anti-republican activities, as this plays into the hands of the reactionary forces and will lead to the collapse of the democratic [Communist] movement in Afghanistan.[5]

On 30 April 1978, Taraki, henceforth the self-styled 'Great Leader of the April Revolution', became both President and Prime Minister of a government which included the two other strong men of the PDPA, Babrak Karmal and Hafizullah Amin (a leading member of the Khalq faction), as, respectively, Vice-President and Deputy Prime Minister. During the summer the Kabul residency reported that 'personality cults' were developing around both Taraki and Amin, with Amin presuming to compare Taraki to Lenin. At a meeting with a KGB delegation, led by the FCD chief, Vladimir Kryuchkov, Taraki dared to liken the April Revolution in Afghanistan to the October Revolution in Russia – a comparison which must have struck Kryuchkov as akin to the crime of *lèse-majesté*. Taraki's pretensions, however, were scarcely more absurd than those of the increasingly decrepit Brezhnev, whose rejuvenated portrait appeared beside that of Lenin on hundreds of thousands of posters inscribed with the slogan 'From Ilyich to Ilyich'. On 5 December 1978 Taraki and Brezhnev signed a Treaty of Friendship and Co-operation. The platitudinous public eulogies bestowed by each side on the other, however, concealed considerable private friction. When asked to release KGB agents and confidential contacts who had been thrown into jail by the Daoud regime, Taraki, who took personal charge of the Afghan security apparatus, proved unco-operative. He declared, in a thinly veiled reference to the KGB, 'Some Soviet specialists, particularly those who worked for many years in Afghanistan under the old regime and have now returned, often have a dated view of the country and do not see, in an objective light, what is happening in the country.'[6]

Cocooned in his own preposterous rhetoric, the 'Great Leader of the April Revolution' showed little grasp of the problems of establishing Communist rule over a staunchly Muslim country. Though Taraki attended Friday prayers at a Kabul mosque and surprised the KGB by beginning his radio broadcasts with the phrase, 'In the Name of the Almighty',[7] he began an assault on traditional Islamic authority, thinly disguised as an attempt to 'clean Islam . . . of the ballast and dirt of bad traditions, superstition, and erroneous belief'. The 320,000 traditionally minded mullahs were treated as an obstacle to 'the progressive movement of our homeland'. Many religious leaders who resisted the 'cleansing' process were tortured and shot – or buried alive.[8] Taraki gave orders for members of the Muslim Brotherhood and followers of Khomeini to be immediately 'eliminated' whenever they were found.[9] Islam became the unifying bond of opposition to the PDPA and its Soviet backers. Afghan resistance to the regime was thus transformed into a *jihad* in defence of Islam whose significance was grossly underestimated by the KGB. None of the reports noted by Mitrokhin even mention the threat of an Afghan *jihad*. The Centre was far more concerned by the vicious power struggle which quickly developed between the Khalq and Parcham factions within the PDPA. If only that internecine warfare could be overcome, the Centre naively believed, the PDPA could become 'the leading and directing force of Afghan society and the force behind its organizational and ideological rebirth'. Taraki, however, turned a deaf ear to the pleas for party unity from the Soviet embassy, the Kabul residency and the KGB liaison mission which arrived in May to help reorganize the Afghan security service. The Kabul residency reported in July, 'Only the leadership of the CPSU can influence the wild [Khalq] opportunists and force them to change their attitude towards the Parcham group.' The 'wild opportunists', however, paid little attention even to the entreaties of Moscow. Large numbers of Parcham supporters were thrown into jail. Their leader, Karmal, who inspired greater confidence in the Centre than Taraki, was sent into exile as ambassador to Czechoslovakia (a job from which he was subsequently sacked).

The main lesson which Taraki believed he had learned from his study of the aftermath of the Bolshevik Revolution was the need for Red Terror. That, he implied, was a lesson which his Soviet comrades seemed to have forgotten. When Puzanov asked him to spare the lives of two Parcham militants who had been sentenced to death, Taraki replied: 'Lenin taught us to be merciless towards the enemies of the revolution, and millions of people had to be eliminated in order to secure the victory of the October Revolution.' Of the twenty-seven alleged conspiracies to topple the regime which Taraki claimed had been uncovered in the four months after the April Revolution, most were probably based on little more than the paranoid tendencies of Taraki and his sycophantic inner circle. Among the supposed ringleaders arrested in August for planning the assassination of Taraki and Amin were the Armed Forces Minister, Major-General Abdul Qadir, a veteran KGB agent codenamed OSMAN, and the Chief of the General Staff, Major-General Shapur Ahmadzai. Taraki claimed that the plot in which they were implicated also involved China, the United States, Iran, Pakistan, Saudi Arabia and the Federal Republic of Germany. Even the show trials at the height of Stalin's Terror had generated few more absurd conspiracy theories. Taraki, however, informed Moscow that a number of the conspirators (doubtless after prolonged torture) had revealed the details of the plot. Ahmadzai, he revealed, was deeply depressed, wept constantly and repeatedly asked to be shot immediately. Many of the other alleged plotters who had been arrested were 'close to committing suicide'.[10]

Taraki was well aware that, having purged most senior officials from the Daoud administration as well as other 'anti-revolutionary, anti-democratic elements', real and imagined, his regime was heavily dependent on Soviet advisers. The Kabul residency, however, reported regular Afghan complaints about the advisers' arrogance and incompetence. The finance minister, Abdel Karim Misaq, told the ministry's chief adviser, N. K. Grechin, 'I beg you not to bring your bureaucratic ways into Afghan ministries! We have enough of our own ... And I would ask you not to take the place of ministers ...'[11]

The advice given by KGB advisers was responsible for at least one deeply embarrassing débâcle in Kabul. On 14 February 1979 the US ambassador, Adolph 'Spike' Dubs, was kidnapped in broad daylight by four Maoist 'guerrillas' and taken at gunpoint to the Hotel Kabul, where they demanded the release of some of their imprisoned comrades from Afghan jails in return for Dubs's release. On the advice of his KGB advisers, Amin ordered an Afghan assault group, armed with Kalashnikovs and wearing Soviet bullet-proof jackets, to storm the hotel. In the shoot-out which followed, Dubs and two of his kidnappers were killed, a third was captured and the fourth escaped. The KGB then embarked on an immediate cover-up to hide their part in the operation and conceal as effectively as possible responsibility for Dubs's death. American security personnel who had come to the hotel were prevented from removing any of the bullet cases from the room. Though the guerrillas had been armed only with a total of three pistols, a gun of unknown origin similar to a Kalashnikov supposedly belonging to the Maoists was planted in the room to give the impression that they had used it to kill the ambassador. In order to prevent the Americans interrogating either of the two guerrillas who had survived, they were told that all four had been killed during the shoot-out. In reality, the captured guerrilla was shot during the night following the kidnap, as was a prisoner who, it was falsely claimed, was the guerrilla who had escaped – thus providing the requisite number of four corpses to show the Americans. Photographs of the three genuine and one bogus Maoists were also published in Afghan newspapers. At the request of Osadchy, the Kabul resident, Amin and other Afghan ministers informed the US embassy, when expressing their condolences, that they had acted entirely on their own initiative and that no Soviet advisers had been involved.[12]

The Taraki regime was also critical of the performance of Soviet military advisers during the early months of operations against the *mujahideen*. According to an official Afghan complaint after the failure of a military operation against rebels in the Kamdesh gorge at the end of 1978:

The Afghan troops led by Adviser Bryaskin have long since shown themselves incapable of eliminating the anti-government bands. We gave your advisers wide powers in the leadership of the Afghan troops. We punish [our] troops severely for any failure to accept the advice of your commanders. This suggests to us that not all your advisers are sufficiently competent. We need experienced generals of whom we know there are many in the USSR. They must increase the fighting capability of the Afghan army and teach it to fight and to use the experience of the Soviet army during the war.[13]

Kabul's tone changed, however, after a major rebellion erupted in Herat on 15 March 1979 and was joined by the 17th Division of the Afghan army. Frenzied, vengeful mobs hunted down Afghan government officials, Soviet advisers and their families, and skinned some of them alive. Body parts of Soviet advisers, their wives and children were triumphantly paraded through the streets. Though Amin remained calm, Taraki panicked, phoning Prime Minister Aleksei Kosygin to appeal for Soviet troops to be sent to Afghanistan in disguise 'to save the revolution'. Taraki flew to Moscow to press his case, but without success. On 1 April the Politburo concluded that the Taraki regime's 'political inflexibility and inexperience' was compounded by its reluctance to take Soviet advice: 'The use of Soviet troops in repressing the Afghan counter-revolution would seriously damage the international authority of the USSR . . . In addition, [it] would reveal the weakness of the Taraki government and would widen the scope of counter-revolution both at home and abroad . . .'

The Politburo, however, made one decision which was to prove of major importance. It set up a commission 'to formulate proposals and co-ordinate actions' on Afghanistan composed of Andropov, Gromyko, Defence Minister Ustinov (all full members of the Politburo), and the head of the Central Committee's International Department, Boris Ponomarev (a non-voting candidate member). It was this commission which had the major role in policy-making on Afghanistan during the nine months which led up to the Soviet invasion. Though the commission, like the Politburo, was not yet ready to agree to Soviet military intervention, it accepted the need for a rapid increase in both military advisers and aid to shore up the Afghan regime against the insurgents. An inspection of the Afghan army by six Soviet generals in April emphasized its low morale along with 'the low level of political training, the extreme religiousness and downtrodden nature of the masses of soldiers'. Over the next two months matters went from bad to worse with the escalation of rebel attacks combined with mutinies and desertions within government forces. After violent demonstrations in the centre of Kabul on 23 June, even Moscow Radio, which usually sought to play down the strength of opposition to the Taraki regime, acknowledged that, 'The Afghan Revolution has encountered strong resistance from its enemies.'[14] On 28 June the Afghanistan Commission reported to the Politburo that 'the measures taken by the [Afghan] government to stabilize the situation have been not very effective'. As well as recommending the despatch of more military advisers to the demoralized regiments of the Afghan army, the commission also agreed on the need to send a parachute battalion disguised as aircraft-maintenance personnel to protect Soviet air squadrons at the Bagram airbase and a KGB detachment of 125–150 men disguised as embassy staff to defend the Soviet embassy.[15]

The ideological blinkers worn by both the Politburo and the Centre leadership prevented them grasping the real nature of the Afghan problem – the impossibility of imposing on a staunchly Muslim and fiercely patriotic country the rule of a Communist regime with little popular support and unreliable armed forces. Instead of addressing the real problem, Moscow blamed the inadequacies of the Taraki government. The Afghanistan Commission concluded in its report of 28 June: 'In the Party and the government . . . all power in fact is concentrated in the hands of N. M. Taraki and H. Amin, who none too rarely make mistakes and commit violations of legality . . .'[16] Matters were made worse by the increasingly vicious infighting between the two. More worryingly still, the far more energetic Amin seemed to be getting the better of the struggle for power. On 27 March, profiting from Taraki's loss of nerve after the gruesome débâcle at Herat, Amin succeeded in replacing him as Prime Minister, though Taraki retained the post of President. On 27 July Amin also became Defence Minister, thus gaining direct control of the Afghan armed forces.[17]

Though the Centre regarded Taraki as vain and incompetent, it had even graver doubts about Amin who, unlike Taraki and Karmal, appears never to have been recruited as a KGB agent.[18] The Kabul residency reported in July that Amin had asked his Soviet financial adviser, P. Y. Dragulis, to try to discover ways in which he could get access to the $400 million of Afghan government funds in foreign bank accounts. The problem, Amin complained, was that withdrawals from these accounts normally required three Afghan official signatures. He asked Dragulis to try 'to arrange it somehow so that I can sign and get the money'. Dragulis told the KGB that he feared that if Amin did manage to 'get the money', he would try to eliminate all those (Dragulis included) who had evidence of his embezzlement.[19]

Far more worrying to the Centre were its exaggerated suspicions of Amin's sympathies for the United States. Though fluent in English, he had not troubled to learn Russian. While a teacher in Kabul twenty years earlier, Amin had won an American scholarship to take a Master's Degree in Educational Administration at Columbia

University. As a Soviet historian wrote later, 'The fact that Amin had studied at Columbia University in New York in his youth whipped up our bestial spy mania.' Even Kim Philby, in an interview a few months before his death in 1988, was still insisting that 'there was more than a suspicion that Amin was dickering with the Americans'.[20] A KGB investigation found no shortage of apparently sinister connections which seemed to support its conspiracy theories. Amin's friends at Columbia had included Nemattula Pazhwak, later Afghan Minister of Education and, according to his KGB file, an anti-Communist. On his way back from New York after his graduation, Amin had stayed with the Afghan ambassador in Bonn, Ali Ahmad Popal, whom the KGB bizarrely believed to be a Western agent. During his early political career in Kabul, Amin had received financial backing from the chairman of the Spinzer joint-stock company, Sarwari Nasher, who was alleged to maintain contact with both the exiled king of Afghanistan and the Americans. After the April 'Revolution', Amin had freed Nasher from prison and provided him with a car and driver.[21] According to KGB defector Vladimir Kuzichkin, alarmist KGB 'investigations showed him to be a smooth-talking fascist who was secretly pro-Western'.[22]

On 1 September a memorandum from the Centre to the Politburo (almost certainly agreed beforehand by Andropov with Gromyko and Ustinov) declared Amin personally responsible for the general failure of Afghan government policy and unjustified mass repression. Ways had therefore to be found of removing Amin from power and persuading Taraki to form a more broadly based government including members of the Parcham faction as well as 'patriotically inclined' clergy, tribal leaders and intellectuals. Ten days later, Taraki visited Moscow on his way back to Kabul from a meeting in Havana of the Non-Aligned Movement (of which Afghanistan was a member). During the stop-over Brezhnev effectively invited him to arrange the removal of Amin from the Afghan government.[23] Amin, meanwhile, was plotting to assassinate Taraki as soon as he returned home. According to a KGB agent report, Amin persuaded the head of the radar section of the Afghan anti-aircraft defence force to arrange for Taraki's plane to be shot down when it entered Afghan airspace on his return from Moscow (presumably by falsely identifying it as a hostile aircraft). The Centre claimed the credit for discovering and thwarting this 'terrorist act'. Amin then attempted to turn the tables by complaining to the Kabul residency that Taraki had tried to assassinate him.[24]

To Moscow's dismay, the struggle for power which followed Taraki's safe return to Afghanistan was won by Amin. On 16 September Kabul Radio announced that the PDPA Central Committee had granted a (fictitious) request from Taraki 'that he be relieved of his party and government positions due to health reasons and physical incapacity which render him unable to continue his work', and had elected Amin to succeed him as Party leader. The Central Committee circulated to Party members a secret resolution denouncing the 'terrorist actions and unprincipled behaviour' of Taraki and his chief supporters from the PDPA, and announcing their expulsion from the Party.[25]

On 17 September General Boris Ivanov, the head of the KGB mission in Kabul, General Lev Gorelov, chief Soviet military adviser, and General Ivan Pavlovsky, Deputy Defence Minister, visited Amin to convey Moscow's insincere congratulations on his election as Party leader. Amin declared that 'he would work very closely with his Soviet friends and that he would take steps to eliminate known faults and to improve the style and methods of his work', and claimed, with equal insincerity, to be doing his best to protect the hated Taraki against demands by the rest of the Party leadership that he be severely punished. The 'Soviet friends' did not, of course, believe a word Amin said. The immediate priority for the KGB was to exfiltrate three of Taraki's leading supporters and former ministers, Sayed Gulabzoy (a long-serving KGB agent), Muhammad Watanjar and Asadullah Sarwari, who had taken refuge in the home of a KGB operations officer. The Kabul residency reported that all three had denounced Amin as an American spy. Despite the lack of documentary proof, their claims were passed by Andropov to Brezhnev and the leading members of the Politburo. Though Amin strongly suspected that the fugitive ministers were being sheltered by the Russians, this was categorically denied by the Kabul residency. All three shaved off their moustaches and dressed in the uniform of the KGB Zenith special forces who were stationed in Afghanistan to protect Soviet installations. They were then secretly transferred to the Zenith base to await exfiltration to the Soviet Union. The cover for the exfiltration, codenamed operation RADUGA ('Rainbow'), was the apparently routine rotation of Zenith personnel. On

18 September ten Zenith troops arrived at the Bagram airbase, sixty kilometres from Kabul, ostensibly to relieve other personnel who were at the end of their tour of duty. With them came an operations group from the Illegals Directorate S, which specialized in constructing bogus identities, and a make-up expert with wigs, hair dye and other disguises. Gulabzoy and Watanjar were given suitably doctored Soviet passports as members of a Zenith unit departing on a Russian aircraft from Bagram airbase to Tashkent on 19 September. Because of the risk that Sarwari, who had become well known as Taraki's security chief, might be identified even in disguise, however, he was smuggled on board the plane in a sealed container with a six-hour oxygen supply. Those who took part in operation RADUGA were given awards and personally congratulated by Andropov. Once in Tashkent, the three former ministers were put up for almost four weeks in a bugged house while their conversation was carefully monitored to check on their reliability. After recording ninety-two tapes, the KGB appears to have been satisfied by what it had heard and transferred them to a secret retreat in Bulgaria.[26]

On 6 October the Afghan Foreign Minister, Dr Akbar Shah Wali, summoned a meeting of ambassadors from the 'socialist states' (China and Yugoslavia included) and, to Moscow's fury, accused the Soviet ambassador Puzanov (subsequently recalled) of conniving at an attempt by Taraki to assassinate Amin on 14 September. Simultaneously, pamphlets entitled 'The attempt on the life of H. Amin by Taraki and the failure of this attempt' were distributed among Party militants and the armed forces. On 9 October Puzanov, Pavlovsky, Gorelov and L. P. Bogdanov of the KGB met Amin to protest against Wali's statement. Bogdanov subsequently reported to the Centre:

During the talks H. Amin was brash and provocative. He sometimes contained his fury with difficulty. He interrupted the Soviet representatives and did not give them a chance to state their point of view calmly. At the same time there were moments when he appeared to collect his thoughts and gave the impression that he did not want to spoil his relations [with the Soviet Union] completely.

Bogdanov also reported that Amin made no mention during the stormy two-hour meeting that Taraki was dead – despite the fact that the Afghan news agency had already distributed an announcement of his death, embargoed until 8 p.m. local time.[27] Next day, 10 October, the *Kabul Times* reported that Taraki 'died yesterday morning of a serious illness, [from] which he had been suffering for some time . . .' In reality, he had been murdered on Amin's orders. Three of Amin's security personnel tied Taraki to a bed and suffocated him with a cushion – presumably to avoid leaving any visible sign of violence on his corpse. Taraki's death throes were said to have lasted fifteen minutes. According to Gromyko, Brezhnev was 'simply beside himself' when told the news: 'To those closest to him he said that he had been given a slap in the face to which he had to respond.'[28] The response which Brezhnev had in mind at this stage, however, was the overthrow of Amin rather than a full-scale Soviet invasion.

The Centre was convinced that there was no time to lose. Amin, it believed, was planning to 'do a Sadat on us'[29] – to expel Soviet advisers as soon as he felt strong enough and turn to the United States. The Kabul residency reported that Amin's brother, Abdullah, had told his supporters, 'It would clearly be sensible for us to follow Egypt's course and treat the Russians as President Sadat did.'[30] In the Centre's conspiratorial imagination, routine meetings between Amin and US diplomats, which in reality the Americans found tedious and unproductive, acquired a deeply sinister significance. Even the FCD's able counter-intelligence chief, Oleg Kalugin, whose grasp of American policy-making was far more sophisticated than that of Andropov and Kryuchkov, 'viewed Afghanistan as a country within our sphere of interest, and thought we had to do whatever possible to prevent the Americans and the CIA from installing an anti-Soviet regime there'.[31] Though the Centre's main fear was of a pro-American Afghanistan, it was also preoccupied in the autumn of 1979 by a second nightmare scenario. The Kabul residency reported, possibly inaccurately, that secret meetings had taken place at the end of September between representatives of Amin and the 'extreme Muslim opposition' at which the possibility of expelling all Soviet officials, releasing all imprisoned Muslim rebels, and ending the civil war had been discussed.[32] To some KGB officers this raised the spectre of 'an Islamic government'.[33] Only by a Soviet invasion did it seem that Afghanistan could be kept within the Soviet sphere of influence.

The first step in the invasion plan was to assemble a dependably pro-Soviet Afghan government-in-waiting to take power after the overthrow of Amin. On 25 October the Centre despatched Aleksandr Vladimirovich Petrov, formerly a Line PR officer at the Kabul residency, to Prague, where Moscow's chosen successor to Amin, Babrak Karmal, was living in exile.[34] While talks with Karmal were proceeding, a series of meetings were held in FCD departments to brief officers on the worsening situation in Afghanistan. The situation, they were told, was intolerable. All of them had to be prepared for the decisive action that would be needed to put things right. To Mitrokhin, as probably to most of those who attended the briefings, it was clear that a Soviet invasion was in the offing. On 30 October, probably prompted by Petrov, Karmal wrote a personal letter to Brezhnev denouncing Amin as an anarchist and declaring: 'The leading members of the [Afghan] Party are prepared to organize and unite Communists, patriots and all the progressive and democratic forces in Afghanistan. The achievement of these aims will be assisted by the fraternal assistance, consultations and advice of our Soviet friends.'

In early November the KGB secretly brought Karmal, the three former ministers exfiltrated from Kabul in September and three other prominent Afghan exiles to Moscow, where they discussed plans to oust Amin from power and set up a new government headed by Karmal. Mitrokhin's notes on the KGB minutes of the meeting record the 'decisive influence' on the Afghans' deliberations of the views of their Soviet comrades.[35]

Within the Politburo the main pressure for invasion came from Andropov and his two habitual allies, Ustinov and Gromyko. Though Ustinov was probably the first to become persuaded of the need for Soviet military intervention, the most influential voice was that of Andropov, who suffered from what some of his colleagues termed a 'Hungarian complex'. As Soviet ambassador in Budapest, he had witnessed the Hungarian Uprising of 1956 at first hand. His insistence then on the supreme necessity of defeating counter-revolution had helped to persuade an initially reluctant Khrushchev to agree to Soviet military intervention. Thereafter Andropov was obsessed with the need to stamp out 'ideological sabotage' wherever it reared its head within the Soviet bloc. In 1968, a year after he became Chairman of the KGB, he was one of the chief advocates of the invasion of Czechoslovakia to crush the Prague Spring. At a

KGB conference in March 1979 he reiterated his view that every outbreak of ideological subversion represented a danger which could not be ignored:

We simply do not have the right to permit even the smallest miscalculation here, for in the political sphere any kind of ideological sabotage is directly or indirectly intended to create an opposition which is hostile to our system . . . and, in the final analysis, to create the conditions for the overthrow of socialism.[36]

By the autumn of 1979 Andropov was convinced that Afghanistan, like Czechoslovakia eleven years earlier, was threatened with 'ideological sabotage' and that only Soviet military intervention could prevent 'the overthrow of socialism'.

Before the invasion could go ahead, however, Andropov and his colleagues on the Politburo Afghanistan Commission had first to win over the ailing Brezhnev. In order to ensure support for the invasion of Czechoslovakia in 1968, Andropov had fed the Politburo with misleading intelligence reports.[37] During the final months of 1979 he was once again economical with the truth. In order not to alarm Brezhnev, Andropov deliberately underplayed the scale of the Soviet military involvement which would be required – initially giving the misleading impression that the overthrow of Amin would be carried out by the Afghan opposition to him rather than by Soviet forces, who would merely provide back-up. He wrote to Brezhnev after the meeting of the Afghan leaders in exile: 'In order to carry out their political programme, the healthy forces of the PDPA intend to come to power by overthrowing the regime. A military committee to plan the military and political operation to eliminate H[afizullah] Amin has been set up.' All that would be involved would be 'a rapid military operation in the capital'. It was therefore in the interests of the USSR to give secret advice and material aid to the 'healthy forces' who were preparing to come to power.[38] Early in December, Andropov sent Brezhnev a further letter, reporting 'alarming information [intelligence] about Amin's secret activities, forewarning of a possible shift to the West', which would result in both the end of Communist rule and a catastrophic loss of Soviet influence. Though still unwilling to mention the possibility of a full-scale Soviet invasion, Andropov reported that Karmal and his comrades had 'raised the question of possible [Soviet] assistance, in case of need, including military' in overthrowing the Amin regime. Andropov added that, though Soviet forces already in Kabul should be 'entirely sufficient for a successful operation', 'as a precautionary measure in the event of unforeseen complications, it would be wise to have a military group close to the [Afghan] border'.[39]

On 12 December, gathering in Brezhnev's office before a Politburo meeting, the members of the Afghanistan Commission – Andropov, Ustinov, Gromyko and Ponomarev – obtained the General Secretary's support for Soviet military intervention. The Politburo then authorized Andropov, Ustinov and Gromyko to oversee the implementation of the decision. The whole affair was treated with such extraordinary secrecy that the document recording this decision was handwritten to avoid informing the Politburo typists, euphemistically entitled 'Concerning the Situation in "A"', and even more euphemistically phrased without any explicit reference either to Afghanistan or to troops. The Politburo members then scrawled their signatures across the handwritten document.[40] While Marshal Akhromeyev and the General Staff operations group in charge of the invasion established their headquarters near the Afghan border in Uzbekistan, the heads of FCD Directorate S (Illegals), Vadim Kirpichenko, and of its Department 8 ('Special Operations'), Vladimir Krasovsky, flew secretly into Kabul to supervise the overthrow of Amin (operation AGAT ['Agate']). Day-to-day control of AGAT was entrusted to Krasovsky's deputy, A. I. Lazarenko. A team from the KGB Seventh (Surveillance) Directorate flew in to monitor Amin's movements. Meanwhile, just as before the invasions of Hungary and Czechoslovakia, elaborate attempts were made to avoid arousing suspicion that invasion was imminent. In an attempt to reassure Amin, his latest requests for military supplies were granted and two radio stations were constructed for him.[41]

Even more secret than the preparations for military intervention was the plan to assassinate Amin drawn up by Department 8. Andropov doubtless hoped that by the time Soviet troops arrived to stabilize the situation in Afghanistan, Amin would be dead and Karmal would have issued an appeal for fraternal assistance from the Red Army to legitimize the invasion. In keeping with the usual procedure for authorizing assassination, Brezhnev was almost certainly informed of the plan. A year earlier the Bulgarian dissident, Georgi

Markov, had been killed in London with a poison pellet fired by a silenced gun concealed inside an umbrella. The poison (ricin) had been provided by the poisons laboratory attached to the KGB OUT (Operational Technical) Directorate, which was under Andropov's personal control.[42] The plan to kill Amin involved the same laboratory, though the poison was different and it was to be administered differently. Department 8 succeeded in infiltrating the illegal Mutalin Agaverdioglu Talybov (codenamed SABIR) into the kitchens of Amin's presidential palace, where he was employed as a chef. As an Azerbaijani brought up close to the Iranian border, Talybov was a fluent Farsi speaker and had previously operated in both Iran and Chechnya-Ingushetiya with Iranian identity documents in the name of Ikhtiar Kesht. In Kabul, he posed as a Farsi-speaking Afghan. While working as a chef, Talybov succeeded in poisoning some of the food prepared for Amin and his immediate entourage.[43]

On 13 December Karmal and five members of his future government were secretly flown from Moscow to Bagram airbase, ready to take over as soon as Amin had been liquidated.[44] On the 17th Amin's nephew and son-in-law, Asadullah Amin, who was also head of the security service, was taken seriously ill with acute food poisoning and, ironically, flown to Moscow for urgent medical treatment.[45] Talybov's main target, however, escaped. According to Vladimir Kuzichkin, then a Line N (illegal support) officer at the Tehran residency, '[Hafizullah] Amin was as careful as any of the Borgias. He kept switching his food and drink as if he expected to be poisoned.'[46] It is quite possible that Asadullah Amin had eaten a dish prepared for Hafizullah. Karmal and his colleagues were forced to fly back from Bagram airbase to the Soviet Union to await the next attempt to overthrow Amin. Since poisoning had failed, the only option which remained was to shoot Amin at the beginning of Soviet military intervention.

On 20 December Amin moved his headquarters to the Darulaman Palace on the outskirts of Kabul, having apparently been persuaded by Soviet advisers that it offered him greater security.[47] The advisers, however, had in mind not Amin's security but the fact that an attack on the Darulaman Palace, conveniently close to the Soviet embassy, would avoid the need for street fighting in the centre of Kabul.[48] On 23 December, the Kabul residency reported that Amin's suspicions had been aroused both by Western reports of Soviet troop movements and by the frequent flights into the Soviet airbase at Bagram. The main invasion began at 3 p.m. local time on 25 December. Two days later 700 members of the KGB Alpha and Zenith special forces, dressed in Afghan uniforms and travelling in military vehicles with Afghan markings, stormed the Darulaman Palace.[49] As the sound of gunfire reverberated from the outskirts of the city, frightened PDPA members at Kabul Radio hid their Party cards behind radiators or flushed them down lavatories in the belief that Amin's government was under attack from anti-Communist *mujahideen*. They were further bemused when they heard a broadcast at 8.45 p.m. purporting to come from their own radio station but, in reality, from the Red Army headquarters at Termez, announcing that Babrak Karmal had assumed power and requested fraternal Soviet military assistance. Fifteen minutes later Soviet paratroops arrived at Kabul Radio and told the confused staff that they had come 'to save the revolution'.[50]

The satisfaction of the Centre at the success of operation AGAT was reflected in a series of awards and promotions: among them those of the head of FCD Directorate S, Kirpichenko, who had overall charge of the operation, from Major-General to Lieutenant-General, and of Lazarenko, who had day-to-day control of AGAT from Colonel to Major-General. Though the Darulaman Palace had been quickly taken and Amin gunned down with his family, however, his guards had put up stiffer resistance than the Centre had expected. Over 100 of the KGB special forces were killed and wounded. Those who died included their commander, Colonel Grigori Boyarinov, commandant of the Department 8 special operations training school at Balashikha, who was posthumously made a Hero of the Soviet Union. The portraits of KGB officers who were killed during operations were normally displayed in black frames in a place of honour at the Centre. Since the fallen heroes of operation AGAT were so embarrassingly numerous, however, Andropov decided not to put their portraits on display.[51]

22

Afghanistan

Part 2: War and Defeat

The report submitted to the Politburo, 'On the Events in Afghanistan on 27 and 28 December 1979', by its Afghanistan Commission (Andropov, Ustinov, Gromyko and Ponomarev) on 31 December was so disingenuous that it effectively amounted to an active measure designed to mislead the rest of the Soviet leadership about the harsh reality of the Afghan situation. Probably composed chiefly for Brezhnev's benefit, the report maintained the fiction that the assassination of Amin had been chiefly the work of the Afghans themselves rather than KGB special forces:

On the wave of patriotic feelings which had overcome fairly broad sections of the Afghan population following the introduction of Soviet troops which was carried out in strict accordance with the Soviet–Afghan treaty of 1978, the forces opposed to H. Amin carried out an armed attack during the night of 27 to 28 December which ended in the overthrow of the regime of H. Amin. This attack was widely supported by the working masses, the intelligentsia, a considerable part of the Afghan army and the state apparatus which welcomed the establishment of the new leadership of the DRA [Democratic Republic of Afghanistan] and the PDPA.[1]

The reality was starkly different. So far from receiving widespread support from both working masses and intelligentsia, the Soviet invasion provoked immediate opposition. Demonstrations against the presence of Soviet troops began in Kandahar on 31 December.[2] The Afghanistan Commission also gave the Politburo an extraordinarily optimistic assessment of the prospects for the new Babrak Karmal government:

Babrak can be described as one of the best-trained leaders of the PDPA theoretically. He is able to take a sober and objective view of the situation in Afghanistan. He has always been noted for his sincere goodwill towards the Soviet Union and is held in great respect in the Party and throughout the country. In this light it is possible to be sure that the new leadership of the DRA will be able to find an effective way to stabilize completely the situation in the country.[3]

If, after the Afghan turmoil of the preceding twenty months, Andropov and his colleagues seriously supposed that the Karmal regime had the capacity 'to stabilize completely the situation', they were living in a fantasy world. That, however, was where Brezhnev preferred to live. The Afghanistan Commission, he declared, 'did its work well'. At his proposal, the Politburo agreed that the Commission should 'continue its work in the same spirit as it conducted it up until now' and 'submit to the Politburo issues which require a decision'.[4]

The Centre's confidence in Karmal's 'sincere goodwill towards the Soviet Union' derived chiefly from his long career as a KGB agent. His mood on taking power appeared reassuringly sycophantic. He asked senior KGB officers in Kabul to assure Comrade Andropov that, as Afghan President, he would unswervingly follow his advice. Karmal was fulsome in his praise for the heroism shown by the KGB special forces who had stormed the Darulaman Palace and other Soviet troops: 'As soon as we have decorations of our own, we would like to bestow them on all the Soviet troops and Chekists [KGB officers] who took part in the fighting. We hope that the government of the USSR will award orders to these comrades.'

Babrak called for the 'severest punishment' of Amin's former associates and the execution of those responsible for the deaths of Soviet troops. He also requested the installation of direct telephone lines to connect him not merely with Brezhnev but also with the four members of the Politburo's Afghanistan Commission (Andropov, Ustinov, Gromyko and Ponomarev) and Kryuchkov.[5] Ponomarev informed the Politburo, 'Babrak Karmal listens very attentively to the advice of our comrades. The leadership of the [Afghan] Party now has a backbone.'[6]

At the beginning of February 1980 Andropov visited Kabul for talks with Karmal and the main members of his regime. It is clear from the tone of his report to the Politburo on his return that Andropov consistently talked down to his fraternal Party comrades:

'... I stressed ... the necessity of a quick correction of all the shortcomings and mistakes which had been tolerated earlier ... I particularly pointed to the correct distribution of his responsibilities by every comrade.' Encouraged by the obsequious tone of the Afghan comrades, Andropov returned in optimistic mood:

First of all, it is necessary to note directly that the situation in Afghanistan is stabilizing now. This is evident from all the data. In the conversation which I had with Com[rade] Karmal, he cited in great detail what has been done in the month since the removal of Amin from power. Although the situation in the country does continue to be complex, and demands the most urgent and pressing measures aimed at its stabilization, the main thing is that now the leadership of Afghanistan understands its fundamental tasks and is doing everything possible so that the situation really does stabilize.

Since Andropov did not doubt that he had correctly identified the measures required 'to liquidate the contradictions which had arisen within the [Afghan] Party and in the country', it only remained for the Karmal regime to implement these measures. Andropov was ideologically incapable of grasping the fundamental obstacles which stood in the way of the imposition of a Communist regime with very little support on a large, staunchly Muslim state. Ustinov's comments on Andropov's report to the Politburo were notably less optimistic. It would, he said, take at least a year, perhaps a year and a half, for the situation in Afghanistan to stabilize.[7]

Andropov's extraordinary misjudgement on the pace of 'stabilization' in Afghanistan was quickly exposed by events in Kabul. From 20 to 23 February, only a fortnight after Andropov's report to the Politburo, there were mass anti-Soviet demonstrations in the capital. Martial law was declared and over 2,000 Soviet troops, more than 1,000 Afghan troops, 73 tanks, 240 personnel carriers (mostly armed) and 207 sorties by Soviet and Afghan aircraft flying low over the city and its environs to intimidate the population were required to restore order. The KGB reported that over 900 demonstrators were arrested.[8] According to other reports, hundreds of demonstrators were killed and thousands arrested (and later executed).[9]

The Kabul demonstration and *mujahideen* attacks elsewhere in the country finally destroyed the illusion that Soviet troops would have to do no more than garrison major cities and provide logistical support while Afghan government troops mopped up local pockets of resistance to the Karmal regime. Most of the countryside, it now recognized, was in the hands of the rebels.[10] In March the Soviet general staff ordered Marshal Sergei Sokolov, who had commanded the invasion forces, to 'commence joint operations with [the Afghan army] with the mission of eliminating armed bands of the opposition . . .' Soviet forces were not equipped for the war which awaited them. They had been trained to fight a modern enemy who would take up defensive positions on the northern European plain. The *mujahideen*, however, declined to dig in and wait to be attacked by Soviet artillery. Not merely were Soviet forces untrained for the problems of fighting Afghan guerrillas; the general staff had barely studied even their own experience of irregular warfare in the Second World War or against post-war Ukrainian and Baltic partisans – let alone the experience of foreign forces. Boots suitable for mountain combat, like clothing and sleeping bags for winter warfare in temperatures as low as minus 30° centigrade, were in short supply. The most prized trophy of war for a Soviet soldier was to capture a Western-manufactured *mujahideen* sleeping bag which, unlike his own, was warm, waterproof and lightweight. Though Soviet military equipment improved in the course of the war, health care remained primitive. Eight times as many soldiers died from infectious diseases as died in hospital while being treated for combat wounds. Over 40 per cent of those who served in Afghanistan contracted viral hepatitis.[11] There were numerous cases also of addiction to easily available opium-based drugs.

The reluctant recognition in March 1980 that the Soviet Union was at war was a major personal embarrassment for the previously rashly optimistic Afghanistan Commission of the Politburo and, in particular, for Andropov, who only the month before had insisted that all available intelligence demonstrated that 'the situation in Afghanistan is stabilizing now'. The Commission report on 7 April made no mention of its earlier errors of judgement. Instead it resorted to specious self-justification. Events since Soviet military intervention had, the Commission insisted, confirmed 'our assessment that this was a timely and correct action'. The Babrak Karmal regime, 'with comprehensive assistance from the Soviet Union', had 'in general correctly outlined the tasks' confronting it. As a result of Soviet and Afghan military operations, 'the counter-revolutionary forces would probably be unable to carry out any large-scale military actions' and engage instead in 'terrorist acts and small group actions' – though there remained the possibility of 'massive uprisings' in some parts of the country. Though the Commission did not explicitly disavow its earlier confident assertion 'that the new leadership of the DRA will be able to find an effective way to stabilize completely the situation in the country', it acknowledged that no solution was yet in sight:

The situation in Afghanistan remains complicated and tense. The class struggle, represented in armed counter-revolutionary insurrections, encouraged and actively supported from abroad, is occurring in circumstances where a genuine unity of the PDPA is still absent, where the state and Party apparatus is weak in terms of organization and ideology, which is reflected in the practical non-existence of local government organs, where financial and economic difficulties are mounting, and where the combat readiness of the Afghan armed forces and the people's militia is still insufficient.

The Commission could not bring itself to mention the glaring personal weaknesses of Babrak Karmal, whom it had eulogized only three months earlier.[12]

The Kabul residency reported that Karmal had developed an absurd sense of self-importance, claiming to be a major world statesman of even greater stature than Fidel Castro. Yet, at the same time, Karmal was plagued with self-doubt, found it difficult to take decisions and had begun to drink heavily. The KGB also disapproved of the fact that Karmal had made Anahita Ratebzad (the only female member of the Politburo), with whom it believed was having an affair, Minister of Education. Nepotism and favouritism towards friends and relations were, it reported, rife within the Party leadership. The Interior Minister, Sayed Gulabzoy, a long-serving KGB agent, expressed surprise to the Kabul residency that Karmal's Soviet advisers seemed unwilling to criticize to his face either his alcoholism or his poor performance as Party leader. As the months passed, Karmal made less and less pretence of seeking to reconcile his Parcham faction of the PDPA with the Khalq. He complained to his Soviet advisers: 'As long as you keep my hands bound and do not let me deal with the Khalq faction, there will be no unity in the PDPA and the government cannot become strong. There can be no organic unity as long as there are Khalqists in the Party. They tortured and killed us. They still hate us. They are the enemies of unity!'

While in Moscow for medical treatment in December 1980, Niyaz Muhammad, the head of the economic department of the PDPA Central Committee, told the KGB that all Afghan officials had been instructed to assure their Soviet advisers that Party unity had been achieved and that Khalq supporters had been punished for revealing the persistence of chronic divisions. Muhammad gave a damning account of the nepotism and incompetence of the Karmal regime: 'Government positions are given to friends. The people do not support the Party at all. The leadership thinks that the USSR will solve all the economic and military problems. All they can think about are motor cars, positions and amusements.'[13]

The KGB's main immediate responsibility in Afghanistan after the installation of the Karmal regime was the creation of a new Afghan security service, Khedamat-e Etala'at-e Dawlati (KHAD), to replace Amin's bloodthirsty secret police. KHAD was trained, organized and largely financed by the KGB.[14] In January 1980 the KGB selected as head of KHAD the energetic, brutal thirty-two-year-old Muhammad Najibullah, a man capable of intimidating opponents by his mere physical presence. Codenamed POTOMOK, he had probably previously been recruited as a KGB agent.[15] Embarrassed by the reference to Allah in his surname, Najibullah asked to be known instead as 'Comrade Najib'. Karmal gave a public assurance that KHAD, unlike its predecessor, would not 'strangle, pressure or torture the people':

On the contrary there will be established within the government framework an intelligence service to protect democratic freedoms, national independence and sovereignty, the interests of the revolution, the people and the state, as well as to neutralize under PDPA [Communist Party] leadership the plots hatched by external enemies of Afghanistan.

KHAD, however, proved even more brutal than its predecessor. In the cruel conditions of an unwinnable counter-insurgency war, the KGB revived on Afghan soil some of the horrors of its Stalinist past.[16] Amnesty International assembled evidence of 'widespread and systematic torture of men, women and children'. A common theme in its reports was the presence of Soviet advisers directing the interrogations, much as they had done during the Stalinist purges in eastern Europe a generation earlier.[17] Najibullah sometimes executed prisoners himself. His preferred method, according to survivors of his prisons, was to beat his victims to the ground, then kick them to death.[18]

As well as taking responsibility for Afghan security and intelligence, the KGB also played a direct part in the war through its special forces – especially the KASKAD ('Cascade') units, each of 145 men, set up to locate, penetrate and destabilize the *mujahideen*.[19] Probably their most successful tactic was to form bogus *mujahideen* groups, sometimes by persuading enemy commanders to change sides, and then to use them to ambush genuine *mujahideen* forces. Early in 1981, for example, a Cascade unit in Herat province made contact through agents with Khoja Shir-Aga Chungara, the Tajik leader of a 250-man enemy force which controlled forty-eight villages and important lines of communication. KGB officers from the unit went unarmed to a meeting with Chungara (henceforth codenamed ABAY) and persuaded him to take up arms against his former associates. Thereafter, Chungara 'diligently carried out all KGB instructions', taking part in twenty-one major joint operations with Cascade units and independently carrying out forty ambushes and killing thirty-one *mujahideen* commanders. Chungara's forces increased to almost 900 and, in his first two years of collaboration with the KGB, were credited with killing 20,500 'enemy' Afghans. In 1982 Cascade units succeeded in turning round four other *mujahideen* groups, who operated in ways similar to Chungara.[20] By the beginning of 1983 there were eighty-six of what the KGB called 'false bands' operating in Afghanistan, posing as *mujahideen* and disrupting the operations of the genuine resistance movement.[21] Some of the clashes between *mujahideen* which paved the way for the far more serious internecine warfare of the 1990s were generated by the KGB.

The long drawn-out Afghan War rescued Department 8 (Special Actions) of FCD Directorate S from the doldrums in which it had languished for most of the 1970s. In 1982 its Special Operations Training School at Balashikha set up a 'Training Centre for Afghanistan', headed by V. I. Kikot, previously a Line F officer in Havana, who was well informed on Cuban methods of irregular warfare. Department 8 also made a detailed study of methods used by

Palestinian guerrillas and terrorists against Israeli targets as well as by the Israelis against Palestinian bases in Lebanon.[22] Balashikha made a significant, though unquantifiable, contribution to devising methods of terrorizing the Afghan civilian population – among them incendiary bombs, napalm, poison gas, miniature mines scattered from the air, and booby-trapped toys which were designed to maim the children who picked them up and so demoralize their parents.

A country riven at the best of times by ethnic and regional rivalry, enduring wartime conditions so terrible that several million of its inhabitants were forced to leave their homes and seek a miserable refuge abroad, was ideal terrain for Service A's well-practised techniques for stirring up mutual suspicion. In addition to using the Cascade units, the Centre exacerbated divisions within the *mujahideen* with the help of agents who were able, at least intermittently, to penetrate their bases inside Pakistan.[23] At the end of 1980 a forged letter from a member of Gulbuddin Hekmatyar's Hizb-i-Islami left in the headquarters of a rival *mujahideen* leader, Muhammad Nabi Muhammadi, by an agent either of the KGB or its KHAD surrogate warned Muhammadi that Hekmatyar was planning to get rid of him. Simultaneously, bogus pamphlets by Muhammadi denouncing Hekmatyar were distributed in Afghan refugee camps in the Peshawar region. Among other Service A forgeries were copies of an apparently compromising letter by Hekmatyar which were distributed to both the Pakistani authorities and other *mujahideen* leaders.[24] Though the bitter divisions among the seven main *mujahideen* groups were not its own creation, the KGB undoubtedly made them more severe. Hekmatyar, in particular, was so prone to attack his rivals that some US intelligence analysts wondered if he might be on the Soviet payroll.[25] Even Zia ul-Haq, his main backer, once ordered the ISI to warn Hekmatyar – to no discernible effect – 'that it was Pakistan who made him an Afghan leader, and it is Pakistan who can equally destroy him if he continues to misbehave'.[26]

The KGB's numerous tactical successes in disrupting *mujahideen* operations, however, could not disguise the fact that, overall, the war was going badly. The Afghan forces, which Brezhnev had been told before the Soviet invasion would bear the main brunt of the brief and victorious struggle to establish the authority of Babrak Karmal, became a liability. According to KGB statistics, 17,000

Afghans had deserted within four months of the Soviet invasion. There were another 30,000 desertions during 1981 and at least as many again in 1982. The Karmal government itself sometimes felt humiliated by the performance of its troops. One KGB report described the outraged reaction of the Afghan Defence Minister, Muhammad Rafi, when he inspected the 11th Division in February 1981, accompanied by the deputy chief Soviet military adviser, V. P. Cheremnykh. While inspecting a barracks, Rafi picked up a dirty blanket from one of the beds and told the commander of the regiment, Muhammad Nadir, that he would personally ram it down his throat unless he established order among his troops. As the inspection continued Rafi completely lost his temper, struck Nadir and ordered him to be tied up and imprisoned in a doubtless filthy latrine until 4 o'clock in the morning, when he sent him in disgrace back to Kabul.[27]

One of the few Afghan leaders to inspire confidence in Moscow was Najibullah. Vadim Kirpichenko's memoirs make no mention of his sadism and pay instead an implausible tribute to him as:

a good organizer, a highly educated person, an opponent of . . . repression in the country, and indeed his [original] profession – a doctor – presupposed a humane quality in his character. Najibullah sincerely desired happiness and prosperity for his people and did everything within his powers to improve . . . the situation in Afghanistan.[28]

During a visit to Afghanistan in 1983, however, Leonov, the head of Service 1, came to realize – as Kirpichenko and others did not – that Najibullah was a fantasist. He boasted that KHAD had 1,300 agents among the *mujahideen*, 1,226 in areas currently under *mujahideen* control, 714 in 'underground counter-revolutionary organizations' and 28 in the various branches of the Pakistani government. Leonov had begun to take notes of Najibullah's account of KHAD achievements but later recalled that, as the account became increasingly fantastic, 'I just put down my pen and ceased to write down what was obvious rubbish.'[29]

The Red Army never deployed sufficient forces to compensate for the military weakness of its Afghan client-state and defeat an elusive guerrilla enemy. In Vietnam US forces at their peak had numbered over half a million. The Soviet Union, burdened by the problems of maintaining 565,000 troops in eastern Europe, 75,000 in Mongolia and 25–30,000 in other Third World countries, never felt able to station much more than 100,000 troops in Afghanistan, a country five times the size of Vietnam.[30] A force of this size could never hope to occupy the whole of Afghanistan. Nor were Soviet forces able to seal the frontiers with Pakistan (and, less importantly, with Iran) and so prevent the *mujahideen* resupplying their forces. As a result, most of the Red Army's successes in driving *mujahideen* from areas of the countryside were only temporary. When Soviet troops withdrew, the *mujahideen* returned. Marshal Sergei Akhromeyev told the Politburo in 1986: 'There is no single piece of land in this country which has not been occupied by a Soviet soldier. Nevertheless, the majority of the territory remains in the hands of rebels.'[31]

In March 1983, after discussing the report of a high-ranking mission of enquiry, the Politburo Afghanistan Commission came close to acknowledging that Soviet military intervention had reached an impasse. Gromyko told the Politburo, 'The number of gangs [*mujahideen* groups] is not decreasing. The enemy is not laying down its weapons.' He struggled none the less to find some grounds for optimism. 'Yes,' he declared, 'the situation is stabilizing.' Gromyko then immediately contradicted himself: 'But the main trouble is that the central authorities have not yet reached the countryside: [they] rarely interact with the masses, about one-third of the districts is not under the control of the central authority, and one can feel the fragility of the state government.'

As the most influential original advocate of the Soviet invasion, Andropov, who had succeeded Brezhnev as General Secretary four months earlier, was anxious both to justify the original decision to intervene and to remind other members of the Politburo of their collective responsibility: 'You remember how arduously and cautiously we decided the question of deploying troops in Afghanistan. L. I. Brezhnev insisted on a roll-call vote by members of the Politburo.'[32] No member of the Politburo presumed to remind Andropov that the real decision to intervene had been taken at a private meeting of himself and the other members of the Afghanistan Commission with Brezhnev, and then rubber stamped by the rest of the Politburo. The sycophantic deference which the Politburo traditionally extended to its General Secretary also ensured that no one drew attention to the striking contradiction between his optimistic assurances at the time of the Soviet invasion and his assessment in March 1983. In December 1979 Andropov had assured Brezhnev that Soviet forces already in Kabul should be 'entirely sufficient for a successful operation'. He had told the Politburo in February 1980 after a visit to Kabul that all available intelligence demonstrated that 'the situation in Afghanistan is stabilizing now'.[33] In March 1983, by contrast, he implied that there had never been any prospect of a rapid victory over the *mujahideen*: 'Miracles don't happen . . . Let us remember our [interwar] fight with [Islamic] *basmachism*. Why, back then, almost the entire Red Army was concentrated in central Asia, yet the fight with *basmachi* continued until the mid-1930s.'[34]

Andropov and the Centre placed most of the blame for the impasse in the war on foreign – especially US and Pakistani – arms supplies and other assistance to the *mujahideen*. For the first three years of the Reagan administration (1981–83) US assistance, mostly chan-nelled by the CIA through Pakistan, ran at a level of about $60 million a year, a sum matched by the Saudis. In 1982 Zia told Reagan's Director of Central Intelligence, Bill Casey, that he thought the existing level of support was about right – though the *mujahideen* lacked the ground-to-air weapons to defend themselves against Soviet and Afghan air attacks. The objective, in Zia's view, should be 'to keep the pot boiling [in Afghanistan], but not [make it] boil over' and provoke a Soviet attack on Pakistan. By 1984, however, both the CIA and Zia believed in the possibility of a *mujahideen* victory. CIA covert aid increased several times over and 'Zia opened the floodgates, taking his chances with Soviet retaliation'.[35]

By the spring of 1983 Andropov privately accepted the need for a settlement which fell well short of a Soviet military victory. He told the UN Secretary-General, Javier Pérez de Cuellar, that the war was damaging the Soviet Union's relations with the West, 'socialist states', Islamic states and the rest of the Third World as well as its internal social and economic development.[36] A way out of the con-flict remained impossible, however, because Andropov saw the war in Afghanistan within the context of a world-wide struggle for influ-ence with the United States. Under existing circumstances with-drawal from Afghanistan would be an unacceptable blow to Soviet prestige. Andropov told the Politburo in March 1983, 'We are fight-ing against American imperialism . . . That is why we cannot back off.'[37] The threat from 'American imperialism', he believed, was greater than at any time since the Cuban missile crisis. During the final year of his life, Andropov was obsessed by the delusion that the Reagan administration had plans for a nuclear first strike against the Soviet Union and insisted that operation RYAN, which was intended to collect intelligence on these non-existent plans, remain the first priority of both the KGB and the GRU.[38]

No solution to the grave problems either of East–West tension or of the war in Afghanistan was possible during the brief and ineffectual period in office of Konstantin Chernenko, who was already gravely ill when he succeeded Andropov as Soviet leader in February 1984.[39] In the spring of that year Leonid Shebarshin, who had been put in charge of Afghan intelligence operations at the Centre in the previous year, accompanied a military mission headed by Marshal Sokolov, then Deputy Defence Minister, on a tour of inspection following what the 40th Army Command in Afghanistan claimed was a major victory over the *mujahideen* forces of Ahmad Shah Massoud in the Panjshir Valley. The mission found the valley deserted, with Soviet and Afghan tanks dotted around fields of unharvested wheat. 'Where is the enemy?' asked Sokolov. 'Is he hiding in the gorges nearby?' 'Yes, Comrade Marshal of the Soviet Union,' the briefing officer replied. 'We have outposts, patrols and helicopters to follow his movements.' He claimed that 1,700 of Massoud's 3,000 'bandits' had been killed. The remainder had fled, carrying with them the bodies of their comrades.[40] Sokolov reported back to Moscow that the 40th Army had inflicted 'a serious defeat' on the enemy and was proving 'a decisive factor in stabilizing the situation in the DRA'.[41] Shebarshin, however, was unconvinced. When he asked the briefer how 1,300 defeated 'bandits' could have carried away 1,700 corpses as well as all their weapons, he received no coherent reply. He later discovered from KGB and KHAD intelligence that Massoud had been forewarned of the 40th Army attack, probably by a sympathizer in the Kabul Defence Ministry, and had pulled most of his fighters and supporters out of the Panjshir Valley ahead of the Soviet sweep, strengthening his reputation as the 'Lion of the Panjshir'. Shebarshin learned to be generally sceptical of 40th Army body counts.[42]

Of all the problems awaiting Gorbachev on his election as General Secretary in March 1985, writes his aide, Anatoli Chernyaev, 'The Afghanistan problem was the most pressing. As soon as the new "tsar" came to power the Central Committee and *Pravda* were flooded with letters. Very few of them were anonymous. Almost all were signed.'[43] With Gorbachev's accession the war in Afghanistan ceased for the first time to be a taboo subject. Under Brezhnev the Soviet media had acted as if there was no war in Afghanistan, publishing pictures and stories of smiling soldiers distributing food and medicine to the grateful Afghan people, but making almost no mention of fighting the *mujahideen*. Some mention of the fighting had been permitted under Andropov and Chernenko but Soviet troops were invariably said to have delivered devastating blows to the perfidious robber bands who were seeking to overturn a popular revolution. At the Twenty-seventh Party Congress in February 1986, however, Gorbachev described the war as 'a bleeding wound'.[44]

At the Politburo on 17 October 1985, Gorbachev had told his colleagues that it was time to come to 'a decision on Afghanistan' – time, in other words, to find a way of bringing the war to an end. By now, following the deaths of Andropov and Ustinov in 1984, Gromyko was the only surviving member of the troika which almost six years earlier had won Brezhnev's consent for a military intervention, the consequences of which he had not begun to comprehend. The change in the Politburo's mood, Chernyaev noted, was evident as soon as Gromyko spoke: 'You had to see the ironic expression of his colleagues – Gorbachev's glare was truly withering. Those looks said it all: "You ass, what are you babbling about, giving us advice? You got us into this dirty business, and now you're pretending that we're all responsible!"'[45]

Though anxious to withdraw from Afghanistan, Gorbachev allowed his forces to make a last major effort to defeat the *mujahideen*. During Gorbachev's first eighteen months as Soviet leader, writes Robert Gates, then Deputy DCI, 'we saw new, more aggressive Soviet tactics, a spread of the war to the eastern provinces, attacks inside Pakistan, and the more indiscriminate use of air power'. These eighteen months were the bloodiest of the war. With massive US assistance, the *mujahideen* held out, but the CIA operatives reported that their morale was being gradually eroded. What the *mujahideen* most lacked was state-of-the-art anti-aircraft weapons. Zia had told Casey in April 1982: 'The Pathans [Pushtun] are great fighters but shit-scared when it comes to air-power.' When the CIA supplied shoulder-launched US Stinger missiles to the *mujahideen* in the summer of 1986, they had a major, perhaps even decisive, impact on the war.[46] On 25 September a group of Hekmatyar's *mujahideen* armed with Stingers shot down three Soviet helicopter gunships as they approached Jalalabad airport. DCI Casey personally showed President Reagan a dramatic video of the attack taken by the *mujahideen*, the soundtrack mingling the sound of explosions with cries of *Allahu Akhbar!* Shebarshin did not immediately grasp the significance of the *mujahideen*'s use of the Stingers. Early in October the GRU obtained two of the missiles from agents in the *mujahideen*, and he expected effective counter-measures to be devised.[47] As the Soviet Defence Ministry complained, the Stingers marked 'a qualitatively new stage in Washington's interference' in the war. 'Although the Soviet and Afghan air forces adjusted their tactics to reduce losses, they effectively lost a trump card in the war – control of the air.'[48] By 1987 the CIA station in Islamabad was co-ordinating the provision of over 60,000 tons per year of weapons and other supplies to the *mujahideen* along over 300 infiltration routes by five- and ten-ton trucks, smaller pick-ups and pack mules. Milt Bearden, the station chief, 'discovered that on an annual basis we needed more mules than the world seemed prepared to breed'.[49]

By the spring of 1986, Gorbachev had decided on the replacement of Karmal as Afghan leader by the much tougher but also more flexible head of KHAD, Muhammad Najibullah, who had the strong backing of the Centre. Early in May Gorbachev bluntly told Karmal that he should hand over power to Najibullah and retire to Moscow with his family. There followed what Anatoli Dobrynin, the only other person present, described as a 'painful' scene in which Karmal 'obsequiously begged Gorbachev to change his mind, promising to perform his duties in a more correct and active way'.[50] Gorbachev refused and Kabul Radio, using a traditional Soviet euphemism for dismissal, announced that the PDPA Central Committee had accepted Karmal's request to resign for 'health reasons' and elected Najibullah in his stead. As a sop to the wounded pride of Karmal and his supporters he was allowed to retain his membership of the PDPA Politburo and to continue to serve as President of the Afghan Revolutionary Council.[51] To Gorbachev's fury, however, Karmal contrived to hold on to some of his former power. He was finally forced to resign from the Politburo and the presidency of the Revolutionary Council in November.[52]

The outcome of the war in Afghanistan was sealed at a dramatic meeting of the Politburo on 13 November 1986. A year earlier, Gorbachev had given the army a last chance to defeat the *mujahideen* or at least to create the illusion of victory. Now he was determined to bring the war to an end and made an unprecedented criticism of the Soviet high command:

We have been fighting in Afghanistan for six years already. Unless we change our approach, we shall continue to fight for another 20–30 years ... Our military should be told they are learning badly from this war ... Are we going to fight endlessly, as a testimony that our troops are not able to deal with this situation? We need to finish this process as quickly as possible.

Gorbachev set a target of two years for withdrawing all Soviet troops, but was anxious to ensure that 'the Americans don't get into Afghanistan' as a result.[53] Chernyaev believed that Soviet troops could have been withdrawn in two months. The reason for the delay was essentially to avoid losing face after the long struggle for influence with the United States in the Third World: 'The Afghan problem, as in the beginning of that adventure, was still seen primarily in terms of "global confrontation" and only secondarily in light of the "new thinking".'[54]

At Gorbachev's proposal, the Politburo appointed a new Afghanistan Commission, chaired by Eduard Shevardnadze, Gromyko's successor as Foreign Minister.[55] Shevardnadze's oral report to the Politburo two months later was, by implication, a devastating indictment of the distortions in previous intelligence and other reports to the leadership which had sought to conceal the extent of the failure of Soviet Afghan policy:

Little remains of the friendly feelings [in Afghanistan] toward the Soviet Union which existed for decades. A great many people have died and not all of them were bandits. Not one problem has been solved to the peasantry's advantage. The government bureaucracy is functioning poorly. Our advisers' aid is ineffective. Najib complains of the narrow-minded tutelage of our advisers.

I won't discuss right now whether we did the right thing by going in there. But we did go in there absolutely without knowing the psychology of the people and the real state of affairs in the country. That's a fact. And everything that we've done and are doing in Afghanistan is incompatible with the moral character of our country.

The Prime Minister, Nikolai Ivanovich Rhyzhkov, praised Shevardnadze's report as the first 'realistic picture' of the situation in Afghanistan: 'Previous information was not objective.' Even the hard-liner Yegor Ligachev agreed that Shevardnadze had provided 'the first objective information' received by the Politburo. Chebrikov, the KGB Chairman, who was a member of the Afghanistan Commission, attempted a half-hearted defence of previous intelligence reporting, claiming that, though the Politburo appeared to have 'received much new material', that material could be found in earlier reports. None the less, he agreed with the conclusions of the rest of the Politburo on the Afghan situation: 'The Comrades have analysed it well.'[56]

As Gorbachev acknowledged, 'They panicked in Kabul when they found out we intended to leave.'[57] In implementing the decision to withdraw, he also had to cope with a rearguard action mounted by some sections of the Centre and the military. He retaliated with a series of public disclosures which revealed that Soviet military intervention had been decided by a small clique within the Politburo that had put pressure on Brezhnev.[58]

In January 1989, a month before the final withdrawal of the last Soviet forces, the Politburo's Afghanistan Commission reported that 'the Afghan comrades are seriously worried about how the situation will turn out'. The comrades were, however, encouraged by the 'strong disagreements' within the *mujahideen*, particularly the mutual hostility between the Pushtun forces of Gulbuddin Hekmatyar and the Tajik forces of Burhanudeen Rabbani and Massoud: 'Armed clashes between detachments of these and other opposition groups are not just continuing, but are taking on wider proportions as well.'[59] Though Mitrokhin retired too early to see KGB files on the later stages of the war, there can be no doubt that promoting divisions within the *mujahideen* and provoking further armed clashes between them remained a major priority of KGB and KHAD operations. While these divisions did not derive from KGB active measures, they were doubtless exacerbated by them. Hekmatyar's publicly stated conviction that, despite supplying him with arms, the

CIA was plotting his assassination[60] has all the hallmarks of deriving from a KGB disinformation operation.

Contrary to a public declaration by Gorbachev, 200 military and KGB advisers secretly remained behind in Kabul after the last Soviet troops had gone. As the Najibullah regime began to crumble in April 1992, having defied all predictions by outlasting the Soviet Union, Boris Yeltsin, the President of the Russian Federation, was surprised to discover the continued presence of the advisers and immediately withdrew them.[61] The fall of Najibullah was swiftly followed by civil war among the *mujahideen*. Much of the chaos which preceded the conquest of Kabul in 1996 by the extreme fundamentalist Taleban was the product of the war which had followed the Soviet invasion in 1979 – and of the secret war in particular. More than any other conflict in history, the war in Afghanistan was shaped by the covert operations of foreign intelligence agencies. The KGB, the CIA, the Pakistani ISI, the Saudi General Intelligence Department and Iranian clandestine services all trained, financed and sought to manipulate rival factions in Afghanistan.[62] These rival factions in turn helped to reduce Afghanistan after fourteen years of disastrous Communist misrule to a chaotic conglomeration of rival warlords.

Africa

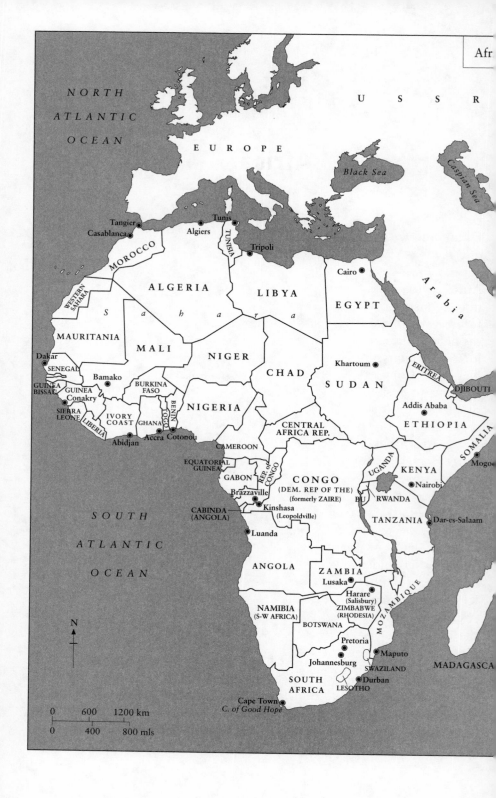

23

Africa: Introduction

Of all the African countries, both Lenin and Comintern were most interested in South Africa. The very first issue of the Marxist newspaper *Iskra*, which Lenin began editing in 1900, mentioned South Africa twice. Like Lenin, Comintern looked to South Africa, the most industrialized and urbanized country on the continent, as the future vanguard of the African Revolution. In 1922 Bill Andrews, the first Chairman of the Communist Party of South Africa (CPSA), joined Comintern's Executive Committee. In 1927 the African National Congress (ANC) elected as its President the pro-Communist Josiah Gumede, who visited Moscow and became head of the South African section of the newly founded Soviet front organization, the League Against Imperialism.[1] During the mid-1920s African and American blacks began to study in Moscow's secret Comintern-run International Lenin School (MLSh) and Communist University of the Toilers of the East (KUTV). All were given false identities during their time in Moscow and their curriculum, like that of the other students, included training in underground work, espionage and guerrilla warfare. The Comintern leadership, however, had low expectations of all but the South Africans. Like other Soviet leaders, Grigori Zinoviev, the Comintern Chairman, knew little about black Africa. When he came to lecture at the KUTV in 1926, an Ashanti student from the Gold Coast, Bankole Awanoore-Renner, asked him about 'Comintern's attitude toward the oppressed nations of Africa'. Zinoviev responded by talking in some detail about the problems of Morocco and Tunisia, but Awanoore-Renner complained that he said nothing about 'the most oppressed people' south of the Sahara. Though Zinoviev pleaded lack of information, Awanoore-Renner thought he detected the stench of racism.

In September 1932 mounting complaints of racism in Moscow by black African and American students led Comintern's Executive Committee to appoint an investigative committee. In January 1933 Dmitri Manuilsky, who had succeeded Zinoviev as Comintern chief, came to the University to listen to their complaints, which included a letter complaining of the 'derogatory portrayal of Negroes in the cultural institutions of the Soviet Union' as 'real monkeys'. The signatures included the name 'James Joken', the Moscow alias of Jomo Kenyatta, later the first leader of independent Kenya.[2] For Kenyatta, as for many radical African students a generation later, life in the Soviet Union was a disillusioning experience. Before he left for Moscow the Special Branch in London believed that he had joined the Communist Party of Great Britain (CPGB) and that a leading British Communist, Robin Page Arnott, had spoken of him prophetically as 'the future revolutionary leader of Kenya'.[3] Kenyatta's lecturers at the KUTV in Moscow were less enthusiastic. Though assessing him as 'a very intelligent and well educated negro', the KUTV lecturers' collective reported that 'He contrasted our school with the bourgeois school, stating that in all respects the bourgeois school is superior to ours. In particular, the bourgeois school teaches [its pupils] to think and provides the opportunity to do so, evidently thinking that our school does not provide this opportunity.' The collective recommended after Kenyatta's graduation in May 1933 that he be given three to four months further 'fundamental' instruction in Marxist-Leninist theory by an experienced teacher before returning to Kenya.[4]

By the early 1930s Comintern's wildly optimistic hopes of a South African revolution had long since evaporated. In 1930 Gumede's Communist sympathies and autocratic leadership style led to his replacement as President of the ANC, which henceforth distanced itself from the CPSA. The CPSA, meanwhile, was in turmoil as a result of both the dictatorial demands of Moscow and its own internal divisions. In 1931 Comintern excommunicated the Party's founders, Sidney P. Bunting and Bill Andrews, who were accused of Trotskyism and 'white chauvinism' (charges dismissed by Bunting in a letter to the Comintern secretariat as 'your wild outburst of lies'). Their removal was quickly followed by the expulsion of the first black Africans to join the CPSA, T. W. Thibedi and Gana Makabeni, both accused of the absurdly named crime of 'Buntingism'. In February 1935 a former Party secretary, Moses Kotane (who was later to become a long-serving general secretary), wrote despairingly to Moscow, pleading for help: 'We are in a state of utter confusion. The Party is disintegrating and the work is practically at a standstill.' Various attempts at reform followed and the CPGB was given 'responsibility for giving constant help to the CPSA'. In February 1939, however, a report to the CPGB concluded that, 'In practice the [South African] Party Centre has not been functioning for the past year' and that Party membership was down to about 200. The vanguard Party of the African Revolution had almost ceased to exist – as indeed had its Comintern overseers in Moscow.[5]

Ironically, Kenyatta's Marxist past made more of an impression during the early years of the Cold War in Nairobi and London than in Moscow. There is no evidence that either the post-war Soviet Foreign Ministry or the KGB ever consulted the files of the defunct pre-war Comintern. The British colonial authorities were alarmed by Kenyatta's record as a Communist or Communist sympathizer in interwar London and his secret trip to study in Moscow, but were unaware of the disillusion generated by his experiences at the KUTV. Kenya's British governor, Sir Evelyn Baring, convinced himself that 'With his Communist and anthropological training, *he knew his people* and was directly responsible [for Mau Mau]. Here was the African leader to darkness and death.'[6]

Outside the Communist University of the Toilers of the East, which was so badly purged that it ceased to function during the Great Terror, African affairs received little attention in either the universities or the intelligence agencies of Stalin's Russia. When Stalin received a letter of congratulation written in Amharic from the Emperor of Ethiopia, Haile Selassie, after Hitler's forces had been halted outside Moscow late in 1941, he asked the Soviet Foreign Ministry for a translation – only to be told, reportedly, that Moscow's only Amharic speaker had died in the defence of the capital. According to Vadim Kirpichenko (head of the FCD African Department from 1967 to 1970), this episode then 'accurately reflected the state of African studies in the country'.[7] Things were little better after the Second World War. When Soviet policy-makers looked at Africa during the early Cold War, many of them saw what one Russian academic called 'a blank sheet of paper'.[8]

Khrushchev's interest in Africa was much greater than Stalin's.

Though he knew little about the Dark Continent, he was favourably impressed by the fiery anti-imperialist rhetoric of the first generation of African post-colonial leaders. A few days before Ghana became the first black African colony to win independence in March 1957, Khrushchev declared enthusiastically, 'The awakening of the peoples of Africa has begun.' A Soviet correspondent at the first Conference of Independent States of Africa a year later reported with equal enthusiasm that 'Africa has spoken for the first time in her history!'[9] The KGB, however, still paid little attention. Not until the summer of 1960, when Khrushchev decided to attend the next session of the United Nations to welcome the admission of sixteen newly independent African states, did the FCD – on instructions from Aleksandr Shelepin, the KGB Chairman – establish a department to specialize in sub-Saharan Africa.[10]

As well as enjoying his own dozen lengthy speeches to the General Assembly in the autumn of 1960, Khrushchev must also have relished the passionate denunciations of Western imperialism by African leaders such as Kwame Nkrumah, who declared:

The flowing tide of African nationalism sweeps everything before it and constitutes a challenge to the colonial powers to make a just restitution for the years of injustice and crime committed against our continent . . . For years and years Africa has been the footstool of colonialism and imperialism, exploitation and degradation. From the north to the south, from the east to the west, her sons languished in the chains of slavery and humiliation, and Africa's exploiters and self-appointed controllers of her destiny strode across our land with incredible inhumanity, without mercy, without shame, and without honour.[11]

Though describing himself as an African socialist rather than a Marxist-Leninist, Nkrumah endorsed Lenin's analysis of imperialism as the 'highest stage of capitalism', still intent on exploiting post-colonial Africa. He claimed Lenin's authority for arguing that 'neo-colonialism . . . can be more dangerous to our legitimate aspirations of freedom and economic independence than outright political control':

[Neo-colonialism] acts covertly, manoeuvring men and governments, free of the stigma attached to political rule. It creates client states, independent in name but in point of fact pawns of the very colonial power which is supposed to have given them independence. This is one of [what Lenin called] the 'diverse forms of dependent countries which, politically, are formally independent, but, in fact, are enmeshed in the net of financial and diplomatic dependence'.[12]

KGB active measures in Africa promoted the same argument.

Some African Communists succeeded in rekindling the idealism of the revolutionary dream which had inspired the early Bolsheviks and captured the imagination of many on the European left in the 1930s. Nelson Mandela, who in 1952 became First Deputy President of the ANC, was one of many non-Communist militants in liberation movements who came to admire the commitment and self-sacrifice of some of his white Communist comrades. Early in his career Mandela's belief that only 'undiluted African nationalism' could end racial oppression led him and some of his friends to break up Communist meetings by storming onto the stage, grabbing the microphone and tearing down Party banners. Gradually, he changed his mind. The Communist most admired by Mandela was an Afrikaner, Bram Fischer, grandson of a Judge-President of the Boer Orange Free State:

In many ways, Bram Fischer . . . made the greatest sacrifice of all. No matter what I suffered in my pursuit of freedom, I always took strength from the fact that I was fighting with and for my own people. Bram was a free man who fought against his own people to ensure the freedom of others.

At the treason trial which sentenced Mandela to life imprisonment in 1964, he told the court:

For many decades the Communists were the only political group in South Africa who were prepared to treat Africans as human beings and their equals; who were prepared to eat with us; talk with us, live with and work with us. Because of this, there are many Africans who today tend to equate communism with freedom.[13]

The feeble response of much of the West to the iniquities of the racist regime in Pretoria strengthened the illusion that the intolerant Soviet one-party state was a force for global liberation. In Africa, as in Europe, however, nothing was so destructive of Communist idealism as the conquest of power. Wherever they emerged, Marxist regimes, despite their rhetoric of national liberation, became oppressive one-party states.

The Centre's Cold War operations in Africa fell into two main phases. The first, beginning in the early 1960s, was prompted by British and French decolonization; the second, starting in the mid-1970s, followed the collapse of the Portuguese Empire in Africa and the overthrow of Haile Selassie in Ethiopia. The former French and British colonies failed to live up to Khrushchev's expectations. Apart from Nkrumah, the only members of the first generation of African leaders to arouse the serious interest of the KGB were the Francophone Marxist dictators of Guinea and Mali, Ahmed Sékou Touré and Modibo Keïta. In all three cases, however, the Centre's hopes were dashed. As well as creating one-party states, Nkrumah, Touré and Keïta wrecked their countries' economies, leaving Moscow wondering whether to pour good money after bad to bail them out. The plentiful SIGINT generated by the KGB's attack on vulnerable African cipher systems doubtless enabled the Centre to follow the calamitous mismanagement of the Nkrumah, Touré and Keïta regimes in depressing detail.[14]

After these disappointments the Centre became increasingly cynical at the Marxist rhetoric of some African leaders, which was often prompted, it believed, not by any real interest in following the Soviet example but chiefly – and sometimes simply – by the hope of securing Soviet economic aid. Leonov noted in his diary on 6 December 1974:

The latest miracle of miracles has occurred. In far-away, impoverished Dahomey, in Cotonou, . . . President Kerekou has proclaimed himself a Marxist-Leninist as of 4 December this year, and his country as going along the path of construction of socialism. He is asking for our help in organizing an army, special [intelligence] services, not to mention the economy. Our ambassador, to whom he [Kerekou] set forth all this, broke into a sweat out of fear, and was incapable of answering either yes or no . . . This action of the Dahomeyans looks absurd . . . 80 per cent of the population of 3 million are illiterate, power is in the hands of a military clique. There is neither industry, nor parties, nor classes.[15]

The end of Portuguese rule and the overthrow of Haile Selassie in 1974, followed by the emergence of apparently committed Marxist regimes in Angola, Mozambique and Ethiopia, created a new wave of optimism in the Centre about its prospects in Africa. Moscow invested far greater hopes and resources in Angola, Mozambique and Ethiopia than it had done in Ghana, Guinea and Mali a decade or more earlier. It also made much more extensive use of its allies, especially Cuba and East Germany, to defend the new Marxist regimes against their opponents than it had ever done before.[16] Castro, in particular, was a willing and at times enthusiastic ally. Some in the Centre later argued that Soviet involvement in Angola was largely the result of Cuban pressure.[17] Even when the Centre's hopes were highest, however, African postings were unpopular with many, if not most, KGB officers. There were a number of embarrassing cases of alcoholism in African residencies.[18]

The high hopes of the mid-1970s disintegrated over the next decade. In Angola and Mozambique, Moscow had to confront the intractable problems caused by a combination of civil war and economic mismanagement. Mengistu's 'Marxist' regime in Ethiopia tried to justify the massacre of its opponents, real and imagined, by referring to Lenin's use of Red Terror during the Russian Civil War. The most enduring Soviet-bloc legacy in many of the post-colonial states of sub-Saharan Africa was the help it provided in setting up brutal security services to shore up their one-party regimes.[19] It is only fair to add, however, that the self-styled Marxist and Marxist-Leninist regimes in Africa had no monopoly of economic mismanagement and brutality (though, in the latter category, none outdid Mengistu). Pro-Western leaders such as Joseph Désiré Mobutu in Zaire, Samuel Doe in Liberia and Hastings Banda in Malawi denounced the sins of their socialist neighbours but differed from them far less in any commitment to democratic values than in their willingness, often for their own personal profit, to allow Western firms to operate in their countries. The legendarily corrupt Mobutu, proprietor of Africa's most notorious 'vampire state', received hundreds of millions of dollars in American aid, much of which disappeared into Swiss bank accounts, simply on the grounds of his committed anti-Communism. While Mobutu accumulated a personal fortune sometimes reckoned to be the size of the Zairean national debt, the inhabitants of a country with some of Africa's finest natural resources became as impoverished as the citizens of Angola and Mozambique.[20]

The only African country which arguably represented something of a KGB success story was South Africa. Though the African National Congress (ANC) was never at any point the Communist stooge which the apartheid regime liked to pretend, Soviet support, channelled through the KGB, helped sustain it in some of its darkest hours.[21] On paper, the rise to power of the ANC after the end of the Cold War appeared to fulfil many of the Centre's earlier hopes. Joe Slovo, the South African Communist Party[22] (SACP) leader, was the most respected of the ANC's white members and the man chiefly responsible for persuading Nelson Mandela to end the armed struggle. Many other ANC militants were also SACP members, among them Mandela's successor, Thabo Mbeki. Mbeki, however, quickly realized that Marxism-Leninism had nothing to offer post-apartheid South Africa. Since succeeding Nelson Mandela, he has co-opted able left-wingers into the government by offering them plum jobs, then entrusted them with Thatcherite reforms. The Centre could never have imagined that at the beginning of the twenty-first century leading South African Communists would find themselves in charge of privatizing state-owned industries, lowering trade barriers and refusing pay rises to public-sector unions.[23]

24

The Cold War Comes to Africa

The most fiercely fought of Africa's wars of liberation was the Algerian Revolution (known in France simply as the Algerian War), which between 1954 and 1962 cost the lives of a million Muslims and led to the expulsion from their homes of about the same number of European settlers. The French authorities, who refused for several years to accept that the revolt of the Front de Libération Nationale (FLN) was a nationalist rebellion against French rule, were quick to see the hand of Moscow behind the beginning of the war. In 1955 the French military commander in the Maghreb, General Jean Calliès, informed the Prime Minister, Edgar Faure, that the outbreak of the rebellion was part of a Cold War strategy 'announced by Stalin himself'.[1] The involvement in the revolt of the Algerian Communist Party, which maintained close links with the staunchly pro-Soviet French Communist Party,[2] seemed further evidence of Soviet involvement. In reality, however, Moscow stayed largely aloof from the conflict. Members of the Algerian Communist Party, which drew much of its support from workers of European origin, were never fully trusted by the overwhelmingly Algerian FLN and frequently found themselves selected for 'suicide missions' against French forces.[3] Though China was quick to recognize the provisional government founded by the FLN in September 1958, it was more than two years before the Soviet Union grudgingly followed suit.[4] Even then a leading Soviet journal published an article by the leader of the Algerian Communist Party claiming that a second revolution was needed to correct the errors in the first, essentially bourgeois revolution.[5] An attempt by Vadim Kirpichenko soon after Algerian independence in 1962 to conclude an agreement on KGB collaboration with the Algerian intelligence chief, Abdelhafid Boussouf, ended in failure.[6]

The KGB's only significant operational successes during the Algerian Revolution were the active measures devised by Service A, chiefly directed against the United States. Service A was able to exploit the willingness of French opinion to blame setbacks during the war on conspiracies by *les Anglo-Saxons*, their American and British allies.[7] In April 1961 the KGB succeeded in planting on the pro-Soviet Italian daily *Paese Sera* a story suggesting that the CIA was involved in the failed putsch mounted by four French generals to disrupt de Gaulle's attempts to negotiate a peace with the FLN which would lead to Algerian independence. Among other media taken in by the story was the leading French newspaper *Le Monde*, which began an editorial on the putsch: 'It now seems established that some American agents more or less encouraged [General Maurice] Challe [one of the coup leaders].'[8] For the remainder of the Cold War bogus CIA plots in Africa, frequently documented by Service A forgeries, were one of the staples of KGB active measures. The credibility of Service A disinformation was greatly enhanced by the fact that, on Eisenhower's instructions, the CIA had prepared a plan to poison Patrice Lumumba, the pro-Soviet prime minister of the Republic of the Congo,* later renamed Zaire. In the event, Lumumba was murdered in December 1960 not by the CIA but by his Congolese rival, Joseph Mobutu, who went on to become one of the most corrupt of independent Africa's kleptomaniac rulers.[9] Before expelling the KGB resident in Kinshasa, Boris Sergeyevich Voronin, Mobutu amused himself by putting Voronin up against a wall and personally staging a mock execution.[10] Soviet propaganda continued to portray Lumumba as the victim of American imperialism. Khrushchev announced the foundation in his honour of the Patrice Lumumba Friendship University to provide higher education in Moscow for students from Africa, Asia and Latin America. The University's first vice-rector and a number of its staff were KGB officers who used the student body as a recruiting ground for Third World agents.[11]

In the summer of 1961 Khrushchev and the CPSU Central

---

* The former Belgian Congo became independent in 1960 as the Republic of the Congo and was successively renamed the Democratic Republic of the Congo in 1964 and Zaire in 1971, reverting in 1997 to Democratic Republic of the Congo. It is often known as Congo (Kinshasa) to distinguish it from the former French colony, the Congo Republic, which is also known as Congo (Brazzaville).

Committee approved a new and aggressive KGB global grand strategy to use national liberation movements in the Third World to secure an advantage in the East–West struggle. That strategy, however, was focused not on Africa but on Central America.[12] Cuban enthusiasm for the prospects of African revolution predated that of the Soviet Union by over a decade. Ahmed Ben Bella, first president of newly independent Algeria, visited Havana in the midst of the missile crisis of October 1962 to be greeted by what he immodestly called 'indescribable scenes of popular enthusiasm'. After the crisis was over and Soviet missile bases were being dismantled, Ben Bella echoed Castro's indignant complaints that Khrushchev 'had no balls'[13] and exchanged 'very tough words' with the Soviet ambassador in Algiers. When the Algerian Revolution had to face what Ben Bella considered its 'first serious threat' during a Saharan border conflict with Morocco in October 1963, it was Castro not Khrushchev who came to his rescue, sending a battalion of twenty-two Soviet tanks and several hundred Cuban troops ready to take on the Moroccans if the desert war continued, though in the event they were not needed. According to Ben Bella:

The tanks were fitted with infra-red equipment that allowed them to be used at night. They had been delivered to Cuba by the Soviet Union on the condition that they were not to be made available to third countries, even Communist countries such as Bulgaria, in any circumstances. Despite these restrictions from Moscow, the Cubans defied all the taboos and sent their tanks to the assistance of the endangered Algerian revolution without a moment's hesitation.

Convinced that sub-Saharan Africa was 'imperialism's weakest link', Che Guevara began using Algiers as a base from which to make ineffective revolutionary forays to Angola and Congo (Brazzaville). After each of his forays he spent many hours in conversation with Ben Bella, recounting his adventures and denouncing the passive attitude of pro-Moscow Marxist parties, whose own assessments of the immediate prospects for revolution were more realistic than his own.[14] After an 'extremely chilly' meeting with Eduardo Mondlane, the leader of the Mozambique national liberation movement, FRELIMO, Guevara patronizingly declared that, '[Sub-Saharan]

Africa had a long way to go before it achieved real revolutionary maturity'.[15]

The Algerian border conflict with Morocco enabled Moscow to mend some of its fences with Ben Bella. Before the conflict, the United States and France had supplied arms to Morocco but refused them to Algeria. The conspiratorially minded Ben Bella became convinced that the United States had prompted what he regarded as Moroccan aggression.[16] Moscow seized its opportunity. Despite Castro's unauthorized loan of Soviet tanks, it began substantial arms shipments to Algeria on long-term credit agreements.[17] The KGB, meanwhile, fed Ben Bella's suspicion of the United States by channelling to him Service A forgeries which purported to reveal American plots to overthrow his and other African socialist regimes.[18] Moscow also set out to pander to Ben Bella's growing personality cult, inviting him to Moscow in May 1964 and giving him a hero's welcome at the Kremlin, where he was presented with both the Lenin Peace Prize and the medal of Hero of the Soviet Union. Only a year later, to Moscow's dismay, he was overthrown in a military coup.[19]

The Soviet Union's closest relationships with leaders of other newly independent African states were also short lived. Moscow's main hopes of extending its influence in sub-Saharan Africa were initially centred on Ghana, which in 1957 became the first black African state to achieve independence under the charismatic leadership of Kwame Nkrumah, widely hailed as the prototype of the new educated African statesman committed to both democracy and socialism. Once in power, however, Nkrumah's rhetoric of liberation was rapidly contradicted by his intolerance of dissent. Though he claimed to be creating a specifically African brand of socialism rather than subscribing to Marxism-Leninism, his speeches became increasingly pro-Soviet. As he and his sycophantic supporters in the Convention People's Party (CPP) transformed Ghana into a corrupt one-party state, Soviet and East German military, security and technical advisers arrived in increasing numbers. A KGB-trained National Security Service oversaw a huge network of informers. According to a Ghanaian white paper published after Nkrumah's overthrow: 'Nkrumah's security officers, both men and women, were placed everywhere – in factories, offices, drinking bars, political rallies and even in churches, not forgetting the taxi drivers, bus drivers, shop assistants, peddlers and seemingly unemployed persons who were all acting as informants.'[20]

Among the many paradoxes in Nkrumah's volatile personality was the fact that, despite his anti-American rhetoric, he was deeply distressed by President Kennedy's assassination and had a warm personal friendship with Kennedy's ambassador, William P. Mahoney, and his family.[21] Encouraged by KGB active measures, however, his suspicions of the CIA deepened and darkened. Like Ben Bella, Nkrumah was taken in by Service A forgeries.[22] After an assassination attempt against him in 1962 Nkrumah became obsessed by the belief that the Agency was plotting his overthrow, frequently giving visitors copies of a book denouncing CIA conspiracies.[23] In February 1964 he became so incensed by a bogus letter fabricated by Service A, supposedly written by a disillusioned US military intelligence officer, which purported to reveal the hostile operations of both the CIA and SIS against his regime, that he wrote a personal letter of protest to President Lyndon Johnson, accusing the CIA of devoting all its energies to 'clandestine and subversive activities among our people'. To emphasize the importance of his protest, Nkrumah instructed the Ghanaian ambassador in Washington to deliver it in person.[24]

Over the next few months, in other active-measures operations codenamed DEFEKTOR 3 and DEFEKTOR 4, the KGB used similar tactics to deceive the Francophone Marxist dictators of Guinea and Mali, Ahmed Sékou Touré and Modibo Keïta. The KGB's influence operations were assisted by penetrations of both the Guinean and Malian intelligence services.[25] The paranoid strain in Sékou Touré's brutal and intolerant personality made him particularly susceptible to rumours of plots against him from almost any source.[26] In May a US intelligence report, supposedly leaked by another disillusioned American intelligence officer but in reality fabricated by Service A, purported to reveal a plot to overthrow Sékou Touré, who reacted by dismissing those of his officials he believed were conspiring with the CIA.[27] A few months later Ben Bella passed on to Keïta similar disinformation planted on him by the KGB, again deriving from a bogus US intelligence report, on an alleged plot by French intelligence and Mali opposition leaders to assassinate him. In order to encourage Keïta to denounce the plot publicly, the report inaccurately declared that he enjoyed such widespread popularity in Mali that the secret opposition to him was afraid to come out into the open. Keïta duly did as Service A had hoped and, in a speech in Bamako, angrily denounced the imperialist conspiracy to undermine Mali's construction of a socialist society.[28]

KGB active measures had similar successes among African delegations at the United Nations. Racism in the United States presented Service A with an easy target which it was quick to exploit. In the segregated Southern states during the early 1960s blacks and whites still could not sit together on buses, eat together in restaurants, or attend the same schools. Pictures of state police beating peaceful civil-rights demonstrators with batons or soaking them with water cannon made front-page news around the world. Despite the passage of the Civil Rights Act in 1964, outlawing racial discrimination, and Martin Luther King's charismatic leadership of a non-violent campaign to implement those rights, rioting in August 1965 in the Los Angeles black ghetto of Watts, which left thirty-six dead and over 1,000 injured, began a series of long hot summers of racial conflict in the inner cities. KGB officers in New York, wearing gloves to avoid leaving fingerprints on their forged letters, simultaneously bombarded African diplomats at the UN with racially insulting correspondence purporting to come from US white supremacists. Oleg Kalugin, who was stationed at the New York residency in the early 1960s, recalls that, 'I lost no sleep over such dirty tricks, figuring they were just another weapon in the Cold War.'[29] The 'dirty tricks' continued for some years. At the twenty-fifth session of the UN General Assembly in 1970, 100 copies of an abusive leaflet, supposedly from an American racist group but in reality fabricated by Service A, were sent to African delegates.[30]

Despite the success of KGB active measures in promoting anti-American conspiracy theories in Africa, the Soviet Union was powerless during the 1960s to prevent the overthrow of two of the African regimes with which it had closest relations. In 1966, due chiefly to his calamitous mismanagement of the supposedly socialist Ghanaian economy and a disastrous fall in world cocoa prices, Kwame Nkrumah was overthrown in a military coup. The new government expelled over 1,000 Soviet advisers and over the next few years terminated all military-assistance agreements with Moscow.[31] With the Politburo's approval, the Accra residency provided secret financial support for a number of former members and supporters of the

Nkrumah regime.[32] In 1968, amid wild rejoicings in the Mali capital Bamako, the brutal, bankrupt 'socialist' regime of Modibo Keïta, winner of the Lenin Peace Prize, was also overthrown by a military coup.[33] In exile in Guinea, probably influenced by further KGB active measures, Nkrumah blamed his overthrow not on his own betrayal of the hopes of the Ghanaian people but on a conspiracy by the CIA which, with the assistance of British and West German intelligence, had sought out 'quislings and traitors' to overthrow him. The African-American US ambassador in Ghana, Franklin Williams, who had succeeded Mahoney, was alleged to have personally offered the chief quislings $13 million and to have tried to persuade them to assassinate Nkrumah at Accra airport – a plan they were said to have rejected as impracticable. The street celebrations in Accra which followed Nkrumah's overthrow were, he improbably claimed, forced by the Americans on a reluctant populace: 'Banners and posters, most of them prepared beforehand in the US embassy, were pushed into the hands of the unwilling "demonstrators".'[34]

The most important lesson drawn by Nkrumah from his overthrow was 'that independent African states must pursue a policy of all-out socialism if they are to survive'.[35] That his host in Guinea, Sékou Touré, survived in power, however, was due not to 'all-out socialism' but to the pervasiveness of his reign of terror which left even the army too cowed to attempt a military coup. The prisoners brought from their homes in the early hours for interrogation at Camp Boiro and other prison camps constructed with assistance from the East German Stasi and the Czechoslovak StB were tortured until they confessed to the usually imaginary conspiracies with which Sékou Touré was obsessed.[36] The KGB turned a blind eye to the horrors of the Guinean regime, preferring instead to exploit its leader's paranoid tendencies by active measures designed to convince him that the CIA was plotting to overthrow him. On at least one occasion (and probably on others not noted by Mitrokhin), the Centre heightened the dramatic impact of Service A's forgeries by sending a senior KGB officer to Conakry, the Guinean capital, to deliver them in person. When shown the forgeries, Sékou Touré became – according to a KGB report – highly emotional, exclaiming angrily, 'The filthy imperialists!' The CIA officers responsible for the (non-existent) plot would, he declared, be expelled within twenty-four hours: 'We highly appreciate the concern shown by our

Soviet comrades.'[37] Active measures, however, were powerless to change Guinean economic realities. The Soviet aid and imports which poured into Guinea in the early years of independence achieved little. A Radio Moscow correspondent visiting Conakry complained, 'We gave them what they wanted and they didn't know what to do with it.' But much of the blame lay with Moscow itself for embarking on a series of grandiose prestige projects which collapsed in disarray: among them a city-wide Conakry public address system which was soon switched off and never used again; a giant printing plant which operated at less than 5 per cent of capacity; a huge outdoor theatre which was abandoned half-completed; a 100kW radio station which was erected over a vein of iron ore and never functioned properly; and a national airline equipped with nine Ilyushins which were usually grounded.[38] Most remarkable of all was a report that Soviet snow ploughs had arrived in Conakry – a report which was widely disbelieved until a British academic discovered them rusting away at the end of the airport runway.[39] In 1978, after almost two decades of supposedly socialist construction, Sékou Touré was finally forced to seek help from the West to bail out his bankrupt economy.[40]

Though the initial priorities of KGB active measures in Africa were operations in newly independent 'progressive' regimes designed to strengthen their suspicion of the United States and their trust in the Soviet Union, the apparent success of Service A's forged documents purporting to reveal CIA plots led to their use in almost every (perhaps every) country on the continent. In operation ANDRO-MEDA, for example, the military ruler of Nigeria, General Yakubu 'Jack' Gowon, President of the Organization of African Unity (OAU) in 1973–74, was sent a fabricated letter in March 1973 supposedly written by a patriotic junior army officer, anxious to alert him to Agency subversion in the armed forces:

Sir! I urge you to take urgent and just actions to defend the nation from the dangerous activities of certain American diplomats in this country, who are trying with all their might to deceive our soldiers and reduce our nation again to chaos. I am well acquainted with Mr H. Duffy, an officer in the US embassy whom I regard with great respect. It is always pleasant to spend time with him, and I usually visited him whenever I came to Lagos. Some time ago Mr Duffy informed me that their First Secretary, Mr Jack

Mauer, wanted to consult with me. He described Mr Mauer as an influential person who could offer me assistance in arranging a trip to study at a US military college. I agreed and was introduced to Mr Mauer at a lawn tennis club. We agreed to meet in the evening. At the appointed time Mr Mauer arrived at the place where I was waiting for him. He was with a friend from the embassy who, as I understood it, was the owner of the car in which they arrived (LR 2229) and in which they drove me home to my brother's house. They began to question me in detail about several young officers in our battalion, and asked me to inform them about the ones who were stealing weapons from our warehouse. I in fact do suspect that at least three of our soldiers and officers are concealing many weapons. I promised to help Mr Mauer and his friend (I do not know his name), but am not about to do anything for them, since I understood what it is they want. But I thought that no one knows how many others might take their bait.

In the name of peace and order in this country, I urge you to stop them before they go too far. God bless you![41]

In Morocco two years later, operation EKSPRESS brought to the attention of King Hassan II a forged report from a CIA agent on an Agency plot to overthrow him. To add plausibility to the forgery, the report correctly identified the head of the CIA station, Charles 'Chuck' Cogan. Three US businessmen and a Rabat notable whom the KGB wished to discredit were also – probably falsely – named as working for the CIA.[42]

Following the Sino-Soviet split in the early 1960s, the KGB also embarked on a major programme of active measures designed to discredit Mao's regime. The Chinese message to the newly independent African states which alarmed Moscow was succinctly summarized in a verse by the Gambian poet Lenrie Peters:

> The Chinese then stepped in . . .
> We're Communist brothers
> To help you build Black Socialism.
> Only you must kick out the Russians.[43]

After some early successes, however, the Chinese overplayed their hand. In May 1965 Kenyan security forces seized a convoy of Chinese arms *en route* via Uganda to rebel forces in Congo (Kinshasa).[44] While on a visit to Tanzania in June, the Chinese Prime

Minister, Zhou Enlai, declared that Africa was now 'ripe for revolution'. African leaders were so indignant ('Revolution against whom?') that, despite having been welcomed in a number of their capitals over the previous two years, Zhou found nowhere else willing to receive him after he left Tanzania. The Kenyan authorities refused even to allow his plane to refuel on its journey home. Chinese pledges of aid to Africa dropped from $111 million in 1964 to $15 million in 1965.[45] The Centre, which referred to the Chinese in Africa by the demeaning codename 'Ants' (MURAVYI),[46] claimed much of the credit for the expulsion of PRC missions from Burundi, the Central African Republic, Dahomey, Tunisia and Senegal between 1965 and 1968.[47] As frequently happened, the KGB probably claimed more credit than it was due. Burundi's decision to 'suspend' diplomatic relations with the PRC in January 1965 appears to have been motivated by the belief of Mwami (King) Mwambutsa that the Chinese had been implicated in the assassination of the Prime Minister, Pierre Ngendnadumwe.[48] Though KGB active measures may well have encouraged Mwambutsa's suspicions, however, some historians conclude that the assassins did indeed have links with the PRC.[49] In January 1966 Colonel Jean Bedel (later self-styled 'Emperor') Bokassa, who had just seized power in the Central African Republic, broke off diplomatic relations with China following the discovery of documents which allegedly revealed a plot by an underground Armée Populaire Centrafricaine controlled by 'Chinese or pro-Chinese'.[50] Though proof is lacking, the emergence of these documents has all the hallmarks of a Service A fabrication. When the Dahomey regime of General Christophe Soglo also broke off relations with Beijing in January 1966, it gave no reasons and no evidence is available on the influence – if any – of Soviet active measures.[51] The breaking of diplomatic relations between Tunisia and the PRC in September 1967 followed a bitter polemic between the two countries in which President Habib Bourguiba had accused China of seeking 'to provoke difficulties, to aggravate existing contradictions, to arm and train guerrillas against the existing [African] regimes'.[52] The KGB reported that the polemic had been fuelled by a bogus Chinese letter, fabricated by Service A, which was sent to Bourguiba's son containing personal threats against him as well as attacking the regime.[53] While KGB active measures may have reinforced President Bourguiba's suspicions of

China, however, they are unlikely to have been at the root of them. Though Kenya did not break off relations with the PRC, it expelled four Chinese officials in two years, the last of them the chargé d'affaires, Li Chieh, who was declared persona non grata in June 1967.[54] Though not publicly stated, the main reason for the expulsions was the PRC's support for the left-wing Deputy President of the ruling KANU Party, Oginga Odinga, who had secretly told the Chinese in 1964 that President Jomo Kenyatta should be overthrown.[55] Odinga, who had also been courted by the Russians,[56] was replaced as Deputy President in 1966 and lost a trial of strength with Kenyatta over the next year. As evidence of Chinese machinations, Kenyan newspapers published extracts from an inflammatory pamphlet entitled 'New [Chinese] Diplomats Will Bring the Great Proletarian Cultural Revolution to Africa'. Though published in the name of the New China News Agency, the pamphlet appears to have been forged.[57] The most likely forger was Service A. Fabrications designed to discredit the Chinese in West Africa included a pamphlet attacking the regime of President Léopold Senghor in Senegal supposedly issued by pro-Chinese Senegalese Communists and bogus information about Chinese plots which was sent to Senghor's government. On the basis of such active measures, the KGB claimed the credit for the expulsion from Senegal in 1968 of two New China News Agency correspondents.[58] In neighbouring Mali the KGB reported also in 1968 that it had brought about the dismissal of the Minister of Information after an active-measures operation, codenamed ALLIGATOR, had compromised him as a Chinese stooge.[59] There can have been few long-serving African leaders who were not at various times fed fabricated evidence of both Chinese and CIA conspiracies against them. Occasionally, however, the fabrications were based on fact – as in the case of the evidence of Chinese plots communicated to President Mobutu.[60] After the later improvement of relations between the PRC and Zaire, Mao personally told Mobutu during his visit to Beijing, 'I wasted a lot of money and arms trying to overthrow you.' 'Well, you backed the wrong man,' replied Mobutu.[61] The case of Mobutu illustrates the complexity of KGB active measures in some African states. As well as being warned of Chinese plots against him, other active measures spread stories of his collaboration with the CIA.[62]

The undoubted decline of Chinese influence in Africa during the mid- and late 1960s, however, was due less to Soviet active measures than to the excesses of the Cultural Revolution. Beginning in 1966, experienced ambassadors were withdrawn from Africa, often to be paraded in dunces' hats and abused by Red Guards in Beijing, leaving in charge of PRC embassies fanatics who engaged in hysterical public adulation of Chairman Mao and denunciations of his opponents. Huge quantities of Mao's writings and portraits flooded some African capitals. In Mali, for example, an estimated 4 million copies of Mao's *Little Red Book* were distributed – one per head of the population. And yet not a single African leader publicly echoed Chinese attacks on the Soviet leadership.[63]

As elsewhere in the Third World, the KGB's greatest successes in African intelligence collection were probably obtained through SIGINT rather than HUMINT. Between 1960 and 1967 the number of states whose communications were decrypted by the KGB Eighth Directorate increased from fifty-one to seventy-two.[64] The increase was doubtless due in part to the growing number of independent African states. Because of the comparative lack of sophistication of their cipher systems, many were, without realizing it, conducting open diplomacy so far as the KGB and other of the world's major SIGINT agencies were concerned. The small SIGINT section of the Rhodesian Central Intelligence Organization, for example, found little difficulty in breaking the codes of its neighbours – except for South Africa which, like the Soviet Union, used the theoretically unbreakable one-time pad for its diplomatic traffic as well as state-of-the-art cipher technology.[65] The work of Soviet codebreakers was simplified by the KGB's recruitment of cipher personnel at African embassies around the world.[66]

The hardest African target for agent penetration as well as for SIGINT was probably the Republic of South Africa, where the KGB lacked either a legal residency or any other secure operational base.[67] In April 1971, however, a senior military counter-intelligence officer, subsequently codenamed MARIO, contacted the KGB residency in Lusaka and offered information about the South African intelligence community. A certain indication of the importance attached to MARIO by the FCD was that it briefed both Andropov and Brezhnev personally on him. Over the next two years his KGB case officers had meetings with him in Zambia, Mauritius, Austria and East Germany. His military intelligence was also highly rated by the

GRU. In 1973, however, it was discovered that MARIO had left military counter-intelligence some time before he approached the Lusaka residency. The fact that he successfully deceived the KGB for two years is evidence of its lack of other sources able to provide reliable information on South African intelligence.[68]

Until the mid-1970s Moscow had only modest expectations of the prospects for national liberation movements in sub-Saharan Africa. The Soviet Union had maintained contact with the [South] African National Congress (ANC), mostly through the South African Communist Party (SACP), since the 1920s. In 1961 the SACP's influence in the liberation movement was increased by the decision of the ANC, which had been banned a year earlier, to abandon its previous insistence on an exclusively non-violent campaign. The ANC and SACP co-operated in founding Umkhonto we Sizwe ('Spear of the Nation') to begin an armed struggle. Unlike the ANC, Umkhonto, which was supplied with Soviet arms and military training, was multiracial and thus open to SACP members, many of whom were of non-African ethnic origin. In 1963 the Soviet Presidium instructed Vladimir Semichastny, the KGB Chairman, to begin transmitting secret subsidies to the ANC – initially $300,000 a year – in addition to the traditional payments to the SACP, then running at $56,000.[69]

Despite Soviet assistance, however, the first fifteen years of Umkhonto operations posed no significant threat to the South African apartheid regime. By the mid-1960s, most leading ANC and SACP militants had been imprisoned or forced into exile. The SACP leadership, based mainly in London, had lost touch with those Party members who remained in South Africa.[70] In 1969, after long and heated debate, the ANC agreed to admit anti-apartheid South African exiles of all ethnic backgrounds, thus opening its doors to an influx of SACP members. Moscow also welcomed the ANC decision to set up a multiracial Revolutionary Council to direct Umkhonto's armed struggle, with Oliver Tambo, the ANC Chairman (in exile in Tanzania), as its head and Yusuf Dadoo, the SACP Chairman (in London), as his deputy. When the Tanzanian government began to object to the growing ANC military presence on its territory, Umkhonto was evacuated to the Soviet Union and remained there for several years.[71]

The Zimbabwe African People's Union (ZAPU), founded in late

1961, and the rival Zimbabwe African National Union (ZANU), which broke away from ZAPU in 1963, had for the first decade of their existence no greater success in their struggle against Ian Smith's white-settler regime in Rhodesia, which declared itself independent of Britain in 1965. Moscow chose what proved to be the less successful faction. Robert Mugabe, the Marxist leader of ZANU, who was to become the first Prime Minister of independent Zimbabwe in 1980, committed the unforgivable sin of describing himself as a 'Marxist-Leninist of Maoist thought'. The Kremlin therefore backed ZAPU, led by the 'bourgeois nationalist' Joshua Nkomo, who was arrested in 1964 and spent the next decade in prison while his chief lieutenants bickered among themselves. In 1967 ZAPU formed a military alliance with the ANC but suffered serious losses after the entry into the conflict of helicopter-borne South African police forces on the side of the Rhodesian security forces. During the early 1970s ZAPU operations posed little threat to the Rhodesian security forces and its military alliance with the ANC disintegrated.[72]

Like Umkhonto in South Africa, the Angolan Movimento Popular de Libertação de Angola (MPLA) began its armed struggle against Portuguese colonial rule in 1961.[73] In 1962, the Centre instructed the residency in Leopoldville (later renamed Kinshasa) to establish secret contact with a member of the MPLA leadership, Agostinho Neto, a protégé of the Portuguese Communist leader Álvaro Cunhal, a hard-line Soviet loyalist who in 1968 was to be the first Western Party leader to support the crushing of the Prague Spring.[74] Oleg Ivanovich Nazhestkin, the KGB officer who met Neto in Leopoldville, where he was living in exile, wrote later that he had expected to encounter a 'dashing, decisive commander' but found instead a shy, mild-mannered intellectual who spoke slowly and became lost in thought for long periods before suddenly producing a lucid analysis of the issues under discussion. Though uncompromisingly hostile to the United States and Western imperialism, Neto seemed uncertain about the MPLA's political aims. He told Nazhestkin:

Our programme sets just, humane, noble, but too distant goals. Now is not the time to be talking about the creation of elements of a communist society in the conditions of African reality. The main task is to produce as broadly based a union as possible of patriotic forces, first and foremost within Angola ... And what is communism [in African conditions]? Help me to come to grips with this question. After all, you're a communist and you must understand it well. Help me to obtain the necessary literature.

Though impressed by Neto's honesty and commitment to Angolan liberation, Nazhestkin was left wondering whether he had the self-belief required to lead an 'uncompromising armed struggle'.[75] Neto, however, retained the strong backing of Cunhal, who arranged for him to visit the Soviet Union in 1964. Following his visit, Moscow publicly announced its support for the MPLA. Neto paid further visits to the Soviet Union in 1966 and 1967.[76]

The Frente de Libertação de Moçambique (FRELIMO), led by the US-educated Eduardo Mondlane, was slower to pose a threat to Portuguese rule in Mozambique than the MPLA in Angola and did not begin guerrilla warfare until 1964. Though the Centre was unimpressed by Mondlane, it had more confidence in a younger member of the FRELIMO leadership, codenamed TSOM, until recently a student in Paris. TSOM was given military training in the Soviet Union in 1965, and thereafter maintained contact with the International Department of the Central Committee on behalf of FRELIMO as well as with the KGB. In 1970 a proposal by the Centre to recruit him as an agent was vetoed by the International Department but he remained a KGB confidential contact who provided information on FRELIMO and Mozambique.[77]

Early in 1967 a four-man interdepartmental mission of enquiry – two from the International Department, a senior diplomat and Vadim Kirpichenko representing the KGB – set off from Moscow to gather information in Dar-es-Salaam, Lusaka and elsewhere on the progress of the national liberation movements in Portuguese Africa. Kirpichenko, as Nazhestkin had been six years earlier, was intrigued by his discussions with Neto but left with mixed feelings:

Neto would constantly shift conversations about the internal situation in Angola – the positions of various parties and prospects for their unification into a single movement, specific MPLA military actions – to the external aspects of the Angolan problem, which we already knew about. At the same time Neto made no attempt to exaggerate the merits of his party and was quite moderate with regard to the assistance expected from us. The impression left by the meetings with him was pleasant, and were it not for the colour of his skin, one might have taken Neto for a somewhat phlegmatic European rather than a temperamental African.[78]

In July 1967, after receiving the report of the mission of enquiry, the Politburo instructed the KGB to provide training for the 'progressive nationalist organizations' fighting for independence in Portugal's African colonies: the MPLA, FRELIMO, and a smaller guerrilla group in Guinea-Bissau, the Partido Africano da Independência da Guiné e Cabo Verde (PAIGC).[79]

The Centre was initially dismayed by the quality of the FRELIMO guerrillas. Between 1966 and 1970 the KGB provided training for twenty-one specialist FRELIMO saboteurs, but found all of them ideologically 'primitive' and ignorant of the Soviet Union save as a source of arms and money.[80] Serious divisions within FRELIMO's ranks led in 1968 to riots in Dar-es-Salaam, the sacking of its offices, the killing of one of its Central Committee, and the closure of the FRELIMO school. In the following year Mondlane was assassinated by a parcel bomb delivered by FRELIMO dissidents. The Centre undoubtedly welcomed his replacement as head of FRELIMO by Samora Machel, whose aim was to make Mozambique 'Africa's first Marxist state'. Machel claimed that his Marxist convictions derived 'not from writing in a book. Nor from reading Marx and Engels. But from seeing my father forced to grow cotton and going with him to the market where he was to sell it at a low price – much lower than the Portuguese grower.'[81]

While FRELIMO was locked in an internal power struggle, the MPLA had emerged as a significant threat to Portuguese rule, though its claims to control one-third of Angola were greatly exaggerated. Following Neto's election as MPLA President in 1969, the MPLA was riven by internal disputes similar to those which had previously disrupted FRELIMO. Reports reached the Centre from supposedly 'reliable sources' that Neto was embezzling Soviet funds and salting them away in a Swiss bank account. His first case officer, Oleg Nazhestkin, tried to defend Neto against these charges:

'Allow me to point out,' I said, 'that as a condition of our assistance we demanded of Neto that no more than one to two individuals within the MPLA should know about it, that only he should personally decide all questions linked with our assistance. And where is he supposed to keep the hard-currency funds, in his desk drawer or in a knapsack on his back during trips out to the liberated regions?'[82]

During the early 1970s Portuguese intelligence reported, somewhat prematurely, that the MPLA no longer represented a military threat. There is some evidence that by 1973 Moscow was shifting support to the MPLA eastern commander, Daniel Chipendra, who had emerged as a challenger to Neto's leadership. Soviet support for the MPLA was reduced to a trickle.[83] FRELIMO, by contrast, had largely recovered from its earlier infighting. In 1973 it forced the closing of Gorongosa National Park, world famous as a big-game hunting ground for wealthy tourists.[84] Simultaneously, Machel led a FRELIMO delegation to Moscow.[85] The Dar-es-Salaam residency maintained covert contact with both Machel and TSOM.[86]

The Centre's principal hopes of influence in sub-Saharan Africa in the early 1970s, however, were centred on Somalia. In October 1969 Somalia's unpopular civilian government was toppled by a military coup which established a Supreme Revolutionary Council (SRC), composed of officers and headed by the army commander General Muhammad Siad Barre. The KGB residency was given advance notice of the coup (codenamed KONKORD) by one of the chief plotters, codenamed KERL, who had visited Moscow and became a member of the SRC.[87] According to KERL's file, he continued after the coup to influence Siad Barre along lines approved by the KGB.[88] Though Mitrokhin's notes give no details, KERL may have had – or at least told the KGB that he had – some influence on Siad Barre's early decision to invite the Soviet navy to visit Somali ports and his simultaneous expulsion of the whole of the American Peace Corps and half the US embassy staff.

The SRC suspended the constitution, abolished the National Assembly, banned political parties and renamed the country the Somali Democratic Republic (SDR). Though poorly educated and little acquainted with Marxism, Siad Barre declared on the first anniversary of the coup that the new regime would be based on 'scientific socialism'. On public occasions, the streets were festooned with heroic images of himself as the 'Victorious Leader', flanked by portraits of Marx and Lenin. The Victorious Leader's notion of 'scientific socialism', however, was somewhat eccentric. Siad Barre claimed to have synthesized Marx with Islam, and produced a little blue-and-white book reminiscent of Mao's little red book, which contained a platitudinous mixture of pontifications and exhortations. In 1971 he announced that the SDR was to be transformed into a one-party state, an ambition eventually fulfilled with the creation of the Somali Revolutionary Socialist Party (SRSP) five years later.[89]

The Centre had far greater confidence in KERL than in Siad Barre. Such was his importance in KGB eyes that during visits to Moscow he had discussions with Andropov, KGB Vice-Chairman Semyon Tsvigun and Brezhnev. KERL was used for a considerable variety of KGB operations: among them a meeting with Muammar al-Qaddafi in Tripoli at the Mogadishu residency's request in 1969 as part of an influence operation; the expulsion of five US diplomats in the spring of 1970 and the cancellation of a visit by the US navy to Mogadishu; active-measures articles in the Somali press; and the purchase for Moscow of US and other Western technology whose export to the Soviet Union was banned under COCOM regulations.[90] KERL's motives were both ideological and mercenary. After obtaining US technology from an Italian source for onward transmission to Moscow in 1972, he was given $5,000.[91] KERL's fellow member of the SRC, Lieutenant-Colonel Salah Gaveire Kedie (codenamed OPERATOR), who had trained at the Frunze Military Academy in Moscow, was recruited as a KGB agent. In 1971, however, Gaveire Kedie was accused with Vice-President Muhammad Ainanche of plotting Siad Barre's assassination. Both were found guilty of treason and executed in public.[92]

The most obvious influence of the KGB on the newly established Somali Democratic Republic was its guiding role in setting up the National Security Service (NSS), headed by Siad Barre's son-in-law Ahmad Sulaymaan Abdullah, which had what the police chief Jama Muhammad Ghalib later acknowledged were 'unlimited powers of search, arrest, detention without trial and torture . . . The promotion of Siad Barre's slogans and the harassment of dissidents, real and imagined, soon became daily routine.'[93] The Centre doubtless failed to appreciate the brutal irony of the arrest of the KGB agent Gaveire Kedie by the Somali security service it had trained. It was, however, able to feed disinformation to the NSS, designed to exacerbate its distrust of the United States. With the assistance of Service A, the Mogadishu residency concocted reports that the CIA was collecting intelligence on the Somali army to pass on to Ethiopia, with which Somalia was in conflict over the Somali-speaking Ethiopian region of Ogaden. The KGB claimed that the purpose of a visit by the US ambassador with a member of the CIA station in Mogadishu to Addis Ababa in the spring of 1972 was to pass on this intelligence.[94]

Later in 1972 Andropov made a personal tour of inspection in Somalia – a certain indication of the importance which he attached to it as a field of KGB operations. In 1973 he invited Sulaymaan for talks in Moscow. By 1974 there were approximately 3,600 Soviet advisers in Somalia, about 1,600 of them military personnel. On 11 July 1974 the Soviet Union and Somalia signed a Treaty of Friendship and Co-operation, the first between Moscow and a black African state, which gave the Soviet fleet access to the strategic port of Berbera. By 1976 Soviet military aid had turned little Somalia into the fourth most heavily armed state in sub-Saharan Africa (after the far larger Nigeria, Zaire and Ethiopia). In a speech to the Twenty-fifth Congress of the CPSU in Moscow in February 1976, Siad Barre declared that Somalia was 'an inseparable part of the world revolutionary movement'. Somalia's place within the Soviet orbit, however, was less secure than his rhetoric suggested. Muslim Somali-speakers had historically seen themselves as of Arab descent, and in 1974 Somalia joined the Arab League, sponsored by Saudi Arabia, one of Moscow's *bêtes noires*. The Somali 'revolution' progressed little beyond the level of revolutionary rhetoric. Though most of Moscow's doubts were expressed in private, one Soviet commentator observed publicly in 1976 that, despite some Somali nationalizations, 'the activity of the private sector did not lessen'.[95] Castro reported after a visit to Somalia in March 1977 that 'The power and influence of the rightist group continue to increase. The Interior Minister [and security chief], Sulaymaan, is doing everything possible to bring Somalia closer to Saudi Arabia and the imperialist countries.'[96] Soon afterwards the Soviet Union effectively abandoned the position it had built up in Somalia in favour of what seemed to be more promising prospects elsewhere in the Horn of Africa.

25

From Optimism to Disillusion

By the mid-1970s the KGB's main hopes of African revolution
were centred on the former Portuguese colonies of Angola and
Mozambique. In Angola, the richest of Portugal's colonies, the end
of Portuguese rule was followed by civil war in which the Marxist
Movimento Popular de Libertação de Angola (MPLA) was opposed
by the non-Marxist Frente Nacional de Libertação de Angola
(FNLA) and União Nacional para a Independência Total de Angola
(UNITA), which had different regional strongholds.[1] In the early
1970s, save for a hard core of Neto supporters among the Centre's
Africanists, Moscow had largely lost confidence in his leadership of
the MPLA. As Neto later acknowledged, the loss of most Soviet
support had brought the MPLA to the verge of defeat.[2] After the
'Revolution of the Red Carnations' in Portugal in April 1974, however, the Portuguese Communist leader and pro-Soviet loyalist,
Álvaro Cunhal, who joined a socialist-led coalition government,
urged Moscow to resume arms deliveries to the MPLA.[3] Failure to
do so might result in the victory of the FNLA, which had earlier
been supported by both the United States and China, and of UNITA,
which had also had Chinese backing in the past and would shortly
win support from South Africa. KGB residencies in Algiers, Bamako,
Brazzaville, Dakar, Dar-es-Salaam, Lusaka, Mogadishu, Nairobi
and Rabat were urgently instructed to send agents and confidential
contacts to Angola and Mozambique to obtain first-hand information on the situation.[4]

In December 1974 the Politburo approved proposals to supply
the MPLA with heavy weapons and ammunition through Congo
(Brazzaville). The Soviet ambassador in Brazzaville, however,
warned against the dangers of becoming embroiled in a civil war
in which, he predicted, US and Chinese support would give the

'reactionaries' of the FNLA and UNITA the upper hand. Moscow threw its weight instead behind attempts by African leaders to persuade the three Angolan liberation movements to join in negotiations with the Portuguese for an orderly transfer of power. These negotiations led to the Alvor Agreement of January 1975 by which Portugal agreed to hand over power on 11 November to a coalition government of MPLA, FNLA and UNITA representatives. None of the three groups, however, took the idea of a coalition government seriously, and from early spring Castro, a strong personal supporter of Neto, put increasing pressure on Moscow to provide armed support for the MPLA. By early summer about 250 Cuban officers had been sent to Angola, where they functioned as a kind of general staff for Neto in planning operations as well as training MPLA forces. Castro looked upon Angola as an opportunity both to establish himself as a great revolutionary leader on the world stage and to revive flagging revolutionary fervour at home. In July President Ford and his 'Forty Committee', which oversaw covert action, authorized large-scale CIA covert support for the FNLA and UNITA through Zaire and Zambia, both hostile to the MPLA. In early August the first South African forces crossed into southern Angola. By the middle of the month, the MPLA was on the defensive, retreating towards the capital, Luanda.[5]

Castro responded by sending a personal appeal to Brezhnev for large-scale support for the MPLA and despatching the first Cuban combat troops to Luanda in the autumn. Many in Moscow, however, continued to see Neto as a maverick. The Soviet Deputy Foreign Minister, Vasili Kuznetsov, said privately in 1975, 'We only need him for a certain period. We know he's been sick . . . And psychologically he's not all that reliable.'[6] The Politburo, like the Foreign Ministry, was reluctant to take the risks of full-scale involvement in the Angolan civil war, and clung to the unrealistic hope that the Alvor Agreement could be resuscitated and the three liberation movements persuaded to settle their differences.[7] The task of conveying this message to Neto was entrusted in October not to a diplomat but to his first case officer, Oleg Nazhestkin, then head of the FCD Angolan desk. Before he left, Nazhestkin was urged by both the Foreign Ministry and the International Department, whose views he found 'narrow and blinkered', to 'convince' Neto of the advantages of uniting with the FNLA and UNITA – a policy which Nazhestkin himself believed was wholly impracticable. By the time Nazhestkin reached Brazzaville *en route* for Luanda, however, the intensification of the civil war had produced a change of heart in Moscow – despite continued scepticism in the Foreign Ministry.[8] An FCD report to the Politburo, countersigned by Viktor Chebrikov, Deputy Chairman of the KGB, warned that without outside support the MPLA would be unable to hold on to Luanda. A telegram from the Centre authorized Nazhestkin to tell Neto that the Soviet Union was prepared to open diplomatic relations on 11 November with an MPLA government which contained no FNLA or UNITA representatives and to give it military assistance. Nazhestkin flew from Brazzaville to Luanda on 2 November and found a city under siege. On arrival he was driven to the Tivoli Hotel, where the MPLA's foreign supporters were housed free of charge and fed with bean soup once a day. Nazhestkin's first problem was to find Neto, who had not been warned of his arrival and was living at a secret location outside Luanda, protected by Cuban troops. A *Pravda* reporter staying in the Tivoli, however, knew some of the Cuban military mission, had recently interviewed Neto and drove Nazhestkin to Neto's head-quarters. Though it was the middle of the night, Neto was still at work in his office and asked him whether he had come to make another attempt to persuade him to 'unite with the enemies of the Angolan revolution'. Nazhestkin decided that unless he was frank he would not recover Neto's trust. There were, he admitted, officials in the Foreign Ministry and International Department who had asked him to do precisely that before he had left Moscow, but wiser counsels had since prevailed and he was authorized to offer an independent MPLA government full support. Neto shed what Nazhestkin describes as a few 'manly' tears of joy, then told him, 'Finally, finally, we've been understood. That means we will work together, work together and struggle together. The Cubans, dear friends, are helping us, but without the Soviet Union it was very, very difficult for us. Now we are sure to be victorious.' The two men carried on talking until daybreak.[9]

A massive Soviet airlift of Cuban troops and Soviet arms made it possible to turn the tide of the civil war. The withdrawal of US support for the MPLA's opponents was of equal importance. On 13 December, CIA covert action in Angola suddenly ceased to be covert. A front-page story in the *New York Times* revealed both the scale of the Agency's operation to support the FNLA and UNITA and the fact that five months earlier Nathaniel Davis, Assistant Secretary for African Affairs at the State Department, had resigned in protest against it. Congress responded by voting to cut off all US covert assistance to any faction in Angola. For the first time in American history a President was forced to stop a covert operation abroad to which he was personally committed. In an angry off-the-record briefing, Henry Kissinger condemned Ford for allowing Congress to ride roughshod over his foreign policy.[10] The CIA's humiliation was greeted with jubilation in the Centre. According to the senior Soviet diplomat (and later defector), Arkadi Shevchenko, Moscow drew the conclusion that 'the United States lacked will in Africa', just as it had lost the will to fight in Vietnam: 'After its humiliation in Vietnam in 1975, America was increasingly portrayed by Party militants as a diminished rival in the Third World. Although some experts took a more cautious line, the Soviet leaders judged that, in addition to the "Vietnam syndrome", the United States now had an "Angola syndrome".'[11] Neto made the same analogy. He declared on 27 July 1976: 'Our fight must go on until FNLA is defeated as the Americans were in Vietnam.'[12] Success in Angola was later to make Moscow much more willing than it would other-wise have been to intervene in Ethiopia.

Though the FNLA virtually collapsed after the withdrawal of US backing, UNITA was able to continue fighting from its tribal homeland in south-eastern Angola with support from South Africa, which was terrified by the prospect of having a Soviet satellite on its doorstep. UNITA's alliance with the apartheid regime represented an enormous propaganda victory for both Moscow and the MPLA. At the OAU summit in January 1976, member states were initially deeply split over which side to recognize in the Angolan civil war. When it was revealed that South African forces were fighting alongside UNITA, however, its African backers faded away. On 10 February 1976 the OAU officially recognized the People's Republic of Angola.[13]

Huge amounts of Soviet propaganda as well as arms were airlifted to Angola, among them a plane-load of brochures of Brezhnev's speech to the Twenty-fifth (1976) Party Congress and two plane-loads of anti-Mao pamphlets. The Soviet embassy in Luanda claimed unconvincingly that it had put this turgid material to good use, but must have found it difficult to dispose of sets of Lenin's collected works which were mistakenly sent in French rather than Portuguese translation. By the summer of 1976 the embassy had run out of Lenin portraits and dutifully requested further supplies from Moscow.[14] To help Neto control dissent, advisers from the East German Stasi set up a brutal security service, the Direção de Informação e Segurança de Angola (DISA), under his personal control, which carried out repeated purges of his opponents, real and imagined.[15]

In October 1976, Neto visited Moscow to sign a Treaty of Friendship and Co-operation with the Soviet Union, pledging both signatories to mutual military co-operation and giving Soviet forces the right to use Angolan airports and Luanda harbour. 'Soviet aid', Neto declared, 'has been the key factor in our historical development, in achieving independence and in the country's reconstruction.'[16] While Moscow publicly hailed Neto as a hero, he continued to be distrusted in both the Foreign Ministry and the International Department. Though the Luanda residency maintained private contact with Neto, probably its most important source for monitoring Neto's militant intentions in 1976 was a female political assistant. Codenamed VOMUS by the KGB, she became a confidential contact of the Luanda residency, which claimed that she exerted a 'favourable' – doubtless pro-Soviet – influence over Neto and others in the MPLA leadership, probably in countering Maoist ideology. In June 1977, however, she was arrested, probably because she sympathized with an almost successful coup by the MPLA Minister of the Interior, Nito Alves, a more orthodox pro-Soviet Marxist, and the chief political commissar in the armed forces, José Van Dúnem.[17] Moscow's reaction to the coup was hesitant. Doubtless to Neto's indignation, it waited four days before condemning the plotters. The most likely explanation is that it had decided to see who emerged victorious before choosing sides but, like VOMUS, would not have been displeased if Neto had been replaced at the head of the MPLA.[18]

Oleg Nazhestkin is adamant that Neto was unfairly dealt with by the Party bureaucrats of the International Department 'who wanted to make Neto into an obedient instrument of their own not always well-conceived policy for building socialism in Africa':

He was not an obedient figure in the hands of our party apparatchiks. He always had his own opinion, his own views on how to operate, how to conduct the struggle, how to act in one or another case. And these opinions of his were far from always coinciding with ours, but he knew how to uphold his own positions. He did not understand, for example, why it was necessary to engage in empty anti-imperialist chatter, to come out with declarations in support of Soviet foreign policy, certain actions of which he, incidentally, did not always agree with, and constantly to sign his name under various appeals and addresses, many of which did not have a concrete, realistic meaning.[19]

Like Moscow, the Soviet embassy in Luanda had greater faith in Nito Alves,[20] and also regretted that his coup had failed. Neto several times complained to Nazhestkin that the International Department was rummaging through his 'dirty linen', trying to find compromising material to use against him.[21]

In contrast to the war of liberation in Angola, in which the MPLA had to contend with the rival FNLA and UNITA, the only movement which fought against Portuguese rule in Mozambique was the Frente de Libertação de Moçambique (FRELIMO). In September 1974 FRELIMO and the Portuguese revolutionary government in Lisbon signed an accord providing for independence in June 1975. Two months after the accord, posing as an *Izvestia* correspondent, the KGB officer Boris Pavlovich Fetisov arrived in Mozambique on a tour of inspection.[22] The KGB and the Stasi were the dominant influences in the formation in 1975 of Samora Machel's brutal security service, the Serviço Nacional de Segurança Popular (SNASP), which began a reign of terror against Machel's opponents real and imagined. The equally brutal Resistência Nacional Moçambicana (RENAMO), originally created by the Rhodesian Central Intelligence Organization (CIO) in 1977, was able to exploit widespread rural opposition to the FRELIMO regime in a long drawn-out civil war.[23]

The collapse of the Portuguese Empire inaugurated what the Tanzanian President Julius Nyerere called the 'second scramble' for Africa. Moscow's enthusiasm for the scramble greatly exceeded that of Washington. During the five-year period beginning in January 1976, the value of Soviet arms transfers to black Africa was to total almost $4 billion, ten times the value of US arms supplies.[24] The emergence of Soviet-backed Marxist regimes in Angola and

Mozambique, together with the CIA's humiliation in Angola, persuaded Andropov to order a major stepping up of the KGB's African operations. In August 1976 the FCD informed its African residencies:

One of the main requirements which SVIRIDOV [Andropov] has demanded for our work in Africa consists of directing the residencies towards major political problems. This means working more persistently to undermine the position of the Americans and British in Africa, and to strengthen Soviet influence on the continent. It is necessary to establish firm positions and channels of influence within the ruling circles, governments and intelligence services, in order to obtain reliable prognoses concerning the situation in the country and the region as a whole, and on the activities of the Americans, the British and the Chinese, and to carry out wide-ranging measures against them.[25]

Andropov's optimism on the prospects for undermining US and British influence in Africa and for advancing that of the Soviet Union derived not merely from the establishment of Marxist-Leninist one-party states in Angola and Mozambique but also from increasing evidence that Ethiopia was following in the same direction.[26]

The pro-Western regime in Ethiopia collapsed at almost the same moment as the Portuguese Empire. On 12 September 1974 Haile Selassie, Emperor of Ethiopia, Elect of God and Conquering Lion of the Tribe of Judah, was arrested by Lieutenant-Colonel Mengistu Haile Mariam and a group of young army officers and taken off to prison in the back seat of a Volkswagen. Haile Selassie was later placed under house arrest in his palace where, a year later, he was strangled, probably by Mengistu himself, and buried beneath a latrine in the palace garden.[27] Power passed to a military junta known as the Derg (Amharic for committee). Radio Moscow declared that the changes in Ethiopia were 'not just an ordinary military coup'.[28] *Pravda* praised the revolutionary implications of the land nationalization of 1975. But when the Derg asked for Soviet arms later in the year, Moscow temporized and hinted that the presence of 'pro-Western' members of the Derg made such a decision difficult.[29] On 20 April 1976 the Derg announced a detailed political programme, the 'National Democratic Revolution', which formed the basis of a working alliance with the pro-Soviet Marxist MEI-

SON (an Amharic acronym for All Ethiopian Socialist Movement) dedicated to the creation of a 'people's democratic republic'. Despite this optimistic rhetoric, however, Ethiopia itself seemed on the verge of disintegration, with separatist movements in several border provinces, a series of local rebellions elsewhere and several thousand arrests in Addis Ababa for counter-revolutionary activity. At this critical moment, when Ethiopia was close to civil war, the Derg found crucial support in Moscow. The visit by a high-level Derg delegation to Moscow in July 1976 was followed five months later by a secret agreement for the supply of Soviet arms.[30]

Mengistu, meanwhile, had consolidated his power within the Derg by murdering, one by one, his rivals both real and imagined.[31] In September 1976 the Derg announced the introduction of summary execution for 'counter-revolutionaries'. Mengistu's paranoid tendencies were further inflamed by an attempt on his life in October. Moscow was unfazed by the bloodbath which followed. *Pravda* reported that, faced with an inevitable 'intensification of the class struggle', the progressive government in Addis Ababa was successfully 'liquidating counter-revolutionary bands' with the support of the mass of Ethiopian society.[32] In a speech on 17 April 1977 Mengistu launched a frenzied attack on the 'enemies of the revolution', and in an extraordinary piece of paranoid theatre broke three glass flagons containing what appeared to be blood. The broken flagons and the blood spilled from them symbolized, he declared, the three enemies which the revolution must exterminate: imperialism, feudalism and capitalism. A month later the Save the Children Fund reported that the supposedly counter-revolutionary victims of Mengistu's bloodbath included not merely adults but 1,000 or more children, mostly aged between eleven and thirteen, whose bodies had been left lying in the streets of Addis Ababa. Amnesty International later estimated that a total of half a million people perished during the Red Terror of 1977 and 1978. The families of the victims were frequently required to pay the cost of the bullets which had killed them.[33]

Mengistu's paranoid strain was easily exploited by KGB active measures designed to exacerbate his fears of CIA plots against him. Operation FAKEL used a series of bogus documents supposedly emanating from the CIA station in Nairobi (in reality almost certainly concocted by Service A) to reveal a non-existent imperialist plot involving Sudan, Saudi Arabia, Somalia, Egypt and Kenya as well as the United States to overthrow the Mengistu regime, assassinate its leaders and invade Ethiopia from both Sudan and Kenya. Doubtless to the delight of the Centre, in September 1977 an agitated Mengistu personally appealed to the Soviet ambassador in Addis Ababa for 'the necessary political and military support at this critical moment' to deal with the plot. The ambassador succeeded in keeping a straight face throughout his meeting with Mengistu and passed on the request to Moscow.[34]

Moscow had hoped to avoid having to choose between the two rival self-proclaimed Marxist regimes in the Horn of Africa, believing that, as arms supplier to both Ethiopia and Somalia, it would be in a position to broker a settlement between the two. In March a Soviet proposal for a Marxist-Leninist confederation of Ethiopia, Somalia, South Yemen and Djibouti (which was due to become independent in June) was welcomed by Mengistu but rejected by Siad.[35] The Somalis had already begun to support a liberation movement in south-eastern Ethiopia. In June 1977, frightened by the Soviet supply of arms to Ethiopia and gambling on the prospect of US military support, Mogadishu launched an invasion which pushed deep into Ethiopian territory. Forced to decide between Ethiopia and Somalia, Moscow opted for Ethiopia. Its motives had more to do with realpolitik than with ideology. Ethiopia had ten times the population of Somalia and an even more important strategic location commanding sea-lanes for oil shipments from the Persian Gulf to the West.[36] In July 1977 the Soviet Union withdrew its 1,000 advisers from Somalia. In November Somalia announced that it had abrogated its Treaty of Friendship and Co-operation with the Soviet Union and that it had suspended diplomatic relations with Cuba.[37]

Though the Somali invasion enabled Mengistu to mobilize support for the war from virtually all sections of Ethiopian society, without massive military aid from the Soviet Union and its allies the Derg could not have survived.[38] At the height of Soviet arms deliveries to Ethiopia during the winter of 1977–78, at a critical point in its war with Somalia, Soviet military transport aircraft reportedly landed every twenty minutes over a period of three months. An estimated 225 planes were involved in an operation co-ordinated via a Soviet military reconnaissance satellite. Simultaneously, 17,000 Cuban forces were airlifted from Angola to join 1,000 Soviet military advisers and 400 East Germans who were training intelligence and internal security units.[39] By March 1978 the Somalis had suffered a decisive defeat. Among the KGB agents apparently alienated by Soviet support for Mengistu was RASHID, one of Somalia's leading journalists whose contacts included Siad Barre. Mitrokhin's notes record the strenuous efforts by the KGB to maintain his allegiance:

In 1978, the residency drilled into RASHID the elementary facts that only the USSR advocated international détente and peaceful co-existence and supported Arab interests. The political errors of the Somali leadership in solving territorial disputes with Ethiopia and Kenya were pointed out to him, the true position in the area of the Horn of Africa was outlined and he was shown the aggressive nature of US policy relating to the solution of this problem, and the role of Saudi Arabia, as the spear-head of the struggle against the National Liberation Movement on the African continent.

RASHID seems to have been unconvinced, and contact with him was broken off.[40]

Mengistu's loyalty to Moscow, by contrast, appeared complete. Every May Day, his troops paraded through Addis Ababa under giant portraits of Lenin. Even years later in exile after the fall of the Soviet Union, Mengistu recalled nostalgically the first time Brezhnev had enfolded him in a bear hug: 'From that moment Brezhnev was like a father to me. We met another twelve times, always in the Soviet Union. Each time, before telling him about our problems, I would say, "Comrade Leonid, I am your son, I owe you everything." And I truly felt that Brezhnev was like a father.'

On 12 September 1978, the fourth anniversary of the overthrow of Haile Selassie, Mengistu presided over the celebrations enthroned in solitary splendour in a gilded chair upholstered in red velvet. While Fidel Castro, as guest of honour, sat in an armchair to his right, the other members of the Derg, for the first time at an official occasion, were relegated to the side-stands. Castro's presence appeared to consecrate Mengistu's dictatorship. Both Havana and Moscow turned a blind eye to the bloodbath which was one of the distinguishing features, under his leadership, of the People's Democratic Republic of Ethiopia.[41] At least one of the KGB's most valuable contacts in Addis Ababa, DYUK, however, told the residency that he blamed the Soviet Union for propping up Mengistu's brutal dictatorship.[42]

The sudden and dramatic rise of Marxist regimes in Angola, Mozambique, Guinea-Bissau and Ethiopia gave new impetus to the attempt to overthrow Ian Smith's white-settler regime in Rhodesia. Moscow continued to back ZAPU, led by Joshua Nkomo, who was released from prison in 1974, rather than Mugabe's ZANU. Though Nkomo was no Marxist, he took a prominent part in Soviet front organizations as a member of the Executive of the Afro-Asian Peoples' Solidarity Organization (AAPSO) and later Vice-President of the World Peace Council.[43] Mitrokhin's incomplete and fragmentary notes on ZAPU identify nine KGB penetrations, at least eight of whom had received military training or had studied in Russia and appear to have been recruited there. The most important ZAPU agent identified by Mitrokhin was NED, a member of the five-man War Council, headed by Nkomo, which took all strategic decisions. Though Mitrokhin gives no details of the intelligence supplied by NED, it was highly valued by the Centre. Presumably because most of NED's intelligence was military, he was passed to GRU control in 1976 – but, most unusually, the KGB was also authorized by the Central Committee to remain in touch with him (a certain sign of the importance attached to him by the Centre).[44] There were probably other GRU penetrations of ZAPU. The only other ZAPU agent identified by Mitrokhin, ARTUR, who was recruited while on a military training course at Simferopol, broke contact with the KGB after his return to Africa.[45] The remaining seven ZAPU recruits appear to have been classed as confidential contacts rather than agents. The fact that, like ARTUR, three of them (POL,[46] SHERIF[47] and SHIRAK[48]) broke contact when they returned to Africa suggests they resented the pressure put on them during their military training to co-operate with the KGB, but felt unable to refuse until they had left the Soviet Union. The most productive of the confidential contacts who remained in touch with the KGB appears to have been RIK, who, though only in the middle ranks of the ZAPU leadership, was reported to be close to Joshua Nkomo and his military chief of staff. According to Mitrokhin's notes on his file, RIK was 'conspiratorial, honest and conscientious in his work. For the information that he provided he was paid not more than 5,000 Mozambique Escudos, as well as some presents.'[49]

Nkomo conducted most of the negotiations for Soviet arms supplies to ZAPU's armed wing, the Zimbabwe People's Revolutionary

Army (ZIPRA), through the Soviet ambassador in Lusaka, Vasili Grigoryevich Solodovnikov, who, as Nkomo later acknowledged in his memoirs, was generally believed to be 'associated with the KGB'. Solodovnikov was one of the leading Soviet experts on Africa but appears to have been only an occasional co-opted collaborator of the KGB, rather than an intelligence officer. According to Nkomo, 'He was a very nice fellow, and we got on very well on the personal level. Moreover, he was entirely professional about his work, and if you discussed a request with him you could be sure that it would soon get on to the agenda of the right committee in Moscow, and the decision would come back without much delay.' Nkomo had 'extensive correspondence' and at least one meeting with Andropov, at which he discussed the 'training of [ZAPU] security operatives'. The Cuban DGI also provided ZAPU with intelligence advisers.[50]

Moscow's inside information and influence on ZAPU, however, proved of little avail because it urged on ZIPRA a mistaken strategy which diminished its influence in favour of its ZANU rival, the Zimbabwe African Liberation Army (ZANLA). On Soviet advice, ZIPRA attempted to turn itself into a conventional force capable of launching a cross-border invasion which would gain control of enough Rhodesian territory to give it major political leverage in determining the peace settlement. In so doing, however, it set up military camps in Zambia, Tanzania and Angola which were far easier targets for attack by Rhodesian security forces than more mobile and elusive guerrilla groups. In a series of cross-border raids in the spring and summer of 1979, the Rhodesian army and air force destroyed ZIPRA's capacity to operate effectively inside Rhodesia before the cease-fire at the end of the year.

ZANLA, by contrast, had much greater success with a strategy based on infiltrating guerrilla groups from its Mozambique bases across the Rhodesian border and winning support in the countryside. Though militarily superior, the Rhodesian security forces lost control of the rural population and with it the war. As one observer noted, 'The real problem is that the Rhodesian military have misunderstood the nature of the war which they are fighting. They have failed to realize that the war is essentially political rather than military and that the guerrillas have no immediate need to be militarily efficient.'[51]

During 1977, wrote the Rhodesian intelligence chief Ken Flower,

'The country had passed the point of no return in its struggle against African nationalism – no political settlement, no answer to the war.' For the white-settler government of Ian Smith, Flower's intelligence 'was unwelcome because it was unpalatable'.[52] In 1979, however, Rhodesia's white minority finally accepted the inevitable and voted for majority rule. To the dismay of both Moscow and the ANC, Mugabe's ZANU rather than Nkomo's ZAPU won an outright victory at the 1980 elections. On the eve of the elections, Nkomo's intelligence chief, Dumiso Dabengwa, had written to Andropov to request his continued backing against ZANU.[53] After Zimbabwe became independent in April 1980, however, the Centre was fearful that Mugabe would bear a grudge over the support it had given to his rival. It sent circular telegrams to residencies in Africa, London and elsewhere calling for detailed intelligence on his policy to the Soviet Union.[54]

Zimbabwean independence left the apartheid regime in South Africa and its colony in South-West Africa (in theory a League of Nations mandate conferred in 1919)[55] as the continent's only remaining white minority regime. After the MPLA victory in 1975, the South-West Africa People's Organization (SWAPO) was able to set up guerrilla bases in Angola which were supplied with Soviet arms and training. In 1976 the SWAPO leader, Sam Nujoma (later the first President of independent Namibia), paid two visits to Moscow.[56] At about this time, the KGB succeeded in recruiting two major agents inside SWAPO: a relative of Nujoma codenamed KASTONO, who later also operated as a Cuban agent;[57] and a member of the SWAPO Central Committee codenamed GRANT, who was recruited in Zambia and paid for intelligence on liberation movements in southern Africa, and on the activities of the Chinese and Western countries in the region.[58] In 1977 Nujoma received a hero's welcome and the usual revolutionary bear hug from Castro during two visits to Cuba. SWAPO was allowed to open an office in Havana and the Cubans provided military training in both Cuba and Angola. In 1981 Nujoma attended the CPSU Congress in Moscow.[59]

There was an authoritarian ring to Nujoma's assertion of SWAPO's right to rule. He declared in 1978: 'We are not fighting even for majority rule. We are fighting to seize power in Namibia, for the benefit of the Namibian people. We are revolutionaries. We are not counter-revolutionaries.'[60] From 1976 onwards there were recurrent purges of mostly innocent SWAPO members suspected of treachery by Nujoma and others in the leadership. As one authoritative study concludes, 'More and more of the movement's brightest and most critical minds disappeared from their posts.'[61] At the military level, SWAPO was no match for the South African Defence Force. Namibia owed its independence less to the guerrilla war than to changes within South Africa which eroded Pretoria's will to retain control of it.[62]

In June 1976 riots in the Soweto townships outside Johannesburg, brutally put down by police firing live ammunition, made South Africa's racial tensions front-page news around the world. So far from being organized by the ANC, however, the Soweto rising was a spontaneous protest begun by schoolchildren demonstrating against government orders that half their lessons should be in Afrikaans. The anger of young urban blacks, frustrated by the third-rate education and dismal job prospects to which they were condemned by the racist regime in Pretoria, boiled over. Only Durban among South African cities escaped the riots which spread across the country and led to over 600 deaths. The authority of the apartheid state never quite recovered its previous self-assurance.

The ANC's guerrilla war took four more years before it was able to dent the confidence of the South African security forces. The SACP sought to maintain the morale of the Party underground by circulating secret pamphlets which declared that 'Secrecy has helped us outwit the enemy':

The enemy tries to give the impression that it is impossible to carry out illegal work. The rulers boast about all our people they have killed and captured. They point to the freedom fighters locked up in the prisons. But a lot of that talk is sheer bluff. Of course it is impossible to wage a struggle without losses. The very fact, however, that the South African Communist Party and African National Congress have survived years of illegality is proof that the regime cannot stop our noble work. It is because we have been mastering secret work that we have been able, more and more, to outwit the enemy.

The main training in 'secret work' was provided by the KGB, as is indicated by the instructions on underground operations circulated within Umkhonto we Sizwe, which followed classic Soviet intelligence tradecraft. Success in the underground war, it was emphasized, required 'everyone [to] strictly follow the organizational and personal rules of behaviour' set out in the instructions. Infiltrators must be 'eliminated – where they pose serious danger to the survival of comrades and there is no other way'.[63]

In June 1980 the Umkhonto we Sizwe Special Operations force, commanded by Joe Slovo, a Moscow loyalist who six years later became Secretary-General of the SACP,[64] launched four simultaneous attacks on oil storage tanks and a refinery, causing huge fires which blazed for a week and were visible for miles around. The team which led the attack was commanded by another SACP member, Motso Mokgabudi (better known by his alias Obadi), who had received extensive military training in the Soviet Union and ran an ANC sabotage training camp in Angola, assisted by Soviet advisers.[65] As in the case of other liberation movements, the KGB (and doubtless the GRU) used the military training courses for the ANC in the Soviet Union as an opportunity to try to recruit confidential contacts and agents. The pressure it exerted on at least some of the potential recruits proved, as on ZAPU training courses, to be counterproductive. Mitrokhin made brief notes of the files of two ANC members recruited while being trained at Simferopol, ALEKS[66] and POET.[67] Both broke contact with the KGB after leaving the Soviet Union.

Though anxious to recruit agents among non-Communist members of the ANC, the KGB was forbidden to do so in the SACP. Relations with the SACP, as with other fraternal parties, were the primary responsibility of the International Department of the CPSU Central Committee. The KGB, however, was used to transmit funds to both the ANC and the SACP. Oleg Gordievsky, who was posted to the London residency in the summer of 1982, personally handed to Yusuf Dadoo, the SACP Secretary-General, over the next six months the equivalent in US dollars of £118,000 for the ANC and £54,000 for the SACP. Instead of putting the money in a briefcase, Dadoo stuffed it into all the pockets of his suit and overcoat. Gordievsky watched as Dadoo's thin frame filled out with dollar bills before he left the Soviet embassy on foot, apparently unconcerned with the risk of being robbed on his way home. Like the rest of the SACP leadership, Dadoo was a committed Moscow loyalist, untainted by

Euro-Communist heresy, who had supported the Soviet invasions of Hungary in 1956 and Czechoslovakia in 1968 but was also totally devoted to the liberation struggle in southern Africa.[68]

After Dadoo's death in 1983, the London residency ceased to handle the transmission of funds to the ANC and SACP. The main west European capital where the KGB maintained contact with its ANC agents and confidential contacts was Stockholm, where the ANC had its largest office outside Africa and received both public support and generous funding from the Swedish Social Democratic Party for its struggle against apartheid. As the West gradually became less feeble in its opposition to apartheid, the Centre became afraid that the ANC might increasingly be tempted to turn westwards. By the early 1980s KGB residencies in Stockholm, London, New York, Paris, Rome and those African capitals where the ANC maintained offices were regularly bombarded with instructions to monitor Western contacts with the ANC leadership and threats to SACP influence. The Centre was quick to show alarm at the slightest ideological shift. In 1982, for example, the London office of the ANC started showing resistance to the tedious articles supplied to it by a KGB officer working under cover as a Novosti news agency correspondent for publication in African newspapers. Unwilling to accept that the problem lay in the pedestrian quality of the articles it produced, the Centre instructed the London residency to redouble its efforts to track down the source of increasing Western influence within the ANC.[69]

In an attempt to exacerbate African suspicions of the West, the Centre maintained a stream of active measures designed to demonstrate that the United States and its allies were giving aid and comfort to the apartheid regime. Operation CHICORY in 1981 used Service A forgeries designed to demonstrate that the US arms embargo was a sham and spread the sensational fiction that the CIA and West German intelligence were plotting to supply South Africa with nuclear weapons. Operation GOLF in 1982, which also fabricated evidence of secret American arms supplies, was based on a forged letter to the US ambassador to the UN, Jeane Kirkpatrick, from a counsellor at the South African embassy in Washington conveying 'best regards and gratitude' from the head of South African military intelligence, purporting to accompany a birthday present sent 'as a token of appreciation from my government'. The use of the word 'priviously' [*sic*] in the letter indicates that, as sometimes happened with its forgeries, Service A had forgotten to check its English spelling. The letter was none the less published by the Washington correspondent of the New Statesman, Claudia Wright, who used it as the centrepiece of an article attacking Jeane Kirkpatrick, entitled 'A Girl's Best Friend'.[70] Among Service A's fabrications in 1983 was a bogus memorandum by President Mobutu's Special Adviser in the Zaire National Security Council reporting on a secret meeting between US and South African envoys to discuss ways, with Mobutu's assistance, of destabilizing the MPLA Angola government. As well as being sent to the ANC and SWAPO, the forgery was widely circulated to the media and successfully deceived some Western as well as African journalists, becoming the centrepiece of a story in the Observer, headlined 'US and S. Africa in Angola Plot'. Though reporting American claims that the document was fabricated, the Observer gave greater weight to supposed evidence for its authenticity.[71] Further Service A forgeries purporting to reveal covert collaboration between Washington and Pretoria continued into the Gorbachev era, among them a 1989 letter from the South African Foreign Minister, 'Pik' Botha, referring to a (non-existent) secret agreement concluded with the United States.[72] Apart from fabricating secret links between Washington and the apartheid regime, the most successful Soviet active measure in Africa was to blame the devastating Aids epidemic sweeping through the continent on a secret American biological warfare offensive.[73]

During the early 1980s, despite the continuing success of KGB active measures, there was a dramatic change of mood in Soviet policy to Africa. In 1980 Andropov was still defiantly optimistic about the prospects for 'liberated' Angola, Mozambique and Ethiopia. Within a few years Andropov's optimism had evaporated.[74] At the end of the 1970s the civil war in Angola had seemed to be winding down, and Angola's huge oil resources encouraged optimism about its economic prospects. During the early 1980s, however, thanks to South African support for UNITA, fierce fighting flared up once more. In only two years (1981–82) Angolan GNP fell by 20 per cent. On a visit to Angola in 1981 a KGB delegation led by Vadim Kirpichenko, though accommodated in the relative luxury of a government mansion, experienced regular interruptions to the electricity and water supply and some of the other daily hardships endured by even the more privileged sections of the Luanda population. Kirpichenko found DISA, the Angolan version of the KGB, in 'primitive' condition, despite the training provided by Stasi advisers:

One could sense poverty and scarcity everywhere, even in the external appearance of the senior heads. The level of education of the leaders, too, was then extremely low. When the Minister [for State Security] introduced the [KGB] delegation to the leading personnel of the ministry, we saw the head of one department wearing a jacket with one sleeve about ten centimetres longer than the other. We never did understand why he did not shorten the longer sleeve, which would not have required too much effort. We were surprised to discover three local Portuguese amongst the leading personnel of the ministry. After the ceremonial introductions, I began, at the request of the Minister, to outline some of our assessments of current problems of the international situation. I had barely spoken two words before the leading personnel of the ministry began to sink into a sweet sleep.

Kirpichenko insists that this discourteous response was 'in no way a reflection of the quality of my speech'.[75]

While Angola remained a drain on the ailing Soviet economy, it depended even more heavily on export earnings from US oil companies. Ironically, the MPLA was forced to use Cuban troops to defend American oil installations from UNITA attack.[76] In Mozambique as in Angola, Moscow had to confront the intractable problems caused by a combination of civil war and economic mismanagement. According to Markus Wolf, the long-serving head of the Stasi's foreign-intelligence arm, 'Internal power struggles in the [FRELIMO] government were exacerbated by debates between the Soviet military and the KGB over the proper way to handle a conflict that was careering out of control.'[77] Dmitri Volkogonov, the first historian to gain access to Andropov's papers as General Secretary, concludes that he 'had no idea what to do about such "allies"'. It was harder still to deal with Ethiopia, where Mengistu continued his orgy of violence against all opposition, much of it a figment of his paranoid imagination. When the political commissar of Mengistu's army, Asrat Destu, was asked during his visit to Moscow in 1984 why the bloodbath continued, he replied, 'We are doing what Lenin did. You cannot build socialism without red terror.' A fortnight after Destu returned to Addis Ababa, he was killed in a shoot-out at a meeting of Mengistu's Revolutionary Council.[78]

In March 1984, a month after Andropov's death, the Centre was taken by surprise when Samora Machel and the South African President, P. W. Botha, signed the Nkomati non-aggression agreement (so called after the town in Mozambique where the signing took place). Photographs of the tall figure of the notoriously short-tempered Botha, nicknamed *die Groot Krokodil* ('the Great Crocodile'), towering over the much smaller Machel seemed to symbolize the triumph of Pretoria's bullying power. In return for FRELIMO's agreement to cease providing bases for the ANC, Pretoria promised to withdraw support for RENAMO (though, in reality, South African military intelligence continued to provide it with some covert assistance). A dismayed ANC declared that the agreement had 'surprised the progressive world'.[79] Soon afterwards N. V. Shishlin, foreign affairs consultant to the International Department (and later to Gorbachev), told the London embassy and KGB residency in a private briefing that 'saving Mozambique' was beyond Moscow's power; its economy had virtually collapsed and FRELIMO was riven with internal rivalries. Shishlin also described Angola's economic problems as catastrophic and its political leadership, like that of Mozambique, as divided and incompetent. He feared that the MPLA, like FRELIMO, might be forced to come to terms with South Africa. The KGB residency in London (and doubtless other capitals) was instructed to collect intelligence on what the Centre feared were a series of potential threats to Soviet influence: among them US plans to undermine the Soviet position in southern Africa; US pressure on its allies to deny economic assistance to Angola and Mozambique; the danger that Angola and Mozambique might move into the Western sphere of influence; SWAPO's willingness to compromise on a Namibian settlement; and Western attempts to undermine the ANC or weaken its Marxist base.[80]

There were deep contradictions at the heart of Soviet policy towards southern Africa. Despite its uncompromising denunciation of apartheid, Moscow maintained top-secret contacts with Pretoria over the regulation of the world market in gold, diamonds, platinum and precious minerals, in which the Soviet Union and South Africa between them had something approaching a duopoly. Because of the extreme sensitivity of these contacts and the outrage which their public disclosure would provoke in black Africa, the KGB took a prominent part in arranging them. In 1984, just as the South African economy was on the verge of a serious crisis, the Kremlin decided to step up secret discussions with Pretoria on the regulation of the market. As a preliminary, KGB residencies in the United States, Britain, West Germany, France and Switzerland were asked to collect intelligence on a whole series of South African financial institutions and businesses.[81] In the mid-1980s De Beers Corporation in South Africa was paying the Soviet Union almost a billion dollars a year for the supply of high-quality diamonds. Moscow's lucrative secret agreements with Pretoria to keep mineral prices high did not prevent it attacking South Africa's Western business partners for doing business with apartheid.[82]

The Gorbachev era was marked by a growing sense that involvement in sub-Saharan Africa represented an unacceptable drain on Soviet resources, by deepening pessimism about the region's revolutionary potential, and by an increasing conviction that its manifold problems were peripheral to Soviet interests.[83] The leadership of the SACP, hitherto staunch defenders of the Moscow line, found it difficult to hide their frustration. In the ill-concealed quarrel between Gorbachev and Castro, who increasingly saw himself as the defender of Marxist-Leninist orthodoxy against Soviet revisionism,[84] the SACP was unmistakably on Castro's side – choosing to hold its Seventh Party Congress in July 1989 not in Moscow but Havana. Within the Soviet bloc in central and eastern Europe, the SACP leadership now looked not to Gorbachev's revisionist regime but to Erich Honecker's hard-line East Germany for inspiration. At the Havana conference it announced its ambition to 'build East Germany in Africa' after the end of apartheid.[85] Over the next few months, however, the fall of the Berlin Wall and the disintegration of the Soviet bloc persuaded the SACP to take a more flexible view.

By a fortunate irony, the Soviet one-party state and the South African apartheid regime began to crumble away at almost the same time. Gorbachev's unwillingness to devote time or money to the South African struggle helped to turn the ANC toward negotiations. The end of the Cold War pushed Pretoria in the same direction. Early in 1989 South Africa agreed to a deal – jointly brokered by the United States and the Soviet Union – to give independence to Namibia (South-West Africa) in return for the withdrawal of Cuban troops from Angola. In July the imprisoned Nelson Mandela, the commanding figure (though not yet the President) of the ANC, had a secret meeting with President P. W. Botha. Mandela had heard 'many accounts of his ferocious temper': 'He seemed to me the very model of the old-fashioned, stiff-necked, stubborn Afrikaner who did not so much discuss with black leaders as dictate to them.' To Mandela's surprise, he found Botha in conciliatory mood: 'He had his hand out and was smiling broadly, and in fact, from that very first moment, he completely disarmed me.' Far more important than Botha's change of heart, however, was the immense moral authority and capacity for uniting the South African people which Mandela had, amazingly, preserved during over twenty-seven years in jail. Mandela's leadership did more than Umkhonto's surprisingly ineffective guerrilla war to bring about the new post-apartheid South Africa. In December 1989, a month after the Berlin Wall came down, Mandela met Botha's successor as President, F. W. de Klerk, for the first time. Immediately after the meeting, Mandela wrote to the exiled ANC leadership in Lusaka, echoing Margaret Thatcher's words about Gorbachev five years earlier, that de Klerk was a man he could do business with.[86] On 2 February 1990 de Klerk announced to parliament the unbanning of the ANC and – to an audible gasp from those present in the chamber – of the SACP also. On 11 February Mandela walked free through the prison gates. In August he announced that the ANC was unilaterally suspending the armed struggle begun almost thirty years before. Ironically, the man who persuaded Mandela that the time had come to take this historic step was none other than the former pro-Soviet hard-liner Joe Slovo, leader of the SACP. Less than three years later the ANC won South Africa's first democratic elections.[87]

The crumbling of the Soviet system ultimately did far more than Soviet Cold War policy to persuade the apartheid regime that its time was up. For the ANC, none the less, Soviet support in the early stages of the armed struggle, at a time when the United States and many of its allies held it at arm's length, was of real significance in sustaining it during its most difficult years. 'The cynical', said Mandela later, 'have always suggested that the Communists were using us. But who is to say that we were not using them?'[88] Ultimately, the ANC gained more than Moscow from the once close relationship between them.

26

Conclusion:
The KGB in Russia and the World

Only a decade before the Soviet Union fell apart, the Centre leadership still remained optimistic about the success of its forward policy in the Third World. Andropov confidently told the Vietnamese interior minister, Fam Hung, during his visit to Moscow in October 1980:

The Soviet Union is not merely talking about world revolution but is actually assisting it. The USSR is building up a powerful military and economic potential which is a reliable defence for the socialist countries and other progressive forces in the world ... Why did the USA and other Western countries agree on détente in the 1970s and then change their policies? Because the imperialists realized that a reduction of international tension worked to the advantage of the socialist system. During this period Angola, Mozambique, Ethiopia and Afghanistan were liberated.[1]

The future DCI, Robert Gates, noted at the same time, 'The sense that the Soviets and their surrogates were "on the march" around the world was palpable in Washington'[2] as well as in Moscow. The victorious Sandinistas in Nicaragua secretly informed Moscow of their intention to turn themselves into a Marxist-Leninist 'vanguard party' which, in alliance with Cuba and the Soviet bloc, would spread the revolution through Central America.[3] Andropov was in no mood to suspend the onward march of 'world revolution' in the hope of restoring the détente of the early 1970s. His hostility to, and suspicion of, the United States reached an extraordinary climax after Ronald Reagan's inauguration as President in January 1981. Four months later the KGB and GRU jointly embarked on operation RYAN, the largest Soviet intelligence operation of the Cold War, designed to detect the – in reality non-existent – plans of the Reagan administration for a nuclear first strike.[4]

By the time RYAN began, Brezhnev did little more than rubber-stamp policies decided by others. When Valeri Boldin became assistant to Mikhail Gorbachev in 1981, he was shocked to observe Brezhnev at Politburo meetings sitting with a vacant stare:

More often than not he would read out a note prepared for him by his assistants, printed in very large characters on a special typewriter. He often got so confused that he read the same sentences over and over again, and then looked around pathetically, as if acknowledging his helplessness.[5]

As Brezhnev entered the final, demeaning phase of his long physical and mental decline, Andropov was driven by the determination to succeed him as Soviet leader, end the 'era of stagnation' (as it was later called) at home, stand up to the supposed nuclear menace of the Reagan regime, and consolidate the Soviet victory over the Main Adversary in the Third World. To prepare for the more dynamic era which he intended to inaugurate, Andropov took the unprecedented decision to embark on what were in effect the first Soviet active measures ever to be implemented against a Soviet leader. Andropov cynically proposed that Brezhnev's personal authority should be enhanced by more frequent appearances on television – with the real intention of exposing the increasing infirmity and confusion of the General Secretary to public view and thus demonstrating the need for his own more vigorous leadership. Brezhnev's decrepitude became the dominant theme in the privately circulated political jokes which for most Soviet citizens were the only available form of political dissent. Among them was this version of Brezhnev's daily schedule:

9 a.m.: reanimation
10 a.m.: breakfast
11 a.m.: awarding medals
12 noon: recharging his batteries
2 p.m.: lunch
4 p.m.: receiving medals
6 p.m.: signing important documents
8 p.m.: clinical death
9 p.m.: reanimation

As well as having more opportunities to observe the General Secretary's failing health, Western journalists and intelligence services were also fed sensational stories revealing that the KGB was investigating members of Brezhnev's family and inner circle for corruption. Brezhnev's daughter Galina, for example, was reported to be having an affair with a Moscow playboy nicknamed 'Boris the Gypsy', who was alleged to be part of a diamond-smuggling ring including members of the Moscow State Circus. Galina's husband, General Yuri Churbanov, was sacked as Deputy Minister of the Interior, and rumours were spread of suicides and even murders among those caught up in the web of corruption.[6]

When Brezhnev finally expired in November 1982, Andropov became the first KGB chief to be elected Party leader by the Politburo.[7] He began, as tradition demanded, by paying a hypocritical tribute to the dear, departed Leonid Ilyich, whose reputation he had been secretly undermining: 'We, his close friends who worked with him in the Politburo, saw the great charm he possessed, the great force that bound us together in the Politburo, the great authority, love and respect that he enjoyed among all Communists, among the Soviet people and the peoples of the world.'

Andropov's own health, however, was already failing fast. Within three months he was in considerable physical discomfort, receiving regular dialysis for kidney failure and forced to do much of his work sitting in a dentist's chair with a button in the armrest which allowed him to shift his position frequently in an attempt to ease the pain. The seriousness of his illness was a closely guarded secret. 'Soviet ambassadors,' recalls Dobrynin, 'myself included, had no idea how grave his illness was.'[8] Andropov's fourteen months of power, so far from marking, as he had intended, the climax of Soviet success among developing nations, marked the moment when the Centre's cherished belief that the Cold War could be won in the Third World began to disintegrate. Soviet forces were bogged down in Afghanistan in a war they could not win and Soviet Third World allies, especially in Africa, were visibly unable to turn their socialist rhetoric into reality. Andropov's own mood had changed dramatically since the beginning of the decade. In June 1983, in one of his last speeches before ill-health forced him to disappear completely from public view, he told the Central Committee Plenum:

It is one thing to proclaim Socialism as one's aim and quite another thing to build it. For this, a certain level of productive forces, culture and social consciousness are needed. Socialist countries express solidarity with these progressive states [in the Third World], render assistance to them in the sphere of politics and culture, and promote the strengthening of their defence. We contribute also, to the extent of our ability, to their economic development. But on the whole, their economic development, just like the entire social progress of those countries, can (of course) only be the result of the work of their peoples and of a correct policy of their leadership.[9]

The Soviet forward policy in the Third World, however, was held back not merely by the low level of local 'productive forces, culture and social consciousness', but also by the catastrophic failure, whose scale Andropov could not bring himself to acknowledge, of the Soviet economy. The widespread hopes in the Third World during the 1950s and 1960s that the Soviet model offered a blueprint for the modernization of their own economies had all but disappeared.[10] Andropov's supposedly reformist leadership merely continued Brezhnev's 'era of stagnation'. The election as Party leader after Andropov's death in February 1984 of Brezhnev's former crony, the seventy-two-year-old, terminally ill Konstantin Chernenko, the very model of an unreconstructed apparatchik with none of Andropov's intellectual gifts, epitomized the sclerosis of the system. At Andropov's funeral, Chernenko was barely able to stumble through the short graveside speech which had been written for him. Dr David Owen, who attended the funeral as leader of the British Social Democratic Party, correctly diagnosed that he was suffering from emphysema.[11] Chernenko had only thirteen months to live. The physical decrepitude of the Politburo as a whole had become probably the dominant theme in underground Soviet political humour; for example:

Question: What has four feet and twenty-four teeth?
Answer: A crocodile
Question: What has twenty-four feet and four teeth?
Answer: The Politburo

The physical weariness of much of the Politburo seemed to match the mood of Soviet policy towards the Third World. Under Andropov and Chernenko, Moscow increasingly saw its Third World friends and allies as burdens on its over-stretched economy rather than allies marching towards the global triumph of socialism. Nikolai Leonov, once a confident supporter of a Soviet forward policy in the Third World, had come to regard Soviet aid to developing countries as 'a cancerous tumour, sapping the strengths of the ailing organism of our own state'.[12]

It took the rise to power in March 1985 of an energetic and relatively youthful reformist, Mikhail Gorbachev, for this growing disillusion with the Third World to be reflected in a fundamental change of Soviet policy. There is no more convincing evidence of Gorbachev's 'new thinking' in foreign policy during his first year as General Secretary than his denunciation of the traditional bias of FCD reporting. The fact that the Centre had to issue stern instructions at the end of 1985 'on the impermissibility of distortions of the factual state of affairs in messages and informational reports sent to the Central Committee of the CPSU and other ruling bodies' is a damning indictment of the KGB's subservience to the standards of political correctness expected by previous Soviet leaders.[13] Henceforth it became easier for FCD reports to acknowledge the futility of much of the Soviet aid to its friends and allies. Gorbachev was well aware that the forward policy in the Third World over the previous quarter-century had imposed unacceptable strains on the ailing Soviet economy as well as doing serious damage to relations with the United States.

Even Gorbachev did not immediately interrupt the ruinously expensive flow of arms and military hardware to Afghanistan, Nicaragua, Vietnam, Syria, South Yemen, Ethiopia, Angola, Algeria and elsewhere. In May 1986, over a year after he became General Secretary, the Politburo agreed 'to supply free of charge uniforms, food and medical supplies to 70,000 servicemen of the Sandinista army' – despite the fact that the Sandinista regime already owed the Soviet Union $1.1 billion.[14] The 1986 CPSU programme, however, barely mentioned the Third World.[15] Gorbachev's decision in November 1986 to withdraw all Soviet troops from Afghanistan by 1988 signalled a major reassessment of Third World policy.[16] One of the main reasons for not announcing an immediate withdrawal, he told the Politburo in February 1987, was to limit the extent of the Soviet Union's humiliation in the eyes of its friends in the Third World:

'India would be concerned, and they would be concerned in Africa. They think this would be a blow to the authority of the Soviet Union in the national liberation movement. And they tell us that imperialism will go on the offensive if you flee from Afghanistan.'[17] Gorbachev still hoped to salvage as much as possible of the Soviet Union's prestige in the Third World, but did not know quite how it was to be done.

By the time the last Soviet troops left Afghanistan, the Centre leadership sensed that its international network of intelligence friends and allies had begun to crumble. At the final meeting of Soviet-bloc intelligence services (also attended by the services of Cuba, Mongolia and Vietnam) in East Berlin in October 1988, the speeches included examples of black humour unthinkable before. One delegation leader asked the question, 'What is socialism?' – then gave the politically incorrect answer: 'The most difficult and tortuous way to progress from capitalism to capitalism.' Only a decade earlier, a Czechoslovak minister who had dared to display disrespect to a hagiography of Brezhnev and other official propaganda by discarding them in his Moscow hotel room had been reported to Andropov personally, as well as to the KGB liaison officer in Prague so that he could make an official complaint.[18] Though the 1988 intelligence conference was held over a year before the fall of the Berlin Wall, the mood was already so pessimistic that, for the first time, no date or location was fixed for the next meeting. On the final evening, as participants were treated to a boat trip on the canals and lakes around Berlin, they were already gloomily aware that they might not meet again. 'In many cases', recalls Kirpichenko, 'one was saying farewell for ever. The commonwealth of intelligence services of socialist countries had ended its existence.'[19]

Soon after becoming US Secretary of State early in 1989, James A. Baker III noted privately that the Soviet Union was 'showing signs of willingness to be part of the solution rather than part of the problem' in the Third World. Moscow was using its influence to persuade Vietnam to withdraw its troops from Cambodia and to bring to an end the long and destructive civil wars in Namibia and Angola.[20] In April 1989, during a state visit to Cuba, previously the chief ally of the Soviet forward policy in the Third World, Gorbachev formally announced that Moscow had renounced its traditional policy of exporting socialism in favour of the principle of non-intervention. He declared in a speech in Havana, 'We are resolutely opposed to any theories and doctrines justifying the export of revolution or counter-revolution.' An outraged Castro retaliated in public with a barrage of misleading statistics on Cuba's socialist achievements and in private with barbed comments on Soviet workers' fear of unemployment and the strange absence of sugar (Cuba's main export) from Soviet shops. Though Gorbachev and Castro had clasped each other in the usual ritual embrace at the beginning of the visit, the two leaders exchanged only a frosty handshake when they said goodbye.[21]

In October 1989, only a few weeks before the fall of the Berlin Wall, the Soviet Foreign Minister, Eduard Shevardnadze, formally acknowledged in a major policy speech to the Supreme Soviet that Soviet intervention in Afghanistan had violated accepted norms of international relations and human behaviour. Withdrawal from Afghanistan was merely the most striking example of a more general retreat from the Third World. During the final years of the Soviet Union, maintaining influence with impoverished former ideological allies from Angola to Nicaragua had lower priority than strengthening relations with wealthier countries outside its sphere of influence such as Brazil, Japan, South Africa and Thailand, which had more to offer as trading partners.[22]

In the immediate aftermath of the disintegration of the Soviet bloc, a disoriented KGB continued to go through the sometimes surreal motions of maintaining its Third World connections. In 1990 Vadim Kirpichenko led a KGB delegation to celebrations marking the fifteenth anniversary of the founding of DISA, the Angolan KGB. He found DISA, and the Ministry of State Security which ran it, better organized with 'more order and discipline' than during his previous visit nine years earlier and reconciled to the need for negotiations with UNITA to bring the long-running civil war to an end. In keeping with the traditional KGB rituals on such occasions, Kirpichenko solemnly handed over a painting of Red Square to his hosts as if nothing in Moscow had changed. When Kirpichenko had made a speech to the Angolan Ministry of State Security nine years earlier, he had been annoyed that much of his audience quickly nodded off. On this occasion, the Minister of State Security spoke for two hours to an audience sitting in the full glare of the tropical sun. The KGB delegation tried to remain politely attentive while –

according to Kirpichenko – privately longing for shade and cold beer, but suffered afterwards from severe sunburn.[23]

In October and November 1990 Kirpichenko led another delegation to Ethiopia to discuss intelligence co-operation. On the outskirts of Addis Ababa stood the shell of the unfinished Stasi-designed training centre of the Ethiopian KGB, whose construction had been abandoned after the collapse of the GDR. Kirpichenko seemed unaware of the surreal nature of the negotiations between the intelligence services of two doomed regimes, noting merely that:

The negotiations took place in a businesslike atmosphere. The Ethiopians always accepted our modest help with gratitude, attended to our advice, but at the same time, which is completely natural, reserved the right to complete independence and freedom of actions . . . Nobody could accuse us of ever . . . pushing the Ethiopian security services into any actions . . . harmful to their national interests.

On 1 November Kirpichenko became the last Soviet representative to have a meeting with President Mengistu, both seated on high-backed red leather chairs decorated with the hammer and sickle. 'What is happening in the USSR?' demanded Mengistu. 'Do Soviet–Ethiopian relations have a future? We are no longer counting on your economic help, but we would ask you to maintain at least military assistance.' Without that assistance, declared Mengistu, he would be unable to put down the rebellion which threatened his regime. At the end of the meeting, he threw out a final reproach: 'You yourselves oriented us towards the socialist path of development, and now you are turning your backs on us!'[24]

Nothing in Kirpichenko's account of the meeting betrayed any awareness that he was dealing with an unhinged mass murderer who in 1977–78 had killed half a million of his adult subjects in the name of Marxism-Leninism even as he forced many of their children to dress in uniforms modelled on those of Soviet young pioneers, and had reduced many others to starvation in order to equip the most powerful army in Africa with Soviet planes, missiles and tanks worth $12 billion. Six months after bidding farewell to Kirpichenko, Mengistu was forced to flee to exile in Zimbabwe. The looters who entered his private study found on the mantelpiece a photo of Mengistu posing with a grinning, back-slapping Fidel Castro, on the desk a bust of Lenin together with a Bob Marley LP, and on the bookshelf Marxist-Leninist texts side by side with histories of British kings and queens which had once belonged to Haile Selassie. In the garden was a starving lion in a cage.[25]

By the time Mengistu went into exile in May 1991, reproaching his former Soviet friends for failing to support his supposedly Marxist-Leninist regime, the Soviet Union had begun to crumble too. The KGB leadership, as they witnessed the wreckage of their hopes both for the Soviet Union and for its place in the world, were almost as disoriented as Mengistu. Though all had come to recognize that there were flaws within the Soviet system, they also blamed its disintegration on an imperialist plot masterminded by the United States. Leonov, head of KGB intelligence assessment as the Soviet Union began to fall apart, warned Gorbachev and the rest of the Soviet leadership that the United States had become a 'vulture swooping over the Soviet Union', plotting to 'incite our people to hate each other' and 'pour oil on the flames of our internal discontent'. When the General Secretary paid no attention to his alarmist classified reports, Leonov made his warnings public, dramatically comparing Gorbachev's refusal to heed KGB admonitions on the threat from the American 'vulture' to Stalin's failure to heed intelligence on the mortal danger from Nazi Germany half a century before.[26] A number of other senior KGB officers also publicized previously classified conspiracy theories about alleged American plots to subvert the Soviet Union and undermine its global influence. In December 1990 the KGB Chairman, Vladimir Kryuchkov (former head of the FCD), blamed some of the appalling failures of Soviet grain storage on (non-existent) CIA operations to infect grain imports. In February 1991 Viktor Grushko, First Deputy Chairman of the KGB (previously deputy head of the FCD), attributed Soviet financial problems to an equally improbable plot by Western banks to undermine the ruble: a conspiracy theory quickly taken up by the newly appointed Prime Minister, Valentin Pavlov. Speaking to a closed session of the Supreme Soviet in June 1991, Kryuchkov sought to justify the belief of the KGB old guard in a deep-laid Western conspiracy to sabotage the Soviet system by reading out a classified FCD report circulated to the Politburo by Andropov fourteen years earlier. The report claimed that the CIA, 'regardless of cost', was recruiting agents within the Soviet economy, administration and scientific research, and training them to commit sabotage. Some of the Soviet Union's current problems, Kryuchkov declared, derived from this secret sabotage offensive.[27]

These and other fantastic conspiracy theories reflected the state of disorientation and denial within the Centre's leadership produced by the collapse and global humiliation of the political system of which they were a part. The failure was so immense that their ideological blinkers made it impossible for them to comprehend it. Kryuchkov showed the extent of his incomprehension by taking the lead in organizing the failed hard-line coup of August 1991 which, though intended to shore up the Soviet Union, merely accelerated its disintegration. Among those who shared his incomprehension was the Soviet Union's most dependable Third World ally over the previous generation, Fidel Castro. In June, while Kryuchkov was in the final stages of planning the coup, he flew to Havana, where his welcome was as warm as Gorbachev's two years earlier had been frosty. Castro, like Kryuchkov, blamed Gorbachev for 'destroying the authority of the [Communist] Party'. *Izvestia* later claimed, probably correctly, that Kryuchkov and Castro had concluded secret agreements on repairing the damage to the Soviet–Cuban alliance caused by Gorbachev. In July Kryuchkov's co-conspirator, Vice-President Gennadi Yanayev, soon to become 'Acting President' during the August coup, sent Castro a secret letter assuring him that, 'Soon there will be a change for the better.' News of the coup, hinted at in Yanayev's letter, was greeted by the Cuban leadership with a euphoria which gave way to deep dismay when it collapsed a few days later.[28]

Though the KGB had won a series of tactical victories over the West in Africa, Asia, Latin America and the Middle East, its Cold War operations ended in strategic defeat well before the Soviet Union itself collapsed in the wake of the failed August coup. By the mid-1980s the grand strategy of a victorious struggle against the Main Adversary in the Third World which would determine 'the destiny of world confrontation between the United States and the Soviet Union, between capitalism and socialism'[29] was in ruins. The KGB's grand strategy failed chiefly because the Soviet system failed. Though good intelligence can sometimes act as a 'force-multiplier', magnifying the diplomatic and military strength of those states which use it effectively, it cannot compensate for the weaknesses of a system as fundamentally flawed as that of the Soviet Union. Attempts to transplant elements of the inefficient Soviet command economy and collectivized agriculture to other continents were uniformly disastrous. A Harvard economist, Jeffrey Sachs, has estimated that if Africa had followed the free-market policies of East Asian governments, its average growth rate per head between 1965 and 1990 would have reached 4.3 per cent, trebling incomes. The actual figure was a mere 0.8 per cent.[30]

After the invasion of Afghanistan, the rhetoric of Soviet solidarity with national liberation movements rang more hollow than ever before. By the 1980s, with both the one-party state and the command economy in irreversible decay, the Soviet Union had nothing of importance to offer the Third World save for arms which most of the recipients could not afford to buy and Moscow could no longer afford to subsidize (though it frequently did). From Peru to Afghanistan vast Soviet arms exports destabilized both the economies and the societies of their Third World recipients. The continent which suffered the most serious consequences was Africa, where the Soviet Union was the major force behind an unprecedented arms boom from the mid-1970s to the mid-1980s. The value of weapons imports into sub-Saharan Africa rose from an annual average of about $150 million (at constant 1985 US dollar prices) in the late 1960s to $370 million in 1970–73 and $820 million in 1974–76, before reaching a peak of almost $2,500 million in 1977–78, chiefly as a result of the massive Soviet arms shipments to Ethiopia during its war with Somalia. During the period 1980–87, annual weapons imports remained fairly constant at some $1,575 million, but with the end of the Cold War fell dramatically to $350 million in 1989–93; the 1993 figure was the lowest since the mid-1960s.[31] As the African historian Professor John Clapham has argued, the ultimate effect of these huge arms imports was not to strengthen the states which received them, but to weaken and, in some cases, eventually to destroy them. Africa's major Cold War arms recipients in the 1970s and 1980s became the main failed and collapsed African states of the 1990s.[32]

Given how little the Soviet Union had to offer the Third World, it enjoyed – sometimes assisted by its friends – some striking public relations successes. In 1979 its most dependable and eloquent supporter in the Third World, Fidel Castro, was elected Chairman of the Non-Aligned Movement for the next three years – despite the fact that Cuba, so far from being non-aligned, was closely aligned with the Soviet bloc. Castro was quick to exploit his flair for anti-imperialist publicity by travelling to New York in October with impressive quantities of rum and lobsters for a huge reception at the twelve-storey Cuban mission to the United Nations (the largest UN mission save for those of the US and USSR), then made an impassioned two-hour plea at the General Assembly for 'wealthy imperialists' (first and foremost the United States) to give developing countries $300 billion over the next decade.[33] At least at a rhetorical level, anti-Americanism and anti-imperialism had a greater global appeal than anti-Communism, an appeal which was central to both Soviet official propaganda and KGB active measures.

Though the United States possessed the world's largest concentration of public relations experts, it found it difficult to project a favourable – or even balanced – image of its policies to the Third World. And yet, unlike the Soviet Union, the United States had much that the rest of the world wanted. American music, films, TV, IT, casual clothes, fast food and soft drink were all part of the most pervasive popular culture in world history. The United States was the most sought-after destination for both economic migrants and university students from the Third World, few of whom preferred to work or study in the Soviet bloc. America was also one of the world's leading centres for a series of progressive causes – among them human rights, gay liberation, feminism and environmentalism – which were persecuted in the Soviet Union. And yet in international meetings with a strong Third World participation it was usually the United States which found itself cast in the role of scapegoat-in-chief. The Vancouver Assembly of the World Council of Churches in 1983 condemned Western capitalism as the main source of injustice in the world, responsible for the evils of sexism, racism, 'cultural captivity, colonialism and neo-colonialism'. By contrast, the Assembly took a compassionate view of the Soviet predicament in Afghanistan, calling for a Soviet withdrawal only 'in the context of an overall political settlement between Afghanistan and the USSR' (conveniently forgetting that the Kabul regime had been installed by the Soviet invaders) and 'an end to the supply of arms to opposition groups from outside' (in other words, the denial of arms to those resisting the Soviet invaders).[34]

In the climate of the Cold War one of the greatest strengths of American culture – its ability to criticize itself – became a foreign-policy weakness. While the Soviet Union tried hard to keep its failings secret, the United States exposed its own to public view. By the years of the Vietnam War, many of the most effective critics of US policy in the Third World were American. The 'Year of Intelligence' in 1975 also began a period of fierce public criticism of the CIA. No intelligence service had ever been exposed to such public examination of its failings. During the 1976 US presidential election campaign, Jimmy Carter condemned the national disgraces of 'Watergate, Vietnam and the CIA'.[35] Though the abuses of the KGB were at a greater level of iniquity than those of the CIA, they were also far less publicized and attracted far less global attention. The iniquities of American foreign policy and covert operations were further magnified by conspiracy theorists who found a ready market inside as well as outside the United States. Since a majority of Americans believed or suspected that the CIA was involved in the assassination of President Kennedy, it is scarcely surprising that so many in the Third World thought that the CIA was out of control.

KGB active-measures campaigns against the Main Adversary were thus directed against an easy target. Though it is impossible to quantify their success, they probably produced at least a modest increase in the amount of anti-Americanism, especially in the Third World, and introduced some novel variations into anti-US conspiracy theories. Without Service A forgeries, it is unlikely so many Third World leaders and opinion-formers would have believed that they and their countries were being targeted by the CIA. Nor is it likely that allegations of American responsibility for Aids and trafficking in 'baby parts' would have spread so successfully without KGB assistance. The KGB was also strikingly successful in using CIA operations, both real and imagined, to divert attention from its own. Covert action in Africa during the Cold War, for example, is still frequently seen as a monopoly of the Agency. Nelson Mandela's usually fair-minded and forgiving memoirs condemn the CIA's 'many contemptible activities in its support of American imperialism',[36] but make no criticism of the role of the KGB or any other Soviet-bloc intelligence agency in, for example, training the brutal intelligence agencies of Africa's Marxist regimes.

Many former Soviet intelligence officers still take pride in the record of the KGB. Leonid Shebarshin, probably the ablest of all its foreign intelligence chiefs, insists that 'Soviet intelligence was the best in the world.' 'Why', he asks, 'did we have such an advantage [over the CIA]? Because most of our officers were passionate about what they were doing . . . The KGB was really about enthusiasm and dedication.'[37] Nikolai Leonov, one of the most successful KGB officers in the Third World, continues both to defend the record of Soviet foreign intelligence and to maintain that Soviet political and military influence in the Third World outstripped that of the United States. But for the internal collapse of the Soviet system, he argues, it would have achieved 'final victory' over the West abroad.[38]

Shebarshin and Leonov, like other former senior FCD officers, still cannot bring themselves to recognize that the KGB, so far from being the victim of a failed system, was at the heart of its most monstrous abuses. Under Stalin the NKVD made possible the surveillance and repression of dissent – both real and imaginary – on a scale unparalleled in the peacetime history of Europe. In the less brutal post-Stalin era, the KGB was central to a system of social control so pervasive that even the possibility of dissent occurred only to a heroic but tiny minority of dissidents. Because of their inability to come to terms with the real record of Soviet intelligence, many of its veterans find it impossible to recognize the motives of secret dissidents within their own ranks, such as Vasili Mitrokhin and Oleg Gordievsky, who recognized the KGB for what it was and set out to undermine its authority. Western historians of intelligence find no difficulty in grasping the fact that there were ideological 'moles' in both East and West during the Cold War. Not so the apologists for the FCD. While idealizing the motives of Soviet ideological agents in the West, they usually refuse to admit that there were any Western ideological agents in the Soviet Union. Yevgeni Primakov, one of the leading intellectuals in Russian foreign intelligence who had close, long-standing links with the FCD before becoming the first head of its post-Soviet successor, the SVR, still clings to an improbably romanticized image of the Cambridge 'mole', Donald Maclean, whom he knew personally, as 'a Scottish lord' (despite the fact that, though the son of a knight, he had no title) who gave up a fortune large enough to meet the entire running costs of Soviet foreign intelligence (a preposterous exaggeration) in order to work as a penetration agent 'for purely ideological reasons'.

By contrast, Primakov denies that Gordievsky, despite the fact that he put his life repeatedly at risk for a cause in which he profoundly believed, was motivated by ideological rejection of the Soviet system.[39] Like Primakov, Vadim Kirpichenko, now chief consultant to the head of the SVR, continues to insist that no Western agents in the Soviet Union ever worked for ideological motives: 'There have never been any purely ideological warriors for the wonderful capitalist system.' Hence Kirpichenko's insistence that Mitrokhin, Gordievsky and others who risked their lives to expose the vices of the KGB were no more than 'traitors' motivated by 'various types of vices' – 'psychological instability', 'family discord', hypochondria, the desire 'to get their boss into trouble' or financial greed.[40]

Such attitudes are a legacy of the mindset of the Soviet one-party state, which always refused to accept that any dissident acted from principle. As well as being monstrous, the KGB's Cold War obsession with what it called 'ideological subversion' reached levels of absurdity comparable with Brezhnev's medal-mania. Even taking an interest in abstract paintings or listening to the wrong kinds of music was regarded as potentially subversive. The KGB Moscow Directorate and Fifth Directorate (which dealt with ideological subversion) proudly reported in 1979 that their agents in the artistic community had succeeded in 'preventing seven attempts by avant-garde artists to make provocative attempts to show their pictures'. Provincial KGBs went to enormous pains to monitor the role of Western popular music in encouraging ideological subversion among the young. The KGB in Dnepropetrovsk oblast, where Brezhnev had begun his career as a Party apparatchik, warned that, 'Even listening to musical programmes gave young people a distorted idea of Soviet reality and led to incidents of a treasonable nature.' Such reports are a reminder of how the hunt for ideological subversion destroyed all sense of the absurd among those committed to the holy war against it. The Centre's in-house journal *KGB Sbornik* regularly celebrated counter-subversive triumphs which were, by any objective standards, of the most trivial importance. One such 'triumph' was the hunt for a subversive codenamed KHUDOZHNIK ('Artist'), who in 1971 began sending anonymous, handwritten letters attacking Marxism-Leninism and various Party functionaries to CPSU and Komsomol committees. Despite the fact that none of his letters became public and he represented no conceivable threat to the regime, the resources deployed to track him down comfortably exceeded those devoted in the West to most major murder enquiries. Because some of KHUDOZHNIK's letters were sent to military Komsomols, there was an immense trawl through the records of people dismissed from military training establishments and the files of reserve officers. In Moscow, Yaroslavl, Rostov and Gavrilov-Yam, where his letters were posted, the Postal Censorship Service searched for many months for handwriting similar to KHUDOZH-NIK's. Numerous KGB agents and co-optees were also shown samples of his writing and given his supposed psychological profile. A further enormous research exercise was undertaken to identify and scrutinize official forms which KHUDOZHNIK might have filled in. In 1974, after a hunt lasting almost three years, his writing was finally found on an application to the Rostov City Housing Commission and he was unmasked as a Rostov street committee chairman named Korobov, tried and imprisoned. This surreal investigation was entirely in accord with Centre policy. Andropov told a conference of the Fifth Directorate in 1979 that the KGB could not afford to ignore the activities of a single dissident, however obscure.[41] Oleg Kalugin, once the youngest general in Soviet foreign intelligence, who, after disagreements with Kryuchkov, was moved from the FCD to become deputy head of the Leningrad KGB in 1980, quickly realized that most of its work was 'an elaborately choreographed farce', in which it tried desperately to discover enough ideological subversion to justify its bloated size and resources.[42]

Apologists for Soviet foreign intelligence frequently seek to distance its operations from the abuse of human rights by the domestic KGB. In reality, as volume 1 of *The Mitrokhin Archive* showed, the struggle against ideological subversion at home and abroad was carefully co-ordinated. Just as hunting down Trotsky and other 'enemies of the people' abroad became the main priority of foreign intelligence operations during the 'Great Terror' before the Second World War,[43] so 'agent operational measures' against some leading dissidents during the 1970s were jointly agreed by Kryuchkov, the head of the FCD, and internal security chiefs. Early in 1977 a total of thirty-two jointly devised active-measures operations intended to discredit and destabilize Andrei Sakharov ('Public Enemy Number One', as Andropov described him) were either already underway or about to begin both at home and abroad.[44] There was similar co-operation between the foreign and domestic arms of the KGB in their obsessive campaign against 'Zionist subversion' and Jewish refuseniks.[45] Until the closing years of the Cold War the FCD set out to prevent all Soviet dissidents and defectors achieving foreign recognition – even in fields entirely divorced from politics (at least as understood in the West). Enormous time and effort were devoted by the Centre to devising ways to damage the careers of Rudolf Nureyev, Natalia Makarova and other defectors from Soviet ballet. After the great cellist Mstislav Rostropovich and his wife, the singer Galina Vishnevskaya, went into exile in the West, the Centre appealed to all Soviet-bloc intelligence services for help in penetrating their entourage and ruining their reputations. Preventing dissident chess players winning matches against the ideologically orthodox was another priority of KGB foreign operations. A team of eighteen FCD operations officers was sent to the 1978 world chess championship in the Philippines to try to ensure the defeat of the defector Viktor Korchnoi by the Soviet world champion Anatoli Karpov.[46]

Abroad as well as at home, the KGB played a central role in the worst Cold War Soviet violations of human rights: among them the suppression of the Hungarian Uprising of 1956,[47] the crushing of the Prague Spring in 1968,[48] the invasion of Afghanistan in 1979[49] and the pressure on the Polish Communist regime to strangle the democratic Solidarity movement in 1981.[50] Export of Soviet systems of oppression had begun between the wars. Mao's security chief, Kang Sheng, learned in Stalin's Russia during the Great Terror some of the brutal methods of liquidating ideological subversion which he later introduced in China.[51] After the Second World War, Communist rule within the newly established Soviet bloc in eastern and central Europe depended on systems of surveillance and repression implemented by local security services created in the image of the KGB.[52] During the Cold War elements of these systems were exported to many of the Soviet Union's friends and allies in other continents. One of the most malign aspects of the foreign operations of the KGB and other Soviet-bloc intelligence services was the assistance which they provided to leaders of one-party states in the Third World from Afghanistan to Ethiopia in crushing opposition to their rule.

Since the governments of one-party states regard dissent as

illegitimate, all require systems of secret surveillance and social control to monitor its progress and keep it in check, though the permissible limits vary from state to state. Only when the vast apparatus of Soviet social control began to be dismantled under Gorbachev did the full extent of the KGB's importance to the survival of the USSR become clear. The manifesto of the hard-line leaders of the August 1991 coup, of which Kryuchkov was the chief organizer, implicitly acknowledged that the relaxation of the campaign against ideological subversion had shaken the foundations of the one-party state: 'Authority at all levels has lost the confidence of the population . . . Malicious mockery of all the institutions of state is being implanted. The country has in effect become ungovernable.' What the plotters failed to grasp was that it was too late to turn back the clock. 'If the *coup d'état* had happened a year and a half or two years earlier', wrote Gorbachev afterwards, 'it might, presumably, have succeeded. But now society was completely changed.' Crucial to the change of mood was declining respect for the intimidatory power of the KGB, which had hitherto been able to strangle any Moscow demonstration at birth. The most striking symbol of the collapse of the August coup was the toppling of the giant statue of the founder of the Cheka, Feliks Dzerzhinsky, from its plinth in the middle of the square outside KGB headquarters. A large crowd, which a few years earlier would never have dared to assemble, encircled the Lubyanka and cheered enthusiastically as 'Iron Feliks' was borne away, dangling in a noose suspended from a huge crane supplied by the Moscow City Government.[53]

As well as suppressing civil liberties at home, the KGB degraded Soviet policy-making abroad. Despite the FCD's numerous successes in intelligence collection, its politically correct assessments of the Main Adversary and its allies served to reinforce rather than to correct the misunderstandings of the Soviet leadership. Even on the eve of the Gorbachev era, the Politburo would have learned more from reading leading Western newspapers than from top-secret Soviet intelligence reports. Kryuchkov's assessment of the international situation in the FCD Work Plan for 1984, for example, declared that 'The imperialist states are pursuing their intrigues over Poland and Afghanistan', but made no reference to the mass opposition to Communist rule and Soviet domination which was at the root of the crisis in both countries. Similarly, Kryuchkov's biennial report early in 1984 on KGB operations and international affairs over the previous two years arrived at the alarmist conclusion that 'the deepening social and economic crisis in the capitalist world' had reached such desperate straits that the imperialists were seriously considering thermonuclear war 'as an escape from the difficulties they have created'. But there was, of course, no mention of the far more intractable economic problems of the Soviet bloc.[54] KGB influence on Soviet foreign policy has been frequently underrated. Even horrendously mistaken intelligence reports – such as those in the early 1960s and early 1980s claiming that the United States was planning a nuclear first strike – were capable of having an important influence on policy if, as happened in both cases, policy-makers took them seriously.[55]

As volume 1 of *The Mitrokhin Archive* sought to demonstrate, scientific and technological intelligence (S&T) from the West, which suffered far less from the demands of political correctness, was put to far more effective use than political intelligence. The plans for the first US atomic bomb obtained for Moscow by British and American agents were the most important military secret ever obtained by any intelligence service. As in the case of nuclear weapons, the early development of Soviet radar, rocketry and jet propulsion was heavily dependent on the covert acquisition of Western technology. The enormous flow of Western (especially American) S&T throughout the Cold War helps to explain one of the central paradoxes of a Soviet state which was once famously described as 'Upper Volta with missiles': its ability to remain a military superpower while its infant mortality and other indices of social deprivation were at Third World levels. The fact that the gap between Soviet weapons systems and those of the West was far smaller than in any other area of economic production was due not merely to their priority within the Soviet system but also to the remarkable success of S&T collection in the West. For most of the Cold War, American business proved much easier to penetrate than the federal government. Long before the KGB finally acquired a major spy in the CIA with the walk-in of Aldrich Ames in 1985, it was running a series of other mercenary agents in American defence contractors, as well as intercepting many of their fax communications. The Pentagon estimated in the early 1980s that probably 70 per cent of all current Warsaw Pact weapons systems were based on Western technology. Both sides in the Cold

War – the Warsaw Pact as well as NATO – thus depended on American know-how. Outside the defence industry, however, the inefficient Soviet command economy was unable to put to good use most of the huge amount of S&T obtained from the West.[56]

Ridiculed and reviled at the end of the Soviet era, the Russian intelligence community has since been remarkably successful at re-inventing itself and recovering its political influence. The last three prime ministers of the Russian Federation during Boris Yeltsin's presidency – Yevgeni Primakov, Sergei Stepashin and Vladimir Putin – were all former intelligence chiefs. Putin, who succeeded Yeltsin as President in 2000, is the only FCD officer ever to become Russian leader.[57] According to the head of the SVR, Sergei Nikolayevich Lebedev, 'The president's understanding of intelligence activity and the opportunity to speak the same language to him makes our work considerably easier.'[58] No previous head of state in Russia, or perhaps anywhere else in the world, has ever surrounded himself with so many former intelligence officers.[59] Putin also has more direct control of intelligence than any Russian leader since Stalin. According to Kirpichenko, 'We are under the control of the President and his administration, because intelligence is directly subordinated to the President and only the President.' But whereas Stalin's intelligence chiefs usually told him simply what he wanted to hear, Kirpichenko claims that, 'Now, we tell it like it is.'[60]

The mission statement of today's FSB and SVR is markedly different from that of the KGB. At the beginning of the 1980s Andropov proudly declared that the KGB was playing its part in the onward march of world revolution.[61] By contrast, the current 'National Security Concept' of the Russian Federation, adopted at the beginning of the new millennium, puts the emphasis instead on the defence of traditional Russian values:

Guaranteeing the Russian Federation's national security also includes defence of the cultural and spiritual-moral inheritance, historical traditions and norms of social life, preservation of the cultural property of all the peoples of Russia, formation of state policy in the sphere of the spiritual and moral education of the population . . .

One of the distinguishing characteristics of the Soviet intelligence system from Cheka to KGB was its militant atheism. In March 2002, however, the FSB at last found God. A restored Russian Orthodox church in central Moscow was consecrated by Patriarch Aleksi II as the FSB's parish church in order to minister to the previously neglected spiritual needs of its staff. The FSB Director, Nikolai Patrushev, and the Patriarch celebrated the mystical marriage of the Orthodox Church and the state security apparatus by a solemn exchange of gifts. Patrushev presented a symbolic golden key of the church and an icon of St Aleksei, Moscow Metropolitan, to the Patriarch, who responded by giving the FSB Director the Mother of God 'Umilenie' icon and an icon representing Patrushev's own patron saint, St Nikolai – the possession of which would formerly have been a sufficiently grave offence to cost any KGB officer his job. Though the FSB has not, of course, become the world's first intelligence agency staffed only or mainly by Christian true believers, there have been a number of conversions to the Orthodox Church by Russian intelligence officers past and present – among them Nikolai Leonov, who half a century ago was the first to alert the Centre to the revolutionary potential of Fidel Castro. 'Spirituality' has become a common theme in FSB public relations materials. While head of FSB public relations in 1999–2001, Vasili Stavitsky published several volumes of poetry with a strong 'spiritual' content, among them *Secrets of the Soul* (1999); a book of 'spiritual-patriotic' poems for children entitled *Light a Candle, Mamma* (1999); and *Constellation of Love: Selected Verse* (2000). Many of Stavitsky's poems have been set to music and recorded on CDs, which are reported to be popular at FSB functions.[62]

Despite their unprecedented emphasis on 'spiritual security', however, the FSB and SVR are politicized intelligence agencies which keep track of President Putin's critics and opponents among the growing Russian diaspora abroad,[63] as well as in Russia itself. During his first term in office, while affirming his commitment to democracy and human rights, Putin gradually succeeded in marginalizing most opposition and winning control over television channels and the main news media. The vigorous public debate of policy issues during the Yeltsin years has largely disappeared. What has gradually emerged is a new system of social control in which those who step too far out of line face intimidation by the FSB and the courts. The 2003 State Department annual report on human rights warned that a series of alleged espionage cases involving scientists, journalists and environmentalists 'caused continuing concerns regarding the lack of due process and the influence of the FSB in court cases'. According to Lyudmila Alekseyeva, the current head of the Moscow Helsinki Group, which has been campaigning for human rights in Russia since 1976, 'The only thing these scientists, journalists and environmentalists are guilty of is talking to foreigners, which in the Soviet Union was an unpardonable offence.'[64] Though all this remains a far cry from the KGB's obsession with even the most trivial forms of ideological subversion, the FSB has once again defined a role for itself as an instrument of social control.

Russian espionage in the West appears to be back to Cold War levels.[65] In the post-Soviet era, however, the disappearance beyond the horizon of the threat of thermonuclear conflict between Russia and the West, the central preoccupation of intelligence agencies on both sides during the Cold War, means that Russian espionage no longer carries the threat which it once did. Early twenty-first-century intelligence has been transformed by the emergence of counter-terrorism as, for the first time, a greater priority than counter-espionage. In the 1970s the KGB saw terrorism as a weapon which could, on occasion, be used against the West.[66] The FSB and SVR no longer do. While Russia and the West still spy on each other, they co-operate in counter-terrorism. Given the transnational nature of terrorist operations, they have no other rational option. The head of the SVR, S. N. Lebedev, declared a year after 9/11, 'No country in the world, not even the United States with all its power, is now able to counter these threats on its own. Co-operation is essential.'[67] Today's FSB and SVR have formal, if little-advertised, liaisons with Western intelligence agencies. In 2004 at the holiday resort of Sochi on the Black Sea the FSB hosted a meeting of intelligence chiefs from seventy foreign services (including senior representatives of most leading Western agencies) to discuss international collaboration in counter-terrorism. In the course of the conference, delegates watched an exercise (codenamed NABAT) by Russian special forces to free hostages from a hijacked plane at Sochi airport.[68]

Despite their public emphasis on 'spiritual security', both the FSB and SVR look back far less to a distant pre-revolutionary past than to their Soviet roots, holding an annual celebration on 20 December, the date of the founding of the Cheka six weeks after the Revolution as the 'sword and shield' of the Bolshevik regime. The FSB continues to campaign for the replacement of the statue of the Cheka's founder, Feliks Dzerzhinsky, on the pedestal outside its headquarters from which it was removed after the failed coup of August 1991. The SVR dates its own foundation from 20 December 1920, when the Cheka's foreign department was established. It celebrated its seventy-fifth anniversary in 1995 by publishing an uncritical eulogy of the 'large number of glorious deeds' performed by Soviet intelligence officers 'who have made an outstanding contribution to guaranteeing the security of our Homeland'.[69] A multi-volume history, begun by Primakov as head of the SVR and still in progress, is similarly designed to show that, from the Cheka to the KGB, Soviet foreign intelligence 'honourably and unselfishly did its patriotic duty to Motherland and people'.[70] Much as Russian intelligence has evolved since the collapse of the Soviet Union, it has yet to come to terms with its own past.

Appendix A
KGB Chairmen, 1917–91

1917–26
Feliks Edmundovich Dzerzhinsky
(Cheka/GPU/OGPU)

1926–34
Vyacheslav Rudolfovich
Menzhinsky
(OGPU)

1934–36
Genrikh Grigoryevich Yagoda
(NKVD)

1936–38
Nikolai Ivanovich Yezhov
(NKVD)

1938–41
Lavrenti Pavlovich Beria
(NKVD)

1941 (February–July)
Vsevelod Nikolayevich Merkulov
(NKGB)

1941–43
Lavrenti Pavlovich Beria
(NKVD)

1943–46
Vsevelod Nikolayevich Merkulov
(NKGB/MGB)

1946–51
Viktor Semyonovich Abakumov
(MGB)

1951–53
Semyon Denisovich Ignatyev
(MGB)

1953 (March–June)
Lavrenti Pavlovich Beria
(MGB)

1953–54
Sergei Nikiforovich Kruglov
(MGB)

1954–58
Ivan Aleksandrovich Serov
(KGB)

1958–61
Aleksandr Nikolayevich Shelepin
(KGB)

1961–67
Vladimir Yefimovich Semichastny
(KGB)

1967–82
Yuri Vladimirovich Andropov
(KGB)

1982 (May–December)
Vitali Vasilyevich Fedorchuk
(KGB)

1982–88
Viktor Mikhailovich Chebrikov
(KGB)

1988–91
Vladimir Aleksandrovich
Kryuchkov
(KGB)

1991 (August–December)
Vadim Viktorovich Bakatin
(KGB)

Appendix B
Heads of Foreign Intelligence, 1920–2005

1920–21
Yakov Kristoforovich Davtyan
(Davydov)
(Cheka)

1921
Solomon Grigoryevich Mogilevsky
(Cheka)

1921–30
Mikhail Abramovich Trilisser
(Cheka/GPU/OGPU)

1930–36
Artur Khristyanovich Artuzov
(OGPU/NKVD)

1936–38
Abram Abramovich Slutsky
(NKVD)

1938
Zelman I. Pasov
(NKVD)

1938
Sergei Mikhailovich Shpigelglas
(NKVD)

1938–39
Vladimir Georgiyevich Dekanozov
(NKVD)

1939–46
Pavel Mikhailovich Fitin
(NKVD/NKGB/NKVD/MGB)

1946 (June–September)
Pyotr Nikolayevich Kubatkin
(MGB)

1946–49
Pyotr Vasilyevich Fedotov
(Deputy Chairman, KI, 1947–49)

1949–52
Sergei Romanovich Savchenko
(Deputy Chairman, KI, 1949–51)

1952–53
Yevgeni Petrovich Pitovranov
(MGB)

1953 (March–June)
Vasili Stepanovich Ryasnoy
(MGB)

1953–55
Aleksandr Semyonovich
Panyushkin
(MGB/KGB)

1956–71
Aleksandr Mikhailovich
Sakharovsky
(KGB)

1971–74
Fyodor Konstantinovich Mortin
(KGB)

1991–96
Yevgeni Maksimovich Primakov
(SVR)

1974–88
Vladimir Aleksandrovich Kryuchkov
(KGB)

1996–2000
Vyacheslav Ivanovich Trubnikov
(SVR)

1988–91
Leonid Vladimirovich Shebarshin
(KGB)

2000–
Sergei Nikolayevich Lebedev
(SVR)

Appendix C

The Organization of the KGB in the later Cold War

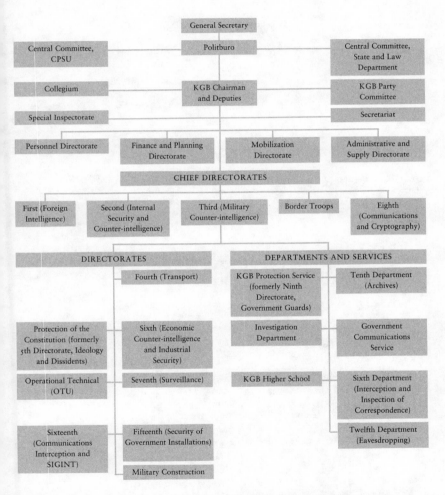

General Secretary

Central Committee, CPSU — Politburo — Central Committee, State and Law Department

Collegium — KGB Chairman and Deputies — KGB Party Committee

Special Inspectorate — Secretariat

Personnel Directorate | Finance and Planning Directorate | Mobilization Directorate | Administrative and Supply Directorate

CHIEF DIRECTORATES

First (Foreign Intelligence) | Second (Internal Security and Counter-intelligence) | Third (Military Counter-intelligence) | Border Troops | Eighth (Communications and Cryptography)

DIRECTORATES | **DEPARTMENTS AND SERVICES**

Fourth (Transport) | KGB Protection Service (formerly Ninth Directorate, Government Guards) | Tenth Department (Archives)

Protection of the Constitution (formerly 5th Directorate, Ideology and Dissidents) | Sixth (Economic Counter-intelligence and Industrial Security) | Investigation Department | Government Communications Service

Operational Technical (OTU) | Seventh (Surveillance) | KGB Higher School | Sixth Department (Interception and Inspection of Correspondence)

Sixteenth (Communications Interception and SIGINT) | Fifteenth (Security of Government Installations) | | Twelfth Department (Eavesdropping)

Military Construction

Source: Desmond Ball and Robert Windren, 'Soviet Signals Intelligence (Sigint): Organisation and Management', *Intelligence and National Security*, vol. 4 (1989), no. 4; Christopher Andrew and Oleg Gordievsky, *KGB: The Inside Story of Its Foreign Operations from Lenin to Gorbachev*, paperback edition (London: Sceptre, 1991); and Mitrokhin.

499

Appendix D

The Organization of the KGB First Chief Directorate (Foreign Intelligence)

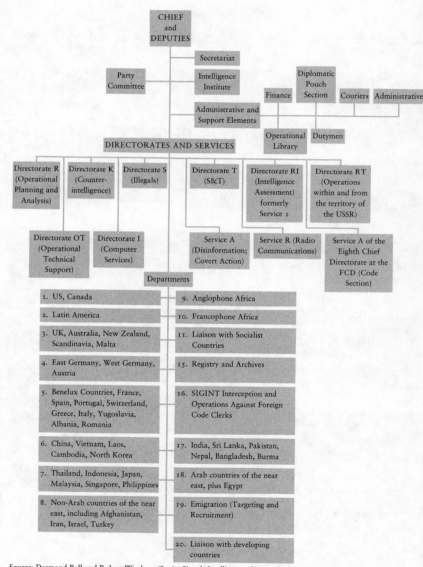

Source: Desmond Ball and Robert Windren, 'Soviet Signals Intelligence (Sigint): Organisation and Management', *Intelligence and National Security*, vol. 4 (1989), no. 4; Christopher Andrew and Oleg Gordievsky, *KGB: The Inside Story of Its Foreign Operations from Lenin to Gorbachev*, paperback edition (London: Sceptre, 1991); and Mitrokhin.

Appendix E

The Organization of a KGB Residency

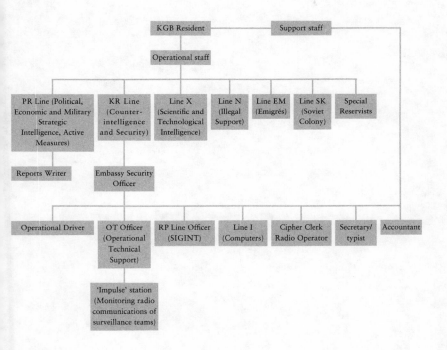

KGB Resident — Support staff

Operational staff

PR Line (Political, Economic and Military Strategic Intelligence, Active Measures) · KR Line (Counter-intelligence and Security) · Line X (Scientific and Technological Intelligence) · Line N (Illegal Support) · Line EM (Emigrés) · Line SK (Soviet Colony) · Special Reservists

Reports Writer · Embassy Security Officer

Operational Driver · OT Officer (Operational Technical Support) · RP Line Officer (SIGINT) · Line I (Computers) · Cipher Clerk Radio Operator · Secretary/ typist · Accountant

'Impulse' station (Monitoring radio communications of surveillance teams)

Notes

Foreword: Vasili Mitrokhin and His Archive

1. Andrew and Mitrokhin, *The Sword and the Shield*, p. 1.
2. Intelligence and Security Committee, *The Mitrokhin Inquiry Report*, p. 4.
3. *Nezavisimaya Gazeta*, 10 Dec. 1966; Reuter reports, 10 Dec. 1966.
4. Though Dr Kennedy-Pipe mentions the KGB's role in the invasion of Afghanistan, she devotes only two sentences to other KGB Cold War operations; Kennedy-Pipe, *Russia and the World, 1917–1991*, pp. 163–4, 168, 203.
5. The article on 'Intelligence' is similarly overwhelmingly concerned with US rather than with Soviet or Russian intelligence. Krieger (ed.), *The Oxford Companion to Politics of the World*, pp. 122, 396–7.
6. Andrew and Mitrokhin, *The Sword and the Shield*, ch. 1; there are some further details in the introduction to the paperback edition.
7. Russian literature, unsurprisingly, is much richer in winter-forest poetry than English literature. Among the poems which best capture Mitrokhin's sense of the magic of the winter forest is one by the nineteenth-century Slavophile Fyodor Tyutchev (translated by F. Jude):

> The forest is entranced
> by Winter the Magician.
> Under velvet snow
> it's mute, immobile, glistening
> wondrously with life,
> standing enchanted,
> neither dead nor alive,
> entranced by a magic dream . . .

8. When Mitrokhin began his career, the foreign intelligence arms of the MGB and the GRU (Soviet military intelligence) were temporarily combined in the Committee of Information (KI).
9. Andrew and Mitrokhin, *The Sword and the Shield*, chs. 19, 20, 28.

10. Ibid., p. 367– 8.
11. Ibid., pp. 10–11.
12. Intelligence and Security Committee, *The Mitrokhin Inquiry Report*, p. 4.
13. Before her retirement, Mrs Mitrokhin had worked as an oto-rhino-laryngologist, attending several medical congresses in the West.
14. Mitrokhin later found similar plans in KGB files to injure and end the dancing career of another celebrated defector from the Kirov Ballet, Natalia Makarova. Andrew and Mitrokhin, *The Sword and the Shield*, pp. 369 – 70.
15. On my early meetings with Mitrokhin, see the introduction to the paperback edition of volume 1.
16. Further details of the various sections of Mitrokhin's archive are given in the Bibliography (p. 595). The extensive endnotes make clear the contribution both of the archive and of other sources to each chapter of the book.
17. Andrew and Mitrokhin, *The Sword and the Shield*, p. xviii.

1. Introduction

1. Rubinstein, *Moscow's Third World Strategy*, pp. 16–17.
2. Pipes, *Russia under the Bolshevik Regime*, ch. 4.
3. Carr, *Foundations of a Planned Economy*, vol. 3, chs. 84–5; Weiner, 'Comintern in East Asia', pp. 168–79; Andrew and Gordievsky, *KGB*, pp. 126–7.
4. Carr, *Foundations of a Planned Economy*, vol. 1, pp. 296–307; Howe, *Anticolonialism in British Politics*, pp. 71–3. On Münzenberg's flair for front organizations, see Andrew and James, 'Willi Münzenberg, the Reichstag Fire and the Conversion of Innocents'. On Gumede, see Davidson, Filatova, Gorodnov and Johns (eds.), *South Africa and the Communist International*, vol. 1, p. xxii.
5. Though much of the Comintern archive is now open to researchers in the Russian State Archive of Socio-Political History, its intelligence files remain classified.
6. McDermott and Agnew, *The Comintern*, p. 145; Davidson, Filatova, Gorodnov and Johns (eds.), *South Africa and the Communist International*, vol. 1, pp. 19–22.
7. See below, pp. 270–71.
8. Probably among the first victims, four years before the beginning of the Great Terror, was one of the most able interwar African Communists: Albert Nzula, the first black General Secretary of the Communist Party of South Africa. Jomo Kenyatta recalled seeing him dragged out of a meeting in Moscow, in full view of the participants, by two OGPU officers. He was never seen alive again, and it was officially claimed that he had died from pneumonia after collapsing drunk in the street in sub-zero temperatures.

Kenyatta claimed that Nzula's death had turned him against Communism. Nzula was only twenty-eight at the time of his death. Had he lived, he would undoubtedly have gone on to play a leading role in the early struggle against apartheid. Nzula, Potemkin and Zusmanovich (ed. Cohen), *Forced Labour in Colonial Africa*, pp. 15–16. (We are grateful for this reference to Professor John Lonsdale.) On other South African victims of the OGPU and NKVD, see Davidson, Filatova, Gorodnov and Johns (eds.), *South Africa and the Communist International*, vol. 1, pp. 17–21.

9. McClellan, 'Africans and Blacks in the Comintern Schools', p. 388, n. 64. Though founded by the Commissariat for Nationality Affairs in 1921, the University came under Comintern jurisdiction in 1923.

10. Suchkov, 'Dzhomo Keniata v Moskve', p. 120.

11. McClellan, 'Africans and Blacks in the Comintern Schools', pp. 380–81. On Kenyatta's years in Moscow, see below, p. 424.

12. Rubinstein, *Moscow's Third World Strategy*, pp. 19–20, 238–9.

13. Fieldhouse, *Black Africa 1945–80*, p. 85. Professor Fieldhouse provides a notably balanced analysis of African economic history during this period.

14. Nkrumah, *Africa Must Unite*, pp. 23–4.

15. Volkogonov, *Rise and Fall of the Soviet Empire*, p. 228.

16. Taubman, *Khrushchev*, p. 427.

17. Foot, *Bevan*, vol. 2, pp. 646–7.

18. Andrew, *For the President's Eyes Only*, p. 240.

19. Taubman, *Khrushchev*, p. 378.

20. Khrushchov [*sic*], *World without Arms*, vol. 1, pp. 165–7.

21. The complaints against Russian racism by African and black American students at the interwar Communist University of the Toilers of the East in Moscow were little publicized; McClellan, 'Africans and Blacks in the Comintern Schools'.

22. Attwood, *The Reds and the Blacks*, p. 16. In 1961 Attwood was appointed US Ambassador to Guinea.

23. Rubinstein, *Moscow's Third World Strategy*, pp. 86–7.

24. See, e.g., Khrushchov, *Communism*, vol. 1, p. 152.

25. Taubman, *Khrushchev*, pp. 475–6. The tale of Khrushchev's shoe banging has grown with the telling. It has been wrongly claimed, for example, that he banged his shoe on his desk during an earlier speech to the General Assembly by the British Prime Minister, Harold Macmillan. On that occasion, however, he merely banged his fists repeatedly and suffered a classic Macmillan put-down when the Prime Minister asked to have the banging translated. Though no newsreel film remains of the shoe banging on 13 October 1960, a photo survives of the shoe on Khrushchev's desk. A KGB report confirms the contemporary account of the shoe banging by Benjamin Welles of the *New York Times*, though some have since expressed scepticism about the episode. For a summary of the evidence, see Taubman, 'Nikita Khrushchev and the Shoe'.

26. Beschloss, *The Crisis Years*, p. 60.

27. Hobsbawm, *Age of Extremes*, p. 436.

28. See below, p. 40.

29. On the remarkable achievements of the Soviet intelligence offensive against the United States during the Second World War, see Andrew and Mitrokhin, *The Sword and the Shield*, chs. 6–8.

30. Leonov, Fediakova and Fermandois, 'El general Nikolai Leonov en el CEP'.

31. vol. 1, app. 3.

32. Dobrynin, *In Confidence*, pp. 404–5. In the pre-Gorbachev era, the International Department was chiefly concerned with relations with foreign Communist parties, other parties and movements. In the Third World, however, it was also involved in state-to-state relations. Brown, *The Gorbachev Factor*, pp. 213–14.

33. Shevchenko, *Breaking with Moscow*, pp. 138, 292; Dobrynin, *In Confidence*, pp. 404–5. Suslov's increasing age steadily decreased his chances of succeeding Brezhnev. He died in January 1982 at the age of 79, leaving the way open for Andropov to become General Secretary after Brezhnev's death ten months later.

34. Leonov, *Likholet'e*, p. 141.

35. Dobrynin, *In Confidence*, pp. 408, 209–10.

36. Willetts, *The Non-Aligned Movement*, pp. 33–4.

37. 'Chief Conclusions and Views Adopted at the Meeting of Heads of Service [FCD]', 1 Feb. 1984; Andrew and Gordievsky, *Instructions from the Centre*, p. 7.

38. Andrew, *For the President's Eyes Only*, pp. 336, 354–5. 'Active measures' ranged from covert media manipulation to assassination.

39. Leonov, *Likholet'e*, pp. 152–4. Many Soviet diplomats were also 'deeply surprised at America's acceptance of this final humiliation'; Shevchenko, *Breaking with Moscow*, pp. 350–51.

40. Ford, *A Time to Heal*, p. 256.

41. During a discussion between the 'free officers' who seized power in Egypt in 1952, Nasser declared, 'The people only know British imperialism. Why should we confuse them by talking about the Americans?' 'American imperialism', he said, was 'a phrase used by the communists only'. El-Din, *Memories of a Revolution*, p. 60.

42. Rubinstein, *Moscow's Third World Strategy*, p. 245.

43. Russell, *War Crimes in Vietnam*, pp. 112, 117–18; Hollander, *Anti-Americanism*, pp. 347–8, 374–5.

44. Warren, *Imperialism*, p. 1.

45. The three volumes of key texts on imperialism edited by Peter Cain and Mark Harrison, though including numerous non-Russian Marxist analyses, contain nothing by any Soviet writer since Lenin.

46. Warren, *Imperialism*, pp. 2–3.

47. Dobrynin, *In Confidence*, pp. 265, 281–2, 303.

48. *Soviet Covert Action*, p. 69.

49. In 1971 Andropov had informed his fellow hard-liner Ustinov that the United States was using the SALT talks to try 'to preserve definite advantages in the most important kinds of strategic weapons'; Andropov to Ustinov, 19 April 1971, 'More Documents from the Russian Archives', p. 69.

50. See below, chs. 6, 21 and 25. The KGB was not, however, enthused by the victory of the Khmer Rouge and the establishment of the Pol Pot regime in Cambodia.

51. Leonov, *Likholet'e*, p. 131.

52. Volkogonov, *Rise and Fall of the Soviet Empire*, p. 324.

53. Gates, *From the Shadows*, pp. 116–17.

54. Volkogonov, *Rise and Fall of the Soviet Empire*, pp. 324–6.

55. Rubinstein, *Moscow's Third World Strategy*, pp. 271–2.

56. vol. 3 pak, app. 3, item 410.

57. Andrew, *For the President's Eyes Only*, pp. 402–4.

58. Andrew and Mitrokhin, *The Sword and the Shield*, ch. 14; Holland, 'The Lie that Linked CIA to the Kennedy Assassination'.

59. According to opinion polls in 1992 on the thirtieth anniversary of Kennedy's assassination, three-quarters of Americans believed the CIA had murdered the President; Moynihan, *Secrecy*, pp. 219–20. Oliver Stone's film version of the conspiracy theory, *JFK*, was enormously influential. One enthusiastic US historian claimed that *JFK* probably 'had a greater impact on public opinion than any other work of art in American history' save *Uncle Tom's Cabin*: Toplin (ed.), *Oliver Stone's USA*, p. 174.

60. vol. 6, ch. 14, part 3.

61. See below, p. 326.

62. Mitrokhin, 'KGB Active Measures in Southwest Asia', pp. 193–4.

63. Bittman, *The Deception Game*, p. 23.

64. *Moscow News*, 1992, no. 25.

65. Gromyko and Ponomarev (eds.), *Soviet Foreign Policy*, vol. 2, p. 641.

66. vol. 6, ch. 14, part 4. Oliver Tambo, Chairman of the African National Congress (ANC), for example, sent congratulations to the CPSU 'and Leonid Brezhnev personally' on 'their unparalleled record of historic achievements ... The latest of these achievements is the new constitution of the USSR; its provisions constitute yet one more triumph for the ideas of the Great October Soviet Revolution.' BBC, *Summary of World Broadcasts*, 5 Nov. 1977, reporting English-language broadcasts from Moscow of 3 Nov. 1977.

67. k-9, 82. Brezhnev, unlike any of the other recipients, received two copies. The daily digest appears to have been instituted by Andropov in order to heighten the leadership's appreciation of the KGB's achievements abroad. Mitrokhin, who had a low opinion of the quality of the invariably

politically correct Soviet intelligence analysis, did not note the contents of any of the daily digests. On the delivery of intelligence reports to the political leadership, see Leonov, *Likholet'e*, p. 130.
68. Nechiporenko, 'Na rodine atstekov', pp. 173–4.
69. Some senior KGB officers also aspired to chests full of medals. Vadim Kirpichenko, for example, who became first deputy head of foreign intelligence in 1991, chose for the front cover of his memoirs, *Razvedka: litsa i lichnosti*, published in 1998, a colour photograph of himself in full-dress general's uniform with the left side of his chest entirely covered in decorations; as of 1998 there was still space for a few more medals on the right.
70. k-3, 300.
71. For the lyrics of 'Happy Birthday, Leonid Brezhnev', see http://baez.-woz.org/Lyrics/brezhnev.html.
72. Leonov, *Likholet'e*, pp. 120–22.
73. Ibid., pp. 124–6.
74. See below, p. 479.
75. Leonov, *Likholet'e*, pp. 129–31.
76. Interview with Vadim Kirpichenko, *Vremia Novostei*, 20 Dec. 2004.
77. Andrew and Mitrokhin, *The Sword and the Shield*, p.555. *Izvestia*, 24 Sept. 1991.
78. See below, pp. 81, 83, 155.
79. Andrew and Gordievsky, *KGB*, p. 585.
80. Kissinger, *Diplomacy*, p. 698.
81. Volkogonov, *Rise and Fall of the Soviet Empire*, pp. 318–19, 333.
82. Westad, 'Moscow and the Angolan Crisis, 1974–1976', p. 21.
83. Gates, *From the Shadows*, p. 116.

2. Latin America: Introduction

1. Reagan, *An American Life*, pp. 239, 474.
2. Carr, *Foundations of a Planned Economy*, vol. 3, p. 958.
3. Andrew and Mitrokhin, *The Sword and the Shield*, pp. 86–8.
4. Miller, *Soviet Relations with Latin America, 1959–1987*, p. 6.
5. A few Latin American Communist parties had received subsidies in the Comintern era. The first Cold War subsidy secretly delivered by the KGB was to the Chilean Party in 1955. A similar payment was made to the Uruguayan Party in the following year. In 1957 the Chilean, Mexican and Argentinian parties received subsidies. The number of recipients increased substantially during the next two decades. Ulianova and Fediakova, 'Algunos aspectos de la ayuda financiera del Partido Comunista de la URSS al comunismo chileno durante la guerra fría'.
6. Leonov, *Likholet'e*, p. 60.

7. Hollander, *Political Pilgrims*, pp. 224–5, 231–2, 237.
8. Talbott (ed.), *Khrushchev Speaks*, pp. 490–91. Khrushchev identifies the KGB resident, Alekseyev, only by his cover profession as a journalist.
9. Leonov, 'La inteligencia soviética en América Latina durante la guerra fría'.
10. Leonov, *Likholet'e*, p. 112.
11. Andrew, *For the President's Eyes Only*, chs. 6–9. Ferguson, *Colossus*, p. 103.
12. Hollander, *Anti-Americanism*, pp. 264–5.
13. Andrew, *For the President's Eyes Only*, pp. 487–93.
14. Seventeen per cent found the United States the 'most unappealing' country, 14 per cent Chile and 10 per cent the Soviet Union. The most admired country was Cuba (20.5 per cent), followed by France, then with a socialist government (12 per cent). Hollander, *Anti-Americanism*, ch. 9.
15. Andrew and Gordievsky, *KGB*, p. 631.
16. Hollander, *Anti-Americanism*, p. 363.

3. 'The Bridgehead', 1959–1969

1. The full versions of Latin American names follow the Spanish system of given name, then patronym, followed by mother's surname. Shorter versions give only the patronym.
2. Quirk, *Fidel Castro*, p. 684; Leonov, Fediakova and Fermandois, 'El general Nikolai Leonov en el CEP'.
3. Andrew and Gordievsky, *KGB*, p. 469; Deas, 'Spectacle of the Rats and Owls'.
4. Fursenko and Naftali, *'One Hell of a Gamble'*, pp. 12–13.
5. Leonov, *Likholet'e*, p. 29.
6. Andrew and Gordievsky, *KGB*, p. 469.
7. Courtois et al., *Le livre noir du communisme*, pp. 711–12.
8. Andrew and Gordievsky, *KGB*, p. 469; Fursenko and Naftali, *'One Hell of a Gamble'*, p. 37. Leonov claims that he did not become a KGB officer until 1958. It is difficult to believe, however, that he had no earlier association with the KGB.
9. Fursenko and Naftali, *'One Hell of a Gamble'*, p. 25.
10. Balfour, *Castro*, ch. 4; Domínguez, *To Make a World Safe for Revolution*, pp. 20–21, 248–9.
11. Senate Committee on the Judiciary, *The Role of the Soviet Union, Cuba and East Germany in Fomenting Terrorism in Southern Africa*, pp. 340–41. Ashby, *Bear in the Backyard*, pp. 23–4.
12. Alekseyev's original surname had been Shitov but he was generally known within the KGB by the codename (or 'workname') ALEKSEYEV, which he had adopted during the Great Patriotic War. Szulc, *Fidel*,

pp. 408–9. Fursenko and Naftali, 'One Hell of a Gamble', pp. 25–9; Domínguez, To Make a World Safe for Revolution, pp. 20–21.

13. Leonov, Likholet'e, pp. 47–55.

14. Fursenko and Naftali, 'One Hell of a Gamble', pp. 44–7.

15. Sejna, We Will Bury You, pp. 45–50. General Sejna was in charge of the arrangements for Raúl Castro's visit. He misremembers the date as 1959 rather than 1960.

16. Leonov, Likholet'e, pp. 57–9.

17. Fursenko and Naftali, 'One Hell of a Gamble', pp. 46, 62–3; Dobrynin, In Confidence, pp. 71–2; Andrew and Gordievsky, KGB, p. 471.

18. Leonov, Likholet'e, p. 60. On the structure of the FCD, see Appendix D.

19. Fursenko and Naftali, 'One Hell of a Gamble', pp. 51–5; Andrew and Mitrokhin, The Sword and the Shield, pp. 180–1, 607–8(n. 31).

20. Geyer, Guerrilla Prince, p. 222.

21. Castañeda, Compañero, pp. 146–7, 188–9.

22. Leonov, Likholet'e, pp. 65–6.

23. Andrew, For the President's Eyes Only, pp. 257–67; Thomas, Cuba, ch. 106.

24. Shelepin to Khrushchev, Memorandum no. 1861-Sh, 29 July 1961. Decree no. 191/75-GS; vol. 6, ch. 5, part 5. Cf. Zubok, 'Spy vs. Spy', pp. 28–30; Zubok and Pleshakov, Inside the Kremlin's Cold War, pp. 253–5.

25. vol. 6, ch. 5, part 5. Fonseca was co-founder of the FSLN, initially called the National Liberation Front. 'Sandinista' was added, chiefly at Fonseca's insistence, in 1962 in honour of the interwar anti-imperialist hero, General Augusto César Sandino.

26. Quoted in Valenta and Durán (eds.), Conflict in Nicaragua, pp. 7, 72–3. Hodges, Intellectual Origins of the Nicaraguan Revolution, pp. 161–7.

27. 'Inside Perspective on the Legacy of Che Guevara: Piñeiro's Last Interview'; Manuel Piñeiro Losada became head of the DGI on its creation in 1961. http://pw1.netcom.com/~hhenke/news4.htm.

28. Zimmermann, Sandinista, pp. 183, 193.

29. vol. 6, ch. 5, part 5. In 1945 Torres (PIMEN) had been exiled from Nicaragua to Guatemala, where he occupied a succession of posts in the Ministry of Education until the overthrow in 1954 of the left-wing regime of President Jacobo Arbenz Gúzman in a coup organized by the CIA.

30. Zimmermann, Sandinista, pp. 55, 87, 94.

31. Mitrokhin's notes do not identify LOT.

32. vol. 6, ch. 5, part 5.

33. Ibid.; t-7, 320.

34. vol. 6, ch. 5, part 5.

35. Ibid.

36. Ibid.

37. Interview with Piñeiro, Tricontinental [Cuba], Dec. 1997. On the organ-

ization of the DGI, see FAS Intelligence Resource Program: http://www. fas.org/irp/world/cuba/dgi/ .

38. k-11, p. 170. In the mid-1950s Grinchenko had to be withdrawn successively from the United States and France after breaches of security (Andrew and Mitrokhin, *The Sword and the Shield*, p. 170). Thereafter he seems to have been used as an illegal trainer.

39. Fursenko and Naftali, *'One Hell of a Gamble'*, pp. 172–89; Dobrynin, *In Confidence*, pp. 72–3; Andrew and Mitrokhin, *The Sword and the Shield*, pp. 237–41; Castañeda, *Compañero*, pp. 182–4.

40. Fursenko and Naftali, *'One Hell of a Gamble'*, p. 292; Castañeda, *Compañero*, p. 229.

41. Quirk, *Fidel Castro*, pp. 456–70.

42. Speech by Castro in Red Square, 28 April 1963. The text of this and other of his speeches cited in this chapter is available on the Castro database http://lanic.utexas.edu/la/cb/cuba/castro.html.

43. Fursenko (ed.), *Prezidium TsK KPSS. 1954–1964*, p. 724.

44. Andrew and Gordievsky, *KGB*, p. 511.

45. Castañeda, *Compañero*, pp. 236–41. On Che's ineffective attempts to spread revolution in Africa, see below, pp. 433–4.

46. Borge, 'La formación del FSLN', p. 31; Black, *Triumph of the People*, pp. 47, 77–8.

47. Mitrokhin's notes identify PIMEN as 'one of the leaders of the ISKRA Group', but his exact relationship with it is unclear; t-7, 320.

48. vol. 6, ch. 5, part 5; t-7, 318, 320.

49. Fursenko and Naftali, *'One Hell of a Gamble'*, p. 353.

50. Miller, *Soviet Relations with Latin America, 1959–1987*, p. 94.

51. Castañeda, *Compañero*, pp. 331–4.

52. Mitrokhin's notes contain statistics on the passports and identity documents used by 327 of the Cuban illegals deployed through Czechoslovakia between 1962 and 1966. Of these, 140 were Venezuelan, 70 Dominican, 60 Argentinian, 50 Colombian, 5 Peruvian, one American and one British (k-20, 61). During a visit to Moscow in 1972, the deputy head of the Cuban Illegals Directorate told the KGB, 'In the past, the Cuban illegal operations had primarily engaged in helping the nationalist freedom movement in the Latin American countries . . .' (k-20, 62).

53. k-11, 130.

54. Semichastnyi, *Bespokoinoe serdtse*, pp. 285–93.

55. Domínguez, *To Make a World Safe for Revolution*, p. 116.

56. vol. 6, ch. 5, part 5; t-7, 318, 320.

57. Black, *Triumph of the People*, pp. 80–81.

58. vol. 6, ch. 5, part 5; t-7, 318, 320.

59. Pezzullo and Pezzullo, *At the Fall of Somoza*, pp. 111–15.

60. Horne, *Small Earthquake in Chile*, pp. 251–2.

61. Castañeda, *Compañero*, ch. 10.

62. Gerassi (ed.), *The Speeches and Writings of Ernesto 'Che' Guevara*, p. 268.
63. Ashby, *Bear in the Backyard*, p. 46; Andrew and Gordievsky, *KGB*, pp. 512–13.
64. Castañeda, *Compañero*, chs. 10, 11; Quirk, *Fidel Castro*, chs. 19, 20; Ryan, *The Fall of Che Guevara*.
65. Balfour, *Castro*, p. 90. Quirk, *Fidel Castro*, pp. 590–91.
66. vol. 6, ch. 5, part 5; Andrew and Mitrokhin, *The Sword and the Shield*, pp. 363– 4.
67. Andrew and Mitrokhin, *The Sword and the Shield*, chs. 15, 16.
68. Speech by Castro, 26 August 1968.
69. Quirk, *Fidel Castro*, ch. 20.
70. Lockwood, *Castro's Cuba, Cuba's Fidel*, p. 260.
71. Quirk, *Fidel Castro*, pp. 601–3, 649.
72. Hollander, *Political Pilgrims*, pp. 260–61.
73. Levinson and Brightman (eds.), *Venceremos Brigade*; quotation from p. 31.
74. Ibid., p. 249.
75. k-20, 62.
76. Amuchastegui, 'Cuban Intelligence and the October Crisis', p. 110.
77. [US] Senate Committee on the Judiciary, Subcommittee to Investigate the Administration of the Internal Security Act, testimony of Orlando Castro Hidalgo, 16 Oct. 1969, pp. 1423–9; Senate Committee on the Judiciary, *The Role of Cuba in International Terrorism and Subversion*, pp. 11, 24.
78. Ashby, *Bear in the Backyard*, pp. 57–8; FAS Intelligence Resource Program: http://www.fas.org/irp/world/cuba/dgi/.

4. 'Progressive' Regimes and 'Socialism with Red Wine'

1. Minute by Andropov, 5 Jan. 1972; k-22, 92.
2. k-22, 64.
3. Leonov, 'La inteligencia soviética en América Latina durante la guerra fría'.
4. Horne, *Small Earthquake in Chile*, p. 26.
5. Ibid., ch. 4.
6. The analysis of the role of the IPC and other US-owned businesses in Peru in Clayton, *Peru and the United States*, ch. 7, provides a convincing case study of the inadequacy of dependency theory.
7. Compensation, however, was agreed five years later.
8. Masterson, *Militarism and Politics in Latin America*, pp. 243–61. On the Velasco regime's reform programme, see McClintock and Lowenthal (eds.), *The Peruvian Experiment Reconsidered*.

9. Leonov, 'La inteligencia soviética en América Latina durante la guerra fría'; Leonov, *Likholet'e*, pp. 108–11.

10. Masterson, *Militarism and Politics in Latin America*, pp. 243–61; Horne, *Small Earthquake in Chile*, ch. 4.

11. t-7, 192. Operations officers in the Lima residency increased in number from two on its foundation in 1969 to twenty in 1976; k-22, 184.

12. k-22, 233.

13. Horne, *Small Earthquake in Chile*, p. 92.

14. k-22, 226.

15. k-22, 31.

16. k-22, 42. By 1972 the residency had five Line PR agents and nine confidential contacts. Three years later Line PR was running ten agents. k-22, 21, 99, 184.

17. Horne, *Small Earthquake in Chile*, pp. 328–9.

18. k-22, 184, 192, 233. The CPSU Central Committee resolution was No. P 7/77-OP, dated 14 June 1971.

19. k-22, 188.

20. k-22, 74.

21. k-22, 233.

22. k-22, 99.

23. k-22, 184, 202. A KGB memorandum (No. 979-A) setting out details of co-operation with Peruvian military intelligence was approved by the CPSU Central Committee on 22 April 1975; k-22, 184. Gallegos has been described as 'the "model" Peruvian army progressive of the Velasco era'. From 1974 to 1976 he was Minister of Agriculture, charged with overseeing the programme of agrarian reform. Masterson, *Militarism and Politics in Latin America*, p. 249.

24. k-22, 225.

25. k-22, 99.

26. k-22, 184.

27. k-22, 233.

28. k-22, 188.

29. k-22, 99.

30. k-22, 187, 188.

31. k-22, 233.

32. Masterson, *Militarism and Politics in Latin America*, pp. 258–9; Rudolph, *Peru: The Evolution of a Crisis*, p. 58.

33. k-22, 99.

34. Horne, *Small Earthquake in Chile*, pp. 88n., 90, 329.

35. Klarén, *Peru*, pp. 359–65.

36. t-7, 192. Maoism in Peru, however, was far from dead. During the 1980s Sendero Luminoso established itself as the world's most aggressive Maoist guerrilla force, responsible for approximately 25,000 deaths.

37. Mitchell, *The Legacy of Populism in Bolivia*, ch. 6; Horne, *Small Earthquake in Chile*, ch. 12.

38. k-22, 287–8.

39. Horne, *Small Earthquake in Chile*, pp. 272–3.

40. k-22, 290.

41. Ibid.

42. Horne, *Small Earthquake in Chile*, pp. 258, 262–3, 330–31; Mitchell, *The Legacy of Populism in Bolivia*, pp. 114–18.

43. k-22, 46.

44. Andrew and Mitrokhin, *The Sword and the Shield*, pp. 162–3, 357–8.

45. Bird, *Costa Rica*, p. 133.

46. k-22, 46. Mitrokhin's notes give no indication of whether or how the loan was repaid.

47. t-7, 126.

48. Figueres's file describes the confidant as his 'trusted representative'; t-7, 126.

49. t-7, 126.

50. k-22, 79.

51. t-7, 126.

52. k-22, 79.

53. Record of conversation on 15 August 1976 between Piñeiro and Vladimir Konstantinovich Tolstikov, then head of the FCD's Second Department; k-22, 9–11, 39.

54. k-22, 46.

55. k-12, 160.

56. Miller, *Soviet Relations with Latin America, 1959–1987*, p. 128.

57. k-22, 368. Though Mitrokhin's notes do not specify Kuznetsov's cover on this occasion, on other missions he operated as a Novosti correspondent; k-22, 343.

58. k-22, 368.

59. k-22, 110.

60. Davis, *The Last Two Years of Salvador Allende*, p. 4.

61. Haslam, *The Nixon Administration and the Death of Allende's Chile*, pp. 2–3.

62. k-12, 160.

63. Davis, *The Last Two Years of Salvador Allende*, pp. 48–53; Quirk, *Fidel Castro*, p. 685.

64. k-22, 368.

65. Gustafson, 'CIA Covert Action and the Chilean Coup', ch. 4.

66. Andrew, *For the President's Eyes Only*, pp. 370–72; Davis, *The Last Two Years of Salvador Allende*, pp. 4–5.

67. k-12, 160.

68. Ulianova and Fediakova, 'Algunos aspectos de la ayuda financiera del

Partido Comunista de la URSS al comunismo chileno durante la guerra fría'. Mitrokhin's notes detail some of the complexities in transmitting the secret subsidies. In 1965, for example, at least $100,000 of the subsidy was transmitted via the KGB residency in Montevideo; t-7, 90.

69. Politburo decision No. P-170/31 of 27 July 1970; k-12, 160. Mitrokhin's notes resolve a conundrum posed by the records of payments to foreign Communist parties in the archives of the CPSU Central Committee. According to one document, in 1970 the Chilean Communist Party received the fourth highest of the secret subsidies given to fraternal parties. The list of 1970 allocations, however, puts the Chilean Party in sixth place (Ulianova and Fediakova, 'Algunos aspectos de la ayuda financiera del Partido Comunista de la URSS al comunismo chileno durante la guerra fría'). The discrepancy is explained by the additional payment to the Chilean Communist Party authorized by the Politburo on 27 July 1970.

70. The Chilean Communist Party leader, Luis Corvalán, records in his memoirs that Allende had asked the Party to request $100,000 from Moscow for him to use in his presidential election campaign. Corvalán adds, 'The reply, which was negative, seemed to us so terrible and unpresentable to our candidate [Allende] that we decided to use our own reserves to provide him with US$100,000 . . . in the name of the Soviet Communists.' Corvalán was clearly unaware that Allende also received $50,000 from Moscow via the KGB. Corvalán, De lo vivido y lo peleado, p. 108; Ulianova and Fediakova, 'Algunos aspectos de la ayuda financiera del Partido Comunista de la URSS al comunismo chileno durante la guerra fría'.

71. k-22, 41.

72. Mitrokhin notes simply, 'A report signed by Andropov, under reference No. 2591-A of 23 September 1970, informed the CPSU Central Committee of the part played by the KGB in the electoral campaign and of the outcome.' The fact that Andropov chose to report on the role of the KGB in the election, however, undoubtedly means that he did so in positive terms; k-12, 160.

73. k-12, 160. Allende's KGB file, DOR No. 90526, fills three volumes for the period up to his election.

74. Andrew, For the President's Eyes Only, pp. 270–71; Gustafson, 'CIA Machinations in Chile in 1970'.

75. k-22, 368.

76. The US economic offensive against the Allende government was conducted not in Chile itself but through attempts to influence international lending markets and the Paris club of major creditor nations. Falcoff, Modern Chile 1970–1989, pp. 217–30; Gustafson, 'CIA Covert Action and the Chilean Coup'. On Allende's economic mismanagement, see Haslam, The Nixon Administration and the Death of Allende's Chile, ch. 5.

77. k-22, 344. In reality, Davis opposed a request by the Santiago CIA station for more funds for covert action in February 1973, and tendered

his resignation over CIA covert action in Angola in 1975. Davis, *The Last Two Years of Salvador Allende*, pp. 308, 387–8. Kuznetsov also gave Allende the names of seventeen other real or alleged CIA officers in Chile.
78. k-22, 341.
79. k-22, 362, 366, 371. In two of these notes from KGB files, Miria Contreras Bell is incorrectly referred to as 'Miria de Ropert', no doubt as a result of her previous marriage to the Socialist Party militant, Enrique Ropert Gallet, some details of whose career were published in the Santiago journal *El Periodista*, vol. 2, no. 44, 14 September 2003. The third reference gives her name as 'Maria [*sic*] Contreras Ropert'. There was some confusion in KGB files when recording Spanish names as a result of the Spanish and Latin American system of giving the Christian forename, then the patronym, followed by the mother's surname, but omitting the last in shorter versions.
80. Davis, *The Last Two Years of Salvador Allende*, p. 50.
81. k-22, 366.
82. See below, p. 77.
83. Beatriz (commonly known as 'Taty') followed her Cuban husband, Luis Fernández Oña, to Havana after the 1973 coup, and committed suicide four years later, apparently suffering from depression. Pérez, 'Salvador Allende, Apuntes sobre su Dispositivo de Seguridad'; Horne, *Small Earthquake in Chile*, p. 352; Miller, *Soviet Relations with Latin America, 1959–1987*, p. 142; Quirk, *Fidel Castro*, p. 664.
84. Interview with senior CIA officer who has requested anonymity; cited in Gustafson, 'CIA Covert Action and the Chilean Coup'.
85. See above, p. 22.
86. k-22, 372.
87. k-22, 367.
88. k-22, 363.
89. The Politburo resolved: '1. Adopt the proposal of the KGB, as stated in Memorandum No. 3075-A/L, dated 7 December 1971. 2. Approve the plan in the USSR Council of Ministers Resolution to allocate the KGB the necessary funds for carrying out special measures (attached).' Council of Ministers Resolution No. 2691-RS, dated 20 December 1971, decreed: 'Via the State Bank of the USSR, allocate to the USSR Council of Ministers Committee on State Security [KGB] $130,000 to carry out special measures, charged to expenses designated by the USSR State Bank's foreign currency plan.' k-22, 367.
90. k-22, 344.
91. k-22, 245.
92. k-22, 370. On Basov, see Davis, *The Last Two Years of Salvador Allende*, pp. 391–2.
93. k-22, 373.
94. k-22, 341. According to Mitrokhin's notes, while in the sanatorium,

the Kuznetsovs were 'involved in an operation [probably an influence operation]' against the Allendes.

95. k-22, 377.

96. k-22, 92. Andropov's memorandum was a response to a report of 5 January 1972 by Sergei Kondrashev, Deputy Head of the FCD, on the work of the Second (Latin American) Department. Mitrokhin did not note Kondrashev's report.

97. k-22, 92.

98. Mitrokhin notes that contact with Torres was 'formalized in the USSR [presumably during a visit by Torres] in November–December 1975', but gives no further details. KGB contact with Torres was maintained by B. P. Kolomyakov, V. Y. Ryabov and V. I. Denisyuk; k-2, 94.

99. k-22, 92.

100. Miller, *Soviet Relations with Latin America, 1959–1987*, p. 132; Horne, *Small Earthquake in Chile*, pp. 345–6. On evidence of CIA funding for the Truckers' Strike, see Haslam, *The Nixon Administration and the Death of Allende's Chile*, p. 171.

101. k-22, 375.

102. k-22, 365.

103. k-22, 377.

104. k-22, 77.

105. Davis, *The Last Two Years of Salvador Allende*, pp. 192, 236.

106. Ibid., ch. 6.

107. Memorandum No. 687-A, 27 March 1973; k-22, 348. As well as being leader of the Venezuelan Movimento Electoral del Pueblo, Beltrán Prieto was a distinguished educationalist and prolific author, publishing more than seventy books on topics ranging from politics to poetry.

108. Leonov, 'La inteligencia soviética en América Latina durante la guerra fría'; Leonov, *Likholet'e*, pp. 125–6.

109. k-22, 110.

110. Ibid.

111. Davis, *The Last Two Years of Salvador Allende*, pp. 171–5; Horne, *Small Earthquake in Chile*, pp. 347–8. Pinochet became army commander on 23 August.

112. Horne, *Small Earthquake in Chile*, pp. 346–7.

113. Davis, *The Last Two Years of Salvador Allende*, pp. 172–4, 204.

114. k-22, 108.

115. The other members of the junta were General Gustavo Leigh of the air force, Admiral José Toribio Merino of the navy and General César Mendoza of the Carabineros; Constable and Valenzuela, *A Nation of Enemies*, p. 53.

116. k-22, 110.

117. Davis, *The Last Two Years of Salvador Allende*, pp. 171–5; Horne, *Small Earthquake in Chile*, chs. 10–11.

118. Horne, *Small Earthquake in Chile*, pp. 353–7.
119. k-22, 82.
120. Leonov, 'La inteligencia soviética en América Latina durante la guerra fría'.
121. k-22, 82.
122. Amnesty International, *The Case of General Pinochet*.
123. The full text of the 2004 Chilean government report is accessible at http://www.comisiontortura.cl/.
124. vol. 5, sec. 12; k-8, 533.
125. Horne, *Small Earthquake in Chile*, p. 361. In 1976 the *New York Times* published only three articles referring to human rights abuses in Cuba.
126. The text in the Appendix is an English translation of the Russian version copied by Mitrokhin. He did not note the Spanish text of the forgery.

5. Intelligence Priorities after Allende

1. k-22, 116.
2. Ibid. It is unclear from Mitrokhin's notes whether or not this is a quotation from the Politburo minutes.
3. Leonov, 'La inteligencia soviética en América Latina durante la guerra fría'.
4. Andrew and Gordievsky, *KGB*, p. 515.
5. k-19, 389.
6. k-22, 106. Mitrokhin's notes include no reference to participation by Méndez Cominches in any conference of Soviet bloc intelligence chiefs before 1973. Since these notes are not comprehensive, however, the possibility that he took part in an earlier conference cannot be excluded.
7. Andrew and Gordievsky, *KGB*, p. 514.
8. k-22, 106. A list of DGI residencies in 1977 noted by Mitrokhin mentions New York, Ottawa, Montreal, Toronto, Mexico, Peru, Venezuela, Guyana, Panama, Jamaica, Britain, France, West Germany, Italy, Portugal, Spain, Japan and thirteen African cities not individually listed by Mitrokhin; k-22, 161. This list, however, appears to be slightly incomplete. A note by Mitrokhin on a 1976 file mentions a DGI residency in Ecuador; k-22, 6.
9. k-20, 345.
10. k-22, 6, 161.
11. k-22, 8, 149.
12. k-20, 62.
13. k-20, 345.
14. For details of KGB SIGINT operations during the Cold War, see Andrew and Mitrokhin, *The Sword and the Shield*, ch.21; details of

running costs for the major radio intercept stations in KGB residencies are given on p. 670.

15. Ball, 'Soviet Signals Intelligence (SIGINT)', pp. 27–9; Rosenau, 'A Deafening Silence', pp. 723–5.
16. vol. 6, ch. 7, part 4.
17. k-22, 146, 106.
18. k-19, 528.
19. k-19, 526.
20. k-19, 529.
21. k-19, 530.
22. k-19, 532.
23. k-18, 527.
24. *Izvestia*, 9 Feb. 1974.
25. t-7, 182.
26. k-19, 267.
27. vol. 6, ch. 8, part 4.
28. Andrew and Gordievsky, *KGB*, pp. 556–7. Though the CIA provided covert funding for UNITA against the MPLA, in the aftermath of the Vietnam War Washington had no stomach for a serious challenge to the Cuban military presence in Africa.
29. Balfour, *Castro*, pp. 129–30.
30. Westad, 'Moscow and the Angolan Crisis, 1974–1976', pp. 26–8.
31. k-19, 389.
32. k-19, 390.
33. k-22, 150. The DGI carried out a similar operation, at the request of the KGB, against the Venezuelan embassy in Havana.
34. k-19, 386.
35. k-19, 388.
36. See below, ch. 6.
37. Andrew and Gordievsky, *KGB*, pp. 559–60.
38. Quirk, *Fidel Castro*, pp. 776–9.
39. 'Russian and East German Documents on the Horn of Africa, 1977–78', pp. 93–4.
40. k-19, 391.
41. k-22, 37.
42. k-22, 89. Posing as the representative of Sovfilmeksport and using the alias Sergei Sergeyevich Konstantinov, Tolstikov had been deputy resident in Argentina from 1955 to 1960 and resident in Mexico from 1962 to 1966; k-22, 376.
43. Miller, *Soviet Relations with Latin America, 1959–1987*, p. 155.
44. k-22, 89.
45. k-14, 710, 711. On Gelbard and the financing of the Argentinian Communist Party see Gilbert, *El Oro de Moscu*, ch. 12.
46. k-22, 78.

47. Milenky, *Argentina's Foreign Policies*, pp. 154–5.

48. k-22, 115.

49. Milenky, *Argentina's Foreign Policies*, pp. 155–7; Miller, *Soviet Relations with Latin America, 1959–1987*, pp. 154–6.

50. Miller, *Soviet Relations with Latin America, 1959–1987*, pp. 149, 156–8.

51. k-22, 115.

52. In 1974–75 the Lima residency tried to stem the right-wing shift by collecting 'compromising material' on General Javier Tantaleán Vanini, whom it identified as an important right-wing influence on Velasco; k-22, 186, 189. Tantaleán's movement, La Misión, allied with Morales Bermúdez in the 1975 coup; McClintock, 'Velasco, Officers and Citizens', p. 281.

53. k-22, 200.

54. k-22, 185.

55. k-22, 184.

56. k-22, 8.

57. k-22, 9. On the origins of the Departamento de América, see above, p. 56.

58. k-8, 525; k-14, 383; k-22, 48, 101, 118.

59. Miller, *Soviet Relations with Latin America, 1959–1987*, pp. 181–2; Smith, 'Mexico since 1946', p. 367. Though these episodes do not appear in Mitrokhin's notes, it would have been wholly out of character if the KGB had failed to claim credit for them.

60. k-22, 101; k-8, 522. Mitrokhin's notes also mention the use for active measures of a Mexican publication identified only by its codename VESTNIK ('Herald').

61. Kalugin, *Spymaster*, pp. 191–2.

62. vol. 6, ch. 14; vol. 6, app. 1, part 22. Andrew and Mitrokhin, *The Sword and the Shield*, pp. 230 – 1.

63. vol. 6, app. 1, pp. 610a, b.

64. Agee, *Inside the Company*, pp. 522–3, 628.

65. vol. 6, app. 1, pp. 610a, b. Echeverría's successor, José López Portillo, was faced with an immediate economic crisis to which he responded by announcing an economic policy based on austerity and monetarism. In January 1977 he signed a three-year agreement with the IMF which was heavily criticized by the left. Abroad, however, he expressed public sympathy with a number of revolutionary causes. The files noted by Mitrokhin claim that the Mexico City residency 'used its contacts and its agents to conduct conversations of influence' with López (k-8, 525), but imply less easy access than under Echeverría. The residency was criticized, for example, for providing inadequate intelligence on Mexican–US relations in 1978–79 and on President Carter's visit to Mexico in 1979 (k-22, 176).

66. k-22, 116.

67. k-22, 128. Since Mitrokhin had no access to the KGB Sixteenth (SIGINT) Directorate, he was unable to note the contents of any decrypts.

68. IZOT is the highest-ranking Brazilian agent identified in the files noted by Mitrokhin. He provided recruitment leads on three fellow diplomats, including the ambassador of a NATO country in Prague. IZOT had himself been talent-spotted for the KGB by another Brazilian ambassador, an agent codenamed ALEKS; k-22, 235–7.

69. k-22, 235–7; k-8, 551.

70. Skidmore, 'Brazil's Slow Road to Democratization', pp. 9–19.

71. Alves, *State and Opposition in Military Brazil*, pp. 48–9, 142, 170–71, 173.

72. In May 1980 Prestes was succeeded as leader of the Brazilian Communist Party by Giocondo Dias. In December Dias sent his thanks to Moscow, via the Brasilia residency, for allowing him, like his predecessor, to nominate Party members for free visits to Soviet sanatoria and holiday homes; k-26, 399.

73. Golbery do Couto e Silva, *Conjuntura politica nacional*, section 'Geopolítica do Brasil', p. 52; Alves, *State and Opposition in Military Brazil*, pp. 24–5.

74. k-22, 1, 3.

75. vol. 6, ch. 5, part 5.

76. Miller, *Soviet Relations with Latin America, 1959–1987*, pp. 174–8.

77. Skidmore, 'Brazil's Slow Road to Democratization', pp. 25–7; Alves, *State and Opposition in Military Brazil*, p. 222.

78. Dix, *The Politics of Colombia*, p. 198.

79. k-22, 91. The Centre was doubtless privately embarrassed by the fact that, like President Echeverría of Mexico, López had previously been the target of a KGB active measure; Agee's *Inside the Company* (pp. 190–91) had claimed that López's party, the MRL, had been financed by the CIA's Bogotá station.

80. k-22, 91. On Tolstikov's meetings with Perón see above, pp. 98–9.

81. k-22, 91, vol. 6, ch. 5, part 5.

82. k-22, 376.

83. k-22, 181.

84. vol. 6, ch. 5, part 5. In 1978 López was succeeded as President by Julio César Turbay Ayala, who followed a very different foreign policy and actively blocked Cuba's attempts to secure a Security Council seat.

85. Leonov, 'La inteligencia soviética en América Latina durante la guerra fría'.

86. vol. 6, ch. 5, part 5.

87. Leonov, 'La inteligencia soviética en América Latina durante la guerra fría'.

88. Torrijos admitted in a meeting with Graham Greene in 1979 that he had been visited by a KGB officer who was 'very cultivated' and spoke 'excellent Spanish'; Greene, *Getting to Know the General*, p. 179. Leonov has acknowledged that the reference is to him; Leonov, 'La inteligencia soviética en América Latina durante la guerra fría'.

89. vol. 6, ch. 5, part 5.

90. vol. 6, misc. footnote material, p. 20.

91. The two main US accounts of the negotiation of the treaties and subsequent struggle to secure ratification are: Vance, *Hard Choices*, ch. 8; Carter, *Keeping Faith*, pp. 152–87.

92. Koster and Sánchez Borbón, *In the Time of the Tyrants*, pp. 199–200.

93. In his memoirs, published in 1982, Carter continued to insist that the charges against Torrijos were false; Carter, *Keeping Faith*, p. 167.

94. vol. 6, ch. 5, part 5.

95. Hearing of US Senate Committee on Foreign Relations, Subcommittee on Terrorism, Narcotics and International Operations, 10 Feb. 1988. Koster and Sánchez Borbón, *In the Time of the Tyrants*, pp. 185, 288–9.

96. Carter, *Keeping Faith*, p. 173.

97. vol. 6, ch. 5, part 5.

98. Carter, *Keeping Faith*, p. 179.

99. vol. 6, ch. 5, part 5.

100. Koster and Sánchez Borbón, *In the Time of the Tyrants*, p. 235.

101. vol. 6, ch. 5, part 5.

102. Kempe, *Divorcing the Dictator*, p. 73.

103. vol. 6, ch. 5, part 5. For details of Torrijos's cigars, see Greene, *Getting to Know the General*, p. 30.

104. vol. 6, ch. 5, part 5.

105. Ibid. Torrijos's moves towards parliamentary democracy in the final years of his dictatorship were largely cosmetic; Koster and Sánchez Borbón, *In the Time of the Tyrants*, ch. 8.

106. vol. 6, ch. 5, part 5.

107. Koster and Sánchez Borbón, *In the Time of the Tyrants*, pp. 140–47.

108. vol. 6, ch. 5, part 5.

109. Koster and Sánchez Borbón, *In the Time of the Tyrants*, pp. 233–5, 248–9.

110. Ibid., pp. 236–9.

111. vol. 6, ch. 5, part 5. Mitrokhin's notes wrongly give the date of Torrijos's death as 2 Aug. 1981 (possibly the date of the KGB report on it). The claim, doubtless encouraged by KGB active measures, that the CIA had killed Torrijos was also widely believed in Panama; Hollander, *Anti-Americanism*, p. 363.

6. Revolution in Central America

1. Quirk, *Fidel Castro*, pp. 794–5.

2. k-22, 153. Later in 1979, del Valle was replaced as Interior Minister by the tough Ramiro Valdés (himself a former Interior Minister), probably because Castro believed him better capable of coping with public discon-

tent. Both del Valle and Valdés were purged in 1985. Quirk, *Fidel Castro*, pp. 794–5, 825.

3. Gates, *From the Shadows*, pp. 123–4.

4. Crozier (ed.), *The Grenada Documents*, pp. 39–40; Romerstein, 'Some Insights Derived from the Grenada Documents'.

5. k-18, 323.

6. Gilbert, *Sandinistas*, p. 11.

7. Miranda and Ratliff, *The Civil War in Nicaragua*, p. 13. The basis of the FSLN reunification was the creation of a National Directorate of nine *comandantes* representing the three main factions: Humberto Ortega Saavedra, Daniel Ortega Saavedra and Victor Tirado López of the Insurrectional Tendency (Terceristas); Jaime Wheelock, Carlos Núñez, Luis Carrión of the Proletarian Tendency; Tomás Borge, Henry Ruiz and Bayardo Arce of the Prolonged Popular War Tendency.

8. Miranda and Ratliff, *The Civil War in Nicaragua*, p. 99; Gates, *From the Shadows*, pp. 126–7; Brown, *The Real Contra War*, p. 80. The KGB residency in San José reported that 280 Costa Rican Communists joined the victorious Sandinista offensive; k-26, 379, 395.

9. Quirk, *Fidel Castro*, p. 795.

10. Speech by Castro, 26 July 1979.

11. Gates, *From the Shadows*, pp. 127–8.

12. vol. 6, ch. 12, part 4.

13. Opening speech by Castro at Havana conference of Non-Aligned Movement, 3 Sept. 1979.

14. Leonov, 'La inteligencia soviética en América Latina durante la guerra fría'.

15. See above, pp. 37–8, 45.

16. Leonov, *Likholet'e*, pp. 227–9.

17. The other leading Sandinistas with whom Leonov had talks were Victor Tirado López, Sergio Ramírez, Bayardo Arce, Alfonso Robelo and Miguel D'Escoto; vol. 6, ch. 5, part 5.

18. vol. 6, ch. 5, part 5.

19. Miranda and Ratliff, *The Civil War in Nicaragua*, pp. 4–5, 14–15, 73. The 'Seventy-Two-Hour Document' was drawn up by the nine *comandantes* of the FSLN National Directorate.

20. k-26, 397.

21. k-26, 396.

22. Miller, *Soviet Relations with Latin America, 1959–1987*, p. 192.

23. Geyer, *Guerrilla Prince*, p. 355. Speech by Castro in Managua, 19 July 1980.

24. Miranda and Ratliff, *The Civil War in Nicaragua*, pp. 116–17.

25. Miller, *Soviet Relations with Latin America, 1959–1987*, p. 192.

26. vol. 6, ch. 5, part 5. In 1970, inspired by the example of the Vietnam War, Carpio had left the PCS and founded the breakaway Fuerzas Populares

de Liberación (FPL), with the intention of beginning a popular war of liberation based on the Vietnamese model.

27. vol. 6, ch. 5, part 5.
28. Bracamonte and Spencer, *Strategy and Tactics of the Salvadoran FMLN Guerrillas*, p. 4.
29. vol. 6, ch. 5, part 5.
30. Ibid. Handal's travel notes on his arms-collection mission were captured and published by the State Department in 1981 (Waller, *The Third Current of Revolution*, pp. 31–2, 95–7). Though Salvadoran revolutionaries and their supporters, backed by KGB active measures, claimed that the notes were forged, the corroboration provided by the KGB file on the mission noted by Mitrokhin shows that they were genuine.
31. vol. 6, ch. 5, part 5.
32. Waller, *The Third Current of Revolution*, pp. 32–3.
33. k-20, 92.
34. Haig, *Caveat*, ch. 6.
35. Miller, *Soviet Relations with Latin America, 1959–1987*, pp. 192–3.
36. Miranda and Ratliff, *The Civil War in Nicaragua*, p. 117.
37. k-20, 113.
38. Miranda and Ratliff, *The Civil War in Nicaragua*, p. 117.
39. Quirk, *Fidel Castro*, pp. 811–12.
40. k-20, 113.
41. k-20, 99.
42. k-20, 113.
43. Andrew and Mitrokhin, *The Sword and the Shield*, pp.528–32. In December 1982 the Polish Deputy Prime Minister, Mieczysław Rakowski, visited Cuba and briefed Castro personally on the situation in Poland since the declaration of martial law a year earlier. 'The PUWP [Communist Party]', he acknowledged, 'could not fulfil its role; the army therefore occupied a dominant position in the country'. k-19, 323.
44. k-20, 118.
45. k-20, 113.
46. vol. 6, ch. 5, part 5.
47. *The Challenge to Democracy in Central America*; Ashby, *The Bear in the Backyard*, pp. 130–31.
48. Crozier (ed.), *The Grenada Documents*, p. 64.
49. Bracamonte and Spencer, *Strategy and Tactics of the Salvadoran FMLN Guerrillas*.
50. vol. 6, ch. 5, part 5.
51. Waller, *The Third Current of Revolution*, pp. 23–37. On KGB contact with the CPUSA leadership, see Andrew and Mitrokhin, *The Sword and the Shield*, pp. 288– 93.
52. Waller, *The Third Current of Revolution*, pp. 38–9.
53. The public relations disaster was compounded by Washington's ignor-

ance of the internal peasant-based resistance movement against the Sandinistas, the Milicias Populares Anti-Sandinistas (People's Anti-Sandinista
Militia) or MILPAS, which had begun in Nicaragua's remote central highlands as soon as the Sandinistas took power in July 1979. The CIA made
contact instead, on Reagan's orders, with far less numerous groups of exiled
former members of Somoza's Guardia Nacional. Even when the exiles
allied with MILPAS in the Fuerza Democratica Nicaragüense (FDN), the
dominant world-wide media image of the Contras was of former Guardia
Nacional thugs of the Somoza dictatorship. Brown, *The Real Contra War*.

54. Reagan, *An American Life*, p. 471.

55. Andrew, *For the President's Eyes Only*, pp. 466–7, 470–71; Shultz,
Turmoil and Triumph, pp. 288–9.

56. Miller, *Soviet Relations with Latin America, 1959–1987*, p. 199; Gilbert, *Sandinistas*, p. 170.

57. Andrew and Mitrokhin, *The Sword and the Shield*, pp.213–14, 457;
Andrew and Gordievsky, *KGB*, pp. 584–99; Andrew and Gordievsky,
Instructions from the Centre, ch. 4.

58. Andrew, *For the President's Eyes Only*, p. 475.

59. Andrew and Mitrokhin, *The Sword and the Shield*, pp. 214–15;
Andrew and Gordievsky, *KGB*, pp. 599–603; Andrew and Gordievsky,
Instructions from the Centre, pp. 85–90. Remarkably, though its priority
was downgraded, operation RYAN continued until November 1991, when
it was cancelled by Yevgeni Primakov, first head of the SVR, who described
it as 'a typical anachronism'; Primakov, *Russian Crossroads*, p. 97.

60. Miranda and Ratliff, *The Civil War in Nicaragua*, ch. 9; Glenn Garvin,
'We shipped weapons, Sandinistas say', *Miami Herald*, 18 July 1999. There
is some evidence that the leading hard-liner in the Politburo, Marshal
Ustinov, who died in December 1984, remained in favour of supplying the
MiG-21s.

61. Gilbert, *Sandinistas*, p. 170.

62. Andrew, *For the President's Eyes Only*, pp. 478–80. The text of Gates's
memo of 14 Dec. 1984 was published in the *New York Times*, 20 Sept.
1991, p. A14.

63. Andrew, *For the President's Eyes Only*, pp. 480–93, 497.

64. Volkogonov, *The Rise and Fall of the Soviet Empire*, p. 495.

65. Miller, *Soviet Relations with Latin America, 1959–1987*, pp. 215–16.

66. Glenn Garvin, 'We shipped weapons, Sandinistas say', *Miami Herald*,
18 July 1999.

67. Andrew and Gordievsky, *KGB*, p. 642.

68. Interview with Major Aspillaga on Radio Martí, 7 August 1987.

69. Quirk, *Fidel Castro*, pp. 824–36; Balfour, *Castro*, pp. 162–8.

7. The Middle East: Introduction

1. Gromyko and Ponomarev (eds.), *Soviet Foreign Policy*, vol. 2, p. 393.
2. Hollander, *Anti-Americanism*, p. 364.
3. Rubinstein, *Moscow's Third World Strategy*, p. 237.
4. On KGB SIGINT operations, see Andrew and Mitrokhin, *The Sword and the Shield*, ch. 21.
5. Ibid., p. 337.
6. Mitrokhin had no access to the files of either the Eighth Chief Directorate (Communications and Cryptography) or the Sixteenth Directorate (SIGINT). The FCD files to which he had access, however, included some documents from both directorates.
7. Dzhirkvelov, *Secret Servant*, pp. 211–14.
8. See below, pp. 202–3.
9. See below, p. 155.
10. It is impossible, however, to exclude the possibility that there may have been some major KGB penetration in Saddam Hussein's Baghdad which was not recorded in the files seen by Mitrokhin.
11. Nasser's tribute was proudly quoted in the official history of Soviet foreign policy; Gromyko and Ponomarev (eds.), *Soviet Foreign Policy*, vol. 2, p. 289.
12. See below, p. 153.
13. See below, p. 151.
14. Taubman, *Khrushchev*, p. 610.
15. See below, pp. 175, 178, 201–2, 208–10.
16. See below, pp. 232–3.
17. Gromyko and Ponomarev (eds.), *Soviet Foreign Policy*, vol. 2, p. 506.
18. See below, pp. 236, 243.
19. See above, pp. 48, 53.
20. See below, pp. 253–4, 256.
21. Fear that the Official IRA might not preserve the secrecy of its KGB connection led to a delay of almost three years in responding to its 1969 request for a secret arms delivery; Andrew and Mitrokhin, *The Sword and the Shield*, pp. 384–5.
22. Ibid., pp. 387–9. The KGB reluctantly became involved in the assassination of the Bulgarian dissident Georgi Markov in London in 1978 only because it felt it could not refuse an urgent plea for assistance from the Bulgarian leader, Todor Zhivkov.
23. It is impossible, however, to exclude the possibility of a continuing connection with the PFLP which was not recorded in files seen by Mitrokhin.
24. See below, pp. 253–6.
25. Clarridge, *A Spy for All Seasons*, pp. 335–6.

26. Andrew and Mitrokhin, *The Sword and the Shield*, p .392. The KGB files noted by Mitrokhin do not reveal how far – if at all – Andropov sought to influence the use made of Palestinian terrorists by his Soviet-bloc allies.

27. Follain, *Jackal*, ch. 15.

28. Najib, 'Abu Nidal Murder Trail Leads Directly to Iraqi Regime'.

29. Gromyko and Ponomarev (eds.), *Soviet Foreign Policy*, vol. 2, pp. 501, 505.

30. See below, p. 259.

8. The Rise and Fall of Soviet Influence in Egypt

1. Nasser, *The Philosophy of the Revolution*, p. 41.

2. Talbott (ed.), *Khrushchev Speaks*, p. 432.

3. Kirpichenko, *Razvedka*, p. 156. *Razvedka*, published in 1998, is an extended version of an earlier edition of Kirpichenko's memoirs, *Iz arkhiva razvedchika*, published five years earlier.

4. Ibid., pp. 34, 40–41. Mitrokhin noted almost no KGB files on agent penetration of Egypt during the Nasser era. Most of his material deals with the post-Nasser period.

5. Heikal, *Sphinx and Commissar*, p. 60. The Presidium agreed to extensive further arms supplies in November 1955. Khrushchev acknowledged that supplying arms was risky but told the Politburo that it was worth the risk. Fursenko (ed.), *Prezidium TsK KPSS. 1954–1964*, pp. 61, 63, 903 n. 9.

6. Kirpichenko, *Razvedka*, pp. 41–3. Shepilov's term as Foreign Minister lasted only from June 1956 to May 1957. He was sacked on suspicion of having supported an attempted coup against Khrushchev.

7. Barron, *KGB*, pp. 69–73; Sakharov, *High Treason*, p. 193; Kuzichkin, *Inside the KGB*, p. 88. Sharaf's official position was that of Minister of State for Presidential Affairs. His life in the shadows meant that he was virtually unknown to the Egyptian public; Beattie, *Egypt during the Sadat Years*, pp. 40–41. On Nasser's 'keen interest' in intelligence, see el-Din, *Memories of a Revolution*, p. 240.

8. Kirpichenko, *Razvedka*, p. 318. Following the usual practice of memoirs by KGB officers (other than defectors), Kirpichenko's memoirs do not identify any of the agents whom he ran.

9. Ibid., p. 121.

10. Sharaf added a long quotation from 'the great leader Lenin'. Heikal, *Sphinx and Commissar*, pp. 226–7.

11. Fursenko (ed.), *Prezidium TsK KPSS. 1954–1964*, pp. 152–203, 954–6.

12. The assassination plot seems never to have progressed beyond the

planning stage. Aldrich, *Hidden Hand*, pp. 479–85; Wright, *Spycatcher*, pp. 84–5.

13. Kirpichenko, *Razvedka*, pp. 108–9.

14. Ibid., pp. 70–73.

15. On the evolution of Nasser's relations with the Soviet Union, see Heikal, *Sphinx and Commissar*, and Dawisha, *Soviet Foreign Policy towards Egypt*, chs. 2, 3.

16. Kirpichenko, *Razvedka*, pp. 73–6, 104.

17. Andrew and Mitrokhin, *The Sword and the Shield*, p. 363.

18. Shelepin to Khrushchev, 29 July 1961; Zubok, 'Spy vs. Spy', p. 33 n. 42.

19. Khrushchev informed the Presidium on 26 May 1964, after his return from a visit to the UAR: 'Egyptian leaders are conducting a quite progressive policy. They have nationalized enterprises [and] banks. They've taken the land away from the feudal lords, but they don't know what to do with the land.' Fursenko (ed.), *Prezidium TsK KPSS. 1954–1964*, pp. 822–3.

20. H. A. R. ['Kim'] Philby, 'Nasser's Pride and Glory', the *Observer*, 22 July 1962. Though Philby did not formally admit in his memoirs working as a KGB agent in Beirut, he gave the broadest of hints: 'If it would have been odd of SIS not to take advantage of my presence in the Middle East, it would have been odder still if the Soviet Intelligence service had ignored me.' Philby, *My Silent War*, p. 178.

21. Dawisha, *Soviet Foreign Policy towards Egypt*, chs. 2, 3.

22. vol. 6, ch. 9.

23. Andropov also insisted that the KGB 'must know not only what is happening in the country of the enemy, but it must take offensive actions and force the enemy into combat under unfavourable conditions, thus paralysing the enemy's activities'; vol. 6, ch. 9, n. 6.

24. Andrew and Mitrokhin, *The Sword and the Shield*, pp. 13, 550–51, 562–63. Primakov, *Russian Crossroads*, pp. 17–19, 44, 89. Primakov was appointed Director of the Moscow Institute of Oriental Studies in 1977 and of the Institute of World Economy and International Relations (IMEMO) in 1985.

25. Andrew and Gordievsky, *KGB*, p. 501.

26. Kirpichenko, *Razvedka*, pp. 101–4, 282–3. Though refuting claims that Primakov was a KGB agent, Kirpichenko acknowledges that he maintained 'close working contact' with him during his Middle Eastern travels, including a 'constant exchange' of political information. The FCD provided Primakov with what Kirpichenko calls 'the necessary assistance'.

27. The transcript of the meetings between Nasser and Podgorny after the Six-Day War is published in Farid, *Nasser: The Final Years*, ch. 1; quotation from p. 5.

28. Aburish, *Nasser*; Beattie, *Egypt during the Nasser Years*; Pryce-Jones, 'Under His Spell'.

29. Heikal, *Sphinx and Commissar*, pp. 282–3.

30. Sadat, *In Search of Identity*, p. 231.

31. Gromyko, *Memories*, p. 270.

32. Heikal, *Sphinx and Commissar*, p. 216.

33. Sadat, *In Search of Identity*, p. 206.

34. Kirpichenko, *Razvedka*, pp. 120–22.

35. Sadat, *In Search of Identity*, pp. 223–4.

36. Leonov, *Likholet'e*, p. 145. Leonov had access to the file on the 'crocodiles" plot as deputy head of Service 1.

37. Kirpichenko, *Razvedka*, p. 113.

38. Beattie, *Egypt during the Sadat Years*, p. 56.

39. Andrew and Mitrokhin, *The Sword and the Shield*, p. 635 n. 63.

40. By 1967 the KGB was decrypting 152 cipher systems employed by 72 states; Andrew and Mitrokhin, *The Sword and the Shield*, p. 337. Though no statistics are available, the number had doubtless increased further.

41. Beattie, *Egypt during the Sadat Years*, pp. 60–61. For another example of tapes of bugged conversations being passed to the Soviet embassy, see ibid., p. 124.

42. Kirpichenko, *Razvedka*, pp. 114–17.

43. Sadat, *In Search of Identity*, pp. 206, 223–4.

44. Leonov, *Likholet'e*, p. 145; Leonov, 'La inteligencia soviética en América Latina durante la guerra fría'.

45. Kirpichenko, *Razvedka*, pp. 122–3.

46. Sadat, *In Search of Identity*, p. 225.

47. Report on the activities of the Cairo residency in 1972–76 by FCD Directorate R (Operational Planning and Analysis); k-18, 485.

48. Andrew and Gordievsky, *KGB*, p. 503.

49. Sadat, *In Search of Identity*, p. 284.

50. Sakharov, *High Treason*; Barron, *KGB*, ch. 2.

51. k-26, 87. Mitrokhin's notes do not indicate whether the money was passed on via the KGB residency; this, however, was common practice.

52. Ismael and El-Sa'id, *The Communist Movement in Egypt, 1920–1988*, p. 129.

53. k-26, 87, 89.

54. The first payment recorded in Mitrokhin's notes was of $15,000 handed by the KGB resident in Baghdad to the leader of the Iraqi Communist Party on 27 May 1974 for onward transmission to SOYUZNIK; k-26, 77.

55. Bregman and el-Tahri, *The Fifty Years War*, p. 112.

56. Sadat, *In Search of Identity*, p. 230.

57. Ayubi, *Nasser and Sadat*, pp. 76–7, 192–3.

58. Andrew and Gordievsky, *KGB*, p. 503.

59. Report on the activities of the Cairo residency in 1972–76 by FCD Directorate R (Operational Planning and Analysis); k-18, 485. The residency, however, was allowed to continue to recruit and run non-Egyptian

agents in Egypt. These included ZAMIL and NAUM, attachés at, respectively, the Syrian and South Yemen embassies, and IND, an intelligence officer at the Indian embassy; k-18, 48.

60. k-18, 482.

61. Dobrynin, *In Confidence*, p. 276.

62. k-18, 482.

63. Dobrynin, *In Confidence*, p. 276.

64. Andrew, *For the President's Eyes Only*, pp. 390–92.

65. Gates, *From the Shadows*, p. 41. Mitrokhin's notes contain only fragmentary information on KGB penetration of the Egyptian armed forces and intelligence services. KGB sources in 1973 included FEDOR (k-14, 530), an army colonel, and the intelligence officer ELDAR (k-27, 150). No information is available on GRU penetration of Egyptian armed forces. As usual, Kirpichenko's memoirs contain no reference to the use of agents but briefly refer to the role of 'radio intercepts'; Kirpichenko, *Razvedka*, p. 126.

66. t-7, 315; vol. 6, ch. 9.

67. k-18, 374.

68. vol. 6, ch. 9. Marwan's career as adviser to Sadat continues intermittently to excite media attention. In 2003 he denied claims by an Egyptian newspaper that he had been a Mossad agent and by an Israeli historian that he had, on the contrary, fed disinformation to Mossad. Yossi Melman, 'Double Trouble', *Ha'aretz*, 20 Jan. 2003.

69. Kazakov was doubtless selected for the mission because of his expertise on the CIA; k-14, 565.

70. k-14, 565; t-7, 220; vol. 6, ch. 8.

71. k-24, 448.

72. k-18, 486.

73. Sadat, *In Search of Identity*, p. 13. Sadat wrongly claimed that he was twelve, rather than fourteen, when Hitler took power.

74. Finklestone, *Anwar Sadat*, p. 16.

75. k-18, 486; vol. 6, ch. 8.

76. vol. 6, ch. 8.

77. vol. 6, ch. 9, app. 3.

78. Ismael and El-Sa'id, *The Communist Movement in Egypt, 1920–1988*, pp. 132–3. The fraternal messages to the CPSU and Arab Communist parties were handed by an emissary of the Communist leader Khaled Mohieddin to the Soviet ambassador for onward transmission; k-26, 83.

79. k-18, 373.

80. The NPUP began in 1976 as an alternative, officially permitted, policy platform within the ruling ASU and became an independent party in the following year.

81. These amounts were handed to Mohieddin on 5 June 1976; k-26, 11, 15.

82. k-14, 562. Mitrokhin noted, after reading a 1974 file relating to the

Cairo residency, 'The recruitment of intelligence officers and contacts as KGB agents was permitted in exceptional circumstances and with special permission from the leadership of the Centre' (k-18, 49). The submission by Kryuchkov and Dushin was presumably drafted in the light of this provision. Mitrokhin's notes, however, contain no example of such 'special permission' being given between 1974 and Sadat's assassination in 1981.

83. k-14, 530.

84. k-5, 176. Among others who showed declining enthusiasm for contact with the KGB was KHALIL, an Egyptian ambassador who, while a counsellor at the embassy in Moscow, had been seduced by a KGB swallow codenamed VIKHROVA. In 1973–74, with KGB assistance, he made three secret journeys without a visa from the foreign capital in which he was based to renew contact with VIKHROVA. On one of these visits KHALIL concluded a bigamous marriage with her, which was subsequently dissolved. Since he was based outside Egypt, he retained his agent status. KHALIL's file records, however, that though expressing gratitude 'from the bottom of his heart' in 1975 for the understanding shown by the KGB during his affair and marriage with, as well as divorce from, VIKHROVA, he refused to supply classified information (k-24, 300).

85. k-14, 339.

86. Andrew and Gordievsky (eds.), *More Instructions from the Centre*, pp. 82–5; k-12, 394.

87. Report on the activities of the Cairo residency in 1972–76 by FCD Directorate R (Operational Planning and Analysis); k-18, 485.

88. Baker, *Sadat and After*, pp. 118–25.

89. k-26, 78.

90. k-26, 14.

91. k-26, 16.

92. Gromyko and Ponomarev (eds.), *Soviet Foreign Policy, 1917–1980*, vol. 2, pp. 607–8.

93. Andrew and Gordievsky, *KGB*, pp. 546–7.

94. Finklestone, *Anwar Sadat*, ch. 23.

95. k-13, 241.

96. Baker, *Sadat and After*, pp. 159–61.

97. The allocation for the Egyptian Communist Party in 1978 was $100,000 (k-26, 17); the Cairo residency requested and probably received an additional $20,000 in December (k-26, 19). In 1979 the allocation was again $100,000 (k-26, 21), raised to $120,000 in 1980 (k-26, 22). Mitrokhin's notes give few details of the allocations to the NPUP.

98. k-26, 18.

99. k-13, 241. Without the knowledge of Mohieddin and the Egyptian Communist Party, the KGB also made contact in 1980 with Communist splinter groups; k-26, 26.

100. Kassem, *In the Guise of Democracy*, p. 123.

101. k-24, 45. A third target of Syrian intelligence and the PFLP was an adviser of King Khalid of Saudi Arabia.
102. Andrew and Gordievsky, *KGB*, p. 547.
103. Gromyko, *Memories*, pp. 222–3.
104. Kassem, *In the Guise of Democracy*; quotation from p. 107.

9. Iran and Iraq

1. vol. 2, ch. 1. On the deportation and liquidation of 'anti-Soviet elements' across the Soviet border, see Andrew and Mitrokhin, *The Sword and the Shield*, pp. 101 – 2.
2. Kuzichkin, *Inside the KGB*, p. 263.
3. Andrew, *For the President's Eyes Only*, pp. 202–6; Roosevelt, *Countercoup*, chs. 12, 13.
4. Shlaim, *The Iron Wall*, p. 195.
5. vol. 2, ch. 6, p. 41.
6. The Centre claimed improbably that the Americans blamed the forgery not on the KGB but on the British, who were said to be jealous of the strength of US influence in Iran; vol. 2, ch. 6, pp. 41–2. On the Shah's susceptibility to conspiracy theory, see Pipes, *Hidden Hand*, pp. 78–80.
7. Shawcross, *The Shah's Last Ride*, p. 83.
8. vol. 2, ch. 6, pp. 43–4.
9. vol. 2, ch. 3, p. 18.
10. Pahlavi, *An Enduring Love*, pp. 68–9. Tafazoli had no part in the subsequent stages of the Shah's courtship of Farah Diba, which are described in these memoirs.
11. Ibid., pp. 66–7. The friend refused to seek the Empress's help to get her out of jail.
12. vol. 2, ch. 3, p. 18.
13. Pahlavi, *An Enduring Love*, p. 67.
14. Shawcross, *The Shah's Last Ride*, pp. 97–8.
15. Ibid., pp. 85, 160–61. The KGB reported that Bakhtiar had 'displayed exceptional harshness towards communists'. It later claimed that Service A fabrications, brought to the attention of the Shah's regime in 1969–70, led to his 'liquidation'; vol. 2 misc., item 14.
16. Kuzichkin, *Inside the KGB*, pp. 216–18. Mitrokhin's brief note on Kuzichkin's defection confirms that he had 'a lot of information about illegals' (vol. 2, ch. 1).
17. Andrew and Mitrokhin, *The Sword and the Shield*, p. 362. After 1962 the Soviet leadership abandoned assassination as a normal instrument of policy outside the Soviet bloc, resorting to it only on rare occasions such as the killing of President Hafizullah Amin of Afghanistan in December 1979; see below, pp. 401–2.

18. Andrew and Mitrokhin, *The Sword and the Shield*, pp. 359–61, 363–5.
19. vol. 2, ch. 2.
20. Andrew and Mitrokhin, *The Sword and the Shield*, p. 374.
21. vol. 2, ch. 2.
22. Andrew and Mitrokhin, *The Sword and the Shield*, pp. 382–3.
23. Little, 'A Fool's Errand'.
24. Milani, *The Persian Sphinx*, pp. 229–30.
25. Shawcross, *The Shah's Last Ride*, p. 206.
26. t-7, 140.
27. t-7, 143.
28. In November 1971, for example, President Bakr's National Charter, which proposed a 'national coalition in which . . . all progressive forces will participate', was enthusiastically received in Moscow, despite serious reservations by the ICP. Smolansky and Smolansky, *The USSR and Iraq*, pp. 114–15.
29. Ibid., pp. 114–17.
30. k-24, 54–7.
31. Smolansky and Smolansky, *The USSR and Iraq*, pp. 22, 70–91; Hiro, *Desert Shield to Desert Storm*, p. 51.
32. British Embassy, Baghdad, to FCO, 15 Nov. and 20 Dec. 1969, FCO 17/871, The National Archives, Kew (copies on National Security Archive website).
33. Sebag Montefiore, 'Stalin and Saddam'; Coughlin, *Saddam*, pp. 47–8, 75–6, 174.
34. Smolansky and Smolansky, *The USSR and Iraq*, pp. 28, 128–9; Karsh and Rautsi, *Saddam Hussein*, pp. 97–8, 131. On the April 1978 coup in Afghanistan, see below, p. 386.
35. k-26, 116.
36. k-13, 221.
37. k-13, 224.
38. Dulaymi, 'Stop the Repressions and Persecution'; Smolansky and Smolansky, *The USSR and Iraq*, pp. 129–30, 137, 139–40.
39. Mogarebi had been drawn into intelligence work in 1944 by the Soviet agent Lieutenant Colonel Makhmud (codenamed IMAM), leader of a group of Tudeh [Communist] sympathizers within the Iranian army, who acted as his controller. After Makhmud's death in 1954, Mogarebi was run directly by the Tehran residency; vol. 2, ch. 3, p. 21.
40. Kuzichkin, *Inside the KGB*, p. 198.
41. In 1976 the residency communicated with Mogarebi on eighteen occasions by radio from a residency car, five times by personal meetings and twice by dead letter-box. Mogarebi refused to travel further from his home for personal meetings or to conduct car-to-car radio communications; vol. 2, ch. 3, p. 21.

42. Ibid.

43. Kuzichkin, *Inside the KGB*, p. 196.

44. The radio signals used to communicate with Mogarebi from a residency car were known as the 'Close Information Link' system; ibid., pp. 196–7. A KGB damage assessment arrived at four possible explanations for SAVAK's detection of Mogarebi: (1) inadequate attention by Mogarebi to his security; (2) an intelligence leak which led SAVAK to conclude that the KGB had a source in the General Staff; (3) mistakes by the Tehran residency in making contact with Mogarebi; or (4) Mogarebi's past association with Iranian Communists and, in particular, with the KGB agent Lieutenant Colonel Makhmud (IMAM); according to Mogarebi's KGB file, he had been arrested in 1954 but released because of lack of evidence; vol. 2, ch. 3, p. 21.

45. vol. 2, ch. 3, p. 23. The KGB remained in contact with ZHAMAN until August 1982; vol. 2, ch. 3, p. 24.

46. vol. 2, ch. 5, p. 24. Hoveyda saw the report while Court Minister for a month after his resignation as Prime Minister in August 1977. SAVAK seems to have forgotten that its report to the Shah would also be seen by Hoveyda as Court Minister.

47. Kuzichkin, *Inside the KGB*, p. 238.

48. vol. 2, ch. 5, p. 38.

49. The FCD 'work plan' for 1974 had included an operation designed 'to establish contact with Ayatollah Khomeini, an Iranian émigré in Iraq with a large number of supporters amongst the clergy in Iran and the opposition to the Shah, and to assess his possibilities'. Mitrokhin noted that the operation 'was not very successful'; vol. 2, ch. 5.

50. Andrew, *For the President's Eyes Only*, pp. 438–41.

51. Mogarebi was shot in December 1978. The residency's proposal to help his family was turned down by the Centre as too risky; Kuzichkin, *Inside the KGB*, pp. 196–200.

52. vol. 2, ch. 5, p. 24.

53. vol. 2, ch. 1. Mitrokhin's notes do not record what retaliation against the Iranian embassy in Moscow actually occurred.

54. vol. 2, ch. 2.

55. Andrew and Mitrokhin, *The Sword and the Shield*, pp. 365, 370–2. Though Mitrokhin noted the precise location of the Swiss and some other European caches, he did not record details of the DLB in the Tehran suburbs.

56. Shawcross, *The Shah's Last Ride*, p. 275. Mitrokhin's notes identify Kazakov as a KGB officer operating under diplomatic cover in the consular section of the Tehran residency; vol. 2, app. 2, item 57.

57. Taheri, *The Unknown Life of the Shah*, pp. 242, 262.

58. Kuzichkin, *Inside the KGB*, p. 230.

59. vol. 2, ch. 6, pp. 49–50; Fadeykin's career is summarized in vol. 2, app. 2, item 43.

60. Rafizadeh, *Witness*, p. 264.
61. vol. 2, ch. 6, p. 49.
62. Pipes, *Hidden Hand*, pp. 80 – 81.
63. vol. 2, ch. 5, p. 38.
64. Taheri, *The Unknown Life of the Shah*, p. 244.
65. Andrew, *For the President's Eyes Only*, pp. 440–41.
66. Kuzichkin, *Inside the KGB*, pp. 256–7.
67. Milani, *The Persian Sphinx*, pp. 338–40.
68. vol. 2, ch. 3, p. 24.
69. vol. 2, ch. 6, p. 54.
70. Pipes, *Hidden Hand*, pp. 81–2; Moin, *Khomeini*, p. 204.
71. vol. 2, ch. 6, pp. 52–3.
72. Shebarshin had become resident following the death in office of Fadeykin; vol. 2, app. 2, items 43, 53. Less than a decade later, Shebarshin, who had already served as resident in New Delhi, was to become head of the FCD.
73. Shebarshin, *Ruka Moskvy*, pp. 127–8.
74. Wright, *In the Name of God*, p. 96.
75. vol. 2, ch. 6, p. 53.
76. Unusually, Mitrokhin did not record KOLCHIN's real name.
77. vol. 2, ch. 6, p. 54.
78. The Tehran residency believed that Qotbzadeh's hostility to the Soviet Union went back to his years as a student in the United States when he had been briefly recruited as a GRU agent but had quarrelled with his controller. Kuzichkin, *Inside the KGB*, pp. 302–3; Smolansky and Smolansky, *The USSR and Iraq*, p. 233.
79. vol. 2, ch. 6, p. 56.
80. Kuzichkin, *Inside the KGB*, p. 304.
81. vol. 2, ch. 6, p. 53.
82. Moin, *Khomeini*, pp. 252–3.
83. Abrahamian, *Tortured Confessions*, pp. 129–31.
84. Shebarshin, *Ruka Moskvy*, pp. 102–3, 134–5, 166. Shebarshin identifies the head of Line PR only as 'Vladimir G'; his name does not appear in Mitrokhin's notes from the files.
85. Ustinov, the Defence Minister, and Ponomarev, the head of the International Department, also served on the Iran Commission; Shebarshin, *Ruka Moskvy*, p. 133.
86. Ibid., pp. 133–6. On the failure of the attempt to rescue the US hostages, see Andrew, *For the President's Eyes Only*, pp. 451–3.
87. Karsh and Rautsi, *Saddam Hussein*, pp. 112–16.
88. Shemesh, *Soviet–Iraqi Relations, 1968–1988*, p. 149.
89. vol. 2, ch. 5, p. 39. In March 1980 STOGOV was arrested in Tehran and accused of secret links with the KGB. He was released in September and allowed to leave Iran after requests from the PLO prompted by the KGB; vol. 2, ch. 5, p. 40.

90. vol. 2, ch. 5, p. 39. The PUK had been founded in 1975 as a breakaway movement from the KDP, then headed by Mullah Mustafa Barzani (see above, pp. 175–6), which it claimed was a 'rightist tribalist command'. The PUK's declared aim was 'to join all the progressive, Leftist nationalist forces in Iraq' in order to liberate the country from 'the economic and political chains of neo-imperialism'. Smolansky and Smolansky, *The USSR and Iraq*, pp. 91–2. In 2005 Talabani became President of Iraq.

91. k-26, 142.

92. k-26, 144.

93. k-26, 139.

94. k-26, 117.

95. k-26, 138.

96. Karsh and Rautsi, *Saddam Hussein*, pp. 2, 136, 151.

97. Though he had no previous military record, in 1976 Saddam had persuaded Bakr to make him a four-star general; he subsequently promoted himself field marshal. Baram, 'Saddam Husayn, the Ba'th Regime and the Iraqi Officer Corps', pp. 211–23.

98. k-26, 147. Mitrokhin's notes do not make clear exactly how much money was sent to the ICP during 1981. A first instalment of $200,000, however, was given to Aziz Muhammad on 13 March 1981 by the Damascus resident; k-26, 120. During the same month the KGB residency in Lebanon handed over another $100,000 of Soviet funds and a further $68,185 collected from Iraqis in the USSR to Kerim Ahmad of the ICP Politburo; k-26, 122.

99. Shemesh, *Soviet–Iraqi Relations, 1968–1988*, p. 222.

100. Ibid., pp. 223–5; Smolansky and Smolansky, *The USSR and Iraq*, pp. 236–7; Karsh and Rautsi, *Saddam Hussein*, pp. 158–9.

101. Shebarshin, *Ruka Moskvy*, pp. 166–8.

102. Information from Sir Nicholas Barrington.

103. Shebarshin, *Ruka Moskvy*, p. 168.

104. Wright, *In the Name of God*, pp. 124, 235–6; Moin, *Khomeini*, p. 255. Shebarshin was succeeded as resident by Anatoli Nikolayevich Kocheskov (codenamed CHIZHOV), previously resident in Belgium; vol. 2 misc., item 2.

105. Abrahamian, *Tortured Confessions*, ch. 4.

106. Beschloss and Talbott, *At the Highest Levels*, chs. 12, 13; Baker, *The Politics of Diplomacy*, pp. 396–8.

107. Gates, *From the Shadows*, p. 502.

108. Primakov, *Russian Crossroads*, p. 51.

109. Baker, *The Politics of Diplomacy*, p. 398.

110. Though Kryuchkov and Yazov were among the leading coup plotters, Primakov was opposed to it.

111. Primakov, *Russian Crossroads*, pp. 63–4.

112. Pipes, *Hidden Hand*, p. 16.

10. The Making of the Syrian Alliance

1. Ramet, *The Soviet–Syrian Relationship*, pp. 33–6.
2. k-12, 201; t-1, 174.
3. k-5, 254; k-2, 14.
4. Aldrich, *The Hidden Hand*, pp. 583–5.
5. vol. 6, ch. 8, part 3, pp. 314–15.
6. vol. 6, ch. 8, part 3, p. 315.
7. vol. 6, ch. 12, part 10, p. 497.
8. Ramet, *The Soviet–Syrian Relationship*, p. 38.
9. k-26, 148, 165, 173.
10. See above, pp. 151–2.
11. Seale, *Asad of Syria*, pp. 142–3. Jundi committed suicide in March 1969, probably to avoid arrest and execution for his various crimes and atrocities; ibid., pp. 151–2.
12. Ibid., pp. 117, 145–8; Roberts, 'The USSR in Syrian Perspective', p. 214.
13. k-24, 58. Mitrokhin's notes contain no reference to KERIM after April 1968.
14. Asad's friend 'Abd al-Halim Khaddam (thought to have operated previously as his spy in the entourage of Salah Jadid) served successively as Foreign Minister and Vice-President (still with major foreign policy responsibilities until 1978) from 1971 to Asad's death in 2001; Mustafa Talas, another old friend of Asad who had become Chief of the General Staff in 1968, was Defence Minister from 1972 to Asad's death; Hikmat Shihabi, head of military intelligence from 1971 to 1974, was Chief of the General Staff from 1974 to 1998.
15. Khuly became head of the BNS only in 1978. In 1987 he was transferred to the post of deputy commander (later commander) of the air force after the scandal caused by the attempt by Syrian intelligence to plant a bomb on an El Al plane at Heathrow Airport. He was finally pensioned off in 1999. Seale, *Asad of Syria*, pp. 181–2, 475–82; Zisser, *Asad's Legacy*, pp. 42, 166, 171.
16. Middle East Watch, *Syria Unmasked*, ch. 4.
17. Ibid., pp. 29–30, 43; Seale, *Asad of Syria*, pp. 177–82, 399–44.
18. Information from Sir Roger Tomkys, British ambassador in Syria 1984–86.
19. t-1, 177.
20. Seale, *Asad of Syria*, pp. 319–20; Zisser, *Asad's Legacy*, pp. 32, 157, 170.
21. t-1, 177. The KGB also claimed that its active measures successfully influenced Rif'at Asad in 1976; k-24, 426.
22. k-12, 185.

23. k-12, 182.
24. See above, p. 195; t-1, 174; k-4, 56; k-12, 201; k-201. Al-Din was killed in an accident in 1980.
25. t-1, 161, 162.
26. t-1, 164.
27. t-1, 160, 169.
28. t-1, 163.
29. t-1, 172.
30. k-24, 61.
31. t-1, 167.
32. t-1, 173, 168.
33. t-1, 176.
34. t-1, 165.
35. Only al-Din (IZZAT) and VATAR are clearly identified as agents.
36. Gromyko, *Memories*, p. 274.
37. Report from Grigori Grigorenko to Andropov, seeking approval for bugging Asad's apartments in the Kremlin, 30 June 1972; approved by Andropov, 3 July 1972; k-6, 168. Though this was the only document relating to the bugging of Asad's apartments during his visits to Moscow transcribed by Mitrokhin, there can be little doubt that this was normal procedure. Mitrokhin was unable to note any of the transcripts of the bugged conversations which were filed in the archives of the Second Chief Directorate.
38. Seale, *Asad of Syria*, p. 192.
39. Ismael and Ismael, *The Communist Movement in Syria and Lebanon*, ch. 7; Ramet, *The Soviet–Syrian Relationship*, pp. 74–7. Bakdash's KGB codename is given in k-26, 172.
40. k-6, 168.
41. Ibid. Mitrokhin's notes do not record whether or not Shaya's confidences to OSIPOV on 12 September 1973 took place during a hunting expedition. On another occasion Shaya told OSIPOV that the former Syrian Foreign Minister, Dr Ibrahim Makhus, had remarked during a shooting party that Arab leaders would do well to try to imitate the efficiency and devotion to duty shown by the gundog.
42. The old Russian calendar was thirteen days behind the Western calendar which was adopted after the October Revolution. Its anniversary thus fell on 7 November rather than 25 October.
43. Ramet, *The Soviet–Syrian Relationship*, pp. 99–102.
44. Ibid., p. 84 n. 35.
45. k-26, 94; k-26, 148.
46. k-26, 94. On 26 March 1975 the General Secretary of the Iraqi Communist Party, Aziz Muhammad, agreed to a similar request.
47. Ramet, *The Soviet–Syrian Relationship*, p. 108.
48. k-22, 442.

49. Ramet, *The Soviet–Syrian Relationship*, pp. 108–12; Roberts, 'The USSR in Syrian Perspective', p. 221.
50. k-26, 221.
51. k-26, 219. Though the files on the July and September 1976 KGB transfers of money via Damascus to the Lebanese Communist Party were the only ones noted by Mitrokhin, there were undoubtedly others.
52. Ramet, *The Soviet–Syrian Relationship*, pp. 112–13, 130–34; Seale, *Asad of Syria*, pp. 286–9. Human Rights Watch includes Jumblatt in a list of foreign assassinations carried out by Syrian intelligence agencies; Middle East Watch, *Syria Unmasked*, p. 153.
53. See above, p. 165.
54. Seale, *Asad of Syria*, p. 305.
55. k-24, 45; see above, p. 167. Though Mitrokhin's notes do not mention Asad, it is scarcely conceivable that discussion of the assassination plan could have gone ahead without his authorization.
56. Ramet, *The Soviet–Syrian Relationship*, pp. 134–5.
57. vol. 6, ch. 8, part 3, p. 314; k-24, 44.
58. Seale, *Asad of Syria*, p. 335.
59. Pipes, *The Hidden Hand*, pp. 59, 71 n.38.
60. Ramet, *The Soviet–Syrian Relationship*, pp. 137, 140–45. On Muhammad, see above, pp. 188–90.
61. See above, ch. 9.
62. k-26, 143. On Carrillo's and Marchais's involvement in Eurocommunism, see Andrew and Mitrokhin, *The Sword and the Shield*, pp. 300–6.
63. Ismael and Ismael, *The Communist Movement in Syria and Lebanon*, p. 202. The Syrian Communist Party split into three groups: the main party led by Bakdash, a group led by his younger rival, Yusuf Faisal, and a breakaway Communist Party-Political Bureau, led by Riyadh al-Turk. Bakdash's and Faisal's groups were members of the ruling National Progressive Front. The Communist Party-Political Bureau was outlawed and viciously persecuted (see below).
64. Al-Turk is known to have been taken to hospital in critical condition in February 1981, January 1982, December 1983, December 1984, December 1987 and November 1988. Middle East Watch, *Syria Unmasked*, pp. 57, 67; Ramet, *The Soviet–Syrian Relationship*, pp. 77–8; Ismael and Ismael, *The Communist Movement in Syria and Lebanon*, pp. 196–7. Amazingly, al-Turk survived to be released from jail in 1998.
65. k-26, 143.
66. The KGB paid the Syrian Communist Party $50,000 in January 1979, $50,000 in April, $45,000 in November, $70,000 and $60,000 in December; k-26, 166. It is possible that further payments are recorded in files not noted by Mitrokhin.
67. k-26, 168.
68. Mitrokhin noted a payment of $30,000 to the Syrian Communist Party

in February 1980 and two much larger payments in December: $100,000 to Bakdash and $199,000 to FARID; k-26, 170, 172.

69. k-26, 164, 197.

70. k-26, 169.

71. k-26, 171.

72. k-26, 151.

73. k-26, 197.

74. Ismael and Ismael, *The Communist Movement in Syria and Lebanon*, pp. 206–25.

75. Shlaim, *The Iron Wall*, pp. 395–410.

76. Seale, *Asad of Syria*, pp. 397–9.

77. 'These conversations', writes Kirpichenko, 'have stuck in my memory by virtue of their seriousness and richness.' However, Asad's questions 'were often difficult to answer because of the incompatibility of our state structures and the specifics of local problems in the security sphere' – a tactful reference to the contrast between the centralized Soviet intelligence system and the chaotic structure of Syria's fifteen overlapping intelligence and security agencies.

78. Kirpichenko, *Razvedka*, pp. 186–8. On Asad and deception, see Pipes, 'Asad's Art of the Double Game'.

79. The most reliable assessment of human rights abuses under the Asad regime is in Middle East Watch, *Syria Unmasked*.

80. See above, pp. 199–200. Rif'at lost most of his influence after an unsuccessful coup attempt during Asad's illness in 1984.

81. 'Europe on alert for Syrian "Hit" Squads', *Sunday Telegraph*, 21 March 1982; 'L'attentat de la rue Marbeuf relance la polémique sur la sécurité', *Le Monde*, 24 April 1982. Others believed to have been the victims of Asad's hitmen abroad in the early 1980s included the former Syrian Prime Minister Salah al-Din al-Bitar, the leading Lebanese journalists Riyad Taha and Salim al-Lawzi, the wife of 'Issam al-'Attar, a leading member of the Muslim Brotherhood, and the French ambassador in Beirut, Louis de la Mar. Middle East Watch, *Syria Unmasked*, pp. 153–4.

82. Volkogonov, *Rise and Fall of the Soviet Empire*, pp. 359–60.

83. Information from Sir Roger Tomkys, British ambassador in Syria 1984–86.

84. Zisser, *Asad's Legacy*, ch. 3.

11. The People's Democratic Republic of Yemen

1. Halliday, 'Soviet Relations with South Yemen'.

2. Vassiliev, *Russian Policy in the Middle East*, pp. 192–3.

3. Golan, *Soviet Policies in the Middle East*, p. 233.

4. Leonov, *Likholet'e*, pp. 142–3.

5. Kirpichenko, *Razvedka*, p. 193.
6. k-12, 373; k-18, 138. Mitrokhin's notes imply, but do not explicitly state, that Muhammad Said Abdalla (codenamed KERIL), the PDRY Minister of State Security, was also present at the meeting with Andropov on 12 May 1972. Mitrokhin had no access to Sixteenth Directorate files and thus provides no information on the KGB's ability to decrypt PDRY communications.
7. k-12, 373; k-18, 138. Mitrokhin's notes do not give the full cost of KGB assistance to the PDRY intelligence agency, but provide some examples: an original allocation of 200,000 convertible rubles in 1972 for the training of PDRY intelligence officers and cipher personnel; 'financial assistance' of 200,000 rubles to PDRY intelligence, approved by the Politburo in February 1975; the supply in May 1975 of 'operational equipment' valued at over 100,000 rubles; and a payment in June 1975 of $100,000 to the PDRY Minister of State Security. It is unclear whether the equipment and money handed over in May and June 1975 were part of, or additional to, the 'assistance' approved by the Politburo in February.
8. Not to be confused with Yasir Arafat, who had the same codename, AREF; see below, p. 250.
9. k-12, 374. The total cost of AREF's treatment at the sanatorium amounted to 2,842 rubles.
10. Kirpichenko, *Razvedka*, p. 193.
11. After the end of Turkish rule in 1918, North Yemen was ruled by an autocratic Imamate from the Zeidi branch of Shia Islam. In 1962 the Imamate was overthrown in a nationalist coup which set up the Yemen Arab Republic. Civil war, however, continued for the remainder of the decade.
12. Almadaghi, *Yemen and the United States*, pp. 90–97.
13. vol. 6, ch. 8, part 3, pp. 316–17.
14. Mitrokhin noted no file on the assassination of al-Hamdi, save for a file on the KGB active measures which it prompted. Al-Hamdi was killed on the eve of a visit to Aden aimed at forging closer links with the PDRY. A variety of theories have been put forward to account for his assassination; Page, *The Soviet Union and the Yemenis*, p. 179.
15. vol. 6, ch. 8, part 3, p. 317.
16. Page, *The Soviet Union and the Yemenis*, pp. 77, 181; Almadaghi, *Yemen and the United States*, pp. 98–9; Golan, *Soviet Policies in the Middle East*, p. 233. The files noted by Mitrokhin contain no information on either assassination.
17. Page, *The Soviet Union and the Yemenis*, pp. 77–8.
18. Almadaghi, *Yemen and the United States*, p. 99.
19. Page, *The Soviet Union and the Yemenis*, p. 183.
20. Vassiliev, *Russian Policy in the Middle East*, p. 194.
21. Page, *The Soviet Union and the Yemenis*, pp. 185–6.

22. vol. 6, ch. 10.
23. Almadaghi, *Yemen and the United States*, p. 113.
24. Halliday, *Revolution and Foreign Policy*, pp. 195–6, 200. Kirpichenko believed that 'the South Yemeni were . . . beginning to tire of constant confrontation with their neighbours, and Ali Nasir Muhammad was feeling out paths of normalization of relations with the rest of the Arab world'. Kirpichenko, *Razvedka*, p. 194.
25. vol. 6, ch. 8, part 3, p. 317.
26. Almadaghi, *Yemen and the United States*, pp. 119–27.
27. Halliday, *Revolution and Foreign Policy*, pp. 41–4.
28. Volkogonov, *The Rise and Fall of the Soviet Empire*, pp. 519–20.
29. Halliday, *Revolution and Foreign Policy*, p. 45.

12. Israel and Zionism

1. *Documents on Israeli–Soviet Relations, 1941–1953*, vol. 1, p. 324.
2. Dzhirkvelov, *Secret Servant*, pp. 246–8; Andrew and Gordievsky, *KGB*, pp. 418–19. Vertiporokh's alias 'Rozhkov' is given in vol. 2, Iran, app. 2, item 71.
3. In 1983, Klingberg was secretly arrested, tried and convicted as a Soviet spy. A news blackout was imposed on his arrest and trial and he was kept in jail under an assumed identity. Not until 1993 was the blackout lifted. Cohen, 'Israel and Chemical/Biological Weapons'; Tsur Batsheva, 'Court Orders Klingberg Freed', *Jerusalem Post*, 4 Sept. 1998. Mitrokhin did not note Klingberg's file.
4. Mitrokhin's notes give no indication of the intelligence supplied by KHAIMOV; k-14, 534.
5. Though Mitrokhin recorded PERETS's real name and date of birth in Sofia, he noted no details of his position in Israel or the intelligence he provided. k-14, 532. Apart from KHAIMOV and PERETS, the only Bulgarian agent in Israel identified by Mitrokhin is ALIALEKH, who joined the Israeli Communist Party and was employed as a manual worker in a dry-cleaning business. Despite his humble employment, ALIALEKH was considered of some significance; he was allowed to visit his relatives in Bulgaria and had meetings with Bulgarian intelligence during his visits; k-14, 533.
6. *Documents on Israeli–Soviet Relations, 1941–1953*, vol. 2, p. 643. During his meetings with Rabinovich, Vertiporokh operated under diplomatic cover as first secretary at the Tel Aviv legation, using his alias Rozhkov; Rabinovich, who reported the meetings to the Foreign Ministry, was unaware that he was dealing with the Soviet resident. The editors of the mostly admirably edited *Documents on Israeli–Soviet Relations* also fail to realize Rozhkov's real identity.

7. *Documents on Israeli–Soviet Relations, 1941–1953*, vol. 2, pp. 868–70. Following a bomb attack on the Tel Aviv legation in February 1953, Soviet–Israeli diplomatic relations were broken off; they were reinstated in July.

8. Black and Morris, *Israel's Secret Wars*, pp. 150–51.

9. *Documents on Israeli–Soviet Relations, 1941–1953*, vol. 2, pp. 579n., 589, 610, 698, 821, 913. In 1953 Sneh and the left-wing faction which he headed were expelled from Mapam; late in 1954 they joined the Israeli Communist Party.

10. Andrew and Mitrokhin, *The Sword and the Shield*, pp. 33– 5.

11. BOKER's successive controllers were Ya. P. Medyanik, V. A. Avdeyenko and I. P. Dedyulya; k-14, 537.

12. Black and Morris, *Israel's Secret Wars*, pp. 157–8.

13. Avni, *False Flag*, chs. 4–10 and 'Postscript' by his interrogator, Yehuda Prag. Avni refutes, among other colourful myths published about his career, the claim that Lenin had stayed with his parents in Switzerland during the First World War.

14. Avni, *False Flag*, chs. 10–11.

15. Mitrokhin's brief notes on Avni refer to him only by the codename CHEKH. Since CHEKH is identified as the Israeli commercial attaché in Belgrade, there is no doubt about his identity. There is, however, a possible ambiguity about the date of Avni's transfer to KGB control. Mitrokhin noted, 'He [CHEKH] was recruited by the KGB', then added a date whose last digit is indistinct but appears to be 1954 (k-4, 89). It is possible but not probable that 1954 refers only to the date at which Avni became commercial attaché in Belgrade, and that his transfer to the KGB occurred earlier. Even when publishing his memoirs in 1999, Avni continued to believe mistakenly that his career in Soviet intelligence had been exclusively with the GRU.

16. As a condition of publishing his memoirs, Avni was not allowed by the Israeli authorities to give details of any Mossad operation – or, apparently, of any of the intelligence about Mossad which he passed on to the GRU and KGB. However, an introduction by Nigel West to the English-language edition (doubtless approved by Avni) gives a few examples of Mossad operations in which he took part; Avni, *False Flag*, pp. xii–xiv.

17. k-4, 90.

18. Avni, *False Flag*, preface and chs. 12–19.

19. Black and Morris, *Israel's Secret Wars*, pp. 158–64; 'Yisrael Beer's Career', *Jerusalem Post*, 16 April 1961. Though published after Beer's arrest, the *Jerusalem Post* simply repeated his fraudulent account of his career before reaching Palestine in 1938.

20. British Military Attaché, Tel Aviv, to Director of Military Intelligence, 14 April 1961; FO371/15746, The National Archives, Kew (I am grateful for this reference to Ronen Bergman).

21. Tel Aviv Embassy to Foreign Office, 17 April 1961; FO371/15746, The National Archives, Kew.

22. 'Yisrael Beer's Career', *Jerusalem Post*, 16 April 1961.

23. British Military Attaché, Tel Aviv, to Director of Military Intelligence, 14 April 1961; FO371/15746, The National Archives, Kew. Peres was, of course, unaware of Beer's KGB connection.

24. Black and Morris, *Israel's Secret Wars*, pp. 162–5; Bergman, 'Spooked', p. 14.

25. Tel Aviv Embassy to Foreign Office, 17 April 1961; FO371/15746, The National Archives, Kew.

26. Among the new KGB agents were DITA, a female journalist in Tel Aviv, and GRANT, a Mapam politician, recruited in, respectively, 1966 and 1967; k-14, 538–9.

27. Black and Morris, *Israel's Secret Wars*, p. 214.

28. vol. 6, ch. 7, part 1, p. 288.

29. Bergman, 'Spooked', p. 15.

30. k-8, 583.

31. Bergman, 'Spooked', p. 15.

32. Mitrokhin noted the figures for the budget of the Jerusalem residency only for the period 1975 to 1980 (k-13, 243–4, 250–51). The figures (in thousands of convertible rubles) were as follows: 13.0 (1975); 14.1 (1976); 16.0 (1977); 16.4 (1978); 20.3 (1979); 25.4 (1980).

33. Among those with whom the KGB lost contact after the Six-Day War were the agents DITA and GRANT and the confidential contact BOY, a Mapam (Israeli Labour Party) journalist; k-14, 538–9, 541.

34. Wolf, *Man without a Face*, p. 257.

35. Sachar, *A History of Israel*, pp. 735–7.

36. Memorandum by Andropov and Gromyko, dated 10 June 1968 and approved by Central Committee on same date; Morozov (ed.), *Documents on Soviet Jewish Emigration*, pp. 65–6.

37. Statistics of Jewish emigration cited in this chapter are taken from Ro'i (ed.), *Jews and Jewish Life in Russia and the Soviet Union*, p. 359.

38. Ro'i, 'Soviet Policy towards Jewish Emigration', pp. 51–6; Morozov (ed.), *Documents on Soviet Jewish Emigration*, p. 359.

39. Andropov to Central Committee, enclosing report by F. D. Bobkov, head of the KGB Fifth Directorate (Dissidents and Ideological Subversion), 17 May 1971; Morozov (ed.), *Documents on Soviet Jewish Emigration*, p. 6.

40. Excerpt from Politburo minutes, 20 March 1973; Morozov (ed.), *Documents on Soviet Jewish Emigration*, pp. 170–76.

41. See above, p. 160.

42. Kalugin, *Spymaster*, pp. 193–4. Kalugin is probably referring to agents infiltrated into Israel after the breach of diplomatic relations. Klingberg, who had emigrated to Palestine in 1947, continued to provide significant intelligence until his arrest in 1983.

43. Wolf, *Man without a Face*, p. 257.

44. t-7, 290.

45. vol. 7, app. 2, 40; k-19, 407; k-16, 76–7; k-18, 135; t-7, 5.

46. k-19, 407; k-16, 75. The spelling of Linov's alias is unclear; Mitrokhin's notes refer to both 'Motl' and 'Mottl'.

47. k-14, 39; k-12, 448.

48. vol. 6, app. 1, p. 590.

49. k-12, 339, 449.

50. t-3, 46; k-12, 10.

51. k-14, 116; k-16, 74.

52. KIM left for the United States, where he remained in contact with the KGB through correspondence containing secret writing and microdots sent to accommodation addresses. In December 1979 he failed to turn up for a meeting in Vienna with G. P. Kapustyan, deputy head of FCD Department 18 (Israel and the Middle East), and may subsequently have broken contact with the KGB; vol. 6, app. 1, p. 590.

53. k-12, 448.

54. k-12, 44.

55. k-14, 116.

56. k-16, 75.

57. k-11, 56; the dates at which YASAI's deployment to Israel was first decided and then cancelled are unclear.

58. k-16, 536; k-24, 76; *Time*, 16 Sept. 1974.

59. k-9, 237.

60. Memorandum by Andropov, 5 June 1975; Morozov (ed.), *Documents on Soviet Jewish Emigration*, pp. 214–15.

61. Andropov, 'Personal for Comrade Chernenko', No. 547-A, 11 March 1975. We are grateful to Vladimir Bukovsky for supplying us with a photocopy of this top-secret communication from his personal collection of KGB documents found in the Kremlin archives.

62. Memorandum by Andropov, 5 June 1975; Morozov (ed.), *Documents on Soviet Jewish Emigration*, pp. 214–15.

63. Shevchenko, *Breaking with Moscow*, p. 375. Shevchenko defected in 1978.

64. A useful chronology of the Jewish Defense League's activities is to be found on the website of the Anti-Defamation League: www.adl.org/extremism/jdf.

65. vol. 6, ch. 14, part 2.

66. Ibid.; Andrew and Mitrokhin, *The Sword and the Shield*, p. 238.

67. k-25, 148.

68. Ibid.

69. vol. 9, ch. 3, paras. 5, 6; t-7, 219; Andrew and Mitrokhin, *The Sword and the Shield*, p. 469.

70. Jakobovits, *'If Only My People . . .'*, ch. 5.

71. The codenames of the agents were VOSTOKOV, LVOV, SHIRO-KIKH, LEVIN, SERGEI, GNOM, ILYIN, MARK, ELEKTRON, PRO-FESSOR and PETROV; k-25, 153.

72. Jakobovits, 'If Only My People . . .', p. 43.

73. k-25, 153.

74. Jakobovits, 'If Only My People . . .', p. 54.

75. Shevchenko, Breaking with Moscow, p. 348.

76. Ro'i, 'Soviet Policy towards Jewish Emigration', pp. 52–3.

77. Politburo minutes, 22 June 1978; Morozov (ed.), Documents on Soviet Jewish Emigration, pp. 228–9.

78. Shcharansky, Fear No Evil, pp. 205–6, 224–5.

79. Dobrynin, In Confidence, pp. 399–400. Shcharansky was freed and allowed to emigrate in 1986; see below, p. 244.

80. Ro'i, 'Soviet Policy towards Jewish Emigration', p. 53.

81. Memorandum by Andropov, 10 May 1981; Morozov (ed.), Documents on Soviet Jewish Emigration, pp. 238–9 (cf. pp. 236–8, 241–5).

82. See below, pp. 131–2.

83. k-9, 112.

84. Andrew and Gordievsky (eds.), More Instructions from the Centre, pp. 91–8.

85. Andrew and Gordievsky (eds.), Instructions from the Centre, p. 7.

86. Ibid., p. 19.

87. Oleg Gordievsky heard Zamoysky put these views in an address to the London KGB residency in January 1985. Zamoysky's conspiracy theories about the Freemasons, who, he claimed, 'have always controlled the upper echelons of government in Western countries', especially the United States ('the most "Masonic" country of all'), were published in 1989 in his book, Behind the Facade of the Masonic Temple.

88. Andrew and Mitrokhin, The Sword and the Shield, pp. 331–2.

89. Ro'i, 'Soviet Policy towards Jewish Emigration', pp. 62, 67 n. 56.

90. Salitan, 'Soviet Emigration Policy, 1968–89', pp. 77–8, 85 n. 38.

91. Remnick, Lenin's Tomb, p. 86.

92. Lewin-Epstein, Ro'i and Ritterbrand (eds.), Russian Jews on Three Continents, appendix, p. 451.

13. Middle Eastern Terrorism and the Palestinians

1. See above, pp. 48, 53.

2. Codename in k-24, 344.

3. Follain, Jackal, pp. 20–21.

4. Mitrokhin's mixture of notes on and extracts from Haddad's file (no. 90248) reveals that the KGB's first contact with Haddad occurred in 1968 but does not identify the month; k-24, 365, para. 50.

5. k-24, 365, para. 51.

6. Follain, *Jackal*, p. 22.

7. k-24, 365, paras. 28–44; Andrew and Mitrokhin, *The Sword and the Shield*, pp. 380–2.

8. k-24, 365, paras. 1–24; Andrew and Mitrokhin, *The Sword and the Shield*, pp. 380–2.

9. vol. 6, app. 1, p. 610.

10. k-24, 59; vol. 6, app. 1, p. 610. It has not proved possible to confirm the English spelling of Korda's name, which appears in the FCD file in Cyrillic transliteration.

11. vol. 6, app. 1, p. 610.

12. Though the KGB accepted this arrangement, it had some reservations from the point of view of security about leaving the choice of the location for these meetings to Haddad; k-24, 365, para. 52.

13. k-24, 365, para. 50.

14. Follain, *Jackal*, pp. 26–8; Dobson and Payne, *War without End*, p. 242.

15. Mortin to Andropov, no. 164/1430, 24 June 1971; k-24, 365, paras. 25, 45–8.

16. Dobson and Payne, *War without End*, p. 160.

17. PLO codename in k-24, 344.

18. k-24, 360. By 1980 Arafat's codename had been changed to BESKOV; vol. 2, ch. 6, para. 47.

19. Rubin and Rubin, *Yasir Arafat*, pp. 42–3. Arafat told a Western intelligence officer that he had first visited Moscow in the 1950s as part of a student delegation.

20. Andrew and Gordievsky, *KGB*, pp. 547–8.

21. GIDAR had been recruited in Moscow in 1968 (possibly during Arafat's visit, though this is not mentioned in Mitrokhin's notes); k-24, 338, 341. Hart, *Arafat* (p. 4), refers to Hasan as 'Arafat's most trusted adviser'.

22. k-24, 360. During his first open visit to Moscow in 1970 Arafat was received not by representatives of the Soviet government or Communist Party but by a front organization, the Afro-Asian Solidarity Committee; Barron, *KGB*, p. 77.

23. Rubin and Rubin, *Yasir Arafat*, ch. 1.

24. Pacepa, *Red Horizons*, chs. 1–2. Pacepa defected to the United States in 1978.

25. k-24, 361.

26. Andrew and Gordievsky, *KGB*, pp. 547–8. See illustrations.

27. Golan, *Soviet Policies in the Middle East*, p. 112.

28. Andropov to Brezhnev, no. 1071, A/OV, 23 April 1975. Manuscript notes on the document record that five other members of the Politburo (Suslov, Podgorny, Kosygin, Grechko and Gromyko) had also been informed, and that approval had been given on 26 April. We are grateful to

Vladimir Bukovsky for supplying us with a photocopy of this top-secret communication from his personal collection of KGB documents found in the Kremlin archives.

29. k-24, 365, paras 54–7. KGB operations in the 1970s to liquidate defectors, whether directly or through the use of proxies, appear to have achieved nothing of significance. The Centre was unwilling either to abandon its traditional policy of executing 'traitors' who had fled abroad or to take the risks necessary to ensure their execution; Andrew and Mitrokhin, *The Sword and the Shield*, ch. 23.

30. k-24, 365, paras. 57–8. Andropov to Brezhnev, no. 1218, A/OV, 16 May 1975. (We are grateful to Vladimir Bukovsky for supplying us with a photocopy of this top-secret communication from his personal collection of KGB documents found in the Kremlin archives. Mitrokhin noted only a summary of the copy in the FCD archives.)

31. k-24, 365, para. 60.

32. k-14, 141.

33. Ibid.; k-24, 351.

34. k-24, 346.

35. Mitrokhin noted a further reference to 'co-operation' with the DFLP and PFLP-GC in 1977; k-19, 313. His notes contain no reference to later contacts with Hawatmeh and Jibril.

36. Mitrokhin's notes record that the KGB was informed of Haddad's plans for 'a petroleum war', but give no further details; k-24, 365, para. 61.

37. Follain, *Jackal*, ch. 1.

38. Had Carlos ever been either an agent or confidential contact, this fact would doubtless have been recorded, following Mitrokhin's normal practice, when Mitrokhin noted his file. The only details noted by Mitrokhin relating to Carlos's period at the Lumumba University were his affair with a Cuban student, Sonia Marine Oriola (by whom, though Mitrokhin's brief notes do not mention this, he had a daughter), and his involvement in a 1969 Moscow demonstration which broke windows at the Iranian embassy; k-3, 67, 133.

39. Follain, *Jackal*, chs. 1–4; quotation from p. 9.

40. Ibid., chs. 5, 6.

41. The course syllabus covered intelligence, counter-intelligence, US intelligence agencies, interrogation, operational equipment, surveillance, organization and conduct of guerrilla warfare, leadership protection, mines, sabotage, military training, Marxism-Leninism, transmission, storage and destruction of secret documents, use of containers, and photography; k-26, 202. Though not mentioned in Mitrokhin's notes, similar courses were probably arranged in subsequent years.

42. k-24, 365, paras. 61–3.

43. k-8, 617.

44. k-24, 365, para. 64.

45. k-8, 617.
46. vol. 6, app. 1, p. 610. On KGB collaboration with Yunis, see above, p. 248.
47. k-24, 365, para. 65. After Haddad's death, his terrorist group fragmented. His former chief lieutenant, Salim Abu Salem (aka Abu Muhammad) founded a breakaway PFLP-Special Command (not to be confused with Jibril's PFLP-General Command), which over the next few years specialized in attacks on Jewish targets, among them in 1980 a Paris synagogue and the Jewish-owned Norfolk Hotel in Nairobi (Dobson and Payne, *War without End*, pp. 160–61).
48. k-3, 67.
49. Follain, *Jackal*, pp. 117, 186–9. Carlos was eventually expelled from Syria in 1991. After a trial in France in 1997, he was sentenced to life imprisonment.
50. Andrew and Gordievsky, *KGB*, pp. 553–4. Qaddafi had earlier provoked the ire of the Centre after publicly endorsing Sadat's expulsion of Soviet advisers and condemning the Soviet–Iraqi Friendship Treaty in 1972. On that occasion the FCD implemented active measures against him; k-2, 298. Mitrokhin noted few files on Libyan matters. The only KGB agent inside the Libyan intelligence community identified in his notes was SERY, who broke contact in 1972; k-14, 434.
51. k-24, 356. Mitrokhin's notes record that Abu Iyad provided intelligence on Egypt, Saudi Arabia and Algeria, but give no details. Markus Wolf acknowledges that he was initially impressed when Abu Iyad 'boasted of his contacts at the heart of the US government, NATO, and the arms trade', but was subsequently generally disappointed by the quality of the intelligence which he provided; Wolf, *Man without a Face*, p. 270.
52. k-14, 143.
53. Andrew and Gordievsky, *KGB*, p. 550.
54. The 1981 report was one of a number captured by the Israelis; Adams, *The Financing of Terror*, pp. 48–9.
55. k-3, 68.
56. Golan, *Soviet Policies in the Middle East*, p. 130.
57. Wolf, *Man without a Face*, p. 271.
58. Shlaim, *The Iron Wall*, ch. 10.
59. Ganor, 'Syria and Terrorism'; Shlaim, *The Iron Wall*, p. 403. Mitrokhin did not see Abu Nidal's file.
60. Rubin, *Transformation of Palestinian Politics*, pp. 4–5.
61. Chernyaev, *My Six Years with Gorbachev*, p. 147; Vassiliev, *Russian Policy in the Middle East*, pp. 318–19.

14. Asia: Introduction

1. Kim Il Sung's refusal to defer to Moscow was not accompanied by strident denunciations of Soviet revisionism on the Chinese model. From the early 1960s he found himself courted by both Moscow and Beijing, and generally tried to avoid taking sides. The lowest point in Kim's relations with the PRC came during the Cultural Revolution when Chinese loud-speakers along the entire length of the Korean border broadcast denunci-ations of North Korean 'revisionism' and there were a number of unpublicized border clashes; Schäfer, 'Weathering the Sino-Soviet Conflict', documents 6, 8.

2. Sebag Montefiore, *Stalin*, pp. 618–20.

3. Weathersby, '"Should We Fear This?"'; Andrew and Elkner, 'Stalin and Intelligence', pp. 83–4.

4. See below, pp. 272–3.

5. Chin et al., 'New Central and East European Evidence on the Cold War in Asia', p. 450.

6. See below, p. 286.

7. Gromyko and Ponomarev (eds.), *Soviet Foreign Policy*, vol. 2, p. 535.

8. See below, pp. 298–9.

9. k-27, 498.

10. Gromyko wrote in January 1967 in a memorandum approved by the Politburo, 'We should go on rendering comprehensive assistance to the DRV [Democratic Republic of Vietnam] in consolidating its defence capacity to resist the [US] aggression, without getting directly involved in the war.' Dobrynin, *In Confidence*, appendix, p. 641.

11. Gromyko and Ponomarev (eds.), *Soviet Foreign Policy*, vol. 2, p. 383.

12. Andrew, *For the President's Eyes Only*, p. 323.

13. Semichastnyi, *Bespokoinoe serdtse*, pp. 331–4. Semichastny 'categori-cally denies' allegations that any US PoW was either sent to the Soviet gulag or interrogated in Moscow during his five years as KGB Chairman.

14. Gaiduk, 'The Vietnam War and Soviet–American Relations', p. 252.

15. k-19, 192.

16. k-19, 195.

17. k-12, 323. The fact that Mitrokhin's notes identify no other agent or confidential contact with access to classified information which compared to that of ISAYEYEV suggests, but does not prove, that KGB sources in Vietnam were generally low-grade. Even ISAYEYEV was categorized as a confidential contact rather than an agent, probably because of the limits which he imposed on his collaboration.

18. See below, pp. 313, 321–2.

19. Gromyko and Ponomarev (eds.), *Soviet Foreign Policy*, vol. 2, p. 400.

20. Shebarshin, *Ruka Moskvy*, p. 73.

21. Rubinstein and Smith (eds.), *Anti-Americanism in the Third World*, p. 138; Hollander, *Anti-Americanism*, p. 346.
22. Shebarshin, *Ruka Moskvy*, p. 79.
23. vol. 3 misc., item 501.
24. Andrew and Mitrokhin, *The Sword and the Shield*, pp. 562–3.
25. UNI report, 4 Aug. 2004.
26. On KGB policy to the Orthodox Church, see Andrew and Mitrokhin, *The Sword and the Shield*, ch. 28.
27. See below, ch. 20.
28. See below, pp. 398–402.
29. Cherkashin, *Spy Handler*, p. 275.
30. Kuzichkin, 'Coups and Killings in Kabul'.
31. See, for example, Leonov, *Likholet'e*.

15. The People's Republic of China

1. Andrew and Gordievsky, *KGB*, pp. 126–7.
2. McKnight, *Espionage and the Roots of the Cold War*, pp. 118–21; 'Communist Activities in China, Federated Malay States, etc. (The "Noulens Case")', box 4, Record Group 262 (records of the British-dominated Shanghai Municipal Police), National Archives, Washington, D.C.
3. Byron and Pack, *The Claws of the Dragon*, parts I and II.
4. Salisbury, *The New Emperors*, pp. 217ff.
5. Leonov, Fediakova and Fermandois, 'El general Nikolai Leonov en el CEP'.
6. Goncharov, Lewis and Litai, *Uncertain Partners*, p. 74.
7. Leonov, Fediakova and Fermandois, 'El general Nikolai Leonov en el CEP'; Zubok and Pleshakov, *Inside the Kremlin's Cold War*, pp. 61, 297 n. 64.
8. Goncharov, Lewis and Litai, *Uncertain Partners*, p. 74.
9. *USSR–China in a Changing World*, p. 74.
10. Semichastnyi, *Bespokoinoe serdtse*, p. 335.
11. k-19, 5.
12. Cradock, *Know Your Enemy*, pp. 164–7.
13. 'Deng Xiaoping's Talks with the Soviet Ambassador and Leadership, 1957–1963', p. 181; Pleshakov, 'Nikita Khrushchev and Sino-Soviet Relations', p. 236.
14. Li Zhisui, *The Private Life of Chairman Mao*, pp. 397–8.
15. Wu, *Laogai*, p. 26.
16. Byron and Pack, *The Claws of the Dragon*, pp. 250–53. On Kang Sheng's return to favour, see ibid., ch. 11, and Salisbury, *The New Emperors*, p. 221.
17. Cradock, *Know Your Enemy*, p. 167.

18. Andrew and Gordievsky, *KGB*, p. 494.
19. 'Deng Xiaoping's Talks with the Soviet Ambassador and Leadership, 1957–1963', pp. 181–2.
20. Byron and Pack, *The Claws of the Dragon*, p. 253.
21. Chang, *Friends and Enemies*, pp. 259–61.
22. Wolf, *Man without a Face*, p. 256.
23. Leonov, Fediakova and Fermandois, 'El general Nikolai Leonov en el CEP'.
24. Zubok and Pleshakov, *Inside the Kremlin's Cold War*, p. 61.
25. During the 1950s Hartvig was used by both Line PR and Line X at the Helsinki residency. Line K later used him for active-measures operations as well as intelligence collection. Though he retired in 1968, he remained in contact with the residency until his death in 1979 (k-14, 756).
26. Andrew and Gordievsky, *KGB*, pp. 494–5.
27. Semichastnyi, *Bespokoinoe serdtse*, p. 335.
28. Directive of the head of the FCD, No. 00156, 2 September 1967; k-19, 4.
29. As Beijing's oldest university, Peking University still keeps its traditional English transliteration.
30. Andrew and Gordievsky, *KGB*, pp. 495–7.
31. k-19, 1, 8.
32. 'Xinjiang, China's Restive Northwest'; Burles, *Chinese Policy toward Russia and the Central Asian Republics*.
33. Short, *The Dragon and the Bear*, p. 186; 'Xinjiang, China's Restive Northwest'.
34. k-19, 9. On the persecution of Mongolians in Inner Mongolia during the Cultural Revolution see Sneath, *Changing Inner Mongolia*, ch. 4.
35. k-27, 420.
36. Politburo resolution No. P122/97, 15 April 1968; k-27, 420.
37. 'Uighhur' [pseud.], 'Sherki Türkestan Evasi'; Tillett, 'The National Minorities Factor in the Sino-Soviet Dispute'.
38. Politburo resolution No. P122/97, 15 April 1968; k-27, 420.
39. Paine, *Imperial Rivals*, p. 354.
40. On the making of the Sino-Soviet frontier, see ibid.
41. Gates, *From the Shadows*, pp. 35–6.
42. Kissinger, *White House Years*, pp. 171–2.
43. Ibid., pp. 174–7.
44. k-27, 421.
45. Andrew and Gordievsky, *KGB*, p. 497; Kissinger, *White House Years*, pp. 183–5.
46. Shevchenko, *Breaking with Moscow*, pp. 218–20.
47. Jian and Wilson, '"All under the Heavens is Great Chaos"'; Jian, *Mao's China and the Cold War*, pp. 245–9; Burr (ed.), *National Security Archive Electronic Briefing Book No. 145*, document 3.

48. Andrew and Gordievsky, *KGB*, p. 497; Dittmer, *Sino-Soviet Normalization*, pp. 192–4.

49. Burr (ed.), *National Security Archive Electronic Briefing Book No. 145*, document 10.

50. Andrew and Gordievsky, *KGB*, pp. 497–8.

51. Li Zhisui, *The Private Life of Chairman Mao*, chs. 74–5. Mitrokhin did not have the opportunity to note the file on the death of Lin Biao, in which Andropov appears to have taken a personal interest; Volkogonov, *The Rise and Fall of the Soviet Empire*, p. 338.

52. Dittmer, *Sino-Soviet Normalization*, p. 192.

53. Li Zhisui, *The Private Life of Chairman Mao*, p. 546.

54. vol. 5 isl., app. 2.

55. k-19, 2.

56. k-19, 12.

57. k-5, 371.

58. k-2, 414. Mitrokhin's notes do not specify the reasons for the failure. Other failed deployments included SENIM, another Chinese agent of the KGB, who crossed the border in August 1972 and was never heard of again; k-18, 72.

59. vol. 6, app. 3, p. 791.

60. k-19, 13.

61. Chang, *Wild Swans*, p. 441.

62. k-19, 20. These difficulties were probably recounted by the agent after his return from a failed mission.

63. k-18, 250.

64. k-19, 78.

65. On 8 April 1978 FENIKS went back to North Korea, but agreed to renew contact if he returned to the PRC or had another foreign posting; k-27, 469. He evidently considered it too dangerous to try to establish contact with the Soviet embassy in Pyongyang.

66. Andrew and Gordievsky (eds.), *Instructions from the Centre*, p. 184.

67. 'On certain national-psychological characteristics of the Chinese and their evaluation in the context of intelligence work', FCD directive no. 822/PR/62, 12 September 1976; text in Andrew and Gordievsky (eds.), *Instructions from the Centre*, pp. 185–94.

68. Short, *The Dragon and the Bear*, p. 215.

69. k-7, 46.

70. 'Plan of requirements on Chinese subjects for 1977', FCD directive No. 891/PR/52, 14 March 1977; text in Andrew and Gordievsky (eds.), *Instructions from the Centre*, pp. 196–203.

71. Short, *The Dragon and the Bear*, pp. 214–15.

72. 'Guidance on measures designed to improve the work against China from third countries', FCD directive No. 16/PR, 12 January 1978; text in Andrew and Gordievsky (eds.), *Instructions from the Centre*, pp. 204–7.

73. 'Basic targets of interest to Line in Hong Kong', FCD directive No. 1734/PR/62, 20 April 1978; text in Andrew and Gordievsky (eds.), *More Instructions from the Centre*, pp. 68–78.

74. 'Guidance on measures designed to improve the work against China from third countries', FCD directive No. 16/PR, 12 January 1978; text in Andrew and Gordievsky (eds.), *Instructions from the Centre*, p. 205.

75. vol. 4 sri, ch. 4, p. 134. A retired Western intelligence officer recalls that, 'Service A clearly made hay with the operational intelligence provided by FENIKS in terms of document format, addresses etc, and I remember some of the forgeries surfacing in Japan in the mid-1970s and being struck by the apparent verisimilitude. (No, we did not swallow them hook, line and sinker!)'

76. vol. 4 sri, ch. 4, p. 134.

77. vol. 4 sri, app. 3, p. 153.

78. k-20, 217. Mitrokhin did not note the file on the implementation of this operation.

79. vol. 4 ind., app. 3, p. 118.

80. Bao and Chelminski, *Prisoner of Mao*, pp. 8–11, 38–9, 99. The book was not, however, a straightforward piece of Soviet propaganda and criticized the insensitivity of Soviet advisers in the PRC during the 1950s. The apparent objectivity of *Prisoner of Mao* subsequently increased Pasqualini's value as a KGB agent of influence.

81. k-14, 19; t-1, 71.

82. vol. 9, ch. 6, p. 53; Andrew and Mitrokhin, *The Sword and the Shield*, p. 471.

83. Pasqualini continued to be an active campaigner against the abuse of human rights in the PRC until his death in 1997. Despite his work as a paid agent of the KGB from 1975 to at least 1979, there is no reason to doubt the sincerity of that campaign.

84. k-14, 27.

85. 'Chief Conclusions and Views Adopted at the Meeting of Heads of Service', FCD directive No. 156/54, 1 February 1984; text in Andrew and Gordievsky (eds.), *Instructions from the Centre*, pp. 4–14.

86. 'Comrade Alyoshin's [Kryuchkov's] instructions on planning the work of sections of the Service and organization abroad in 1984', 2 November 1983; text in Andrew and Gordievsky (eds.), *Instructions from the Centre*, pp. 16–22.

87. Andrew and Gordievsky (eds.), *Instructions from the Centre*, pp. 207–8.

88. 'Work on China', FCD directive no. 11781/X, 7 May 1985; text in Andrew and Gordievsky (eds.), *Instructions from the Centre*, pp. 208–10.

89. Leonov, Fediakova and Fermandois, 'El general Nikolai Leonov en el CEP'.

90. Andrew and Mitrokhin, *The Sword and the Shield*, ch. 21.

91. The budget for the Beijing residency in 1979 of 4,500 hard-currency

rubles puts it in approximately the same league as Athens (4,200) and Tehran (5,000), but well below New York (29,400), Washington (26,000), Rome (15,000), Bonn (11,300), Tokyo (10,400), Paris (10,100) and London (7,100); vol. 6, ch. 9. For further comparative statistics, see Andrew and Mitrokhin, *The Sword and the Shield*, p. 634 n. 63.

92. Mitrokhin noted only the subject of the file; k-20, 124. Though Mitrokhin did not note the date, neighbouring files in the k-20 series refer to the early to mid-1970s.

93. Interview by Christopher Andrew with Viktor Makarov, 1993; Kahn, 'Soviet Comint in the Cold War', p. 10.

16. Japan

1. Andrew and Mitrokhin, *The Sword and the Shield*, pp. 93, 94–5, 281–2; Andrew and Gordievsky, *KGB*, pp. 189–92, 250–52, 281–2; Whymant, *Stalin's Spy*.

2. See below, pp. 304–5.

3. Text of 1951 US–Japanese Security Treaty in Buckley, *Japan Today*, app. 3.

4. Though frequently referred to as one of the four islands, the Habomais were technically an island group.

5. Text of 1960 US–Japanese 'Treaty of Mutual Cooperation and Security' in Buckley, *Japan Today*, app. 4.

6. Scalapino, *The Japanese Communist Movement*, pp. 114–15; Packard, *Protest in Tokyo*.

7. k-8, 599.

8. Ambrose, *Eisenhower*, vol. 2, pp. 581–2. Scalapino, *The Japanese Communist Movement*, p. 115 n. 25. There was, however, little personal hostility during the protest movement to US citizens in Japan.

9. k-8, 599.

10. Ibid.

11. Scalapino, *The Japanese Communist Movement*, pp. 115, 314.

12. Andrew and Mitrokhin, *The Sword and the Shield*, p. 364–5.

13. k-8, 248.

14. vol. 6, ch. 5, part 5.

15. k-8, 251.

16. Andrew and Mitrokhin, *The Sword and the Shield*, p. 374.

17. vol. 6, ch. 5, part 5, pp. 176–7. Mitrokhin's notes on plans for operation VULKAN do not indicate whether or not it was ever implemented. NOMOTO was a Japanese citizen who had emigrated to Russia to work in the Kamchatka fisheries before being recruited as a KGB illegal agent. He was deployed to Japan in 1963 after the closing of the JIMMY residency; k-16, 434.

18. vol. 6, ch. 5, part 5, p. 177. The compromise of KGB sabotage planning after the defection in 1971 of the Line F officer in London, Oleg Lyalin, led to the withdrawal of Line F officers from most Western residencies (Andrew and Mitrokhin, *The Sword and the Shield*, p. 383). It is likely that the Line F officer was also withdrawn from Tokyo. Though Mitrokhin noted a number of plans for 'special actions' in Japan drawn up in 1970, he saw none prepared in later years.

19. Andrew and Mitrokhin, *The Sword and the Shield*, pp. 383.

20. Scalapino, *The Japanese Communist Movement*, pp. 174–8. In May 1964 two prominent JCP members, the deputy Yosio Shiga and his close associate Ichizo Suzuki, were expelled by the Central Committee on charges of 'engaging in conspiratorial activities, such as secretly contacting the Soviet Union, deceiving and betraying our party'. Later in the year Shiga founded a new pro-Soviet breakaway Communist Party, the JCP (Voice of Japan), which survived mainly on handouts from Moscow and never became a significant threat to the JCP. Braddick, *Japan and the Sino-Soviet Alliance*, pp. 206, 210–11.

21. Braddick, *Japan and the Sino-Soviet Alliance*, p. 204.

22. In the wake of the JCP's decision to side with Beijing after the Sino-Soviet split, many of its intellectual supporters broke with the Party or were expelled, significantly reducing its influence on public opinion; ibid., p. 267. In 1969 the JCP made an uncompromising denunciation of the Soviet invasion of Czechoslovakia and demanded the return of the Habomais and Shikotan.

23. One of the illegals in the JIMMY residence, VASILIEV, an ethnic Chinese Soviet citizen, who was operating under cover as a university student, refused to return from Tokyo, apparently because of his wish to marry a Japanese woman; k-12, 416; k-16, 238; k-27, 35.

24. k-27,360. KOCHI was recruited in 1962. There is no indication in Mitrokhin's brief notes on his file that he was able to provide classified documents. According to KOCHI's file, the quality of his intelligence declined significantly after 1967. In 1975, a year after he gave up most of his journalism, he was removed from the agent network.

25. t-7, 247.

26. t-7, 248.

27. Of the 100,000 convertible rubles allocated to the JSP in 1972, 60,000 went to individuals to assist their careers in the Diet and elsewhere, and to promote their roles as agents of influence; 10,000 to strengthen links between the JSP and the CPSU; 20,000 for active measures to damage Japan's relations with the USA and PRC; 10,000 for active measures to prevent any alignment of the JSP with the other main opposition parties, the Clean Government Party (Komeito) and the Democratic Socialist Party (DSP). t-7, 250–51.

28. t-7, 248; k-23, 58. GAVR, whose real name is not included in Mitro-

khin's notes, has been identified by Levchenko as Seiichi Katsumata; Barron, *KGB Today*, p. 174. The payment recorded in Mitrokhin's brief note of his file was doubtless not an isolated one. GAVR was regarded by the KGB as the leader of the centrist faction in the JSP; k-23, 58.

29. t-7, 249, 260. ATOS, whose real name is not included in Mitrokhin's notes, has been identified by Levchenko as Tamotsu Sato; Barron, *KGB Today*, p. 174. Mitrokhin's brief note of his file records a payment to Sato of 400,000 yen, apparently in October 1973, for the publication of articles in JSP periodicals; t-7, 260. There were doubtless other payments.

30. t-7, 249, 260. Mitrokhin noted another payment to ALFONS (doubtless one of a number) of 150,000 yen for the publication of material in *Shakai Shimpo*; t-7, 260.

31. t-7, 249; k-23, 60.

32. t-7, 249.

33. JACK (DZHEK in Cyrillic) was recruited in 1973; k-23, 57.

34. GRACE was probably recruited in 1975; k-8, 600. Though his real name is not included in Mitrokhin's notes, he has been identified by Levchenko as Shigeru Ito. Levchenko also refers to two other JSP agents, RAMSES and TIBR, not mentioned in Mitrokhin's notes (at least by these codenames) on whom no other information is available. Barron, *KGB Today*, pp. 173–4; Levchenko, *On the Wrong Side*, p. 110.

35. k-23, 29.

36. Barron, *KGB Today*, pp. 99–105.

37. k-23, 56.

38. k-8, 600; k-23, 29.

39. k-23, 20.

40. The JSP deputy and KGB confidential contact KERK also had a leading role in the Association; k-23, 56.

41. k-8, 600; k-23, 54. Hara, *Japanese–Soviet/Russian Relations since 1945*, p. 131. Levchenko, *On the Wrong Side*, pp. 89–90; Barron, *KGB Today*, pp. 79–80, 120.

42. *Asahi Shimbun*, 4 Sept. 1973; Levchenko, *On the Wrong Side*, pp. 89–90; Barron, *KGB: The Hidden Hand*, pp. 79–80.

43. Date of Ishida's recruitment in k-8, 600; k-23, 54. Levchenko identifies Pronnikov as his recruiter; *On the Wrong Side*, p. 90; Barron, *KGB Today*, p. 79.

44. The budget for Seventh Department residencies in 1973, in convertible rubles, was as follows: Japan: 203,100; India: 204,600; Pakistan: 54,800; Laos: 19,000; Thailand: 32,500; Cambodia: 26,700; Singapore: 22,600; Malaysia: 23,600; Indonesia: 72,800; Burma: 35,300; Nepal: 12,200; Sri Lanka: 30,600; Bangladesh: 52,900; Reserve: 3,000 (k-18, 65). India, Pakistan, Bangladesh, Burma, Sri Lanka and Nepal later became the responsibility of a new Seventeenth Department; Laos and Cambodia were moved to the Sixth Department. See Appendix D.

45. Politburo resolution No. P 100/U1 of 16 Aug. 1973; t-7, 200.

46. t-7, 200.

47. On Tanaka's visit to Moscow, see Hara, *Japanese–Soviet/Russian Relations since 1945*, ch. 3.

48. k-18, 90.

49. When Mitrokhin saw FEN's file in either 1974 or 1975, his cultivation, which had begun in 1972, was still continuing but had made sufficient progress for plans to be made for his recruitment in 1975; k-8, 260. FEN is almost certainly identical with the fully recruited LDP agent identified by Levchenko after his defection in 1979 as FEN-FOKING; Barron, *KGB Today*, p. 174.

50. k-23, 16.

51. McCargo, *Contemporary Japan*, pp. 106–9; Buckley, *Japan Today*, pp. 37–9.

52. k-5, 74.

53. k-14, 208.

54. k-6, 159.

55. k-27, 454.

56. k-23, 55.

57. k-23, 24. It seems likely, though not certain, that ROY was the agent later identified by Levchenko as ARES (Levchenko, *On the Wrong Side*, pp. 119–27, 154–5). ROY, like ARES, was a journalist recruited in the mid-1960s, run for a time by Line KR, who worked solely for money and had important intelligence connections but was less productive in the mid-1970s after the suspicions of Japanese counter-intelligence had been aroused. Discrepancies between Mitrokhin's notes on ROY and Levchenko's recollection of ARES are probably due chiefly to the fact that Mitrokhin did not see his file after 1977. Levchenko recalls that, from approximately that moment, ARES 'became productive again'.

58. k-14, 208. Mitrokhin's notes identify a further journalist agent, FET (or FOT), but give no additional information; k-18, 87.

59. The print journalists working as KGB agents in 1979 identified by Levchenko were KANT and DAVEY of the *Sankei Shimbun*, KAMUS of the *Tokyo Shimbun* and VASSIN, a former JCP member who ran a newsletter (Barron, *KGB Today*, pp. 174–5; Levchenko, *On the Wrong Side*, p. 111). It is possible that two of these agents may be among those identified in files noted by Mitrokhin under different codenames.

60. Barron, *KGB Today*, pp. 139–42, 174; Glaubitz, *Between Tokyo and Moscow*, p. 165.

61. Recollection of a retired Western intelligence officer stationed in Japan in the 1970s.

62. Glaubitz, *Between Tokyo and Moscow*, pp. 143–57; Berton, 'Two Decades of Soviet Diplomacy and Andrei Gromyko', pp. 79–81.

63. k-27, 27.

64. Braddick, *Japan and the Sino-Soviet Alliance*, p. 237.

65. Hasegawa, 'Japanese Perceptions of the Soviet Union and Russia in the Postwar Period', pp. 274–86.

66. k-16, 523; k-2, 319, 320; k-18, 88; k-14, 484.

67. k-27, 284.

68. MISHA was recruited after a quarrel with LANDYSH (of which no details are given in Mitrokhin's notes) threatened to compromise him; k-2, 321. The probability is that MISHA subsequently worked for money.

69. In an interview with Christopher Andrew in Washington in November 1987, Stanislav Levchenko confirmed that NAZAR had been recruited in the 1970s. Since the interview took place eight years before Andrew first saw the Mitrokhin archive, however, it was impossible during the interview to discuss other evidence which tends to identify MISHA as NAZAR.

70. Levchenko, *On the Wrong Side*, p. 150; Barron, *KGB Today*, pp. 158–9.

71. Two other Foreign Ministry recruitments during the 1970s identified in files noted by Mitrokhin are the diplomat MARCEL and an assistant military attaché, codenamed KONUS, recruited with MARCEL's assistance; k-2, 317–18.

72. Buckley, *Japan Today*, ch. 3.

73. Ibid.; McCargo, *Contemporary Japan*, ch. 3.

74. t-2, 77.

75. TANI's file records that his S&T met the requirements of the foremost authorities (*instantsii*), in effect the Politburo, one of the highest accolades. In addition to his S&T on semi-conductors, he provided important intelligence on integrated circuits for military radar systems; k-2, 82.

76. k-2, 363.

77. The other thirteen Line X agents in senior positions identified in Mitrokhin's notes on KGB files together with their main S&T fields were: ARAM (radio-physics, k-2, 419); ARGUS (radio engineering, k-14, 754); BRAT (scientific research at Tokyo University, t-2, 105); EYR (aerospace R&D, k-14, 755); KANDI (microbiology, k-14, 101); KARI (university physicist, t-2, 80); KISI (university aerospace research, k-14, 477); RIONI (Hitachi, t-2, 79); SAK (Mitsubishi, k-6, 159); SOT (technology exports, k-12, 363); TAIR (infra-red spectroscopy, k-19, 452); TONI (electronic engineering, t-2, 82); and UTI (nuclear physics, k-18, 224).

78. Levchenko, *On the Wrong Side*, p. 104.

79. Ibid., p. 105.

80. On S&T operations against the United States, see Andrew and Mitrokhin, *The Sword and the Shield*, pp. 186–9, 215–20.

81. In 1980 a total of 3,396 Soviet R&D projects were assisted by S&T. Ibid., pp. 215–20; Brook-Shepherd, *The Storm Birds*, p. 260; Hanson, *Soviet Industrial Espionage*; US Government, *Soviet Acquisition of Militarily Significant Western Technology: An Update*.

82. k-8, 338.
83. Levchenko, *On the Wrong Side*, p. 102; Glaubitz, *Between Tokyo and Moscow*, pp. 186–7.
84. Levchenko, *On the Wrong Side*, p. 104.
85. Andrew and Mitrokhin, *The Sword and the Shield*, p. 216; Andrew and Gordievsky, *KGB*, p. 622.
86. Andrew and Mitrokhin, *The Sword and the Shield*, pp. 556–8.
87. Levchenko, *On the Wrong Side*, pp. 157–65.
88. The only two cases of agents put on ice as a result of Levchenko's defection which were noted by Mitrokhin were those of DENIS (k-23, 29) and YAMAMOTO (k-23, 20), neither of whom had been personally handled by Levchenko. There were undoubtedly a substantial number of similar cases not noted by Mitrokhin. It is clear from the accounts of Levchenko's career in Tokyo by himself and John Barron that he knew the names or identifying details of at least a score of KGB agents. The damage-limitation exercise would necessarily have been implemented on the cautious assumption that his knowledge might have been even more extensive. There is, for example, no evidence that Levchenko knew the existence of DENIS, with whom the KGB none the less broke contact.
89. k-27, 27.
90. Ibid.
91. Kimura, 'Japanese–Soviet Political Relations from 1976–1983', p. 97.
92. Glaubitz, *Between Tokyo and Moscow*, p. 88.
93. Haslam, 'The Pattern of Soviet–Japanese Relations since World War II', p. 35. On Gorbachev's visit to Tokyo, see Hara, *Japanese–Soviet/Russian Relations since 1945*, ch. 4.
94. *Asahi Evening News*, 11 Dec. 1982; Glaubitz, *Between Tokyo and Moscow*, pp. 164–5.
95. See above, pp. 131–2.
96. Glaubitz, *Between Tokyo and Moscow*, pp. 188–9.
97. Ibid., p. 198.
98. Andrew and Gordievsky (eds.), *Instructions from the Centre*, pp. 17, 20–21.
99. Chernyaev, *My Six Years with Gorbachev*, p. 28.
100. Haslam, 'The Pattern of Soviet–Japanese Relations since World War II', p. 3.
101. Glaubitz, *Between Tokyo and Moscow*, p. 78; Levchenko, *On the Wrong Side*, pp. 102–3.

17. The Special Relationship with India Part 1

1. Andrew and Gordievsky, *KGB*, p. 504.
2. Gorev, *Jawaharlal Nehru*, pp. 48–9, 54.
3. Mullik, *The Chinese Betrayal*, p. 110.
4. Mullik, *My Years with Nehru*, pp. 60–61. During Khrushchev's visit to India late in 1955, Nehru made clear in private talks that he was aware of 'personal links' between leading Indian Communists and Soviet officials (though he did not mention the KGB by name). These links do not, however, seem to have diminished the warm official welcome given to the Soviet leader. Fursenko (ed.), *Prezidium TsK KPSS. 1954–1964*, p. 909 n. 7.
5. vol. 4 ind., app. 1, item 11.
6. Ibid., item 13; there is no indication in Mitrokhin's notes of the nature of the intelligence provided by RADAR.
7. Ibid., item 12.
8. Decrypts were filed in the archives of the KGB Eighth (and later the Sixteenth) Directorate, to which Mitrokhin did not have access.
9. vol. 4 ind., ch. 3, p. 12. There is no independent corroboration for the KGB conclusion that Promode Das Gupta was an IB agent. In 1964 he became a leading member of the hard-line breakaway CPI (M).
10. vol. 4 ind., ch. 3, para. 12.
11. See below, p. 321.
12. vol. 4 ind., ch. 6, p. 37.
13. vol. 4 ind., ch. 3, p. 13.
14. Fursenko (ed.), *Prezidium TsK KPSS. 1954–1964*, pp. 72–5. Khrushchev's trip, on which he was accompanied by Marshal Nikolai Bulganin, also took in Burma and Afghanistan. He also proposed that decorations and possible salary increases be given to the pilots who had flown him on his travels.
15. Andrew and Gordievsky, *KGB*, pp. 504–5.
16. Gromyko, *Memories*, p. 243.
17. CPSU Central Committee resolution No. ST 23/26-s of 16 May 1962; vol. 4 ind., ch. 5, p. 28.
18. Arora, *Krishna Menon*, pp. 210–11.
19. CPSU Central Committee resolution of 15 Nov. 1962; vol. 4 ind., ch. 5, p. 28.
20. The KGB paid Menon's election expenses totalling 733,000 rupees. vol. 4 ind., ch. 5, p. 28.
21. Ibid., p. 29.
22. Ibid.
23. Frank, *Indira*, pp. 265–6; Arora, *Krishna Menon*, pp. 273–5.
24. vol. 4 ind., ch. 5, p. 29.
25. Frank, *Indira*, p. 290. Mrs Gandhi's KGB codename is given in vol. 4, ch. 5, p. 30.

26. vol. 4 ind., ch. 5, p. 30.

27. Gandhi (ed.), *Two Alone, Two Together*, pp. 592–4.

28. Frank, *Indira*, pp. 238–9.

29. Malhotra, *Indira Gandhi*, p. 93.

30. Mallick, *Indian Communism*, p. 92.

31. vol. 4 ind., ch. 5, p. 29; k-24, 239. Shebarshin describes Mishra in his memoirs as 'extremely influential', though not of course identifying him as a Soviet agent; *Ruka Moskvy*, p. 82. See below, pp. 322–3.

32. k-8, 121.

33. vol. 4 ind., ch. 5, p. 30.

34. Press reports of speech to parliament by Home Minister Y. B. Chavan on 13 Dec. 1967, revealing Modin's part in publicizing the forgeries. Andrew and Gordievsky, *KGB*, pp. 505–6.

35. Barron, *KGB*, p. 237.

36. vol. 4 ind., ch. 5, p. 30.

37. Frank, *Indira*, p. 308. Kamaraj had returned to parliament after winning a by-election; though he remained head of the Syndicate, he was no longer Congress President.

38. Mallick, *Indian Communism*, pp. 123–4, 147. Congress Forum for Social Action codename in vol. 4 ind., ch. 4, p. 16.

39. Frank, *Indira*, p. 317.

40. Ibid., pp. 313–15. The Intelligence Bureau (IB), which had hitherto run both internal and foreign intelligence, was divided in two: the IB, which remained in charge of internal intelligence, and the newly formed Research and Analysis Wing (RAW), which ran foreign intelligence. Revenue Intelligence, hitherto part of the Finance Ministry, was also brought under the direct control of the Prime Minister's Secretariat, headed by Haksar. Malhotra, *Indira Gandhi*, p. 125.

41. Frank, *Indira*, pp. 313, 320.

42. Malhotra, *Indira Gandhi*, p. 126.

43. Frank, *Indira*, pp. 327–9; Mallick, *Indian Communism*, pp. 122–3, 147–8.

44. vol. 4 ind., ch. 4, pp. 25–6. Mitrokhin's probably incomplete notes on the sums paid to RERO record payments of 100,000 rupees in 1971, 1974 and 1977, and a payment of 60,000 rupees in 1976.

45. Kaul, *Reminiscences*, p. 255.

46. Gromyko, *Memories*, pp. 244–5.

47. Shebarshin identifies his source only as a 'well-informed acquaintance' who was banned from maintaining unofficial contacts with foreigners because of his official position. The source must thus have had the status of a KGB 'confidential contact' even if he was not a fully recruited agent. Shebarshin, *Ruka Moskvy*, pp. 72–5.

48. Ibid., pp. 75–6.

49. Singh, *The Yogi and the Bear*, pp. 89–96; Horn, *Soviet–Indian Relations*, p. 73.

50. Andrew and Gordievsky, *KGB*, pp. 509–10.

51. vol. 3 pak., ch. 1, p. 1.

52. Kalugin, *Spymaster*, pp. 126–7. In 1974 Kalugin became the youngest general in the First Chief Directorate.

53. vol. 4 ind., ch. 1, p. 5. KGB agents in Indian intelligence in 1978 included GOPAL (who worked in the Chinese department), PROTON (US department), ZINGER (US department), AVAR, KROT and SARDAR; vol. 4 ind., app. 1, items 34–8, 42.

54. Kalugin, *Spymaster*, pp. 126–7.

55. Malhotra, *Indira Gandhi*, pp. 143ff.

56. k-24, 239; see above, p. 317.

57. vol. 4 ind., ch. 5, pp. 30–31; Shebarshin's codename is given in vol. 3 misc., p. 112.

58. Frank, *Indira*, pp. 350–52, 368.

59. k-24, 239. Mishra's widow doubtless did not realize this was KGB money.

60. Kalugin, *Spymaster*, p. 126.

61. vol. 4 ind., ch. 6, p. 38.

62. The only detailed figures noted by Mitrokhin for the funds channelled to the CPI via the KGB cover the period August 1975 to June 1976 and the early months of 1977. They are as follows: August 1975: three separate payments of 404,157, 136,010 and 440,476 rupees; September 1975: 473,010 rupees; October 1975: 876,486 rupees; November 1975: 444,118 rupees; January 1976: 668,824 rupees; March 1976: 300,000 rupees; April 1976: 666,176 rupees; May 1976: 200,000 rupees; June 1976: two payments of 400,000 and 769,120 rupees; January 1977: two payments of 90,676 and 1,354,015 rupees; February 1977: two payments of 441,176 and 600,000 rupees (vol. 4 ind., ch. 3, p. 15).

63. Ibid. Mitrokhin did not record the date of the fishing trip. The member of the CPI National Council chosen to receive money from the KGB changed in 1975–76 but kept the codename BANKIR; pp. 14–15.

64. Rao was also briefly CPI general secretary in the early 1950s. In 1977 the All-Indian Congress of Trade Unions received 10,000 Swiss francs and 43,750 US dollars; ibid., p. 14. Its leader, S. A. Dange, then CPI chairman and a committed supporter of the Indira Gandhi regime, was a controversial figure. In 1978 he was expelled from the CPI and founded his own All-India Communist Party after the Party abandoned support for Mrs Gandhi; Mallick, *Indian Communism*, p. 152.

65. vol. 3 pak., ch. 5, p. 19; vol. 4, ch. 4, p. 16. A file of 1976 identifies as under KGB control one press agency (TREST), two daily newspapers (RAZUM and VOLNA), eight weekly newspapers (BRIZ, IDEYA, KURYER, PRIBOY, PRILIV, SIGNAL, SVET and ZNANIYE) and four magazines (OVAL, SPEKTR, TRIBUNA and one other). All are identified by name in Mitrokhin's notes; vol. 4 ind., ch. 4, pp. 16–17.

66. vol. 7 ind., ch. 7, p. 51; vol. 3 pak., ch. 5, p. 19. In 1973 the KGB also claimed to have published twenty-eight books and pamphlets in India; Mitrokhin noted no statistics for later years. It is, of course, possible that some journalists extracted money from the KGB for anti-American articles they would have written anyway.

67. In Italy, for example, according to KGB statistics, it planted forty-eight press articles in 1975 and sixty-three in 1976; Andrew and Mitrokhin, *The The Sword and the Shield*, p. 659 n. 172 .

68. k-12, 388; vol. 4 ind., app. 1, items 45, 117. During the late 1940s, Indira Gandhi's husband Feroze had been director of the *National Herald*; Rau later complained of his 'ignorance, inexperience and adventurism'. Frank, *Indira*, pp. 201–2. Rau's books include *India: Portrait of a People* (published by the Ministry of External Affairs in 1981), *History of Indian Journalism*, *The Press in India* and *Nehru for Children*.

69. Dhar, *Indira Gandhi, the 'Emergency', and Indian Democracy*, p. 235.

70. Andrew and Gordievsky, *KGB*, pp. 506–7.

71. Volkogonov, *The Rise and Fall of the Soviet Empire*, p. 281. In 1973 (the only year for which Mitrokhin noted the statistics) the KGB claimed to have organized five demonstrations in India; vol. 3 pak., ch. 1, para. 104.

72. vol. 4 ind., ch. 4, p. 17.

73. vol. 4 ind., ch. 8, p. 72.

74. Cf. above, pp. 17, 21, 94.

75. Shebarshin, *Ruka Moskvy*, pp. 91–3.

76. vol. 4 ind., ch. 8, p. 72.

77. Interview with Shebarshin, *Daily Telegraph*, 1 Dec. 1992.

78. vol. 4 ind., ch. 8, p. 72.

79. Malhotra, *Indira Gandhi*, pp. 163, 291; Frank, *Indira*, pp. 368, 374–5. On Allende's death, see above, p. 85.

80. Malhotra, *Indira Gandhi*, pp. 155–6.

81. Moynihan, *A Dangerous Place*, p. 41.

82. vol. 4 ind., ch. 8, p. 71.

83. Ibid., pp. 72–3.

84. Malhotra, *Indira Gandhi*, p. 167.

85. Frank, *Indira*, ch. 16.

86. vol. 4 ind., ch. 5, p. 32.

87. Mallick, *Indian Communism*, p. 149.

88. vol. 4 ind., ch. 5, p. 32. According to KGB files, the number of articles which it planted in the Indian press none the less declined in 1976 to 1,980, presumably as a result of press censorship during the emergency; vol. 4 ind., ch. 7, pp. 50–51.

89. Frank, *Indira*, pp. 388–9. The conspiracy theory that the CIA was behind the murder of Mujibur Rahman was vigorously promoted by the KGB; see below, p. 351. Mrs Gandhi also sent one of her personal assistants

to ask Shebarshin whether he thought the Chinese were involved in the coup. Shebarshin said he thought not; Shebarshin, *Ruka Moskvy*, pp. 94–5.
90. Ibid., pp. 95–7.
91. vol. 4 ind., ch. 4, pp. 17–18.
92. Bakshi, *Russia and India*, p. 140.
93. vol. 4 ind., ch. 5, p. 32.
94. Bakshi, *Russia and India*, p. 140; Dhar, *Indira Gandhi, the 'Emergency', and Indian Democracy*, p. 329.
95. Frank, *Indira*, pp. 393–5; Dhar, *Indira Gandhi, the 'Emergency', and Indian Democracy*, pp. 325–9. A hand-written note of 27 July 1976 from Mrs Nehru to Dhar about Sanjay's interview is reproduced on pp. 326–8.
96. vol. 4 ind., ch. 4, p. 19.
97. vol. 4 ind., ch. 5, p. 33.
98. Bakshi, *Russia and India*, p. 142; Singh, *The Yogi and the Bear*, pp. 133–4.
99. vol. 4 ind., ch. 5, p. 33.
100. vol. 4 ind., ch. 3, p. 15.
101. vol. 4 ind., ch. 4, p. 19.
102. Frank, *Indira*, pp. 413–14.

18. The Special Relationship with India Part 2

1. vol. 4 ind., ch. 5, p. 33.
2. Ibid., pp. 33–4.
3. Dhar, *Indira Gandhi, the 'Emergency', and Indian Democracy*, pp. 355–6. Frank, *Indira*, pp. 413–14.
4. vol. 4 ind., ch. 3, p. 12. Mitrokhin's notes give no examples of the 'important information' obtained from the CPM leadership in West Bengal.
5. Singh, *The Yogi and the Bear*, p. 134.
6. vol. 4 ind., ch. 4, p. 21.
7. FCD directive approved by Politburo resolution No. P 50/72 dated 24 March 1977; vol. 4 ind., ch. 7, p. 51.
8. Bakshi, *Russia and India*, p. 145.
9. Politburo resolution No. 1638-A/OV (of special importance), 2 Aug. 1977; vol. 4 ind., ch. 4, p. 21.
10. vol. 4 ind., ch. 7, p. 51.
11. vol. 4 ind., ch. 8, pp. 69–70.
12. vol. 7 ind., ch. 7, p. 58.
13. Frank, *Indira*, pp. 431–2.
14. Singh, *The Yogi and the Bear*, pp. 141–2.
15. vol. 4 ind., ch. 5, p. 34.
16. Frank, *Indira*, p. 432.
17. vol. 4 ind., ch. 5, pp. 34–5.

18. vol. 4 ind., ch. 4, para. 31.

19. Singh, *The Yogi and the Bear*, p. 173.

20. vol. 4 ind., ch. 5, p. 36. The Delhi main residency did, however, report that Mrs Gandhi was favourably impressed by the fact that the chief Soviet delegate to the CPI Twelfth Congress in 1982, Eduard Shevardnadze, was a candidate rather than a full member of the Politburo.

21. Singh, *The Yogi and the Bear*, p. 174.

22. Malhotra, *Indira Gandhi*, p. 260.

23. Bakshi, *Russia and India*, p. 157.

24. vol. 4 ind., ch. 8, p. 86.

25. Malhotra, *Indira Gandhi*, p. 235.

26. vol. 4 ind., ch. 8, para. 16.

27. vol. 4 ind., ch. 7, pp. 57–8.

28. The congratulations, approved by Kryuchkov, were signed on 5 May 1982 by the head of the FCD Seventeenth Department, Gennadi Afanasy-evich Vaulin, who had preceded Lysenko as main resident in Delhi from 1977 until early in 1982 (vol. 4 ind., app. 3, item 59; k-24, 252).

29. vol. 4 ind., ch. 7, pp. 58–9.

30. FCD memorandum No. 155/2351, signed by Kryuchkov on 30 Oct. 1982 and approved by Andropov soon afterwards; vol. 3 pak., ch. 5, pp. 46–7.

31. vol. 4 ind., ch. 8, p. 71; Singh, *The Yogi and the Bear*, p. 300 n. 101.

32. Singh, *The Yogi and the Bear*, pp. 199–200. The Soviet Union was also mentioned once, by implication, in a section of the summit communiqué dealing with the responsibilities of the industrialized nations to the developing world.

33. Singh, *The Yogi and the Bear*, pp. 200–201, 308 n. 83.

34. Ibid., pp. 220–21.

35. vol. 4 ind., ch. 7, p. 60.

36. Frank, *Indira*, ch. 21.

37. See, e.g., Yajee, *CIA*, pp. 97–9.

38. Gates, *From the Shadows*, pp. 357–8.

39. US Department of State, *Soviet Influence Activities*; US Information Agency, *Recent Appearances of Soviet Disinformation*; Andrew and Gordi-evsky, *KGB*, p. 630.

40. Bakshi, *Russia and India*, pp. 165–93.

41. US Department of State, *Soviet Influence Activities*; US Information Agency, *Recent Appearances of Soviet Disinformation*; Andrew and Gordi-evsky, *KGB*, pp. 630–31.

42. Andrew and Gordievsky, *KGB*, p. 629.

43. Bakshi, *Russia and India*, pp. 200–201.

19. Pakistan and Bangladesh

1. Gromyko, *Memories*, pp. 246–7.
2. vol. 3 pak., ch. 4, p. 13.
3. The earliest amount of the annual subsidy to the SPC recorded by Mitrokhin was for $20,000; his notes, however, do not mention the date. The SPC received $30,000 in 1974, and $25,000 in 1975 and 1976. The larger sum in 1974 is probably to be explained by the SPC in that year asking for an additional sum to found a bi-monthly newsletter in London; vol. 3 pak., ch. 4, p. 13.
4. vol. 3 ban., ch. 2, p. 96.
5. vol. 3 pak., ch. 4, p. 18.
6. Ibid., p. 14.
7. vol. 3 pak., ch. 2, p. 3.
8. Ibid., p. 6; vol. 6, ch. 3.
9. vol. 3 pak., ch. 2, p. 5. Mitrokhin's notes give no indication of the intelligence GREM supplied.
10. Ibid., p. 3. Mitrokhin's notes give no indication of the intelligence that Hasan supplied. The fact that he had at least five successive FCD controllers (L. V. Shebarshin, N. V. Mardoniyev, G. V. Lazarev, A. V. Korneyev and S. P. Kuznetsov) strongly suggests that his material was of real significance. While Hasan was stationed in Saudi Arabia, where there was no legal KGB residency, the illegal KHALEF and a KGB Fifth Directorate officer masquerading as a pilgrim on the Haj were sent to make contact with him.
11. On the Eighth and Sixteenth Directorates, see Andrew and Mitrokhin, *The Sword and the Shield*, ch. 21. Mitrokhin did not have access to their archives.
12. ALI's other controllers included Leonid Shebarshin; vol. 3 misc., p. 115.
13. Shebarshin later concluded, possibly incorrectly, that Bhutto had been speaking with the approval of Ayub Khan; Shebarshin, *Ruka Moskvy*, pp. 34–6.
14. vol. 3 pak., ch. 7, pp. 55–6.
15. Raza, *Zulfikar Ali Bhutto and Pakistan*, p. 237.
16. vol. 3 pak., ch. 7, paras. 240–47.
17. Shebarshin, *Ruka Moskvy*, pp. 62–3. The resident's codename is given in vol. 3 pak., ch. 7, para. 245. Shebarshin refers to him only as Vasili B.
18. Raza, *Zulfikar Ali Bhutto and Pakistan*, pp. 5–7.
19. Ibid.; Talbot, *Pakistan*, pp. 179–84.
20. vol. 3 pak., ch. 6, para. 205.
21. vol. 3 pak., ch. 7, paras. 246–9.
22. vol. 3 pak., ch. 6, paras. 206–24.
23. Kolbenev, 'Kak Pakistan raskololsia na dva gosudarstva', p. 75.

24. There is, however, no KGB file noted by Mitrokhin which says so explicitly.

25. vol. 3 pak., ch. 7, paras. 248–9. The 'Agartala conspiracy' trial turned into a public relations disaster for Ayub Khan. Evidence emerged that Pakistani police had tortured the alleged conspirators, and one of the defendants was murdered while in custody. The trial also offered Mujib a welcome opportunity to publicize the cause of the Awami League. The trial was never completed and charges were dropped as a precondition to meetings between opposition leaders and Ayub early in 1969. Ziring, *Pakistan in the Twentieth Century*, pp. 310–11.

26. This strategy may be safely deduced from the active-measures operations designed to discredit all the main opponents of the PPP and the Awami League.

27. vol. 3 pak., ch. 5, para. 101.

28. Kolbenev, 'Kak Pakistan raskololsia na dva gosudarstva', p. 79.

29. Raza, *Zulfikar Ali Bhutto and Pakistan*, pp. 251–4; Ziring, *Pakistan in the Twentieth Century*, p. 408.

30. Raza, *Zulfikar Ali Bhutto and Pakistan*, pp. 250–51.

31. Ziring, *Bangladesh*, pp. 88–9.

32. Mascarenhas, *Bangladesh*, p. 28.

33. Ziring, *Bangladesh*, pp. 84–9.

34. vol. 3 ban., ch. 1, para. 415.

35. Ibid.; Directorate of National Security codename in vol. 3 ban., ch. 3, para. 441.

36. vol. 3 ban., ch. 1, para. 416.

37. Politburo resolution No. N 76/VIII OP, 2 Feb. 1973; vol. 3 ban., ch. 3, para. 434.

38. vol. 3 ban., ch. 2, paras. 430–31.

39. Mitrokhin noted no file on the foundation of BAKSAL.

40. vol. 6, ch. 2, part 3. Mitrokhin's notes do not identify the dates of their recruitment or give any information on the operations against the United States in which they were involved.

41. vol. 3 ban., ch. 2, para. 432; ch. 3, paras. 437–9, 442–3.

42. vol. 3 ban., ch. 3, para. 444.

43. Raza, *Zulfikar Ali Bhutto and Pakistan*, p. 226.

44. vol. 3 pak., ch. 5, para. 104.

45. Ibid., para. 120.

46. Ibid., para. 109.

47. Ibid., para. 111.

48. Ibid., para. 109.

49. Ibid., para. 107.

50. Ibid., para. 108.

51. Ibid., para. 103.

52. Raza, *Zulfikar Ali Bhutto and Pakistan*, pp. 250–51, 232–4.

53. Politburo resolution No. P 30/49 of 20 Oct. 1976, 'On our position regarding the proposal of Pakistan that a top-level conference of developing countries be held'; vol. 3 pak., ch. 5, para. 115.

54. vol. 3 pak., ch. 5, paras. 115–18.

55. Anwar, *The Terrorist Prince*, p. 27.

56. vol. 3 pak., ch. 5, para. 119.

57. Zafarullah (ed.), *The Zia Episode*, pp. 127–9, 133–5.

58. vol. 3 ban., ch. 3, para. 444.

59. Ibid., para. 446.

60. Ibid., para. 441.

61. Ibid., paras. 448–51.

62. Ibid., para. 452.

63. Ibid., para. 453.

64. Zafarullah (ed.), *The Zia Episode*, pp. 154–6, 164 n. 1.

65. Arif, *Working with Zia*, pp. 313–14, 412.

66. Gates, *From the Shadows*, pp. 146–8. The Carter administration had secretly decided to give non-military support to the *mujahideen* in July 1979.

67. vol. 3 pak., ch. 5, para. 1; Arif, *Working with Zia*, p. 315.

68. vol. 3 pak., ch. 5, para. 127.

69. Gates, *From the Shadows*, pp. 147–8.

70. vol. 3 pak., ch. 5, paras. 127–45. In operation SARDAR-5, for example, carried out on the evening of 14 to 15 March, a further series of Service A leaflets purporting to come from 'a group of young officers' were distributed by KGB officers in Islamabad, Rawalpindi and Karachi. Other leaflets were distributed by post. All denounced Zia and demanded his overthrow.

71. vol. 3 pak., ch. 5, paras. 127–45.

72. vol. 3 pak., ch. 7, para. 254.

73. vol. 3 pak., ch. 5, para. 127.

74. Ibid., para. 144.

75. Ibid., para. 129.

76. Bradsher, *Afghan Communism and Soviet Intervention*, pp. 181–4; Urban, *War in Afghanistan*, p. 17.

77. Arif, *Working with Zia*, pp. 337–8. In October 1980 Arif visited CIA headquarters at Langley for talks on Afghanistan.

78. Barron, *KGB Today*, pp. 45–6. Mitrokhin did not note any file dealing with the expulsion.

79. vol. 3 pak., ch. 5, para. 128.

80. Anwar, *The Terrorist Prince*, p. 60.

81. vol. 1, ch. 7; Mitrokhin, 'The KGB in Afghanistan', p. 140.

82. Anwar, *The Terrorist Prince*, pp. 43–5, 63–4.

83. vol. 1, ch. 7; Mitrokhin, 'The KGB in Afghanistan', p. 140.

84. On the KGB and KHAD, see below, pp. 408–9.

85. Although on occasion Murtaza spoke mysteriously about possible Russian connections, it is possible that this derived from his habit of unsubstantiated boasting rather than any conscious contact on his part with the KGB; Anwar, *The Terrorist Prince*, p. 75.

86. Ibid., pp. 87–8. Though Mitrokhin's reference to discussions between Murtaza and Najibullah do not specifically mention these terrorist attacks, there can be little doubt that they were agreed between them since KHAD provided the bombs used.

87. vol. 1, ch. 7; Mitrokhin, 'The KGB in Afghanistan', p. 140.

88. Anwar, *The Terrorist Prince*, pp. 95–8.

89. vol. 1, ch. 7; Mitrokhin, 'The KGB in Afghanistan', p. 140.

90. Anahita Ratebzad, codenamed SIMA, appears on a list which Mitrokhin compiled from KGB files of Afghan 'agents and confidential contacts'; vol. 1, app. 1. Unusually, however, the list fails to distinguish between the two categories. On Ratebzad, see below, p. 407.

91. Anwar, *The Terrorist Prince*, pp. 103–5. On Karmal's background as a KGB agent, see below, pp. 387, 403–4.

92. Anwar, *The Terrorist Prince*, pp. 107–9.

93. vol. 1, ch. 7; Mitrokhin, 'The KGB in Afghanistan', p. 140.

94. Anwar, *The Terrorist Prince*, pp. 112–16. Colonel Qaddafi went back on an earlier agreement to allow the hijackers to force the crew to fly the plane to Tripoli.

95. vol. 1, ch. 7; Mitrokhin, 'The KGB in Afghanistan', p. 145.

96. vol. 1, ch. 7; Mitrokhin, 'The KGB in Afghanistan', p. 143. At the suggestion of Najibullah, the KGB recruited Agent FURMAN, on whom no further details are available, to select agents posing as refugees to target Afghan refugee communities in Pakistan and Iran; vol. 1, app. 1. Though Mitrokhin noted no further examples, the KGB doubtless recruited other agents with the same mission as FURMAN.

97. vol. 3 pak., ch. 5, para. 145. On KGB active measures to disrupt *mujahideen* operations, see below, pp. 409–10.

98. vol. 1, ch. 7; Mitrokhin, 'The KGB in Afghanistan', p. 143.

99. See below, pp. 409–10.

100. Kryuchkov to Andropov, no. 155/796, 18 April 1981; vol. 3 pak., ch. 5, para. 150.

101. vol. 3 pak., ch. 5, para. 195.

102. Ibid., para. 143.

103. Anwar, *The Terrorist Prince*, pp. 130–37. Anwar's sources include both the terrorists who had attempted to shoot down Zia's plane with SAM-7 missiles. In 1992 Murtaza Bhutto declared in a newspaper interview, 'I had two attacks carried out against General Zia. Once the computer of the missile fired at him malfunctioned, and the second time he had a hair's breadth escape.' Mitrokhin's brief notes on KHAD/KGB dealings with Murtaza Bhutto unfortunately do not go beyond the 1981 hijack.

104. After a series of abysmally planned, unsuccessful operations in 1984 (none of which seems to have benefited from KHAD support), and with most of Al-Zulfikar's members in jail, Murtaza announced its dissolution in the following year. His stormy career came to a violent end in September 1996 when he was shot dead by Pakistani police outside his Karachi house while his estranged sister, Benazir, was Prime Minister. Anwar, *The Terrorist Prince*, chs. 12–16.

105. Ziring, *Pakistan in the Twentieth Century*, p. 459.

106. vol. 3 pak., ch. 5, para. 264.

107. See above, ch. 18.

108. vol. 3 pak., ch. 5, paras. 281–9. Mitrokhin's notes do not give details of the award to the resident.

109. Talbot, *Pakistan*, pp. 249–50.

110. Arif, *Working with Zia*, pp. 318–19, 334–5, 342.

111. Though the Pakistan air force board of enquiry found that 'the most probable cause' of the air crash was sabotage, a USAF accident-investigation team concluded that the most likely explanation was mechanical failure. Talbot, *Pakistan*, pp. 284–5.

112. Arif, *Working with Zia*, p. 319.

20. Islam in the Soviet Union

1. No single chapter, probably no single volume, can do justice to the complexity of the Soviet Union's Muslim populations, especially in the Caucasus, one of the most ethnically and linguistically diverse areas in the world. Islam and the struggle against Russian and Soviet rule, however, proved strong unifying factors within the predominantly Muslim areas. Gammer, 'Unity, Diversity and Conflict in the Northern Caucasus'.

2. Taheri, *Crescent in a Red Sky*, pp. ix, xiv, 92.

3. Flemming, 'The Deportation of the Chechen and Ingush Peoples'; Smith, *Allah's Mountains*, pp. 58–67; Andrew and Mitrokhin, *The Sword and the Shield*, pp. 101–2.

4. According to a report in 1973 by the leading Soviet expert in 'scientific atheism', V. G. Pivovranov, 52.9 per cent of Chechens (undoubtedly a considerable underestimate) were religious believers, as compared with only 11.9 per cent of ethnic Russians. Bennigsen and Broxup, *The Islamic Threat to the Soviet State*, pp. 33–4; Dunlop, *Russia Confronts Chechnya*, pp. 81–2.

5. Taheri, *Crescent in a Red Sky*, p. xiv.

6. Lewis, *After Atheism*, p. 149.

7. vol. 5 isl., ch. 8, p. 39.

8. On KGB policy to the Orthodox Church, see Andrew and Mitrokhin, *The Sword and the Shield*, ch. 28.

9. vol. 5 isl., ch. 3, pp. 8, 12; ch. 4.

10. Olcott, 'Islam and Fundamentalism in Independent Central Asia', p. 24.

11. vol. 5 isl., app. 1, pp. 42–3.

12. Bennigsen and Wimbush, *Mystics and Commissars*, pp. 2, 43–4.

13. Bennigsen and Broxup, *The Islamic Threat to the Soviet State*, pp. 104–5.

14. vol. 5 isl., ch. 4, p. 17.

15. Bennigsen and Broxup, *The Islamic Threat to the Soviet State*, p. 106.

16. vol. 5 isl., ch. 4, p. 17.

17. vol. 5 isl., ch. 3, para. 38.

18. vol. 5 isl., ch. 4, p. 16.

19. Olcott, 'Islam and Fundamentalism in Independent Central Asia', p. 21.

20. vol. 5 isl., ch. 8, p. 39.

21. Ibid., pp. 37–8.

22. Bennigsen and Wimbush, *Mystics and Commissars*, chs. 1, 2. On the Sufi response to the Tsarist advance in the north Caucasus, see Zelkina, *In Quest for God and Freedom*. The Qadiriya had been brought to the north Caucasus in the 1850s by Sheikh Kunta Haji. The KGB, like the rest of the Soviet bureaucracy, referred to the Qadiriya as the 'Kunta Haji', and it is so described in the files noted by Mitrokhin. As Yaacov Ro'i has argued, much more research is needed to establish the degree to which the Sufi brotherhoods were responsible for the tenacity of Muslim religious practice; Ro'i, 'The Secularisation of Islam and the USSR's Muslim Areas', p. 13.

23. vol. 5 isl., ch. 8, p. 30. Auaev (whose first name was not noted by Mitrokhin) was described in KGB files as leader of the 'Kunta Haji sect'.

24. Bennigsen and Wimbush, *Mystics and Commissars*, p. 31.

25. Mitrokhin's notes do not record the date of Gaziev's death, but the context suggests a date in the mid-1960s.

26. vol. 5 isl., ch. 8, p. 30.

27. Ibid., pp. 32–5.

28. Ibid., p. 35. For examples of similar operations elsewhere in the Soviet bloc, see Andrew and Mitrokhin, *The Sword and the Shield*, chs. 15, 16.

29. The real names of the illegals were as follows: AKBAR: Makhmudzhen Ariudzhanov (k-24, 245); STELLA: real name not recorded by Mitrokhin, but trained with AKBAR in 1970–76; the two operated as a married couple (vol. 2, app. 1, p. 70; k-24, 25); SABIR: Mutalim Agaverdioglu Talybov (k-27, 400; vol. 2, ch. 3, p. 26): ALI: Sebukh Apkaryan (k-5, 115; k-27, 37); STRELTSOV: Murmon Iosivovich Lokhov (vol. 2, ch. 3, p. 25; k-20, 197); MARK: identity uncertain but probably Vyacheslav Petrovich Makarov (k-16, 379) – MARK was one of the commoner KGB codenames used at various times to refer to several different illegals; RAFIEV: no identifying details recorded in Mitrokhin's notes; DEREVLYOV and DEREVLYOVA: Oleg Petrovich and Zinaida Nikiforovna Buryen (vol. 8, ch. 8, p. 33); KHALEF: Shamil Abdullazyanovich Khamsin (vol. 10, ch. 2);

BERTRAND: Georgi Ivanovich Kotlyar (k-21, 17; vol. 6, ch. 5, p. 154).

29. Andrew and Mitrokhin, *The Sword and the Shield*, pp. 312–13.

30. vol. 5 isl., ch. 8, p. 35.

31. Andrew and Mitrokhin, *The Sword and the Shield*, p. 512.

32. vol. 5 isl., ch. 8, pp. 36–7.

33. Ibid., p. 39.

34. Lieven, *Chechnya*, p. 28.

35. Bennigsen and Wimbush, *Mystics and Commissars*, p. 117. The pilgrims referred to were clearly associated with Qadiris rather than the Naqshbandis. The Naqshbandi *zikr* ('remembrance' of God) was a silent collective prayer.

36. vol. 5 isl., ch. 6, p. 21.

37. vol. 5 isl., ch. 3, p. 11.

38. Bennigsen and Broxup, *The Islamic Threat to the Soviet State*, p. 115.

39. See above, p. 186.

40. Bennigsen and Broxup, *The Islamic Threat to the Soviet State*, pp. 116–17.

41. Bennigsen and Wimbush, *Mystics and Commissars*, p. 108.

42. For example, the Khorzhem district in Uzbekistan and Kurgan-Tube in Tajikistan; vol. 5 isl., ch. 3, p. 14.

43. vol. 5 isl., ch. 6, p. 22.

44. Politburo resolution No. P 29/27 of 25 Sept. 1981; vol. 5 isl., ch. 5, p. 19.

45. vol. 5 isl., ch. 5, pp. 19–20.

46. For details of the annual votes in the UN General Assembly, see Rogers, *The Soviet Withdrawal from Afghanistan*, part II.

47. See below, pp. 417–18.

48. Bennigsen and Broxup, *The Islamic Threat to the Soviet State*, pp. 113–15.

49. Liakhovskii, *Plamia Afgana*, pp. 591–2; 'More East-Bloc Sources on Afghanistan', p. 270.

50. Two such conference successes by 'a particularly highly regarded agent of the Azerbaijan KGB' are noted in vol. 5 isl., ch. 6, p. 23.

51. vol. 5 isl., ch. 4, p. 17. It is not suggested that Babakhanov was a KGB agent.

52. Andrew and Gordievsky (eds.), *Instructions from the Centre*, p. 7.

53. Hosking, *A History of the Soviet Union*, pp. 445–6; Taheri, *Crescent in a Red Sky*, p. 130.

54. Remnick, *Lenin's Tomb*, pp. 180–81; Taheri, *Crescent in a Red Sky*, pp. 148, 170.

55. vol. 1, app. 3.

56. vol. 5 isl., app. 2, p. 50.

57. Taheri, *Crescent in a Red Sky*, pp. 147, 154; Remnick, *Lenin's Tomb*, p. 190.

58. k-25, 32.

59. vol. 5 isl., app. 2, p. 61.

60. Vaisman, 'Regionalism and Clan Loyalty in the Political Life of Uzbekistan', p. 116.

61. Remnick, *Lenin's Tomb*, pp. 182, 187, 194; Taheri, *Crescent in a Red Sky*, pp. 149–50.

62. Vaisman, 'Regionalism and Clan Loyalty in the Political Life of Uzbekistan', p. 121 n. 38.

63. Taheri, *Crescent in a Red Sky*, pp. 149–50. Rashidov later made a posthumous return to political popularity. In independent Uzbekistan he is widely regarded as a wily Uzbek patriot who succeeded in outwitting the supposedly more sophisticated Russians. In 1992 a large statue of him was erected in Tashkent and one of the main avenues, formerly Lenin Prospekt, was named after him (Carlisle, 'Geopolitics and Ethnic Problems of Uzbekistan', pp. 82–3; Stephen Kinzer, 'Free of Russians but Imprisoned in Cotton', *Uzbekistan Journal*, 20 Nov. 1997).

64. Kunayev died in 1993 after spending the last seven years of his life under virtual house arrest.

65. Aliyev later made a remarkable political comeback, becoming President of independent Azerbaijan in 1993. During a visit to Baku in 2001 President Putin presented him with his certificate of graduation from the MGB (later KGB) Leningrad Higher School in 1949; *RFE/RL Newsline*, 11 Jan. 2001.

66. On the subsequent history of SADUM and the removal of Kazakhstan from its jurisdiction, see Olcott, 'Islam and Fundamentalism in Independent Central Asia', pp. 26–32.

67. Taheri, *Crescent in a Red Sky*, p. 138.

68. Andrew and Gordievsky (eds.), *Instructions from the Centre*, pp. 218–21.

69. vol. 5 isl., ch. 8, p. 38.

70. Remnick, *Resurrection*, p. 272.

71. Dunlop, *Russia Confronts Chechnya*, pp. 112–13.

72. Chechen and Ingush writers who protested against the fiction of the 'voluntary union' were singled out for persecution by the KGB and lost their jobs; ibid., p. 82.

73. Ingushetiya voted to remain within the Russian Federation, partly to obtain Russian support in settling its territorial disputes with the Chechens and Ossetians, partly to avoid being submerged in a union with the far more numerous Chechens; ibid., p. 122.

74. One of the major influences on Yeltsin's decision to begin the war with Chechnya was the FSK, the post-Soviet successor to the internal directorates of the KGB (Andrew and Mitrokhin, *The Sword and the Shield*, p. 563). For the KGB old guard, some of whom held senior posts in the FSK (subsequently the FSB), the invasion of 1994 was revenge for the humiliation of 1991.

21 Afghanistan Part 1

1. Mitrokhin wrote an account of KGB operations in Afghanistan, mostly on the period 1978 to 1983, based exclusively on material noted and copied by him from KGB files (vol. 1 of his archive). Most of this account (excluding appendices identifying numerous KGB agents) is now available as a Cold War International History Project working paper, 'The KGB in Afghanistan', in both the Russian original and English translation (details in the Bibliography). Page references in the notes which follow are to the English edition.

2. vol. 1, ch. 2; Mitrokhin, 'The KGB in Afghanistan', pp. 24–6.

3. vol. 1, ch. 1; Mitrokhin, 'The KGB in Afghanistan', pp. 16–21. On the origins of the PDPA and the early careers of Taraki and Karmal, see Bradsher, *Afghan Communism and Soviet Intervention*, pp. 1–10.

4. vol. 1, ch. 2; Mitrokhin, 'The KGB in Afghanistan', pp. 17, 21. It is unlikely that Babrak Karmal was recruited before or during his imprisonment from 1949 to 1952. He was, however, a KGB agent by 1957 at the latest.

5. vol. 1, ch. 2; Mitrokhin, 'The KGB in Afghanistan', pp. 18, 21–3.

6. vol. 1, ch. 2; Mitrokhin, 'The KGB in Afghanistan', pp. 29–42.

7. vol. 1, ch. 2; Mitrokhin, 'The KGB in Afghanistan', p. 39.

8. Bradsher, *Afghan Communism and Soviet Intervention*, pp. 41–3.

9. vol. 1, ch. 2; Mitrokhin, 'The KGB in Afghanistan', p. 36. The Muslim Brotherhood was a pan-Islamic society founded in Egypt in 1929 aimed at imposing Islamic law on the Muslim nation.

10. vol. 1, ch. 2; Mitrokhin, 'The KGB in Afghanistan', pp. 29–41.

11. vol. 1, ch. 2; Mitrokhin, 'The KGB in Afghanistan', p. 43.

12. vol. 1, ch. 8; Mitrokhin, 'The KGB in Afghanistan', pp. 154–7.

13. vol. 1, ch. 2; Mitrokhin, 'The KGB in Afghanistan', p. 44.

14. Bradsher, *Afghan Communism and Soviet Intervention*, pp. 48–51; Urban, *War in Afghanistan*, pp. 31–4.

15. 'The Soviet Union and Afghanistan, 1978–1989: Documents', pp. 152–3.

16. Ibid., p. 152.

17. Urban, *War in Afghanistan*, pp. 31, 36–7.

18. There is no indication in the files noted by Mitrokhin that Amin was recruited as a KGB agent. As usual, however, the absence of evidence does not amount to proof.

19. vol. 1, ch. 3; Mitrokhin, 'The KGB in Afghanistan', pp. 46–7.

20. Andrew and Gordievsky, *KGB*, p. 577.

21. vol. 1, ch. 3; Mitrokhin, 'The KGB in Afghanistan', p. 47. A senior Western diplomat who knew Popal dismisses KGB suspicions that he was a Western agent as 'ridiculous': 'Popal was probably pleased with himself for dining with foreign diplomats and, in his view, fooling them.'

22. Kuzichkin, 'Coups and Killings in Kabul'. These 'investigations' are probably best interpreted as a by-product of KGB conspiracy theories about Amin.

23. vol. 1, ch. 3; Mitrokhin, 'The KGB in Afghanistan', pp. 49–50.

24. vol. 1, ch. 3; Mitrokhin, 'The KGB in Afghanistan', pp. 61–2.

25. Bradsher, *Afghan Communism and Soviet Intervention*, pp. 58–9.

26. vol. 1, ch. 3; Mitrokhin, 'The KGB in Afghanistan', pp. 63–81.

27. vol. 1, ch. 3; Mitrokhin, 'The KGB in Afghanistan', pp. 67–71; Dobbs, *Down with Big Brother*, p. 11. From 1972 to 1977 Bogdanov had been resident in Tehran; vol. 2 misc., item 3.

28. Bradsher, *Afghan Communism and Soviet Intervention*, pp. 59–60.

29. Westad, 'Concerning the Situation in "A"', p. 130.

30. vol. 1, ch. 4; Mitrokhin, 'The KGB in Afghanistan', p. 86.

31. Kalugin, *Spymaster*, pp. 230–31.

32. vol. 1, ch. 4; Mitrokhin, 'The KGB in Afghanistan', p. 86.

33. Kalugin, *Spymaster*, p. 233.

34. vol. 1, ch. 4; Mitrokhin, 'The KGB in Afghanistan', p. 87. Petrov had been stationed in Kabul under cover as a Tass correspondent from 1972 to 1978, and had probably become well acquainted with Karmal during these years; vol. 2 to sort, item 6.

35. vol. 1, ch. 4; Mitrokhin, 'The KGB in Afghanistan', pp. 87–8.

36. Andrew and Mitrokhin, *The Sword and the Shield*, pp. 251–2, 255–7, 330.

37. Andropov had similarly supplied the Politburo with misleading intelligence reports to gain their support, initially refused, for the expulsion of Solzhenitsyn in 1974. Andrew and Mitrokhin, *The Sword and the Shield*, pp. 256–7, 317–18.

38. vol. 1, ch. 4; Mitrokhin, 'The KGB in Afghanistan', pp. 87–9.

39. 'The Soviet Union and Afghanistan, 1978–1989: Documents', p. 159.

40. A photocopy of the Politburo memorandum, 'Concerning the Situation in "A"', of 12 Dec. 1979, together with translation and commentary, appears in 'More Documents from the Russian Archives', pp. 75–6.

41. vol. 1, ch. 4; Mitrokhin, 'The KGB in Afghanistan', pp. 90, 93–4. On the deceptions which preceded the Soviet invasion of Hungary in 1956 and of Czechoslovakia in 1968, see Andrew and Mitrokhin, *The Sword and the Shield*, pp. 248–9, 255–7.

42. Andrew and Mitrokhin, *The Sword and the Shield*, p. 389.

43. The main source for Talybov's Afghan mission is information given by the KGB defector Vladimir Kuzichkin to John Barron and *Time* magazine (Barron, *KGB Today*, pp. 15–16; Kuzichkin, 'Coups and Killings in Kabul'). In 1979 Kuzichkin was a Line N (illegal support) officer in the Tehran residency and was therefore informed about Talybov's operations as an illegal in Iran operating with Iranian identity documents. He also learned about Talybov's deployment to Afghanistan. The files noted by

Mitrokhin contain no reference to Talybov's operations after the mid-1970s. (On his deployment to Chechnya-Ingushetiya, see above, pp. 376, 575 n. 29.) Mitrokhin's notes do, however, corroborate two aspects of Kuzichkin's account. First, they confirm the personal details given by Kuzichkin about Talybov, as well as adding others such as his codename and assumed Iranian identity (k-27, 400). Since the real identity of illegals was one of the KGB's most closely guarded secrets, Kuzichkin's accuracy on this point adds to the credibility of the rest of his account. Secondly, Mitrokhin's brief note on Kuzichkin's defection confirms that he had 'a lot of information' about illegals (vol. 2, ch. 1); Mitrokhin also confirms that at least one of Amin's immediate entourage became seriously ill with food poisoning.

44. Bradsher, *Afghan Communism and Soviet Intervention*, p. 77.

45. vol. 1, ch. 4; Mitrokhin, 'The KGB in Afghanistan', p. 102. The date of, though not the explanation for, Asadullah Amin's transfer to a Soviet hospital is given in Bradsher, *Afghan Communism and Soviet Intervention*, p. 78. In 1980 Asadullah Amin was returned to Afghanistan by the Russians and executed by the Karmal regime; ibid., p. 129.

46. Kuzichkin, 'Coups and Killings in Kabul'.

47. For three days before Amin's move, the Darulaman Palace had been protected by Soviet security personnel; vol. 1, ch. 4; Mitrokhin, 'The KGB in Afghanistan', p. 96.

48. Urban, *War in Afghanistan*, p. 46.

49. vol. 1, ch. 4; Mitrokhin, 'The KGB in Afghanistan', pp. 96–9.

50. Urban, *War in Afghanistan*, p. 46.

51. vol. 1, ch. 4; Mitrokhin, 'The KGB in Afghanistan', pp. 99–100. Mitrokhin noted that over 100 of the special forces were 'killed'. Andrew sent him a written query on this point in the autumn of 2003, asking whether he had meant to write 'killed and injured'. His usually robust health, however, had begun to decline rapidly and he died a few months later without responding to the query. It seems likely that Mitrokhin's statistic refers to the numbers injured as well as killed.

22 Afghanistan Part 2

1. vol. 1, ch. 4; Mitrokhin, 'The KGB in Afghanistan', pp. 103–6; 'The Soviet Union and Afghanistan, 1978–1989: Documents', p. 160.

2. Bradsher, *Afghan Communism and Soviet Intervention*, pp. 118–19.

3. vol. 1, ch. 4; Mitrokhin, 'The KGB in Afghanistan', p. 106; 'The Soviet Union and Afghanistan, 1978–1989: Documents', p. 160.

4. 'The Soviet Union and Afghanistan, 1978–1989: Documents', pp. 162–3.

5. vol. 1, ch. 4; Mitrokhin, 'The KGB in Afghanistan', p. 100.

6. 'The Soviet Union and Afghanistan, 1978–1989: Documents', p. 163.

7. Ibid., pp. 165–6.

8. vol. 1, ch. 5; Mitrokhin, 'The KGB in Afghanistan', p. 116.

9. Grau (ed.), *The Bear Went over the Mountain*, p. xxxi.

10. vol. 1, ch. 5; Mitrokhin, 'The KGB in Afghanistan', p. 116.

11. Grau (ed.), *The Bear Went over the Mountain*, ch. 7; Bradsher, *Afghan Communism and Soviet Intervention*, pp. 200–202, 211.

12. 'The Soviet Union and Afghanistan, 1978–1989: Documents', pp. 170–72. As before, the report was signed by Andropov, Ustinov and Gromyko. On this occasion, however, Ponomarev's signature was missing; the report was signed instead by Vadim Zagladin, one of his deputies on the International Department of the Central Committee.

13. vol. 1, ch. 6; Mitrokhin, 'The KGB in Afghanistan', pp. 128–30, 135–6.

14. In 1981, for example, the Centre provided 250 million convertible rubles to pay KHAD salaries; vol. 1, ch. 7; Mitrokhin, 'The KGB in Afghanistan', p. 147.

15. Najibullah appears on a list which Mitrokhin compiled from KGB files of Afghan 'agents and confidential contacts'; vol. 1, app. 1. Unusually, however, the list fails to distinguish between the two categories.

16. Andrew and Gordievsky, *KGB*, pp. 578–9.

17. Amnesty International, *Afghanistan: Torture of Political Prisoners*.

18. Bradsher, *Afghan Communism and Soviet Intervention*, p. 161.

19. In setting up the Cascade units, the Centre drew on the precedent of operations against the Basmachi rebels in central Asia who were finally defeated in the early 1930s. vol. 5 isl., ch. 2; vol. 1, ch. 7; Mitrokhin, 'The KGB in Afghanistan', p. 148.

20. vol. 1, ch. 7; Mitrokhin, 'The KGB in Afghanistan', pp. 145–9.

21. vol. 1, ch. 7; Mitrokhin, 'The KGB in Afghanistan', p. 141.

22. vol. 1, app. 3; k-24, 87, 89; k-8, 590.

23. On KHAD/KGB agent penetration of Pakistan, see above, pp. 357, 360, 363–4.

24. vol. 1, ch. 7; Mitrokhin, 'The KGB in Afghanistan', p. 144.

25. Steve Coll, 'Spies, Lies and the Distortion of History', *Washington Post*, 23 Feb. 2002.

26. Bradsher, *Afghan Communism and Soviet Intervention*, p. 185.

27. vol. 1, ch. 5; Mitrokhin, 'The KGB in Afghanistan', pp. 125–6.

28. Kirpichenko, *Razvedka*, pp. 361–2.

29. Leonov, *Likholet'e*, pp. 269–70. A GRU report described Najibullah as intelligent, vicious, vain and ambitious, and noted his habit of surrounding himself with yes-men chosen 'not for their professional qualities but for their personal devotion to him'; 'More East-Bloc Sources on Afghanistan', p. 250.

30. Rogers, *The Soviet Withdrawal from Afghanistan*, p. 8.

31. 'The Soviet Union and Afghanistan, 1978–1989: Documents', p. 180.

32. Ibid., p. 177.

33. See above, pp. 400, 405.

34. 'The Soviet Union and Afghanistan, 1978–1989: Documents', p. 177.

35. Gates, *From the Shadows*, pp. 251–2, 319–21.

36. Bradsher, *Afghan Communism and Soviet Intervention*, p. 271.

37. 'The Soviet Union and Afghanistan, 1978–1989: Documents', p. 177.

38. See above, pp. 131–2.

39. See below, p. 474.

40. Shebarshin, *Ruka Moskvy*, pp. 178–9; Bearden and Risen, *The Main Enemy*, pp. 231–2.

41. 'More East-Bloc Sources on Afghanistan', p. 249.

42. Shebarshin, *Ruka Moskvy*, pp. 179–80. Bearden and Risen, *The Main Enemy*, pp. 232–3, 534.

43. Chernyaev, *My Six Years with Gorbachev*, p. 25.

44. Galeotti, *Afghanistan*, p. 142.

45. Chernyaev, *My Six Years with Gorbachev*, pp. 42–3.

46. Gates, *From the Shadows*, pp. 251–2, 428–30.

47. Bearden and Risen, *The Main Enemy*, pp. 258–9; Shebarshin, *Ruka Moskvy*, pp. 185–6, 196. There were a number of occasions on which KGB and other Soviet special forces intercepted rebel caravans bringing arms from their supply bases in Pakistan and captured Stingers *en route* to the *mujahideen*. KGB and KHAD agents also succeeded in obtaining a number of Stingers by bribery; Galeotti, *Afghanistan*, p. 196.

48. Bradsher, *Afghan Communism and Soviet Intervention*, pp. 225–6. As head of foreign intelligence from 1991 to 1996, Primakov was taken in by a woefully inaccurate intelligence report that 'the idea of deploying the Stingers was supplied by Osama bin Laden, who had been co-operating closely with the CIA at the time' (Primakov, *Russian Crossroads*, p. 34). This report may well have been an example of 'blow-back' – a story which began as SVR disinformation deceiving an agent who then presented it as authentic intelligence. There is no support in the Mitrokhin material (or any other reliable source) for the claim that the CIA funded bin Laden or any of the other Arab volunteeers who came to support the *mujahideen*. Most were funded through charities and mosques in the Middle East, especially Saudi Arabia and the Gulf States, and were frequently viewed with suspicion by the Afghan *mujahideen*.

49. Most of the mules used to transport arms and other supplies to the *mujahideen* came from China over the Kunjerab Pass; Bearden and Risen, *The Main Enemy*, p. 312.

50. Dobrynin, *In Confidence*, pp. 442–3.

51. Bradsher, *Afghan Communism and Soviet Intervention*, p. 158.

52. Ibid., pp. 158–60; 'The Soviet Union and Afghanistan, 1978–1989: Documents', pp. 178–81.

53. 'The Soviet Union and Afghanistan, 1978–1989: Documents', pp. 178–81.

54. Chernyaev, *My Six Years with Gorbachev*, p. 90.

55. 'The Soviet Union and Afghanistan, 1978–1989: Documents', p. 181.

56. Ostermann (ed.), 'Gorbachev and Afghanistan', pp. 144–5.

57. Ibid., p. 144.

58. Bradsher, *Afghan Communism and Soviet Intervention*, pp. 281, 283, 290.

59. 'The Soviet Union and Afghanistan, 1978–1989: Documents', p. 181. The Committee was still chaired by the Foreign Minister, Eduard Shevardnadze. Its other most influential members were KGB Chairman Vladimir Kryuchkov and Defence Minister Dmitri Yazov, who had succeeded Chebrikov and Sokolov.

60. Bradsher, *Afghan Communism and Soviet Intervention*, p. 331. There was, however, a later CIA attempt on Hekmatyar's life. Having been expelled from Afghanistan by the Taleban in 1995, he returned in 2001 to fight the Americans, and a year later survived attack by a Hellfire missile fired from an unmanned CIA Predator drone; Bearden and Risen, *The Main Enemy*, p. 535.

61. Bradsher, *Afghan Communism and Soviet Intervention*, p. 378.

62. Steve Coll, 'Spies, Lies and the Distortion of History', *Washington Post*, 23 Feb. 2002.

23. Africa: Introduction

1. Davidson et al. (eds.), *South Africa and the Communist International*, vol. 1, pp. xxii, xlv, 2–5.

2. McClellan, 'Africans and Blacks in the Comintern Schools'.

3. Superintendent E. Parker, 'Secret Report on Communist Party Activities in Great Britain Among Colonials', 22 April 1930; cited in Howe, *Anticolonialism in British Politics*, p. 66.

4. Suchkov, 'Dzhomo Keniata v Moskve', pp. 120–21.

5. Davidson et al. (eds.), *South Africa and the Communist International*, vol. 1, pp. xxii, xlv, 12–23; vol. 2, pp. 46, 123, 239–40, 297–9.

6. Lonsdale, 'Jomo Kenyatta, God, and the Modern World', pp. 31–3.

7. Kirpichenko, *Razvedka*, p. 162.

8. G. Vassiliev, quoted in Guimarães, *The Origins of the Angolan Civil War*, p. 161.

9. Heldman, *The USSR and Africa*, p. 44.

10. Kirpichenko, *Razvedka*, p. 162. The Department was later divided into two, the Ninth and Tenth, responsible for, respectively, Anglophone and Francophone Africa; see Appendix D.

11. Nkrumah, *I Speak of Freedom*, pp. 262–3.

12. Nkrumah, *Africa Must Unite*, p. 174.

13. Mandela, *Long Walk to Freedom*, pp. 123–4, 137–8, 436, 562.

14. See below, p. 442.
15. Leonov, *Likholet'e*, p. 144. There is no suggestion that President Kerekou was involved with the KGB. He was unaware that his administration contained a number of KGB agents: LUR, who worked in the presidential office (k-8, 444), whom the KGB vainly hoped might be a future president; DODZH, one of his ministers (t-1, 188); ZINS, an intelligence officer (t-1, 189); and the diplomat DAG (vol. 4 ind., app. 3).
16. See below, pp. 452–9.
17. Leonov, *Likholet'e*, p. 144.
18. Andrew and Gordievsky, *KGB*, p. 557. A GRU resident in Ghana and a KGB resident in Zambia, who were summoned back to Moscow during the Brezhnev era, were among a number of Soviet intelligence officers in Africa who were recalled for drunkenness (k-17, 129; vol. 8, app. 2, item 118).
19. See below, pp. 454, 455, 459, 461.
20. Guest, *Shackled Continent*, pp. 47–8; Andrew and Gordievsky, *KGB*, p. 558.
21. See below, pp. 443, 463–5, 470.
22. Previously the Communist Party of South Africa, it changed its name to the South African Communist Party in 1953.
23. Guest, *Shackled Continent*, p. 231.

24. The Cold War Comes to Africa

1. General Calliès to Premier Edgar Faure, 4 April 1955, Vincennes, Service Historique de l'Armée de Terre, 1H/1103/Dossier (D) 1. We are grateful for this reference to Mathilde von Bülow, author of a path-breaking forthcoming Cambridge University PhD thesis on Franco-German relations and the Algerian War.
2. k-3, 120.
3. Horne, *A Savage War of Peace*, pp. 137–8.
4. Ibid., pp. 404–6.
5. Heldman, *The USSR and Africa*, p. 62.
6. Kirpichenko blames the failure on 'a schism in the leadership of the Algerian revolution' in August 1962. Kirpichenko, *Razvedka*, pp. 79ff.
7. On French suspicions of Anglo-Saxon conspiracies in the French Empire, see Andrew, 'France: Adjustment to Change, ' pp. 337, 339.
8. vol. 6, ch. 14, part 4; Holland, 'The Lie that Linked CIA to the Kennedy Assassination', pp. 5–6. On KGB cultivation of *Paese Sera* and *Le Monde* see Andrew and Mitrokhin, *The Sword and the Shield*, pp. 300, 469–470.
9. Andrew, *For the President's Eyes Only*, p. 253.
10. Kirpichenko, *Razvedka*, pp. 97–8.
11. Barron, *KGB*, p. 323.

12. Shelepin to Khrushchev, memorandum No. 1861-Sh, 29 July 1961; decree No. 191/75-GS; vol. 6, ch. 5, part 5, p. 178. See above, p. 40.

13. On Castro's complaints, see above, pp. 45–6.

14. Ben Bella also allowed Che to set up an Algerian base for Latin American revolutionaries through which arms were secretly channelled to Latin America. Ben Bella, 'Che as I Knew Him'.

15. Cabrita, *Mozambique*, p. 45.

16. Ben Bella, 'Che as I Knew Him'.

17. Grimaud, *La politique extérieure de l'Algérie*, pp. 131–2.

18. The only case noted by Mitrokhin concerned Service A forgeries against the Modibo Keïta regime in Mali; k-8, 555; there were doubtless other examples.

19. Following Ben Bella's overthrow, the KGB lost the services of an agent in his Information Ministry, codenamed AKHMED, who went into exile in France; t-2, 172. For the remainder of the Cold War, Algeria was governed by two military rulers – Houari Boumedienne (1965–78) and Chadli Benjedid (1979–92), whose forces were partly trained and equipped by the Soviet Union but who were wary of too close a relationship with Moscow; Lassassi, *Non-Alignment and Algerian Foreign Policy*, pp. 150–60. The KGB carried out a series of active measures designed to compromise members of their administrations whom it suspected of pro-Western tendencies (vol. 9, ch. 4; k-5, 808; k-8, 601).

20. Barron, *KGB*, pp. 342–5.

21. Rooney, *Kwame Nkrumah*, pp. 230, 241.

22. Mitrokhin records that a series of bogus documents revealing supposed Western plots were passed to Nkrumah via a KGB agent, but identifies only two specific examples: the forged US intelligence report of plots against him which prompted his written protest to President Lyndon Johnson in February 1964 and the supposed attempt by the US military attaché in Somalia to mount a coup against the Somali government in May 1966 (denounced by Nkrumah in *Dark Days in Ghana*, p. 50): k-8, 555; vol. 6, ch. 14, part 2. The other fictitious plots by Western intelligence to overthrow African regimes publicly denounced by Nkrumah, such as an attempted coup in Tanzania, doubtless also either derived from, or were encouraged by, the KGB; Nkrumah, *Dark Days in Ghana*, pp. 48–51.

23. Rooney, *Kwame Nkrumah*, p. 226.

24. k-8, 555. The full text of Nkrumah's letter to Johnson of 26 February 1964, not copied by Mitrokhin, is published in Rooney, *Kwame Nkrumah*, pp. 243–5.

25. The most important agents identified in Mitrokhin's fragmentary notes on Guinea and Mali appear to have been two senior intelligence officers: POZ in Guinea (k-8, 444) and ROK in Mali (k-8, 537).

26. Though the United States and France were the usual targets of Sékou Touré's paranoia, on at least one occasion he also accused the Soviet Union

of plotting against him. In 1962, after African students in France had passed a motion denouncing oppression in Guinea, Sékou Touré bizarrely claimed that the Soviet ambassador in Conakry (who was subsequently withdrawn) had colluded with the French ambassador in Moscow to whip up student agitation against him. Anastas Mikoyan was swiftly despatched from Moscow to mend fences with the Guinean dictator. Kaké, *Sékou Touré*, chs. 5–7; Attwood, *The Reds and the Blacks*, pp. 63–4. On Sékou Touré's main interrogation and torture centre, Camp Boiro, see also: www.campboiro.org.

27. k-8, 555; vol. 6, ch. 12, part 5, p. 450.

28. k-8, 555.

29. Kalugin, *Spymaster*, p. 52.

30. vol. 6, ch. 12, part 5, p. 451.

31. Library of Congress, *Ghana: A Country Study*, ch. 5.

32. The only case noted by Mitrokhin was that of one of Nkrumah's former ministers, a KGB confidential contact codenamed AFORI, who was jailed for a year after the military coup and given $1,000 by the Accra residency after his release (k-14, 545). Mitrokhin did not record the total amount of assistance allocated to former members and supporters of the Nkrumah regime.

33. Sanankoua, *La chute de Modibo Keïta*.

34. Nkrumah, *Dark Days in Ghana*, pp. 30, 49–50, 158–60. The CIA station in Accra was in contact with some of Nkrumah's opponents, but there is no convincing evidence that it was the mainspring of the coup. As President Johnson's adviser Walt Rostow later put it, 'We did not throw a match in the haystack' (Rooney, *Kwame Nkrumah*, pp. 253–4). The claim that the Agency attempted to assassinate Nkrumah is fantasy. Under the military rule of General Ignatius Kutu Acheampong (codenamed GLEN) from 1972 to 1978, KGB hopes of influence in Ghana revived. An officer from the Accra residency, D. A. Dityayev, became Acheampong's unofficial security adviser. With the assistance of LIR, a senior Ghanaian intelligence officer and confidant of Acheampong, the KGB was able to recruit four Ghanaian employees of the US embassy, including a servant, codenamed STEFEN, of the CIA head of station, whose house was bugged (though the bug was later discovered). A leading Ghanaian journalist, KAPRAL, also a confidant of Acheampong, was used to place active-measures articles in the press. With Acheampong's overthrow in 1978 and execution in the following year, however, KGB influence once again went into decline; k-27, 185, 429–30; k-14, 750; vol. 6, ch. 8, part 4, p. 329.

35. Nkrumah, *Dark Days in Ghana*, p. 157.

36. Kaké, *Sékou Touré*, chs. 6–7. On Camp Boiro, see also: www.campboiro.org.

37. vol. 6, ch. 8, part 4, p. 327; Andrew and Mitrokhin, *The Sword and the Shield*, pp. 243–4.

38. Attwood, *The Reds and the Blacks*, pp. 68–77.

39. Clapham, *Africa and the International System*, pp. 146, 290 n. 25.

40. Sékou Touré had sought smaller-scale assistance from the West on a number of previous occasions.

41. vol. 6, ch. 8, part 4, p. 327. Mitrokhin's notes do not record Gowon's reaction to the letter. However, a retired British diplomat has recalled to Christopher Andrew learning of the letter in 1973.

42. k-8, 511. Mitrokhin's notes give no indication of Hassan's reaction.

43. Lenrie Peters, 'Satellites' (1967); cited by Snow, *The Star Raft*, p. 105.

44. Odinga, *Not Yet Uhuru*, pp. 292–3. The precise nature of this arms shipment and Odinga's involvement in it remain obscure.

45. Attwood, *The Reds and the Blacks*, pp. 249, 296; Snow, *The Star Raft*, p. 95. On Zhou's African visits in 1963–64, see Scalapino, *On the Trail of Chou En-lai in Africa*.

46. Mitrokhin noted the regular use of this codename in correspondence between the Centre and the Tanzanian residency (k-17, 85); it is likely to have been also used in communications with other African residencies.

47. k-27, 498. Details of all African states with which the PRC established and broke off diplomatic relations from 1956 to 1970 are given in Larkin, *China and Africa 1949–1970*, pp. 66–7.

48. Larkin, *China and Africa 1949–1970*, p. 127.

49. Robinson, 'China Confronts the Soviet Union'. Further KGB active measures were designed to persuade Mwambutsa not to restore diplomatic relations with Beijing. Forged documents on supposed PRC plots against the Burundi regime were also brought to the attention of President Mobutu of Congo (Kinshasa) in the belief that he would inform Mwambutsa, with whom he was on friendly terms; k-27, 498.

50. Larkin, *China and Africa 1949–1970*, p. 129.

51. Ibid., pp. 130–31.

52. Ibid., pp. 134–5.

53. The active measure was codenamed operation BURNUS; k-13, 354.

54. Larkin, *China and Africa 1949–1970*, pp. 135–6.

55. Snow, *The Star Raft*, p. 97. On relations between Kenyatta and Odinga, see the account by the US ambassador: Attwood, *The Reds and the Blacks*, chs. 18, 19. 'Had [Odinga] loyally served Kenyatta and not tried to build up his own political apparatus', Attwood believes, 'he might have established himself as [Kenyatta's] logical successor.' Kenyatta was a regular target of KGB active measures accusing him of collaboration with the CIA; vol. 6, app. 1, part 2.

56. Mitrokhin's brief notes on KGB operations in Kenya suggest (but, because of their fragmentary nature, do not prove) a low level of success in penetrating KANU. KENT, the only KANU agent of any significance whose file he noted, had his campaign expenses paid by the Nairobi residency in 1974 but failed to be elected. His case officers were Boris Ivanovich Borisenko and Ivor Yanovich Pavlovsky; vol. 7, app. 1, item 98.

57. Larkin, *China and Africa 1949–1970*, pp. 136–7.

58. k-27, 498. Senegal recognized the PRC but did not maintain formal diplomatic relations; its expulsion of New China News Agency correspondents, the main PRC representatives in Senegal, thus amounted to an informal diplomatic breach.

59. k-13, 344; k-27, 498.

60. k-27, 498.

61. Snow, *The Star Raft*, p. 123.

62. vol. 6, app. 1, part 2.

63. Snow, *The Star Raft*, pp. 100–101; Larkin, *China and Africa 1949–1970*, p. 2.

64. Andrew and Mitrokhin, *The Sword and the Shield*, pp. 337–8.

65. Ellert, 'The Rhodesian Security and Intelligence Community', p. 98.

66. In the Kenyan embassy in Paris, for example, both SERZH and RUDOLF (recruited in, respectively, 1967 and 1970) provided cipher material as well as diplomatic documents (k-4, 69; k-5, 252; k-27, 465; t-1, 17; t-7, 42).

67. The Mitrokhin archive casts no light on the curious case of the KGB illegal Yuri Loginov, who was recruited by the CIA in Helsinki in 1961 and moved to South Africa in 1967. Wrongly concluding that Loginov was a KGB plant, the CIA then informed the South African authorities who arrested him. Loginov was later handed back to the Russians in a spy swap in Germany. Wise, *Molehunt*, pp. 214–18, 230–32.

68. k-2, 366. The GRU, however, had at least one agent of real significance: Dieter Gerhardt, a South African naval officer recruited in London during his attachment to the Royal Navy in 1960 who rose to become commander of the Simonstown naval base. Over the next two decades he was allegedly paid a total of $250,000 for naval intelligence. He was arrested in 1983 and sentenced to life imprisonment.

69. Shubin, *ANC: A View from Moscow*, pp. 37, 62–8. In 1965 Moscow supplied $560,000 to the ANC and $112,000 to the SACP. However, these sums appear to have been for a two-year period. There is no record of any further allocation in 1966.

70. Israel, *South African Political Exile in the United Kingdom*, p. 172.

71. Kempton, *Soviet Strategy toward Southern Africa*, pp. 151–74; Ellis and Sechaba, *Comrades against Apartheid*, ch. 2; Johnson, *South Africa*, pp. 169–72.

72. Kempton, *Soviet Strategy toward Southern Africa*, pp. 105–6, 110–11; Andrew and Gordievsky, *KGB*, p. 559.

73. Kempton, *Soviet Strategy toward Southern Africa*, pp. 37–8.

74. On Cunhal see Andrew and Mitrokhin, *The Sword and the Shield*, pp. 283–4.

75. Nazhestkin, 'V ognennom kol'tse blokady', pp. 235–40. Nazhestkin's assessment was very similar to that of a senior Portuguese army officer

who admired Neto's 'generous idea' and 'struggles against fascism and colonialism' but doubted his 'ability to lead the country through such a complex [independence] struggle'; Gleijeses, *Conflicting Missions*, p. 236.

76. Guimarães, *The Origins of the Angolan Civil War*, pp. 165–7.

77. k-12, 269.

78. Kirpichenko, *Razvedka*, pp. 205–8.

79. Politburo resolution No. P-46/KLU of 10 July 1967 and USSR Council of Ministers resolution No. 1657 RS of 10 July 1967; k-14, 38.

80. k-14, 599.

81. Finnegan, *A Complicated War*, pp. 108–13.

82. Nazhestkin, 'V ognennom kol'tse blokady', pp. 240–41.

83. Kempton, *Soviet Strategy toward Southern Africa*, pp. 38–40; Guimarães, *The Origins of the Angolan Civil War*, pp. 99–100, 165–7; Gleijeses, *Conflicting Missions*, p 243.

84. Finnegan, *A Complicated War*, p. 111.

85. Golan, *The Soviet Union and National Liberation Movements*, p. 270.

86. k-12, 600.

87. k-17, 113.

88. Ibid.

89. Despite its revolutionary rhetoric, the SRC was a clan-based regime, sometimes derisively referred to by the acronym MOD: M for Mareehaan (Siad Barre's clan); O for Ogaden (the clan of Siad Barre's mother); and D for Dulbahante (the clan of Siad Barre's son-in-law, Ahmad Sulaymaan Abdullah, head of the NSS). These three clans dominated the government.

90. k-17, 113.

91. Ibid. Whether KERL was an agent or a confidential contact is unclear.

92. k-17, 113–14. Ironically, there was speculation at the time that Ainanche and Kedie were executed 'on the strong advice' of Moscow; Patman, *The Soviet Union in the Horn of Africa*, p. 121.

93. Ghalib, *The Cost of Dictatorship*, p. 127.

94. vol. 6, ch. 14, part 1.

95. Patman, *The Soviet Union in the Horn of Africa*, pp. 113–14, 180–86.

96. 'Russian and East German Documents on the Horn of Africa, 1977–78', p. 58.

25. From Optimism to Disillusion

1. FNLA's main support came from the Kikongo-speaking people in the north, UNITA's from Umbundu speakers in the central plateau. Though the MPLA had a more national appeal, its strongest base was among Kimbundu-speaking people around the capital, Luanda.

2. Nazhestkin, 'V ognennom kol'tse blokady', p. 245.

3. Guimarães, *The Origins of the Angolan Civil War*, pp. 99–100. On

Cunhal and the KGB, see Andrew and Mitrokhin, *The Sword and the Shield*, pp. 283–4.

4. k-14, 601.

5. Westad, 'Moscow and the Angolan Crisis', pp. 24–5; Nazhestkin, 'V ognennom kol'tse blokady', pp. 245–6. On Castro and Angola, see above, pp. 95–6.

6. Shevchenko, *Breaking with Moscow*, p. 365.

7. Westad, 'Moscow and the Angolan Crisis', pp. 25–6.

8. According to Dobrynin: 'The Soviet Foreign Ministry had nothing to do with our initial involvement in Angola and looked at it with some scepticism.' Dobrynin, *In Confidence*, p. 362.

9. Nazhestkin, 'V ognennom kol'tse blokady', pp. 246–55.

10. Andrew, *For the President's Eyes Only*, pp. 411–17; Gates, *From the Shadows*, pp. 65–9.

11. Shevchenko, *Breaking with Moscow*, p. 364.

12. Guimarães, *The Origins of the Angolan Civil War*, p. 105.

13. Ibid., p. 113.

14. Westad, 'Moscow and the Angolan Crisis', pp. 28, 32 n. 60.

15. Courtois et al., *Le livre noir du communisme*, pp. 757–63; Wolf, *Man without a Face*, pp. 265–6.

16. Guimarães, *The Origins of the Angolan Civil War*, p. 170.

17. k-18, 202. VOMUS's case officers in the Luanda residency were Sergei Bodrinskikh and Valentin Yevsenin.

18. Kempton, *Soviet Strategy toward Southern Africa*, p. 59.

19. Nazhestkin, 'V ognennom kol'tse blokady', pp. 239–41.

20. Westad, 'Moscow and the Angolan Crisis', p. 28.

21. Nazhestkin, 'V ognennom kol'tse blokady', pp. 240–41.

22. k-14, 601.

23. Cabrita, *Mozambique*, part II, chs. 3–6, part III, ch. 4; Courtois et al., *Le livre noir du communisme*, pp. 763–7; Wolf, *Man without a Face*, pp. 265–6. During a restructuring of SNASP in 1977, the main responsibility for training its personnel passed from the Stasi to the Cubans; Cabrita, *Mozambique*, pp. 90–91.

24. Krause, 'Soviet Arms Transfers to Sub-Saharan Africa'.

25. vol. 6, ch. 8, part 4, p. 320.

26. Significantly, the FCD directive came one month after a visit to Moscow by a high-level Ethiopian delegation.

27. Orizio, *Talk of the Devil*, pp. 144–5.

28. Patman, *The Soviet Union in the Horn of Africa*, p. 151.

29. Ibid., p. 173.

30. Ibid., ch. 5.

31. Lefort, *Ethiopia*, p. 257.

32. Patman, *The Soviet Union in the Horn of Africa*, pp. 195–6.

33. Courtois et al., *Le livre noir du communisme*, pp. 748–57; Orizio, *Talk of the Devil*, p. 151.

34. 'Russian and East German Documents on the Horn of Africa, 1977–78', pp. 79–81.

35. Patman, *The Soviet Union in the Horn of Africa*, pp. 202–3.

36. The Soviet Union cut off aid to a secessionist group in the north, the Eritrean Peoples' Liberation Front (EPLF), a more genuinely Marxist movement than any in Ethiopia; Donham, *Marxist Modern*, pp. 136–7.

37. Patman, *The Soviet Union in the Horn of Africa*, ch. 6.

38. Ottaway and Ottaway, *Afrocommunism*, p. 175.

39. Ehrlich, 'The Soviet Union and Ethiopia'; Andrew and Gordievsky, *KGB*, p. 560.

40. k-14, 260.

41. Orizio, *Talk of the Devil*, pp. 150–51; Lefort, *Ethiopia*, p. 226.

42. Though Mitrokhin's notes give no details of the information provided by DYUK on the policy of Mengistu and the Derg, he was clearly regarded as an important source. DYUK was given an ISKANDER signal device concealed in the handle of a souvenir knife with which to make contact with the Addis Ababa residency. He had three case officers in the mid-1970s: I. I. Muzykin, A. I. Oroshko, and I. Ya. Pavlovsky; k-12, 528. Other apparently disillusioned KGB agents included the diplomats KHARIS and STRE-LOK. k-12, 251; vol. 6, app. 1, part 27.

43. Kempton, *Soviet Strategy toward Southern Africa*, p. 123.

44. k-18, 413. On the ZAPU War Council, see Brickhill, 'Daring to Storm the Heavens', p. 54.

45. k-17, 27.

46. k-12, 540.

47. k-12, 543.

48. k-17, 28.

49. k-12, 124. The KGB's other confidential contacts in ZAPU were LOR, a ZAPU official who was in Moscow in 1973 and was subsequently based in Tanzania (k-12, 540); COLLINS, a radio announcer (k-12, 486); MOD-EST (k-18, 165) and YAN (k-14, 66), both of the ZAPU External Relations Department.

50. Nkomo, *Nkomo*, pp. 175–6; Andrew and Gordievsky, *KGB*, p. 559. There is no mention of Solodovnikov in the Mitrokhin material.

51. Turner, *Continent Ablaze*, ch. 1; Kriger, *Zimbabwe's Guerrilla War*. For a more sympathetic assessment of ZAPU military strategy, see Brickhill, 'Daring to Storm the Heavens'; Bhebe and Ranger (eds.), *Soldiers in Zimbabwe's Liberation War*, pp. 7–16.

52. Flower, *Serving Secretly*, pp. 173, 185–6.

53. Dabengwa's correspondence with Andropov was later discovered, along with secret arms caches, by Zimbabwean security forces. Ellis and Sechaba, *Comrades against Apartheid*, p. 104.

54. Andrew and Gordievsky, *KGB*, p. 559.

55. In 1966 the UN General Assembly voted to terminate South Africa's

mandate. Five years later, the International Court of Justice ruled that South Africa's continued occupation was a violation of international law.

56. Golan, *The Soviet Union and National Liberation Movements*, pp. 272–3. Small-scale Soviet support for SWAPO had begun a decade earlier.

57. k-14, 492; KASTONO believed he had been recruited by the GRU rather than the KGB.

58. k-27, 486; GRANT became increasingly reluctant to operate as a KGB agent and was discovered to be working for the East Germans. KGB contact with him was suspended, probably in 1982.

59. Golan, *The Soviet Union and National Liberation Movements*, pp. 272–3.

60. Turner, *Continent Ablaze*, p. 99 n. 13.

61. Leys and Saul (eds.), *Namibia's Liberation Struggle*, pp. 55–6, 104–6.

62. Turner, *Continent Ablaze*, pp. 69–84.

63. 'How to Master Secret Work': www.sacp.org.za/docs/history/secretwork.

64. Slovo had been an uncompromising supporter of the Soviet invasions of Hungary in 1956 and Czechoslovakia in 1968. He informed an SACP militant who, after she had visited Hungary in 1955, told him of the corruption and cynicism of the pro-Soviet regime, that she had turned into a reactionary, 'as if that epithet absolved him from any further discussion'. Israel, *South African Political Exile in the United Kingdom*, p. 149.

65. Obadi was killed in a South African cross-border raid in Mozambique in January 1981. Ellis and Sechaba, *Comrades against Apartheid*, pp. 105–7.

66. k-17, 30.

67. k-17, 29.

68. Andrew and Gordievsky, *KGB*, pp. 560–61.

69. Ibid., p. 561.

70. Andrew and Gordievsky (eds.), *Instructions from the Centre*, pp. 100–102. 'A girl's best friend. Claudia Wright explores the often secret relationship between US Ambassador to the UN, Jeane Kirkpatrick, and South Africa' (with photograph of the forged letter to Kirkpatrick), *New Statesman*, 5 Nov. 1982. See illustrations.

71. Godwin Matatu, 'US and S. Africa in Angola Plot' (with photograph of part of the forged document), *Observer*, 22 Jan. 1984; Andrew and Gordievsky (eds.), *Instructions from the Centre*, pp. 138–9. See illustrations.

72. Andrew and Gordievsky, *KGB*, p. 630.

73. See above, p. 340.

74. See below, pp. 471, 473–4.

75. Kirpichenko, *Razvedka*, p. 209.

76. Kempton, *Soviet Strategy toward Southern Africa*, pp. 68–9.

77. Wolf, *Man without a Face*, p. 265.

78. Volkogonov, *The Rise and Fall of the Soviet Empire*, pp. 373, 416–17.
79. Sampson, *Mandela*, p. 332.
80. Andrew and Gordievsky (eds.), *More Instructions from the Centre*, pp. 66–7.
81. Andrew and Gordievsky, *KGB*, p. 562.
82. Campbell, 'Soviet Policy in Southern Africa', pp. 208–9.
83. Ibid., p. 228.
84. See above, p. 135.
85. Johnson, *South Africa*, p. 199.
86. Mandela, *Long Walk to Freedom*, chs. 97–8. Mandela did not formally become President of the ANC, in succession to Oliver Tambo, until Tambo stood down in July 1991.
87. Sparks, *Tomorrow Is Another Country*; Waldmeir, *Anatomy of a Miracle*.
88. Mandela, *Long Walk to Freedom*, p. 113.

26. Conclusion

1. vol. 1, app. 3. Soviet academic experts were equally optimistic. Yuri Semenov wrote in 1980 that as a result of the help provided by the Soviet Union and other 'socialist countries' to former colonial states, 'many of them have adopted a socialist orientation and have entered on the path of non-capitalist development. The existence of a world socialist system provides the nations which are retarded in their development with a realistic possibility of a transition to socialism, which by-passes the long and tormented route by which mankind as a whole has passed.' Semenov, 'The Theory of Socio-economic Foundations and World History', p. 52.
2. Gates, *From the Shadows*, p. 174.
3. See above, p. 121.
4. See above, pp. 132–3.
5. Boldin, *Ten Years that Shook the World*, p. 40. Boldin later became Gorbachev's chief of staff, but took part in the unsuccessful coup against him in August 1991.
6. Gates, *From the Shadows*, pp. 186–7; Volkogonov, *Rise and Fall of the Soviet Empire*, pp. 330–31. On the political jokes of the Brezhnev era, see 'Our Great Leaders and Teachers': www.nctimes.net.
7. In May 1982 Andropov left the KGB for the Central Committee Secretariat to displace his main rival for the succession, Konstantin Chernenko, a long-time Brezhnev crony, apparatchik and sycophant, as effectively second Party secretary to Brezhnev. Proof is lacking for suggestions that Brezhnev favoured Chernenko as his successor.
8. Volkogonov, *Rise and Fall of the Soviet Empire*, pp. 329–30, 358–9; Dobbs, *Down with Big Brother*, p. 106; Dobrynin, *In Confidence*, p. 551.

9. Campbell, 'Soviet Policy in Southern Africa', p. 228. From September 1983, though still working from his sickbed, Andropov, by then terminally ill, was no longer able to chair Politburo meetings; Volkogonov, *Rise and Fall of the Soviet Empire*, p. 384.

10. Rubinstein, *Moscow's Third World Strategy*, p. 238.

11. Volkogonov, *Rise and Fall of the Soviet Empire*, pp. 385–96.

12. Leonov, *Likholet'e*, p. 141.

13. Garthoff, 'The KGB Reports to Gorbachev', pp. 226–7; Andrew and Mitrokhin, *The Sword and the Shield*, pp. 214–15;

14. Volkogonov, *Rise and Fall of the Soviet Empire*, p. 495.

15. Kennedy-Pipe, *Russia and the World*, p. 196.

16. See above, p. 417.

17. Ostermann (ed.), 'Gorbachev and Afghanistan', p. 146.

18. On the misbehaviour of the Czechoslovak minister see Andrew and Mitrokhin, *The Sword and the Shield*, pp. 274–5.

19. Kirpichenko, *Razvedka*, pp. 250–58.

20. Beschloss and Talbott, *At the Highest Levels*, p. 56.

21. Ibid., pp. 57–8. Unlike Gorbachev, Leonov and some other senior KGB veterans were still welcome visitors to Cuba in the early twenty-first century; 'Cuba's Comandante Turned Coma-andante', *Moscow News*, 31 Oct. 2004.

22. Kennedy-Pipe, *Russia and the World*, p. 196.

23. Kirpichenko, *Razvedka*, pp. 190–92.

24. Ibid., pp. 201–3. Details of Mengistu's chairs in Hartley, *The Zanzibar Chest*, p. 138.

25. Orizio, *Talk of the Devil*, pp. 144ff; Hartley, *The Zanzibar Chest*, p. 138. See above, p. 457.

26. Article by Leonov in *Sovetskaia Rossiia*, 26 April 1991. Leonov wrote this article as head of KGB intelligence assessment and made clear that it summarized detailed warnings sent by his department to 'the leadership of this country'. Andrew and Gordievsky (eds.), *Instructions from the Centre*, pp. 219–21.

27. Andrew and Gordievsky (eds.), *Instructions from the Centre*, pp. 218, 221–2. Among those taken in by the conspiracy theories was Gorbachev's chief of staff (formerly his assistant), Valeri Boldin, who took seriously Kryuchkov's claims that the KGB 'had intercepted certain information in the possession of Western intelligence agencies concerning plans for the collapse of the USSR and steps necessary to complete the destruction of our country as a great power'. Boldin, *Ten Years that Shook the World*, p. 263.

28. Remnick, *Lenin's Tomb*, p. 448. See above, pp. 135–6.

29. See above, p. 10.

30. Jeffrey Sachs, quoted in Gary Duncan, 'Economic Agenda', *The Times*, 10 Jan. 2005.

31. Clapham, *Africa and the International System*, pp. 153–4.
32. Ibid., pp. 155–6.
33. Szulc, *Fidel*, pp. 533–4.
34. Andrew and Mitrokhin, *The Sword and the Shield*, pp. 496–7.
35. Andrew, *For the President's Eyes Only*, pp. 425–6.
36. Mandela, *Long Walk to Freedom*, p. 379.
37. Cherkashin, *Spy Handler*, p. 146.
38. Interview with Leonov in *Pravda*, 21 March 2002.
39. Primakov, *Russian Crossroads*, pp. 92, 111. Primakov claims that Gordievsky came 'close to confessing' before his escape from Russia but makes no mention of the fact that Gordievsky, who had not been told he was under suspicion, was invited for a strategy meeting in a KGB dacha, given a drugged Armenian brandy, then suddenly subjected to aggressive interrogation and repeatedly told, as his head reeled from the effect of the drugs, that he had just confessed. The use of the phrase 'close to confessing', however, amounts to an admission that, even in these circumstances, Gordievsky did not in fact confess. On Gordievsky's interrogation and escape, see Andrew and Gordievsky, *KGB*, introduction, and Gordievsky, *Next Stop Execution*, chs. 1, 14.
40. Interview with Kirpichenko, *Vremia Novostei*, 20 Dec. 2004.
41. Andrew and Mitrokhin, *The Sword and the Shield*, pp. 330, 546–7.
42. Kalugin, *Spymaster*, pp. 287–98.
43. Andrew and Mitrokhin, *The Sword and the Shield*, ch. 5.
44. Ibid., chs. 19, 20.
45. See above, ch. 12.
46. Andrew and Mitrokhin, *The Sword and the Shield*, pp. 559–60. Korchnoi lost the championship by a single point.
47. Ibid., pp. 248–9.
48. Ibid., ch. 15.
49. See above, ch. 21.
50. Andrew and Mitrokhin, *The Sword and the Shield*, ch. 30.
51. See above, pp. 270–72.
52. Andrew and Gordievsky, *KGB*, ch. 9.
53. Andrew and Mitrokhin, *The Sword and the Shield*, p. 561.
54. Andrew and Gordievsky (eds.), *Instructions from the Centre*, ch. 1.
55. See above, pp. 38, 135–6.
56. Andrew and Mitrokhin, *The Sword and the Shield*, pp. 215–20, 556–8. On similarities in the East German case, see Macrakis, 'Does Effective Espionage Lead to Success in Science and Technology?'
57. Unlike Putin, Andropov had no background in foreign intelligence; he was a Party apparatchik and diplomat before becoming KGB Chairman in 1967.
58. A list of thirty-three influential former KGB and FSB officers in the

Putin administration was published in *Novaia Gazeta* in June 2003.

59. Nick Holdsworth and Robin Gedye, 'Putin brings back the Cold War spy system', *Daily Telegraph*, 15 July 2004.

60. Interview with Kirpichenko, *Vremia Novostei*, 20 Dec. 2004.

61. See above, p. 471.

62. Elkner, 'Spiritual Security in Putin's Russia'.

63. 'Senior Whitehall and security sources', cited by Jason Bennetto, 'Carry On Spying: Russian Agents Flood UK in Revival of Intelligence Cold War', *Independent*, 26 Oct. 2004.

64. US Department of State, *Country Reports on Human Rights Practices, 2003: Russia*; Anna Badkhen, 'Democracy on the Brink: Spy Mania', *San Francisco Chronicle*, 7 March 2004; Kathy Lally, '"Spy Mania" Strikes Russia', *Baltimore Sun*, 4 Jan. 2004.

65. 'Senior Whitehall and security sources', cited by Jason Bennetto, 'Carry On Spying: Russian Agents Flood UK in Revival of Intelligence Cold War', *Independent*, 26 Oct. 2004. Recent reports of the all-party Intelligence and Security Committee refer more discreetly to concern at the level of 'significant Russian activity in the UK' and the problem of allocating sufficient resources to deal with it; Intelligence and Security Committee, *Annual Report 2003–2004*, pp. 29–30. According to Primakov, though post-Soviet Russian intelligence 'has never hesitated in respect to [S&T] espionage', political intelligence has remained its 'top priority'; Primakov, *Russian Crossroads*, pp. 97–102.

66. See above, pp. 246–50.

67. Interview with Lebedev, *Rossiiskaia Gazeta*, 20 Dec. 2002.

68. RIA Novosti report, 20 May 2004. A year earlier the FSB had hosted a meeting of intelligence agencies from forty-three states to discuss terrorist finance.

69. Samolis (ed.), *Veterany vneshnei razvedki Rossii*, pp. 3–4.

70. Primakov et al., *Ocherki istorii rossiiskoi vneshnei razvedki*, vol. 3, conclusion.

Bibliography

1. Mitrokhin's Archive

Mitrokhin's notes and transcripts are arranged in four sections:
(i) k series: handwritten notes on individual KGB files, originally stored in large envelopes
(ii) t series: handwritten notebooks containing notes on individual KGB files
(iii) vol. series: typed volumes containing material drawn from numerous KGB files, mostly arranged by country, sometimes with commentary by Mitrokhin
(iv) frag. series: miscellaneous handwritten notes
For details of the methods by which Mitrokhin collected and stored his archive, see Andrew and Mitrokhin, *The Mitrokhin Archive*, vol. 1, ch. 1.

2. Books and Articles

Abebe, Ermias, 'The Horn, the Cold War, and Documents from the Former East-Bloc: An Ethiopian View', *Cold War International History Project Bulletin*, nos. 8–9 (1996–97)

Abrahamian, Ervand, *Tortured Confessions: Prisons and Public Recantations in Modern Iran* (Berkeley/Los Angeles, 1999)

Aburish, Saïd K., *Arafat: From Defender to Dictator* (London: Bloomsbury, 1998)

Aburish, Saïd K., *Nasser: The Last Arab* (London: Duckworth, 2004)

Adams, James, *The Financing of Terror* (London: NEL, 1988)

Agee, Philip, *Inside the Company: CIA Diary*, paperback edn (New York: Bantam Books, 1976)

Aldrich, Richard J., *The Hidden Hand: Britain, America and Cold War Secret Intelligence* (London: John Murray, 2001)

Alexiev, Alexander R., 'The Soviet Stake in Angola: Origins, Evolution, Prospects', in Bark, Dennis L. (ed.), *The Red Orchestra*, vol. 2: *The Case of Africa* (Stanford: Hoover Institution Press, 1988)

Almadaghi, Ahmed Norman Kassim, *Yemen and the United States: A Study of a Small Power and Super-State Relationship 1962–1994* (London: I. B. Tauris, 1996)

Alves, Maria Helena Moreira, *State and Opposition in Military Brazil* (Austin: University of Texas Press, 1985)

Ambrose, Stephen, *Eisenhower*, vol. 2: *The President* (New York: Simon & Schuster, 1984)

Amnesty International, *Afghanistan: Torture of Political Prisoners* (London: Amnesty International, 1986)

Amnesty International, *The Case of General Pinochet: Universal Jurisdiction and the Absence of Immunity for Crimes against Humanity*, Amnesty International Report EUR 45/21/98

Amuchastegui, Domingo, 'Cuban Intelligence and the October Crisis', *Intelligence and National Security*, vol. 13 (1998), no. 3

Andargachew, Tureneh, *The Ethiopian Revolution, 1974–1987: A Transformation from an Aristocratic to a Totalitarian Autocracy* (Cambridge: Cambridge University Press, 1993)

Andrew, Christopher, *For the President's Eyes Only: Secret Intelligence and the American Presidency from Washington to Bush* (London: HarperCollins, 1995)

Andrew, Christopher, 'France: Adjustment to Change', in Bull, Hedley, and Watson, Adam (eds.), *The Expansion of International Society* (Oxford: Oxford University Press, 1984)

Andrew, Christopher, and Elkner, Julie, 'Stalin and Intelligence', in Shukman, Harry (ed.), *Redefining Stalinism* (London: Frank Cass, 2003)

Andrew, Christopher, and Gordievsky, Oleg, *KGB: The Inside Story of its Foreign Operations from Lenin to Gorbachev*, paperback edn (London: Sceptre, 1991)

Andrew, Christopher, and Gordievsky, Oleg (eds.), *Instructions from the Centre: Top Secret Files on KGB Foreign Operations, 1975–1985* (London: Hodder & Stoughton, 1990); slightly revised US edn published as *Comrade Kryuchkov's Instructions: Top Secret Files on KGB Foreign Operations, 1975–1985* (Stanford: Stanford University Press, 1993)

Andrew, Christopher, and Gordievsky, Oleg (eds.), *More Instructions from the Centre: Top Secret Files on KGB Global Operations, 1975–1985* (London: Frank Cass, 1991)

Andrew, Christopher, and James, Harold, 'Willi Münzenberg, the Reichstag Fire and the Conversion of Innocents', in Charters, David and Tugwell, Maurice (eds.), *Deception in East–West Relations* (London: Pergamon-Brassey's, 1990)

Andrew, Christopher, and Mitrokhin, Vasili, *The Mitrokhin Archive*, vol. 1: *The KGB in Europe and the West* (London: Penguin, 1999)

Andreyev, Yuri, *Zionism: Preaching and Practice* (Moscow: Novosti, 1988)

Anwar, Raja, *The Terrorist Prince: The Life and Death of Murtaza Bhutto* (London: Verso, 1997)

Arif, General Khalid Mahmud, *Working with Zia: Pakistan's Power Politics* (Karachi: Oxford University Press, 1995)

Arora, K. C., V. K. *Krishna Menon: A Biography* (New Delhi: Sanchar Publishing House, 1998)

Ashby, Timothy, *The Bear in the Backyard: Moscow's Caribbean Strategy* (Lexington, MA: D. C. Heath & Co., 1987)

Association of Soviet Lawyers (ed.), *The White Book: Evidence, Facts, Documents* (Moscow: Progress Publishers, 1981)

Attwood, William, *The Reds and the Blacks: A Personal Adventure* (London: Hutchinson, 1967)

Avni, Zeev, *False Flag: The Soviet Spy Who Penetrated the Israeli Secret Intelligence Service*, paperback edn (London: St Ermin's Press, 2000)

Ayubi, Shaheen, *Nasser and Sadat: Decision Making and Foreign Policy (1970–1972)* (Lanham, MD: University Press of America, 1994)

Baer, Robert, *See No Evil: The True Story of a Ground Soldier in the CIA's War against Terrorism*, paperback edn (New York: Three Rivers Press, 2002)

Baker, James A. III, *The Politics of Diplomacy: Revolution, War and Peace, 1989–1992* (New York: G. P. Putnam's Sons, 1995)

Baker, Raymond William, *Sadat and After: Struggles for Egypt's Political Soul* (London: I. B. Tauris, 1990)

Bakshi, Jyotsna, *Russia and India: From Ideology to Geopolitics 1947–1998* (Delhi: Dev Publications, 1999)

Balfour, Sebastian, *Castro*, 2nd edn (London: Longman, 1995)

Ball, Desmond, *Soviet Signals Intelligence (SIGINT)*, Canberra Papers on Strategy and Defence, no. 47 (Canberra: Australian National University, 1989)

Ball, Desmond, and Windren, Robert, 'Soviet Signals Intelligence (Sigint): Organisation and Management', *Intelligence and National Security*, vol. 4 (1989), no. 4

Bao, Ruo-Wang [Pasqualini, Jean], and Chelminski, Rudolph, *Prisoner of Mao* (London: André Deutsch, 1975)

Baram, Amatzia, 'Saddam Husayn, the Ba'th Regime and the Iraqi Officer Corps', in Rubin, Barry, and Keaney, Thomas A. (eds.), *Armed Forces in the Middle East: Politics and Strategy* (London: Frank Cass, 2002)

Bark, Dennis L. (ed.), *The Red Orchestra*, vol. 2: *The Case of Africa* (Stanford: Hoover Institution Press, 1988)

Barron, John, *KGB: The Secret Work of Soviet Agents* (London: Bantam Books, 1974)

Barron, John, *KGB Today: The Hidden Hand* (London: Hodder & Stoughton, 1984)

Bearden, Milt, and Risen, James, *The Main Enemy: The Inside Story of the*

CIA's Final Showdown with the KGB (New York: Random House, 2004)

Beattie, Kirk J., *Egypt during the Nasser Years* (Boulder, CO: Westview Press, 1994)

Beattie, Kirk J., *Egypt during the Sadat Years* (London: Palgrave, 2000)

Ben Bella, Ahmed, 'Che as I Knew Him', *Le Monde Diplomatique*, October 1997

Bennigsen, Alexandre, and Broxup, Marie, *The Islamic Threat to the Soviet State* (London: Croom Helm, 1983)

Bennigsen, Alexandre, and Wimbush, S. Enders, *Moslems of the Soviet Union* (London: Hurst, 1985)

Bennigsen, Alexandre, and Wimbush, S. Enders, *Mystics and Commissars: Sufism in the Soviet Union* (Berkeley/Los Angeles: University of California Press, 1985)

Bergman, Ronen, 'Spooked', *Ha'aretz Magazine*, 10 April 1998

Berton, Peter, 'Two Decades of Soviet Diplomacy and Andrei Gromyko', in Rozman, Gilbert (ed.), *Japan and Russia: The Tortuous Path to Normalization, 1949–1999* (London: Macmillan, 2000)

Beschloss, Michael R., *The Crisis Years: Kennedy and Khrushchev, 1960–1963* (New York: Edward Burlinghame Books, 1991)

Beschloss, Michael R., and Talbott, Strobe, *At the Highest Levels: The Inside Story of the End of the Cold War* (London: Little, Brown & Co., 1993)

Bhebe, Ngwabi, and Ranger, Terence (eds.), *Soldiers in Zimbabwe's Liberation War* (London: James Currey, 1995)

Bird, Leonard, *Costa Rica: The Unarmed Democracy* (London: Sheppard Press, 1984)

Birmingham, David, 'The Twenty-seventh of May', in Birmingham, David, *Portugal in Africa* (London: Macmillan, 1999)

Bittman, Ladislav, *The Deception Game: Czechoslovak Intelligence in Soviet Political Warfare* (Syracuse, NY: Syracuse University Research Corporation, 1972)

Black, George, *Triumph of the People: The Sandinista Revolution in Nicaragua* (London: Zed Press, 1981)

Black, Ian and Morris, Benny, *Israel's Secret Wars: A History of Israel's Intelligence Services* (New York: Grove Weidenfeld, 1991)

Boldin, Valery, *Ten Years that Shook the World: The Gorbachev Era as Witnessed by His Chief of Staff* (New York: Basic Books, 1994)

Bonavia, David, *Verdict in Peking: The Trial of the Gang of Four* (London: Burnett Books, 1984)

Borge, Tomás, 'La formación del FSLN', in *La Revolución a Traves de Nuestra Dirección Nacional* (Managua: SENAPEP, 1980)

Borovik, Artyom, *The Hidden War: A Russian Journalist's Account of the Soviet War in Afghanistan* (London: Faber and Faber, 1991)

Bracamonte, José Angel Moroni, and Spencer, David E., *Strategy and Tactics of the Salvadoran FMLN Guerrillas: Last Battle of the Cold War, Blueprint for Future Conflicts* (London: Praeger, 1995)

Braddick, C. W., 'The Waiting Game: Japan–Russia Relations', in Takashi, Inoguchi, and Purnendra, Jain (eds.), *Japanese Foreign Policy Today: A Reader* (New York: Palgrave, 2000)

Braddick, C. W., *Japan and the Sino-Soviet Alliance, 1950–1964: In the Shadow of the Monolith* (Basingstoke: Palgrave Macmillan, 2004)

Bradsher, Henry S., *Afghan Communism and Soviet Intervention* (Oxford: Oxford University Press, 1999)

Brass, Paul R., *The Politics of India since Independence* (Cambridge: Cambridge University Press, 1990)

Bregman, Ahron, and el-Tahri, Jihan, *The Fifty Years War: Israel and the Arabs* (London: Penguin/BBC Books, 1998)

Brickhill, Jeremy, 'Daring to Storm the Heavens: The Military Strategy of ZAPU, 1976–79', in Bhebe, Ngwabi, and Ranger, Terence (eds.), *Soldiers in Zimbabwe's Liberation War* (London: James Currey, 1995)

Brook-Shepherd, Gordon, *The Storm Birds* (London: Weidenfeld & Nicolson, 1988)

Brown, Archie, *The Gorbachev Factor* (Oxford: Oxford University Press, 1996)

Brown, T. Louise, *War and Aftermath in Vietnam* (London: Routledge, 1991)

Brown, Timothy C., *The Real Contra War: Highlander Peasant Resistance in Nicaragua* (Norman: University of Oklahoma Press, 2001)

Buckley, Roger, *Japan Today*, 3rd edn (Cambridge: Cambridge University Press, 1998)

Burles, Mark, *Chinese Policy toward Russia and the Central Asian Republics* (Santa Monica: Rand, 1999)

Burr, William (ed.), *National Security Archive Electronic Briefing Book No. 145*, www.nsarchive.org

Byron, John, and Pack, Robert, *The Claws of the Dragon: Kang Sheng – The Evil Genius behind Mao and His Legacy of Terror in People's China* (New York: Simon & Schuster, 1992)

Caballero, Manuel, *Latin America and the Comintern, 1919–1943* (Cambridge: Cambridge University Press, 1986)

Cabrita, João M., *Mozambique: The Tortuous Road to Democracy* (London: Palgrave, 2000)

Cain, Peter J., and Harrison, Mark (eds.), *Imperialism: Critical Concepts in Historical Studies*, 3 vols (London: Routledge, 2001)

Campbell, Keith, *ANC: A Soviet Task Force?* (London: Institute for the Study of Terrorism, 1986)

Campbell, Kurt M., 'Soviet Policy in Southern Africa: Angola and Mozambique', in Campbell, Kurt M., and MacFarlane, S. Neil (eds.), *Gorbachev's Third World Dilemmas* (London: Routledge, 1989)

Carlisle, Donald S., 'Geopolitics and Ethnic Problems of Uzbekistan', in Ro'i, Yaacov (ed.), *Muslim Eurasia: Conflicting Legacies* (London: Frank Cass, 1995)

Carr, Edward Hallett, *Foundations of a Planned Economy*, 3 vols (London: Macmillan, 1976–79)

Carter, Jimmy, *Keeping Faith* (London: Collins, 1982)

Castañeda, Jorge G., *Compañero: The Life and Death of Che Guevara* (London: Bloomsbury, 1997)

The Challenge to Democracy in Central America (Washington, DC: Departments of State and Defense, 1986)

Chang, Gordon H., *Friends and Enemies: The United States, China and the Soviet Union, 1948–1972* (Stanford: Stanford University Press, 1990)

Chang, Jung, *Wild Swans: Three Daughters of China*, paperback edn (London: Flamingo, 1993)

Charen, Mona, *Useful Idiots: How Liberals Got It Wrong in the Cold War and Still Blame America First* (Washington, DC: Regnery, 2003)

Chazan, Naomi, *An Anatomy of Ghanaian Politics: Managing Political Recession, 1969–1982* (Epping: Bowker, 1983)

Cherkashin, Victor (with Feifer, Gregory), *Spy Handler: Memoir of a KGB Officer. The True Story of the Man Who Recruited Robert Hanssen and Aldrich Ames* (New York: Perseus Books, 2005)

Chernyaev, Anatoly S., *My Six Years with Gorbachev* (Pennsylvania: Pennsylvania University Press, 2000)

Chin, Yvette, Domber, Gregory, Gnoniska, Malgorzata, and Munteanu, Mircea, 'New Central and East European Evidence on the Cold War in Asia: Conference Report', *Cold War International History Project Bulletin*, nos. 14–15 (2003–2004)

Clapham, Christopher, *Transformation and Continuity in Revolutionary Ethiopia* (Cambridge: Cambridge University Press, 1989)

Clapham, Christopher, *Africa and the International System: The Politics of State Survival* (Cambridge: Cambridge University Press, 1996)

Clarridge, Duane R., *A Spy for All Seasons: My Life in the CIA* (New York: 1997)

Clayton, Lawrence A., *Peru and the United States: The Condor and the Eagle* (Athens, GA: University of Georgia Press, 1999)

Cohen, Avner, 'Israel and Chemical/Biological Weapons: History, Deterrence, and Arms Control', *The Nonproliferation Review*, vol. 8 (Fall–Winter, 2001), no. 3

Connelly, Matthew, *A Diplomatic Revolution: Algeria's Fight for Independence and the Origins of the Post-Cold War Era* (Oxford: Oxford University Press, 2002)

Connelly, Matthew, 'Taking off the Cold War Lens: Visions of North–South Conflict during the Algerian War for Independence,' *American Historical Review*, vol. 105 (2000), no. 3

Constable, Pamela and Valenzuela, Arturo, *A Nation of Enemies: Chile under Pinochet* (London: W. W. Norton, 1991)

Corvalán, Luis, *De lo vivido y lo peleado: Memorias* (Santiago: LOM Ediciones, 1997)

Coughlin, Con, *Saddam: The Secret Life*, paperback edn (London: Pan Macmillan, 2003)

Courtois, Stéphane, Werth, Nicholas, Panné, Jean-Louis, Paczkowski, Andrzej, Bartosek, Karel, and Margolin, Jean-Louis, *Le livre noir du communisme: crimes, terreur et répression* (Paris: Robert Laffont, 1997)

Cradock, Sir Percy, *Experiences of China* (London: John Murray, 1994)

Cradock, Sir Percy, *Know Your Enemy: How the Joint Intelligence Committee Saw the World* (London: John Murray, 2002)

Crassweller, Robert D., *Perón and the Enigmas of Argentina* (New York: W. W. Norton, 1987)

Crozier, Brian (ed.), *The Grenada Documents* (London: Sherwood Press, 1987)

Davidson, Apollon, Filatova, Irina, Gorodnov, Valentin, and Johns, Sheridan (eds.), *South Africa and the Communist International: A Documentary History*, vol. 1: *Socialist Pilgrims to Bolshevik Footsoldiers 1919–1930* (London: Frank Cass, 2003)

Davidson, Apollon, Filatova, Irina, Gorodnov, Valentin, and Johns, Sheridan (eds.), *South Africa and the Communist International: A Documentary History*, vol. 2: *Bolshevik Footsoldiers to Victims of Bolshevisation 1931–1939* (London: Frank Cass, 2003)

Davis, Nathaniel, *The Last Two Years of Salvador Allende* (Ithaca, NY: Cornell University Press, 1985)

Dawisha, Karen, *Soviet Foreign Policy towards Egypt* (London: Macmillan, 1979)

Deas, Malcolm, 'Spectacle of the Rats and Owls', *London Review of Books*, 2 June 1988

'Deng Xiaoping's Talks with the Soviet Ambassador and Leadership, 1957–1963', *Cold War International History Project Bulletin*, no. 10 (1998)

Devlin, Judith, *The Rise of the Russian Democrats: The Causes and Consequences of the Elite Revolution* (Aldershot: Edward Elgar, 1995)

Dhar, P. N., *Indira Gandhi, the 'Emergency', and Indian Democracy* (New Delhi: Oxford University Press, 2000)

el-Din, Khaled Mohi, *Memories of a Revolution: Egypt 1952* (Cairo: American University of Cairo Press, 1995)

Dinges, John, *Our Man in Panama: The Shrewd Rise and Brutal Fall of Manuel Noriega* (New York: Times Books, 1991)

Dittmer, Lowell, *Sino-Soviet Normalization and Its International Implications, 1945–1990* (Seattle: University of Washington Press, 1992)

Dix, Robert H., *The Politics of Colombia* (New York: Praeger, 1987)

Dobbs, Michael, *Down with Big Brother: The Fall of the Soviet Empire* (London: Bloomsbury, 1997)

Dobrynin, Anatoly, *In Confidence* (New York: Times Books, 1995)

Dobson, Christopher, and Payne, Ronald, *War without End. The Terrorists: An Intelligence Dossier* (London: Harrap, 1986)

Documents on Israeli–Soviet Relations, 1941–1953, edited by the Cummings Center, State Archives of Israel, Foreign Ministry of the Russian Federation and the Foreign Ministry of Israel, 2 vols (London: Frank Cass, 2000)

Domínguez, Jorge I., *To Make a World Safe for Revolution: Cuba's Foreign Policy* (Cambridge, MA: Harvard University Press, 1989)

Donham, Donald L., *Marxist Modern: An Ethnographic History of the Ethiopian Revolution* (Berkeley/Los Angeles: University of California Press, 1999)

Dulaymi, Nazibah, 'Stop the Repressions and Persecution', *World Marxist Review*, vol. 22 (March 1979)

Dunlop, John B., *Russia Confronts Chechnya: Roots of a Separatist Conflict* (Cambridge: Cambridge University Press, 1998)

Dzhirkvelov, Ilya, *Secret Servant: My Life with the KGB and the Soviet Elite* (London: Collins, 1987)

Efrat, Moshe, 'The Soviet Union and the Syrian Military-Economic Dimension: A *Realpolitik* Dimension', in Efrat, Moshe, and Bercovitch, Jacob (eds.), *Superpowers and Client States in the Middle East: The Imbalance of Influence* (London: Routledge, 1991)

Eftimiades, Nicholas, *Chinese Intelligence Operations* (London: Frank Cass, 1994)

Ehrlich, Haggai, 'The Soviet Union and Ethiopia: The Misreading of *Politica Scioana* and *Politica Tigrina*', in Bark, Dennis L. (ed.), *The Red Orchestra*, vol. 2: *The Case of Africa* (Stanford: Hoover Institution Press, 1988)

Elkner, Julie, 'Spiritual Security in Putin's Russia', paper to the British Intelligence Study Group, 4 Feb. 2005 (publication pending in *Intelligence and National Security*)

Ellert, Humphrey, 'The Rhodesian Security and Intelligence Community', in Bhebe, Ngwabi, and Ranger, Terence (eds.), *Soldiers in Zimbabwe's Liberation War* (London: James Currey, 1995)

Ellis, Stephen, and Sechaba, Tsepo, *Comrades against Apartheid* (London: James Currey, 1992)

Falcoff, Mark, *Modern Chile 1970–1989: A History* (London: Transaction Publishers, 1991)

Farah, Nuruddin, *Sweet and Sour Milk* (London: Allison and Busby, 1979)

Farid, Abdel Magid, *Nasser: The Final Years* (Reading, MA: Ithaca Press, 1994)

Faúndez, Julio, *Marxism and Democracy in Chile: From 1932 to the Fall of Allende* (New Haven: Yale University Press, 1988)

Ferguson, Niall, *Colossus: The Rise and Fall of the American Empire* (London: Allen Lane, 2004)

Fieldhouse, D. K., *Black Africa 1945–80: Economic Decolonization and Arrested Development* (London: Allen & Unwin, 1986)

Finklestone, Joseph, *Anwar Sadat: Visionary Who Dared* (London: Frank Cass, 1996)

Finnegan, William, *A Complicated War: The Harrowing of Mozambique* (Berkeley/Los Angeles: University of California Press, 1992)

Flemming, William, 'The Deportation of the Chechen and Ingush Peoples: A Critical Examination', in Fowkes, Ben (ed.), *Russia and Chechnya: The Permanent Crisis* (London: Macmillan, 1998)

Flower, Ken, *Serving Secretly: An Intelligence Chief on Record: Rhodesia into Zimbabwe* (London: John Murray, 1987)

Follain, John, *Jackal: The Secret Wars of Carlos the Jackal* (London: Weidenfeld & Nicolson, 1998)

Fontaine Talavera, Arturo, 'Estados Unidos y la Unión Soviética en Chile', *Estudios Públicos*, no. 72 (1998)

Foot, Michael, *Aneurin Bevan*, vol. 2: *1945–1960* (London: Davis-Poynter, 1963)

Ford, Gerald R., *A Time to Heal* (London: W. H. Allen, 1979)

Frank, Katherine, *Indira: The Life of Indira Nehru Gandhi* (London: HarperCollins, 2001)

Frankel, Glenn, *Rivona's Children: Three Families and the Price of Freedom in South Africa* (London: Weidenfeld & Nicolson, 1999)

Frankel, Jonathan, 'The Soviet Regime and Anti-Zionism: An Analysis', in Ro'i, Yaakov, and Beker, Avi (eds.), *Jewish Culture and Identity in the Soviet Union* (New York: New York University Press, 1991)

Freedman, Robert O. (ed.), *Soviet Jewry in the 1980s: The Politics of Anti-Semitism and Emigration and the Dynamics of Resettlement* (Durham, NC: Duke University Press, 1989)

Freedman, Robert O., 'The Soviet Union and Syria: A Case Study of Soviet Policy', in Efrat, Moshe, and Bercovitch, Jacob (eds.), *Superpowers and Client States in the Middle East: The Imbalance of Influence* (London: Routledge, 1991)

Friedman, Robert I., *The False Prophet: Rabbi Meir Kahane – from FBI Informant to Knesset Member* (London: Faber and Faber, 1990)

Fursenko, A. A. (ed.), *Prezidium TsK KPSS. 1954–1964. Chernovye protokol'nye zapisi zasedanii. Stenogrammy. Postanovleniia / T. 1. Chernovye protokol'nye zapisi zasedanii. Stenogrammy* (Moscow: ROSSPEN, 2003)

Fursenko, Alexander, and Naftali, Timothy, *'One Hell of a Gamble': Khrushchev, Kennedy, Castro and the Cuban Missile Crisis, 1958–1964* (London: John Murray, 1997)

Fursenko, Alexander, and Naftali, Timothy, 'The Pitsunda Decision: Khrushchev and Nuclear Weapons', *Cold War International History Project Bulletin*, no. 10 (1998)

Fursenko, Alexander, and Naftali, Timothy, 'Soviet Intelligence and the Cuban Missile Crisis', *Intelligence and National Security*, vol. 13 (1998), no. 3

Gaiduk, Ilya V., 'The Vietnam War and Soviet–American Relations, 1964–73: New Russian Evidence', *Cold War International History Project Bulletin*, nos. 6–7 (1995–96)

Gaiduk, Ilya V., *The Soviet Union and the Vietnam War* (Chicago: Ivan R. Dee, 1996)

Galeotti, Mark, *Afghanistan: The Soviet Union's Last War* (London: Frank Cass, 1995)

Gammer, Moshe, *Muslim Resistance to the Tsar: Shamil and the Conquest of Chechnia and Daghestan* (London: Frank Cass, 1994)

Gammer, Moshe, 'Unity, Diversity and Conflict in the Northern Caucasus', in Ro'i, Yaacov (ed.), *Muslim Eurasia: Conflicting Legacies* (London: Frank Cass, 1995)

Gandhi, Arun, *The Morarji Papers: Fall of the Janata Government* (New Delhi: Vision Books, 1983)

Gandhi, Indira, *Selected Speeches and Writings of Indira Gandhi*, vols. 1–5 (New Delhi: Ministry of Information and Broadcasting, 1971–86)

Gandhi, Sonya (ed.), *Two Alone, Two Together: Letters between Indira Gandhi and Jawaharlal Nehru, 1940–1964* (London: Hodder, 1992)

Ganor, Boaz, 'Syria and Terrorism', *Survey of Arab Affairs*, 15 November 1991

Garthoff, Raymond L., 'The KGB Reports to Gorbachev', *Intelligence and National Security*, vol. 11 (1996), no. 2

Gates, Robert M., *From the Shadows: The Ultimate Insider's Story of Five Presidents and How They Won the Cold War* (New York: Simon & Schuster, 1996)

Gerassi, J. (ed.), *The Speeches and Writings of Ernesto 'Che' Guevara* (London: Weidenfeld & Nicolson, 1968)

Geyer, Georgie Anne, *Guerrilla Prince: The Untold Story of Fidel Castro* (Boston: Little, Brown & Co., 1991)

Ghalib, Jama Mohamed, *The Cost of Dictatorship: The Somali Experience* (New York: Lilian Barber Press, 1995)

Gilbert, Dennis, *Sandinistas: The Party and the Revolution* (Oxford: Basil Blackwell, 1988)

Gilbert, Isidoro, *El Oro de Moscu: La Historia Secreta de las Relaciones Argentino-Soviéticas* (Buenos Aires: Planeta, 1994)

Gilbert, Martin, *Shcharansky: Hero of Our Time* (London: Macmillan, 1986)

Gitelman, Zvi, '"From a Northern Country": Russian and Soviet Jewish Emigration to America and Israel in Historical Perspective', in Lewin-Epstein, Noah, Ro'i, Yaacov, and Ritterbrand, Paul (eds.), *Russian Jews on Three Continents: Migration and Resettlement* (London: Frank Cass, 1997)

Glaubitz, Joachim, *Between Tokyo and Moscow: The History of an Uneasy Relationship, 1972 to the 1990s* (London: Hurst & Co., 1995)

Gleijeses, Piero, *Conflicting Missions: Havana, Washington and Africa, 1959–1976* (Chapel Hill: University of North Carolina Press, 2002)

Golan, Galia, *The Soviet Union and National Liberation Movements in the Third World* (Boston: Unwin Hyman, 1988)

Golan, Galia, *Soviet Policies in the Middle East from World War Two to Gorbachev* (Cambridge: Cambridge University Press, 1990)

Golbery do Couto e Silva, General, *Conjuntura política nacional, o poder do executivo e geopolitica do Brasil* (Rio de Janeiro: José Olympico, 1981)

Goncharov, Sergei N., Lewis, John W., and Litai, Xue, *Uncertain Partners: Stalin, Mao and the Korean War* (Stanford: Stanford University Press, 1993)

Gordievsky, Oleg, *Next Stop Execution: The Autobiography of Oleg Gordievsky* (London: Macmillan, 1995)

Gorev, Alexander, *Indira Gandhi: Patriot, Fighter, Humanist* (Moscow: Novosti Press Agency Publishing House, 1989)

Gorev, Alexander, *Jawaharlal Nehru: Patriot, Fighter, Humanist* (Moscow: Novosti Press Agency Publishing House, 1989)

Govrin, Yosef, *Israeli–Soviet Relations, 1953–1967: From Confrontation to Disruption* (London: Frank Cass, 1998)

Gozman, Leonid, 'Is Living in Russia Worthwhile?', in Lewin-Epstein, Noah, Ro'i, Yaacov, and Ritterbrand, Paul (eds.), *Russian Jews on Three Continents: Migration and Resettlement* (London: Frank Cass, 1997)

Grau, Lester W. (ed.), *The Bear Went over the Mountain: Soviet Combat Tactics in Afghanistan* (London: Frank Cass, 1998)

Greene, Graham, *Getting to Know the General: The Story of an Involvement* (London: Vintage, 1999)

Grimaud, Nicole, *La politique extérieure de l'Algérie* (Paris: Editions Karthala, 1984)

Gromyko, Andrei, *Memories* (London: Hutchinson, 1989)

Gromyko, A. A., and Ponomarev, B. N. (eds.), *Soviet Foreign Policy, 1917–1980*, 2 vols (Moscow: Progress Publishers, 1981)

Guest, Robert, *The Shackled Continent: Africa's Past, Present and Future* (London: Macmillan, 2004)

Guimarães, Fernando Andersen, *The Origins of the Angolan Civil War: Foreign Intervention and Domestic Political Conflict* (London: Macmillan, 1998)

Gustafson, Kristian, 'CIA Machinations in Chile in 1970', *Studies in Intelligence*, vol. 47 (2003), no. 3

Gustafson, Kristian, 'CIA Covert Action and the Chilean Coup', Cambridge University PhD thesis (due for completion in 2005)

Haghayeghi, Mehrdad, *Islam and Politics in Central Asia* (New York: St Martin's Press, 1995)

Haig, Alexander, *Caveat* (London: Weidenfeld & Nicolson, 1984)

Halliday, Fred, 'Soviet Relations with South Yemen', in B. R. Pridham (ed.), *Contemporary Yemen: Politics and Historical Background* (London: Croom Helm, 1984)

Halliday, Fred, *Revolution and Foreign Policy: The Case of South Yemen, 1967–1987* (Cambridge: Cambridge University Press, 1990)

Hanratty, Dennis M., and Meditz, Sandra W. (eds.), *Colombia: A Country Study* (Washington, DC: Library of Congress, 1990)

Hanson, Philip, *Soviet Industrial Espionage: Some New Information* (London: RIIA, 1987)

Hara, Kimie, *Japanese–Soviet/Russian Relations since 1945: A Difficult Peace* (London: Routledge, 1998)

Hart, Alan, *Arafat: A Political Biography*, revised edn (London: Sidgwick & Jackson, 1994)

Hartley, Aidan, *The Zanzibar Chest: A Memoir of Love and War*, paperback edn (London: HarperPerennial, 2004)

Hasegawa, Tsuyoshi, Haslam, Jonathan, and Kuchins, Andrew (eds.), *Russia and Japan: An Unresolved Dilemma between Distant Neighbours* (Berkeley: University of California Press, 1993)

Hasegawa, Tsuyoshi, 'Japanese Perceptions of the Soviet Union and Russia in the Postwar Period', in Hasegawa, Tsuyoshi, Haslam, Jonathan, and Kuchins, Andrew (eds.), *Russia and Japan: An Unresolved Dilemma between Distant Neighbours* (Berkeley: University of California Press, 1993)

Haslam, Jonathan, *The Nixon Administration and the Death of Allende's Chile: A Case of Assisted Suicide* (London/New York: Verso, 2005)

Haslam, Jonathan, 'The Pattern of Soviet–Japanese Relations since World War II', in Hasegawa, Tsuyoshi, Haslam, Jonathan, and Kuchins, Andrew (eds.), *Russia and Japan: An Unresolved Dilemma between Distant Neighbours* (Berkeley: University of California Press, 1993)

Heikal, Mohammed, *The Road to Ramadan* (London: Collins, 1975)

Heikal, Mohammed, *Sphinx and Commissar* (London: Collins, 1978)

Heldman, Dan C., *The USSR and Africa: Foreign Policy under Khrushchev* (New York: Praeger, 1981)

Henriksen, Thomas H., 'The People's Republic of Madagascar', in Bark, Dennis L. (ed.), *The Red Orchestra*, vol. 2: *The Case of Africa* (Stanford: Hoover Institution Press, 1988)

Henze, Paul B., 'Moscow, Mengistu and the Horn: Difficult Choices for the Kremlin', *Cold War International History Project Bulletin*, nos. 8–9 (1996–97)

Hiro, Dilip, *Desert Shield to Desert Storm: The Second Gulf War* (London: HarperCollins, 1992)

Hobsbawm, Eric, *Age of Extremes*, paperback edn (London: Abacus, 1995)

Hodges, Donald C., *Intellectual Origins of the Nicaraguan Revolution* (Austin: University of Texas Press, 1987)

Hodges, Tony, *Angola: From Afro-Stalinism to Petro-Diamond Capitalism* (Oxford: James Currey, 2001)

Holland, Max, 'The Lie that Linked CIA to the Kennedy Assassination', *Studies in Intelligence*, no. 11 (Fall–Winter 2001–2002)

Hollander, Paul, *Political Pilgrims: Travels of Western Intellectuals to the Soviet Union, China and Cuba* (Oxford: Oxford University Press, 1981)

Hollander, Paul, *Anti-Americanism: Critiques at Home and Abroad 1965– 1990* (Oxford: Oxford University Press, 1992)

Horn, Robert C., *Soviet–Indian Relations: Issues and Influence* (New York: Praeger, 1982)

Horne, Alistair, *A Savage War of Peace: Algeria 1954–1962*, paperback edn (Harmondsworth: Penguin, 1979)

Horne, Alistair, *Small Earthquake in Chile*, revised edn (London: Papermac, 1990)

Hosking, Geoffrey, *A History of the Soviet Union*, paperback edn (London: Fontana, 1985)

Hough, Jerry F., *The Struggle for the Third World: Soviet Debates and American Options* (Washington, DC: Brookings Institution, 1986)

Howe, Stephen, *Anticolonialism in British Politics: The Left and the End of Empire* (Oxford: Clarendon Press, 1993)

Howell, Jude, 'The End of an Era: The Rise and Fall of G.D.R. Aid', *Journal of Modern African Studies*, vol. 32 (1994), no. 2

Hudson, Rex A., and Hanratty, Dennis M., *Bolivia: A Country Study* (Washington, DC: Library of Congress, 1991)

Intelligence and Security Committee [UK], *The Mitrokhin Inquiry Report*, Cm. 4764, 13 June 2000

Intelligence and Security Committee [UK], *Annual Report 2003–2004*, Cm. 6420, 29 June 2004

Ismael, Tareq Y., and El-Sa'id, Rifa'at, *The Communist Movement in Egypt, 1920–1988* (Syracuse, NY: Syracuse University Press, 1990)

Ismael, Tareq Y., and Ismael, Jacqueline S., *The Communist Movement in Syria and Lebanon* (Gainesville, FL: University Press of Florida, 1998)

Israel, Mark, *South African Political Exile in the United Kingdom* (London: Macmillan, 1999)

Israelyan, Victor, *Inside the Kremlin during the Yom Kippur War* (University Park, PA: Pennsylvania University Press, 1995)

Jakobovits, Immanuel, *'If Only My People . . .': Zionism in My Life* (London: Weidenfeld & Nicolson, 1984)

Jian, Chen, *Mao's China and the Cold War* (Chapel Hill: University of North Carolina Press, 2001)

Jian, Chen, and Wilson, David, ' "All under the Heavens is Great Chaos": Beijing, the Sino-Soviet Border Clashes, and the Turn toward Sino-American Rapprochement', *Cold War International History Project Bulletin*, no. 11 (Winter 1998)

Johnson, R. W., *South Africa: The First Man, the Last Nation* (London: Weidenfeld & Nicolson, 2004)

Jonson, Lena, *Vladimir Putin and Central Asia: The Shaping of Russian Foreign Policy* (London: I. B. Tauris, 2004)

Kahn, David, 'Soviet Comint in the Cold War', *Cryptologia*, vol. 22 (1998)

Kaké, Ibrahim Baba, *Sékou Touré: le héros et le tyran* (Paris: Presses Jeune Afrique, 1987)

Kalugin, Oleg, *Spymaster: My 32 Years in Intelligence and Espionage against the West* (London: Smith Gryphon, 1994)

Karsh, Efraim, *Soviet Policy towards Syria since 1970* (London: Macmillan, 1991)

Karsh, Efraim, and Rautsi, Inari, *Saddam Hussein: A Political Biography* (London: Brassey's (UK), 1991)

Kassem, May, *In the Guise of Democracy: Governance in Contemporary Egypt* (Reading, MA: Ithaca Press, 1999)

Kaufman, Edy, *Crisis in Allende's Chile: New Perspectives* (New York/ London: Praeger, 1988)

Kaul, T. N., *Reminiscences Discreet and Indiscreet* (New Delhi: Lancers Publishers, 1982)

Kean, Christopher, *Diez Días en Cuba: Mensaje de la disidencia a la diáspora* (New York: Freedom House, 1992)

Kempe, Frederick, *Divorcing the Dictator: America's Bungled Affair with Noriega* (London: I. B. Tauris, 1990)

Kempton, Daniel R., *Soviet Strategy toward Southern Africa: The National Liberation Movement Connection* (New York: Praeger, 1989)

Kennedy-Pipe, Caroline, *Russia and the World, 1917–1991* (London: Arnold, 1998)

Khrushchov, N. S., *World without Arms, World without Wars*, 2 vols (Moscow: Foreign Languages Publishing House, 1960)

Khrushchov, N. S., *Communism: Peace and Happiness for the Peoples*, 2 vols (Moscow: Foreign Languages Publishing House, 1963)

Kimura, Hiroshi, 'Japanese–Soviet Political Relations from 1976–1983', in Rozman, Gilbert (ed.), *Japan and Russia: The Tortuous Path to Normalization, 1949–1999* (London: Macmillan, 2000)

Kirpichenko, Vadim, *Iz arkhiva razvedchika* (Moscow: Mezhdunarodnye otnosheniia, 1993)

Kirpichenko, Vadim, *Razvedka: litsa i lichnosti* (Moscow: Geiia, 1998)

Kissinger, Henry, *White House Years* (Boston: Little, Brown & Co., 1979)

Kissinger, Henry, *Years of Upheaval* (Boston: Little, Brown & Co., 1982)

Kissinger, Henry, *Diplomacy* (New York: Simon & Schuster, 1994)

Klarén, Peter Flindell, *Peru: Society and Nationhood in the Andes* (Oxford: Oxford University Press, 2000)

Kolbenev, Eduard, 'Kak Pakistan raskololsia na dva gosudarstva', in Karpov, V. N. (ed.), *Vneshniaia razvedka* (Moscow: XXI vek – Soglasie, 2000)

Korey, William, *Russian Antisemitism, Pamyat, and the Demonology of Zionism* (Chur, Switzerland: Harwood Academic Publishers, 1995)

Korey, William, 'The Soviet Public Anti-Zionist Committee: An Analysis', in Freedman, Robert O. (ed.), *Soviet Jewry in the 1980s: The Politics of Anti-Semitism and Emigration and the Dynamics of Resettlement* (Durham, NC: Duke University Press, 1989)

Koster, R. M., and Sánchez Borbón, Guillermo, *In the Time of the Tyrants: Panama, 1968–1990* (London: Secker & Warburg, 1990)

Krause, Joachim, 'Soviet Arms Transfers to Sub-Saharan Africa', in Nation, R. Craig, and Kauppi, Mark V. (eds.), *The Soviet Impact in Africa* (Lexington, MA: D. C. Heath, 1984)

Krieger, Joel (ed.), *The Oxford Companion to Politics of the World*, 2nd edn (Oxford: Oxford University Press, 2001)

Kriger, Norma J., *Zimbabwe's Guerrilla War: Peasant Voices* (Cambridge: Cambridge University Press, 1992)

Kristoff, Nicholas D., and Wudunn, Sheryl, *China Wakes: The Struggle for the Soul of a Rising Power* (New York: Vintage Books, 1995)

Kull, Steven, *Burying Lenin: The Revolution in Soviet Ideology and Foreign Policy* (Boulder, CO: Westview Press, 1992)

Kuzichkin, Vladimir, *Inside the KGB: Myth and Reality* (London: André Deutsch, 1990)

Kuzichkin, Vladimir, 'Coups and Killings in Kabul', *Time*, 22 Nov. 1982.

Larkin, Bruce D., *China and Africa 1949–1970: The Foreign Policy of the People's Republic of China* (Berkeley/Los Angeles: University of California Press, 1971)

Lassassi, Assassi, *Non-Alignment and Algerian Foreign Policy* (Aldershot: Avebury, 1988)

Lefort, René, *Ethiopia: An Heretical Revolution?* (London: Zed, 1983)

Leonov, N. S., *Likholet'e* (Moscow: Mezhdunarodnye otnosheniia, 1995)

Leonov, Nikolai, 'La inteligencia soviética en América Latina durante la guerra fría', *Estudios Públicos*, no. 73 (1999)

Leonov, Nikolai, Fediakova, Eugenia, and Fermandois, Joaquín, 'El general Nikolai Leonov en el CEP', *Estudios Públicos*, no. 73 (1999)

Leung, John K., and Kau, Michael Y. M., *The Writings of Mao Zedong* (Amonk, NY: M. E. Sharpe, 1992)

Levchenko, Stanislav, *On the Wrong Side: My Life in the KGB* (Washington/New York: Pergamon-Brassey's, 1988)

Levinson, Sandra, and Brightman, Carol (eds.), *Venceremos Brigade: Young Americans Sharing the Life and Work of Revolutionary Cuba* (New York: Simon & Schuster, 1971)

Lewin-Epstein, Noah, Ro'i, Yaacov, and Ritterbrand, Paul (eds.), *Russian Jews on Three Continents: Migration and Resettlement* (London: Frank Cass, 1997)

Lewis, David C., *After Atheism: Religion and Ethnicity in Russian Central Asia* (New York: St Martin's Press, 2000)

Leys, Colin, and Saul, John S. (eds.), *Namibia's Liberation Struggle: The Two-Edged Sword* (London: James Currey, 1995)

Li Zhisui, *The Private Life of Chairman Mao* (London: Chatto & Windus, 1994)

Liakhovskii, A. A., *Plamia Afgana* (Moscow: Iskon, 1999)

Library of Congress: Federal Research Division, *Ghana: A Country Study*, http://lcweb2.loc.gov/frd/cs/ghtoc.html

Lieven, Anatol, *Chechnya: The Tombstone of Russian Power* (New Haven: Yale University Press, 1998)

Little, Douglas, 'A Fool's Errand: America and the Middle East', in Kunz, Diane B. (ed.), *The Diplomacy of the Crucial Decade: American Foreign Relations during the 1960s* (New York: Columbia University Press, 1994)

Lockwood, Lee, *Castro's Cuba, Cuba's Fidel* (New York: Random House, 1969)

Lonsdale, John, 'The Labors of *Mwiguithania*: Jomo Kenyatta as Author, 1928–45', *Research in African Literatures*, vol. 29 (1998), no. 1

Lonsdale, John, 'Jomo Kenyatta, God, and the Modern World', in Deutsch, J-G., Probst, P., and Schmidt, H. (eds.), *African Modernities* (Oxford: Currey, 2002)

Macrakis, Kristie, 'Does Effective Espionage Lead to Success in Science and Technology? Lessons from the East German Ministry of State Security', *Intelligence and National Security*, vol. 19 (2004), no. 1

Malashenko, Alexei, 'Does Islamic Fundamentalism Exist in Russia?', in Ro'i, Yaacov (ed.), *Muslim Eurasia: Conflicting Legacies* (London: Frank Cass, 1995)

Malhotra, Inder, *Indira Gandhi: A Personal and Political Biography* (London: Hodder & Stoughton, 1989)

Mallick, Ross, *Indian Communism: Opposition, Collaboration and Institutionalization* (Delhi: Oxford University Press, 1994)

Mandela, Nelson, *Long Walk to Freedom* (London: Little, Brown & Co., 1994)

Mandela, Nelson, and Castro, Fidel, *How Far We Slaves Have Come! South Africa and Cuba in Today's World* (New York/London: Pathfinder, 1991)

Mars, Perry, *Ideology and Change: The Transformation of the Caribbean Left* (Detroit: Wayne State University Press, 1998)

Mascarenhas, Anthony, *Bangladesh: A Legacy of Blood* (London: Hodder & Stoughton, 1986)

Masterson, Daniel M., *Militarism and Politics in Latin America: Peru from Sánchez Cerro to Sendero Luminoso* (New York/London: Greenwood Press, 1991)

McCargo, Duncan, *Contemporary Japan* (London: Macmillan, 2000)

McClellan, Woodford, 'Africans and Blacks in the Comintern Schools', *International Journal of African Historical Studies*, vol. 26 (1993), no. 2

McClintock, Cynthia, and Lowenthal, Abraham F. (eds.), *The Peruvian Experiment Reconsidered* (Princeton, NJ: Princeton University Press, 1983)

McClintock, Cynthia, 'Velasco, Officers and Citizens: The Politics of Stealth', in McClintock, Cynthia, and Lowenthal, Abraham F. (eds.), *The Peruvian Experiment Reconsidered* (Princeton, NJ: Princeton University Press, 1983)

McDermott, Kevin, and Agnew, Jeremy, *The Comintern: A History of International Communism from Lenin to Stalin* (London: Macmillan, 1996)

MacFarquhar, Roderick, and Fairbank, John K. (eds.), *The Cambridge History of China*, vol. 15: *The People's Republic; Part II: Revolutions within the Chinese Revolution 1966–1982* (Cambridge: Cambridge University Press, 1991)

McKnight, David, *Espionage and the Roots of the Cold War: The Conspiratorial Heritage* (London: Frank Cass, 2002)

McMahon, Robert J., *The Cold War on the Periphery: The United States, Pakistan and India* (New York: Columbia University Press, 1994)

McNamara, Robert S., *In Retrospect: The Tragedy and Lessons of Vietnam* (New York: Times Books, 1995)

Middle East Watch, *Syria Unmasked: The Suppression of Human Rights by the Asad Regime* (New Haven: Yale University Press, 1991)

Milani, Abbas, *The Persian Sphinx: Amir Abbas Hoveyda and the Riddle of the Iranian Revolution* (Washington, DC: Mage Publishers, 2000)

Milenky, Edward S., *Argentina's Foreign Policies* (Boulder, CO: Westview Press, 1978)

Miller, Nicola, *Soviet Relations with Latin America, 1959–1987* (Cambridge: Cambridge University Press, 1989)

Miranda, Roger, and Ratliff, William, *The Civil War in Nicaragua: Inside the Sandinistas* (London: Transaction Publishers, 1993)

Mitchell, Christopher, *The Legacy of Populism in Bolivia: From the MNR to Military Rule* (New York: Praeger, 1977)

Mitrokhin, Vasiliy (ed.), *KGB Lexicon: The Soviet Intelligence Officer's Handbook* (London: Frank Cass, 2002)

Mitrokhin, Vasiliy, 'The KGB in Afghanistan', introduced and edited by Christian F. Ostermann and Odd Arne Westad, Cold War International History Project, Working Paper no. 40 (February 2002)

Mitrokhin, Vasiliy, 'KGB Active Measures in Southwest Asia', *Cold War International History Project Bulletin*, nos. 14–15 (2003–2004)

Moin, Baqer, *Khomeini: Life of the Ayatollah* (London: I. B. Tauris, 1999)

'More Documents from the Russian Archives', *Cold War International History Project Bulletin*, no. 5 (1994)

'More East-Bloc Sources on Afghanistan', *Cold War International History Project Bulletin*, nos. 14–15 (2003–2004)

Morozov, Boris (ed.), *Documents on Soviet Jewish Emigration* (London: Frank Cass, 1999)

Moynihan, Daniel Patrick, *A Dangerous Place* (London: Secker & Warburg, 1979)

Moynihan, Daniel Patrick, *Secrecy: The American Experience* (New Haven: Yale University Press, 1998)

Mullik, B. N., *The Chinese Betrayal* (Bombay: Allied Publishers, 1971)

Mullik, B. N., *My Years with Nehru, 1948–1964* (Bombay: Allied Publishers, 1972)

Najib, Mohammed, 'Abu Nidal Murder Trail Leads Directly to Iraqi Regime', *Jane's World Insurgency and Terrorism Report*, 23 August 2002

Nasser, Gamal Abdel, *The Philosophy of the Revolution* (Cairo, 1954)

Nazhestkin, Oleg, 'V ognennom kol'tse blokady', in Karpov, V. N. (ed.), *Vneshniaia razvedka* (Moscow: XXI vek – Soglasie, 2000)

Nechiporenko, Oleg, 'Na rodine atstekov', in Karpov, V. N. (ed.), *Vneshniaia razvedka* (Moscow: XXI vek – Soglasie, 2000)

'New Evidence on North Korea', *Cold War International History Project Bulletin*, nos. 14–15 (2003–2004)

Nkomo, Joshua, *Nkomo: The Story of My Life* (London: Methuen, 1984)

Nkrumah, Kwame, *I Speak of Freedom: A Statement of African Ideology* (London: Heinemann, 1961)

Nkrumah, Kwame, *Africa Must Unite* (London: Heinemann, 1963)

Nkrumah, Kwame, *Dark Days in Ghana* (London: Lawrence & Wishart, 1968)

Nzula, A. T., Potemkin, I. I., and Zusmanovich, A. Z. (ed. Robin Cohen), *Forced Labour in Colonial Africa* (London: Zed, 1979)

Odinga, Oginga (with foreword by Kwame Nkrumah), *Not Yet Uhuru: The Autobiography of Oginga Odinga*, paperback edn (London: Heinemann, 1968)

Olcott, Martha Brill, 'Islam and Fundamentalism in Independent Central Asia', in Ro'i, Yaacov (ed.), *Muslim Eurasia: Conflicting Legacies* (London: Frank Cass, 1995)

Orizio, Riccardo, *Talk of the Devil: Encounters with Seven Dictators* (London: Secker & Warburg, 2003)

Osei, Akwasi P., *Ghana: Recurrence and Change in a Post-Independence African State* (New York: Peter Lang, 1999)

Ostermann, Christian F., 'East Germany and the Horn Crisis: Documents on SED *Afrikapolitik*', *Cold War International History Project Bulletin*, nos. 8–9 (1996–97)

Ostermann, Christian F. (ed.), 'Gorbachev and Afghanistan', *Cold War International History Project Bulletin*, nos. 14–15 (2003–2004)

Ottaway, David, and Ottaway, Marina, *Afrocommunism* (London: Holmes & Meier, 1981)

Ottaway, David, and Ottaway, Marina, *Ethiopia: Empire in Revolution* (New York: Africana, 1978)

Pacepa, Ion, *Red Horizons: The Extraordinary Memoirs of a Communist Spy Chief* (London: Heinemann, 1988)

Packard, George R. III, *Protest in Tokyo: The Security Crisis of 1960* (Princeton: Princeton University Press, 1966)

Page, Stephen, *The Soviet Union and the Yemenis: Influence in Asymmetrical Relationships* (New York: Praeger, 1985)

Pahlavi, Farah, *An Enduring Love*, trans. Clancy, Patricia (New York: Miramax Books, 2004)

Paine, S. C. M., *Imperial Rivals: China, Russia and Their Disputed Frontier* (Armonk, NY: M. E. Sharpe, 1996)

Palmer, David Scott, *Peru: The Authoritarian Tradition* (New York: Praeger, 1980)

Pastor, Robert A., *Condemned to Repetition* (Princeton, NJ: Princeton University Press, 1988)

Pateman, Roy, 'Intelligence Operations in the Horn of Africa', in Sorenson, John (ed.), *Disaster and Development in the Horn of Africa* (London: Macmillan, 1995)

Patman, Robert G., *The Soviet Union in the Horn of Africa: The Diplomacy of Intervention and Disengagement* (Cambridge: Cambridge University Press, 1990)

Payne, Douglas, *Cuba: Systematic Repression of Dissent* (Washington, DC: INS Resource Information Center, 1998)

Pérez, Cristián, 'Salvador Allende, Apuntes sobre su Dispositivo de Seguridad: El Grupo de Amigos Personales (GAP)', *Estudios Públicos*, no. 79 (Autumn, 2000)

Pezzullo, Lawrence, and Pezzullo, Ralph, *At the Fall of Somoza* (Pittsburgh: University of Pittsburgh Press, 1993)

Philby, Kim, *My Silent War*, paperback edn (London: Granada, 1979)

Pinkus, Benjamin, *The Jews of the Soviet Union: The History of a National Minority* (Cambridge: Cambridge University Press, 1988)

Pipes, Daniel, *The Hidden Hand: Middle East Fears of Conspiracy* (London: Macmillan, 1996)

Pipes, Daniel, 'Asad's Art of the Double Game', in Ma'oz, Moshe, Ginat, Joseph, and Winckler, Onn (eds.), *Modern Syria* (Brighton: Sussex Academic Press, 1999)

Pipes, Richard, *Russia under the Bolshevik Regime, 1919–1924*, paperback edn (London: HarperCollins, 1995)

Pleshakov, Constantine, 'Nikita Khrushchev and Sino-Soviet Relations', in Westad, Odd Arne (ed.), *Brothers in Arms: The Rise and Fall of the Sino-Soviet Alliance, 1945–1963* (Stanford: Stanford University Press, 1998)

Primakov, E. M., et al., *Ocherki istorii rossiiskoi vneshnei razvedki* (Moscow: Mezhdunarodyne otnosheniia, 1995–)

Primakov, Yevgeny, *Russian Crossroads: Towards the New Millennium* (New Haven: Yale University Press, 2004)

Pryce-Jones, David, 'Under His Spell', *Sunday Times* (Culture), 1 August 2004

Quirk, Robert E., *Fidel Castro* (New York: W. W. Norton & Co., 1993)

Rafizadeh, Mansur, *Witness: From the Shah to the Secret Arms Deal* (New York: William Morrow, 1987)

Ramet, Pedro, *The Soviet–Syrian Relationship since 1955: A Troubled Alliance* (Boulder, CO: Westview Press, 1990)

Ranuga, Thomas K., *The New South Africa and the Socialist Vision: Positions and Perspectives towards a Post-Apartheid Society* (Atlantic Highlands, NJ: Humanities Press, 1996)

Rao, P. V. Narasimha, *The Insider* (New Delhi: Viking/Penguin Books India, 1998)

Rashid, Ahmed, *Taliban: Militant Islam, Oil and Fundamentalism in Central Asia*, paperback edn (New Haven: Yale University Press, 2001)

Raza, Rafi, *Zulfikar Ali Bhutto and Pakistan, 1967–1977* (Karachi: Oxford University Press, 1997)

Raza, Rafi (ed.), *Pakistan in Perspective 1947–1977* (Karachi: Oxford University Press, 1997)

Reagan, Ronald, *An American Life* (New York: Simon & Schuster, 1990)

Remnick, David, *Lenin's Tomb: The Last Days of the Soviet Empire*, paperback edn (London: Penguin, 1994)

Remnick, David, *Resurrection: The Struggle for a New Russia* (London: Picador, 1998)

Roberts, David, 'The USSR in Syrian Perspective: Political Design and Pragmatic Practices', in Efrat, Moshe, and Bercovitch, Jacob (eds.), *Superpowers and Client States in the Middle East: The Imbalance of Influence* (London: Routledge, 1991)

Robinson, Thomas, 'China Confronts the Soviet Union: Warfare and Diplomacy on China's Inner Asian Frontiers', in Twitchett, Denis, and Fairbanks, John F. (eds.), *The Cambridge History of China*, vol. 15 (Cambridge: Cambridge University Press, 1991)

Rogers, Tom, *The Soviet Withdrawal from Afghanistan: Analysis and Chronology* (Westport, CT: Greenwood Press, 1992)

Ro'i, Yaacov (ed.), *Jews and Jewish Life in Russia and the Soviet Union* (London: Frank Cass, 1995)

Ro'i, Yaacov (ed.), *Muslim Eurasia: Conflicting Legacies* (London: Frank Cass, 1995)

Ro'i, Yaacov, 'The Secularisation of Islam and the USSR's Muslim Areas', in Ro'i, Yaacov (ed.), *Muslim Eurasia: Conflicting Legacies* (London: Frank Cass, 1995)

Ro'i, Yaacov, 'Soviet Policy towards Jewish Emigration: An Overview', in Lewin-Epstein, Noah, Ro'i, Yaacov, and Ritterbrand, Paul (eds.), *Russian Jews on Three Continents: Migration and Resettlement* (London: Frank Cass, 1997)

Romerstein, Herbert, 'Some Insights Derived from the Grenada Documents', in Bark, Dennis L. (ed.), *Red Orchestra*, vol. 1: *Instruments of Soviet Policy in Latin America and the Caribbean* (Stanford: Hoover Institution Press, 1986)

Rooney, David, *Kwame Nkrumah: The Political Kingdom in the Third World* (London: I. B. Tauris, 1988)

Roosevelt, Kermit, *Countercoup* (New York: McGraw-Hill, 1979)

Rosenau, William, 'A Deafening Silence: US Government Policy and the Sigint Facility at Lourdes', *Intelligence and National Security*, vol. 9 (1994), no. 4

Rozman, Gilbert (ed.), *Japan and Russia: The Tortuous Path to Normalization, 1949–1999* (London: Macmillan, 2000)

Rubin, Barry, *Paved with Good Intentions: The American Experience and Iran* (Oxford: Oxford University Press, 1980)

Rubin, Barry, *The Transformation of Palestinian Politics: From Revolution to State-Building* (Cambridge, MA: Harvard University Press, 1999)

Rubin, Barry, and Rubin, Judith Colp, *Yasir Arafat: A Political Biography* (Oxford: Oxford University Press, 2003)

Rubinstein, Alvin Z., *Moscow's Third World Strategy*, paperback edn (Princeton, NJ: Princeton University Press, 1990)

Rubinstein, Alvin Z., 'The Middle East in Moscow's Strategic Prism', in Brown, Carl M. (ed.), *Diplomacy in the Middle East: The International Relations of Regional and Outside Powers* (London: I. B. Tauris, 2001)

Rubinstein, Alvin Z., and Smith, Donald E. (eds.), *Anti-Americanism in the Third World: Implications for U.S. Foreign Policy* (New York: Praeger, 1985)

Rudolph, James D., *Peru: The Evolution of a Crisis* (Westport, CT: Praeger, 1992)

Russell, Bertrand, *War Crimes in Vietnam* (London: Allen & Unwin, 1967)

'Russian and East German Documents on the Horn of Africa, 1977–78', *Cold War International History Project Bulletin*, nos. 8–9 (1996–97)

Ryan, Henry Butterfield, *The Fall of Che Guevara: A Story of Soldiers, Spies and Diplomats* (Oxford: Oxford University Press, 1998)

Sachar, Howard M., *A History of Israel: From the Rise of Zionism to Our Time* (Oxford: Basil Blackwell, 1976)

el-Sadat, Anwar, *In Search of Identity* (London: Collins, 1978)

Sajjadpour, Kazem, 'Neutral Statements, Committed Practice: The USSR and the War', in Rajaee, Farhang (ed.), *Iranian Perspectives on the Iran–Iraq War* (Gainesville, FL: University Press of Florida, 1997)

Sakharov, Vladimir, *High Treason* (New York: Ballantine Books, 1981)

Salisbury, Harrison E., *The New Emperors. Mao and Deng: A Dual Biography* (London: HarperCollins, 1992)

Salitan, Laurie, 'Soviet Emigration Policy, 1968–89', in Lewin-Epstein, Noah, Ro'i, Yaacov, and Ritterbrand, Paul (eds.), *Russian Jews on Three Continents: Migration and Resettlement* (London: Frank Cass, 1997)

Samolis, T. V. (ed.), *Veterany vneshnei razvedki Rossii: Kratkii biograficheskii spravochnik* (Moscow: SVR, 1995)

Sampson, Anthony, *Mandela: The Authorised Biography*, paperback edn (London: HarperCollins, 2000)

Sanankoua, Bintou, *La chute de Modibo Keïta* (Paris: Chaka, 1990)

Sand, G. W., *Soviet Aims in Central America: The Case of Nicaragua* (New York: Praeger, 1989)

Scalapino, Robert A., *On the Trail of Chou En-lai in Africa* (Santa Monica: RAND, 1964)

Scalapino, Robert A., *The Japanese Communist Movement, 1920–1966* (Berkeley/Los Angeles: University of California Press, 1967)

Schäfer, Bernd, 'Weathering the Sino-Soviet Conflict: The GDR and North Korea, 1949–1989', *Cold War International History Project Bulletin*, nos. 14–15 (2003–2004)

Schleicher, Hans-Georg, and Schleicher, Illona, *Special Flights: The GDR and Liberation Movements in Southern Africa* (Harare: SAPES Books, 1998)

Schönwälder, Gerd, *Linking Civil Society and the State: Urban Popular Movements, the Left and Local Government in Peru, 1980–1992* (University Park, PA: University of Pennsylvania Press, 2002)

Seale, Patrick (with McConville, Maureen), *Asad of Syria: The Struggle for the Middle East*, revised edn (London: I. B. Tauris, 1990)

Sebag Montefiore, Simon, *Stalin: The Court of the Red Tsar*, paperback edn (London: Phoenix, 2004)

Sebag Montefiore, Simon, 'Stalin and Saddam: The Twin Tyrants', *Sunday Times*, 4 July 2004

Seely, Robert, *The Russian–Chechen Conflict, 1800–2000: A Deadly Embrace* (London: Frank Cass, 2001)

Sejna, Jan, *We Will Bury You* (London: Sidgwick & Jackson, 1982)

Semenov, Yu. I., 'The Theory of Socio-economic Foundations and World History', in Gellner, Ernest (ed.), *Soviet and Western Anthropology* (London: Duckworth, 1980)

Semichastnyi, Vladimir, *Bespokoinoe serdtse* (Moscow: Vagrius, 2002)

Senate Committee on the Judiciary, *The Role of the Soviet Union, Cuba and East Germany in Fomenting Terrorism in Southern Africa* (Washington, DC: US Government Printing Office, 1982)

Senate Committee on the Judiciary, *The Role of Cuba in International Terrorism and Subversion* (Washington, DC: US Government Printing Office, 1982)

Shawcross, William, *The Shah's Last Ride: The Story of the Exile, Misadventures and Death of the Emperor* (London: Chatto & Windus, 1989)

Shcharansky, Natan, *Fear No Evil* (London: Weidenfeld & Nicolson, 1988)

Shebarshin, Leonid Vladimirovich, *Ruka Moskvy: Zapiski nachal'nika sovetskoi razvedki* (Moscow: Tsentr-100, 1992)

Shemesh, Haim, *Soviet–Iraqi Relations, 1968–1988: In the Shadow of the Iraq–Iran Conflict* (Boulder, CO: Lynne Rienner Publishers, 1992)

Shevchenko, Arkadi N., *Breaking with Moscow*, paperback edn (New York: Ballantine Books, 1985)

Shlaim, Avi, *The Iron Wall: Israel and the Arab World* (London: Allen Lane, The Penguin Press, 2000)

Short, Philip, *The Dragon and the Bear* (London: Hodder & Stoughton, 1982)

Shubin, Vladimir, *ANC: A View from Moscow* (Bellville, South Africa: Mayibuye, 1999)

Shultz, George P., *Turmoil and Triumph: My Years as Secretary of State* (New York: Charles Scribner's Sons, 1993)

Shvets, Yuri B., *Washington Station: My Life as a KGB Spy in America* (New York: Simon & Schuster, 1994)

Simpson, John, *Behind Iranian Lines* (London: Robson Books, 1988)

Singh, S. Nihal, *The Yogi and the Bear: Story of Indo-Soviet Relations* (New Delhi: Allied Publishers Private Ltd, 1986)

Skidmore, Thomas E., 'Brazil's Slow Road to Democratization: 1974–1985', in Stepan, Alfred (ed.), *Democratizing Brazil: Problems of Transition and Consolidation* (Oxford: Oxford University Press, 1989)

Smith, Peter H., 'Mexico since 1946: Dynamics of an Authoritarian Regime', in Bethell, Leslie (ed.), *Mexico since Independence* (Cambridge: Cambridge University Press, 1991)

Smith, Sebastian, *Allah's Mountains: Politics and War in the Russian Caucasus* (London: I. B. Tauris, 1998)

Smith, Wayne S., 'Cuba and the Soviet Union, Cuba and Russia', in Donna Rich Kaplowitz (ed.), *Cuba's Ties to a Changing World* (Boulder, CO/London: Lynne Rienner Publishers, 1995)

Smolansky, Oles M., and Smolansky, Bettie M., *The USSR and Iraq: The Soviet Quest for Influence* (Durham, NC: Duke University Press, 1991)

Sneath, David, *Changing Inner Mongolia: Pastoral Mongolian Society and the Chinese State* (Oxford: Oxford University Press, 2000)

Snow, Philip, *The Star Raft: China's Encounter with Africa* (London: Weidenfeld & Nicolson, 1988)

Sobel, Lester A. (ed.), *Argentina and Peron* (New York: Facts on File, 1975)

Soviet Active Measures, Hearings before the Subcommittee on European Affairs, United States Senate, 99th Congress, 1st Session (Washington: US Government Printing Office, 1986)

Soviet Covert Action (The Forgery Offensive), Hearings before the Subcommittee on Oversight of the Permanent Select Committee on Intelligence, House of Representatives, 96th Congress, 2nd Session (Washington: US Government Printing Office, 1980)

'Soviet Documents on Angola and Southern Africa, 1975–1979', *Cold War International History Project Bulletin*, nos. 8–9 (1996–97)

'The Soviet Union and Afghanistan, 1978–1989: Documents from Soviet and East German Archives', *Cold War International History Project Bulletin*, nos. 8–9 (1996–97)

Sparks, Allister, *Tomorrow Is Another Country: The Inside Story of South Africa's Negotiated Revolution* (Sandton, South Africa: Struik Book Distributors, 1994)

Suchkov, D. I., 'Dzhomo Keniata v Moskve', *Vostok* (1993), no. 4

Swietochowski, Tadeusz, *Russia and Azerbaijan: A Borderland in Transition* (New York: Columbia University Press, 1995)

Szalontai, Balázs, ' "You Have No Political Line of Your Own" : Kim Il Sung and the Soviets', *Cold War International History Project Bulletin*, nos. 14–15 (2003–2004)

Szulc, Tad, *Fidel: A Critical Portrait* (London: Hutchinson, 1987)

Taguieff, Pierre-André (ed.), *Les Protocoles des Sages de Sion*, 2 vols (Paris: Berg International, 1992)

Taheri, Amir, *Crescent in a Red Sky: The Future of Islam in the Soviet Union* (London: Hutchinson, 1989)

Taheri, Amir, *The Unknown Life of the Shah* (London: Hutchinson, 1991)

Talbot, Ian, *Pakistan: A Modern History* (London: Hurst & Co., 1998)

Talbott, Strobe (ed.), *Khrushchev Speaks*, with introduction and commentary by Edward Crankshaw (Boston: Little, Brown & Co., 1970)

Taubman, William, *Khrushchev: The Man and His Era* (London: The Free Press, 2003)

Taubman, William, 'Nikita Khrushchev and the Shoe', *International Herald Tribune*, 26 July 2003

Thomas, Hugh, *Cuba: or The Pursuit of Freedom* (London: Eyre & Spottiswoode, 1971)

Tillett, Lowell, 'The National Minorities Factor in the Sino-Soviet Dispute', *Orbis*, vol. 21 (1971)

Toplin, Robert Brent (ed.), *Oliver Stone's USA: Film, History, and Controversy* (Lawrence, KN: University Press of Kansas, 2000)

Turner, John W., *Continent Ablaze: The Insurgency Wars in Africa, 1960 to the Present* (London: Arms and Armour Press, 1998)

'Uighhur, M. E.' [pseud.], 'Sherki Türkestan Evasi (The Voice of Eastern Turkestan)', *Central Asian Survey*, vol. 1 (1982–83)

Ulianova, Olga, and Fediakova, Eugenia, 'Algunos aspectos de la ayuda financiera del Partido Comunista de la URSS al comunismo chileno durante la guerra fría', *Estudios Públicos*, no. 72 (1998)

Urban, Mark, *War in Afghanistan* (London: Macmillan, 1988)

US Department of State, *Soviet Influence Activities: A Report on Active Measures and Propaganda* (August 1987)

US Department of State, *Country Reports on Human Rights Practices, 2003: Russia*, 25 February 2004, www.state.gov/g/drl/hr/c1470.htm

US Government, *Soviet Acquisition of Militarily Significant Western Technology: An Update* (September 1985)

US Information Agency, *Recent Appearances of Soviet Disinformation* (6 October 1989)

USSR–China in a Changing World: Soviet Sinologists on the History and Prospects of Soviet–Chinese Relations (Moscow: Novosti, 1989)

Vaisman, Demian, 'Regionalism and Clan Loyalty in the Political Life of Uzbekistan', in Ro'i, Yaacov (ed.), *Muslim Eurasia: Conflicting Legacies* (London: Frank Cass, 1995)

Valenta, Jiri, and Durán, Esperanza (eds.), *Conflict in Nicaragua: A Multidimensional Perspective* (London: Allen & Unwin, 1987)

Vance, Cyrus, *Hard Choices: Critical Years in America's Foreign Policy* (New York: Simon & Schuster, 1983)

Vassiliev, Alexei, *Russian Policy in the Middle East* (Reading, MA: Ithaca Press, 1993)

Venâncio, Moisés, and Chan, Stephen, 'War and Gropings towards Peace', in Chan, Stephen, and Venâncio, Moisés (eds.), *War and Peace in Mozambique* (London: Macmillan, 1998)

Verbitsky, Semyon, 'Factors Shaping the Formation of Views on Japan in the USSR in the Postwar Period', in Rozman, Gilbert (ed.), *Japan and Russia: The Tortuous Path to Normalization, 1949–1999* (London: Macmillan, 2000)

Volkogonov, Dmitri, *The Rise and Fall of the Soviet Empire: Political Leaders from Lenin to Gorbachev* (London: HarperCollins, 1998)

Waldmeir, Patti, *Anatomy of a Miracle: The End of Apartheid and the Birth of the New South Africa* (London: Viking, 1997)

Waller, J. Michael, *The Third Current of Revolution: Inside the 'North American Front' of El Salvador's Guerilla War* (Lanham, MD: University Press of America, 1991)

Warren, Bill, *Imperialism: Pioneer of Capitalism* (London: Verso, 1980)

Weathersby, Kathryn, ' "Should We Fear This?" Stalin and the Danger of War with America', Cold War International History Project, Working Paper no. 40 (July 2002), accessible on www.chip.si.edu

Weathersby, Kathryn, 'New Evidence on North Korea: Introduction', *Cold War International History Project Bulletin*, nos. 14–15 (2003–2004)

Weiner, Michael, 'Comintern in East Asia, 1919–39', in McDermott, Kevin, and Agnew, Jeremy, *The Comintern: A History of International Communism from Lenin to Stalin* (London: Macmillan, 1996)

Westad, Odd Arne, 'Concerning the Situation in "A": New Russian

Evidence on the Soviet Intervention in Afghanistan', *Cold War International History Project Bulletin*, nos. 8–9 (1996–97)

Westad, Odd Arne, 'Moscow and the Angolan Crisis, 1974–1976: A New Pattern of Intervention', *Cold War International History Project Bulletin*, nos. 8–9 (1996–97)

Westad, Odd Arne, 'Reagan's Anti-Revolutionary Offensive in the Third World', paper for Oslo Nobel Symposium, June 2002

Westad, Odd Arne (ed.), *Brothers in Arms: The Rise and Fall of the Sino-Soviet Alliance 1945–1963* (Stanford: Stanford University Press, 1998)

Whymant, Robert, *Stalin's Spy: Richard Sorge and the Tokyo Espionage Ring* (London: I. B. Tauris, 1996)

Willetts, Peter, *The Non-Aligned Movement: The Origins of a Third World Alliance* (London: Frances Pinter, 1978)

Wise, David, *Molehunt: The Secret Search for Traitors that Shattered the CIA* (New York: Random House, 1992)

Wistrich, Robert S., *Antisemitism: The Longest Hatred* (London: Thames Methuen, 1991)

Wolf, Markus (with McElvoy, Anne), *Man without a Face: The Autobiography of Communism's Greatest Spymaster* (London: Jonathan Cape, 1997)

Woodward, Ralph Lee, *Central America: A Nation Divided*, 3rd edn (Oxford: Oxford University Press, 1999)

Wright, Peter, *Spycatcher: The Candid Autobiography of a Senior Intelligence Officer* (New York: Viking, 1987)

Wright, Robin, *In the Name of God: The Khomeini Decade* (London: Bloomsbury, 1990)

Wu, Hongda Harry, *Laogai – The Chinese Gulag* (Boulder, CO: Westview, 1992)

'Xinjiang, China's Restive Northwest', *Human Rights Watch Backgrounder*, November 2000

Yajee, Pandit Sheel Bhadra, *CIA: Manipulating Arm of U.S. Foreign Policy* (New Delhi: Criterion Publications, 1987)

Zafarullah, Habib (ed.), *The Zia Episode in Bangladesh Politics* (New Delhi: South Asian Publishers, 1996)

Zamoysky, Lolly, *Behind the Facade of the Masonic Temple* (Moscow: Progress Publishers, 1989)

Zelkina, Anna, *In Quest for God and Freedom: The Sufi Response to the Russian Advance in the North Caucasus* (London: Hurst & Co., 2000)

Zimmermann, Matilde, *Sandinista: Carlos Fonseca and the Nicaraguan Revolution* (Durham, NC: Duke University Press, 2000)

Ziring, Lawrence, *Bangladesh: From Mujib to Ershad, an Interpretive Study* (Karachi: Oxford University Press, 1992)

Ziring, Lawrence, *Pakistan in the Twentieth Century: A Political History* (Karachi: Oxford University Press, 1997)

Zisser, Ayal, *Asad's Legacy: Syria in Transition* (London: Hurst & Co., 2001)

Zubok, Vladislav, 'Spy vs. Spy: The KGB vs. the CIA, 1960–1962', *Cold War International History Project Bulletin*, no. 4 (1994)

Zubok, Vladislav, and Pleshakov, Constantine, *Inside the Kremlin's Cold War: From Stalin to Khrushchev* (Cambridge, MA: Harvard University Press, 1996)

Index

Syria – *cont.*
 Soviet relations with 17, 142,
  201, 206–7, 208, 211, 213,
  215
 Sunnism 211
 and terrorism 142, 144, 211,
  256
 violence and oppression 199,
  208–9, 211–12

Tabari, Ehsan 192
Tafazoli, Djahanguir 172
TAGIR (Syrian KGB contact) 201
Taha, Riyad 540n81
TAIR (Japanese Line X agent)
 559n77
Taiwan 272, 274
Tajikistan 371, 372, 385
Talabani, Jalal 188
TALAN (KGB agent in XUAR)
 280
Talas, Mustafa 208, 537n14
Taleban régime, Afghanistan 419
Talybov, Mutalim Agaverdioglu
 (SABIR) 376, 401
Tambo, Oliver 443, 507n66
Tanaka, Kakuei 300, 301–2
TANI (Japanese KGB agent,
 S & T) 306
Tanzania 439–40, 443, 461
TARAKANY, operation 364–6
Taraki, Nur Muhammad (NUR)
 177, 386–95, 396–7
Tarantel press agency 343–5
TARSHIKH (Ahmad Yunis, Abu
 Ahmad) 248, 255
Tartus 206
Tashkent 279, 371–2, 383,
 396
Tass news agency 110, 181
Tatars 370, 372
Tavrosky, Yuri 271

Tawab, Air Vice-Marshal
 Muhammad Ghulam 354
TAYFUN, operation 184
technology
 COCOM embargo on Soviet
  acquisition of Western 307–8,
  448
 see also scientific and
  technological intelligence
Tehran 169, 174, 179, 186
telephone
 Egyptian tapping 154
 external calls by Soviet Jews
  236–7
Tereshkova, Valentina 20
Termez 401
TERMIT intercept posts, Cuba
 92
terror
 in Afghanistan 389–90, 410
 in Cambodia 88, 264
 in China 264, 270, 487
 in Ethiopia 429, 457, 467–8
 in Guinea 437
 Lenin's use of 429
 Stalinist 264, 270, 484, 487
terrorism 173, 252, 492
 Palestinian 143–4, 246–59
 Syria sponsors 142, 144, 211
 in USA, apparently Zionist
  237–8
 *see also individual organizations
  and terrorists*
Thailand 318, 477, 557–8n44
Thatcher, Margaret 132
Thibedi, T. W. 424–5
Third World, Soviet policy towards
 1–24
 Brezhnev régime and 9–24
 Gorbachev era 477
 KGB's global grand strategy 9,
  40, 150, 432–3, 480–81